Donahue, Quinn & Grandilli

REAL ESTATE PRACTICE IN ONTARIO

SEVENTH EDITION

Donahue, Quinn & Grandilli

REAL ESTATE PRACTICE IN ONTARIO

SEVENTH EDITION

Peter D. Quinn, B.A., LL.B.
Danny C. Grandilli, B.A., J.D.

LexisNexis®

Members of the LexisNexis Group worldwide

Canada	LexisNexis Canada Inc, 123 Commerce Valley Dr. E. Suite 700, MARKHAM, Ontario
Australia	Butterworths, a Division of Reed International Books Australia Pty Ltd, CHATSWOOD, New South Wales
Austria	ARD Betriebsdienst and Verlag Orac, VIENNA
Czech Republic	Orac, sro, PRAGUE
France	Éditions du Juris-Classeur SA, PARIS
Hong Kong	Butterworths Asia (Hong Kong), HONG KONG
Hungary	Hvg Orac, BUDAPEST
India	Butterworths India, NEW DELHI
Ireland	Butterworths (Ireland) Ltd, DUBLIN
Italy	Giuffré, MILAN
Malaysia	Malayan Law Journal Sdn Bhd, KUALA LUMPUR
New Zealand	Butterworths of New Zealand, WELLINGTON
Poland	Wydawnictwa Prawnicze PWN, WARSAW
Singapore	Butterworths Asia, SINGAPORE
South Africa	Butterworth Publishers (Pty) Ltd, DURBAN
Switzerland	Stämpfli Verlag AG, BERNE
United Kingdom	Butterworths Tolley, a Division of Reed Elsevier (UK), LONDON, WC2A
USA	LexisNexis, DAYTON, Ohio

National Library of Canada Cataloguing in Publication

Donahue, D.J.
      Real estate practice in Ontario / D.J. Donahue, P.D. Quinn, D.C. Grandilli. — 7th ed.

Includes index.
ISBN 978-0-433-46770-0 (bound) — ISBN 0-433-46771-7 (pbk.)

1. Real property — Ontario. 2. Conveyancing — Ontario. 3. Real estate business — Law and legislation — Ontario. I. Quinn, P.D. (Peter D.) II. Grandilli, D.C. (Danny C.) III. Title.

KEO271.D65 2011	346.71304'3	C2003-902463-6
KF570.D66 2011		

Printed and bound in Canada.

Preface

It has again been eight years since the last edition (as our publisher has reminded us many times!). The laws continue to change and there is no shortage of material to write about.

It was never our intention to make this a comprehensive textbook about real estate law in Ontario. That book would be far too large and expensive. We apologize for the increasing number of case citations but include them as a starting point for more extensive research by those who feel the need to do so. Of necessity, we have had to be brief and omit many things which sometimes affect daily real estate practice. Nevertheless, we hope this text will continue to provide a handy desktop reference.

Don Donahue has retired from active practice but continues to be interested and was involved in the production of this edition. This book was originally his creation and we are grateful to him for including us and proud to carry on a fine tradition.

We also thank our publisher for its continuing patience and support and, in particular, our readers for theirs.

Donald J. Donahue
Peter D. Quinn
Danny C. Grandilli

Toronto
February 2011

About the Authors

Donald J. Donahue, Q.C., was a partner in the Toronto Real Property and Planning Group of McCarthy Tétrault. With more than 40 years of legal experience in real property law, he is the founding author of this text and has stayed on board for this edition.

Peter D. Quinn, B.A., LL.B., is a partner in the Toronto Real Property and Planning Group of McCarthy Tétrault. Co-author of this book since its second edition, he has more than 35 years of legal experience in a wide range of real property law areas, including commercial leasing, and land development and planning. He has been named in the 2006-2010 editions of the *Canadian Legal Lexpert Directory*, as a leading lawyer in the area of property development. As well, he is listed in all editions of *Chambers Global: The World's Leading Lawyers,* as a leading lawyer in the area of real estate law. Mr. Quinn is also recognized in *Best Lawyers in Canada* in the field of real estate law.

Danny C. Grandilli, B.A., J.D., is a partner in the Toronto Real Property and Planning Group of McCarthy Tétrault. With more than 20 years of legal experience in the fields of commercial real estate and private equity transactions, he has been co-author of this book since its sixth edition. Mr. Grandilli has been listed in the 2004-2010 editions of *Chambers Global: The World's Leading Lawyers* in the area of real estate law. He is also listed as a pre-eminent practitioner in Euromoney Legal Media Group's *Guide to the World's Leading Real Estate Lawyers*.

Table of Contents

CHAPTER 1

The Registry System

REGISTRY ACT, R.S.O. 1990, c. R.20

HISTORY

The system under which titles are recorded is basic to the practice of law in real estate. The Registry system is the older of two systems in use in Ontario. The *Registry Act* was one of the first statutes passed by the Legislature of Ontario when the province was initially established. In principle, the *Registry Act* is now substantially the same as when it was first passed. It has been amended more and more frequently, however, in order that the practice under the Registry system and the Land Titles system may grow more similar and eventually merge into one system. For example, Part I of the *Land Registration Reform Act*, R.S.O. 1990, c. L.4, effective as of November 1, 1984, introduced common registration documents for use under both systems. Part III was later added to provide for the electronic registration of documents.

The fundamental purposes of the system are to give public notice of interests that are claimed in land, to establish priorities between claimants, and to provide an orderly method of recording titles.

While the territory that now comprises the Province of Ontario was being settled from 1780 onwards, the British government was having it surveyed. The province was divided into counties, each county was divided into townships, and these in turn were surveyed into concessions and lots on the concessions.

The basic measurement of these early surveyors was Gunter's Chain. A chain measures 66 feet (20.1168 metres) and is divided into 100 links. All old descriptions measure distances in chains and links. To make sense of them (and to have new descriptions registered under current regulations), you must convert them to feet and inches or feet and decimals thereof by multiplying by 66 feet. Of course, you may also use metric measurements.

Since July 1, 1976, land registry offices have accepted plans and descriptions in either feet and inches or in metres.

Although several patterns were used throughout the province, a typical township was laid out in 14 concessions, being 14 strips of land running from one side of the township to the other, each strip measuring 100 chains or 6,600 feet or 1 ¼ miles (2.0116 kilometres) from front to rear. Dividing each of these strips from the next was a public road allowance measuring one chain in width. The typical Ontario homesteader's lot on that concession had a 20-chain frontage. These farm lots were marked off simply by staking the front two corners of the lot. The settler then had to run the lines back from the road allowance. Every five lots, another one-chain road allowance was laid out. Thus, the 1 ¼-mile grid pattern of roads found in many parts of Ontario was created. Even in the City of Toronto today, this pattern still persists. Running north and south, Yonge, Bathurst, Dufferin, Keele and Jane streets, and running east and west, Queen, Bloor, St. Clair, Eglinton and Lawrence streets are each 1 ¼ miles from the next.

So a typical concession lot had a 20-chain frontage on the road allowance and extended 100 chains back to the next road allowance. That is a 200-acre lot (acreage = length × breadth in chains divided by 10). These were usually patented and subsequently sold in halves for typical Ontario 100-acre farms. "Broken front concessions" are those that have an irregular boundary, such as a river or lake.

All of the land in the province was claimed by the Crown and the only way settlers could get title was to obtain a Crown Patent. This is the document by which title to the land, subject to certain reservations, is passed to the patentees, their heirs and assigns. This document is the basis of title and only by examining the Crown Patent can you ascertain what interests in that land are being retained by the Crown (see the discussion in Chapter 3 on the *Public Lands Act*). Strangely enough, this important information does not appear in the abstract books found in the registry office, except in the case of Crown Patents issued since October 1, 1965. For patents issued prior to that date, you must make a search at the office where copies of every patent issued by the Crown in right of Ontario are on file:

Ministry of Natural Resources
300 Water Street
P.O. Box 7000
Peterborough, ON
K9J 8M5

Title to all lands in Ontario that were reserved as Indian lands was vested in the Crown in right of Canada. Thus, if you are dealing with title to lands that at one time formed part of an Indian reserve, the Crown Patent was issued by the federal government in Ottawa, and not the provincial government in Toronto. For some reason, copies of these patents are kept in two different offices in Ottawa and, apparently, it is impossible to ascertain from the legal description in which of the two offices a copy of the patent for a particular parcel is filed. The offices are the following:

1. Office of the Registrar General of the Department of Consumer and Corporate Affairs, and

2. Office of the Registrar of Indian Lands, Land Entitlement Division of the Department of Indian Affairs and Northern Development.

Under the *Registry Act*, s. 20, whenever a township lot was patented, notice of such patent was forwarded to the land registrar in the appropriate land registry office. A land registry office was established for each county in southern Ontario, usually in the county town beside the court house. Certain counties were divided into ridings and more than one land registry office was created in those counties. In addition, separate land registry offices were established for the cities of Toronto, Ottawa and London. Many of the smaller land registry offices have been closed and registry and land titles offices have merged.

The land registrar, upon receiving notice of the Crown Patent, commenced to keep a public record of subsequent dealings with that township lot by opening a page in the abstract book. Thus, a separate book or series of books was created for each township and a separate page for each township lot in each concession.

After the original entry on that page of notice of the Crown Patent, every document subsequently registered in the land registry office dealing with that lot would be entered on that page in order of registration.

When a plan of subdivision is registered, a new abstract book is opened for that plan and a new page set up for each lot on the plan.

There were three other types of municipalities in Ontario: city, town and village. Upon incorporation of any of these, the land comprising the new municipality was separated from the township of which it was formerly a part and a new series of books opened for all lands within the town, city or village limits.

An innovation in municipal organization in Ontario occurred in the introduction of the "regional municipality". This concept was first established when the Municipality of Metropolitan Toronto was created in 1953. Thereafter, the entire "golden horseshoe" area around the west end of Lake Ontario from Oshawa to Niagara Falls, plus areas around Ottawa, Sudbury, Muskoka and Kitchener-Waterloo, were established as various regional municipalities. Within these regional municipalities, there have been drastic changes in the boundaries of various municipalities, and many historic names of original townships have disappeared entirely.

The creation of these entities creates a problem when describing land in a conveyance: the land must be described in accordance with its present designation. For instance, land formerly described as being "in the Town of Georgetown, in the County of Halton", is now "in the Town of Halton Hills, in the Regional Municipality of Halton".

More recently, the trend has been to consolidate all of the municipalities found within a regional municipality into one single municipal corporation. The municipalities and borough that together constituted the Municipality of Metropolitan Toronto were amalgamated into one municipality designated as the City of Toronto. Similarly, the Regional Municipality of Ottawa-Carleton, which had included various municipalities such as Kanata and Nepean, have been amalgamated into one entity designated as the City of Ottawa.

LAND REGISTRATION REFORM ACT, R.S.O. 1990, c. L.4

Forms

The *Land Registration Reform Act* ("LRRA") changed the practice of real estate law significantly when it became applicable to all land in Ontario on April 1, 1985 (by O. Reg. 35/85). However, its impact was mainly on form, rather than substance. In fact, Part I of the Act is concerned primarily with introducing common documents to both the Registry and Land Titles systems.

Previously, not only were different forms used in the two registration systems, but the same types of transactions had different names. A deed under the *Registry Act* was a transfer under the *Land Titles Act*; similarly, a mortgage was a charge, and a discharge of mortgage was a cessation of charge. Now the same forms with the same names are used under both registration systems. Officially, the terms under both systems are "transfer" (a conveyance of freehold and leasehold land), "charge" (a lien on the chargor's property to secure payment of money or performance of other obligations) and "discharge" (a cancellation of a charge). Also, "document" is the general term equivalent to "instrument" under the *Registry Act*.

The forms themselves (in R.R.O. 1990, Reg. 688) retain both terms. Form 1 is the Transfer/Deed of Land; Form 2 is the Charge/Mortgage of Land, and Form 3 is the Discharge of Charge/Mortgage.

One of these three forms or Form 4, Document General, must accompany any document seeking registration under either the *Land Titles Act*, R.S.O. 1990, c. L.5, or the *Registry Act*. Often (and preferably), completion of one of the forms itself is sufficient for registration. However, other documents may be attached, and often are in the case of a Document General. A schedule (Form 5 may be used) may be attached to any of the other forms to provide additional information.

The Director of Titles, under the LRRA, s. 3(4), does have discretion to permit a document to be registered even if it is not in the prescribed form. Moreover, subs. 3(5) permits an application to be brought before the Superior Court of Justice, with notice to the Director, for an order permitting registration of a document in other than the prescribed form.

Aside from the schedule, the documents are primarily in "box" format, allowing required information to be merely indicated with an "X" or short answer. Note that affidavits are no longer required, though statements under the *Planning Act*, R.S.O. 1990, c. P.13, s. 50(22), and the *Family Law Act*, R.S.O. 1990, c. F.3, s. 21(3), have been incorporated in the forms.

Special Features of the Forms

The LRRA incorporates certain implied covenants in transfers and charges (see s. 5 and s. 7, respectively). These covenants will be deemed to be part of the document unless expressly excluded or varied in a schedule. The covenants inferred in a transfer are similar to those previously implied under the *Conveyancing and Law of Property Act*, R.S.O. 1990, c. C.34 (at least, that was the intention). The usual covenants found in a charge, such as the covenants that the chargor has the right to give the charge and that the chargor, or successors, will pay principal and interest as required by the charge, are implied in the charge document.

Along with the implied covenants, a party may include additional covenants and terms in a schedule to the transfer or charge. The chargee may also register a set of standard charge terms that it intends to use in charges taken in its favour. Most institutional lenders have registered standard charge terms. The Director of Titles has the power to require them to do so. A set of standard charge terms is then incorporated into the prescribed form of charge by reference to its registration number. If the chargee wishes to amend its standard charge terms, he or she files an amended set of terms, which will be given a new number. A chargee may have several sets of standard charge terms to be used as needed.

The discharge of charge/mortgage no longer needs to refer to the mortgage date or parties, as was the case prior to the LRRA. The prescribed form (Form 3) requires only that the registration date and number of the mortgage, assignments and "every other registered instrument relating exclusively to the mortgage" be set out. The latter requirement is meant to cover such things as postponements, extension agreements and collateral assignments of rents, so that they can be ruled out or deleted by the land registrar at the same time as the mortgage.

Form 4, Document General, is to be used for all documents other than transfers, charges and discharges. For example, deposits, notices of lease, construction liens, powers of attorney and court orders would be registered by way of a Document General.

The use of the Form 5 Schedule is permissive, as attachments to the other documents need not be in any particular form.

Reasons for Change

The LRRA is one piece of a larger effort to streamline, automate and computerize the land registration system.

In 1968, the provincial government asked the Law Reform Commission to study the provincial land registration system and make recommendations. The resulting 1971 report urged widespread changes, including total conversion to the Land Titles system; use of province-wide property maps; automation of title records to permit computerized searching and registration of documents; and public use of microfilm instead of paper documents.

While the government accepted the recommendations in principle, it acknowledged that it would take some time (and money) to change the systems.

By introducing documents common to both registration systems through the LRRA, the first step was taken to facilitate the conversion to a complete Land Titles system. Moreover, the compartmentalized arrangement of the forms has speeded up the process of registration at the land registry office. With the required information appearing consistently in the same spot, staff can check documents more quickly for compliance with the legislation. The simplified format has also resulted in fewer pages to microfilm.

Computerization of the Land Registry System

Part II of the LRRA implemented a system of automated recording, retrieval and property mapping to computerize land registration records.

The system referred to in Part II is known as the Province of Ontario Land Registration and Information System ("POLARIS"). In the late 1980s, the Ontario Ministry of Consumer and Commercial Relations began the process of converting paper records into electronic information to be stored on databases. This conversion included all land registration records so that abstracts, plans and instruments pertaining to all lands in a registry office would become electronically accessible.

The County of Oxford was the first area in Ontario where POLARIS was implemented. Following that, properties in the County of Kent and County of Middlesex were converted. At the same time, the decision was taken to convert Land Registry system titles to Land Titles system titles at the same time as they were being computerized. Presently, Part II of the LRRA applies to all lands in Ontario (see section 1, O. Reg. 16/99, as amended) and, in fact, POLARIS has been fully implemented in many registry offices with all land registration records having been fully converted for the purposes of undertaking full searches. As of October 1, 2009, 44 of the 55 registry offices in Ontario had been fully converted, with all documents and maps being electronically accessible. Many of the remaining 11 registry offices are well advanced insofar as automation is concerned. For example, Parry Sound is 94.4 per cent complete and Wentworth 97 per cent complete (both as of October 1, 2009).

With POLARIS, properties governed by the *Registry Act* that are not converted to Land Titles, are parcelized, mapped and assigned a Property Identification Number ("PIN"). The most recent instrument that has apparently resulted in the last change of ownership is referenced for the purposes of providing a legal description. All registrations affecting a property from and after the activation date for the property are then abstracted on the computerized parcel; however, registrations prior to that date are not referenced. As a result, a search of a property under the *Registry Act*, even if assigned a PIN, still requires a search of paper records (for instruments affecting it registered prior to the PIN activation date) and computerized records (for instruments registered thereafter). This system is known as the Parcelized Day Forward Registry ("PDFR"). Eventually, it is the intention to convert all PDFR system properties to the Land Titles system.

Properties that are governed by the *Land Titles Act* (including those properties that have been fully converted) are similarly parcelized, mapped and assigned a PIN. In accordance with the provisions of the *Land Titles Act* (and subject to its qualifications as discussed in Chapter 2), the information obtained when accessing a PIN for Land Titles properties provides the user with the property parcel upon which is listed the legal description, registered owner, registered instruments and qualifications to title that pertain to that property.

Teraview is the software that provides access to POLARIS. It is administered and controlled by Teranet Inc. ("Teranet"), a public-private joint venture that was created in 1991 to accelerate the computerization of the land registration system. With Teraview, authorized users can retrieve POLARIS real property information and, as will be discussed below, complete land transactions from their desktop personal computer.

Electronic Registration

The *Electronic Registration Act (Ministry of Consumer and Business Services Statutes), 1991*, S.O. 1991, c. 44 introduced the legislative framework by which the final stage of the full implementation of the goals that were envisioned when POLARIS was introduced could be achieved. Its purpose, as clearly set out in s. 2, is to require or permit the filing of information under designated statutes in electronic formats and to transmit the information to an electronic database. The result is an all-electronic, paperless system, where documents are created, submitted and maintained in electronic format. Pursuant to O. Reg. 759/93 as amended by O. Reg. 13/99, the LRRA and *Land Titles Act* are designated as statutes to which the *Electronic Registration Act* applies.

Part III of the LRRA was introduced in 1994 to govern electronic registration of documents in registry offices. The impact of its changes on the practice of real estate in Ontario is as significant as the changes to the practice that came with the introduction of the LRRA in the first place.

Pursuant to s. 19(*c*) of the LRRA, the Ministry of Consumer and Business Services may by regulation designate lands as being in an area in which documents must be registered in an electronic format. As of October 1, 2009, the lands included within the boundaries of the Land Registry Offices of Algoma, Brant, Bruce, Cochrane, Dufferin, Dundas, Durham, Elgin, Essex, Haldimand, Halton, Hastings, Huron, Kenora, Lambton, Lanark, Leeds, Lennox, Middlesex, Muskoka, Niagara North, Niagara South, Nipissing, Norfolk, Northumberland, Ottawa-Carleton, Peel, Perth, Prince Edward, Rainy River, Peterborough, Simcoe, Sudbury, Thunder Bay, Timiskaming, Toronto, Waterloo, Wellington and York Region have been so designated.

Teranet, in consultation with the Ministry of Government Services, has developed and finalized the procedures and formats to be used for the electronic registration of documents and incorporated them into Teraview. Authorized users access Teraview to prepare conveyancing documents on personal computers using a series of prompts that Teranet has programmed into the system. As a document is prepared, Teraview automatically completes portions of the document from information accessed as soon as the PIN is recognized. Once the document is complete, it is e-mailed to the solicitor for the other party to the transaction for his or her approval. Once the document is settled, each lawyer must approve the document on Teraview and electronically "sign" the document to indicate its settlement. On the date scheduled for the completion of the transaction, each lawyer must again "sign" the document electronically to confirm that it can be released upon which it is electronically registered in the POLARIS database.

To further streamline the electronic registration process, supporting documentation that would accompany a conveyancing document in the paper registration system (such as the affidavits that accompany a transfer under a power of sale in a mortgage) is replaced by compliance with law statements. The lawyer for the party that would have had to produce an affidavit or other supporting evidence makes the statement in the document that all requirements have been satisfied for the conveyance to occur. If you are acting for the party who is receiving the conveyance and would normally have expected to receive and review the affidavit and other evidence supporting it (such as in the power of sale example), you can rely on the other lawyer's compliance with law statement and not review the supporting evidence.

To protect the integrity of the electronic registration system, the Director of Land Registration requires that all users apply for and obtain a licence from Teranet to access the system. If granted a licence, the user is issued an encryption key that must be used in effecting registrations electronically and that identifies the user by reference back to that key. Section 23.1 of the LRRA allows the Director to suspend any licence if there are grounds to believe the user is electronically registering documents without authorization from the holder of the interest affected by the registration. Bulletin 2009-01 outlines in further detail the access requirements applicable to Teraview.

The sufficiency of electronically registered documents to deal with interests in land is reinforced by Part III of the LRRA. Section 21 provides that notwithstanding s. 2 of the *Statute of Frauds Act*, R.S.O. 1990, c. S.19, s. 9 of the *Conveyancing and Law of Property Act*, R.S.O. 1990, c. C.34 (each of which requires agreements that affect interests in land to be in writing) and any other statute or any rule of law, an electronic document that deals with an interest in land is not required to be in writing or to be signed by the parties thereto and has the same effect for all purposes as a document that is in writing. Similarly, s. 22 provides that if a document is registered in an electronic format and the document exists in a written form that is not a printed copy of the electronic document, the electronic document prevails.

Section 24 of the LRRA is the statutory basis for compliance of law statements. Pursuant to s. 24(2), evidence in an electronic format made in accordance with the LRRA is deemed to comply with any requirement under a statute to provide written evidence in the form of an affidavit, declaration or other written statement despite the fact that the evidence is not in writing or signed by the person you would have expected to sign it.

Note that pursuant to s. 28, the implied covenants contained in s. 5 and s. 7 of the LRRA apply to transfers and charges registered electronically. Also note that pursuant to s. 32, Part III of the LRRA and any regulation made thereunder prevail where there is a conflict between such provision and any provision of the *Land Titles Act*, the *Registry Act* or the *Electronic Registration Act*.

Finally, it is important to review the provisions of O. Reg. 19/99, as amended, which sets out rules, procedures and formats that govern electronic registration. These requirements have been reflected in Teraview as evidenced by the prompts and fields to be completed when preparing electronic documents. Some of the significant provisions of this regulation are as follows:

s. 2 — prohibits unregistered users from registering or searching electronically;

s. 4 — prescribes requirements for every document that is submitted for electronic registration;

s. 5 — prescribes requirements for the electronic registration of a transfer;

s. 6 — prescribes requirements for the electronic registration of a charge;

s. 7 — prescribes requirements for the electronic registration of a discharge of charge or other interest;

s. 8 — prescribes requirements for the electronic registration of all other documents (to deal with documents that would have previously been registered by document general); and

s. 13 — prescribes requirements for the electronic registration of estate-related applications.

The remaining sections in the same regulation list additional requirements for the electronic registration of: foreclosure applications (s. 19), transfers under power of sale (s. 20), transfers of charge (s. 21), postponements (s. 22), applications under s. 71 of the *Land Titles Act* (s. 23), cautions pertaining to agreements of purchase and sale and options (s. 24), leases (s. 25), powers of attorney (s. 39.1), *etc.* Special procedures relating to the electronic registration of powers of attorney have been enacted to discourage the use of such documents in fraudulent conveyances. Please see the discussion on those procedures in Chapter 2.

Section 40 is also noteworthy. It provides that certain compliance of law statements identified in the regulation can only be made by an Ontario solicitor. If there is a statement of fact included within any prescribed statement that only a solicitor can make, the statement of fact shall be made on the advice of the party to the document who has knowledge of the fact on whose behalf it is made.

RELEVANT SECTIONS OF THE REGISTRY ACT

The following is a review of those sections of the *Registry Act* that most often affect the average practitioner.

Sections 3 to 21 — Administration

These sections deal with the appointment and duties of land registrars and their deputies. They also set out the various records and indices that the land registrar must maintain.

Note s. 15(4), which requires a land registrar to produce for inspection and supply a copy of any document, instrument, book or public record relating to land that is registered, deposited or maintained in a registry office. As a consequence of Parts II and III of the LRRA, this section offers the land registrar the alternative of providing a "facsimile" of any of the foregoing materials rather than the original itself. "Facsimile" is defined in s. 1 to include "a print from microfilm and a printed copy generated by or produced from a computer record". Under s. 15(4)(c), it is possible to obtain a copy of any document or instrument certified by the land registrar.

The provisions in s. 15(4) replace provisions that had appeared in s. 14, s. 15 and s. 17 requiring the land registrar to furnish a Registrar's Abstract, which had constituted *prima facie* evidence of the registration of the instruments found on the abstract against title to the lands described therein.

Pursuant to s. 18(8), the land registrar is required to maintain an index known as the "General Register Index" where the documents listed in s. 18(6) are to be registered. The types of documents listed in s. 18(6) include estate administration documents (wills, letters probate), documents that relate to corporate name changes (articles of amendment, amalgamation) and orders in council, among others. Note the addition of s. 18(6)18 allowing general conveyances and transfers of assets of a corporation to another corporation to be registered in this index to provide evidence and facilitate transactions involving bulk conveyances of interests in land.

With the implementation of POLARIS and the extension of the provisions of Part II of the LRRA to all lands in Ontario (s. 1 of O. Reg. 16/99), the Director of Titles must divide all properties in a registry office into blocks and assign a PIN to each property. Property maps must also be prepared to illustrate all such properties (s. 21). Once this is done, a land registrar must create an automated index under a PIN assigned to a property and record every instrument that affects a property thereon, which index is known as an abstract index. In practice, once a property has been fully integrated in the POLARIS system and is assigned a PIN, registrations affecting that property after its POLARIS implementation date can be searched by referring to the automated abstract index; registration before that date must be searched manually in the non-automated abstract index organized by lots and concessions rather than PINs. Eventually, as lands are converted and brought into the Land Titles system, the paper abstract index will inevitably disappear.

Sections 22 and 23 — Instruments to Be Registered

Any of the instruments defined in s. 1 may be registered, subject to the requirements of Part I of the LRRA and other provisions of the *Registry Act* itself. The concept of registration has been broadened to accommodate electronic registration by providing that "delivery" of a document to the land registrar includes "delivery by direct electronic transmission". Note that, under s. 22(3), documents purporting to affect unpatented Crown land have no effect under the *Registry Act*. In fact, until the land is patented, the land registrar cannot assign a PIN to it and cannot create an index for it.

Pursuant to s. 23, the land registrar may refuse to register documents that will not microfilm properly or that do not, in his or her opinion, relate to an interest in land. This latter power creates problems for the registration of debentures with equipment lists and for the registration of use restrictions, for example.

Section 22(7) and (8) — Notices of Leases and Agreements

While s. 22(6) prohibits registration of a document which refers to an unregistered document, subs. (7) specifically allows registration of a notice of lease, amendment of lease, sublease, assignment of lease, *etc.* (see R.R.O. 1990, Reg. 995, Form 10). Subsection (8) allows for registration of a notice of an agreement of purchase and sale or an option to purchase (Form 12). However, pursuant to subs. (9), such a registration expires in one year unless a renewal notice is registered. In addition, please note that when registering an agreement pursuant to subs. (8), a statement of good faith must accompany that registration to assert that the registration of the agreement is not being done for any fraudulent or improper purpose (see Form 15 and s. 23 of R.R.O. 1990, Reg. 995).

You can protect your client's interest in land by registering a notice of agreement or option. Registration of such notices also overcomes the problems faced when the original agreement is not in registrable form. It should be noted, however, that land transfer tax must be paid at the time of registration of such notice, as the definition of "convey" in s. 1(1) of the *Land Transfer Tax Act*,

R.S.O. 1990, c. L.6, includes "agreeing to sell land in Ontario, or the giving of an option". In the case of a notice of an agreement of purchase and sale, tax must be paid on the entire purchase price. In the case of an option, tax need only be paid on the price paid for the option, with tax on the full price being payable only after the exercise of the option and registration of the ensuing transfer.

Section 25 — Legal Description

This section prohibits registration of an instrument unless it contains a short description of the land, or where a registrable description is not already recorded in the abstract index, a full registrable description plus, in those areas of the province where a PIN has been assigned, the property identifier.

As always, there are exceptions to this requirement for description. An obvious one is a plan of subdivision. Certain other documents such as wills, court orders, powers of attorney and corporate letters patent do not have descriptions of land as they are registered in the general register, as discussed above.

Section 25(3)(*d*) is very useful to remember. If you have an instrument, such as an agreement affecting lands that are described only by municipal address, it would not be registrable because it does not contain a description acceptable under the LRRA or the regulations. When, to protect your client's interest, it is essential that such instrument be registered, you may attach a statement by any party to the instrument, or by the solicitor, confirming that the instrument affects lands as described in the declaration and the instrument must then be accepted for registration. (See R.R.O. 1990, Reg. 995, Form 15, for the form of statement.)

For more detail on the requirements under the regulations for descriptions, see Chapter 17.

Section 29 — Affidavit of Subscribing Witness Not Required

As part of the move to streamline the title-search system and cut down on paper storage, most affidavits previously required under the *Registry Act* have been dispensed with. For example, an affidavit of subscribing witness is no longer required for registration purposes. If one is included, the document may be refused registration.

Nevertheless, some mortgagees are requiring affidavits of subscribing witness in order to avoid a potential subsequent denial of execution. These affidavits must be held in your file as they cannot be registered.

Of course as properties continue to be integrated into POLARIS and electronic registration is mandated for more and more registry offices, affidavits will rarely be required as compliance with law statements replace affidavit evidence. Materials that substantiate such statements will be kept in solicitors' files (as discussed in Chapter 17), but they will no longer be registered.

Section 37 — Corporate Seal

While a corporate seal was previously a prerequisite to registration of a document by a corporation, that is no longer the case.

Use of the corporate seal is now optional. If it is not used, the document must state that the signatories have the authority to bind the corporation.

Section 38 — Court Orders

A judgment or court order affecting land may be registered providing a solicitor's statement accompanies the registration confirming that the judgment or order is in full force and effect and has not been stayed and that it affects the land mentioned in it. For foreclosure orders and orders discharging liens, a description of the land and the registration number of the mortgage pursuant to which the foreclosure was instituted or registration number of the lien and certificate of action, respectively, must be included in the body of the order. Note that it is no longer necessary to produce the original court order or judgment when registering a notarial copy of same.

Section 46 — Power of Attorney

If an instrument is signed by someone under a power of attorney, the instrument must indicate the date of registration and the registration number of the original power of attorney so that it can be checked by any subsequent searcher. If the original power of attorney cannot be produced for registration, you must apply to the court for authorization to register the instrument without evidence of registration.

Documents executed using a power of attorney require a statement to be included to the effect that the authorizing power of attorney was in force and effect and not revoked and, additionally, that the attorney's principal was at least 18 years old (R.R.O. 1990, Reg. 995, s. 30).

Insofar as electronic registration is concerned, special procedures have been implemented to regulate transactions that rely on powers of attorney as the basis of the authority to effect the transaction. Those procedures have been enacted in an attempt to avoid fraudulent transactions, which sometimes use forged powers of attorney to perpetrate a fraud. Please see the discussion on these procedural requirements in Chapter 2.

Section 47 — Affidavits of Age and Spousal Status

Affidavits of age and spousal status are no longer required or permitted. Instead, in the LRRA forms and electronic formats for registering, the transferors or chargors are required to certify that they are at least 18 years old. A blank space follows for the purpose of including a statement of spousal status and of the status of the property as a matrimonial home (see Chapter 6).

Section 48 — Description of Transferee

An individual must be described by surname, followed by first name in full, and by "another given name, if any, in full". Initials are not permitted. Persons with additional names are permitted to use all of their given names. Prior to passage of the LRRA, the old rules required "at least" one given name in full and it did not matter whether it was the first given name.

The purpose of this amendment was to assist in building a list of owners' names so that writs of execution might, in the future, be filed directly against title, rather than as general liens. For the same reason, the LRRA forms, both paper and electronic, also require the transferee's birth date to be shown.

It should be noted that failure to comply with these requirements does not invalidate registration.

Section 48(2) also prevents registration of a deed in favour of a partnership or a name under which one carries on business without giving the actual name of the partners. A corporation may, of course, take title in its own name.

Sections 49 and 50 — Evidence of Registration

As presently enacted, s. 49 requires a land registrar to consecutively number all instruments and stamp the date and time of registration thereon. Priority of registration is determined by the registration particulars. However, alternate provisions to replace the foregoing, which have yet to be proclaimed into force, are included within s. 49. The future provisions will not require the date or time of registration to be included on an instrument and priorities will be determined solely on the basis of registration numbers.

Section 50 has also been amended to dispense with the document that all real property solicitors treated as tangible evidence of registration, namely the endorsement and delivery by the land registrar of a duplicate copy of the instrument registered. Instead, the land registrar's only obligation is to register the instrument in the appropriate index and cause it to be microfilmed or electronically scanned.

Section 53 — Registration of Wills

A will (including a holograph will) itself may be registered under subs. (1)(*a*) when accompanied by evidence of death and a statement of subscribing witness. The normal practice today is to have the will probated in the appropriate court and then to register a notarial copy of the probate (formally called the certificate of appointment of estate trustee with a will) in the general register in the land registry office in which any land referred to in the will is situate. The certificate is itself the evidence of death as well as proof that the will is the last will and testament of the deceased and not some previously revoked document.

The will (with attendant documentation), letters probate or letters of administration are attached to Form 4, Document General, for registration.

The practice of registering the will itself rather than having it probated was more common in the earlier part of the twentieth century, probably because of the expense involved in obtaining probate and because land was then much less valuable. Recently, the practice has somewhat revived because of significant increases in the estate administration tax. The law is clear that the power of the estate trustee (formerly called the executor) derives from the will and not from its probate. There have been cases that have raised doubts as to whether the registration of a will alone would support the conveyance of a marketable title. However, the ability to rely on a registered will without probate as the basis for conveyance of a good title was confirmed by Zalev J. in *Prinsen v. Balkwill*, [1991] O.J. No. 3645, 2 O.R. (3d) 281 (Gen. Div.). One should be aware of the restrictions on registration of a will in Land Titles (see Chapter 2).

Until April 10, 1979, the Ontario government claimed a lien under the *Succession Duty Act*, R.S.O. 1970, c. 449, against lands standing in the name of a deceased person for any duty that was payable. When an executor filed the necessary tax returns and paid tax, if any, the Minister of Revenue issued a certificate that could be registered against the land saying no lien is claimed. Under subs. (3)(c), if such certificate was not issued, or if consent to registration was not endorsed right on an instrument, "any land so conveyed does not vest in the person beneficially entitled thereto or his assigns or any person claiming under him". Because succession duty is no longer payable in Ontario, subs. (8) states that subss. (3) to (7) do not apply where the deceased person died prior to January 1, 1970, or after April 10, 1979.

Section 55 — Requirement for Recital of Registration of Probate

An instrument dealing with the land of a deceased person cannot be registered unless it refers to the date and number of registration of the letters probate, letters of administration or will under which the persons executing the instrument purport to act.

Section 56 — Discharge of Charge

When producing a discharge of charge/mortgage in Form 3 (R.R.O. 1990, Reg. 688) for registration under the *Registry Act*, you are no longer required to produce the duplicate original charge/mortgage and any assignment thereof or include a statement that "the duplicate original charge/mortgage cannot be produced".

Note that s. 56(7) requires that where the land described in the mortgage has been subdivided by the registration of a plan of subdivision, the discharge must also contain a description of the land as it is presently described, *i.e.*, giving the numbers of the lots and the plan affected. Without the additional information, the land registrar will have no way of locating the registration of the charge in the abstract book for each of the lots so affected. With lands in the POLARIS system, the PIN for each lot is required in the discharge.

The discharge must list the registration number of the charge/mortgage and any assignment, as well as that of "any other instrument relating exclusively to the mortgage" (subs. (8)). This requirement permits the registrar to delete, not only the mortgage itself when discharged, but also all related documents (for example, an assignment of rents, extension agreements). To accommodate properties that have been converted to the Parcelized Day Forward Registry, subs. (8)(b) authorizes the land registrar to make an entry in the automated abstract index that the mortgage and related instruments are deleted. Pursuant to subs. (11), such an entry is effective to free the land described from any claim under the mortgage and other instruments discharged.

Subsection (11) states that a mortgage (and related documents) no longer affects land where the abstract index shows that a discharge has been registered for more than 10 years but the mortgage has not been deleted from the index. This provision was intended to provide a transition from the time when mortgages were not deleted upon registration of a discharge. Without it, a title searcher would have to inspect the discharge as well as the original mortgage to confirm that it was properly discharged.

The discharge of notices of lodgement of title documents, which were historically registered pursuant to the provisions of s. 30, now repealed, can now be registered in the same manner that a discharge of mortgage is registered (see s. 58(12) and s. 66).

Section 58 — Mortgage-of-a-Mortgage

Neither a mortgage-of-a-mortgage nor a discharge of a mortgage-of-a-mortgage may be registered without a judge's fiat. If one wishes to charge or pledge a mortgage as security for the repayment of moneys advanced, it must be done by way of an assignment of mortgage containing a provision for reassignment to the assignor upon payment of the moneys due. Then, when the moneys are repaid, the mortgage is reassigned to the original mortgagee. A discharge of a mortgage-of-a-mortgage does not operate as a discharge of the original mortgage either with or without a judge's fiat. Except for the specific cases set out in s. 58(3), there must always be a reassignment of the mortgage to the original mortgagee, and then a discharge of the mortgage.

Section 63 — Statutory Reconveyance

The registration of a discharge of charge formerly acted as a reconveyance to the mortgagor of the original estate in the lands described in the mortgage. As a charge is no longer considered a "conveyance" under the LRRA, there is no longer any statutory reconveyance on the registration of a discharge.

Section 64 — Deeds to Uses

A wife's right to dower is now a dated concept, but the history behind this device to avoid dower rights may still be relevant.

Deeds to uses were used for two centuries to avoid a wife's right to dower in her husband's land, but there was always some doubt as to whether a grantee to uses could exercise the power of appointment a second time after using it to give a mortgage on his land. Also, until this section was enacted, the benefit of the deed to uses could be lost if a husband gave a mortgage and, before he exercised his power of appointment, a discharge of that mortgage in statutory form was registered. Such discharge had the effect of vesting in the mortgagor the legal estate free from the uses. It was, therefore, subject to dower. See *Re Hazell*, [1925] O.J. No. 49, [1925] 3 D.L.R. 661 (C.A.).

Following that decision, many conveyancers in Ontario employed a "long uses clause" in deeds establishing title to uses. The clause was an attempt to circumvent the *Hazell* decision, and it usually stated that the granting of a mortgage would not "exhaust" the use and the power of appointment could still be validly exercised, notwithstanding the registration of a discharge of mortgage in statutory form. Despite the use of this clause, doubt still persisted. Section 59, which came into force on January 1, 1967, put an end to the confusion arising out of *Hazell* with regard to deeds registered after that date.

Subsection (2) states that "a mortgage made by a grantee to uses does not exhaust the grantee's power of appointment", and subs. (3) states that, notwithstanding the registration of a discharge of a mortgage, whether made by the grantee to uses or made prior to taking title, "the grantee to uses may exercise the power of appointment as though the mortgage had not been made".

A deed to uses in no way affects a spouse's rights under family law legislation; the device is therefore no longer used. Even though a man holds title to uses, his spouse's consent to the transaction is required on the face of Forms 1 and 2 and on the electronic counterpart to such forms. Also, as lands in the Registry system are converted and transferred into the Land Titles system, exceptions as to title contained in s. 44 of the *Land Titles Act* relating to dower rights are specifically excluded.

Section 67 — Deletion of Certain Instruments

Pursuant to s. 67, where instruments purporting to validly discharge certain registrations (including a certificate of pending litigation, a claim for a construction or mechanic's lien, a conditional sales contract, an oil or gas lease, a registered notice of security interest, *etc.*) have been registered for at least two years, the land described in the discharging instrument is not affected by any claim under the original instrument and the land registrar may delete it from the abstract index. This can be a useful provision in simplifying a cluttered title that still has references to registered interests and corresponding discharges for them. The ability exists in subs. (5) to request that the land registrar delete an instrument on the basis of a registered discharge prior to the expiry of the two-year period.

Sections 70 to 77 — Effect of Registration

Sections 70 and 74 form the basis of the whole Registry system:

70(1) After the grant from the Crown of land, and letters patent issued therefor, every instrument affecting the land or any part thereof shall be adjudged fraudulent and void against any subsequent purchaser or mortgagee for valuable consideration without actual notice, unless the instrument is registered before the registration of the instrument under which the subsequent purchaser or mortgagee claims.

(2) This section does not extend to a lease for a term not exceeding seven years where the actual possession goes along with the lease, but it does extend to every lease for a longer term than seven years.

74(1) The registration of an instrument under this or any former Act constitutes notice of the instrument to all persons claiming any interest in the land, subsequent to such registration, despite any defect in the proof for registration, but nevertheless it is the duty of a land registrar not to register any instrument except on such proof as is required by this Act.

If an instrument is not registered, it is void against a subsequent purchaser for valuable consideration without actual notice. That means that if a person owns some land and gives another a mortgage that the second person does not register, and the first person sells the land to a third party who has not heard of the second person's mortgage, then the second person's mortgage no longer has any effect on the land. The third party may ignore it. However, if the second person had registered the mortgage, then, by s. 74, the third party would be subject to the mortgage even if he or she had not bothered to search title. Registration constitutes notice to all persons claiming an interest in the land. Nevertheless, the second person must have registered the mortgage before the third party registers the deed. It will be no use if the second party comes along two or three weeks later to register the mortgage because, by then, the third party will have registered the deed. Note, however, the important case of *Babcock v. Archibald*, [1981] O.J. No. 3102, 34 O.R. (2d) 65 (H.C.J.), which held that a person who buys land knowing of another's (unregistered) claim to it, but is informed and reasonably believes that the claim is invalid, does not have "actual notice" of the other's interest.

To take another example, consider first, second and third mortgages. They are first, second or third simply because of the order in which they are registered. Assume a mortgagor borrows $100,000 on the security of his or her house and gives the mortgagee a mortgage that is supposed to be a first mortgage, but the mortgagee holds on to the instrument without registering it. Then suppose the mortgagor borrows a further $50,000 and gives another mortgage that this mortgagee registers immediately. In that case, the second lender has a first mortgage and the first lender has a second. If the first lender does not hurry and register the instrument, the mortgagor may arrange a further mortgage or sell the lands and the first lender's mortgage would have no effect against the *bona fide* purchaser for value without notice. See *King v. McMillan*, [1982] O.J. No. 669, 137 D.L.R. (3d) 368 (H.C.J.) and *Comay Planning Consultants Ltd. v. Starkman*, [1986] O.J. No. 1121, 57 O.R. (2d) 223 (H.C.J.).

There is one situation where priority of registration will not prevail. If A is to buy land from B and is to give back to B a mortgage for part of the purchase price, a mortgage from A to C executed and registered before A is actually the registered owner will not have priority over the purchase money mortgage to B, even though it was registered first. This can easily happen if a purchaser is borrowing money to finance a purchase in addition to giving back to a vendor a mortgage for part of the purchase price. Although it is common practice for mortgagees to register their mortgage before advancing funds, it would be most unwise to register a mortgage from a purchaser of land before the deed is registered. If, at the time of registration of the deed, a mortgage back to the vendor is also registered, the subsequent mortgage would have priority over the earlier registered mortgage, provided of course that the vendor/mortgagee had no actual notice of the earlier registered mortgage. For a further discussion of this problem, see the Court of Appeal decision in *Durbin v. Monserat Investments Ltd.*, [1978] O.J. No. 3414, 20 O.R. (2d) 181.

Note that any lease for a term exceeding seven years that is not registered on title or notice of which is not registered on title "shall be adjudged fraudulent and void against any subsequent purchaser or mortgagee for valuable consideration without actual notice" (s. 70). However, subss. 74(4) and (5) must be borne in mind when registering notice of a lease or an agreement of purchase and sale under subss. 22(7) and (8). Registration constitutes notice only of those particulars contained in the notice, and registration of an agreement of purchase and sale shall not constitute notice after the expiry date of such notice pursuant to s. 22(8) (one year unless renewed).

Section 78 — Plans of Subdivision

This section and those following deal with the registration of plans of subdivision generally. Note that by subs. (3), the endorsing of a mortgagee's consent on a plan of subdivision discharges from the mortgage all land shown on the plan as a street or highway, and that, by subs. (5), the plan shall not be registered by the land registrar until all mortgagees' consents have been endorsed thereon, although a plan which does not dedicate any land as a public highway does not require the mortgagee's consent (subs. (6)).

Subsection (9) prohibits the registration of any further plans of subdivision under the Registry system in areas where the Land Titles system is available. This is another means by which the two land registry systems are being consolidated.

Section 80 — Reference Plans

This section has greatly simplified the searching of titles. It prohibits the registration of a deed or mortgage if the land described therein is anything less than the entire parcel owned by the grantor or mortgagor, unless:

1. the land is the whole of a lot or block on a registered plan of subdivision, or

2. the land is the whole of a "Part" according to a reference plan.

Because of this section, there are fewer cumbersome metes and bounds descriptions, since every time land is subdivided in any way, a reference plan illustrating the parcel as a "Part" must first be obtained and deposited in the land registry office.

There is provision under subs. (2) for the land registrar to exempt a specific transaction "having regard to the circumstances". Sometimes the land registrar will accept an instrument for registration if the party tendering the instrument undertakes to produce and deposit the required reference plan within a specified period of time. (See *Holmes v. Graham*, [1978] O.J. No. 3538, 21 O.R. (2d) 289 (C.A.).) In other cases, an instrument will be accepted for registration with a stamped notation that it will not be accepted for any future dealings with the land.

Section 81 — Vague Descriptions

Even where an instrument deals with the entire parcel of land owned by the grantor or mortgagor, the land registrar may require the deposit of a reference plan if the description of the land is complex or vague. However, there is provision for the acceptance of a sketch drawn to scale if the land registrar is satisfied that it would be unreasonable to require a reference plan.

Sections 100, 101.1 and 102 — Orders and Regulations

It is worth noting the addition of s. 100, s. 101.1 and the amendment of s. 102. The *Registry Act* creates three levels of directives that can be issued to introduce and specify procedures and to add requirements that must be observed. First, the Director of Titles has the right to make orders in respect of matters governed by certain sections of the Act. Second, the Minister of Consumer and Business Services may make orders as to other matters (see s. 101.1). Finally, the Minister may make regulations prescribing and designating various requirements. Solicitors must be mindful of all three levels of directive, especially the Director's and Minister's orders, which are not as widely accessible as they are not updated or reported in the same manner or to the same extent as are statutes and regulations.

Sections 105 to 110 — Deposits

Under these sections, one may deposit any "document", defined in s. 105, in the land registry office. The document itself need not contain a registrable description of the land. It may be a letter giving evidence of some fact relating to title; often, it is a statutory declaration. The document is attached to a requisition setting out the name of the party, the particulars of the document, and a description of the land it affects that complies with the requirements of s. 25(2). The requisition and document are then attached to a completed Form 4, Document General (R.R.O. 1990, Reg. 688), and filed.

Note that by s. 106(2), deposit of a document is not deemed registration. Therefore, you do not get the benefit of s. 74, whereby registration constitutes notice. As a practical matter, however, the document will come to the attention of any competent title searcher.

Sections 111 to 115 — Investigation of Titles

Sections 111 to 115 were incorporated into the *Registry Act* on January 1, 1967. Prior to that date, they formed *The Investigation of Titles Act*, R.S.O. 1950, c. 186, which was repealed (S.O. 1964, c. 48). These sections and their predecessors form the basis of the "40-year rule".

The *Registry Amendment Act, 1981*, S.O. 1981, c. 17, which came into effect on August 1, 1981, made important amendments to these sections. The entire Part III of the *Registry Act* was repealed and a new Part III substituted (by s. 4) with the stated intention by the Ministry "that it is not necessary to search title for more than a forty-year period", except in cases specified in the amendment. It was also intended to clarify "that a claim will only affect land for forty years".

This amendment was intended to put an end to the practice of searching back beyond the 40-year period to find an unsupported root of title. Prior to this amendment, many conveyancers would not accept as a root an executor's deed or a deed that purported to be given under power of sale contained in a mortgage. They would insist on going beyond that instrument to find a root that stood by itself, although the Court of Appeal in *Algoma Ore Properties Ltd. v. Smith*, [1953] O.J. No. 678, [1953] O.R. 634, at 642, stated that:

> The purchaser is entitled to rely on the form of the instruments registered and is not bound to inquire into their substance and if the instrument on which he relies as the root of title ... is on its face sufficient to convey the fee, ... he is entitled to rely upon it.

Note that the term "root of title" does not appear in s. 112. The term "title search period" is defined as the 40 years immediately preceding the day of dealing with the land. Section 112(1) states:

> A person dealing with land shall not be required to show that the person is lawfully entitled to the land as owner thereof through a good and sufficient chain of title during a period greater than the forty years immediately preceding the day of such dealing, except in respect of a claim referred to in subsection 113(5).

The exceptions in s. 113(5) include claims by the Crown reserved by the original Crown Patent, or by the Crown in lands forfeited to the Crown by cancellation of letters patent, or by the Crown or a municipality in a public highway or lane, or under s. 113(5)(*a*)(iv) of a person to an unregistered right of way, easement or other right that the person is openly enjoying and using. They also include any claim arising under any Act (see Chapter 4 for statutory liens) and the claim of any railway company to its right of way, where such right of way was acquired after July 1, 1930.

Section 112(2) states:

> Where there has been no conveyance, other than a mortgage, of the freehold estate registered within the title search period, the chain of title commences with the conveyance of the freehold estate, other than a mortgage, most recently registered before the commencement of the title search period.

Thus, in the case where nothing has been registered within the 40 years immediately preceding the closing of the current transaction, the "root of title" is the conveyance most recently registered before the commencement of the 40 years.

Section 112(3) states:

> A chain of title does not depend upon and is not affected by any instrument registered before the commencement of the title search period except,
>
> (*a*)   an instrument that, under subsection (2), commences the chain of title;
>
> (*b*)   an instrument in respect to a claim for which a valid and subsisting notice of claim was registered during the title search period; and
>
> (*c*)   an instrument in relation to any claim referred to in subsection 113(5).

Solicitors in Ontario have resisted following the language of s. 112, and previous editions of this book recommended that a title search commence with the first deed prior to the 40-year period even where there are transfers registered within the 40-year period. However, two decisions of the Court of Appeal have concluded that this is not necessary.

Grange J.A., speaking for the Court of Appeal in *Ontario Hydro v. Tkach*, [1992] O.J. No. 2001, 10 O.R. (3d) 257, at 262, commented on the portions of the Act relevant to this appeal:

> As I read the Act now, it is clear that there is no need to go beyond the 40-year period unless there has been no conveyance within the 40-year period [pursuant to s. 112(2)]. Then, and then only, an earlier root of title must be found; otherwise the title searcher and the solicitor certifying title can safely rely on the instruments within the 40-year period.

More recently, the Court of Appeal in *Fire v. Longtin*, [1994] O.J. No. 542, 17 O.R. (3d) 418, validated title to lands based on a chain of title that commenced with a grant in 1975 from a grantor who did not have any title to convey; nothing else had been registered on that title within the 40-year period. McKinlay J.A., at 427 O.R., stated:

> It is my view that when Part III of the Act was passed in 1981 one of its specific purposes was to clear up title problems of this sort, and support titles on which successive grantees may have relied. As commented by Grange J.A. in the *Tkach* case, the application of Part III may result from time to time in apparent injustices to persons with claims to real property which are older than 40 years. However, the legislature has weighed that possibility against the expectations of persons more recently dealing with the land. In the final result it has opted for legislation which, although it may appear to favour more recent grantees, still contains many safeguards of the rights of those claiming under more ancient conveyances.

The Supreme Court of Canada confirmed this result in dismissing the appeal: see [1995] S.C.J. No. 83, [1995] 4 S.C.R. 3. It is now clear that searches need only be for the last 40 years.

Apart from establishing a title search period of 40 years pursuant to which practitioners could confirm the validity of title to real property as discussed above, ss. 111 to 115 also provide for an expiry period of 40 years insofar as claims affecting title are concerned. A "claim" is broadly defined in s. 111 as any "right, title, interest, claim or demand" such as mortgages, liens, easements, *etc.* The Court of Appeal in *1387881 Ontario Inc. v. Ramsay*, [2005] O.J. No. 2727, 77 O.R. (3d) 666; supplementary reasons, [2005] O.J. No. 3850 (C.A.); leave to appeal refused (see [2005] S.C.C.A. No. 482, 41 R.P.R. (4th) 208) describes the relationship between the title search period and the expiry of claims period as follows (at 673 O.R.):

> The expiry period, also called the registration or notice period, is the period of time after which affected claims expire. While the expiry period runs forward in time for 40 years from the date of registration of a claim, the title search period runs backward in time from the date of dealing for 40 years. While the expiry period invalidates claims not renewed within its period, the title search period

deems irrelevant any claims registered before its period. Thus, the expiry period and the title search period, while different, complement each other.

In other words, the *Registry Act* created a regime, insofar as claims were concerned, that limited the currency of a claim to 40 years from its date of registration and required the claim holder to renew a claim before its expiry. Notwithstanding the seemingly strict 40-year limit on the currency of a claim and the requirement to "refresh" it by registering a notice of claim before the 40 years expire, ambiguities contained within ss. 111 to 115 as they relate to claims have prompted many lawyers to accept the validity of a claim that was more than 40 years old and not "refreshed" by a notice of claim as long as details of the claims were otherwise subsequently noted on title, usually in subsequent conveyances. The most common example that illustrates the reasoning behind this approach is with easements. It was often the case that once an easement was registered, a subsequent transfer of the lands that were subject to the easement would specifically refer to the title being qualified by that easement and give the registration particulars thereof. The recital of the easement particulars in the subsequent transfer was viewed as being akin to filing a notice of claim and resetting the 40-year expiry date applicable to that easement.

The validity of this approach was the exact issue under consideration in *Ramsay* and it was held by the Court of Appeal to be correct, largely based on the broadness of the definition of claim in s. 111. The fact that the particulars relating to the original registration of a claim were recited in a subsequent transfer represented a "true acknowledgement" of the claim and allowed the 40-year expiry period for that claim to run therefrom.

The government of the Province of Ontario passed the *Ministry of Government Services Consumer Protection and Service Modernization Act, 2006*, S.O. 2006, c. 34 to remove the ambiguities contained in ss. 111 to 115 of the *Registry Act*, on which the Court in *Ramsay* was relying, in order to make the operation of the expiry period more clear. This Act amends the *Registry Act* to provide that only a notice in the form prescribed by the *Registry Act* and its regulations will constitute a "notice of claim". As a result, the expiry period for a claim starts either with the registration of the original instrument that first created the claim, or with the registration of a prescribed notice of claim. Recitals of the particulars of a claim in a subsequent transfer are no longer effective to start the expiry period anew. In addition, s. 113(2) of the *Registry Act* provides that a claim does not expire once the 40-year period lapses unless there is the registration of a transfer to a purchaser made in good faith for valuable consideration. While this added clarification is helpful, the message these amendments send to real estate practitioners is that notices of claim in the prescribed form must be used to keep claims such as easements in force and that such notices should be registered within the 40-year expiry period.

As noted earlier, it should be recognized that there are exceptions to the 40-year expiry period rule contained within the *Registry Act*, even as amended. One is found in s. 114, which was added to the Act by the enactment of the *Easement Statute Law Amendment Act, 1990*. This section retroactively preserved municipal public utility easements and easements in favour of the Ministry of Government Services ("MGS") until December 3, 1999 even though rights that were created by such easements may have expired after July 31, 1981. In other words, public utility easements of municipalities and easements of the MGS that existed on July 31, 1981 continued until December 31, 1999 notwithstanding that they were not protected by the filing of a notice of claim pursuant to s. 113(2) prior to the *Easement Statute Law Amendment Act, 1990* coming into force. After the 1999 deadline however, this grace period expired and s. 113 applied.

Notwithstanding the provisions of s. 114, one should also remember that municipalities and other persons can still claim valid easement rights that are not registered by application of s. 113(5)(*a*)(iv), which provides that the provisions of the *Registry Act* relating to investigations of title does not apply to a claim to an unregistered right of way or easement that a person is openly enjoying and using. The case of *Grittani v. Marcilio*, [1992] O.J. No. 1151 (Gen. Div.) demonstrates the application of this section. In this case, the court held that a right of way, last mentioned on title to a property by reference in a deed registered in 1949, had expired as no notice had been filed to renew it pursuant to s. 113(2). However, that result did not affect the rights of the person who had the benefit of the right of way to advance a claim under s. 113(5)(*a*)(iv). If a person could demonstrate that a right was openly enjoyed or used, the failure of that person to renew a registration in such circumstances would not affect the rights of that person afforded by s. 113(5)(*a*)(iv) as that section does not require the registration of such rights on title to a property to make the rights effective.

Finally, note s. 194(3) of the *Municipal Act*, R.S.O 1990, c. M.45 (now s. 91(3) of the *Municipal Act, 2001*, S.O. 2001, c. 25), which provides that Part III of the *Registry Act* does not apply to a claim of a person relating to any municipal public utility constructed on land before June 21, 1990 (being the date this section was added to the *Municipal Act*) with the consent or acquiescence of the owner of the land. The 40-year search rule, therefore, does not apply to claims relating to such rights prior to June 21, 1990, provided the consent of the owner was obtained or the owner otherwise acquiesced.

CERTIFICATION OF TITLES ACT, R.S.O. 1990, c. C.6

This Act, first passed in 1958, was a step by the legislature toward ending the tedious procedure of searching titles for 40 years. An owner of land could voluntarily apply to the Director of Titles to have the title to any land in Ontario under the registry system investigated and certified. Section 78(10) of the *Registry Act* required that, in those areas of the province that the Lieutenant Governor in Council has designated as "certification areas", it is compulsory to have the title to land included in any new plan of subdivision investigated and certified. No new plan of subdivision can be accepted for registration in those areas until title has been so certified. By R.R.O. 1990, Reg. 993, originally O. Reg. 825/81, which came into force on January 1, 1982, the whole of the Province of Ontario was designated as a certification area.

Upon registration of a Certificate of Title under this Act, the Certificate is conclusive evidence as of the time stated in the certificate (not the time of registration) that the person named therein as owner has absolute title to the lands described in the certificate, subject only to the exceptions and encumbrances shown in the schedules attached to the certificate (see s. 14). A new root of title is thus created and there is no need to search behind it. This certificate is not updated as in the Land Titles system; from the date of the certificate to the present date, you make your title search in the usual way in the land registry office, thus avoiding a long search prior to the date of the certificate.

Pursuant to the *Good Government Act, 2009*, S.O. 2009, c. 33 (see s. 2(1) of Schedule 17 thereof) this statute has been repealed. All applications for title certification can only be made under the *Land Titles Act* as either an application for first registration, or an application for an absolute title. However, this statute made complementary amendments to the *Registry Act* (see s. 71.1) to confirm the validity of Certificates of Title in existence prior to December 15, 2009 (the date this recent statute received Royal Assent). Section 116.1 of the *Registry Act* confirms the continued access to The Land Titles Assurance Fund should a person incur a loss as a result of an error in a Certificate of Title.

CHAPTER 2

The Land Titles System

LAND TITLES ACT, R.S.O. 1990, c. L.5

Land Titles is the second of the two systems of title registration in Ontario. In most of northern Ontario, it is the only system available. In some counties of southern Ontario, it has not yet been introduced. However, the areas in which the system is available are being constantly expanded. Many of the land registry offices in which the Land Titles system is in force are now combined offices for both the Registry system and the Land Titles system.

In those areas to which the *Land Titles Act* does apply, registered owners of lands under the Registry system may apply to put their land into the Land Titles system. This is referred to as an "application for first registration". If owners propose to register a plan of subdivision or to develop a condominium, they must first have the land brought into the Land Titles system (see s. 144 of the *Land Titles Act* and s. 78(11) of the *Registry Act*, R.S.O. 1990, c. R.20). In addition, as part of the increased implementation of the Province of Ontario Land Registration and Information System (POLARIS), Teranet is converting lands whose titles are in the Registry system to the Land Titles system as qualified titles ("LTCQ") as described in Chapter 1. For these reasons, the land covered by the Land Titles system is constantly expanding. And while expanding, the Act and the regulations are constantly being amended with the stated purpose of evolving a merger of the Registry system and the Land Titles system and fully implementing POLARIS and electronic registration. (See, for example, the discussion of the POLARIS conversion and the *Land Registration Reform Act*, R.S.O. 1990, c. L.4 ("LRRA"), in Chapter 1.)

The Ministry of Government Services issues bulletins from time to time for the guidance of land registrars and the public. These bulletins usually indicate any change of practice in the land registry offices. Copies of all such bulletins may be accessed from the Province of Ontario's website at <www.ontario.ca>.

The basis of the system is that the *Land Titles Act* establishes title to land by declaring under a guarantee of indemnity that it is vested in a named person. If, by error, someone is deprived of an interest in land by reason of the land being brought into this system, a claim may be made against the Land Titles Assurance Fund for the amount of the loss (see Part V of the Act).

In theory, under this system, a person wishing to search the title to lands registered under the *Land Titles Act* goes to the local land registry office and requests the examination of the register for the parcel of land or, if the lands have been assigned a Property Identification Number ("PIN"), accesses the Teraview database and retrieves the automated register for the lands. The interested searcher then examines the register for that parcel and the register alone shows who the registered owner is and what encumbrances are outstanding. The searcher need not examine the transfer to that person to see if it is valid, nor is it necessary to trace the chain of title back to be sure there are no missing links as in the Registry system. Unfortunately, there are many exceptions to the Land Titles certificate (less so with LTCQ titles, as discussed later) so that, in practice, one must do almost as many searches under this system as under the Registry system.

The entries in the Land Titles register are binding when signed by the land registrar or, in the case of lands that have been included in POLARIS, when the land registrar has certified the entry of the registration as complete by noting a "C" opposite the instrument on the parcel register. The accuracy of the entries is guaranteed by the Assurance Fund.

If the owner of property located in an area to which the *Land Titles Act* applies decides to register a parcel of land under the Land Titles system, the owner makes application to the land registrar. The applicant must provide a solicitor's abstract of title containing a full 40-year search of the title to that parcel of land together with the certificate of title in Form 5. The owner must also provide tax certificates and execution certificates to satisfy the land registrar as to the validity of the title. The land registrar notifies adjoining landowners of the application so that they have an opportunity to oppose the application if they feel the applicant is attempting to encroach upon their lands. If all the evidence of the applicant's title produced is satisfactory, the land registrar will create a new parcel register for this new parcel of land and assign it a PIN. The first entry is the certificate that the applicant is the owner with an absolute title subject only to the encumbrances that are listed and to the exceptions and qualifications in the Act (see s. 44). When that owner subsequently sells, mortgages or deals with the land in any way, the instrument effecting such sale or mortgage in prescribed form is taken or submitted electronically to the land registry office for that Land Titles division for registration. The forms, records and procedures on first registration are set out in ss. 2-12.1 of R.R.O. 1990, Reg. 690, as amended by O. Reg. 25/99.

Under the Registry system any document can be registered as long as it is in the prescribed form and the land is properly described. You could even register a deed from John Doe to yourself of your neighbour's land. It would not have much legal effect, but it could be registered and it certainly would create a cloud on your neighbour's title. Under the Land Titles system however, only a very limited number of types of documents may be registered. They must follow strictly the forms prescribed by the Act. They will not be accepted for registration unless properly executed by the person shown on the register or electronically submitted on behalf of that person as the owner. The document is very carefully examined and when finally accepted, a new entry is made on the register and certified by the land registrar setting out what change has occurred in the state of the title by reason of the registration of that document. This new entry has the effect of cancelling, varying or modifying the previous entries. Thus the state of the title to a parcel is always immediately apparent from a glance at the register.

As mentioned in Chapter 1, the *Land Titles Act* must be read together with the LRRA to fully understand the statutory requirements governing this system of land registration. This is especially important for lands in the Land Titles system as, at present, it is only lands in this system to which Part III of the LRRA (dealing with the electronic registration of documents) applies.

The *Land Titles Act* is even longer than the *Registry Act*. The following are a few of the sections that a practitioner deals with from day to day.

RELEVANT SECTIONS OF THE LAND TITLES ACT

Section 3 — Areas Affected by the Act

The Act no longer lists those parts of the province in which the Land Titles system is available; the areas are now designated by regulation (see O. Reg. 428/99).

All land in northern Ontario, except for the very few parcels of land in that area patented prior to 1875, is under the Land Titles system. Thus, the Act applies to every provincial judicial district. In southern Ontario, the Land Titles system is available but not compulsory in some counties and regional municipalities. In the remainder of southern Ontario, the Land Titles system will not be available until it is extended to those areas by regulation.

Section 23 — Inhibiting Orders

This section entitles a land registrar to attach a "no further dealing" indicator on a parcel to prevent any person from registering any instrument in respect of that parcel until a dispute or irregularity is resolved. Any person who has an interest in the parcel may give notice to the Director of Titles or land registrar alleging an error, omission or irregularity and, if the allegation merits investigation, it may prompt an entry to be made on the parcel register inhibiting further dealing until the matter is resolved. An application for such an entry must be in Form 44 and accompanied by the affidavit required as in Form 34 (see R.R.O. 690, as amended by O. Reg. 25/99).

Section 36 — Possessory Title

This section sets out one reason why someone would voluntarily expend the time and cost of putting land into the Land Titles system:

(2) Subject to the approval of the Director of Titles, an applicant for first registration whose claim to ownership is based upon length of possession of the land may be registered as the owner in fee simple with an absolute title of the land.

Even if a clear chain of title for 40 years cannot be established by a search in the land registry office, but uninterrupted possession for upward of 10 years can be established, the Director of Titles has the discretion to accept and certify the title. Although a possessory title is a good title in the Registry system that can be forced on an unwilling purchaser, it is difficult to establish and is always open to question, particularly if new evidence comes to light. However, after certification by the Director of Titles under this section, the title is put beyond question and no one need go behind this certificate to worry over any prior deficiencies.

Section 38 — Leasehold Land

This section provides for a separate register of leasehold lands. In applying for the creation of such a parcel, it must be demonstrated that at least 21 years remain in the term of the lease at the time of the application. Examples of leasehold parcels will be found in titles to certain large office buildings in downtown Toronto. The owner of the parcel of land on which the project is to be constructed has the title registered in the normal freehold register. The owner then grants to the developer of the building a "ground lease", *e.g.*, for 99 years, and the developer may then apply under this section for a separate leasehold title. The interest of the lessee in the land will then appear in the leasehold register.

This means the owner of the leasehold title obtains the title guarantee afforded by the Act that is not otherwise available to a lessee. In addition, both the freehold and leasehold titles are simplified by having recorded against them only those interests that directly affect each; for example, the leasehold title will not show a charge of the freehold and vice versa. This will help avoid confusion and reduce the cost to each owner of transactions involving their respective titles.

Section 41 — Procedure on First Registration

Pursuant to s. 30(1), any person may apply to be registered under the *Land Titles Act* as an owner of land; under this section are found the requirements for such first registration. Note that the rules set out under this section grant discretion to the land registrar. Rule 3 is a good example of this:

> If the land registrar, upon the examination of any title, is of the opinion that it is open to objection but is nevertheless a title *under which the holding will not be disturbed*, the land registrar may approve of it ... [emphasis added].

Often in searching a Registry system title, you will find some defect or cloud on the title that you can say with some assurance will not interfere in any way with an owner's possession or holding of the land, for example, an old restriction imposed by a defunct company or a minor discrepancy in description. This is known as a "good holding title". But you must advise your clients that when they come to sell the land they will probably be faced with a requisition to remove the defect or cloud. This is the sort of problem that the land registrar may accept and certify the title without recording any exception. (See *Ennisclare on the Lake Ltd. v. Preston Glen Corp.*, [1982] O.J. No. 3497, 39 O.R. (2d) 154 (Co. Ct.).) For this reason, almost all land assemblies of urban lands go into the Land Titles system. Future dealings with the project, either through sale or financing, will not be delayed by niggling title problems that would have continued except for the land registrar's certificate of title. Nevertheless, sufficient opportunity must be given to persons wanting to object to any first registration and the land registrar must hear and determine the legitimacy of any objections and, in contentious cases, refer the objection to the Divisional Court.

Section 42 — Notice to Adjoining Landowners

A notice of an application for first registration must be served upon each owner and mortgagee or assignee of lands adjoining the parcel for which application for first registration has been made. This notice is served by registered mail, addressed to the address shown on the registered transfer or charge or, if no address is shown, to the solicitor's address as shown. This gives the neighbouring landowners and mortgagees an opportunity to oppose the application for first registration if, for any reason, the new application appears to encroach upon their lands.

Section 44 — Liabilities, Rights and Interests Outstanding

This section contains a list of 13 liabilities, rights and interests to which land registered under the Land Titles system remains subject. It is a formidable list and should always be kept in mind when giving an opinion as to title to land registered under the Land Titles system. Remember that on every Land Titles parcel dealing with an absolute title the following words appear:

The title of the said owner is subject to:

1.   The exceptions and qualifications in the Land Titles Act.

The following is a review of some of these exceptions as contained in s. 44.

Paragraph 1 makes all land in Land Titles subject to provincial taxes and succession duties and municipal taxes. (See Chapter 4 for the tax lien provisions.) You must, of course, obtain a tax certificate from the local municipality.

Paragraph 3 makes title subject to encroachments and possessory rights that an owner in any adjoining land has acquired before the lands were brought into the Land Titles system. However, pursuant to s. 44(3), this exception to absolute title does not apply if adjoining owners were served with notice of the application for first registration and no objection was filed by them within the prescribed time limits.

Note that paragraph 4 makes title subject to unregistered leases for terms less than three years where there is actual occupation. Thus, if you are acting for a client who has a lease of lands registered under the Land Titles system for a term longer than three years, notice of that lease must be registered to protect your client's interest.

Paragraph 6 makes title subject to any construction lien where the time within which it must be registered has not expired.

Paragraph 7 makes title subject to rights of the Crown by authority of any statute. Remember that s. 244 of the *Business Corporations Act*, R.S.O. 1990, c. B.16 states that all land owned by a corporation when it ceases to exist escheats to the Crown. Therefore, it is essential that you confirm the status of every corporation in the chain of title. For Ontario corporations, this investigation need include only corporate owners in the last 20 years (even prior to first registration) to ensure that each corporation was in existence when it conveyed the land (see p. 167).

Paragraph 11 makes all land in Land Titles subject to the provisions of ss. 50 and 50.1 of the *Planning Act*, R.S.O. 1990, c. P.13. This exception creates a serious flaw in the Land Titles system. Chapter 5 discusses these sections of the *Planning Act* in detail. For now, just remember that s. 50 prohibits the conveying, transferring, mortgaging or charging of any parcel of land (other than a whole lot on a registered plan) where the grantor or mortgagor retains the fee or the equity of redemption in land abutting the land that is being conveyed or mortgaged (s. 50(3)(*b*)) without the consent of the local committee of adjustment or land division committee. The penalty for ignoring this section is severe: s. 50(21) states that if the section is not complied with, the deed or mortgage "does not create or convey any interest in land". In other words, it is void.

Thus, you have the land registrar's certificate stating that John Jones is the owner in fee simple with an absolute title; yet, if the person conveying to Jones retained the fee or equity of redemption in land abutting Jones' parcel and did not obtain the consent of the local committee of adjustment or land division committee to the conveyance, then that conveyance is a nullity. The land registrar's certificate is meaningless because it is subject to the exceptions contained in s. 44 of the *Land Titles Act*. To emphasize this problem, consider s. 71 of the *Planning Act*, which states that "[i]n the event of conflict between the provisions of this and any other general or special Act, the provisions of this Act prevail".

When dealing with lands other than a whole lot on a registered plan of subdivision you must ensure that the provisions of the *Planning Act* have been complied with. To do so, you must search the abutting lands to make sure that the transferor in any transfer did not retain abutting lands, and this not just for the most recent transfer but possibly all transfers back through the chain to June 15, 1967 (see p. 136). This could be a very time consuming search since under the Land Titles system, unlike the Registry system, it has often been difficult to ascertain the parcel numbers of adjoining lands. The advance of POLARIS implementation and the mapping of all lands affected does alleviate some of this difficulty, though. Even the previous requirement (now repealed by the *Land Registration Reform Act*) that all transferors and chargors or their solicitors swear an affidavit that the transferor or chargor did not retain the fee or the equity of redemption in any lands abutting is no assurance that the transfer or charge is not a nullity. There was nothing to prevent a person swearing such an affidavit from making a mistake or even committing perjury. The land registrar made no investigations of adjacent lands. If the affidavit proves to be incorrect it in no way validates the void transfer.

The LRRA introduced an optional scheme whereby specific statements may be made by the grantor, the grantor's solicitor and the solicitor for the grantee in Blocks 13 and 14 of a transfer/deed. Where these statements are made, any contravention of s. 50, or its predecessors, does not prevent the conveyance of any interest in the land (subs. (22)). Where the statements are included in a transfer/deed the need for searching the prior conveyances is alleviated.

The exception contained within s. 44(1)13 relating to the *Rental Housing Protection Act*, R.S.O. 1990, c. R.24, has been repealed as a result of the repeal of that statute.

It once was possible to apply to have title registered free of those interests listed in the first few paragraphs of s. 44(1), but this right was repealed by s. 3 of *The Land Titles Amendment Act, 1980*, S.O. 1980, c. 49.

Section 45 — *Effect of First Registration*

First registration of a person as owner of land which is referred to in the *Land Titles Act* as "an absolute title" vests in that person an estate in fee simple, free from all interests except those set out in s. 44 and any encumbrances entered on the register.

Section 49 is a similar provision dealing with registration of a person as first registered owner of leasehold land.

Section 46 — *Qualified Title*

As mentioned in Chapter 1 and earlier in this chapter, in fully implementing the POLARIS system, Teranet is in the process of transferring most properties in the province from the Registry system to the Land Titles system pursuant to s. 32 of the *Land Titles Act*. The owner of the land does not initiate this transfer; indeed the owner is not even notified. The Teranet staff make such searches as they deem advisable and, if satisfied, will transfer the property to Land Titles with a qualified title, which has become known as an "LTCQ" (Land Titles Conversion Qualified) title. One of the standard qualifications is that the staff searchers have not satisfied themselves as to inconsistencies in the description of the property and adjoining properties and as a result, an LTCQ title is subject to "the rights of a person who would, but for the *Land Titles Act*, be entitled to the land or any part of it through length of adverse possession, prescription, misdescription or boundaries settled by convention". Accordingly, the solicitor acting for anyone interested in the property must make investigations to cover this qualification and ensure there are no issues as a result thereof. In addition, an LTCQ title also is qualified as to any rights that arise in respect of "any lease to which subs. 70(2) of the *Registry Act* applies", which qualification was necessary in order to reconcile the differences in the length of a term of a lease that each of the *Registry Act* and *Land Titles Act* provide before registration is required (seven years versus three years, respectively).

In other respects, the qualified title created under this section may be superior to the absolute title referred to in s. 45. The Ministry of Government Services has determined that, because of the searches it does in connection with the transfer, it will mark the title register as not being subject to the following exceptions that would otherwise apply pursuant to s. 44:

1. dower and spousal rights;
2. contraventions of s. 50 of the *Planning Act* prior to the implementation date of the parcel from the Registry system to the Land Titles system;
3. provincial succession duties; and

4.   escheats to the Crown following dissolution of a corporate registered owner.

Note, however, that the exclusion of these qualifications is effective only up to the date of registration under the Land Titles system. In other words, the exceptions will apply in circumstances arising afterwards. Therefore, appropriate searches in subsequent transactions must be performed back to the date of first registration in the Land Titles system.

Please also note the provision found in s. 119.1 of the *Land Titles Act* relating to dower, which allows any person entitled to such an estate to apply to the land registrar to register notice of such estate if the applicant has satisfied the land registrar as to the legitimacy of the claim.

If the staff searchers find material title problems in their search of a property, the practice has been not to convert that parcel to LTCQ but to leave it in the Registry system. If staff searchers find title problems that do not preclude the property's conversion, they will convert the property but note the problems on the parcel register as qualifications. Bulletin 2008-05 issued by the Ministry sets out recommended procedures to be followed to have such qualifications deleted. Once a property is converted, title is guaranteed and anyone whose claim against the property has been missed by the staff searchers will be protected by the Assurance Fund.

The provisions of s. 46(2) of the *Land Titles Act* permit the registered owner of land with an LTCQ title to apply to the land registrar to be registered as an owner of land with an absolute title. An owner may want to upgrade its title if the owner intends to register a plan of subdivision or a condominium. Lands included in such plans must have an absolute rather than LTCQ title. Owners may also want to convert their title to resolve boundary disputes or adverse possession claims.

Title to a property that is upgraded from LTCQ pursuant to s. 46(2) is known as "LT Plus". An LT Plus title will have different title qualifications from both LTCQ and absolute title parcels. The first difference is that the LTCQ qualifications relating to adverse possession would be removed as the process by which title is upgraded requires adjoining landowners to be served and affords such parties with a period to raise objections. Another difference relative to absolute title parcels is that the benefit of the exceptions to the qualifications contained in s. 44(1) relating to dower, succession duties, the *Planning Act* and escheats originally found on the LTCQ parcel are carried forward into the LT Plus parcel. As a result, conversion to an LT Plus title can indeed be considered an upgrade as the resulting title is superior to both an absolute and LTCQ title as there are fewer qualifications affecting it and a corresponding greater guarantee afforded by the Act.

The Ministry of Government Services has published a Client Guide dated August 2001, which details the procedures that must be followed in converting an LTCQ title to LT Plus. It can be obtained from registry offices or from the Real Property Registration Branch of the Ministry.

Section 51 — No Title by Adverse Possession

This is an important difference from the Registry system. There can be no title by adverse possession acquired after land is registered in the Land Titles system. Under common law, you may acquire possessory title to lands simply by moving in and occupying them for a period of 10 years without using force, without acknowledging anyone else's claim to the land, and without hearing of any objection by the legal owner to your possession. However, once land is registered under Land Titles this cannot happen. Similarly, under common law, you can establish a right of way just by walking across your neighbour's lot for 20 years without any interruption. But in Land Titles there is no way you can establish a right of way except by obtaining a grant of easement from the registered owner and registering it on title.

Section 62 — No Notice of Trusts

The *Land Titles Act* refuses to recognize the existence of trusts. If an owner of land registered in Land Titles is described as a trustee, this does not impose on any person the duty of making an inquiry as to the power of the person so described to deal with the land in any way. The owner may deal with the land as if there had been no mention of a trust.

The decision of the Ontario Court (General Division) in *Randvest Inc. v. 741298 Ontario Ltd.*, [1996] O.J. No. 3182, 30 O.R. (3d) 473 confirmed the intent of the *Land Titles Act* in s. 62 not to recognize trusts. In this case, the solicitors for a purchaser had searched title and noted that the land transfer tax affidavit appended to the last transfer indicated that the registered owner held title to the property in trust for a third party. As a result, the solicitors for the purchaser submitted a title requisition requesting a transfer of the apparent beneficial owner's interest in the property. The vendor's solicitors replied that good title could be conveyed regardless of the trust. In deciding that the requisition of the purchaser had been satisfactorily answered, the court confirmed that s. 62 allowed all parties interested in a property to ignore all references to a trust, regardless of where the references appeared.

Section 67 — Name

The description of a registered owner follows the same rules as set forth in s. 48 of the *Registry Act* — surname first, followed by first given name in full and any other given name, in full. No other person, other than a corporation, may be shown as the registered owner in any other manner.

Section 69 — Vesting Orders

The *Land Titles Act* recognizes that registered title or an interest therein may be ordered to be changed by virtue of a court decree. Pursuant to s. 100 of the *Courts of Justice Act*, R.S.O. 1990, c. C.43, a court may vest in any person an interest in real property that the court has the authority to order be dealt with. Vesting orders are quite common in bankruptcy and insolvency proceedings. Section 69 of the *Land Titles Act* provides that once a vesting order is issued, the current registered owner remains the owner until the vesting order is registered, or until the existing owner transfers the property to the person entitled to the land by the vesting order.

The decision of the Ontario Court of Appeal in *HSBC Bank of Canada v. Deloitte & Touche Inc.*, [2004] O.J. No. 2744, 71 O.R. (3d) 355 considered the character of vesting orders as court orders which effect a conveyance of lands. The court acknowledged that a vesting order was like any other order in that once issued, it could be subject to an appeal. However, given that a vesting order also served as a conveyancing instrument, the registration of a vesting order was final and could not be reversed unless another order was issued prior to the vesting order's registration which stayed the vesting order. The filing of a notice of appeal did not stay the order and the registration of a vesting order in the face of an appeal had no affect on the validity of a conveyance resulting from its registration.

Section 70 — Powers of Attorney

The use of powers of attorney is also consistent with the requirements that exist in the *Registry Act*. Pursuant to the provisions of s. 70, the provisions of R.R.O. 1990, Reg. 690 (as amended by O. Reg. 25/99) and the provisions of O. Reg. 26/99, an instrument purporting to be signed under power of attorney will not be registered unless the actual power of attorney, or a notarial or certified copy thereof, is first registered and a statement is included in the instrument that: (a) the person who granted the power of attorney was at least 18 years old and had the capacity to grant the power of attorney; and (b) the power of attorney is in full force and effect at the time of registration.

Note the additional requirements contained in ss. 4(i), 4(i.1) and 39.1 of O. Reg. 19/99 under the LRRA when registering a power of attorney electronically. These requirements are further discussed at the end of this chapter in the context of the *Ministry of Government Services Consumer Protection and Service Modernization Act, 2006*, S.O. 2006, c. 34.

Section 71 — Registration of Notices of Unregistered Interests

Apart from recognizing the rights that any person may have in land as an owner or mortgagee, the Act provides a mechanism by which persons with more varied interests in land, whose interests have been created outside of the registration system, may register a notice of such rights on title. Unregistered rights are created by agreements of purchase and sale, general assignments of rents, cost-sharing agreements, easement agreements and many other different and often complex agreements.

It is often necessary to register notice of the rights created in such agreements on title to protect the rights. Pursuant to s. 71(2) where such a notice is registered, every owner and every person to whom that owner conveys an interest in the land (other than persons who already have a prior registered interest against title) are deemed to be affected with notice of the unregistered interest. As a result, parties who subsequently acquire an interest in the same lands acquire that interest subject to the rights of any person who has registered a prior notice in respect of its unregistered interest.

As s. 71 was drafted in a broad manner to allow parties with varied interests to apply for registration of all of their interests, procedures have been implemented to assist registry office staff in ensuring that registrations are not made in respect of matters or rights that do not affect an interest in land. Bulletin No. 96001 dated July 10, 1996 was issued by the Ministry of Consumer and Commercial Relations to set out those procedures. Bulletin 2002-2 was subsequently issued to clarify that registration of non-disturbance agreements is permitted pursuant to s. 71.

Any registration under s. 71 must be submitted using either Form 16 contained in R.R.O. 1990, Reg. 690 or the alternate Form 16 that is appended as appendix "A" to this Bulletin. If the prescribed form is used then, except in the limited cases described in the Bulletin, the pre-approval of the Director of Titles will be necessary before the document is accepted for registration. If the form attached to the Bulletin is used, that pre-approval process will not normally be required. The main difference in the two forms is that the new form requires an application for registration under s. 71 to be made by the solicitor for the applicant who must state that the notice relates to an interest in land. A time period after which the notice will expire must also be specified and the application must contain an instruction that authorizes the land registrar to delete the notice automatically after the time period expires. While an "indeterminate" time period may be specified, that choice will make the requirements for releasing that interest from title in the future much more onerous. The format of the "new" form forces an applicant to make statements and agree to the future removal of the document from title in an attempt to address past problems with s. 71 registrations — ensuring that they really deal with interests in land and that they can easily be removed from title in the future.

Section 71(1.1) of the *Land Titles Act* deals with the registration of a caution to protect an interest created by an agreement of purchase and sale (this replaces s. 134, which has been repealed). Bulletin 2000-2 dated July 21, 2000 was issued to detail procedural requirements for the registration of such a caution. Form 16 is again used. Note that the date of closing set out in the purchase agreement must be specified. In addition, authorization must be given to the land registrar to delete the caution 60 days after such closing date. This caution cannot be renewed; however, if the closing date is extended, another caution may be registered based on the new date. It should also be noted that the registration of a caution under s. 71(1.1) will not prohibit dealings with the parcel.

The requirements of the Electronic Registration regulation under the LRRA (O. Reg. 19/99) must again be consulted for any registrations under s. 71 or s. 71(1.1) for lands in districts where electronic registration is mandatory. Section 23 of the Regulation deals with s. 71 and its requirements are consistent with the description of the "new" Form 16 referenced above. Section 24 details what information is needed for purchase agreement cautions and for notices of purchase options. It includes the date of the agreement, the date the sale is to be completed or that the option expires, a statement as to any renewal rights and a statement that the applicant will, within 14 days of receiving a request, produce the relevant agreement for inspection by any person, failing which the land registrar is authorized to cancel the registration.

Section 72 — Effect of Unregistered Instruments

No person, other than the parties thereto, is deemed to have any notice of the contents of any instrument if that instrument is not mentioned in the appropriate register, *i.e.*, if it has not been duly registered. However, the courts have held that a person having actual notice of a contrary claim may not simply rely on the register; he or she will be subject to the contrary claim (see *Roboak Developments Ltd. v. Lehndorff Corp.*, [1987] O.J. No. 1108, 47 R.P.R. 275 (Div. Ct.)).

As a particular example of the application of this principle, consider *Gawalko v. Sullivan*, [1990] O.J. No. 658, 38 O.A.C. 318, in which the Ontario Court of Appeal held that a purchaser (Gawalko) of land registered in Land Titles was bound by an unregistered agreement entered into by Gawalko's predecessor providing for an easement across the purchased land. A road had been constructed across the land and Brooke J.A. held that the purchaser had "actual notice of the roadway" and therefore, by implication, the unregistered agreement.

Subsections (2) and (3) should be noted: you are on notice of any instrument registered in the "highways register" and the "Trans-Canada Pipe Line register" even if the instrument is not recorded on the parcel.

Section 75 — Amending the Register

This section of the Act facilitates the registration of documents that evidence changes in fact that must be reflected on the parcel register. For example, any change in the name of an owner, whether the owner is an individual or corporation, requires an application under s. 75 accompanied by supporting documentation. For an individual, the evidence could be a marriage certificate. For a corporation, the evidence could be articles of amendment or amalgamation.

Similarly, applications are made pursuant to this section to register court orders that effect changes to the identity of a person who is the registered owner of an interest in land. An example of such an order would be a foreclosure judgment granted to a mortgagee. Other types of court orders that are commonly registered include orders to cause or effect discharges of a registered charge, support orders enforceable under the *Family Law Act* and vesting orders.

Pursuant to O. Reg. 26/99, applications under s. 75 must be consistent with Form 18 and be accompanied by documentary evidence supporting the change requested, and where the evidence is a court order or judgment, an original, certified or notarial copy of the order or judgment must be presented together with an affidavit of a solicitor deposing that the order is in full force and effect and has not been stayed and that the order affects the land referred to in the application.

Sections 30 and 31 of O. Reg. 19/99 under the LRRA specify the requirements for electronic registration of the same documents. For changes to the parcel as a result of court orders, either the order itself or the particulars of the date and court file numbers of the order must be included. If one chooses to register the actual order, or a certified or notarial copy thereof, it will be necessary to first "index" the order in order to complete the necessary field on the electronic document.

Indexing is used in the electronic registration system in order to provide evidence to the land registry office and pre-approve the eventual registration to be made on the basis of that evidence. Indexing requires that the paper evidence be physically brought to the applicable registry office in advance of the actual registration of the instrument. If accepted, the land registry office will assign an index number to it, which number will be referenced in the actual registration to be electronically made. The document that is filed in this index is not available remotely; it is microfilmed and retained at the land registry office.

Finally, compliance with law statements will have to be made depending on the nature of the registration. For example, the affidavit one would file in the non-electronic system that a court order is in full force and effect is replaced with a statement to that effect in the electronic system.

Section 78 — Time of Registration

Section 78(5) outlines the basis upon which priorities are to be determined among registered instruments and specifies that priority is determined according to the order in which the instruments are registered and not according to the order in which they were created. It is therefore important to register an instrument that affects an interest in land as soon as possible to avoid priority being lost to other interests that get registered sooner.

As also discussed in the context of s. 72, the courts have held that s. 78(5) applies only to registered interests in land and does not negate the applicability of the principle of actual notice with respect to unregistered interests (*United Trust Co. v. Dominion Stores Ltd.*, [1976] S.C.J. No. 99, [1977] 2 S.C.R. 915). In other words, where a purchaser becomes the registered owner of land and takes title with actual notice of a pre-existing unregistered interest in that same property, the purchaser takes title subject to that unregistered interest and cannot rely on s. 78(5) to argue that he or she has priority as s. 78(5) can only be used to establish priority between registered instruments (see the discussion of the law on this section in *DeGasperis Muzzo Corp. v. 951685 Ontario Inc.*, [2000] O.J. No. 3218, 35 R.P.R. (3d) 243 (S.C.J.) affirmed [2001] O.J. No. 2583, 42 R.P.R. (3d) 63 (C.A.)).

The *DeGasperis* case cited above is very interesting and revealing in its demonstration of the operation of the actual notice and registered notice principles as applied to establish priority of claims under s. 78. In this case, a mortgagee registered its mortgage on title having actual notice of a long-term lease that was not registered. Given its actual notice, the lender's mortgage was acknowledged as being subsequent in priority to the lease. Thereafter, in order to protect its priority in the lease against persons who might subsequently acquire an interest in the lands without actual notice of its lease, the tenant registered a notice of lease on title. In considering the priorities between the tenant and the mortgagee, which had been considered settled due to the mortgagee's actual notice of the lease, the Court of Appeal ruled that by operation of s. 78(5), registered interests rank according to the order in which they are registered. As a result, the tenant, by virtue of registering its lease, could no longer assert priority over the mortgagee on the basis of actual notice.

Note that registration of an instrument is complete only when the entry in the proper register is certified by the land registrar. You may have tendered an instrument for registration and completed a transaction based upon its receipt by the clerk at the counter in the land registry office or by its electronic transmission via Teraview; however, until the instrument and its execution have been checked and entered in the register and the entry certified, the instrument is not in fact registered and has no effect under the *Land Titles Act*.

In the western provinces of Canada, where systems similar to our Land Titles system are in use, closings take place in escrow until the instruments are actually registered. Here, despite the risks created by s. 78, current practice is to complete purchases and mortgage advances just as one would do under the Registry system and not await the certification of the instrument. This approach is taken in spite of the provisions in s. 78(2), which allows the land registrar to decline the registration of a document within 21 days after it was received where the land registrar decides that the document contains an error, omission or deficiency. Before the document is declined, however, a period of time not exceeding 30 days must be given to the party that registered the document to remedy the problem.

As mentioned in connection with the discussion relating to the *Registry Act* in Chapter 1, alternate provisions that have yet to be proclaimed are included in s. 78, which will replace the date and time stamping of instruments that are registered with registration numbers alone, which registration numbers shall be determinative of the priority among registered documents.

Finally, the right of the land registrar to refuse the registration of a document because it is illegible, not microfilmable or contains material that does not affect or relate to an interest in land appears in the *Land Titles Act* (s. 81) to the same degree as in the *Registry Act*.

Sections 86 to 91 — Transfers

Transfers of freehold or leasehold parcels are governed by the above provisions in the *Land Titles Act*. These provisions must be read together with the LRRA, which sets out requirements for the registration of transfers in both an electronic and non-electronic format. Section 5 of the LRRA lists covenants that are implied in every transfer of land, whether the transfer is electronic or non-electronic.

For registrations of transfers where electronic registration is not yet mandatory, Form 1 prescribed by R.R.O. 1990, Reg. 688 is used and must be completed in accordance with the regulations contained within the LRRA.

Transfers under the electronic registration system must be completed in accordance with the requirements in s. 4 and s. 5 of the Electronic Registration regulations (O. Reg. 19/99). When accessing a transfer form on Teraview, a user must identify the type of transfer required (*i.e.*, general transfer, transfer by executor, transfer under power of sale, *etc.*) after which Teraview will present fields to be completed and offer choices to assist in the completion of the form. As with Form 1, statements as to spousal status, *Planning Act* compliance, corporate authority and as to capacity to transfer the lands must be made, as applicable. Finally, once the transfer is completed, an electronic land transfer tax affidavit is provided by Teraview to complete the process.

Section 92 — Transfers to Uses

This section, which has the same effect as s. 64 of the *Registry Act*, is similarly now irrelevant in view of the abolition of dower under the *Family Law Reform Act*, R.S.O. 1980, c. 152. The section provides that a transfer to uses may be registered. An appointment by way of a charge by an owner to uses does not exhaust the owner's power of appointment and notwithstanding the registration of a cessation of charge, the owner to uses may exercise this power of appointment again as if the charge had not been made.

Sections 93 and 101 to 104 — Charges

These sections deal with the form, registration, transfer and cessation of charges or mortgages. It also provides (in s. 93(5)) for the registration of trust deeds as a charge upon lands and subs. (8) provides for discharge of a trust deed by registration of a standard form of cessation.

Section 93(2) requires that a charge that secures the payment of money must state the principal amount that it secures. Previously, this section also required the rate of interest, maturity date and payment periods to be included, but those additional requirements have been repealed. Sections 94 to 98 of the Act (which had dealt with covenants to be implied in all charges) have also been repealed as they became unnecessary as the applicability of the LRRA was extended to all lands in Ontario.

Section 93(4) creates a security upon the lands against which a charge is registered to the extent of the money actually advanced under it but in no event exceeding its stated principal amount. This security interest binds the owner of the lands and all persons subsequently obtaining an interest in the same lands even if the money is not advanced by the chargee at the time the charge is registered. In other words, a chargee who is granted a charge on lands for a stated principal amount is given priority for that amount even if the chargee advances the moneys under that charge after another charge is registered.

The registration of a charge against lands that are within the boundaries of a registry office where electronic registration has not yet been mandated occurs by the completion and execution of Form 2 prescribed by R.R.O. 1990, Reg. 688, pursuant to the LRRA.

Charges to be registered against land where electronic registration is compulsory must comply with ss. 4 and 6 of the Electronic Registration regulations under the LRRA. The charge must contain and information must be provided as to: (a) the principal amount of the charge; (b) the rate of interest and periods of payment; (c) the maturity date; (d) the interest or estate charged (freehold or leasehold); (e) any applicable standard charge terms reference; (f) a statement that the chargor charges the land; (g) statements as to age of majority and spousal status, if applicable; and (h) a statement that the chargor acknowledges receipt of a copy of the charge.

When accessing a charge form on Teraview, the user will be asked to choose between a freehold and leasehold charge. Trust deeds, debentures and crystallized floating charges are all considered freehold charges by Teraview. The system will then present fields to be completed and will automatically complete other fields by accessing information from the parcel to which the PIN relates. Options are also presented to the user that allow the user to customize the charge where, for example, a certain undivided interest rather than all of the lands are being charged, or where it is necessary to delete or modify the implied covenants deemed to be included in a charge.

Section 101 of the *Land Titles Act* permits the registration of an assignment or transfer of a charge. Upon registration of a transfer of a charge, the transferee becomes the owner of the charge; however, s. 101(7) acknowledges situations where a charge is transferred to another person as security and in such circumstances, the Act permits a provision to be inserted into the transfer of charge requiring the charge to be transferred back to the transferor upon satisfaction of the obligations owed to the transferee. Regulations governing the electronic and non-electronic forms and procedures to be used for registration of a transfer of charge are found in the *Land Titles Act* and LRRA.

Finally, please note s. 104 of the *Land Titles Act*, which provides for a mechanism by which the land registrar may delete/cancel an entry on the register relating to an old construction lien or mechanics lien where the land registrar is satisfied that the lien is no longer effective. This provision is useful in removing liens from title that have not been preserved and perfected.

Section 99 — Power of Sale

This section allows for the registration of a transfer under a power of sale contained within a charge. In order to effect such a transfer, a chargee must register evidence specified by the Director of Titles concerning the conduct of the sale and related matters.

Bulletin 98007, dated December 18, 1998, issued by the Real Property Registration Branch of the Ministry of Consumer and Commercial Relations, had specified the evidence needed to satisfy s. 99(1). That Bulletin has since been revoked and replaced by Bulletin 2003-1, which, like its predecessor, gives two alternatives as to the evidence required. Bulletin 2003-1 emphasizes that Land Registry Offices can accept evidence in accordance with the first or the second alternative, but not a combination of both. The second alternative is more in keeping with the intent of electronic registration in doing away with paper evidence and replacing it with compliance of law statements.

The first alternative is to attach statutory declarations as specified to the transfer, including declarations of personal knowledge, of notice and service and that the power of sale was exercised in accordance with specified legislation. The second alternative is to use specified statements in the transfer, including that the sale is authorized under the charge and the *Mortgages Act*, that notice of the sale was given when the charge was in default and that the sale proceedings and transfer comply with specified legislation. Additional statements are specified if writs of execution have been filed. If there are no registered encumbrances subsequent to the charge, a statement must be made to that effect. If there are subsequent encumbrances that are to be deleted, this must be specified in a statement. Finally, a statement of spousal status is required.

If a chargee satisfies either of the alternative evidentiary requirements specified by the Director of Titles then, pursuant to s. 99(1.1), that evidence is conclusive proof of compliance with Part II and Part III of the *Mortgages Act*, as applicable, and registration of a transfer under s. 99 is sufficient to give good title to a purchaser. The registration of that transfer also entitles the land registrar (pursuant to s. 99(2)) to delete the entry of any instrument from the parcel appearing to rank subsequent to the charge under which the land is sold. There are, of course, exceptions to the authority given to the land registrar to delete entries of certain instruments once a transfer under power of sale is registered (for example, in the case of construction liens) where additional evidence will be required before the land registrar will be satisfied that the interest or instrument can be deleted.

Section 111 — Leases

This section of the *Land Titles Act* allows for the registration of notices pertaining to leases against a freehold parcel. It is to be compared to s. 38, which allows for the creation of a separate leasehold parcel where the term of a lease is at least 21 years. Generally speaking, s. 38 leasehold parcels are usually created in ground lease situations where land is leased on a long-term basis and the tenant will be developing the lands and needing to charge its leasehold interest and eventually granting subleases once improvements are constructed. In these cases, a separate leasehold parcel simplifies the land registration process by allowing all registrations that only affect that leasehold interest to be registered in one place without cluttering the title to the landlord's freehold interest, which is shown on another parcel.

Where the remaining term of a lease is less than 21 years or the need for a leasehold parcel is not warranted (which is the case for most leases), s. 111 permits the registration of a notice of lease against a freehold parcel. Once a notice of lease has been registered, a party may then register the following notices, as applicable, that relate to that lease registration: a sublease, an amendment of the lease, an assignment of the lease, a charge of the lease, an assignment of the lessor's interest in the lease or a determination of the lease (s. 111(6)).

The reason for registering a notice of lease or of an interest in a lease on title is usually to give notice of that interest to third parties and to protect one's priority in that leasehold interest against others. In the review of s. 44, earlier in this chapter, it was noted that the *Land Titles Act* only protected the interest of a tenant in respect of a lease where the term then remaining is less than three years. If the term of a lease is three years or more, registration is required to protect one's interest.

The registration of the actual lease (or a "short form" of lease) is no longer required. Section 111(4) only requires a notice to be registered listing certain details. In fact, in this case, the *Land Titles Act* has been amended to accord with the practice of registering notices of leases in the *Registry Act*. Such a notice need only provide: the identity of the parties, the date of the lease, the term and expiry date of the lease, a reference to any purchase options and renewal rights and a statement that the applicant is prepared to produce the actual lease for inspection to anyone who has an interest in the same lands (see Bulletin 98008 dated December 18, 1998 and Bulletin 2003-2). The requirements for completing a Document General for registration, in a non-electronic format, of a notice of an interest in a lease are found in Forms 31 and 32 of R.R.O. 1990, Reg. 690.

Electronic registration of a notice of an interest in a lease must comply with the Electronic Registration regulations under the LRRA (see s. 25). The requirements are similar to those for the registration of the same notice in the non-electronic format. The fields to be completed and questions that Teraview requires to be completed will, as usual, be customized based on the particular interest in a lease with which the user is concerned. There is, however, an interesting difference in the statement respecting production of the lease. In the electronic registration system, the statement that must be included is that the actual lease will be produced within 14 days of a request by a party who has an interest in the lands and that the applicant consents to the cancellation of the document on proof being presented to the land registrar that the lease was not produced upon such a request. Given the "built-in" sanction provided for in the e-reg system, the obligation to produce leases upon request must be strictly observed, by clients and their solicitors.

Finally, regardless of whether a notice pursuant to s. 111 is being made in an electronic or non-electronic format, a land transfer tax affidavit must be completed and submitted with the registration. A statement must be included in that affidavit confirming whether the term of the lease, including renewal and extension options, can or cannot exceed 50 years. If the term can exceed 50 years, land transfer tax is exigible.

Sections 113 to 116 — Certificates of Ownership

At one time land registrars were authorized to issue a Certificate of Ownership to the first registered owner or any transferee, and to issue a Certificate of Ownership of Charge to the owner of any charge. Both were impressive documents containing the land registrar's certificate of title with a large red seal, which some clients liked to have. Some mortgagees insisted. However, they were not essential; they told you only what appeared in the register and you were reporting that to your client anyway.

By s. 32 of *The Land Titles Amendment Act, 1979*, S.O. 1979, c. 93, the sections in the Act dealing with the issuance of such certificates were repealed.

Sections 118 and 119 — Registration of Restrictions

These sections give authority for the registration of restrictive covenants annexed to land. Section 118 permits an owner to impose restrictions on transferring or charging lands it owns. Upon the registration of these types of restrictions, the land registrar usually attaches a "no further dealings" indicator on the parcel for the affected lands.

Section 119 permits restrictions to be registered that prohibit building upon land, that regulate the way land is or is not to be used or that impose other controls capable of being legally annexed to land. However, note the qualification contained in subs. 119(6), which requires a person who is registering restrictions to be mindful of the common law prerequisites of creating restrictions. This section provides that "the entry on the register of a condition or covenant as running with or annexed to land does not make it run with the land" if the nature or type of the restriction or the manner in which it is expressed would not allow it to be considered as a valid restriction.

Subsections 119(8) and (9) are of interest to solicitors wishing to clear up titles. Subsection (8) gives the land registrar the right to delete from the register an entry relating to a restrictive covenant running for a specific period of time if the period plus 10 years has expired. Subsection (9) gives authority for the deletion of restrictive covenants having no expiry date but which have been registered for more than 40 years. Pursuant to subs. 119(12), subs. (9) does not apply to a covenant or easement under the *Conservation Land Act*, R.S.O. 1990, c. C.28.

Sections 120 to 127 — Death of a Registered Owner

See Chapter 6.

Sections 128 to 133 — Cautions

These sections are important and unique to the Land Titles system. Under the Registry system anyone can register any type of agreement or claim against land; however, under the Land Titles system the only method by which a person, other than the registered owner of land, can register notice of a claim is to proceed under s. 71 (discussed above), or under s. 128:

> (1) A person claiming to have an interest in registered land or in a registered charge of which the person is not the registered owner may apply to the land registrar for the registration of a caution to the effect that no dealing with the land or charge be had on the part of the registered owner or other person named in the caution without the consent of the cautioner.

The language used in subs. 128(1) is very specific. It only permits persons claiming an interest in the land or in a charge to apply for cautions; no other interest in land is recognized. For the sake of clarity, subs. 128(3) explicitly denies a person interested under a lease the right of applying for a caution.

The registration of a caution in a non-electronic format is accomplished using a Document General and by completing the information specified in Form 33 of R.R.O. 1990, Reg. 690. Pursuant to s. 131 of the *Land Titles Act*, every caution must be supported by affidavit material or a statement that establishes the nature of the person's claim and the land purported to be affected. The requirements for that affidavit are set out in Form 34 of Reg. 690.

In the e-reg system, the formalities of s. 36 of O. Reg. 19/99 have been incorporated into Teraview which, as in all other e-reg cases, guides the user through the process of completing the form. The user will be asked to choose from a list of different types of cautions and to insert the PIN for the lands affected. Upon making these selections, the e-reg system will automatically complete certain information and will then organize the fields of information to be completed that are relevant to the particular registration. A statement must be made by the applicant that he or she is entitled to register the caution.

Once registered, a caution is effective for 60 days from the date of its registration and cannot be renewed. During that 60-day period, the land registrar cannot allow any further dealings with the land without the consent of the cautioner; however, the cautioner is obliged to serve a copy of the caution and a notice setting forth the particulars of its registration on the owner and other persons interested in the lands. Pursuant to s. 129(7), the land registrar shall delete the caution from title when the caution ceases to have effect (after 60 days) or when the cautioner withdraws the caution.

The above provisions significantly change the approach taken with respect to cautions in the past. Previously, caution registrations were effective for five years and could be renewed. There was no obligation on the cautioner to serve the owner with notice; instead, once (and if) the owner became aware of the caution, the owner could apply to the land registrar to remove the caution, the land registrar would serve the cautioner with the objection and a hearing would be held among all parties. The new approach of the Act is to place the onus on a cautioner to demonstrate to a court that the claims it has advanced are legitimate and to have a court issue a certificate of pending litigation before the caution expires. As the Ministry of Consumer and Commercial Relations observed in Bulletins 98009 and 2000-2, which list further procedural requirements relating to cautions, land registrars' decisions on cautions under the previous regime were regularly appealed with the effect that lands were left subject to cautions for long periods of time before judicial intervention scrutinized the legitimacy of the claim that led to the registration of the caution. The new approach forces the cautioner to "convert" the caution into a certificate of pending litigation within 60 days or else risk losing the benefit of the registration.

Section 130 does allow a second caution to be registered in respect of the same claim with the permission of the land registrar; however, given the very deliberate changes in these provisions made with a view to forcing cautioners to the court system, it is unlikely that this section will often be used.

Transitionary provisions remain in the Act to deal with cautions registered prior to June 18, 1999, which are governed by the old provisions and are effective for five years, after which they may be deleted by the land registrar without application. In *Bowgray Investments Ltd. v. Fournier*, [1988] O.J. No. 3120, 67 O.R. (2d) 173 (H.C.J.), the court held that where a caution was registered more than five years before, a purchaser may take title without actual or constructive notice of the cautioner's alleged interest. Unfortunately, the Court of Appeal, while upholding the decision ([1991] O.J. No. 3130, 3 O.R. (3d) 384*n*), noted that the purchaser had not pulled the caution to examine it and declined therefore to express any opinion as to whether the caution could provide actual notice of a claim if it had been inspected.

Section 136 — Executions

When dealing with land registered under the Registry system, you must always search for executions filed in the office of the sheriff of the judicial district in which the land is situate against the registered owner and predecessors in title. Such is not the case in the Land Titles system.

When you submit a transfer for registration in the land registry office, it will not be accepted until the land registrar has made a search of the executions filed. Only if the land registrar finds no executions against the transferor will the title of the transferee be entered in the register free of executions. If there is such an execution on file, the land registrar will show on the register that the title of the transferee is subject to that execution. The result is that historical execution searches against predecessors in title are unnecessary; only searches against the present owners are required (see s. 44(6)).

The practice relating to the filing of executions under the Land Titles system has changed though. Previously, sheriffs forwarded writs of execution that affected land to the land registrar in the applicable registry office who had the responsibility of recording and organizing that information for the purposes of searching. Now, subs. 136(1) requires the sheriff to organize such information. Upon receiving the necessary fees and direction from a judgment creditor, the sheriff must enter a writ in the sheriff's electronic database for writs, indicate in the database that the writ affects lands governed by the *Land Titles Act*, assign each writ a number and a date of receipt and finally, give the land registrar for each land titles division that falls within the sheriff's territorial jurisdiction access to the electronic database of writs. No land is bound by a writ of execution until the sheriff has complied with all of these requirements, which are found in subs. 136(1).

Subsections 136(6) and (7) cover issues surrounding the name that appears on a writ in comparison to the name by which an owner chooses to hold title to a property. If a person is known by more than one name, subs. 136(6) provides that the name found on a writ of execution must match the name used by the same person to hold property for the writ to be effective against those lands. If the names differ, the fact that the two names identify the same person is not relevant and no process exists to notify the land registrar of the dual identity in an attempt to have the writ extend to the debtor's lands as had previously been the case under subs. 136(6).

In a situation where the name of the execution debtor shown on a writ is identical to the name shown as the owner on a parcel register but the two are not the same person, such a writ does not bind the land if the land registrar decides that the two names do not represent the same person and the land registrar either issues a certificate to that effect or, in the case of a transfer, allows a transfer to be registered free of the writ (in other words, without noting the writ as outstanding on the parcel register for the property). Bulletin 98003 dated December 14, 1998 clarifies the rules relating to similar names and the applicability or non-applicability of writs in such circumstances. Note in particular the clearance procedures set out in the Bulletin, which allow an affidavit by a registered owner stating that he or she is not the same person as a judgment debtor named in a writ of execution to be acceptable to allow title to be shown free and clear of the writ provided that the judgment debt is less than $50,000. It is also acceptable for the solicitor for the owner to make an unequivocal statement that their client is not the same person as the party identified in the writ, which approach will be accepted for writs that are both above and below the $50,000 threshold.

Sections 140 to 142 — Descriptions

As discussed in Chapter 1 in the context of the *Registry Act*, the above sections of the *Land Titles Act* require that lands be described in a manner consistent with POLARIS. All lands are to be divided into blocks and properties and assigned PINs. Property maps are to be prepared and as new properties are converted into the Land Titles system or existing properties are subdivided, new PINs are to be assigned. Automated parcel registers are to be created and all instruments that affect that register are to be entered thereon. Pursuant to s. 142(2)(*d*), a PIN must be used in describing a property.

Section 150 — Reference Plans

If your client proposes to transfer or charge either a portion of a lot or block on a registered plan of subdivision or a portion of a registered parcel, the instrument will not be accepted for registration unless a plan of survey, certified by an Ontario Land Surveyor, illustrating such portion has been deposited. These plans of survey are known as reference plans. They are numbered in each land registry office in order of their filing, and the number is preceded by the number of that particular land registry office and by the capital letter R. For example, in the Land Registry Office for the Land Titles Division of Toronto, such a plan would be 66R-1234. This designation is used to distinguish a reference plan from a registered plan of subdivision under the Land Titles system where the plan number is preceded by the capital letter M.

Once such a plan has been filed, there is no necessity to describe the land by metes and bounds. The parcel would be described as follows:

> Part of Lot 15, Plan 43M-1234, City of Mississauga, Regional Municipality of Peel, being Part 1, Plan 43R-5678.

Sections 163 to 165 — General

As in the *Registry Act*, the *Land Titles Act* provides for three levels of directives to be issued and practitioners must recognize this and keep themselves informed as to changes implemented in this manner. First, pursuant to subs. 163(1), the Minister of Government Services may make regulations, as has always been the case. Second, pursuant to subs. 163(2), the Director of Titles may make regulations prescribing forms and providing for their use. Third, pursuant to subs. 163.1, the Minister may make orders as to various matters. In 2006, a new directive was added to the *Land Titles Act* permitting the Lieutenant Governor in Council to make regulations governing the publication of information regarding fraud or suspected fraud in the Land Titles system. It is also likely that the bulletin system of delivering guidelines as to the registration process will continue to be used by the Ministry. As a result, practitioners must keep themselves up-to-date with changes that originate from all of these sources of directive. Insofar as electronic registration is concerned, every practitioner should obtain a copy of the *Electronic Registration Procedures Guide* published by the Real Property Registration Branch of the Ministry. Copies can be obtained from Teranet by e-mail at <www.teranet.ca>.

MINISTRY OF GOVERNMENT SERVICES CONSUMER PROTECTION AND SERVICE MODERNIZATION ACT, 2006, S.O. 2006, c. 34 (BILL 152)

This statute received Royal Assent on December 20, 2006 and insofar as real property law is concerned, was the Government of Ontario's statutory response to address issues related to real estate fraud. Bill 152, among other amendments, brought about changes to the LRRA and the *Land Titles Act* to respond to the perceived vulnerability of the Teraview electronic registration system to fraud and to address perceived injustices in then recent Ontario court decisions that left defrauded property owners either without their properties, or with properties that were now encumbered by mortgages that fraudsters had caused to be registered against them.

The changes to the *Land Registration Reform Act* brought about by Bill 152 are aimed at allowing the Director of Land Registration to revoke the rights of a person who is allowed to submit documents for registration electronically where there are reasonable grounds to believe that person is not authorized to register such documents (see s. 23.1). To complement this change, the Ministry has implemented an enhanced clearance protocol for issuing licences to practitioners to allow them to use Teraview; this is detailed in Ministry Bulletins 2009-01 and 2009-02. The intent of the changes is to ensure that all persons who make registrations electronically are identified and approved, have financial resources to compensate victims of fraud and have the appropriate qualifications and integrity to use Teraview.

The changes to the *Land Titles Act* in Bill 152 are focused on amending parts of s. 78 that certain courts had relied on in not fully returning title to defrauded parties in the state that existed before the fraud (see ss. 4.1 and 4.2) and in allowing the Director of Titles to rectify the register to restore ownership to the rightful owner (see s. 57(13)). These changes align the *Land Titles Act* with the decision of the Ontario Court of Appeal in *Lawrence v. Wright*, [2007] O.J. No. 381, 51 R.P.R. (4th) 1, where the Court acknowledged that the *Land Titles Act* should be interpreted in accordance with the doctrine of deferred indefeasibility of title. This doctrine provides that any purchaser or mortgagee who, in good faith, deals with a party who fraudulently holds itself as the registered owner, does not acquire an indefeasible title; the innocent purchaser or mortgagee's title only becomes indefeasible once the property is sold or mortgaged anew, hence the "deferred" nature of its title in the interim. Where, as in *Lawrence*, a fraudster pretends to be the registered owner and proceeds to mortgage the property and run away with the proceeds, the application of the doctrine of deferred indefeasiblity allows the innocent property owner who has been defrauded to have the mortgage deleted from title. This admittedly leaves the mortgagee, who is also an innocent party, with no mortgage. Its recourse will be against the Land Titles Assurance Fund. The obvious message to mortgagees, with the acceptance of the doctrine of deferred indefeasibility by the Ontario courts and the Ontario legislature, is that the undertaking of proper due diligence in assessing the identity and authority of mortgage applicants is vital in protecting mortgagees from fraudulent acts such as those that occurred in the *Lawrence* case.

Bill 152 also amended the provisions of the *Land Titles Act* that address compensation from, and recourse to, the Land Titles Assurance Fund by: (i) simplifying applications to the Fund with a view to rectifying titles and providing compensation quickly in straightforward cases (in fact, the Province's website, which provides information on the Fund, suggests a decision can be reached in three months); (ii) deleting the requirement that a defrauded person must have exhausted his or her remedies against others before applying for compensation from the Fund; (iii) prohibiting title insurers from claiming compensation from the Fund where they make payments to policy holders based on fraud; (iv) preventing mortgage lenders from claiming against the Fund where they have not exercised the "requisite due diligence" (see the Order of the Director of Titles 2007-02, which defines this term); and (v) increasing penalties for fraud-related offences.

One final noteworthy change was brought about by Bill 152 through amendments to regulations to the LRRA and the issuance of policy bulletins by the Director of Titles and Director of Land Registration, all with a view to further combatting fraud. This change relates to powers of attorney. Due to increased use of forged powers of attorney in certain cases to assist fraudsters in having registered title transferred and mortgages registered, O. Reg. 76/08, made under the LRRA, was passed, amending O. Reg. 19/99, being the general electronic registration regulation. Sections 4(*i*) and 4(*i*.1) of the amended regulation, which deal with registration requirements for instruments that rely on powers of attorney, now provide as follows:

> 4. A document submitted for electronic registration, other than a power of attorney or a revocation of a power of attorney, shall contain,
>
> (*i*)   if the document is made by an attorney acting under a power of attorney given by a donor that is not a corporation,
>
> (i)   a statement by the attorney that, to the best of the attorney's knowledge and belief,
>
> (A)   the donor was at least 18 years old and had the legal capacity to give the power when giving it, and
>
> (B)   the power is in full force and effect,
>
> (ii)   a statement by the solicitor submitting the document confirming that the solicitor has reviewed the power with the attorney who has confirmed that,
>
> (A)   the attorney is the lawful party named in the power,
>
> (B)   the attorney is acting within the scope of the authority granted by the power,
>
> (C)   to the best of the attorney's knowledge, information and belief, the power was lawfully given and has not been revoked, and

         (D) if the attorney is a corporation, the person signing the document at the time the document was made was in the stated position at the corporation and had the authority to bind the attorney, and

    (iii) the registration number and date of the power;

(*i*.1) if the document is made by an attorney acting under a power of attorney given by a donor that is a corporation,

    (i) a statement by the attorney that,

        (A) to the best of the attorney's knowledge and belief, the power is in full force and effect,

        (B) the attorney is acting within the scope of the authority granted under the power, and

        (C) the attorney has the authority to bind the donor, and

    (ii) the registration number and the date of the power;

Insofar as the content of the power of attorney itself, s. 39.1 of the amended regulation provides as follows:

39.1(1) A power of attorney submitted for electronic registration shall contain,

(*a*) a statement of the type of the document;

(*b*) statements setting out the effect of the document;

(*c*) the date that the preparation of the document was completed;

(*c*.1) a statement by the party completing the document that the party has the authority to complete the document;

(*d*) the date that the land registrar received the document for registration;

(*e*) the names of the parties to the document;

(*e*.1) a statement by the party who applies to have the document registered electronically specifying whether the party is the donor or the donee of the power;

(*f*) an address for service, including the postal code, for the person claiming or obtaining an interest under the document or for the person's solicitor;

(*g*) the name, address, telephone number and fax transmission number of the person who prepared the document;

(*h*) the name, address, telephone number and fax transmission number of the person who submitted the document;

(*i*) if the document is made by a corporation, a statement by the person acting for the corporation that the person is authorized to bind the corporation;

(*j*) all other information that the Director considers necessary to establish the interest claimed by the parties to the document;

(*k*) a statement whether the power is for a limited purpose or a general purpose; and

(*l*) an image, in electronic format, of the original executed and witnessed power or of a notarial or certified copy of the original.

Following closely after the passing of the revised regulations on powers of attorney, Bulletins 2009-01 and 2009-02 were issued by the Ministry to detail the practical implementation of the regulations and to help practitioners understand what Teraview would require in order for powers of attorney to be registered and for documents that rely on a power of attorney to be registered. One of the most noteworthy changes is the introduction of a power of attorney index for each registry office. Powers of attorney and any partial or total revocation of a power of attorney must be registered in this index. Upon registration, the document is given a registration number; that number is then recited in the document being registered on title, which relies on the authority of the power of attorney. Practitioners must now review any power of attorney by searching the index to retrieve the power of attorney referenced in any document and to ensure a revocation has not subsequently been filed in the index. Searches can be conducted in the index by reference to instrument number, donor name and attorney name.

CHAPTER 3

Other Statutes Affecting Real Estate in Ontario

In addition to the *Registry Act* (R.S.O. 1990, c. R.20), the *Land Titles Act* (R.S.O. 1990, c. L.5), the *Land Registration Reform Act* (R.S.O. 1990, c. L.4) and certain other statutes dealt with in subsequent chapters, there are a number of other statutes dealing exclusively with real estate, and a further group of statutes which affect real estate. The statutes selected in this chapter are listed alphabetically. This list is not intended to be exhaustive. The statutes and the sections discussed have been arbitrarily selected by the authors as those that are most likely to affect your day-to-day practice.

ASSIGNMENTS AND PREFERENCES ACT, R.S.O. 1990, c. A.33

Pursuant to s. 4 of this Act, any transfer of property, whether for consideration or as a gift, made by a person when insolvent or when the person knows that their insolvency is imminent, and where the transfer is made with the intent to defeat creditors is void as against such creditors. Similarly, any transfer given to a specific creditor in such circumstances with the intent to give a creditor an unjust preference over other creditors is also void against such other creditors. A transfer to a creditor that has the effect of giving that creditor a preference over others is presumed to have been made with the intent of giving such creditor an unjust preference whether or not the transfer was made to such creditor voluntarily or under pressure.

Section 4 does not prohibit or restrict any transfer made in good faith in the ordinary course of business to an innocent purchaser or a transaction where the consideration paid has a fair and reasonable "relative value" to the property transferred. However, such a transfer, even when the test of value is met, does not allow a transfer of property to creditors as such a transfer is still considered an unjust preference.

The *Fraudulent Conveyances Act*, R.S.O. 1990, c. F.29 is a complementary statute imposing further restrictions in similar circumstances. Pursuant to s. 2, every conveyance of real property made with the intent to defeat creditors is void unless the property is sold for good consideration and in good faith to a person not having notice or knowledge of the intent to defraud creditors. It is important to note the payment of a realistic consideration is not enough to avoid the sanctions of this Act; there must also be good faith and evidence of a lack of knowledge of the vendor's intent by the purchaser. The Ontario Court of Appeal in *Perry, Farley & Onyschuk v. Outerbridge Management Ltd.*, [2001] O.J. No.

1698, 54 O.R. (3d) 131 (C.A.) held that an action to set aside a fraudulent conveyance under this statute cannot be statute-barred pursuant to the provisions of the *Limitations Act*, R.S.O. 1990, c. L.15, s. 45. The issue of whether actions to set aside fraudulent conveyances are subject to the *Limitations Act, 2002*, S.O. 2002, c. 24, which came into force on January 1, 2004, has not yet been litigated. Section 4 of the new Act sets a basic two-year limitation period, while s. 15 prohibits commencement of proceedings in respect of any claim after the 15th anniversary of the day on which the act or omission on which the claim is based took place.

BANKRUPTCY AND INSOLVENCY ACT, R.S.C. 1985, c. B-3

This is a very complicated and involved statute governing matters of the insolvency and bankruptcy of persons generally. For the purposes of this summary, only certain provisions relating to security enforcement and landlord and tenant rights are explored. Refer to Chapter 20 for a greater review.

Section 244(1) of the Act provides that, prior to enforcing any security against any property of an insolvent person, a secured party must send a prescribed form of notice of that intention to the insolvent person. Pursuant to s. 124 of the *Bankruptcy and Insolvency General Rules*, a notice of intention to enforce security must be in a prescribed form and sent by registered mail or courier or, if agreed to by all parties, by electronic transmission. Form 86 dictates the form to be used, as established by the *Rules*. A secured creditor must wait at least 10 days from the date the notice is sent before enforcing its security, unless the insolvent person consents to earlier enforcement. While the notice need only be sent to an "insolvent person" and not to any debtor, if a secured creditor's loan is in default, it is more likely than not that the debtor is not meeting its liabilities as they become due making that person an "insolvent person" and entitling it to the notice. Once the notice is received, a debtor may, of course, file a notice of intention to file a proposal which allows the debtor a 30-day period during which a stay of proceedings is imposed on all creditors. During that period, no creditors may take any action against a debtor, meaning that, in the case of a mortgagee, no foreclosure action or notice of sale under mortgage may be issued.

Sections 65.1 and 65.2 of the Act deal with the rights and remedies of landlords and tenants upon the insolvency or bankruptcy of tenants. Section 65.1 prevents any creditor, including a landlord, from terminating any agreement, including a lease, where a debtor files either a notice of intention to file a proposal or an actual proposal, or by reason that the tenant has not paid rent prior to filing either the notice of intention or the proposal. Furthermore, a landlord cannot terminate a lease or claim any accelerated rent on the basis that a tenant is insolvent, even if the tenant is in default in the payment of rent. These provisions in the Act override anything contained in a lease to the contrary.

Pursuant to s. 65.2, at any time after a notice to file a proposal is made, an insolvent tenant may disclaim a commercial lease on giving 30 days' notice to a landlord. It had been the case that once such a disclaimer was made, a landlord was entitled to a payment equal to the lesser of six months' rent or the rent remaining for the term of the lease. Now, pursuant to s. 65.2(4), a landlord may file a proof of claim for its actual losses resulting from the disclaimer equal to the lesser of (i) the aggregate of the next year's rent due and 15 per cent of the rent for the remainder of the term; and (ii) the next three years' rent. A landlord may also challenge in court any disclaimer of a lease; however, pursuant to s. 65.2(3), no such challenge can succeed if the court is satisfied that the insolvent person would not be able to make a viable proposal without the disclaimer of the lease.

Once a bankruptcy occurs, a landlord's rights against a tenant are stayed (see s. 69.3). The landlord cannot terminate the lease or exercise a distraint remedy. The landlord is given a preferred claim for arrears of rent for a period of three months of arrears of rent and three months of accelerated rent for the periods before and after the bankruptcy, respectively. The total amount payable cannot exceed the realization from the property under lease, and any payment respecting accelerated rent is to be credited against the amount payable for occupation rent (see s. 136(1)(*f*)). Pursuant to s. 146 of the Act, all other rights of landlords in such circumstances are left to be governed by provincial jurisdiction and accordingly, one must turn to the *Commercial Tenancies Act*, R.S.O. 1990, c. L.7 in Ontario for further details on post-bankruptcy rights of landlords and trustees-in-bankruptcy.

Pursuant to s. 38(2) of the *Commercial Tenancies Act*, a trustee-in-bankruptcy for the tenant may occupy the premises demised by a lease for the three-month period following bankruptcy and then elect to either terminate the lease, retain the lease or assign the lease. If the trustee elects to assign the lease, all rent arrears must be paid in full to the landlord and any assignee of the lease must execute an assumption agreement, agree to conduct a business that is not of a more objectionable or hazardous nature than that of the former, now bankrupt, tenant and be approved by the court as "a person fit and proper" to be allowed into possession. As you can expect, there are many court decisions reported dealing with the application of this test in s. 38(2). The decision in *Sunys Petroleum Inc. (Trustee of) v. 653120 Ontario Ltd.*, [2000] O.J. No. 1105, 130 O.A.C. 365 (C.A.) is an interesting case where the court refused to accept an assignee of a lease as a "fit and proper person".

BEDS OF NAVIGABLE WATERS ACT, R.S.O. 1990, c. B.4

You would do well to keep this Act in mind when giving an opinion on title to a farm or a cottage property which has a frontage on a lake, or across which a stream flows. Unless there is an express grant in the Crown Patent of the bed of a navigable body of water or stream bordering on or passing through a parcel of land, title to the bed of that body of water or stream does not pass with the title to the adjacent land; it remains in the Crown in right of Ontario. Thus, if the body of water is navigable, the boundary of land bordering it is the low water mark; if it is non-navigable, the boundary of the land is the centre of the body of water.

There is no definition in the Act of a navigable water or stream. The question of navigability and the right of the public to use navigable waters has been the subject of many reported court cases in Canada. Perhaps Doherty J. best summarized the test of navigability in *Canoe Ontario v. Reed*, [1990] O.J. No. 1293, 69 O.R. (2d) 494 at 501 (H.C.J.), as follows:

(i)   Navigability in law requires that the waterway be navigable in fact. It must be capable in its natural state of being traversed by large or small craft of some sort.

(ii)   Navigable also means floatable in the sense that the river or stream is used or is capable of use for floating logs or log rafts or booms.

(iii)   A river may be navigable over part of its course and not navigable over other parts.

(iv)   To be navigable, a river need not in fact be used for navigation so long as it is realistically capable of being so used.

(v)   A river is not navigable if it is used only for private purposes or if it is used for purposes which do not require transportation along the river (*e.g.*, fishing).

(vi)   Navigation need not be continuous but may fluctuate with the seasons.

(vii) Where a proprietary interest asserted depends on a Crown grant, navigability is initially to be determined as at the date of the Crown grant.

In the Supreme Court of Canada case, *Simpson Sand Co. v. Black Douglas Contractors Ltd.*, [1964] S.C.J. No. 15, [1964] S.C.R. 333, the Court held that the creation of a large bay along the St. Lawrence River by the excavation of gravel created a body of navigable water, and that the owner of the land under that water could not prevent others from passing over it.

The Act does not, however, apply to mill ponds or small lakes that have no navigable outlet or inlet; they have been found to be not navigable and the boundaries of lots on which such bodies of water are located follow the original lot lines notwithstanding the water lying thereon (see *Williams v. Salter and Karwick*, [1912] O.J. No. 282, 23 O.W.R. 34 (Div. Ct.)). It also does not apply where, in "the absence of an express grant" of the "bed of a navigable body of water or stream, a patent from the Province of land bordering on a navigable body of water or stream, is deemed not to pass the bed of such body of water" (see *Saker v. Middlesex Centre (Township) Chief Building Official*, [2001] O.J. No. 5473, 57 O.R. (3d) 496 (S.C.J.)).

If a body of water is navigable, then it may be used by any member of the public who has a legitimate reason to pass over it, including particularly other owners of land fronting on that water. Anyone who attempts to build an impediment to the use of such water without approval of the Minister of Transport will be in breach of the *Navigable Waters Protection Act*, R.S.C. 1985, c. N-22. This includes construction of docks. Section 5(1) states:

(1) No work shall be built or placed in, on, over, under, through or across any navigable water without the Minister's prior approval of the work, its site and the plans for it.

Section 6(1) states that "[i]f any work ... is built or placed without having been approved ... the Minister may ... order the owner of the work to remove or alter the work".

It should be noted that the Crown, through the Ministry of Natural Resources, in the 1980s, embarked on a "Water Lot Program". Sections 13 and 26 of the *Public Lands Act*, R.S.O. 1990, c. P.43 make it an offence for anyone to erect a building or make an improvement on Crown land without authority. The Ministry took inventory of all boathouses with living accommodations built into navigable waters and required the owners to apply for a lease, licence of occupation or land use permit. At this time, the Ministry is not requiring authority for docks or boathouses "where the total surface area of the supporting structure (e.g. pipes, cribs) placed on the bed of the water body is less than 15 square metres" *per* the work permit section of the Ontario Ministry of Natural Resources website: <www.mnr.gov.on.ca/>.

A landowner who can establish actual possession alone or through predecessors of a part of the bed of the lake or stream for more than 60 years need not apply for authorization. Section 3 of the *Limitations Act*, R.S.O. 1990, c. L.15 (now section 3(1) of the *Real Property Limitations Act*, R.S.O. 1990, c. L.15) protects such an owner against action by the Crown, and s. 17 of the *Public Lands Act* authorizes the Minister of Natural Resources to issue a quit claim to such person.

BOUNDARIES ACT,
R.S.O. 1990, c. B.10

This Act provides a procedure whereby the owner of land may apply to the Director of Titles to have the survey boundaries of the land confirmed or have the land surveyed where doubts or errors exist as to the true location of the boundaries.

On receipt of a report from a surveyor appointed by the Director, a hearing is held after advertisement and the Director may dispose of any objections in such manner as seems just and equitable. The Director may order that the survey be amended or confirm it. There are provisions for appeal. A certificate of confirmation of the survey is conclusive and the boundaries as shown on that survey become the true boundaries. The certified plan of survey is then deposited in the land registry office and supersedes all former plans and descriptions.

This Act is most often used by the Ministry of Transportation and Communications and by municipal corporations, pursuant to s. 13(2), to confirm the true location of the boundaries of public highways. Once the certified plan of survey has been registered, no instrument that affects any parcel that adjoins the confirmed boundary may be registered unless the description both conforms and refers to that plan.

BROWNFIELDS STATUTE LAW AMENDMENT ACT, 2001, S.O. 2001, c. 17

This statute effects amendments to several existing statutes with a view to creating a regime to encourage the redevelopment of "brownfields", which is a term used to describe lands that are environmentally contaminated as a result of historical industrial use and that are often in a state of disuse or abandonment.

The Act received Royal Assent on November 2, 2001 and most, but not all, of its provisions were proclaimed in force on December 1, 2002. The other provisions of the Act have since been proclaimed, resulting in amendments to the *Education Act*, R.S.O. 1990, c. E.2, the *Environmental Protection Act*, R.S.O. 1990, c. E.19, the *Municipal Act*, R.S.O. 1990, c. M.45, the *Planning Act*, R.S.O. 1990, c. P.13, and other statutes identified therein. These amendments attempt to address perceived barriers to brownfields redevelopment. The first and foremost of these is environmental liability. The Act creates Part XV.1 of the *Environmental Protection Act* providing for the establishment of an Environmental Site Registry. Owners of properties may file a site condition report for a property in the Registry if it meets specific criteria as to quality and thoroughness. These criteria and the regime associated with them are contained in the Records of Site Condition — Part XV.1 of the Act Regulation (O. Reg. 153/04). If there are existing contaminants, a "qualified person" must certify that the property meets prescribed standards and meets standards specified in a risk assessment accepted by the Ministry of Environment. The Ministry may then issue a certificate of property use that requires an owner to take certain specific actions or to refrain from using the property in a certain manner or from constructing specific improvements.

The preparation and filing of a record of site condition in respect of a property is not mandatory unless there is an intention to change the use of land, as specified by the Regulation. For example, the conversion of lands once used as a manufacturing facility to a residential use will require the developer to obtain a record of site condition as a precondition thereto. That being said, with the introduction of this regime, there is no doubt that third parties interested in a property may require an owner to "voluntarily" file a record of site condition as a prerequisite to their involvement as a lender, insurer or developer thereof.

Once a record of site condition is filed in the Register and accepted by the Ministry, certain remedial orders that could otherwise be issued under the *Environmental Protection Act* cannot thereafter be made against any of: the owner of that property, a subsequent owner, a person in occupation of the property or a person who has "charge, management or control of the property".

Part XV.2 is also introduced by the Act to form part of the *Environmental Protection Act* and contains several provisions that provide protection to municipalities, secured creditors, receivers, trustees-in-bankruptcy and fiduciaries against environmental orders in respect of properties that they are involved with from a development or lending perspective. For secured creditors, protection continues if they become an owner of a property as a result of foreclosure.

Part III of the Act amends the *Municipal Act* to allow municipalities to provide tax relief to offset environmental rehabilitation costs. Part VII of the Act amends the *Planning Act* to allow municipalities to make loans or grants to owners and tenants of brownfields for the purpose of carrying out "community improvement plans". The total aggregate amount of all loans, grants and tax relief provided to a property cannot exceed the cost of effecting the environmental remediation.

All of the provisions of this statute must be carefully reviewed in advising a purchaser, lender or other interested party on any proposed involvement with a brownfields site. In addition, professional environmental advice from qualified engineers and other experts will be needed to assess the results and impact of the mandatory reports required by the statute for any brownfields redevelopment.

BULK SALES ACT,
R.S.O. 1990, c. B.14

This Act does not deal directly with real estate but you must keep it in mind when you are involved in the sale of a business.

By s. 2, the Act applies to every sale in bulk except a sale in bulk by an executor, administrator, trustee in bankruptcy and certain other exceptions. A sale in bulk is defined in s. 1 as "a sale of stock in bulk out of the usual course of business or trade of the seller".

Thus, if you are involved in the sale of a store or hotel or any other type of business in which the stock-in-trade is being sold along with the real estate (or even without the real estate), you must comply with this Act.

The idea behind this Act is to protect creditors of a business against the risk of the sale of the business and the owner disappearing with the proceeds, leaving the creditors with no right of action against the purchaser.

Section 4 requires that a buyer, before paying over the proceeds of the sale (other than a 10 per cent deposit) "shall demand of and receive from the seller, and the seller shall deliver to the buyer, a statement verified by the affidavit of the seller" in prescribed form listing the names and addresses of all creditors, both secured and unsecured, together with the amount of indebtedness to each.

Thereafter, the buyer may complete the purchase only if:

1. the claims of unsecured creditors do not exceed $2,500 and the claims of secured creditors do not exceed $2,500; or

2. the seller delivers an affidavit showing that all claims have been paid in full; or

3. adequate provision has been made for immediate payment in full of all claims unless the creditor files a waiver. The only adequate provision for payment that you should accept is the actual payment to the creditors of their claims out of the proceeds of the sale by certified cheque.

If the total debt exceeds the proceeds of the sale, there is provision for the appointment of a trustee and the payment of the proceeds to the trustee for distribution to creditors *pro rata*, but only if 60 per cent of the unsecured trade creditors consent.

Remember s. 16: if the buyer does not comply with this Act, the sale is voidable and the buyer is personally liable to pay off the creditors of the vendor. If the buyer complies, then the purchased assets are free and clear of the debts.

There is provision in s. 3 that a judge may make an order exempting a sale in bulk from the application of this Act upon being satisfied that the sale will not impair the ability of the seller to pay the creditors in full.

You should keep this Act in mind when you are preparing the agreement of purchase and sale; it should be a condition of the agreement that the provisions of the *Bulk Sales Act* be complied with. It is, however, not uncommon practice in many transactions involving a sale in bulk for the purchaser to agree to accept the vendor's indemnity against claims by the vendor's creditors in lieu of the vendor obtaining an order exempting the sale. One should remember, however, that this indemnity is only as good as the vendor's ability to pay the creditors; therefore, advise your client accordingly. In effect, the purchaser by accepting such an indemnity is agreeing that adequate provision has been made for the payment of the creditors (presumably because of the vendor's creditworthiness).

In such a situation, you must also comply with the *Retail Sales Tax Act*, R.S.O. 1990, c. R.31, s. 6:

> (1) No person shall dispose of his, her or its stock through a sale in bulk to which the *Bulk Sales Act* applies without first obtaining a certificate in duplicate from the Minister that all taxes collectable or payable by such person have been paid or that such person has entered into an arrangement satisfactory to the Minister for the payment of such taxes or for securing their payment.
>
> (2) Every person purchasing stock through a sale in bulk to which the *Bulk Sales Act* applies shall obtain from the person selling such stock the duplicate copy of the certificate furnished under subsection (1), and, if the person who is purchasing the stock fails to do so, that person is responsible for payment to the Minister of all taxes collectable or payable by the person who is disposing of the stock through a sale in bulk.

Note the decision of the Supreme Court in *National Trust Co. v. H & R Block Canada Inc.*, [2003] S.C.J. No. 70, [2003] 3 S.C.R. 160, where the Court commented on the underlying purpose of the Act. The Court ruled that a purchaser's duty to account must be interpreted in light of the true purpose of the Act and of commercial realities. Specifically, the Court noted, the Act has two main purposes: (1) to protect the interest of creditors whose debtors have disposed of all or substantially all of their assets; and (2) to ensure the fair distribution of the proceeds of a sale in bulk among the seller's creditors, based on their priority ranking. The intent is to deter fraud and ensure the proper payment of creditors. The Act is not intended to be punitive in nature.

CONSERVATION AUTHORITIES ACT, R.S.O. 1990, c. C.27

No one may place or remove fill within a flood plain or alter a waterway under the jurisdiction of a local Conservation Authority without its permission. You also require permission to construct a new building, add to an existing one or reconstruct a destroyed one within a flood plain. The Act permits the Conservation Authority to order removal of offending structures or unauthorized fill.

You should write to the local Conservation Authority to determine if the land concerned is under its jurisdiction, or you can review the applicable regulations under the Act, although this will be difficult unless you know the elevations of the land in which you are interested. It may be very important to your client to know that permission of the Conservation Authority is required, particularly if any kind of development activities are contemplated.

CONVEYANCING AND LAW OF PROPERTY ACT, R.S.O. 1990, c. C.34

In general, the various sections of this Act are unrelated to one another. They originate in early English legislation and modify or overcome ancient common law rules concerning conveyancing. The language in many sections was adopted directly from ancient statutes and is very difficult to interpret. Fortunately, most of these sections have little practical application.

RELEVANT SECTIONS OF THE ACT

The following are some of the important sections:

Section 13 — Tenants in Common

Where land is conveyed to two or more persons, the section states that they shall take as tenants in common unless it is stated in the document that they will take as joint tenants. Hence, you see the words in the granting clause and *habendum* (now Box 11 of the Transfer/Deed of Land) of thousands of deeds to A and B "as joint tenants and not as tenants in common". If the deed is silent as to the manner of holding title, the grantees will be tenants in common.

Section 15 — Easements

Every conveyance of land includes (unless specifically excluded) all houses, edifices, trees, water-courses, privileges, easements, *etc.*, appertaining to the lands. Bear this in mind when dealing with land to which an easement has been validly annexed (see Chapter 7). The easement is conveyed whether specifically referred to in the conveyance or not.

Sections 16 and 17 — Mining Rights

You can sever the mining rights, meaning the ores, mines and minerals on or under the ground, from the surface rights. Remember that surface rights means all rights in the land other than the ores, mines and minerals.

Section 22 — Restrictions

Every covenant made after March 24, 1950, that restricts the sale, ownership, occupation or use of land because of the race, creed, colour, nationality, ancestry, or place of origin of any person is void and of no effect.

Section 23 — Implied Covenants

Under s. 23, certain covenants as contained in the *Short Forms of Conveyances Act*, R.S.O. 1980, c. 472, were deemed to be included in a deed whether specifically set out or not, *i.e.*, right to convey, quiet enjoyment, freedom from encumbrances and further assurance.

However, by S.O. 1984, c. 32, s. 17, this section was repealed for conveyances made under the *Land Registration Reform Act*, R.S.O. 1990, c. L.4. The implied covenants in a transfer are listed in s. 5 of the *Land Registration Reform Act*.

Section 37 — Lien for Improvements

This is an interesting provision that, if you make lasting improvements on land believing that it is your own (for instance, build part of your house on it), you and your assigns may have a lien on that land for the value of the improvements. In addition, the court may in its discretion direct a conveyance of the land to you upon payment of compensation.

Section 41 – Conveyance to Oneself

This section provides that a person may convey property to themselves in the same manner that property can be conveyed to another person. In practice, one often encounters such conveyances where a party changes a joint tenancy tenure to a tenancy-in-common or where a party obtains a severance of lands and registers a "self-conveyance" in order to preserve the severance and have it be effective in respect of the lands for which it was obtained.

Section 61 — Discharge of Restrictive Covenants

Under s. 61, if there are restrictive covenants annexed to land preventing the use of the land in a particular manner, you may apply to a judge of the Ontario Superior Court of Justice for an order modifying or discharging such covenant.

The applicant must show that the benefit from such a modification or discharge will far outweigh any possible detriment to any person objecting to the application.

COURTS OF JUSTICE ACT,
R.S.O. 1990, c. C.43

Only s. 103 of the *Courts of Justice Act* is reviewed for the purposes of this chapter, being the section dealing with the issuance of certificates of pending litigation. Given changes to the *Land Titles Act* which permit cautions relating to agreements of purchase and sale to be automatically deleted within 60 days of closing and which provide cautions generally will otherwise expire within 60 days, parties will be forced to quickly obtain certificates of pending litigation to protect any interest they purport to have in lands where there is a dispute with the owner.

Under s. 103, a party may apply to the court for the issuance of a certificate. There are several reported cases exploring circumstances where a court will issue a certificate, but generally speaking, entitlement to a certificate requires that an interest in land be legitimately and reasonably claimed by a plaintiff. Where a court is convinced of such a claim, it may issue the certificate which will then be registrable on title to the land. However, pursuant to s. 103(4), a party who registers a certificate without a reasonable claim to an interest in land is liable for damages sustained by any person as a result of the registration. This section mirrors that contained in the *Land Titles Act* (see s. 132).

THE DOWER ACT,
R.S.O. 1970, c. 135

This statute was repealed effective March 1, 1978, by s. 70 of *The Family Law Reform Act, 1978*, S.O. 1978, c. 2, as was the common law right to dower. It will still, however, be of interest to know about dower when dealing with old titles and also because of the possibility of dower rights that were preserved because they vested before *The Dower Act* was repealed.

The language of s. 1 of *The Dower Act* is rather quaint, having been taken directly from a long line of English statutes commencing with *Magna Carta* in 1215:

> A widow, on the death of her husband, may tarry in his chief house for forty days after his death, within which time her dower shall be assigned her ... and for her dower shall be assigned to her the third part of all the lands of her husband whereof he was seized at any time during coverture, except such thereof as he was so seized of in trust for another.

The original intention of the barons at Runnymede and of subsequent legislatures in perpetuating this legislation was apparently to protect a widow against the danger of her husband making no provision for her in his will.

In today's language, it meant that a widow was entitled to one-third of a life interest in the total value of any land that her husband had legal title to during their married life. When required, the present value of this right was established using actuarial tables of life expectancy.

It was established that in order to determine the present value of a dower right, you had to use Cameron's Tables, which were prepared in the late nineteenth century. Their outdated life expectancy tables and unrepresentative interest rates were discarded by the decision in *Re Casselman*, [1974] O.J. No. 2223, 6 O.R. (2d) 742 (C.A.), which is authority for the calculation of a dower interest using current life expectancies and interest rates. The monetary result was thus very significantly increased.

The Act contained many exceptions to the right of dower which are dealt with on pp. 155-56, but basically you must remember that if a man executed a deed or transfer of land, he was required to swear whether he was married or unmarried. If married, his wife had to join in the deed to bar her dower, *i.e.*, release the right given to her under this Act. If she did not sign the deed, then her right to dower remained outstanding even though the property was subsequently sold several times over. Note that by s. 19, the wife's right to dower was effectively barred if she signed the deed or transfer even though the document did not contain words specifically relating to dower. Note also that by s. 20, a married woman under 21 years of age could bar her dower by joining with her husband in a deed or transfer containing a release or bar of dower.

If a wife who had a right to dower did not sign and her husband died before March 31, 1978, her dower interest in the land remains until her death, or until she releases it.

See the commentary that follows on s. 25 of the *Real Property Limitations Act* for a practical answer to many dower problems arising out of a search of title.

ELECTRICITY ACT, 1998, S.O. 1998, c. 15, Sched. A

Searches that are normally undertaken by practitioners on a property acquisition to ascertain the existence of unregistered hydro easements are still required as a result of this Act. Before this statute was enacted, s. 48 of the *Power Corporation Act*, R.S.O. 1990, c. P.18 provided that where any right or easement has been or in the future is acquired by Ontario Hydro in respect of any land, the land continues to be subject to that right and is binding on subsequent owners, whether or not the right or easement is registered on title. Section 48 has been repealed; however, pursuant to s. 46 of the *Electricity Act, 1998*, the provisions of s. 48 continue to have effect as it is provided that if before the repeal of s. 48 land was subject to a right or easement by operation of that section, the land continues to be subject to the right or easement until it expires or is released. In addition, the benefit of these rights can be transferred to several different entities described in subs. 46(2), being entities which the *Electricity Act, 1998* now permit to be involved in the transmission and distribution of electricity. Pursuant to subs. 46(3), an entity that has a right or easement that is protected by the Act must reply to inquiries as to the existence, term and extent of such rights within 21 days after receipt of a request of an owner or other person acquiring an interest in the lands. The failure to reply to such an enquiry exposes the entity to liability for any loss or damage suffered as a result of that failure.

Please also note the terms of s. 113 of the Act, which creates the Electrical Safety Authority to administer the Electrical Safety Code. This agency can issue compliance orders with respect to facilities for the transmission, generation and use of electricity. If such orders are not complied with, the person to whom the order was issued is, on conviction, guilty of an offence and liable to pay a fine of up to $50,000, or to imprisonment for not more than one year, or both, plus a further fine of up to $5,000 a day for each day during which the non-compliance continues.

ENVIRONMENTAL PROTECTION ACT, R.S.O. 1990, c. E.19

It is important that a client considering the purchase or sale of property, the lending of money on a mortgage of property or even the leasing of property be aware of the potential liability for environmental contaminants on, under or emanating from that property (see, for example, *Montague v. Ontario (Ministry of the Environment)*, [2005] O.J. No. 868, 196 O.A.C. 173 (S.C.J.); and *Karge v. Ontario (Ministry of Environment and Energy)*, [1996] O.E.A.B. No. 51 (Ontario Environmental Appeal Board)). Many recent cases and Environmental Appeal Board decisions have been reported where the owner of land has been ordered to clean up a site at a cost even greater than the purchase price, even where there was no prior knowledge of the contaminants, pollutants, wastes, dangerous goods, toxic substances or hazardous materials found thereon. In addition, statutory responsibility for contamination has been extended to an owner, a person in occupation or a person having the charge, management or control of a source of a contaminant. This broad responsibility allows the Ministry of the Environment to pursue a range of persons who may have had varying degrees of connection to a property in its attempt to remediate contamination or enforce the various orders the Ministry may issue pursuant to this Act.

It is clear that a search of title will not of itself reveal the presence of such environmental hazards, although evidence of prior occupation of the property by, for example, a smelter, or oil refinery or gasoline service station should alert a purchaser to potential problems. Unfortunately, historical searches of past ownership of properties will become less frequent and more difficult as more properties governed by the Registry system are converted into Land Titles and electronic searching and registration is fully implemented.

It is not possible to obtain a certificate from the Ministry of the Environment that a property is clear of contaminants. The Ministry does maintain records of certain types of contaminants known to them and has published the following inventories that should be reviewed:

1. Ministry of the Environment Waste Disposal Site Inventory dated June 1991 which lists active and closed waste disposal sites;

2. Inventory of Industrial Sites Producing or Using Coal Tar and Related Tars in Ontario dated November 1988; and

3.   Ontario Inventory of Approved PCB Storage Sites dated July, 1992.

Pursuant to s. 19, the Ministry is also required to maintain an index of the names of all persons against whom orders or approvals under the Act are issued. The Ministry must, upon the request of any person, search the index and inform any person making a request as to whether or not the name of a particular person appears in the index. Finally, the Ministry must allow the inspection of the actual order or approval. Note that the index is not organized by property but by person; also, note that once an order or approval has expired or is revoked or set aside, the Ministry must remove the person's name from the index. As a result, it is not possible to obtain historical information on past orders and approvals.

There are several types of orders that may be issued under the Act. They include:

1.   *Control orders* to cause a responsible person to take actions and implement procedures to control and limit sources of contamination (see s. 7 and s. 124);

2.   *Stop orders* to cause a responsible person to immediately stop the discharge of contamination into the environment (see s. 8 and s. 128);

3.   *Remedial orders* to cause a person to take actions to repair or to act to prevent further contamination; if water supplies are threatened by the contamination, the order may force the person to provide alternate sources of water (see s. 17);

4.   *Preventative measure orders* requiring a person to implement procedures and have machinery and staff available to implement the measures specified in the order to address specific contamination (see s. 18);

5.   *Waste removal orders* requiring a person to remove waste and restore the site to a satisfactory condition (see s. 43);

6.   *Spill orders* requiring a person to do everything practicable and necessary to ameliorate the adverse effects caused by the spill of a contaminant (see s. 97).

The applicable regional office of the Ministry of the Environment which has jurisdiction over the property you may be concerned with must be contacted to have a search of the index of orders completed.

There are other sections in the *Environmental Protection Act* with which real estate practitioners should be familiar. Section 46 of the Act prohibits any use of land which has been used for the disposal of waste within 25 years of the date on which the land ceased to be so used, without the approval of the Minister. This prohibition applies to sites used formally, or informally, for the disposal of waste. Usually, nothing is registered on title to indicate that a particular property has been so used. If there is any doubt, you should review the waste disposal site inventory referred to above and write to the Ministry of the Environment Approvals Branch to ascertain whether any certificates of approval for waste disposal sites have been issued at:

2 St. Clair Avenue West
Floor 12A
Toronto, ON
M4V 1L5

The Minister and Director may take any action they consider necessary in respect of any environmental matter where an order has been issued, whether or not the order has been stayed (see s. 146 and s. 147). This allows the Ministry to be proactive where a person ordered to do so is not remediating contamination. Please be aware that pursuant to s. 154(2), the Ministry may recover costs expended by it in remediating contamination by instructing the municipality in which the property is located to recover the said amounts and granting the municipality a lien on the property for such amounts which are deemed by this section to constitute municipal property taxes and are afforded the same priority as property taxes.

One other especially noteworthy provision in the *Environmental Protection Act* is s. 197. This section authorizes the Ministry to make an order requiring any person to give a copy of any order or decision affecting the property to anyone acquiring an interest therein. Pursuant to subs. 197(2), a certificate setting out a requirement may be registered on title under specified circumstances. In addition, pursuant to subs. 197(4), dealings with property by persons subject to a requirement are voidable by the person who was not given a copy of the order or direction before acquiring an interest in the affected lands.

It will be obvious that enquiries with respect to environmental matters with public authorities and the review of published inventories will not produce any assurance that a property is free of contaminants. The most effective means of finding if environmental problems exist is to have an environmental audit conducted by an engineering consultant. In the jargon of the industry, initially a "Phase 1" audit is performed, which consists generally of a superficial visual inspection, review of available records and enquiries about existing and prior uses. That study may result in recommendations for further, more detailed investigations, including taking soil or other samples and analyzing them for contamination; this is usually known as a "Phase 2" audit.

ESCHEATS ACT, R.S.O. 1990, c. E.20

As most practitioners are aware, this statute confirms the common law doctrine of escheat, which causes property of an intestate individual without heirs, or a dissolved corporation, to vest immediately in the Crown.

Due to the various liabilities a property owner can incur in owning real estate, the Government of Ontario recently enacted changes to this Act to ensure the Province did not inherit such liability simply as a result of a property being escheated to it.

Section 1(3) of the Act now provides that if land has escheated or been forfeited to the Crown due to the dissolution of a corporation, the Crown is not deemed to have taken possession of the property until the Public Guardian and Trustee registers notice of taking possession with the land registry office. Similarly, s. 7(1) now provides that where land has escheated, the Crown is not required to maintain or manage the property or take any action in relation to it, and no action or proceeding can be commenced against the Public Trustee and Guardian in respect of the property.

FIRE PROTECTION AND PREVENTION ACT, 1997, S.O. 1997, c. 4

This statute is the basis for the establishment of the Ontario Fire Code, which is contained within O. Reg. 388/97, as amended, passed pursuant to this Act. Pursuant to s. 21 of this Act, a Fire Chief may issue orders to an owner or occupant of lands requiring them to remediate conditions that constitute fire hazards and to effect improvements toward fire safety and compliance with the Fire Code. Orders may also be issued in certain circumstances to close premises and remove all persons from it and to keep premises vacant until corrective measures are taken to the satisfaction of the Fire Marshal or a Fire Chief. Any order issued can be appealed within 15 days to the Fire Safety Commission but such an appeal does not necessarily stay the order while the appeal is in progress.

Pursuant to Part VII of the Act, a person who refuses or neglects to obey an order under s. 21 is liable, on conviction, to a fine of not more than $20,000 for every day during which the default continues. The imposition or payment of the fine does not relieve the person from complying with the order.

The Act also permits a Fire Chief or the Fire Marshal to apply to the Fire Safety Commission for authorization to undertake whatever work or activity is necessary to remedy a condition for which there is an outstanding work order. Where that authorization is obtained and work is undertaken, all costs incurred plus interest on such amounts constitute a lien against the property in favour of the local municipality which, pursuant to s. 38(3), has priority lien status, as described in s. 1 of the *Municipal Act, 2001* or s. 3 of the *City of Toronto Act, 2006*, S.O. 2006, c. 11, Sched. A, and shall be added by the treasurer of the municipality to the tax roll.

HEALTH PROTECTION AND PROMOTION ACT, R.S.O. 1990, c. H.7

The framework of this statute is similar to that discussed above in respect of the *Fire Prevention and Protection Act*. Orders may be issued to owners and occupiers of premises in respect of any matter relating to occupational or environmental health and safety requiring that corrective action be taken, and also forcing premises and businesses to be closed until the corrective actions have been completed. A medical officer of health may also cause the local board of health to take the initiative and take independent actions to eliminate or decrease a health hazard. Where such actions are taken, all costs incurred are recoverable by a board of health from an owner or occupier and if not paid within 60 days, can be added to the tax roll for the property. Such amounts may then be collected by the local municipality in the same manner as real property taxes.

Part IX of the Act contains provisions which expose owners, occupiers and corporate officers and directors to fines on conviction for failing to obey work orders issued under this Act.

LIMITATIONS ACT, 2002,
S.O. 2002, c. 24, Sched. B

The new Act governing limitations came into force on January 1, 2004 and replaced the limitation periods in the previous Act and several other statutes as well. Note that many provisions of the former Act, namely, those provisions governing limitations applicable to real estate interests, were not repealed. These unrepealed provisions continued in full force and effect and are now found in the new *Real Property Limitations Act*, which you will find summarized later in this chapter.

Pursuant to s. 4 of the Act, a basic two-year period is established as the time limit to bring an action in Ontario, being a reduction from the six years that had often been the previous governing limitation. At the same time, the Act preserves certain limitation periods in 46 Ontario statutes, which are named in the Schedule to the Act. Practitioners need to be aware of these exceptions to the two-year period.

Pursuant to s. 5, the Act adopts the discoverability principle for most claims. Specifically, a proceeding cannot be commenced in respect of a claim after the second anniversary of the day on which the claim was discovered. There is a four-part test set out in para. 5(1)(*a*) for determining when a claim is discovered, but otherwise, there is a presumption in subs. 5(2) that a plaintiff discovered a claim on the day that the act or omission took place unless the contrary is proven. Note that the further presumption in subs. 5(3) pertaining to claims in relation to demand obligations provides that the day on which injury, loss or damage occurs is the first day on which there is a failure to perform an obligation once a demand is made. This is a recent change to the Act brought about in 2008 to ease concerns that for a demand obligation, the two-year limitation period would start to run before an actual demand was made by the lender.

Pursuant to s. 11 of the Act, the running of the limitation period is suspended where an independent third party, such as an arbitrator or mediator, is retained to resolve the dispute. There must be an actual agreement with the third party to retain them in connection with a dispute in order to take advantage of the suspensive effect of s. 11; an agreement containing a clause that simply anticipates the use of such third party is not enough.

A significant change introduced by the Act is an ultimate limitation period of 15 years. No proceeding shall be commenced in respect of any claim after the 15th anniversary of the day on which the act or omission on which the claim is based took place (see s. 15).

The most controversial provision of the Act was s. 22, which originally provided that the limitation periods of two years and 15 years could not be varied by contract. This precluded parties, especially sophisticated commercial parties, from shortening or extending limitation periods in the context of a particular transaction, something that is routinely done in contracts governing many commercial matters. As a result of strenuous objections, amendments have been enacted to modify this provision. Pursuant to subss. 22(2) and (3), the Act now recognizes that any agreement entered into before January 1, 2004 may, by contract, vary or exclude the two-year limitation period provided for in the Act. Pursuant to subss. 22(3) and (4), the 15-year ultimate limitation period may, by agreement made on or before October 19, 2006, be suspended or extended if the relevant claim has been discovered. Most significant are the provisions of subss. 22(5) and (6). They provide that where a business agreement is concerned, the two-year limitation period may be varied or excluded by contract, and the 15-year limitation period may be varied by contract, but only suspended or extended if a claim has been discovered. A "business agreement" is defined as any "agreement made by parties, none of whom is a consumer" as defined in the *Consumer Protection Act, 2002*, S.O. 2002, c. 30, Sched. A. That statute defines a "consumer" as "an individual acting for personal, family or household purposes and does not include a person who is acting for business purposes".

One final noteworthy section in the Act insofar as real estate practitioners are concerned is s. 2(1), which provides that the Act does not apply to proceedings that the *Real Property Limitations Act* covers, meaning that the two-year and 15-year periods can be ignored when dealing with claims relating to adverse possession, prescriptive easements, *etc.*

LINE FENCES ACT, R.S.O. 1990, c. L.17

Where the owner of land wants to construct, repair or reconstruct a boundary fence, fence-viewers can be appointed by the local municipality to view and arbitrate as to what portion of the fence the owner and the next door neighbour shall construct, reconstruct or repair, as well as maintain and keep up. The fence-viewers' award may be registered on title. If the adjoining landowner fails to comply with the award, the fence-viewers will prepare a certificate as to default, which may also be registered on title. The amount owing may be collected as municipal taxes and, until paid, is a charge on the land (see s. 12(7)). Pursuant to s. 98(1) of the *Municipal Act, 2001*, S.O. 2001, c. 25, a municipality may provide that this Act does not apply within all or any part of its boundaries.

MUNICIPAL ACT, R.S.O. 1990, c. M.45

This is a summary of certain sections from this repealed statute to assist in understanding the past application of certain sections when reviewing title and earlier development matters concerning parcels of real property. There are also useful case law references that are still applicable to the interpretation of municipal law concepts. Effective January 1, 2003, this Act was repealed and replaced with the *Municipal Act, 2001*, S.O. 2001, c. 25, which received Royal Assent on December 12, 2001 and is reviewed next in this chapter.

ROAD ALLOWANCES

Often when searching titles, you will find that a portion of the parcel being searched has at some time formed a part of an original road allowance or a public highway. In order to give your opinion on title, you must satisfy yourself that the road allowance or highway has been properly closed.

If you are acting for someone who is assembling land for redevelopment, which includes a highway or road allowance, your advice on the procedure of closing that highway or road allowance will be required. Before dealing with the closing of a highway, consider what a "highway" is and how it became one. The term "highway" is defined in s. 1(1) as "a common and public highway, and includes a street". Highways include an original road allowance even though it has never actually been opened up as a road.

Section 261 states that a public highway is established by the expenditure of public money thereon. However, such roadway must have been dedicated by the owner.

The title to soil or freehold in a trespass or diversion road does not pass from the registered owner to the municipality unless there is clear evidence of an intention to dedicate. (See *Macoomb v. Welland (Town)*, [1907] O.J. No. 95, 13 O.L.R. 335 (C.A.) and *Reed v. Lincoln (Town)*, [1974] O.J. No. 2185, 6 O.R. (2d) 391 (C.A.).)

Section 57 of the *Surveys Act*, R.S.O. 1990, c. S.30, states that every road allowance, highway, street, lane, walk and common that is laid out on a registered plan of subdivision is a public highway. Please note that "lane" was not included in this section until the amendment of the *Surveys Act* of June 4, 1920, which appears as S.O. 1920, c. 48, s. 13(2). There is some question whether a lane shown on a plan registered prior to that date is, without some other act of dedication, a public highway. Lerner J., in *Alfrey Investments Ltd. v. Shefsky Developments Ltd.*, [1974] O.J. No. 2178, 6 O.R. (2d) 321 (H.C.J.), held that it was not. McDermid Co. Ct. J., in *Aihoshi v. St. Thomas (City)*, [1981] O.J. No. 2260, 22 R.P.R. 149 (Co. Ct.), reviewed many cases and concluded that Lerner J. was mistaken and that a lane shown on a plan prior to 1920 was still a public highway.

Municipal streets are often widened by expropriation or purchase of a strip of land from the adjoining landowner. Between the date of the registration of a plan of expropriation or the transfer and the date of registration of a by-law dedicating the strip as a public highway, there is often delay. The question arises as to whether the adjoining landowner then has right of access across the strip. There is a helpful provision in s. 23(7) of the *Regional Municipalities Act*, R.S.O. 1990, c. R.8, which states: "where the Regional Corporation acquires land for the purpose of widening a regional road, the land so acquired ... forms part of the road". Because of the exception in subs. (12), this provision does not apply to the Regional Municipalities of York and Niagara.

A similar provision appears in s. 82 of the *Municipality of Metropolitan Toronto Act*, R.S.O. 1990, c. M.62 (now repealed): "When land abutting on a metropolitan road is dedicated for highway purposes for ... the widening of the metropolitan road, the road so dedicated is part of the metropolitan road".

CLOSING ROAD ALLOWANCES

Section 297(l)(c) of the *Municipal Act* gives the council of every municipality the power to pass by-laws "for stopping up any highway or part of a highway".

So the first step must be that a by-law closing the highway be passed by council. This will not be done without notice being published in a local newspaper once a week for four weeks and posted in a conspicuous place near the highway, or portion thereof, to be closed (s. 300). An opportunity will be given to any person who applies to be heard by council.

Section 298 prohibits the passing of a by-law closing a highway if the effect of such closing will be to deprive any person of the means of ingress or egress to and from that person's land, unless that person consents and an alternate way of access is provided.

The procedures for closing a road allowance in a township were amended by S.O. 1978, c. 101, s. 15. Under the old s. 443(6)(c), R.S.O. 1970, c. 164, the by-law of a township council closing a highway "does not have any force until confirmed by a by-law of the council of the county in which the township is situated passed at an ordinary meeting of the council held not later than one year after the passing of the by-law by the council of the township".

Now since 1978, under subss. 297(6), (7) and (8), when a township council intends to close a highway, it must notify the clerk of the county in which the township is situated. Then the county council has 60 days in which to notify the township that it objects and thereafter the by-law shall not be passed "except by agreement between the council of the county and the council of the township and, failing agreement, the Municipal Board, upon application, may determine the matter and its decision is final" (subs. 297(7)). If the county council does not object or if it passes a by-law consenting to the proposed by-law, "the council of the county shall have no further right of objection" (subs. 297(8)).

If the highway being closed is part of an original road allowance, which either runs along the bank of any river or stream or along or on the shore of a lake or leads to the bank of any river or stream or to the shore of a lake, subs. 297(3) states that a by-law closing a road allowance passed by any municipality does not take effect until it has been approved by the Minister of Municipal Affairs. Note that subs. 297(3) was repealed in 1999.

If the highway being closed is part of a highway laid out on a registered plan of subdivision registered after March 27, 1946, subs. 297(10) states that the by-law does not take effect until it has been approved by the Minister of Municipal Affairs. This subsection was also repealed in 1999.

If the highway gives access to a King's Highway (see pp. 88-89), the approval of the Minister of Transportation is required before it may be closed: see the *Public Transportation and Highway Improvement Act*, R.S.O. 1990, c. P.50, subs. 24(3).

Lastly, subs. 297(11) states that a by-law passed by any municipality for the closing of a highway does not take effect until it has been registered in the land registry office for the land titles division or registry division in which the land is situate. A copy of the by-law certified by the clerk under the seal of the municipality is acceptable for registration without further evidence.

Now, after all that has been accomplished, the highway is closed but title to the land on which the highway is situate is still vested in the municipality (see s. 262). The municipality cannot sell the land unless it complies with s. 315. (See *Tonks v. Reid*, [1966] S.C.J. No. 62, [1967] S.C.R. 81, affg [1965] O.J. No. 991, [1965] 2 O.R. 381 (C.A.).)

First, council must set a price for which the land is to be sold. Then the council must offer the land at that price to the owner or owners of the land abutting the closed highway. Only if those abutting landowners do not exercise their right to buy can the municipality proceed to sell to any other person. That sale should also be authorized by a by-law of the municipality.

In order to perfect title to a road allowance, you should register on title, in addition to the deed from the municipality, a copy of the by-law authorizing the closing and the sale together with evidence of the appropriate approvals, and a statutory declaration of the municipal clerk as to the proper giving of notice.

POSSESSION AND USE OF UNOPENED ROAD ALLOWANCES

Sections 299, 316 and 317 will be of assistance to parties through whose lands a diversion of an original road allowance has been constructed. In rural or cottage areas it was often impossible because of the terrain to construct a road within the boundaries of the road allowance laid out in the original survey (see p. 1).

Section 299(1) states the following:

> (1) A person in possession of and having enclosed with a lawful fence that part of an original allowance for road upon which the person's land abuts that has not been opened for public use by reason of another road being used in lieu of it or of another road parallel or near to it having been established by law in lieu of it shall, as against every person except the corporation the council of which has jurisdiction over the allowance for road, be deemed to be legally possessed of such part until a by-law has been passed by such council for opening it.

This section clearly gives the abutting landowner legal possession against everyone but the municipality, but it does not give title. There are a number of old cases dealing with the legal maxim "once a highway, always a highway". They are reviewed in *Nash v. Glover*, [1876] O.J. No. 313, 24 Gr. 219 (Ont. Ch. Ct.).

These cases seem to be in conflict with the language of ss. 316 and 317. In those cases where a road was opened in the place of the original road allowance and the owners of the land over which the new roadway passed received no compensation, those owners, or their successors in title if they own land abutting the original road allowance, are entitled to "the soil and freehold of it and ... to a conveyance of it" (s. 316(1)). *Gibson v. Trafalgar (Township)*, [1923] O.J. No. 135, 53 O.L.R. 340 at 343 (H.C.) states that if the owners of such land can bring themselves, by evidence, within the provisions of this section, the strip of land comprising the original road allowance is theirs as if they had directly obtained the patent thereof from the Crown. The absence of a deed does not affect the owners' title; title vests by reason of the provisions of this section. It may, however, be difficult to obtain evidence that no compensation was paid because most of such diversions were constructed long ago.

Note that members of the public may not improve an unopened road allowance to access their property without permission of the municipality. (See *Goudreau v. Chandos (Township)*, [1993] O.J. No. 2070, 14 O.R. (3d) 636 (Gen. Div.).)

TAX SALES

Until enactment of the *Municipal Tax Sales Act, 1984*, S.O. 1984, c. 48 (see p. 80), sales by municipalities for arrears of taxes were governed either by the *Municipal Act* or the *Municipal Affairs Act* (see p. 78). For sales under the *Municipal Act*, a municipality could sell land for taxes only when taxes had been in arrears for at least three years. In summary, the Act required that the municipality publish notice of a sale of lands for arrears of taxes once in the Ontario *Gazette* and once a week for 13 weeks in a local newspaper, and that it post notice in a public place at the place where council met. If, prior to the date noted in such notices, the arrears of taxes had not been paid, the treasurer of the municipality could sell the lands by public auction. If the treasurer was unable to sell for the amount required to pay off the arrears of taxes and the costs of the sale, the municipality could purchase the lands for the amount due.

When a sale had been effected, the treasurer had to deliver to the purchaser a certificate of sale (s. 433 of the *Municipal Act*, R.S.O. 1980, c. 302). Within 90 days of the sale, the treasurer had to search in the land registry office and in the sheriff's office to ascertain the name and address of the registered owner and any encumbrancers. Within the same period, the treasurer was required to forward to the owner and each encumbrancer a notice of the sale by registered mail, which notice gave the owner and encumbrancers one year from the date of sale to redeem the land by paying the amount owing for taxes plus costs. A similar notice was registered against the land in the land registry office.

If the land was redeemed by the owner or encumbrancer, the treasurer issued a receipt for the amount paid. A copy of the receipt was registered and that was the end of the tax sale.

If the land was not redeemed within the one-year period specified in the notice, the treasurer delivered a tax deed to the purchaser (s. 442(10)).

Section 445 prescribed the form of the tax deed and stated that it had "the effect of vesting the land in the purchaser, his heirs, assigns and legal representatives, in fee simple". Section 448 stated that "[w]here land is sold for taxes and a tax deed thereof has been executed, the sale and the tax deeds are valid and binding, to all intents and purposes, except as against the Crown". Thus, a tax deed was accepted by many solicitors as a good root of title with no need to search further back in time. Two cases, however, indicate that further searches are required and that one cannot rely on a tax deed alone.

Even if all the requirements for a tax sale as set out in the *Municipal Act* had been fulfilled, the tax deed might still be null and void if in fact there were no arrears of taxes: see *Canada (Attorney General) v. Faith*, [1957] O.J. No. 515, [1957] O.W.N. 492 (C.A.). You must, therefore, satisfy yourself from the material registered on title or otherwise that taxes were due and payable when the tax sale proceedings were taken by the municipality.

You must also satisfy yourself that the proper person has been assessed and billed for taxes. In the case *Kirton v. Frolak*, [1972] O.J. No. 2061, [1973] 2 O.R. 185 (H.C.J.), the tax deed was held to be invalid because the assessment was invalid. The municipality had assessed a person for taxes on a property because that person had obtained and registered a deed to the property. A proper search of title would have shown that the grantor in that deed did not have title. The actual owner had not been assessed and was able to obtain an order quieting title free and clear of the claim of the purchaser under the tax deed.

By s. 445(2), a tax deed was not valid unless there was affixed a statutory declaration of the treasurer that notice had been sent to the owner and encumbrancers as provided in s. 442. Therefore, if you find a tax deed on title for a sale conducted under the *Municipal Act*, you must carefully check this declaration.

Further, a tax deed did not affect the interest of the Crown (see s. 429(2)); nor did it affect any easement or restrictive covenant (see subss. 471(1) and (2)). So for these reasons also you must still complete a full 40-year search to ascertain if any such interests are outstanding.

Under s. 429, a sale of land for taxes was the sale only of the interest in the land of the person who was liable for payment of taxes and it did not affect the interest or rights of the Crown or of any tribe or body of Indians or any member thereof in the land sold. A tax deed gave the purchaser only the rights and interest of the person whose interest was being sold. It might be wise to check the patent to see if any reservations in favour of Indians were contained therein before giving an opinion on the title.

Note that the treasurer referred to in these sections was the treasurer of the county in which the municipality was located. The tax deed from a township had to be signed by the warden and the treasurer of the county. However, in towns and cities the mayor and treasurer were authorized to perform these duties by s. 462. In addition, s. 604 stated that a county council might by by-law authorize the reeve and treasurer of any township or village within that county to perform these duties.

If your title is based on a tax sale under these provisions (or as previously contained in the *Assessment Act*) or under the *Municipal Affairs Act*, and if the deed from the municipality was registered prior to July 1, 1973, it will be comforting to examine *The Tax Sales Confirmation Act, 1974*, S.O. 1974, c. 90. By that Act, the legislature repeated a practice that was common in the 1930s of passing legislation from time to time to overcome any deficiency in form or content or procedure in tax sales up to a specific date. All these statutes declare and confirm tax sales prior to a specific date to be legal, valid and binding. The 1974 Act was almost identical in form to the last such legislation passed in 1946. The effectiveness of this Act to give good title to a purchaser even through proper procedures had not been followed in the tax sale was confirmed by *Hunt Estate v. Renfrew (County)*, [1990] O.J. No. 3304, 75 O.R. (2d) 310 (Gen. Div.).

RENT PAYABLE TO MUNICIPALITY FOR ARREARS OF TAXES

Section 384 of the *Municipal Act*, R.S.O. 1990, c. M.45, gives the municipality the right, where taxes are due upon any land occupied by a tenant, to require the tenant to pay the rent to the municipality from time to time until the taxes are paid. This right has begun to be exercised more frequently by municipalities.

MUNICIPAL ACT, 2001, S.O. 2001, c. 25

Effective January 1, 2003, the *Municipal Act, 2001* replaced several statutes, including the *Municipal Act* that has just been reviewed in this chapter, and the *Municipal Tax Sales Act*, discussed later on. As with its predecessor, this is a very long statute dealing with several aspects of municipal practice and procedure and outlining general and specific municipal powers and authority. As in the earlier review of the *Municipal Act*, this commentary will deal with the provisions of the *Municipal Act, 2001* that will be most relevant to practitioners.

RELEVANT SECTIONS OF THE ACT

Section 31 — Highways

A municipality is authorized to establish a highway by passing a by-law to that effect. A "highway" is defined by the Act as a "common and public highway" and includes any other structure forming part of a highway, such as a bridge. Section 31(2) is a change that is worth noting as it provides that after January 1, 2003, land may only become a highway if a municipality has passed a by-law to that effect; land cannot become a highway by virtue of the activities of a municipality or any other person in relation to such lands, including the spending of public money. Thus, the intention of the legislature is that the decision to establish highways may only be made by elected municipal officials, and cannot, for example, be imposed on the municipality by the Ontario Municipal Board or otherwise inferred (*Mattamy (Rouge) Ltd. v. Toronto (City)*, [2003] O.J. No. 4829, 68 O.R. (3d) 677 (S.C.J.); supp. reasons [2004] O.J. No. 801 (S.C.J.)). This alters the approach taken in s. 261 of the former Act, which made the spending of public money a factor in confirming that a road was a highway. There are exceptions to the general provision that a road may only be established as a highway by by-law. They are contained in s. 26, which lists the following as highways in all cases: highways that existed on December 31, 2002; highways transferred to a municipality pursuant to the *Public Transportation and Highway Improvement Act*; road allowances made by Crown surveyors that are located in municipalities; and road allowances, highways, streets and lanes shown on a plan of subdivision.

Section 31(6) is a useful provision in eliminating certain legal access concerns that may arise in reviewing access rights to lands. It provides that where a municipality acquires land for the purposes of widening a highway, the land acquired immediately forms part of the highway to the extent of the widening without the requirement of a by-law being first enacted.

Sections 34 to 39 — Closing Highways

The permanent closing of a highway by a municipality requires that a public notice be given before it passes a by-law to that effect. Once the notice is given and a municipality proceeds to pass a by-law closing a highway, the by-law does not take effect until a certified copy of the by-law is registered in the applicable land registry office. Note that any by-law permanently closing a highway which abuts land owned by the Crown in right of Canada requires the consent of the federal government.

Insofar as the sale of land which comprised part of a highway that has been closed, there is no provision in the new Act similar to s. 315 in the old Act, which contained separate procedures and entitlements to the purchase and sale of closed highways. In particular, there is no requirement in the new Act to first offer any land representing a closed highway to the owners of property which abut the closed road. The authority of the municipality to sell such lands is governed by the general provisions contained in the new Act (discussed below) governing the sale of municipal lands generally.

Section 91 — Easements

Pursuant to s. 91(2) any easement of a public utility provided by a municipality does not have to be appurtenant or annexed to any specific parcel of land to be valid. Only the servient tenement needs to be identified.

Section 91(3) is identical to s. 194(3) of the old *Municipal Act*, which stipulates that the notice provisions of Part III of the *Registry Act* do not apply in respect of a municipal public utility constructed before June 21, 1990 with the consent of the owner (see the discussion on this provision found in Chapter 1).

Section 144 — Site Alteration Work Orders

Pursuant to s. 142 of the Act, a municipality may pass by-laws regulating the placing of fill, the removal of topsoil, the grading of lands and the rehabilitation of lands affected by such activities. If any regulation is contravened, a work order may be issued pursuant to subs. 144(5) requiring an owner of lands to remedy the contravention. If such remediation does not occur within a specified time period, the municipality may do the work at the owner's expense and, pursuant to subs. 144(12), recover the costs incurred, plus interest, from the owner of the land either by an action or as if such amounts constituted realty taxes. Section 1(3) of the Act entitles the municipality to a priority status for such costs if the municipality chooses to collect such remediation amounts as taxes.

The same regime is contained within s. 427 of the Act which generally provides that where any person is in default of any legal requirement ordered to be observed by a municipality, the municipality may do the work and add the cost incurred by it, plus interest, to the tax roll and collect them in the same manner as realty taxes.

Section 268 — Sale of Municipal Lands

The purchase and sale of any lands owned by a municipality, including closed highways, is governed by the provisions contained in s. 268. Subsection 268(1) requires every municipality to enact a by-law to set forth the practice and procedure it will follow, including what notice it will give to the public, for land sales. In addition, in respect of every land sale, a municipality must first declare, by by-law or resolution, that the land to be sold is surplus, then obtain at least one appraisal of the land's fair market value and finally give notice to the public of the sale. A municipality is also required to give notice pursuant to para. 268(3)(*c*). Failure to give notice will not render an agreement of purchase and sale void and unenforceable in every circumstance (*Doherty v. Southgate (Town)*, [2006] O.J. No. 2910, 271 O.L.R. (4th) 59 (C.A.)). Pursuant to subs. 268(4), as long as a municipality satisfies these conditions, follows the procedures set out in its general by-law for the sale of the lands and acts in good faith, then the manner in which any particular sale of land is completed is not open to review by a court.

On the closing date for the sale of any municipal land, the clerk of the municipality will normally issue a certificate verifying that the requirements of the municipality's by-law and of s. 268 have been complied with. Such a certificate shall be appended to the transfer/deed and, pursuant to subs. 268(7) "shall be deemed to be sufficient proof that this section has been complied with" unless the purchaser has actual notice to the contrary.

It is interesting to note that a municipality's obligation to obtain a fair market value appraisal of the lands being sold does not apply where certain classes of lands are being sold. These exclusions are noted in subs. 268(8). In particular, subs. 268(8)2 provides that an appraisal is not needed to sell closed highways if the lands are sold to an owner of land abutting the closed highway. This allows municipalities to sell such highway lands to abutting land owners at less than fair market value, recognizing the practicality of conveying closed roads to abutting landowners and giving a municipality the flexibility to do so.

An interesting case dealing with the obligation of a municipality in connection with 0.3-metre reserves can be found in *Ontario Mission of the Deaf v. Barrie (City)*, [2004] O.J. No. 1269, 70 O.R. (3d) 394 (S.C.J.). In this case, the defendant municipality was unsuccessful in halting a property owner's development and was ordered by the Ontario Municipal Board to grant site plan approval for the development. Along the boundary of the plaintiff's lands, the municipality had a 0.3-metre reserve that separated the lands from municipal services and municipal roads. As most practitioners are aware, these reserves are often taken by, or transferred to, a municipality as a means of controlling the development of a property and ensuring an owner satisfies municipal requirements in relation thereto. In this case, the City of Barrie refused to lift the 0.3-metre reserve it held to give the plaintiff access to the municipal roads and services until the development issues, which they were dissatisfied with and which were the subject of the OMB hearing that the City had lost, were resolved. The Court held that while municipalities had discretion in dealing with reserves, that discretion had to be based on proper planning principles. The ownership of reserve blocks was not governed by principles applicable to other municipal property where the

City could consider its own personal interests in considering a specific action; rather, it held ownership of reserves to ensure orderly development, after which it was intended that the reserve be released and become part of the street. In the case at hand, the Court held that there was no legitimate planning purpose for the City's refusal to lift the reserve and ordered same.

Sections 371 to 389 — Tax Sales

Part XI of the new *Municipal Act* contains the statutory provision governing the sale of land by a municipality to recover realty tax arrears. It replaces the regime contained in the *Municipal Tax Sales Act*, R.S.O. 1990, c. M.60, which was repealed effective January 1, 2003.

The procedures to be followed by a municipality in conducting tax sales pursuant to Part XI is very similar, and often identical, to that contained in the *Municipal Tax Sales Act*. Pursuant to s. 373, where taxes are in arrears for land on January 1 in the third year following that in which the taxes become owing, the municipality may register a tax arrears certificate against title to the lands. The alternative two-year time frame that had been included in the *Municipal Tax Sales Act* for tax arrears relating to unimproved lands has been deleted.

The tax arrears certificate will provide that the lands described in it will be sold if the cancellation price is not paid within one year of the certificate's registration.

Within 60 days of the registration of the tax arrears certificate, the municipality must send notices to the owner of the land, execution creditors of the owner, other persons having an interest in the land and the spouse of the owner, if applicable. The requirement that had existed in s. 4(1)2 of the *Municipal Tax Sales Act* to also send such notice to tenants in occupation of the lands has been deleted. Once these notices are sent out, the municipality must prepare a statutory declaration as to service and make it available for inspection. This statutory declaration no longer is registered on title.

Pursuant to s. 375, before the expiry of the one-year period specified by the tax arrears certificate, any person may pay the amounts owing and require the municipality to cancel the tax arrears certificate. If the arrears have been paid by a person to whom notice of the arrears was sent (other than the owner or his or her spouse), that person is entitled to a lien on the land for the amount paid, which lien is confirmed in the tax arrears cancellation certificate registered by the municipality, and which lien is given priority over the interest of all other persons who were originally served with notice of the tax arrears in the first instance.

If the tax arrears noted in the tax arrears certificate are still not paid 280 days after the registration of the tax arrears certificate, the municipality must, within 30 days of the expiry of the 280-day period, send new notices to all of the persons who have an interest in the land, as was previously done, indicating that the land will be advertised for sale unless the arrears are paid before the one-year period expires.

Subsection 379(2) contains the procedures that must be followed in advertising the lands for sale, which are practically identical to the procedures under the *Municipal Tax Sales Act*. If there is a successful purchaser, a tax deed is prepared and registered; if there is no successful purchaser, the municipality may prepare and register a notice vesting the lands in the municipality. In either case, the municipality shall prepare a statement to accompany the tax deed or notice of vesting confirming the matters set forth in subs. 379(6) of the Act that relate to following the formalities in Part XI as preconditions to any sale. Once the tax deed is registered, it vests in the person an "estate in fee simple in the land, together with all rights, privileges and appurtenances and free from all estates and interests" save and except for: (a) easements and restrictive covenants; (b) interests of the Crown; and (c) any interest acquired by any abutting landowner by adverse possession.

If a tax deed or notice of vesting is not registered within one year after a public sale is conducted and at which there was no successful purchaser, the tax arrears certificate is deemed to be cancelled; however, this does not preclude the municipality from registering a new tax arrears certificate in the future.

Pursuant to s. 380, proceeds received from a tax sale by a municipality are applied first to pay the tax arrears, second to pay persons, other than the owner, who have an interest in the land in order of their respective priorities in the land and lastly to the owner. If there is any dispute among these parties, the municipality is authorized to pay excess moneys into court. Cases decided under s. 380 relate to establishing right to the excess moneys and, in particular, to establishing ownership or an interest in the land. The courts have determined that a beneficial owner did not have entitlement (*St. Louis v. Thunder Bay (City)*, [2005] O.J. No. 6017, 39 R.P.R. (4th) 109 (S.C.J.), while an abutting landowner with possessory title did (*Murray Township Farms Ltd. v. Quinte West (City)*, [2006] O.J. No. 2956, 50 R.P.R. (4th) 266 (S.C.J.)).

Finally, as in s. 13(1) of the *Municipal Tax Sales Act*, s. 383 of this Act stipulates that, subject to proof of fraud, every tax deed and notice of vesting when registered, is final, binding and not subject to any challenge for any reason. Furthermore, no action may be brought for the recovery of the land after the registration of the tax deed or notice of vesting as long as the statements required by s. 379(6) have been included and registered therewith.

MUNICIPAL AFFAIRS ACT, R.S.O. 1990, c. M.46 (FORMERLY THE DEPARTMENT OF MUNICIPAL AFFAIRS ACT)

This statute establishes the powers and duties of the Ministry of Municipal Affairs. It also used to contain a simple procedure for tax sales in certain limited circumstances until the passage of the *Municipal Tax Sales Act*, which consolidated the rules for tax sale under both this Act and the *Municipal Act*. To a large extent, the procedures under this Act were adopted in the *Municipal Tax Sales Act, 1984*. Nevertheless, for the purposes of reviewing title, it is still important to know the procedures that applied under this Act.

During the Great Depression in the 1930s, many municipalities found that their tax revenues were not sufficient to cover their expenditures. Many of them could not honour their debentures. The Ontario government had to take over these debts and in those municipalities the Department of Municipal Affairs took over effective operation of the business of the municipality. In any municipality where this had ever happened, the Act's simplified procedures for tax sales remained in effect until enactment of the *Municipal Tax Sales Act, 1984*, even though the Department had long since handed back control to the elected council.

Where the *Municipal Affairs Act* applied, the treasurer simply registered a tax arrears certificate when taxes were unpaid for three years. Thereupon the land described in the certificate vested in and became the property of the municipality in fee simple, free and clear of any other interest subject only to the right of redemption. The treasurer then sent, by registered mail, to anyone having an interest in the property as shown by searches in the land registry office and the sheriff's office, a notice in prescribed form of the registration of the certificate and of the right of redemption. The redemption period was one year. If it was redeemed, the treasurer registered a redemption certificate which cancelled the tax arrears certificate and title went back as it was. But if it was not redeemed, the municipality became the owner and could sell it by deed just as it could sell any other land it owned. This deed might be authorized by by-law and, if so, proof of the passage of that by-law, *i.e.*, a certified copy, should be registered on title. However, such a by-law was not essential. Many solicitors were of the opinion that a municipality could not validly sell land without passing a by-law authorizing such sale. They were relying on the *Municipal Act* (ss. 101(1) and 191(1)):

> 101(1) Except where otherwise provided, the jurisdiction of every council is confined to the municipality that it represents and its powers shall be exercised by by-law.

> 191(1) The council of every corporation may pass by-laws for acquiring or expropriating any land required for the purposes of the corporation, and for erecting and repairing buildings thereon, and for making additions to or alterations of such buildings, and may sell or otherwise dispose of the same when no longer so required.

Waterous Engine Works Co. v. Palmerston (Town), [1892] S.C.J. No. 82, 21 S.C.R. 556, and *John Mackay and Co. v. Toronto (City)*, [1920] A.C. 208 (P.C.) are cases that provided further authority for the proposition that actions taken by a municipality not authorized by by-law were void.

However, neither of those cases dealt with the sale of land. Lerner J., in his judgment in *Biggs v. Egremont (Township)*, [1974] O.J. No. 1793, 5 O.R. (2d) 72 (H.C.J.), vard [1976] O.J. No. 2086, 12 O.R. (2d) 18 (C.A.), ruled that the powers of the municipality to acquire or expropriate land by by-law are disjunctive and not conjunctive with the words of the statutory authority to "sell or otherwise dispose of lands". Therefore, a municipality may sell land without a by-law.

Clearly, a by-law of the municipality was not required to authorize a tax sale under the provisions of the *Municipal Act*, since title to the land under those provisions did not vest in the municipality; that statute specifically authorized the treasurer and the warden to execute and deliver a tax deed that vested the land in the purchaser.

Under the *Municipal Affairs Act*, the treasurer was required to register a statutory declaration on title to the lands setting forth the names and addresses of all persons to whom notice had been sent. A copy of the notice had to be attached as an exhibit.

The deed from the municipality had to have the consent of the Minister of Intergovernmental Affairs endorsed on it. Note that, as in the procedure under the *Municipal Act*, the land remained subject to easements and to any interest of the Crown. *The Tax Sales Confirmation Act, 1974*, S.O. 1974, c. 90, s. 2, confirms the vesting of clear title in the municipality in the case of tax arrears certificates registered prior to July 1, 1973, notwithstanding deficiencies of form or procedure.

MUNICIPAL TAX SALES ACT, R.S.O. 1990, c. M.60

The tax sale provisions of the *Municipal Act* and the *Municipal Affairs Act* were repealed when this Act was passed, effective November 27, 1984. After that date, if there are arrears of taxes of more than three years, the treasurer may register a tax arrears certificate on title. That certificate states that the land will be sold by public sale if the cancellation price (tax arrears and other amounts owing) is not paid within one year of the registration of the certificate. All parties with an interest in the land are sent notice of the certificate by registered mail.

If the cancellation price is paid within one year, the certificate is cancelled and its cancellation is registered. If, however, a year passes and the arrears are still outstanding, the treasurer puts the land up for public sale. If the land is not sold, it vests in the municipality.

If the cancellation price is paid by someone other than the registered owner who was entitled to notice of the sale, that person has a lien on the land for the amount paid. The cancellation certificate shall clearly state that the person named has a lien. That lien has priority over the interest of any other person who received notice of the arrears.

If the land is sold, the treasurer registers a tax deed (or a notice of vesting, if the land goes to the municipality) along with a statutory declaration verifying that proper procedure has been followed. A registered deed or notice of vesting vests the estate in fee simple in the land in the person (or municipality) named.

Subject to proof of fraud, every tax deed and notice of vesting, when registered, is final, binding and conclusive, and not subject to challenge for any reason. No action may be brought for recovery of land after the registration of a tax deed or notice of vesting, provided the statutory declaration has also been registered. This result has been confirmed by the decision in *Hunt Estate v. Renfrew (County)*, [1990] O.J. No. 3304, 75 O.R. (2d) 310 (Gen. Div.). It is still possible to bring an action for damages against the municipality, however.

Effective January 1, 2003, this Act was repealed and municipal tax sales is now governed by the *Municipal Act, 2001*, which is reviewed and discussed earlier in this chapter.

OCCUPIERS' LIABILITY ACT,
R.S.O. 1990, c. O.2

This statute imposes a duty of care on "occupiers" to take such care as is reasonable in the circumstances to ensure that persons entering onto premises are reasonably safe while on the premises. The duty imposed by this Act replaces the rules established at common law in respect of such duties but, to the extent a greater obligation is owed by any other statute or "rule of law", that higher standard is deemed to apply (see s. 9).

An "occupier" is defined as including any person in physical possession of a property or who has responsibility and control over a property's condition, the activities carried on at a property or over what persons are allowed onto a property. Pursuant to s. 3(3), the duty of care owed under this Act may be modified or excluded by an occupier.

Section 4 stipulates that the duty of care provided for does not apply in respect of risks willingly assumed by a person entering onto a property as long as the occupier does not deliberately or recklessly create unsafe conditions. Courts have held that to take advantage of this provision, an occupier must demonstrate that a person assumed a risk with full knowledge of the risk and waived their right against the occupier with respect thereto (see *Waldick v. Malcolm*, [1989] O.J. No. 1970, 70 O.R. (2d) 717 (C.A.), affd by the Supreme Court of Canada [1991] S.C.J. No. 55, 83 D.L.R. (4th) 114).

Section 8 of the Act also creates a duty of care that landlords must observe toward tenants and any other person allowed onto premises. Such a duty is only owed where the landlord is responsible for the maintenance and repair of the premises and fails to carry out that responsibility.

ONTARIO NEW HOME WARRANTIES PLAN ACT,
R.S.O. 1990, c. O.31

This Act applies to all new homes sold in Ontario. A "home" is defined under the Act to include a self-contained one-family dwelling, whether detached or attached, a building composed of not more than two self-contained, one-family dwellings, a residential condominium unit and any other dwelling prescribed by regulation. The Act is administered by Tarion Warranty Corporation, which may be contacted at:

> 5150 Yonge St.
> Concourse Level
> Toronto, ON
> M2N 6L8

> Website: <http://www.tarion.com>

Section 6 of the Act requires registration of a vendor or builder before any person can act as such of a new home. This registration may be revoked if a person "has a record of breaches of warranties or of failure or unwillingness to complete performance of contracts" (see s. 8(2)). Section 12 requires that no builder may even commence construction of a home until Tarion has been notified and the prescribed fee has been paid. The fee goes toward creation of a guarantee fund. A prospective purchaser should always ask for a builder's registration number and for the enrolment number of the particular home. Where a builder is not registered under the Act but enters into agreements to sell homes, the courts have held that prior to closing and while the builder remains unregistered, the purchase agreement is voidable at the option of the purchaser (see *Beer v. Townsgate I Ltd.*, [1997] O.J. No. 4276, 36 O.R. (3d) 136 (C.A.)).

The Act and its regulations have several significant functions that can be summarized as follows:

DEPOSITS

If a builder goes bankrupt or fundamentally breaches a purchase or construction agreement in relation to a home purchase entered into before February 1, 2003, the purchaser is entitled to be paid out of the guarantee fund the amount of the deposit paid to the builder to a maximum of $20,000. After February 1, 2003, the maximum payable is $40,000. For condominiums, the maximum amount payable out of the guarantee fund is $20,000 plus interest. Any deposit over and above the specified amounts is not protected. A purchaser must receive from the builder a deposit receipt in proper form as evidence of payment of the deposit (see s. 14(1) of the Act and s. 6 of R.R.O. 1990, Reg. 892, as amended).

WARRANTIES

Every vendor of a new home is deemed to give to every purchaser several warranties that will be honoured by the Corporation if the vendor fails to honour them provided that a claim is filed by the purchaser with the Corporation within the time period applicable to each warranty, which time periods start running from the date of the issuance of the certificate of completion and possession (discussed below). Those warranties are as follows:

1. The home is constructed in a workmanlike manner, is free from defects in materials, is fit for habitation and is constructed in accordance with the Ontario Building Code. This warranty has a duration of one year and is meant to cover the deficiencies listed in the certificate of completion and any other issues that arise thereafter before the year expires. Pursuant to s. 6(3) of R.R.O. 1990, Reg. 892, the maximum claim that can be advanced in respect of matters to which this warranty applies is either $100,000, $150,000 or $300,000, depending on the date of the agreement and the date that possession to the home is given; if a warranty claim relates to incomplete items, s. 6(7) of the same regulation limits the liability of the Corporation to 2 per cent of the sale price or $5,000, whichever is greater. Note also that s. 13(2) of the Act lists 12 exclusions to this warranty.

2. There will be no water penetration through the basement or foundation of the house and: (i) the home is constructed in a workmanlike manner and is free from defects in materials such that the building

envelope prevents water penetration; (ii) the electrical, plumbing and heating systems are free from defects; (iii) all exterior cladding is free from defects; and (iv) the home is free from Ontario Building Code violations affecting safety (see s. 14 and s. 15(2) of R.R.O. 1990, Reg. 892). These warranties have a duration of two years and the maximum claims are the same as for claims under paragraph 1 above.

3. The home is free of major structural defects. Pursuant to s. 16 of Reg. 892, this warranty has a duration of seven years from the date of the executed certificate of completion and possession and, as with the prior warranties, is limited to a claim for up to $300,000 (see s. 6(3) of Reg. 892). What constitutes a "major structural defect" is described in great detail in s. 1 of Reg. 892 and includes failure of the load-bearing walls, defects that materially and adversely affect the use of the home for the purpose for which it was intended, damage due to soil movement, major cracks in basement walls, collapse or distortion of joints or roof structure and other items.

SUBSTITUTION OF MATERIALS

Pursuant to s. 18 of Reg. 892, every vendor of a new home warrants that it will not make any substitutions in any items of construction or finishing for which the purchaser has a right of selection pursuant to the terms of the purchase agreement. Time periods are provided for in the regulation within which a purchaser must select a substitution, failing which the vendor or builder may select an alternate item; nevertheless, all substitutions, whether selected by the vendor or purchaser or whether they involve items that the purchaser has a right or no right to select, must be items of equal or better quality than the items being replaced. Any claim advanced by a purchaser to the Corporation of a purported breach of these "no substitution" provisions must be made within one year from the date of the certificate of completion.

CONCILIATION

Section 17 of the Act provides for a conciliation process between the builder and the purchaser in respect of disputes as to warranty matters and a 15-day "cooling-off" period before either of them can start an action against one another in order to allow the Corporation to invoke its conciliation function. Any decision by the Corporation relating to a warranty matter may be appealed by the purchaser to the Licence Appeal Tribunal. Note the decision in *Griffin v. T & R Brown Construction Ltd.*, [2006] O.J. No. 4724, 53 R.P.R. (4th) 104 (S.C.J.); supp. reasons [2007] O.J. No. 527 (S.C.J.) where the Court allowed a home buyer who was dissatisfied with the conciliation decisions of the Corporation, and who did not appeal to the above Tribunal, to avail himself of remedies at common law for breach of the purchase agreement notwithstanding the builder's position that the Act provided the homebuyer with statutory redress for his complaints.

DELAYS IN COMPLETION

Another necessary function of the Act is to deal with delays that prevent new homes from being transferred to purchasers on the originally scheduled completion date. Section 12 of R.R.O. 1990, Reg. 894 requires that every agreement of purchase and sale for a new home include a mandatory addendum prescribed by the regulation. The addendum creates a regime to deal with closing date extensions and offers purchasers rights of termination and compensation in certain circumstances.

The addendum contains the agreement of the builder/vendor to take all reasonable steps to construct the dwelling without delay. If the vendor cannot close the transaction on the date originally set for closing because additional time is required to complete construction, the vendor is required to extend the closing date for any period or periods it requires which, in the aggregate, cannot exceed 120 days. Be aware that this provision is subject to contractual modification where, for example, a purchaser is able to obtain the agreement of the vendor that no extensions are permitted.

If the home is still not complete after the 120-day extension period, then the purchase agreement shall either be: (i) terminated by the purchaser with the delivery of a notice to that effect within 10 days of the expiry of the 120-day period; (ii) extended for an additional 120 days where the purchaser has not delivered a termination notice; and (iii) finally terminated if after 240 days (the sum of the two extension periods), the home is still not completed, unless the vendor and purchaser then agree to some other arrangement.

Note that the vendor may exclude delays resulting from strikes or from other events beyond the vendor's control in calculating the above time periods. To take advantage of the right to further extend the closing date as a result of these events, the vendor must give notice to a purchaser of the circumstances within 20 days and provide an estimate of the likely delay. Once the strike or other event has concluded, the vendor has 20 days to notify the purchaser of the facts surrounding the event that caused the delay and the new closing date that is in effect as a result thereof.

Pursuant to s. 2(4) of O. Reg. 165/08, where delays have occurred, a purchaser is entitled to compensation for additional living costs caused by the delay in an amount equal to $100 per day but not exceeding $5,000 in the aggregate. Such compensation is payable if closing occurs after the scheduled closing date, as it may have been extended, subject to certain other limitations set forth in the regulation which allow a vendor to avoid such claims where sufficient notice of the anticipated delay was given to a purchaser. However, closing must occur for a purchaser to make such a claim for reimbursement of living expenses.

CONDOMINIUMS

The above sections of the Act that have been reviewed often contain different provisions where the home at issue is a residential condominium unit. For example, the addendum described above does not apply to the sale of condominiums; instead, the Act allows vendors of such units greater latitude to estimate occupancy dates and extend closings. For condominiums, s. 3 of O. Reg. 165/08 requires a vendor selling a condominium unit to specify in the purchase agreement a tentative or fixed occupancy date. If only a tentative date is given, the vendor must provide a fixed date for occupancy within 30 days after the completion of the roof of the building and at least 120 days before the scheduled tentative date. If no notice is given as to the fixed occupancy date at least 90 days prior to the tentative date, then the tentative date becomes the fixed date for occupancy. Subject to rights to extend occupancy for periods that are similar to those which apply to non-condominiums, the Act does not give a condominium purchaser a right to rescind the purchase agreement if occupancy dates are not achieved due to construction delays. Purchasers are left to claims for compensation of living expenses.

Insofar as warranties are concerned, all time periods for individual units start to run from the date the purchaser takes occupancy, and not the date the certificate of possession is signed.

Insofar as the common elements of a condominium are concerned, the basic one-year warranty contained in s. 13(1) of the Act is provided to the condominium corporation, which warranty runs from the date of the registration of the declaration for the condominium. Pursuant to s. 6(8) of Reg. 892, the maximum amount recoverable out of the guarantee fund in respect of claims relating to the common elements is the lesser of $2,500,000 or $50,000 per number of units in the building.

It is essential that every purchaser complete the Certificate of Completion and Possession before completing the purchase. It provides a space for unfinished items or deficiencies to which the builder must still attend. It also gives the two numbers referred to above and it is a prerequisite of any claim under the Act.

For further discussion of this Act, see Chapter 14.

ONTARIO WATER RESOURCES ACT, R.S.O. 1990, c. O.40

The *Ontario Water Resources Act* ("OWRA") is, in many ways, a complementary statute to the *Environmental Protection Act* and many of its provisions mirror those that were reviewed earlier in this chapter in connection with the *Environmental Protection Act*.

As the title suggests, the OWRA contains provisions directed at protecting that part of the environment comprised of rivers, lakes, watercourses and other natural and artificial bodies of water and at controlling their use by the public. To that end, the Ontario Clean Water Agency is created by the OWRA to issue orders, directions, approvals and reports pertaining to the use and abuse of water. Orders may be issued pursuant to s. 16, s. 16.1, s. 16.2, s. 17 and other sections of the Act in respect of contraventions of the OWRA which require persons to comply with directions, take preventative measures to lessen water quality impairment, effect changes to water or sewer works and to cause persons to cease the use of their properties until water pollution is eliminated. Pursuant to the now repealed s. 13 of the OWRA, the Minister of the Environment was required to maintain a record of all orders, approvals, requirements and reports issued under the Act and provide information to the public as to same and allow inspections of all such materials. Pursuant to the new s. 13.1, which came into force on June 4, 2007, the Ministry maintains alphabetical index records of the names of all persons to whom instruments are directed under the Act. The new section permits inspection of any instrument directed to the named person, and also requires the Ministry to search the index record and inform any person making a request as to whether the name of a specified person appears.

Pursuant to ss. 80 to 84 of the OWRA, the Minister or Director under the Act may cause anything to be done to a property as a result of any outstanding order or direction if it is in the public interest to do so. All costs incurred in undertaking any such initiative are recoverable with interest from the person to whom the order was issued. Pursuant to s. 88, if an order has been issued to a person who owns land in a municipality, the Director may instruct the municipality to recover the costs incurred by the Agency in relation to that land and the municipality shall have a lien on the land for such amounts which are deemed to be municipal taxes and be added to the tax rolls and be collected in the same manner and enjoy the same priority as municipal taxes.

Section 103 of the OWRA contains the same provisions found in s. 197 of the *Environmental Protection Act* discussed earlier in this chapter which allows the Agency to register restrictions on title to a property which prohibit the owner from dealing with the property without first giving a purchaser a copy of all outstanding orders issued under the Act. If a person does not give copies of such orders to a purchaser, a subsequent dealing with the land is voidable at the instance of the person who was not given a copy of all orders before the applicable property transaction was completed.

Certain other provisions of the OWRA regulate the taking of water, the construction of wells, the establishment of water works and the operation of sewage works. Section 34 limits the taking of water from any public source to no more than 50,000 litres a day without permit, subject to the exceptions mentioned therein. Pursuant to s. 36, a permit is required to construct or establish a well in prescribed areas.

Sections 53 to 62 of the Act deal with sewage works. In part, they replace Part VIII of the *Environmental Protection Act* that had dealt with sewage works but has since been repealed. "Sewage works" are any works for the collection, treatment and disposal of sewage. No sewage works can be established, altered or replaced without an OWRA approval. Section 53(6) makes it clear that these provisions also regulate the use, installation and replacement of septic tanks which makes this part of the Act relevant for residential and recreational property purchases where septic tanks are in use. A purchaser should check to make sure a certificate of approval has been issued under the OWRA and has not been revoked. The local health unit or Ministry of the Environment office will be able to advise whether such approvals have been issued.

PARTITION ACT, R.S.O. 1990, c. P.4

If two or more joint tenants, tenants-in-common or partners have a dispute over the land which they jointly own, any such party may make application to the Ontario Superior Court of Justice for the partition of the land, or if the land is not readily divisible, for the sale of the property and division of the proceeds. The proceeding is available to anyone who has an interest in land, including, for example, a mortgagee. The courts have consistently held that a tenant-in-common has a *prima facie* right under the *Partition Act* to compel the sale of a property that it owns in common with a co-tenant: *Greenbanktree Power Corp. v. Coinamatic Canada Inc.*, [2002] O.J. No. 1786, 59 O.R. (3d) 449 (S.C.J.), affd [2003] O.J. No. 3878, 69 O.R. (3d) 784 (Div. Ct.), affd [2004] O.J. No. 5158, 75 O.R. (3d) 478 (C.A.). Pursuant to *Greenbanktree*, partition and sale applications will be dismissed only where the application is brought with malicious, oppressive or vexatious intent. Other cases have held that serious hardship that will arise upon sale or partition may be sufficient on its own to allow a judge to dismiss the application: see the cases listed in *Lagoski v. Shano*, [2007] O.J. No. 159, 53 R.P.R. (4th) 295 (S.C.J.), revd [2007] O.J. No. 5348, 232 O.A.C. 21 (Div. Ct.).

Like any court proceeding, this one involves considerable time and expense. Therefore, it is common, and indeed recommended, that co-owners acquiring land enter into some form of co-ownership agreement. Such agreement should provide a mechanism for the sale of the land in the event of disagreement between the co-owners. Often this will take the form of a "shotgun" clause under which one party may name a price for either buying or selling the land. The other party may choose which to do but must do one or the other. In agreeing to such a resolution mechanism, it is also advisable to specifically preclude the co-owners from being allowed to make an application under the *Partition Act* for the partition and sale of the property. The courts have held that an explicit provision to this effect in a co-owners agreement will preclude a co-owner from an entitlement to the partition and sale of the property where an alternate mechanism (such as a buy-sell or "shotgun") is included in the co-owners agreement (see *Capannelli v. Muroff*, [2002] O.J. No. 191 (C.A.).

PUBLIC LANDS ACT,
R.S.O. 1990, c. P.43

This Act deals generally with the granting of Crown lands and gives jurisdiction for Crown lands to the Ministry of Natural Resources. It is under this Act that Crown patents are issued, creating the original title to land.

The major problem arising out of any consideration of Crown patents is the effect and meaning of the reservations from the grant.

Section 15(6) requires all Crown grants for summer resort locations to reserve all mines and minerals thereunder. The minerals reservation means that if gold, silver, lead, iron or another mineral is found under your client's cottage, it belongs to the Crown. A separate grant must be obtained to obtain title to the minerals. However, note that by s. 61, where lands were patented before May 6, 1913, minerals pass to the grantee whether reserved or not and, in the case of Crown grants after that date, minerals pass unless expressly reserved.

Subsection 58(2), as passed in 1970, states that a reservation of all timber and trees or any class or kind of trees in a Crown grant for a summer resort location is void, and subs. 58(3) states that the reservation of all timber and trees or any class or kind of trees contained in a Crown grant dated on or before April 1, 1869, is void. This will do away with the reservation found in most old patents for "all white pine trees".

Reservations in letters patent that dealt with the Surveyor-General of Woods, or that required a patentee to erect a dwelling thereon or a transferee to take an oath prescribed by law, were all repealed by the *Public Lands Amendment Act*, S.O. 1957, c. 99.

By s. 65, all patents shall reserve to the Crown the right to construct roads without compensation.

These Crown patent reservations create a problem when dealing with cottage properties. Although there is no set rule, you will usually find that there is a 66-foot allowance reserved along the shoreline of a lake. Sometimes, the strip is characterized as a "road allowance", in which case title in the strip is in the local municipality and it can be closed in the usual way. However, most of such road allowances have not been closed; neither have they been opened as actual roadways. But the reservation of that strip of land remains outstanding as a problem to you and your client. The cottage property does not actually front on the water; the general public has a right to pass along the strip; the municipality may decide to open a road along the waterfront; and any buildings erected on the strip could be removed. In many cases, the problems are intensified because the water-line today is so different than it was when the first surveys were drawn. Parts of the 66-foot road allowance reserved in an old Crown patent may now be under water. You must rely on a surveyor to establish exactly where the road allowance is.

Another reservation in Crown grants for land fronting on navigable waters is the right of mariners and fishermen to use the "foreshore"; this right allows people on the water to land in cases of emergency, but it does not give to anyone the right to enter the foreshore from the land.

These Crown patent reservations are confusing and each title must be interpreted after a careful examination of the actual patent. Patents are not usually found in the normal search of title. The first entry in a land registry office abstract will give you the date and name of the original patentee. To look at particulars of the grant and the reservations, you must attend at the office of the Ministry of Natural Resources where copies of every patent in Ontario are on file (see p. 2).

PUBLIC TRANSPORTATION AND HIGHWAY IMPROVEMENT ACT, R.S.O. 1990, c. P.50

You must always advise of the implications of ss. 31 and 34 of the *Public Transportation and Highway Improvement Act* when your client is purchasing land abutting a provincial highway. It is interesting to note also that although our head of state is now and has been since 1952, Her Majesty Queen Elizabeth, a provincial highway in Ontario is still designated as "the King's Highway" (see s. 7); any reference to a Queen's Highway in a description of land is in error.

Section 31(1)(*b*) prohibits the construction of any entrance or access to any King's Highway, except in accordance with the conditions of a permit issued by the Ministry of Transportation. Thus, although your client may have good title to a piece of land abutting a highway, access to it is denied until a permit from the Minister has been obtained. That permit will be specific as to the location of the entrance. The reason for this requirement is to prevent an entranceway on a curve or just over the brow of a hill.

Section 34 restricts your client even further. "No person shall, except under a permit therefor from the Minister" erect or alter any building, fence, gasoline pump, tree, shrub, hedge or other structure or road within 45 metres of any limit of a King's Highway or within 180 metres of the centre point of an intersection. Nor can a sign be displayed within 400 metres of the limit of a King's Highway other than a 60-centimetre by 30-centimetre sign giving the owner's name and occupation. Also, certain uses, such as shopping centres, stadiums or any other uses that cause people to congregate in large numbers, must be set back 800 metres.

Naturally the restrictions on lands abutting "controlled access highways", *e.g.*, the 400 series highways and the Queen Elizabeth Way, are even more stringent; no buildings, *etc.*, within 45 metres of any limit or 395 metres of the centre of an intersection (see s. 38(2)). Note that these sections do not absolutely prohibit these uses on lands abutting King's Highways, but they do require that you apply to the Minister of Transportation and Communications for a permit which may be issued subject to such terms and conditions as are deemed proper.

Subsections 34(6) and 38(5) authorize the Minister to require an owner of land to remove any building, fence, gasoline pump or sign erected in contravention of these sections.

REAL PROPERTY LIMITATIONS ACT, R.S.O. 1990, c. L.15

This Act establishes the time periods during which action to enforce various rights in relation to real property may be taken. Note that effective January 1, 2004, the title of the Act was changed from the *Limitations Act*, by S.O. 2002, c. 24, Sched. B, s. 26(2).

CERTAIN SECTIONS OF THE ACT

Section 4 — Ten-Year Possessory Title

No person can bring an action to recover land or rent except within the 10 years following the time at which the right first arose. This is the basis of the 10-year possessory title. By s. 13, if any acknowledgment in writing has been given to the person entitled to the land by the person in possession, then the 10-year period runs from the date of this acknowledgment. Thus, all you have to do to preserve your title to lands that are occupied by someone else is to obtain written acknowledgment from the occupant once every 10 years.

The courts will not lightly interfere with the title of a registered owner. The rule has always been to construe the limitations in the very strictest manner and any small act indicating possession is sufficient to protect the interests of the paper title holder: see *Masidon Investments Ltd. v. Ham*, [1982] O.J. No. 3541, 39 O.R. (2d) 534 (H.C.J.), affd [1984] O.J. No. 3139, 45 O.R. (2d) 563 (C.A.).

For a good discussion of the current law on adverse possession, see *Elliott v. Woodstock Agricultural Society*, [2008] O.J. No. 3708, 92 O.R. (3d) 711 (C.A.). In this case, the Court confirms that pursuant to ss. 4 and 15 of this Act, persons claiming a possessory title must establish: (1) actual possession for the statutory period of 10 years by themselves and those through whom they claim; (2) that the possession was with the intent of excluding from possession the actual owner; and (3) that there has been discontinuance of possession for the statutory period by the owner. On the facts of *Elliott*, the Court ruled that the third test was not satisfied where the owner held lands as inventory for future development, even though the claimant easily demonstrated and satisfied the first two parts of the test.

For other valuable discussions of the law, see *Bradford Investments (1963) Ltd. v. Fama*, [2005] O.J. No. 3258, 77 O.R. (3d) 127 (S.C.J.); and *Cantera v. Eller*, [2007] O.J. No. 1899, 56 R.P.R. (4th) 39 (S.C.J.), affd [2008] O.J. No. 5220, 74 R.P.R. (4th) 162 (C.A.).

Before proceeding with a claim based on adverse possession, you must satisfy yourself that the land is registered under the *Registry Act* and not the *Land Titles Act*. Section 51 of the *Land Titles Act* makes it clear that no rights can be acquired by adverse possession in lands after they have been registered under that Act (see *Gatz v. Kiziw*, [1958] S.C.J. No. 63, [1959] S.C.R. 10, and *Wigle v. Vanderkruk*, [2005] O.J. No. 3032, [2005] O.T.C. 638 (S.C.J.); supp. reasons [2005] O.J. No. 3676 (S.C.J.)).

You should also check the chain of title to the land in question to make sure that no tax deed has been registered within the 10-year period of possession. A conveyance by tax deed operates to extinguish every claim based upon possession, except for claims perfected by more than 10 years' possession prior to registration of the tax deed (see *Raynor v. Gaspini*, [1982] O.J. No. 3488, 39 O.R. (2d) 51 (H.C.J.)).

Section 16 — Road Allowances

This section states that nothing in ss. 1 to 15 applies to lands included in any road allowance where the freehold in any such road allowance or highway is vested in the Crown or in a municipal corporation. Thus, no matter how long one maintains an encroachment over a portion of a road allowance, the municipality is not barred from bringing an action for possession, and the occupant cannot obtain title by adverse possession.

This section was added in 1922. However, even if it could be established that a predecessor in title was in open and exclusive possession of an unopened road allowance for 10 years prior to 1922, it was not possible to acquire possessory title to an original road allowance against a municipality because title to road allowances did not vest in municipalities until the enactment of the *Municipal Act, 1913*. See *Di Cenzo Construction Co. v. Glassco*, [1978] O.J. No. 3524, 21

O.R. (2d) 186 (C.A.). See also *Household Realty Corp. v. Hilltop Mobile Home Sales Ltd.*, [1982] O.J. No. 3344, 37 O.R. (2d) 508 (C.A.), which distinguishes an original road allowance from one created by the registration of a plan of subdivision.

Section 25 — Dower

This section provides a convenient answer to some dower problems. An action to enforce a dower right must be brought within 10 years from the death of the husband of the doweress. Unfortunately, s. 26 complicates that somewhat:

> Where a doweress has, after the death of her husband, actual possession of the land of which she is dowable, ... the period of ten years ... shall be computed from the time when such possession of the doweress ceased.

If you find an old dower interest outstanding on title that has not been barred or otherwise avoided, it is not enough to establish that the husband has been dead more than 10 years; you must also establish by affidavit evidence that the doweress has not been in possession during the last 10 years.

Section 31 — Easements

This section establishes that an easement that has been enjoyed for 20 years without interruption or consent is absolute and indefeasible. Such an easement is known as a "prescriptive" easement or one acquired by prescription or adverse possession. Where consent was once granted but 20 years have passed without that consent being renewed or restated, a claim to a right of way by adverse possession is established (see *Adrian v. McVannel*, [1992] O.J. No. 2401, 11 O.R. (3d) 137 (Gen. Div.)).

Section 35 — Easements for Wires and Cables

Notwithstanding the provisions of s. 31, no easement in respect of wires or cables running through or over land can be acquired by prescription.

ROAD ACCESS ACT,
R.S.O. 1990, c. R.34

This statute, which came into force in 1978, gives statutory protection to persons using what might otherwise be referred to as a right of way of necessity. In other words, it protects the access rights of property owners who would otherwise have landlocked parcels were it not for the access provided by an access road. An "access road" is defined in s. 1 as "a road located on land not owned by a municipality and not dedicated and accepted as, or otherwise deemed at law to be, a public highway, that serves as a motor vehicle access route to one or more parcels of land".

Section 2 prohibits any person from placing or maintaining an obstacle or barrier over an access road that, as a result, prevents all access to a parcel of land or a boat docking facility unless authorized by a judge's order or by written agreement of all persons affected by such barrier or unless the closure is temporary in nature for purposes of effecting repairs to same.

Subsections 2(3) to (6) set out the procedure for making application for closure of an access road.

Section 7 provides that a knowing contravention of s. 2 is an offence, and the Court "may order the person to remove the barrier or other obstacle" (s. 7(2)).

There have been many recent cases surrounding this Act and disputes between landowners burdened by access roads on their lands and landowners relying on such roads for access. For example, in *2008795 Ontario Inc. v. Kilpatrick*, [2007] O.J. No. 3248, 86 O.R. (3d) 561 (C.A.), the Court considered what constituted and qualified as the only access to lands and whether alternate access arrangements qualified as proper roads to permit the burdened land owner to disallow future access. This case also generally explores the history of this Act and its practical interpretation.

SHORT FORMS OF LEASES ACT, R.S.O. 1990, c. S.11

SHORT FORMS OF CONVEYANCES ACT, R.S.O. 1980, c. 472

SHORT FORMS OF MORTGAGES ACT, R.S.O. 1980, c. 474

Under the *Land Registration Reform Act, 1984*, the *Short Forms of Conveyances Act* and the *Short Forms of Mortgages Act* no longer apply to land in Ontario; standard covenants are now implied in transfers and changes. However, you should know these two Acts in order to interpret deeds and mortgages found in a chain of title prior to 1984. The *Short Forms of Leases Act* is still in force.

The three statutes follow a similar pattern. Their object is to reduce the length of conveyances, leases and mortgages. In each of the three statutes you will find as Schedule A the basic form of the document in question. Then, in Schedule B there are two columns. If a document is in the form shown in Schedule A and those words set out in Column One of Schedule B are included, the document has the same effect as if the much longer wording found in Column Two of Schedule B had been used.

Each Act specifically allows express exceptions or qualifications to be added to the prescribed wording in Column One, and the same exceptions or qualifications are deemed to have been added to the extended wording in Column Two.

But to obtain the advantage of the extended wording the basic form found in Schedule A must be used. This will explain why, aside from lawyers' basic conservatism, there has been such uniformity in deeds, mortgages and leases over the years.

Of course, nothing prevents adding other clauses to a document. Nor is there any reason to adhere to the short form document at all. Each Act states that, even if the document does not have the benefit of this Act, it is nevertheless binding.

SURVEYS ACT,
R.S.O. 1990, c. S.30

This is a long Act dealing with the technical aspects of surveys and is of interest mainly to surveyors. However, consider s. 57, dealing with roadways shown on a plan of subdivision. Even if never used, they are, by virtue of being laid out on the plan of subdivision, public roads until closed. And by the act of consenting to the registration of a plan of subdivision, a mortgagee of the lands comprising that plan of subdivision discharges its mortgage against all lands laid out as streets or highways (s. 78(3) of the *Registry Act* and s. 151(2) of the *Land Titles Act*).

TECHNICAL STANDARDS AND SAFETY ACT, 2000,
S.O. 2000, c. 16

This Act replaced several statutes and consolidated and imposed a consistent regulatory regime to govern the use and operation of amusement devices, boilers and pressure vessels, elevating devices, hydrocarbon fuel facilities and other enumerated matters. By its enactment, the previous *Amusement Devices Act*, *Boilers and Pressure Vessels Act*, *Elevating Devices Act*, *Energy Act* and *Gasoline Handling Act*, among others, were repealed.

The Technical Standards and Safety Authority ("TSSA") is given authority for the administration of the Act pursuant to s. 1.1 of O. Reg. 159/97 promulgated pursuant to the *Safety and Consumer Statutes Administration Act, 1996*, S.O. 1996, c. 19. It is a non-profit corporation that is not part of the Government of Ontario or a Crown agency. Instead, its board of directors is composed of representatives from the regulated industries, from government and from public interest groups. As a result, this essentially private authority created by statute assumes control of all enforcement and administrative matters in respect of the subjects identified above that had previously been overseen by the Ministry of Consumer and Commercial Relations.

Pursuant to s. 14 of the Act, an order may be issued to any person with respect to any matter regulated by the Act involving safety. The order may require that an apparatus be shut down, used with restrictions or not used at all. Orders may also be issued pursuant to s. 21 of the Act requiring a person to comply with a provision of the Act or any safety code or regulation made thereunder. Any person who fails to comply with the Act, the regulations or any order is guilty of an offence and on conviction is liable to a fine of up to $50,000 and/or to imprisonment for up to a year. A corporation is liable to be fined up to $1,000,000. Directors and officers are personally liable if they do not take all reasonable care to prevent a corporation from committing an offence and are subject to the same penalties as a person.

Pursuant to O. Reg. 223/01, various codes are adopted and incorporated by reference into the regulations. Real property practitioners involved in purchase, mortgage and lease transactions will be most concerned with any orders issued under the Act due to non-compliance with the safety codes relating to elevators, boilers and fuel storage tanks and to the issuance of licences for same.

The Liquid Fuels Handling Code merits some specific discussion. Pursuant to s. 1.1.4 of the Code, the owner of a facility as defined therein, must turn over to a purchaser or lessee of the facility all fuel handling records that an owner must maintain pursuant to the Code. The Code also regulates in detail the specifications, installation, repair and maintenance of fuel tanks. Insofar as the removal and closure of underground or above ground fuel tanks is concerned, the Code provides that:

- all leaks must be immediately contained;

- a tank not used for up to 180 days must be regularly inspected;

- a tank not used for more than 180 days requires that all product be removed from it and the tank be locked; and

- a tank not used for more than two years must be removed.

Any permanent removal of a tank requires the owner to notify the TSSA, the Ministry of the Environment and the local municipality within 90 days of its removal. Part 7 of the Code imposes environmental restoration obligations on owners as a result of the removal of tanks or due to any leaking from tanks. Such obligations include the preparation of assessment reports and decommissioning evaluations.

Effective September 1, 2007, the Liquid Fuels Handling Code, 2007, was adopted under Director's Order FS-107-07. Major changes between the 2001 and 2007 Codes include a new section on leak detection, a revised environmental section that requires that assessment reports be submitted to the TSSA when removing an underground tank or a large aboveground tank, and a new requirement that facilities must replace single-wall piping within 12 months of discovering a leak in the pipe. The Code is available from the Canadian Standards Association at 1-800-463-6727, or <http://www.ShopCSA.ca>.

The Fuel Oil Regulation (O. Reg. 213/01), as amended by a Director's Order issued on June 28, 2001, required all underground fuel tanks to be registered with the TSSA by May 1, 2001 failing which fuel oil will not be deliverable to the tank. Note that a fuel oil tank in a home is not an underground tank for the purposes of this regulation unless it is buried. In addition, the regulations provide for a timetable to be observed insofar as the removal or upgrading of existing tanks is concerned. For example, an underground tank 25 years old or older, or of unknown age, that was not specifically protected from corrosion, was required to be removed or upgraded by October 1, 2006. Other timelines apply to tanks that are not so old.

Information as to orders, licences and compliance matters can be obtained from the TSSA at:

14th Floor, Centre Tower
3300 Bloor Street West
Toronto, ON
M8X 2X4

The TSSA's website is <http://www.tssa.org> and can be consulted for further information.

TRESPASS TO PROPERTY ACT, R.S.O. 1990, c. T.21

It is an offence under this Act to enter without permission on land under cultivation or land enclosed so as to keep people out or animals in. Furthermore, an owner may post signs or give oral or written notice to the individuals concerned to prohibit entry or specific activities on the property (such as "No hunting or fishing" on a farmer's property or "No ball playing" in a public park) or requiring a person to leave premises already entered upon. An offender is liable to be arrested and fined.

Of course, any entry without permission on another person's land is also actionable at common law and the trespasser is liable for damages.

VENDORS AND PURCHASERS ACT, R.S.O. 1990, c. V.2

This is a short Act, and it is of much practical importance.

RELEVANT SECTIONS OF THE ACT

Section 1 — Rules

This section contains four rules that regulate the rights and obligations of the parties to an agreement of purchase and sale.

Rule 1, which deals with 20-year recitals, is of great assistance to a conveyancer:

1. Recitals, statements and descriptions of facts, matters and parties contained in statutes, deeds, instruments or statutory declarations twenty years old at the date of the contract, unless and except in so far as they are proved to be inaccurate, are sufficient evidence of the truth of such facts, matters and descriptions.

Thus, if when searching title you find in a deed 20 years old a recital stating that a grantor was unmarried, or that a joint tenant has died, or even where a party is described as "unmarried" or "widower", you do not have to look for any further evidence of that fact as you would in a more recent instrument; you are entitled under this "20-year recital" rule to depend on the facts and descriptions set out in the instrument.

Section 3 — Vendor and Purchaser Applications

This is the most often used and most important section of the Act. This section provides for an application to the Superior Court of Justice to settle a dispute between a vendor and a purchaser or their solicitors as to a requisition or objection to title.

If you are acting for the purchaser and you have searched the title and found something which you believe to be wrong with the title, you will requisition from the solicitor for the vendor the correction of this defect in title. The vendor's solicitor in turn will answer your letter of requisitions. There may be an explanation of facts or law for your requisition which, in the vendor's solicitor's opinion, is sufficient but which you do not choose to accept. Thus, the agreement between your respective clients may be on the verge of collapsing, and probably there will be two unhappy clients. They are not interested in such fine legal arguments; they just want to buy and sell property. Yet the solicitor for the purchaser must be able to give a clear opinion on title.

To settle this type of problem, either party can apply to the court for a ruling as to whether or not the requisition has been validly answered. If the court rules that it is a proper answer, then you register a certified copy of that court order on title and the problem is solved forever.

Since any requisition or answer to a requisition might go before a court for a ruling under this section, they should always be carefully worded so that it is clear what is being asked and what the reply is. The certified copy of the court order may contain both the question and the answer together with the court's decision as to whether the answer is sufficient.

It should be remembered that an order under this Act is usually considered to be a judgment *in personam*, not a judgment *in rem*; it deals with a particular answer to a requisition on a particular parcel of land and is binding on all subsequent purchasers of that parcel of land. In *Ferguson v. Niagara Falls (City)*, [1994] O.J. No. 4423, 21 O.R. (3d) 776 at 781 (Gen. Div.), Fleury J. stated regarding a ruling made by him under the Act:

> It is declaratory of the state of the title. The same objection as to title can never be raised after such an order has been granted. The judgement binds the land.

However, such an order may not be binding on purchasers of other land in similar circumstances because it is only the order of a single judge, and while it has persuasive value for another judge, it is not binding.

Many people learned this to their distress when they relied on the judgment of Fraser J. in *Carter v. Congram*, [1969] O.J. No. 1538, [1970] 1 O.R. 800 (H.C.J.), and used the device described therein to avoid s. 26 (now s. 50) of the *Planning Act*. In a newspaper report of the proceedings in the Supreme Court of Canada in *Forfar v. East Gwillimbury (Township)*, [1972] S.C.J. No. 38, 28 D.L.R. (3d) 512, Spence J. is quoted as having asked, "[i]f John Brown chooses to rely on a single court judgment that holds valid a scheme that is avowedly worked out to go around a statute, don't you think he was pretty bold?" This leaves a solicitor in a quandary in the many situations where the only law available is a single court judgment.

Section 4 — Implied Terms of Agreement of Purchase and Sale

This section is often overlooked. It states that if an agreement of purchase and sale is silent as to certain things, they shall be deemed to be included nonetheless. Each one of these clauses is included in all standard printed forms of agreement of purchase and sale, but in a handwritten agreement prepared by laymen or an agreement prepared by a careless solicitor there might be an omission. It is comforting to know that the law implies these provisions. They include the time for making requisitions on title, the time for answering them, and the items that are to be adjusted on closing.

VETERANS' LAND ACT,
R.S.C. 1970, c. V-4

This is one of the very few federal statutes referred to in this book and it gives rise to a constitutional problem. The Act was passed by the Parliament of Canada originally to assist veterans of military service to establish themselves on farms. The Director, The Veterans' Land Act, bought parcels of land and then sold them to veterans on very attractive terms. The deed to the veteran was delivered only upon payment of the total purchase price. The purpose of the Act was extended over the years so that veterans could borrow money on the security of land owned by them at very low cost. In each case, title in the land was conveyed to The Director, The Veterans' Land Act, until the loan was repaid. At that time the Director would either reconvey the lands to the veteran or as otherwise directed.

The only significance any of this has to our subject is s. 5(3) of the Act:

> (3) All conveyances from the Director constitute new titles to the land conveyed and have the same and as full effect as grants from the Crown of previously ungranted Crown lands.

Therefore, if you are searching a title and discover in the chain of title a deed from The Director, The Veterans' Land Act, you should not have to look behind it since this is said to be as good as an original Crown Patent.

Unfortunately, some lawyers refuse to accept this on the grounds that the federal government, under the division of powers in the *British North America Act*, does not have the power to deal with property and civil rights and, therefore, s. 5(3) is *ultra vires* and unconstitutional. We would refer you to *Armstrong v. Van Der Weyden*, [1965] 1 O.R. 68, 46 D.L.R. (2d) 629 (H.C.J.). This case was an application under the *Vendors and Purchasers Act* and Stewart J. considered that this section was a sufficient answer to requisitions concerning the chain of title prior to the deed from the Director.

See, however, *Patterson v. Gallaugher*, [1983] O.J. No. 3299, 46 O.R. (2d) 567, where the High Court of Justice expressed *in obiter* its grave doubts concerning the constitutional validity of s. 5(3).

CHAPTER 4

Statutory Liens and Tax Statutes Affecting Real Estate

In addition to the various liens that are established by common law and statute which are revealed by a search of registered title, there are a series of liens established by statute which may require further investigation outside the sheriff's office and the land registry office. You may find no reference to these liens on title but the land is encumbered by them nonetheless. There are also statutes that provide for amounts to be added to, and collected in the same manner as municipal taxes; and still others that provide relief from municipal taxes. Certain of these statutes are reviewed below.

BANKRUPTCY AND INSOLVENCY ACT, R.S.C. 1985, c. B-3

Section 14.06(7) of the Act provides that where any environmental condition or damage to a property is remedied or corrected by the federal or provincial government, the property of a debtor benefitting from such work is subject to a charge for the costs incurred in respect of such work. The charge is automatically created without the need for any registration on title. Such a charge is enforceable in the same manner as any mortgage or other security interest registered against property in accordance with the law of the jurisdiction in which the property is situate. The charge ranks ahead of any other claim, right or charge against the property notwithstanding any other federal or provincial law.

BROWNFIELDS FINANCIAL TAX INCENTIVE PROGRAM

The Brownfields Financial Tax Incentive Program is a provincial program that provides tax relief to eligible owners of brownfield properties. "Brownfield" properties are generally properties where contamination has rendered a site vacant, under-utilized, unsafe, unproductive or abandoned.

The Program is authorized by s. 365.1 of the *Municipal Act, 2001*, S.O. 2001, c. 25 and is conditional on a participating municipality enacting, by by-law, a complimentary brownfield tax incentive program. For example, the City of Toronto has a Brownfields Remediation Tax Assistance initiative, which offers brownfield property owners tax relief against certain remediation costs incurred where properties are remediated with a view to develop a site for uses that provide employment (not including retail).

To the extent that eligibility requirements are met, the Program provides tax relief by cancelling or deferring the educational tax component of municipal taxes. The amount of the cancellation or deferral will usually match the amount of the assistance being given by the municipality under its own municipal initiative.

Owners of brownfield properties cannot apply directly to the Program; rather, a municipality must make application to the Ministry of Municipal Affairs and Housing on behalf of the owner. This ensures that the property owner has first qualified for inclusion in the applicable municipality's brownfield initiative before making application to the Program.

Note that based on the current terms of the Program, tax assistance under the Program may be discontinued once a property that is enrolled in the Program is transferred or subdivided.

CONSERVATION LAND TAX INCENTIVE PROGRAM

Pursuant to s. 13.1 of the *Ministry of Natural Resources Act*, R.S.O. 1990, c. M.31, the Ministry of Natural Resources allows owners of eligible conservation lands to apply for a property tax exemption. Such lands must be "provincially significant" and include: (1) wetlands; (2) areas of natural and scientific interest; (3) habitats of endangered species; (4) certain lands within the Niagara Escarpment Plan; and (5) community conservation land. In each case, the parcel of land must be at least 1/5 of a hectare.

A commitment must be made to the Ministry by owners who receive an exemption to maintain their property in its natural state and to refrain from carrying out activities that would cause the property to lessen or lose its natural attributes. The Ministry reserves the right to recover taxes which would have otherwise been payable for up to five prior years where an owner has not honoured its commitment.

This is an annual program requiring an application anew in each year.

CORPORATIONS TAX ACT,
R.S.O. 1990, c. C.40

Section 99(1) of the Act states:

> 99(1) Any amount payable or required to be remitted under this Act by any person is, upon registration by the Minister in the proper land registry office of a notice claiming a lien and charge conferred by this section, a lien and charge on any interest the corporation liable to pay or remit the amount has in the real property described in the notice.

It was once necessary to list all corporations in the chain of title and write to the Ministry of Revenue to obtain a certificate that the Ministry claimed no lien for corporation tax. In 1979, by S.O. 1979, c. 89, s. 1, the lien provision was amended to dispense with an automatic lien for arrears. The lien is now effective only upon registration by the Minister of a notice of lien on title. Therefore, the tedious procedure of writing and waiting for clearances is no longer necessary.

DEVELOPMENT CHARGES ACT, 1997, S.O. 1997, c. 27

Many municipalities levy a charge on any new development and construction undertaken within their jurisdiction. Such a charge is also levied by regional municipalities and by both public and separate school boards pursuant to the *Education Act*.

The charges levied are usually calculated by reference to a development charges by-law passed by a municipality pursuant to s. 26. Alternatively, a separate agreement may be entered into with a developer pursuant to s. 27. In either case, the area or density of the new development often determines the amount of the charge.

The Act permits a municipality to withhold a building permit from a developer if development charges are not paid. If a municipality chooses to issue a building permit without payment in full of the development charges, s. 32(1) of the Act allows the municipality to add the unpaid amounts to the tax rolls for the property and collect such amounts in the same manner and with the same priority as realty taxes. The *Education Act* contains complimentary provisions in respect of those development charges levied by public and separate school boards in the municipality.

ESTATE TAX ACT, R.S.C. 1970, c. E-9

Section 47 (repealed, S.C. 1983-84, c. 40, s. 26(1)) stated:

> 47(1) Any amount payable as tax, interest or penalties under this Act ... shall ... be ... a lien ... in favour of Her Majesty.

The lien provision in *The Succession Duty Act* was so effective that the federal government decided they too would impose a lien. After the passage of the *Estate Tax Act*, S.C. 1958, c. 29, on January 1, 1959, it was necessary to register an *Estate Tax Act* release on title also. These are little blue release documents that were registered or attached to the instrument before the land could be conveyed.

The *Income Tax Act*, which came into force January 1, 1972, contains a provision that the *Estate Tax Act* does not apply to any person whose death occurred after 1971. Therefore, no estate tax release was available or required in the case of persons dying after December 31, 1971.

Because of certain complicated arrangements between the Government of Ontario and the Government of Canada, estate tax releases are no longer required, and the Department of National Revenue will not issue releases even for property owned by a person who died between 1959 and 1971.

Section 47(3) of the *Estate Tax Act* stated that no lien for estate taxes could be imposed in a province that had entered into an agreement with the Government of Canada under which no transfer may be made without registration of a consent. In 1969, pursuant to P.C. 1969-2097, s. 12(B) of the Estate Tax regulations was amended to prescribe Ontario as one of the provinces that had entered such an agreement. Therefore, from that date forward there was no lien for estate tax in Ontario.

FAMILY RESPONSIBILITY AND SUPPORT ARREARS ENFORCEMENT ACT, 1996, S.O. 1996, c. 31

Pursuant to s. 42 of this Act, a support order issued by a court may be registered on title to the land of the person identified as the payor in the order and upon its registration, the order constitutes a charge on that property. Such a charge may be enforced by the sale of the property in the same manner as a sale to realize on a mortgage. Note that pursuant to s. 42(3) any discharge or postponement of the support order requires a court order.

The registration of a support order under this Act is subject to any encumbrances registered in priority to it at the time of its registration.

THE FARM PROPERTY CLASS TAX RATE PROGRAM

Under the *Ministry of Agriculture, Food and Rural Affairs Act*, R.S.O. 1990, c. M.16, s. 7, authority exists for the creation of programs, one of which is the Farm Property Class Tax Rate Program. Pursuant to this initiative, an owner of property that meets all prerequisites is entitled to be taxed at a rate that is 25 per cent of the municipal residential tax rate. One of the prerequisites is that there be an operating farm on the land from which agricultural products having a gross value of at least $7,000 have been produced in the year. The farm may be run by the owner of the land or by a tenant; in either case, the owner becomes entitled to the lower tax rate.

Other prerequisites include: (1) the property has been assessed as farmland; (2) more than one-half of the ownership is held by a Canadian citizen or permanent resident; and (3) a valid Farm Business Registration number has been issued for the farm business operation on the land.

HARMONIZED SALES TAX

The federal goods and services tax ("GST") was introduced on January 1, 1991, and is levied pursuant to Part IX of the *Excise Tax Act*, R.S.C. 1985, c. E-15, as amended. The rate remained unchanged until July 1, 2006, when it was reduced from 7 to 6 per cent; it was further reduced to 5 per cent effective January 1, 2008.

Effective July 1, 2010, Ontario harmonized its retail sales tax with the GST to create a harmonized sales tax ("HST") at the rate of 13 per cent, with 5 per cent being the federal component originating from the GST and with 8 per cent being the provincial component originating from the Ontario *Retail Sales Tax Act*, R.S.O. 1990, c. R.31. Accordingly, going forward and subject to transitionary provisions required to cover overlaps in the supply of goods and services during the phasing in of this new tax, HST replaces the GST in Ontario.

The application of HST is extremely complex, so the following is of necessity a very brief summary of its effect on real estate transactions. That being said, in most cases the transition from the GST regime to the HST regime will not result in any significant difference, other than, of course, the higher rate!

The general rule is that HST must be paid on all purchases made in Canada unless the supply is exempt. If the purchase is by someone who intends to use the supply in commercial activities, the purchaser is entitled to an "input tax credit" — in effect, a rebate of the tax paid. If the purchaser is a registrant under the Act or the vendor is a non-resident, then the purchaser is required to file a special HST return and pay the net tax (*i.e.*, net of input tax credits) directly to the Canada Revenue Agency ("CRA"). Otherwise, the purchaser is required to pay the appropriate percentage of the purchase price to the vendor and the vendor remits that amount to the Receiver General.

The exemptions are found in Part 1 of Schedule V of the Act. The main exemption is the sale of "used housing", which includes residential condominium units. Thus, the majority of real estate transactions involving the purchase and sale of a previously occupied house are exempt from HST. Other exemptions include homes built by owner-occupiers, the sale of recreational properties (including non-commercial hobby farms) by an individual, certain sales of farmland and certain sales of vacant lands sold by an individual who is not doing so in the course of a business.

For purchase of real property such as apartment buildings, the property being acquired will usually similarly qualify as the sale of used housing and therefore be exempt. In these circumstances, it is necessary to obtain assurances from the vendor that such is the case; it is common to obtain representations, warranties and declarations to that effect.

If a purchaser of non-exempt property (*e.g.*, commercial real estate, whether new or used) is registered for HST purposes, the vendor is not required under s. 221(2)(*b*) to collect and remit the HST. When acting for the vendor of commercial real property, you should obtain proof from the purchaser by way of a statutory declaration that the purchaser is a registrant accompanied by a copy of the purchaser's certificate of registration, which will include the registration number. Obtaining this information is essential in order to avoid the liability under the Act that comes with failing to otherwise collect the tax. Non-registration of the transferee (which is often different from the purchaser named in the agreement of purchase and sale) is frequently a problem encountered at closing on account of the amount of potential tax, particularly because it is common to use a newly incorporated company to purchase property intended for commercial use. Therefore, a vendor is advised to warn the purchaser of the need for registration well in advance of closing and to monitor progress to avoid the difficulties that will exist at closing if the transferee is not registered. Note that pursuant to s. 221(*b*.1), vendors will also not be required to collect and remit HST where they and the recipient have made an election under s. 2, Part I, Schedule V of the Act in respect of the supply.

Note that the CRA maintains a website allowing vendors to ascertain whether an HST number that a purchaser provides is valid. That website must be consulted by practitioners to verify the accuracy of the purchaser's HST number. In *Lee Hutton Kaye Maloff & Paul Henriksen v. Canada*, [2004] T.C.J. No. 429, 2004 G.T.C. 439, the Court held that a vendor could not rely on a purchaser's misrepresentation as to its GST registration status and was held not to be relieved of its obligation to collect GST in the circumstances.

Insofar as a purchaser is concerned, after providing the evidence required by a vendor that removes any obligation on the vendor to collect the HST, the purchaser must still remember to report the transaction to Revenue Canada. In the past, this required a purchaser to file a Form 60 wherein it would claim an input tax credit in an amount equal to the HST that would otherwise have been payable in connection with the purchase. Presently, this report can be included on the purchaser's regular HST return that the purchaser is required to file in connection with its business dealings generally. In any event, no amount is actually paid due to the offset.

Similarly, a purchaser should ensure that real property being sold as an "exempt supply" (*i.e.*, not subject to tax) in fact meets the qualifications. The necessary information may be available only to the vendor and therefore obtaining a statutory declaration from the vendor will be important in many circumstances.

With respect to the purchase of new houses and new residential condominium units, HST will be payable by a purchaser at the full rate. However, s. 254 of the *Excise Tax Act*, R.S.C. 1985, c. E-15 contains a new housing rebate applicable to the GST component of the HST. This rebate reduces the GST component of the tax but does not totally eliminate it. The rebate available varies depending on the price paid for the new home. Where the price is up to $350,000, a purchaser is entitled to an amount equal to the lesser of $7,560 and 36 per cent of the total GST paid. If the price is over $350,000, the rebate is calculated by multiplying the lesser of $7,560 and 36 per cent of the total GST by the amount of $450,000 subtracted by the total consideration paid divided by $100,000. Purchasers of homes costing over $450,000 are not eligible for the rebate. Note that this rebate will only apply if individuals are purchasing a new home. In practice, the builder will apply for the rebate and show it on the statement of adjustments as a credit.

In addition to the federal new housing rebate, a provincial new housing rebate has been introduced, which is available to buyers of new homes in Ontario. This rebate applies to the 8 per cent component of the HST, which originates from the Retail Sales Tax harmonization into the GST. The same types of new residential properties that qualify for the federal rebate will also qualify for the provincial one. The administration of both rebates will be undertaken by the CRA.

The provincial rebate is equal to 75 per cent of the provincial component of the HST on the price of a new home. In no event, however, can the rebate exceed $24,000. Effectively, this entitles new home purchasers to a rebate calculated against the first $400,000 of the purchase price of a new home.

Purchasers of new homes that have a price in excess of $400,000 still qualify for the rebate; again, this rebate is limited to the first $400,000. Accordingly, for a new home priced at $400,000, the provincial rebate is calculated by multiplying the provincial component of the HST, being 8 per cent, against the $400,000, being $32,000. The rebate is then 75 per cent of that amount, being $24,000.

Finally, insofar as rental payments are concerned, rents payable for the lease of residential premises for a term in excess of one month do not attract HST; however, as a general principle, HST is exigible and must be collected by landlords on rents and any amounts characterized as additional rents (*i.e.*, operating costs and a tenant's share of realty taxes) for leases of non-residential premises.

HERITAGE PROPERTY TAX PROGRAM

The tax incentive program pertaining to heritage buildings is contained within s. 365.2 of the *Municipal Act, 2001*. Pursuant to that section, a municipality may pass a by-law to establish tax relief programs for heritage properties. Note that this program is optional and a municipality may not opt to establish such a program.

Where the program is in place, the amount of tax relief a municipality may allow to an eligible heritage property must be between 10 and 40 per cent of municipal taxes. An "eligible heritage property" is one that is so designated under Part IV of the *Ontario Heritage Act*, R.S.O. 1990, c. O.18, or one that is part of a heritage conservation district under Part V of that Act. In addition, the property must be subject to an easement agreement pursuant to the terms of s. 22 or s. 37 of that Act.

It is worth noting that pursuant to s. 365.2(13) of the *Municipal Act, 2001*, an owner of an eligible heritage property may retain the benefit of any tax reduction or refund obtained under s. 365.2 despite the provisions of any lease or other agreement relating to the property.

If an owner of an eligible heritage property demolishes it or breaches the terms of any easement agreement relating to the property's heritage designation, the municipality may require the owner to repay all or part of any past tax benefits provided to the owner under this program, together with interest accruing from the date of the tax reduction or rebate. If an owner defaults in that repayment obligation, the amounts owing can be collected by the municipality as realty taxes with the same rights and priorities as if they were amounts owing on account of realty taxes.

HOUSING DEVELOPMENT ACT,
R.S.O. 1990, c. H.18

The Minister of Housing may make grants or loans to a municipality or any person to assist in the repair, improvement or conversion of real property for residential purposes. Where loans are made, the amount of the loan together with interest may be added to the tax roll for the property for which the loan was made and collected in the same manner as realty taxes over the term of the loan.

In addition, the Act contemplates the registration of a certificate on title to the property evidencing the amount and terms of the loan.

INCOME TAX ACT,
R.S.C. 1985, c. 1 (5th Supp.)

Subsection 116(1) requires any non-resident person (which includes a corporation) intending to sell property to give notice to the Minister of National Revenue. The notice must describe the property, give the name and address of the purchaser, set out the amount of proceeds of the sale and the amount of the adjusted cost base to the vendor of the property at the time of sending the notice. This information is declared on Form T2062 obtainable from any District Taxation Office. The purpose of the section is to provide a method of enforcing payment of Canadian income tax by a non-resident on any capital gain resulting from the sale of Canadian property.

If the non-resident vendor pays to the Receiver General of Canada 25 per cent of the amount by which the sale price exceeds the vendor's adjusted cost base for the property or furnishes security to the Minister of National Revenue, the Minister shall issue to the non-resident vendor and to the purchaser a certificate, Form T2064, fixing the sale price at the amount shown in the said notice — the "certificate limit".

Subsection 116(5) imposes liability on a purchaser where it acquires property from a non-resident vendor and does not follow the withholding obligations set forth therein. A purchaser is liable to pay to the Receiver General as a tax, a prescribed percentage of the amount, if any, by which the cost to the purchaser of the property exceeds the certificate limit fixed by the T2064 certificate, if any such certificate is issued unless:

(a) after reasonable inquiry, the purchaser had no reason to believe that the non-resident person was not resident in Canada; or

(b) a T2064 certificate has been obtained from the Minister of National Revenue.

In other words, a purchaser must either obtain evidence that the vendor is not a non-resident or be provided with the above-mentioned certificates with a certificate limit noted thereon that matches the purchase price. If no certificate is obtained and no evidence of vendor residency is obtained, the liability of the purchaser is to pay a prescribed percentage of the purchase price to the Receiver General. If a certificate has been obtained but the certificate limit is less than the purchase price, the liability will be for the prescribed percentage of the difference.

The prescribed percentage varies depending on whether the property is depreciable or non-depreciable. For real property other than depreciable property, the prescribed percentage is 25 per cent (subs. 116(5)). For depreciable property, the prescribed percentage is 50 per cent (subs. 116(5.3)).

This places a substantial onus on the solicitor for a purchaser to satisfy himself or herself that no tax liability will arise under s. 116. First, the solicitor must make reasonable enquiry as to whether or not the vendor is and will be at the time of sale a resident of Canada for the purposes of the *Income Tax Act*. If there is no reason to believe that the vendor is a non-resident, then the sale can proceed without further regard to s. 116. But if, after enquiry, it is determined that the vendor is a non-resident, production of the Minister's certificate under subs. 116(4) or subs. 116(5.2) is required. That certificate must be carefully examined to make sure that the purchase price does not exceed the "certificate limit". Only then can the purchase be safely completed.

Information Circular No. 72-17R5 dated March 15, 2005, issued by the Department of National Revenue purported to address the issue of what constitutes "reasonable inquiry":

> The purchaser incurs no obligation to pay tax if, after reasonable enquiry, there was no reason to believe the vendor was a non-resident of Canada. There is a question as to what constitutes "reasonable inquiry". The purchaser must take prudent measures to confirm the vendor's residence status. The CRA will review each case on an individual basis whenever a purchaser assessment is being considered. The purchaser may become liable if, for any reason, the CRA believes that the purchaser could have or should have known that the vendor was a non-resident or did not take reasonable steps to find out the vendor's residence status. The CRA will not make inquiries on behalf of a purchaser in this regard.

This is a rather open-ended statement that does not provide the certainty to resolve questions of residency one would expect in light of the liability to the purchaser of making an incorrect determination. Standard practice is to request a statutory declaration at closing that the vendor is not a non-resident within the meaning of s. 116. One should observe the same caution in relying on this declaration as on any other "self-serving" declaration.

If you are acting for a vendor who is clearly a non-resident, you should, as soon as you receive the agreement of purchase and sale, file Form T2062 with the District Taxation Office.

Although it is not related directly to conveyancing of property, you should be able to advise your client as to the provisions of para. 40(2)(*b*) of the *Income Tax Act* concerning the disposition of property that falls within the definition in s. 54 of "principal residence". As you are aware, and subject to certain exceptions contained in the Act, taxpayers do not generally have to include in their income any capital gain achieved from the sale of their principal residences. Until the budget of November 1981, a husband and wife could have two principal residences. Interpretation Bulletin IT-120 dated September 14, 1973, indicated that a husband and wife could each designate separate principal residences even when they did not live apart. It was then advisable that, where a couple owned a house and a cottage, the house be registered in the name of one party and the cottage in the name of the other party. Paragraph 6 in that Interpretation Bulletin stated:

> Where the taxpayer claiming the principal residence status has occupied the residence for only a short period of time during a taxation year (such as a seasonal residence occupied during a taxpayer's vacation or a house which was sold early or bought late in a taxation year), it is the Department's view that the taxpayer "ordinarily inhabited" that residence in the year provided that the principal reason

for owning the property was not for the purpose of gaining or producing income therefrom.

The Bulletin also indicated that the principal residence status would not be lost even though a taxpayer received incidental rental income from the cottage.

However, in the November 1981 budget, this was considered one of the "loopholes" that the Minister of National Revenue wanted to close, and now a husband and wife can have only one principal residence.

Please also note the "super-priority" provisions contained in s. 227(4.1) of the Act, which provide that where amounts are owed under the Act, or amounts are withheld by a person for remittance to the CRA and not paid, such amounts are deemed to represent trust moneys held by that person for the CRA. This deemed trust is similar to a floating charge against a person's property that remains outstanding while amounts continue to be owed to the CRA. However, the trust does not attach to any specific assets of the tax debtor to prevent their sale. The owner is free to alienate his or her property in the ordinary course, in which case the trust no longer attaches to the property once sold, but instead attaches to the proceeds of sale. Accordingly, a purchaser need not enquire as to a vendor's state of compliance with the CRA insofar as such remittances are concerned.

Furthermore, the Crown's claims to such trust moneys take priority over all other claims, including existing security interests. As a result, unless a security holder possesses a "prescribed security interest", all claims of the CRA for these outstanding amounts have priority over the security of any secured creditor. Complimentary changes to the federal legislation governing Canada Pension Plan and unemployment insurance remittances reflect the same priority for unpaid amounts.

Section 2201 of the Income Tax Regulations provides that a mortgage is a "prescribed security interest" and accordingly, a mortgagee does not lose priority to the CRA insofar as its interest in the real property of the debtor is concerned. However, the CRA is given first priority over all other secured creditors in respect of all of the other property of the debtor. Note that there are certain qualifications contained in s. 2201 relating to mortgages and the priority they retain over the Crown. One of these relates to mortgages that secure revolving lines of credit. Amounts that are undrawn on a line of credit at the time a deemed trust comes into existence in favour of the Crown for unpaid remittances, are not given priority over the said trust moneys when the undrawn amounts are subsequently drawn. Also, if a secured creditor holds other security from the same borrower in addition to a mortgage, the value of that additional security is deducted from amounts owing under the mortgage in determining the priority between the Crown and the secured creditor for amounts due under the mortgage. The Supreme Court of Canada has clarified and upheld the super-priority provisions in the Act in *First Vancouver Finance v. M.N.R.*, [2002] S.C.J. No. 25, [2002] 2 S.C.R. 720. See also *Canada (Attorney General) v. Community Expansion Inc.*, [2004] O.J. No. 5493, 72 O.R. (3d) 546 (S.C.J.), affd [2005] O.J. No. 186 (C.A.).

LAND TRANSFER TAX ACT, R.S.O. 1990, c. L.6

This statute governs the tax payable to the Province upon the registered or beneficial disposition of an interest in land. Recently, authority was given to the City of Toronto to levy a similar tax for lands within the City. Please see the section in this chapter entitled "Municipal Land Transfer Tax" for a summary of those taxing provisions.

FORM OF AFFIDAVIT

Land transfer tax is calculated upon the total value of consideration paid for the land and buildings conveyed in the instrument being tendered for registration. The Act provides that every such instrument should have attached to it an affidavit setting out the value of consideration entitled "Affidavit of Residence and Value of the Consideration".

The form of this affidavit is prescribed by regulation. It may be sworn by the purchaser, the purchaser's solicitor or by an agent authorized in writing by the purchaser, but it is recommended that the purchaser personally swear this affidavit. You will note that the total consideration is to be allocated first between realty and chattels and then to moneys paid in cash, the balance of existing mortgages being assumed by the purchaser, the amount of any mortgages being given back on closing to the vendor and various other headings. The land registrar multiplies the total consideration as shown in that affidavit by the current rate of tax and the result is payable to the Minister of Finance but submitted to the land registrar in the land registry office along with the registration fee. Transfers registered electronically require different procedures for payment, as described later in this section. Alternatively, land transfer tax may be paid directly to the Ministry of Finance, Land Transfer Tax Section, in which case the transfer will be stamped with evidence of payment. The address is as follows:

Land Transfer Tax Section
Ministry of Finance
33 King Street West
Oshawa, ON
L1H 8H9

Many people choose to pay the tax at this office so that their transfers as registered in the local land registry office will not contain the Affidavit of Residence and of Value of the Consideration and thus the amount paid for the property will not be readily available for inspection. They should be made aware, however, that the information in the affidavit is still available to the public upon enquiry at the Ministry of Finance office in Oshawa.

DEFINED TERMS

There are several defined terms in the Act that practitioners should become familiar with to fully understand the scope of the Act and its applicability to various real estate transactions. In reading s. 2 and s. 3 of the Act, which impose land transfer tax on registered and unregistered dispositions, respectively, the use of the terms "convey", "land" and "value of consideration" must be understood to determine how the Act applies to a particular transaction.

"Convey" is defined as including the "granting, assigning, releasing, surrendering, leasing or disposing" of any land and also includes "agreeing to sell land" or "the giving of an option upon or with respect to any land ... or the registration of a caution or notice of any kind" that signifies the existence of an agreement by which the land will be conveyed. As is readily apparent, this definition is very broad and extends to the following transactions: sales, leases, surrenders of lease, agreements of purchase and sale, options, *etc.*

"Land" is also broadly defined and includes:

> lands, tenements and hereditaments and any estate, right or interest therein, a structure to be constructed on land as part of an arrangement relating to a conveyance of land, a leasehold interest ... the interest of an optionee, the interest of a purchaser under an agreement to sell land, or goodwill attributable to the location of land or to the existence thereon of any building or fixture, and fixtures.

It is important to recognize that fixtures constitute land and that, as a result, a distinction is often necessary as to whether a certain component of a building is a fixture or is simply equipment or a chattel that does not fall within the definition of land. Where a purchaser is buying a business that includes lands, buildings, fixtures and chattels, it will often be necessary to consider the common law approach to distinguishing between chattels and fixtures to determine whether land transfer tax applies to those components.

The most involved definition in the Act is for "value of the consideration" where different types of transactions are considered and different approaches to the calculation of consideration for each of them is included. For a typical purchase and sale, the value of the consideration is:

> the gross sale price or the amount expressed in money of any consideration given or to be given for the conveyance by or on behalf of the transferee and the value expressed in money of any liability assumed or undertaken ... as part of the arrangement relating to the conveyance and the value expressed in money of any benefit of whatsoever kind conferred directly or indirectly by the transferee on any person as part of the arrangement relating to the conveyance. ...

Again, this definition is broadly drafted with a view to ensuring that any consideration paid as part of the "arrangement relating to the conveyance" is caught. This wording allows the Ministry to charge land transfer tax not only on the cash paid or debt assumed for the land, but also for all other benefits passing to the transferor, whether those benefits directly or indirectly accrue to the transferor's benefit. *Assaly v. Ontario (Minister of Revenue)*, [1986] O.J. No. 797, 41 R.P.R. 309 (H.C.J.), affd [1988] O.J. No. 3022, 48 R.P.R. 177 (C.A.) and *472601 Ontario Ltd. v. Ontario (Minister of Revenue)*, [1987] O.J. No. 2600, 47

R.P.R. 91 (H.C.J.) are cases where the Ministry of Finance successfully argued that land transfer tax was payable on the value of the services to be provided by a transferor to a transferee pursuant to a construction contract and management contract, respectively, as those contracts were an integral part of the arrangement relating to the conveyance of the lands and should be considered assumed liabilities.

Assistance with calculating the "value of the consideration" with respect to the purchase of new homes is provided in Bulletin LTT 1-2006, dated March 2006. This Bulletin was issued to warn purchasers that the Land Transfer Tax Branch viewed components of new home purchases, such as upgrades, extras, installations and similar arrangements, as forming part of the value of consideration for the home against which land transfer tax is payable.

Bulletin LTT 1-2010 was issued by the Land Transfer Tax Branch to clarify the effect of the Ontario Harmonized Sales Tax on the value of consideration concepts in the Act. First, the Bulletin acknowledges that where HST actually applies and is payable on the purchase of property, the value of consideration does not include the amount of HST. Accordingly, land transfer tax is not payable on the HST paid. Second, insofar as HST rebates available from federal and provincial programs on the purchase of new homes, the Land Transfer Tax Branch has stipulated that where the rebate is assigned to the vendor/builder and the purchaser pays the difference in the net HST payable after applying the rebate, no land transfer tax is payable on the rebate. However, if the purchaser pays the entire HST and assigns the HST rebate to the vendor/builder without any credit, then land transfer tax is payable on the rebate.

The definition of "value of the consideration" contains alternate provisions covering specific transactions which require that different calculations be made in determining land transfer tax liabilities, examples of which are as follows:

Foreclosures (and Quit Claims in lieu thereof) — the lesser of the amount owing under the mortgage and the fair market value of the lands at the time of registration (see Bulletin LTT 5-2000);

Leases — where the term, including renewals, exceeds 50 years, the fair market value of the land to which the lease pertains;

Corporate transfers — where land is transferred to a corporation and part of the consideration consists of the corporation's shares, or where a corporation transfers property to any shareholder of the corporation, the value of consideration is deemed to be the property's fair market value (see Bulletin LTT 3-2000);

Options — tax is payable based on the amount actually paid at the time for the option. If the option is exercised, tax will be paid on the purchase price on the registration of a transfer (see Bulletin LTT 1-2001);

Agreements of purchase and sale — tax is payable on the entire purchase price noted in the agreement upon its registration (see Bulletin LTT 1-2001);

Fractional Ownership Resorts — tax is payable on the purchase price or value of consideration paid (see Bulletin LTT 1-2009); and

Easements — tax is paid on the actual consideration paid (see Bulletin LTT 1-2001).

Pursuant to Bulletin LTT 10-2000, it is recognized that a gift of land is not taxable on the basis that no value of consideration is paid. However, if land is gifted and the transferee assumes a mortgage or other financial obligation, tax will be payable on the amount owing under the obligation even though no other consideration passed. This approach differs from that set out in R.R.O. 1990, Reg. 696 relating to transfers between spouses.

DISPOSITION OF BENEFICIAL INTEREST

Spurred on by huge increases in the tax payable caused not only by rate increases but also by inflation in land values, a variety of practices developed in the 1980s to avoid payment of land transfer tax. One such scheme involved a registered owner of land conveying registered title to land to a trustee corporation for no consideration while retaining the beneficial interest in the land. No tax was payable on the registration of the conveyance because the consideration was nil. Then, the beneficial owner would convey the beneficial interest in the land to a purchaser by an unregistered transfer and would transfer the shares in the registered owner trustee corporation to that purchaser. The purchaser would then own all the shares of the registered owner of the land and would be the beneficial owner, incurring no liability for land transfer tax because no transfer for which consideration was paid was tendered for registration.

Section 3 of the *Land Transfer Tax Act* was added effective July 18, 1989, imposing tax at the same rates as in s. 2 upon any disposition of beneficial interest in land even though a transfer is not tendered for registration. That tax is payable within 30 days after the date of the disposition. If the tax has not been paid at the registry office, the purchaser is required to file a return and pay the tax to the Ministry of Finance in Oshawa.

Subsection 3(1) of the Act broadly characterizes a beneficial disposition as a sale, transfer or assignment of a beneficial interest and "any change in entitlement to or any accretion to a beneficial interest in land". There is an exception in para. 3(1)(g) that makes it clear that an agreement of purchase and sale, while constituting a conveyance, is not taxable as a beneficial disposition where the consideration specified in the agreement has yet to be paid, as will be the case in most instances.

It is the Land Transfer Tax Branch's position, as set forth in Guide Notes issued on s. 3 of the Act, that a person holding units in a limited partnership or trust that owns real property in Ontario holds a beneficial interest in that real property. In other words, the Branch "looks through" the trust and partnership and deems the unitholders to be akin to co-owners of the property. Any transfer by persons of their units in such a trust or limited partnership is deemed to be a beneficial disposition that is taxable. Pursuant to O. Reg. 70/91, an exemption is recognized for the disposition of an interest in a mutual fund trust. An exemption is also recognized for the disposition of an interest in a partnership if the entitlement to profits applicable to the interest being disposed of does not increase by more than 5 per cent from the profits applicable to that interest at the beginning of the partnership's fiscal year.

RATE OF LAND TRANSFER TAX

The rate of land transfer tax has increased considerably — by more than 500 per cent in the last 25 years. At present, for both registered and unregistered dispositions, the rate is ½ of one per cent on the first $55,000 of consideration, 1 per cent on that part of the consideration between $55,000 and $250,000 plus 1 ½ per cent on the balance. Where the property being conveyed contains at least one, but not more than two single family dwellings and the total consideration exceeds $400,000, the tax is 2 per cent on the excess.

The following is a quick formula for calculating tax payable:

1. if price is less than $250,000:

   consideration × 0.01 - $275 = tax payable;

2. if price is less than $400,000 or if property is non-residential:

   consideration × 0.015 - $1,525 = tax payable;

3. if price for residential property is greater than $400,000:

   consideration × 0.02 - $3,525 = tax payable.

As a result of a practice that developed where a purchaser would have a vendor execute several separate transfers for undivided interests in a property, which together, when all registered, still transferred 100 per cent of the property to the purchaser but individually reflected a value of consideration of less than $55,000 in order to attract the lowest rate of tax, s. 2.3 was added to the Act to allow the Minister to charge land transfer tax as if the series of conveyances were only one conveyance. This section applies to all conveyances, whether registered or unregistered.

Also note that there is a provision in s. 2(2) of the Act allowing an apportionment of consideration to be made where a property consists of a residential property and of additional lands that are not necessarily used as part of that residential property (such as a farm). This apportionment avoids a sale of a farm property, where the total purchase price is greater than $400,000, attracting land transfer tax at the higher rate of 2 per cent for the amount in excess of $400,000, where it can be shown that the residential portion of the farm has a value below the $400,000 threshold.

RETAIL SALES TAX

The form of land transfer tax affidavit that is signed in order to certify the value of consideration paid requires an allocation of that consideration between land, buildings, fixtures and goodwill as one category, and chattels as a second category. This allocation allowed the Ministry of Revenue to levy and collect land transfer tax on the value allocated to the first category, and provincial or retail sales tax on the value allocated to the second category.

As of July 1, 2010, the Province of Ontario has harmonized its provincial sales tax with the federal goods and services tax resulting in an HST of 13 per cent. With that harmonization, the statutory regime that was contained in the *Retail Sales Tax Act* for determining when that tax was payable has been replaced with the statutory regime under the *Excise Tax Act*, which governs the federal goods and services tax.

As a result of these changes, there is no Retail Sales Tax to be paid on amounts allocated to chattels. At the time of writing, the land transfer tax affidavit and the regulations under the *Land Transfer Tax Act* still require the completion of an affidavit that sets out the value between the two categories. Presumably, that will be amended in due course as the allocation is no longer relevant.

As summarized earlier in this chapter, in the context of the discussion on the HST, the sale of "used housing" is an exempt supply for HST purposes. Accordingly, no HST is payable on the purchase of resale homes. That exemption extends to any chattels purchased as an incidental part of the transaction involving the purchase of the home. Those same principles would also apply to any chattels purchased as incidental to a real estate transaction where the type of property being acquired is exempt, such as apartment buildings. Where real property is acquired that does not fall within an exempt category under the *Excise Tax Act*, the payment of HST on any chattels acquired as incidental to that transaction would be handled the same way as payment of HST on the real property itself. Usually, no HST will be payable at the closing of the transaction if a purchaser is an HST registrant and agrees to self-assess, as described in the section in this chapter on the HST.

As the HST had only recently come into effect as of the date of writing of this edition, it is expected that clarification and amendments to current procedures and forms under the *Land Transfer Tax Act* will be implemented to remove references to provisions that are based on *Retail Sales Tax Act* rules that no longer apply. In the interim, the Ministry of Revenue has issued newsletters confirming that while chattel allocations will still need to be set out in a land transfer tax affidavit, no retail sales tax will be payable or collected.

NON-RESIDENTS OF CANADA

Prior to May 1997, the rate of land transfer tax that was payable by a person who was a non-resident of Canada was 20 per cent of the total consideration. Any person, whether a citizen of Canada or not, who had not sojourned in Canada for at least 366 days in the previous 24 months, and any corporation, 50 per cent of whose common shares are owned by non-residents, or 25 per cent of whose common shares are owned by any one non-resident person, was required to pay land transfer tax at a rate equal to 20 per cent of the purchase price of any land in Ontario other than "unrestricted land".

"Unrestricted land" included land zoned as commercial or industrial and land assessed or lawfully used for commercial, industrial or residential use.

The intent of the Act had been to require non-residents to pay tax at 20 per cent on the purchase of farmland, woodlands and recreational properties.

These non-residency provisions have been repealed and are no longer applicable.

INTER-CORPORATE TRANSFERS

Special provisions are set forth in subss. 3(9) to (15) to allow inter-corporate beneficial dispositions of land without the payment of tax. Pursuant to these provisions, the land transfer tax that would otherwise be payable is deferred and eventually cancelled. In order to take advantage of this exemption, the following rules must be observed:

1. The transfer must not be registered.

2. The transfer must be from a corporation to another corporation that are affiliates (as defined in s. 3(15)).

3. The transferor and transferee must remain affiliated for at least three years from the date of the transfer.

4. The transferee must give an undertaking that it will remain an affiliate of the transferor during the three-year deferral period and post security for the tax (usually in the form of a bond or letter of credit) that would have otherwise been payable (together with interest therein at a prescribed rate compounded over a 38-month period) in case the foregoing conditions are not met.

The security will be returned (and the deferred tax cancelled) at the end of the three years upon proof (in the form of an affidavit) that the conditions have been met. Remember, however, that the transfer can never be registered or the tax will then be payable. In this regard, practitioners should be aware of s. 13.1 of the Act, which deems the registration of conveyance of legal title to the land to the beneficial owner or to a trustee of the beneficial owner to be evidence of the registration of transfer, attracting full land transfer tax.

The security will also be returned if the land is sold within the three-year period to an arm's-length purchaser who pays tax on that purchase.

The Ministry has published Ontario Tax Bulletin LTT 3-2000 in April 2000 containing detailed procedures relating to obtaining a tax deferral and eventual cancellation of tax for such transactions. Note that the conditions in the deferral provisions of the Act will be strictly applied by the courts in determining whether a conveyance qualifies for the deferral as in *Dam Investments Inc. v. Ontario (Minister of Finance)*, [2007] O.J. No. 2674, 61 R.P.R. (4th) 51 (C.A.).

OTHER EXEMPTIONS FROM LAND TRANSFER TAX

There are several exemptions and/or exceptions to the payment of land transfer tax for certain conveyances. Certain of these are listed below:

1. *Leases* — Pursuant to s. 1(6), no tax is payable in respect of a conveyance involving a lease where the term of the lease, including renewal or extension options, cannot exceed 50 years in the aggregate. A land transfer tax affidavit must still be filed with any such conveyance though, in which a statement as to the term must be included.

2.   *Amalgamations* — Pursuant to Bulletin LTT-3-2000, the Ministry has clarified that where two or more companies amalgamate and land belonging to each of them thereby becomes owned by the amalgamated company, that transaction is not viewed as a conveyance for the purposes of the Act.

3.   *Transfers between Spouses* — Pursuant to R.R.O. 1990, Reg. 696, as amended, transfers among spouses are not taxable where the conveyance is for "natural love and affection", even if a mortgage is assumed as part of the conveyance. The land transfer tax affidavit must include information enabling the Minister to determine that the provisions of this regulation have been met.

4.   *Family Corporations* — Pursuant to R.R.O. 1990, Reg. 697, as amended, transfers of land from an individual or individuals, each of which is a member of a family, to a family farm corporation or family business corporation, are exempt. To obtain the exemption, a special affidavit must be filed in which it must be demonstrated that prior to the conveyance, the land was used primarily as a farm or for an active business by the individual who is a member of the family, and that the land is being conveyed to allow that individual to continue running the farm or active business under the direction of other individuals who are family members. There are additional conditions to be met for conveyances to a family business relating to the amount of income generated from the business, which cannot be examined or satisfied until the end of the taxation year for the business and, as a result, a person or persons claiming this exemption must file security with the Minister for the amount of the tax otherwise payable at the time of the conveyance. The security can be reclaimed at the end of the taxation year if the additional conditions are satisfied. Note that the conditions of the regulation will be strictly applied by the courts to determine whether a conveyance qualifies for the exemption as in *Upper Valley Dodge Chrysler Ltd. v. Ontario (Minister of Finance)*, [2005] O.J. No. 6123, 42 R.P.R. (4th) 147 (C.A.).

5.   *Employee to Employer Dispositions* — Pursuant to O. Reg. 71/91, no tax is payable on an unregistered disposition of land from an employee or his or her spouse, to his or her employer if the disposition is pursuant to a relocation program offered by the employer as part of the employee's terms of employment. In practice, an employee being relocated is paid for his or her home by the employer in return for which the employer receives a transfer/deed for the home signed by the employee but with the name of the transferee left blank. The employer then has 180 days to sell the house to a third party, who is not an employee of the employer, and that party then pays land transfer tax upon completion of the sale.

6. *Land as Capital* — Pursuant to Bulletin LTT 3-2000, the Ministry has acknowledged that where a shareholder of a corporation transfers land to a corporation for no consideration representing that shareholder's contribution of capital to the corporation, no land transfer tax is payable.

7. *First-Time Home Purchase Rebates* — Pursuant to s. 9.2 of the Act, the first-time purchaser of a resale home, existing home or a newly constructed home who has never owned a home anywhere in the world and whose spouse has similarly not owned a home anywhere in the world, is entitled to a refund of land transfer tax on the purchase of such home provided the purchaser occupies the home as his or her principal residence within nine months of the home's purchase. The maximum refund available for new homes purchased is $2,000. To be eligible, a purchaser cannot have previously received an Ontario Home Ownership Savings Plan based refund of land transfer tax. A separate refund affidavit, entitled Ontario Land Transfer Tax Refund Affidavit for First-Time Purchasers of Eligible Homes, must be filed with the usual land transfer tax affidavit (please see Bulletin LTT 1-2008).

8. *Natural Love and Affection* — Pursuant to Bulletin LTT 8-2000, the Ministry treats a conveyance by one individual to another, regardless of their relationship, that occurs for natural love and affection, as one where land transfer tax is not payable, provided there is no outstanding mortgage registered on title to the property being conveyed. If there is a mortgage, land transfer tax is payable on the principal amount outstanding. New provisions that are found in s. 13.1 of the Act appear to remove this exemption for transfers among related persons and impose a tax based on the fair market value of the property transferred; however, the Ministry has explained that this new section does not take away the inter-spousal exemption or natural love and affection exemption. This section was added to enable the Ministry to recoup tax in situations where a person who fails to pay tax on a conveyance attempts to transfer the property a second time to a relative on the basis of this exemption in an effort to thwart the Ministry in registering a lien on the property for the tax owing on the first transaction. In such a situation, tax can be collected on the second transfer to a relative by the Ministry.

9. *Trusts* — Pursuant to Bulletin LTT 1-2005, conveyances involving trusts are recognized as not being taxable if the conditions detailed therein are met. The basis for the exception is that the value of consideration is deemed to be nil. The requirements to be satisfied to evidence a nil value of consideration are quite involved and cover trust conveyances from a trustee to its beneficial owner, from a trustee to another trustee for the same beneficial owner and from a beneficial owner to a trustee.

REFUND APPLICATIONS

Tax Bulletin LTT 2-2006, dated November 2006, outlines the procedures to apply for refunds of land transfer tax. In addition to the first-time homebuyer described above, refunds may also be obtained where tax is overpaid or when no transfer has taken place. Tax may be overpaid due to failure to obtain an exemption as described above or simply due to calculation errors. In any circumstance, it is necessary to follow the appropriate steps to apply for a refund, and to take note of the time limits for submitting such applications.

There is no standard application form for refunds of land transfer tax. The Ministry requires that applicants forward written requests providing the reasons for the refund, accompanied by supporting documentation. Required supporting documentation includes evidence that the tax was paid, a copy of the agreement of purchase and sale, a copy of the statement of adjustments, and other specified documents depending on the reason for the request. For example, first-time purchasers are also required to include a copy of the Ontario New Home Warranty Certificate, and an original sworn Land Transfer Tax Refund Affidavit for First-Time Purchasers of Eligible Homes.

ELECTRONIC REGISTRATION

With the implementation of mandatory electronic registration in certain registry offices pursuant to the provisions of the *Land Registration Reform Act*, and the increasing frequency of electronic registration generally, the *Land Transfer Tax Act* has been amended to provide for the land transfer tax affidavit to be filed electronically. Section 2.1 of the Act, which was repealed in 2004, originally made it clear that any document registered electronically still attracted tax at the same rate as if the document was manually registered. Section 5(1.1) of the Act now provides that any conveyance tendered for registration as an electronic document is to contain information provided as a statement in the form and manner approved by the Minister.

As with other forms of electronically registered documents, accessing the land transfer tax affidavit on Teraview presents the user with mandatory fields for completion and optional fields depending on the nature of the transaction. In some cases, supplementary information will have to be presented in person at the registry office before registration can take place (for example, where tax is prepaid or where exemptions are claimed in complicated situations such as a family corporation transfer). Tabs exist whereby the user can access categories of "explanations" and "exemptions" to allow the user to provide statements needed to file affidavits in some of the situations discussed in this chapter. Generally speaking though, the electronic affidavit is similar to the non-electronic affidavit. Practitioners should require their clients to swear a paper copy of the land transfer tax affidavit to provide the basis for the submission of an electronic version through Teraview.

Insofar as logistics are concerned, when registering with Teranet as a registered Teraview user, the account holder must designate an account from which Teranet is authorized to withdraw registration fees and land transfer tax payable upon submitting documents for registration. The account agreement provides that whenever a user submits instructions for registration of a document electronically, Teranet is authorized to debit the user's designated account for the registration fees and land transfer tax payable. As a result, a user will have to ensure funds are received from clients and deposited in the designated account in advance to allow this pre-authorized debiting of land transfer tax amounts to proceed.

NON-PAYMENT OF LAND TRANSFER TAX

Section 15.1 creates a lien for unpaid tax. The Ministry must register a notice of lien for the lien to be enforceable, and once registered, the lien has priority over all subsequent registered encumbrances. There is also a penalty imposed equal to 5 per cent of the tax when no affidavit is filed and no tax paid and a penalty of 5 per cent of the shortfall where only part of the tax is paid (see s. 5). This is in addition to interest on unpaid amounts levied pursuant to s. 17. Section 5(13) of the Act also imposes an additional penalty ranging from 25 per cent of the tax to twice the tax if a person is convicted of an offence under the Act.

THE MANAGED FOREST TAX INCENTIVE PROGRAM

The Managed Forest Tax Incentive Program is administered by the Ministry of Natural Resources and provides lower property taxes to participating owners that agree to conserve and manage forests they own. Lands that qualify for this program are reassessed and taxed at 25 per cent of residential tax rates. In order to qualify, the following requirements must be met: the land must be owned by a Canadian citizen or corporation, the land must encompass an area of at least 4 hectares (excluding residences), the land must be under one roll number, there must be a minimum number of trees per acre on it and the land cannot be subject to a registered plan of subdivision. If the land qualifies, an application must be submitted to the Ontario Forestry Association or the Ontario Woodlot Association. It will be necessary to submit a Managed Forest Plan with a long-term horizon with your application, which plan must be first approved by a forestry expert recognized by these associations as having expertise in the area. If the application is accepted, the lands will be reassessed subject to a review in five years where a new forestry plan will have to be prepared in order to maintain the lower tax assessment under the program. Note that upon a sale of the property that participates in this program, the new owner will not benefit from the lower tax rate unless, within 90 days of the purchase, they update the Managed Forest Plan and have the plan approved anew.

MUNICIPAL ACT,
R.S.O. 1990, c. M.45

Section 382 of the Act states:

> The taxes due upon any land with costs ... are a special lien on the land in priority to every claim, privilege, lien or encumbrance of every person except the Crown. ...

This is the lien for municipal realty taxes. Before completing any purchase or mortgage transaction or giving any opinion on title, you should write to the Treasurer of the municipality in which the land is situate asking for a tax certificate. You send with your request a legal description of the lands in question and a cheque to cover the Treasurer's fee. These fees vary from municipality to municipality. The certificate will inform you of any arrears of taxes and of the status of the current year's taxes.

Pursuant to s. 221(27), unpaid water and sewer charges may also be added to the tax rolls of a municipality and recovered in the same manner and with the same priority as municipal taxes.

The municipality also has the right under s. 384 of the *Municipal Act*, where realty taxes are due upon any land occupied by a tenant, to require the tenant to pay the rent to the municipality from time to time until the taxes are paid.

As mentioned in Chapter 3, the *Municipal Act* and *Municipal Tax Sales Act* were repealed with effect as at January 1, 2003 and were replaced by the *Municipal Act, 2001*, which is reviewed below.

MUNICIPAL ACT, 2001,
S.O. 2001, c. 25

This Act became effective as at January 1, 2003 and replaced the *Municipal Act* and *Municipal Tax Sales Act*. The provisions reviewed for this chapter, however, are very similar to those reviewed above in connection with the *Municipal Act*.

Pursuant to s. 349(3), "taxes are a special lien on the land in priority to every claim, privilege, lien or encumbrance of every person except the Crown, and the lien and its priority are not lost or impaired" for any reason. Accordingly, the same regime that existed relating to taxes in the old *Municipal Act* is continued.

Similarly, s. 398(2) provides that where any public utility is supplied to a property and not paid for, the charges can be added to the tax rolls and collected as if they were taxes. "Public utility" is defined in s. 1(1) of the Act and includes the provision of water, sewage services, fuel, energy (excluding electricity), heating and cooling and telephone services. The inclusion of these provisions in this Act effective as of January 1, 2003 coincides with the repeal of portions of the *Public Utilities Act*, R.S.O. 1990, c. P.52, specifically, s. 31 of that Act, which provided for a lien for non-payment of public utilities. The lien is now found in the *Municipal Act, 2001*. Please note, however, that the lien created by

s. 398(2) attaches to the property to which the public utility was supplied, which differs from the approach taken by s. 31 of the *Public Utilities Act*, where the lien attached to the real and/or personal property of the owner or occupant to whom the utility was supplied. See the discussion that follows in this chapter on the *Public Utilities Act* for further details.

The effect that an owner's unpaid realty taxes may have on tenants of that property is set forth in s. 350. If taxes are outstanding, a municipality may give a notice requiring tenants to pay their rent to the municipality rather than the landlord. If a tenant does not pay, the Act gives the municipality all of the remedies of a landlord *vis-à-vis* that tenant. If a tenant does pay, s. 350(3) makes it clear that the tenant may deduct the amounts paid from the rent due to the landlord.

One final section that will be reviewed is s. 364, which entitles an owner of a commercial or industrial building to a tax rebate if a building has been vacant. This rebate is available where all or part of the building has been vacant for 90 consecutive days in a calendar year. In order to apply for a rebate, an owner must make an application by February 28 in the following year and provide information as to the vacancies.

MUNICIPAL LAND TRANSFER TAX

Pursuant to s. 267 of the *City of Toronto Act, 2006*, S.O. 2006, c. 11, Sched. A, the City of Toronto was given authority to impose new taxes through the passing of by-laws. One of the first new taxes the City chose to implement was a municipal land transfer tax ("MLTT"). That tax was introduced by the enactment of By-law 1423-2007 on December 13, 2007, with effect as at February 1, 2008.

MLTT is charged on the value of consideration paid on a conveyance of registered and beneficial interests in land, just like the provincial land transfer tax. The graduated tax rates are as follows:

(a) for properties containing at least one, but not more than two, single-family residences:

0.5% on the first $55,000 of consideration;

1.0% on the consideration between $55,000 and $400,000; and

2.0% on the consideration above $200,000

(b) for all other properties:

0.5% on the first $55,000 of consideration;

1.0% on the consideration between $55,000 and $400,000;

1.5% on the consideration between $400,000 and $40,000,000; and

1.0% on the consideration above $40,000,000.

The *City of Toronto Act, 2006* exempts certain entities from paying MLTT. Those exempted include: the Crown and its agencies, school boards, post-secondary education institutions, hospitals, every long-term care home (as defined by the *Long-Term Care Homes Act, 2007*, S.O. 2007, c. 8) and authorities, boards, commissions, corporations and organizations, a majority of whose directors, members or officers are appointed or chosen by or under the authority of the Lieutenant Governor in Council or a member of the Provincial Executive Committee. Section 760-14 of By-Law 1423-2007 contains additional exemptions for nursing homes, charitable homes for the aged, rest homes, transactions involving any of the City of Toronto, Toronto Economic Housing Corporation and Toronto Economic Development Corporation, local boards and persons and entities entitled to exemptions under the *Land Transfer Tax Act*.

Rebates are available for MLTT for first-time home purchasers of both new and existing residential properties. A "first time purchaser" is defined under By-Law 1423-2007 as an individual who is 18 years of age or older and who has never owned an eligible home anywhere in the world and whose spouse has not owned an eligible home anywhere in the world while he or she was a spouse of that person. The By-law also requires occupancy of the home within nine months of its acquisition. The maximum amount of the rebate is $3,725, which is the MLTT otherwise payable for a residential property whose price is $400,000. If the purchase price exceeds $400,000, the rebate is capped at $3,725. For homes that are less than $400,000, the rebate eliminates the payment of the MLTT.

Payment of MLTT is effected in the exact same way as provincial land transfer tax. On registration, Teranet will require the payment of MLTT before it will allow the electronic registration of the conveyance. A person entitled to a first-time home rebate can receive credit for the rebate at the time of registration and avoid having to pay MLTT and later applying for the rebate.

Where there is an unregistered beneficial conveyance of an interest in land, MLTT is payable within the same time period as provincial land transfer tax, namely, within 30 days. However, the filing is not effected at the Ministry of Finance – Land Transfer Tax Branch office; rather, By-Law 1423-2007 requires payment to the City of Toronto's Chief Financial Officer at Toronto City Hall or the North York Civic Centre.

Very generally speaking, By-Law 1423-2007 is otherwise consistent with the approach on land transfer tax that the *Land Transfer Tax Act* mandates. There is explicit recognition in the By-law that the City may refer to bulletins and guidelines issued by the Land Transfer Tax Branch. At the same time, the MLTT does create a second taxing authority, so matters such as assessments and appeals will have to be pursued with both municipal and provincial authorities separately.

POWER CORPORATION ACT, R.S.O. 1990, c. P.18

Most of this Act has been repealed. In particular, s. 89 of the Act, which created a lien in favour of Ontario Hydro for unpaid power supplied to an owner, and which gave that lien the same priority as municipal taxes, has been repealed. As a result, no such lien exists for the provision of power by Ontario Hydro, which is consistent with the Government of Ontario's initiative to privatize all aspects of the transmission and distribution of electricity. As this industry will be run by the private sector and no longer by the government, it is not entitled to a lien for unpaid charges in priority to any other lien claimant in the private sector.

PROVINCIAL LAND TAX ACT, 2006,
S.O. 2006, c. 33,
Sched. Z.2

Regions in Ontario that have not yet been organized into municipalities fall under the scope of this statute insofar as the payment of realty taxes are concerned. Pursuant to s. 2, all land situate in unorganized territories is liable to taxation, subject to certain exceptions. These taxes are payable directly to the Ministry of Finance. If taxes are not paid, s. 12(3) of the Act contains the same provisions found in the *Municipal Act* deeming the unpaid amounts to be a lien on the property in priority to all other encumbrances. Section 15 contains a regime for forfeiture and sale similar to that in the *Municipal Act*.

The *Local Roads Board Act*, R.S.O. 1990, c. L.27 is a similar statute to the now-repealed *Local Improvements Act*. In an unorganized territory, landowners can petition the Ministry of Transportation to create or improve roads with the cost of same shared by such owners and repayable over time as part of realty taxes. The Ministry is given the same lien and priority rights against any owner who does not pay their share of the costs.

PUBLIC UTILITIES ACT,
R.S.O. 1990, c. P.52

Effective January 1, 2003, Part III of the *Public Utilities Act* was repealed by s. 482(2) of the *Municipal Act, 2001*, S.O. 2001, c. 25. As a result, s. 31, which is described below, is no longer applicable. Liens for the supply of public utilities are governed by the *Municipal Act, 2001*, which is effective as of January 1, 2003, as discussed earlier in this chapter.

THE SUCCESSION DUTY ACT,
R.S.O. 1970, c. 449

Section 21 of the old *Succession Duty Act* stated:

21(1) Where any duty is levied on property passing on the death of the deceased, such duty or so much thereof as remains unpaid, with interest thereon, is and remains a first lien and charge on such property until paid or a certificate is given under section 40 discharging such property.

This statute was repealed by *The Succession Duty Repeal Act, 1979*, S.O. 1979, c. 20, s. 1, which came into force April 11, 1979, but by s. 1 thereof, it continues to affect the property of a person who died prior to April 10, 1979. And by a previous amendment, the lien does not apply where the deceased died prior to January 1, 1970. By O. Reg. 44/78 the interests of a deceased person in property held in joint tenancy with a spouse and in property passing upon registration of a discharge of mortgage were exempted from the requirement for consent.

Where a search of title shows that a person who died between January 1, 1970 and April 10, 1979, was at the time of death an owner of land, you must assure yourself that an Ontario Succession Duty release has been registered on title to that land properly describing same. Remember that aside from the lien against the lands, s. 53(3) of the *Registry Act*, R.S.O. 1990, c. R.20, invalidates any dealing with the lands if such release has not been issued.

TILE DRAINAGE ACT, R.S.O. 1990, c. T.8

Section 11(2) of this Act creates a lien against a property where a municipality has paid for the installation of weeping tiles to control water run-off. The municipal costs are added to the owner's realty taxes and collected in the same manner and with the same priority as realty taxes.

The provisions of the *Drainage Act*, R.S.O. 1990, c. D.17 are identical where a municipality constructs improvements relating to drains, natural water courses, regulating the water table, dams and other protective water works.

WORKPLACE SAFETY AND INSURANCE ACT, 1997, S.O. 1997, c. 16, Sched. A

This Act creates an insurance fund used to compensate workers for losses they suffer as a result of workplace accidents. Employers are required to pay premiums in amounts determined by the Act in order to maintain the insurance fund. Any person who fails to pay such amounts is subject to enforcement proceedings under s. 139 pursuant to which the Workplace Safety and Insurance Board may issue a default certificate and file the certificate with the courts resulting in an execution to be issued against that person.

Pursuant to subss. 140(2) and (3), if an employer does not pay amounts owing under this Act, the Board may deliver a certificate of the amounts owing to the municipality in which the employer owns property. The municipality shall then add the amounts to the tax rolls for the property, which allows it to collect the amounts as if they were taxes. A municipality may add a 5 per cent surcharge to compensate it for its services. Section 140(4) allows the Board to pursue the remedies available to it in s. 139 and s. 140 simultaneously.

Section 145 provides that the certificate issued pursuant to s. 139, when filed with the court, causes the amounts set forth therein to constitute a first lien, after municipal taxes, upon the property of the employer. The lien is only effective if a notice is filed by way of a writ in the office of the sheriff for the area in which the affected property is situate and a copy of the writ is delivered to the proper land registrar.

Note that the lien created by filing the writ of execution does not create any special priority over other liens and encumbrances previously in existence. See *Crown Trust Co. v. Ontario (Workmen's Compensation Board)*, [1975] O.J. No. 2219, 7 O.R. (2d) 466 (H.C.J.), where Houlden J. held in reviewing similar provisions in the predecessor statute to the Act, that this lien was subject to prior encumbrances.

One other important provision of this Act that real estate practitioners should be aware of is s. 141. That section provides that a person who hires a contractor or subcontractor to do work is deemed to be the employer of the employees of the contractor and subcontractor for the purposes of the Act and, as a result, is liable to pay the premiums payable under the Act that the contractor and subcontractor should be paying in respect of the employment of such employees. In other words, an owner of property who hires someone to undertake any work thereon, is directly liable to the Board for premiums payable under the Act by the person hired to do the work and similarly subject to the Board's remedies described above if they also do not pay. Subsections 141(3) and (5) allow an owner to set-off amounts paid to the Board against amounts owing to a contractor where an owner has been required to make good a contractor's default in the payment of premiums.

The Board's operational policies implemented pursuant to s. 131 of the Act provide that the Board will issue a clearance certificate whereby it waives a person's liability with respect to a contractor's premium obligations under the Act. These certificates may be obtained by contacting any Board office and submitting an application form. This will cause the Board to review its records to determine whether the contractor is in good standing in respect of its statutory obligations under the Act.

As a result of this clearance procedure, owners or other principals hiring contractors often require such a clearance certificate to be presented by a contractor as a precondition to payment of accounts tendered by the contractor.

CHAPTER 5

Governmental Controls on the Use and Disposition of Land

There was a time, not so long ago, when landowners could do whatever they wanted on their land and with their land as long as their actions did not cause physical damage to their neighbours. In that case, the neighbours' remedy was to sue privately. Governments were not concerned generally unless it became a police matter. While there were private developments of land in which the developer imposed restrictions by way of restrictive covenants, municipal and provincial governments kept out of this field.

Around the end of the Second World War, however, when there was a sudden increase in urban growth, municipal governments began to realize that something had to be done to control the haphazard growth that was taking place and also to protect the citizens from unpleasant uses of neighbouring property.

At the same time, development began to move out from the cities along the roadways then in existence. Farmers were selling off small parcels of land along the frontage of their farms to eager purchasers who erected houses, factories and service stations in haphazard pattern. Long strips of this type of development began to appear along every concession road around the urban areas of Ontario. These new landowners began to demand municipal services for the taxes they were paying. They wanted water, sewers, fire protection, schools and all the other advantages of urban living. Various municipalities and the Ontario government realized that this was a most impractical and expensive type of development. There were huge gaps between built-up areas and whole sections between the roads with no development, yet the municipalities were being requested to build miles of sewers and water mains and street lights for just those few people living along the strips of development. Something had to be done.

The answer to these problems adopted by government came in two parts, both within the *Planning Act*, R.S.O. 1990, c. P.13. The methods of control employed in the Act have not changed substantially since the Act was first passed in 1946. To regulate undesirable uses within developed areas, municipal councils were given the power under Part III (now Part V) of the Act to control the use of land within their municipalities by means of restricted area by-laws, commonly known as "zoning" by-laws. To restrict undesirable new development, particularly in rural areas, local planning boards (now committees of adjustment or land division committees) were empanelled to decide upon applications to sever existing parcels of land.

The following part of this chapter is an attempt to summarize the themes of subdivision control and zoning under the Act with the emphasis on the former because of its devastating consequences for conveyancing practice.

SUBDIVISION CONTROL

Section 50(3) of the *Planning Act*, reproduced in part below, contains a general prohibition against all transfers of any interest in land excepting only those transactions specifically mentioned in the Act:

> 50(3) No person shall convey land by way of a deed or transfer, or grant, assign or exercise a power of appointment with respect to land, or mortgage or charge land, or enter into an agreement of sale and purchase of land or enter into any agreement that has the effect of granting the use of or right in land directly or by entitlement to renewal for a period of twenty-one years or more unless ...

The theory of this part of the Act is that if you control severances of land you then control the size of parcels, their location and the resulting density of population. In this regard, the Act is designed to be self-policing, that is, the onus to ensure compliance has been placed on the person who should care most: the purchaser. If a breach occurs, then the purchaser suffers most by failing to obtain any title at all. On the other hand, many people view subdivision control as an obstacle to be circumvented in the face of their desire to acquire a specific parcel of land. The result is often a mutual effort by a vendor and purchaser to circumvent the Act.

As a result, the history of subdivision control under the *Planning Act* has been one of constant change in terms of loopholes discovered by ingenious conveyancers, exceptions created by sympathetic judges, and statutory amendments enacted by vigilant legislators to plug the loopholes and the exceptions.

The judicial interpretation of the *Planning Act* varies from time to time between a strict construction and a remedial approach. In *Ontario (Attorney General) v. Yeotes*, [1981] O.J. No. 2495, 31 O.R. (2d) 589, leave to appeal refused [1981] S.C.C.A. No. 210, 37 N.R. 356, the Ontario Court of Appeal held that a transaction is not illegal merely because it is contrary to the policy of the *Planning Act*. On the other hand, in *Cait v. Lemrac Holdings Ltd.*, [1969] O.J. No. 1356, [1969] 2 O.R. 544, the High Court of Justice invalidated a group of simultaneous conveyances holding that they were not a *bona fide* transaction but a mere device designed to circumvent the requirements of the *Planning Act*. In *Forfar v. East Gwillimbury (Township)*, [1971] O.J. No. 1636, [1971] 3 O.R. 337, the Court of Appeal refused to exercise its discretion to order the issue of building permits for lots created by a "checkerboarding" scheme. Schroeder J.A. held, at 344 O.R., that "it is the substance rather than the form of the transaction which is relevant". His view was later confirmed by the Supreme Court of Canada ([1972] S.C.J. No. 38, 28 D.L.R. (3d) 512n).

The courts have consistently held that a transfer or any other document in contravention of the *Planning Act* is a nullity. Section 50(21) states that they do not "create or convey any interest in land". Therefore, it is essential that you be fully conversant with the permitted and prohibited types of transactions and that you ensure that the *Planning Act* has been complied with.

WHOLE LOTS ON A PLAN OF SUBDIVISION

Part of a grantor's land may be conveyed if the part conveyed consists of a whole lot on a plan of subdivision. This conclusion is reached by reading subss. 50(3)(a) and 50(5)(a) together. Subsection (3)(a) permits any conveyance of land within a plan of subdivision, even though it is only part of what the grantor owns. Subsection (5)(a) prohibits the conveyance of part of a lot if the grantor owns abutting land which is not a whole lot. Therefore, a whole lot may be conveyed because it is within a plan of subdivision and, being a "whole lot", its conveyance is not prohibited by subs. (5)(a).

The municipality, under subs. 50(7), may pass a by-law that the part lot control provisions of subs. (5) do not apply to a particular plan of subdivision. This by-law, when registered, will leave you only with the restriction imposed by subs. (3)(a). Thereafter, so long as you describe the land in accordance with the plan (for example, "Part of Lot __ Plan __"), you may convey whatever you want. You should be aware, however, that an exempting by-law is not retroactive; it will not operate to cure previous breaches (see *Canada Permanent Trust Co. v. Mortgage Insurance Co. of Canada* (1981), 10 A.C.W.S. (2d) 179 (Ont. C.A.)).

The municipality may also, under subs. (4), pass a by-law deeming an existing plan "not to be a registered plan of subdivision". Then, you will not be able to convey even a whole lot because it will be as if the plan did not exist at all.

There is sometimes confusion as to what constitutes a "registered plan of subdivision". Many years ago, plans were registered primarily for description and conveyancing purposes without much consideration of planning principles. Nevertheless, these are "registered plans of subdivision" for the purposes of the Act. On the other hand, a compiled plan prepared by a municipality in 1954 was held not to be a registered plan of subdivision. In *Elrick v. Hespeler (Town)*, [1966] O.J. No. 1123, [1967] 2 O.R. 448 at 450 (C.A.), MacKay J.A. said:

> The plan does not subdivide lands of any registered owner, it merely locates the lands of such owner on the plan and assigns a lot number to each parcel.

Similar reasoning could be applied to plans prepared by land registrars and judges pursuant to ss. 83 and 88 of the *Registry Act*, R.S.O. 1990, c. R.20.

However, in *Alron Investments Ltd. v. Greenvest Holdings Ltd.*, [1977] O.J. No. 2354, 16 O.R. (2d) 822 (Co. Ct.), the town plan of Wingham was found to be a registered plan on the basis that it actually subdivided what was previously one parcel of land. In both *Courneyea v. Smith*, [1977] O.J. No. 2286, 16 O.R. (2d) 269 (H.C.J.) and *Theriault v. Beaulieu*, [1982] O.J. No. 2301, 23 R.P.R. 154 (Co. Ct.), compiled plans registered prior to the enactment of the *Planning Act* in 1946 were held to be registered plans. See also *Tyrrell v. Pemberton*, [1983] O.J. No. 2186, 31 R.P.R. 11 (Co. Ct.) and *James O'Malley Construction Ltd. v. Lyle West Electric Ltd.*, [1980] O.J. No. 3640, 29 O.R. (2d) 116 (Co. Ct.). Nevertheless, in view of the *Elrick* decision, you should be careful when dealing with lands that are included in plans that are not undeniably registered plans of subdivision.

NO FEE IN ABUTTING LAND

Owners may always convey their land if they do not retain the fee simple or equity of redemption (legal terms for ownership) in any land abutting the land being conveyed. This exemption from the general prohibition in the preamble to s. 50 is found under subss. (3)(*b*) and (5)(*a*). It includes mortgages and agreements affecting the land.

Definition of "Abutting Land"

While there is no definition of "abutting land", it is clear that to be "abutting", it must have some common boundary with the land being conveyed. Land that touches only at a corner does not "abut" (see *Herman v. Kalbfleisch*, [1972] O.J. No. 1785, [1972] 2 O.R. 720 (Co. Ct.)). Likewise, two parcels of land that only share a common right of way do not abut (see *Starbuck v. Thibault*, [1982] O.J. No. 2319, 23 R.P.R. 230 (Co. Ct.) and *Hamilton v. Reed*, [1984] O.J. No. 3421, 49 O.R. (2d) 97 (H.C.J.)). There is no problem with an owner selling off the mineral or air rights of the land; s. 50(2) deems land not to be abutting if it abuts on a horizontal plane only. In *Cardiniere Atlantic Investment and Shipping Co. S.A. v. British Economic Insurance Co.* (1980), 1 A.C.W.S. (2d) 360 (Ont. Co. Ct.), O'Leary Co. Ct. J. held that a lease of an above-grade floor of a building for more than 21 years did not require consent. No consent will be required where the grantor holds only an easement in abutting land (see *Vasey v. Tribee Investments Ltd.*, [1970] O.J. No. 1680, [1971] 1 O.R. 477 (H.C.J.)).

Dominion over the Fee

The courts have often applied a broad concept of ownership for the purposes of the *Planning Act*, including persons who have "dominion over the fee", that is, persons who control the disposition of the land: *Forfar v. East Gwillimbury (Township)*, [1972] S.C.J. No. 38, 28 D.L.R. (3d) 512*n*, affg [1971] O.J. No. 1636, [1971] 3 O.R. 337 (C.A.). Thus, people granting land may not do so if they control the disposition of the adjacent land, for example where they are the beneficial owner of abutting land registered in the name of their trustee: *G. Roger Rivard Construction Ltd. v. East Gwillimbury (Town)*, [1979] O.J. No. 4457, 27 O.R. (2d) 34 at 40 (Div. Ct.); *Captain Developments Ltd. v. Marshall*, [1979] O.J. No. 3155, 11 R.P.R. 87 (Co. Ct.); *Pattison v. Sceviour*, [1983] O.J. No. 3165, 43 O.R. (2d) 229 (H.C.J.). In *Brendon v. ClubLink Properties Ltd.*, [2001] O.J. No. 3904, 23 M.P.L.R. (3d) 317 (S.C.J.), ClubLink had agreed to purchase all of a 65-acre property with the promise to reconvey 62 acres to the vendor once it had transferred a 3-acre parcel to the Ministry of Transportation. The Court found this arrangement contravened s. 50 because the vendor at all times retained control over the 62-acre parcel.

Although the *Planning Act* does not offer protection to innocent purchasers, the courts have held on a number of occasions that purchasers will be protected where they did not have actual notice that the abutting landowner was a trustee for the grantor to them: *Reference re Certain Titles to Land in Ontario*, [1973] O.J. No. 1948, [1973] 2 O.R. 613 (C.A.); *Cohen v. McClintock*, [1978] O.J. No.

3356, 19 O.R. (2d) 623 (H.C.J.). Likewise, where a mortgagee had no notice that the mortgagor had an interest in the abutting land, its interest was protected: *Sleightholme Estates Ltd. v. Bank of Montreal*, [1984] O.J. No. 3359, 48 O.R. (2d) 217 (H.C.J.). Because, under the *Land Titles Act*, R.S.O. 1990, c. L.5, a trustee registered as owner is treated as the absolute owner, the beneficial owner will not be found to hold the fee: *Wood v. Dennett*, [1976] O.J. No. 2404, 15 O.R. (2d) 576 (H.C.J.). In one case, the vendor of a parcel resided on abutting land that he had previously conveyed to The Director, The Veterans' Land Act. The Court held that the vendor's interest in the abutting land was a personal one only and that no consent was required because he did not hold the "fee": *Juska v. Courtnage* (1980), 1 A.C.W.S. (2d) 317 (Ont. Co. Ct.).

Simultaneous Conveyances

One of the devices attempted in the past to circumvent the prohibition against retaining abutting land was to make simultaneous conveyances to separate individuals, for example, by enclosing two deeds in one envelope or two grants in one deed. The argument made was that the grantor did not retain the fee in abutting land even for an instant since all that was owned was conveyed at once. Section 50(15) was enacted to close this loophole by deeming that the grantor retained the fee in abutting land. The courts have made it clear that this prohibition only applies to simultaneous conveyances to different purchasers: *Pierotti v. Lansink* (1979), 25 O.R. (2d) 656 at 660 (C.A.). Where the land is partly in the Land Titles system and partly in the Registry system, a separate transfer and deed of the respective parts to a single purchaser will not contravene the *Planning Act*: *Szegho v. Baril*, [1978] O.J. No. 3284, 19 O.R. (2d) 95 (H.C.J.).

Identity of "Grantor"

The courts have consistently applied a strict definition to the term "grantor" used under the *Planning Act*, holding that in order to apply the prohibition against the grantor retaining the fee in abutting land, the owner of that abutting land must be identical to the grantor. Thus, if A and B own parcel 1 and A alone owns parcel 2, which abuts the first parcel, no consent will be required for A to convey parcel 2 or for A and B to convey parcel 1. It does not matter in what capacity A and B hold the land, whether as partners, as joint tenants or as tenants in common. A few of the many decisions regarding this issue follow: *MacDonald v. Yates*, [1974] O.J. No. 1993, 4 O.R. (2d) 547 (H.C.J.) (partners); *Murray v. Clark*, [1974] O.J. No. 2050, 5 O.R. (2d) 261 (H.C.J.) (joint tenants); *Langford v. Sorenson* (1980), 5 A.C.W.S. (2d) 301 (Ont. Co. Ct.) (tenants-in-common). However, this line of cases opened a loophole. If A and B owned a parcel jointly, A could convey his undivided interest in the east half to B with the result that the parcel was now divided into two parts that could be conveyed separately. The first conveyance was all right, because when A conveyed the east half to B, the abutting land (being the west half) was owned by A and B. Although never given judicial blessing, this scheme was outlawed by s. 50(19).

The courts have also decided that consent will not be required if the owners of abutting parcels do not hold the land in identical capacities. For example, A was the first mortgagee of land abutting land that A owned; no consent was required to a conveyance of the land A owned even though A technically held the legal title to both parcels: *Redmond v. Rothschild*, [1970] O.J. No. 1670, [1971] 1 O.R. 436 (C.A.).

In *Fralick v. Derushie*, [1981] O.J. No. 2256, 21 R.P.R. 281 (Co. Ct.), no consent was required for an executrix to sell land pursuant to a will under which she was the sole beneficiary, even though she personally owned abutting land.

CONSENT OF THE LAND DIVISION COMMITTEE

Under s. 53(1) of the *Planning Act*, the municipal council may grant consents to conveyances or other transactions that result in a severance of the grantor's land holdings. In most cases, the municipal council has delegated the authority to the committee of adjustment or land division committee that held that power under the previous version of the Act. These committees are independent bodies appointed by the council. For those parts of Ontario that do not have an organized municipal government, the Minister of Municipal Affairs is empowered to grant consents. A summary of the procedure in obtaining a consent is found later in this chapter (see p. 143-44); for this part, we will consider the effect of a consent.

Consent Must Be Final

Subsections (3)(*f*) and (5)(*f*) both exempt from the general prohibition of s. 50 those transactions that have received a "consent", which is defined in subs. (1) to be a consent given by a municipal council or the Minister of Municipal Affairs, as the case may be. It has been decided that the requirement for a consent means a "final" consent, that is, one where all appeal periods have expired and no appeal remains outstanding (see *Smale v. Van der Weer*, [1977] O.J. No. 2427, 17 O.R. (2d) 480 (H.C.J.) and *Blair v. Crawford*, [1989] O.J. No. 1917, 70 O.R. (2d) 748 (H.C.J.)).

Compliance with Conditions

The land division committee has power to make its consent subject to compliance with conditions imposed by the committee. Most commonly, the conditions include the payment of realty taxes to date, the payment of special levies to the municipality, or the donation of a strip of land for road-widening purposes. Once imposed, the condition cannot later be modified or waived by the committee (see *Wimpey Developments Ltd. v. Frontenac (County) Land Division Committee*, [1979] O.J. No. 4305, 25 O.R. (2d) 350 (Div. Ct.)). The only two ways to avoid an undesirable condition are to appeal to the Ontario Municipal Board or to reapply to the committee. A vendor who must apply for consent should consider inserting provisions in the agreement of purchase and sale, which would limit responsibility for complying with conditions imposed by the committee; it has been held that a vendor cannot withdraw from the transaction simply because a condition of the consent is too expensive or otherwise onerous (see *E. Filice Construction Ltd. v. V. Cambone Construction Ltd.*, [1977] 2 A.C.W.S. 825 (Ont. H.C.J.) and *John E. Dodge Holdings Ltd. v.*

805062 Ontario Ltd., [2003] O.J. No. 350, 63 O.R. (3d) 304 (C.A.), where the vendor was ordered to comply with a condition to build a road).

Note s. 53(41) of the *Planning Act*: where a consent is conditional, the applicant has one year from the giving of notice of the conditions to perform them. If the conditions are not performed within this time limit, the decision to give consent lapses and there is instead a deemed refusal of the application.

Lapsing of Consent

Section 53(43) provides that a consent given under the Act automatically lapses two years after the date of the certificate, unless a shorter period is stipulated in the decision. To be effective, the consent must be used within that period. However, it is not necessary to register a conveyance in order to avoid the lapsing of a consent — execution and delivery of the deed is sufficient (see *Carey v. LaPrise*, [1978] O.J. No. 3688, 23 O.R. (2d) 299 (Co. Ct.)).

Note that the two-year limitation on the consent does not start to run until the date of the certificate. Although s. 53(41) of the Act requires that conditions imposed on a consent be fulfilled with one year of the giving of notice of the decision, there is no specific limitation on when the certificate itself can be given or dated. In *McCann v. Renfrew (County) Land Division Committee*, [1978] O.J. No. 3317, 19 O.R. (2d) 349, the Divisional Court ordered the Committee to stamp the applicant's deed with a certificate confirming the consent given more than two years before the deed was presented to the Committee for stamping. The Committee had a policy requiring the stamp to be affixed within two years but had failed to notify the applicant. Today, a committee could limit the time by making it an express condition of the consent that the transfer or charge (or applicable document) be stamped within a specified time limit.

Conveyance of Wrong Parcel

Many owners believe that what you apply for under the *Planning Act* is a severance, that is, permission to create two or more separate parcels of land somewhat in the manner of a plan of a subdivision. In fact, the consent is to convey or otherwise deal with a specific parcel of land. This misunderstanding has led some owners to apply for and obtain consent to convey the wrong parcel, the one they intended to retain. This happens, it seems, particularly with farmers who are often granted a special status under a municipality's official plan allowing them the right to retain a retirement lot. Frequently, the farmer wants to sell the retirement lot while continuing to reside in his traditional home.

It is well established, however, that the consent, to be effective, must be for the parcel to be conveyed: *Faion v. Bonnydon Ltd.*, [1974] O.J. No. 2058, 5 O.R. (2d) 314 (Co. Ct.); *Radford v. Bartliff* (1979), 2 A.C.W.S. 119 (Ont. Co. Ct.). In order to alleviate this problem, s. 50(6) was introduced, allowing the conveyance of the remaining parcel, provided its conveyance occurs before the "consented to" parcel is conveyed: *Baker v. Belleville Collectors Market Ltd.*, [1987] O.J. No. 2629, 60 O.R. (2d) 157 (Dist. Ct.). This provision, while helpful, often presents difficulty to the purchaser; conditions to the consent may not be satisfied or the consent may not be used in time, in which case the consent will lapse and the supposed exemption for the conveyance of the "remaining" parcel may evaporate. The purchaser will, of course, not have any control over this turn of events.

A decision of the Ontario Court of Appeal illustrates the difficulty with this section. In *1390957 Ontario Ltd. v. Acchione*, [2002] O.J. No. 22, 57 O.R. (3d) 578, one owner had obtained a consent to convey part of her land and registered a transfer to herself with the consent stamped on the transfer. A month later, she transferred the other part to Ms. Acchione. In a subsequent transaction, the purchaser alleged that Ms. Acchione did not have good title. Rosenberg J.A., in overturning the Superior Court of Justice (who had held the transfer to be valid because it would otherwise result in an absurdity), found that the plain wording of the Act required the part not subject to the consent to be conveyed *before* the part that was consented to, in order to be able to take advantage of s. 50(6) of the Act.

"Once a Consent, Always a Consent"

Section 50(12) of the *Planning Act* was added, effective March 31, 1979, to provide that no further consent was required to deal with a parcel of land that had been conveyed by deed or transfer with a consent under s. 50. By giving a consent, the committee in effect creates a parcel of land that is the equivalent of a whole lot on a plan of subdivision. The committee may, however, stipulate that subdivision control continues to apply to the parcel. The stipulation must be included in the certificate of consent so that a subsequent purchaser will be warned.

A question still exists whether this section applies to consents given before the section came into force on March 31, 1979. A number of decisions have held that it does: *Jackson v. Brennan* (1981), 6 A.C.W.S. (2d) 450 (Ont. Co. Ct.); *Ord v. Ramsden* (1981), 9 A.C.W.S. (2d) 113 (Ont. Co. Ct.); *R & R Eastern Estates Ltd. v. Van Heurn*, [1986] O.J. No. 2969, 57 O.R. (2d) 168 (Dist. Ct.); and *Ochitwa v. Biddulph (Township)*, [1992] O.J. No. 105, 6 O.R. (3d) 793 (Gen. Div.).

At least two decisions reached the opposite conclusion, both based on the well-established principle that statutes are not retroactive unless expressly made so. In both *Thompson Estate v. London (City)*, [1997] O.J. No. 4572, 36 O.R. (3d) 572 (Gen. Div.) and *Imrisek v. D'Ermo*, [1993] O.J. No. 1969, 14 O.R. (3d) 774 (Gen. Div.), the Court concluded that s. 50(12) was not retroactive because there was no opportunity prior to this amendment for committees in granting consents to stipulate that subdivision control would continue to apply.

In *Zurich Indemnity Co. of Canada v. Anchelle Holdings Inc. (in Trust)*, [1995] O.J. No. 1453, 38 O.R. (3d) 26 (Gen. Div.), Lane J. reviewed the cases both for and against and expressed his preference for those favouring retroactivity. In his view "the legislature intended that a consent, once given, should suffice to authorize the continued conveyance of the identical parcel of land".

At least some solicitors have concluded that the *Anchelle Holdings* approach is the correct one and have been prepared to put the issue to rest with respect to individual properties by signing the *Planning Act* statements in the transfer (see p. 142-43 below). They believe that the *Imrisek* decision can be distinguished on the basis that the transfer was to The Director, The Veteran's Land Act and was therefore in essence merely a consent to a mortgage. Further, the *Acchione* case was not referred to in the *Thompson Estate* decision and was therefore "not based on the whole of the jurisprudence" (*per* Lane J. in the *Anchelle Holdings* decision at 32 O.R.). In any event, all these decisions are at the trial level only. One hopes that someday the Court of Appeal will side with those favouring retroactivity.

Consent Cures Previous Breaches

Section 50(14) of the *Planning Act* provides in part that a consent given to a conveyance, mortgage or charge cures any previous contravention of the *Planning Act*. The section is clearly retroactive with respect to breaches occurring prior to December 15, 1978, when this section was added to the Act. That result has been confirmed by the Court of Appeal in *Bluestone v. Enroute Restaurants Inc.*, [1994] O.J. No. 1214, 18 O.R. (3d) 481. Indeed, a new consent to a transfer or mortgage will cure a prior breach even though the breach related to a different configuration of the land (see *Kafco Homes Ltd. v. Norlington Industries Inc.*, [1995] O.J. No. 317, 22 O.R. (3d) 57 (C.A.)).

This section creates perhaps the simplest, cheapest and quickest method to correct a contravention of the Act. An owner can apply for a new consent and then convey the parcel with that consent. Section 41 of the *Conveyancing and Law of Property Act*, R.S.O. 1990, c. C.34 specifically recognizes a conveyance from a grantor to himself or herself as being effective (see *Tessis v. Scherer*, [1982] O.J. No. 3496, 39 O.R. (2d) 149 (C.A.), leave to appeal to S.C.C. refused (1982), 39 O.R. (2d) 616*n*, 26 R.P.R. 41*n*).

Section 50(14) even allows a transaction to be completed before the consent becomes final provided of course that the consent is eventually obtained: see, for example, *Bizzarro v. Marina Bay Development Corp.*, [1991] O.J. No. 1311, 4 O.R. (3d) 258 (Gen. Div.), where two mortgages were given on adjoining parcels some months before the conditions of the consent were satisfied.

CONDITIONAL UPON COMPLIANCE WITH SECTION 50

The general prohibition in s. 50 against persons dealing with their land extends even to agreements of purchase and sale. However, subs. 50(21) exempts agreements that are made expressly conditional upon compliance with s. 50 of the Act. The standard real estate board forms all contain language to this effect and also require the vendor to apply for any necessary consent.

The failure to include a condition in an agreement of purchase and sale when the vendor owns abutting land may result in the agreement being unenforceable by either the purchaser or the vendor (see *Rogers v. Leonard*, [1973] O.J. No. 2130, 1 O.R. (2d) 57 (H.C.J.)). In one case, where the agreement did not contain a condition when it should have, the vendor actually obtained the consent of the committee of adjustment to the resulting conveyance and then refused to close. The court dismissed the action by the purchaser on the ground that the agreement was a nullity (see *Dunn v. Rogers*, [1974] O.J. No. 530 (C.A.)).

The courts have on many occasions been anxious to avoid this harsh result. The decision in *Davmark Developments Ltd. v. Tripp*, [1974] O.J. No. 2028, 5

O.R. (2d) 17 (H.C.J.), held that no special wording was required so long as the intention was clear that the contract is conditional on compliance. In *Ludlow v. Beattie*, [1978] O.J. No. 3442, 20 O.R. (2d) 363 (H.C.J.), the Court ordered rectification of an agreement of purchase and sale by inserting the condition that the solicitor forgot to include. In other cases, the courts have read in a condition where the parties' pre-contractual conduct or words indicated, even vaguely, an intention to comply with the *Planning Act*.

Notwithstanding the courts' desire at times to alleviate against a harsh result, it is important that the condition be explicit. In *Dical Investments Ltd. v. Morrison*, [1990] O.J. No. 2160, 75 O.R. (2d) 417, the Court of Appeal held that a general expression that all governmental requirements would be complied with in an agreement granting an option to purchase lots on a proposed plan of subdivision was not sufficient compliance with s. 50(21) and, therefore, the option was unenforceable. Similarly, in *Morgan Trust Co. of Canada v. Falloncrest Financial Corp.*, [2006] O.J. No. 4603, 218 O.A.C. 71, the Court of Appeal followed the *Dical* decision in finding as void an option to purchase a residence upon "registration of any plan of subdivision on the lands, or the severance of the lands". Although the intention of the parties seemed clear, the Court rejected the concept of an "implied agreement" to make the contract conditional on compliance with s. 50 of the Act — the condition must be expressly set out.

CURES FOR CONTRAVENTIONS

As previously discussed (p. 116), a contravention of s. 50 of the *Planning Act* results in the transfer or other instrument being a nullity. This means that all persons claiming an interest in the property subsequent to the contravention will receive nothing, even though they may have paid over all their money in good faith. While the cures are limited, there are a number of which you should be aware:

The Planning Amendment Act, 1967, S.O. 1967, c. 75

Section 10(3) states that the contravention before June 15, 1967, of s. 29 (as it then was) or its predecessor "does not have and shall be deemed never to have had the effect of preventing the conveyance or creation of any interest in land". This is an awkward way of saying that even though s. 29(18) said that a deed created no interest in land, the legislature realized that a lot of mistakes were made in the first few years, so they wiped the slate clean as of June 15, 1967. You may therefore safely ignore any previous non-compliance with s. 29 (now s. 50).

Certificate of Validation

If you have a contravention of the *Planning Act*, you may apply under s. 57 to the local land division committee (or the Minister of Municipal Affairs where the land is not within an organized municipality) for a certificate of validation. A certificate of validation, once issued, cures all prior contraventions of the *Planning Act* affecting the parcel of land in question. Previous to this amendment in 1996, an order had to be obtained from the Minister and published in the Ontario *Gazette*, a difficult, expensive and time-consuming process. Now, however, the application is very similar to an ordinary application for a consent and should, therefore, be the remedy of choice. However, note that a validation certificate cannot be issued unless the land conforms to the municipality's official plan and zoning by-law. This can be a serious impediment, especially if the use of the land is a legal, non-conforming use because its use predated changes in the official plan and zoning by-law.

New Consent

As discussed previously (see p. 135), a conveyance or mortgage with a consent has the effect, under s. 50(14), of forgiving previous breaches of the Act. Thus, you may always apply to the committee of adjustment for a new consent and then convey the land, if only to yourself, in order to cure a previous contravention of the Act.

Plan of Subdivision

Section 50(14) forgives any breach of the Act that has occurred prior to the registration of a plan of subdivision. Because proper planning principles will have been applied to the land covered by the plan, it does not matter what happened before.

Land Titles "Qualified Title"

As discussed at p. 31, the registration of a person as first registered owner with a qualified title under the *Land Titles Act*, R.S.O. 1990, c. L.5, is not subject to s. 50 of the *Planning Act*, and, therefore, any previous breaches may be ignored.

CONVEYANCES TO GOVERNMENTAL AUTHORITIES

Conveyances to and from governmental authorities, such as a municipality or the governments of Ontario or Canada, are exempted from subdivision control by subss. (3)(*c*) and (5)(*b*) of s. 50. Crown agencies are included within this exemption, for example, Canada Mortgage and Housing Corporation and the Ontario Development Corporation (see *McGruer v. Clark Ltd.*, [1976] O.J. No. 2219, 13 O.R. (2d) 385 (H.C.J.); *Bevark Holdings Ltd. v. Toronto Harbour Commissioners*, [1987] O.J. No. 23, 58 O.R. (2d) 87 (H.C.J.), affd [1988] O.J. No. 1811, 66 O.R. (2d) 521 (C.A.)). However, many organizations that you might think would be exempted are not, for example, Boards of Education and Bell Canada.

TRANSMISSION AND UTILITY LINES

Paragraph (3)(*d*) of s. 50 exempt from subdivision control conveyances for electrical and hydrocarbon transmission lines as defined in the *Ontario Energy*

Board Act, 1998, S.O. 1998, c. 15, Sched. B (Part VI). In addition, para. 50(5)(*c*) exempts "utility lines", which includes hydro and gas pipeline easements. Note, however, that this exemption applies only where the land is within a plan of subdivision. In both cases, the acquiror must make a declaration that it is being acquired for such purpose (the declaration should be included in the transfer or deposited on title).

MORTGAGES

Subsection 50(8) of the *Planning Act* permits a purchaser to give back to a vendor a mortgage of the property purchased, even though the purchaser owns abutting land and the mortgage would otherwise be void.

On the other hand, a mortgagee may not give a partial discharge of the land covered by a mortgage unless a consent to convey the same land has been given, or it is a whole lot on a plan of subdivision or the discharge is given to a government (subs. 50(17)). For these purposes of the Act, the mortgagee is treated as a grantor and is deemed under subs. 50(16) to hold the fee in any abutting land retained under the mortgage.

Under subs. 50(18), a mortgagee may not exercise a power of sale or a right of foreclosure with respect to a part only of the land covered by the mortgage unless: (a) the part is a whole lot on a plan; or (b) the part does not abut any other land covered by the mortgage; or (c) the parcel to be conveyed was previously consented to or is the remaining part of a parcel that had a consent; or (d) the approval of the Minister of Municipal Affairs or the land division committee has been obtained.

LEASES

As has been noted, subss. 50(3) and 50(5) prohibit agreements that are for the use of land for periods of 21 years or more (including rights of renewal) unless they are covered by one of the available exemptions, such as a consent by a land division committee or an agreement covering the whole of the grantor's land. On this basis, leases of parts of an owner's land are covered by the *Planning Act*. The theory is, of course, that a long-term lease is equivalent to ownership and should therefore be subject to the application of proper planning principles and policies.

However, it became apparent that it was ridiculous to apply this restriction to leases in office buildings and the like; there were no planning issues at stake and the process of obtaining consent to long-term leases was expensive and wasteful of the time of land division committees and other municipal officials. Accordingly, subs. 50(9) was added, which exempted agreements granting the use of a part of a building or structure for any period of years.

While this addition solved the problem for most office leases, a question still remains whether the inclusion in the lease of ancillary rights to use of other parts of the landlord's land (for example, for outdoor parking) meant that a consent is still required. This question arises most frequently in the shopping centre context where the leases either explicitly, or even implicitly, almost always include rights to the exterior of buildi ngs, whether for parking, outdoor selling rights or merely access.

In these cases, most careful solicitors will insist on a consent being obtained, either prior to the lease being entered into or as soon thereafter as reasonably possible. In this latter case, it is common to provide that, until the consent is obtained, the term of the lease is limited to a period of 21 years less one day.

A decision that is helpful in this regard is found in *Sears Canada Ltd. v. Scarborough Town Centre Holdings Inc.*, [1996] O.J. No. 5419, 45 O.R. (3d) 474. The Ontario Court (General Division) upheld the validity of a number of long-term anchor leases in various shopping centres on the basis that "the outdoor selling rights and use of the parking lot are merely ancillary to the essential lease provisions and do not change the character of it" (at 477 O.R.). MacFarland J. was clearly influenced by the fact that these properties "were located in urban centres and had been through a plethora of approval processes" (at 477 O.R.).

EASEMENTS

Like long-term leases, easements are "agreements for the use of land" and require consent if they cover only part of the owner's land. In certain situations, this requirement can be addressed either by limiting the easement to a term of 21 years less a day (at least until the consent is obtained) or by obtaining a blanket easement covering all of the owner's land.

One special (and helpful) exception to the general rule is found in s. 9(3) of the *Condominium Act, 1998*, S.O. 1998, c. 19, which provides that s. 50 of the *Planning Act* does not apply to easements transferred by or reserved to a condominium corporation. Another exception is found in s. 40(5) of the *Land Titles Act*, which exempts easements created by a condominium declaration.

Note that a release of an easement does not require consent. The giving of a release or quit claim of an easement is not the entering into of an "agreement that has the effect of granting the use of land"; rather, it is the opposite.

A note of caution however — a conveyancer might try to circumvent the need to obtain a consent to an easement over a specific part of a parcel of land by having a blanket easement granted over the whole parcel, and then releasing the easement, except for the specific part required. While not tested, remember the cases discussed at p. 128, where the Court looked at the "substance rather than the form of the transaction" to find against transactions designed to circumvent the *Planning Act*.

PARTITION ORDERS

The *Planning Amendment Act, 1981*, S.O. 1981, c. 15, added a provision to close a loophole created by the decision in *Ontario (Attorney General) v. Yeotes*, [1981] O.J. No. 2495, 31 O.R. (2d) 589 (C.A.), leave to appeal refused [1981] S.C.C.A. No. 210, 37 N.R. 356. In that case the Court of Appeal ordered partition of a single parcel among several co-owners pursuant to the *Partition Act*, R.S.O. 1990, c. P.4, reasoning that the *Planning Act* prohibited only certain types of transactions which create severances, not all kinds. Section 50(20) now provides that a partition order will have no effect unless the result is otherwise in compliance with the *Planning Act.*

Note, however, that s. 50(20) does not apply to orders for partition made under s. 10(1) of the *Family Law Act,* R.S.O. 1990, c. F.3 (*Pulzoni v. Pulzoni,* [1982] O.J. No. 2302, 25 R.P.R. 72 (Ont. H.C.J.)), nor to vesting orders made by a court (*Brankston v. Wright,* [1985] O.J. No. 2529, 50 O.R. (2d) 666 (H.C.J.); *Holmsten v. Karson Kartage Konstruction Ltd.,* [1997] O.J. No. 1352, 33 O.R. (3d) 54 (Gen. Div.)).

WILLS

A number of judicial decisions held that severances that result from the provisions of a will were not prohibited under s. 50 on the basis that the devise was not a conveyance and therefore not prohibited under s. 50. There appeared to be a growing practice of using this approach in estate planning. Therefore, the *Planning Statute Law Amendment Act, 1991,* S.O. 1991, c. 9, was passed to prohibit subdivision by will as of July 26, 1990 (s. 50.1). As a transitional measure, the Minister of Municipal Affairs could make orders giving effect to subdivision provisions in wills for persons who died after July 26, 1990 and prior to the Act receiving Royal Assent; a number of such orders were made.

POSSESSORY TITLE

Quit-claim deeds given by adjacent owners will not require consent under the *Planning Act* when they are given to confirm a possessory title that has already been acquired: *Duthie v. Wall,* [1979] O.J. No. 4150, 24 O.R. (2d) 49 (H.C.J.); *MacMain v. Hurontario Management Services Ltd.,* [1980] O.J. No. 2810, 14 R.P.R. 158 (Co. Ct.). It will be necessary to deposit evidence on title, presumably in the form of statutory declarations, to support the conclusion of possessory title and thereby avoid the suspicion that the transaction may be a sham to avoid subdivision control.

It has also been held that the doctrine of adverse possession will operate after 10 years of possession to assure title to a purchaser who received a deed that breached the *Planning Act* and, therefore, conveyed no title: *OAS Management Group Inc. v. Chirico,* [1990] O.J. No. 260, 9 O.R. (3d) 171 (Dist. Ct.).

On the other hand, an agreement between neighbours regarding the location of a fence, entered into in order to avoid subsequent claims of possessory title, has been found to be void because it was an agreement without a termination date and therefore granted the use of land for a period of more than 21 years: *Bea v. Robinson,* [1977] O.J. No. 2463, 18 O.R. (2d) 12 (H.C.J.). In drafting a boundary agreement like this, you should limit it to a fixed term of no more than 21 years less one day in order to avoid this result. The owners at the time the agreement expires may renew it if they wish.

CORRECTING AND QUIT-CLAIM DEEDS

Several cases have made it clear that s. 50 applies only to substantive transactions and does not prevent deeds or other instruments given to remove clouds from title.

In *Turner v. Turner Funeral Home Ltd.*, [1971] O.J. No. 1917, [1972] 2 O.R. 851 (Co. Ct.); *Lance v. Jones*, [1980] O.J. No. 3725, 30 O.R. (2d) 13 (H.C.J.); and *Consortium Capital Projects Ltd. v. Blind River Veneer Ltd.*, [1988] O.J. No. 103, 63 O.R. (2d) 761 (H.C.J.), affd [1990] O.J. No. 3318, 72 O.R. (2d) 703*n* (C.A.), the courts have decided that s. 50(3) was never intended to affect deeds given to correct an error made in a description (known as "correcting deeds").

Nor will you require consent for a quit-claim deed given merely to remove a cloud from the title of an adjacent owner or to confirm title in some way (see above regarding possessory title). Section 50 will not apply as long as the quit-claim does not result in an actual conveyance.

IMPORTANT DATES

It is important to know a number of dates when various changes under the *Planning Act* were effected. Except when you have a new consent or a plan of subdivision, both of which cure previous defects (see p. 137), a conveyance that contravenes s. 50 of the Act will result in the failure of the entire title thereafter. Thus, it is essential that you ensure compliance with the Act for all transactions after the last general forgiveness amendment on June 15, 1967. The following is a list of the important dates to keep in mind when reviewing titles.

1. June 15, 1967: The *Planning Act* was amended (S.O. 1967, c. 75) to forgive all previous contraventions of the Act (see p. 136).

2. May 2, 1968: The Act was amended (S.O. 1968, c. 96) to remove the 10-acre exemption, *i.e.*, conveyances where the resulting parcels were all in excess of 10 acres. This exemption is the reason for the numerous parcels of land in rural Ontario, which are just slightly larger than 10 acres.

3. June 27, 1970: This was the date when subdivision control was imposed on all of Ontario (S.O. 1970, c. 72, s. 1(2)). Before this date, subdivision control only applied if the municipality had passed a "subdivision control by-law" that was registered against title or if the Minister of Municipal Affairs had registered an order to the same effect. In addition, prior to June 27, 1970, even if there was a subdivision control by-law, you could subdivide any land within a plan of subdivision unless the municipality had passed and registered a part-lot control by-law.

4. March 31, 1979: The predecessor to s. 50(12) was deemed in force providing that a parcel created by a conveyance with a consent could subsequently be dealt with without requiring a further consent even though the grantor owned abutting land (see p. 134). Assuming this amendment (S.O. 1979, c. 59) is not retroactive, this subsection will only apply to conveyances after this date.

5. August 1, 1983: The *Planning Act, 1983*, S.O. 1983, c. 1 was proclaimed in force. Section 50(6) was introduced, containing the exemption for conveyance

of the remaining parcel where consent has been obtained to convey the abutting parcel.

6.   July 26, 1990: Severance by will is prohibited. As a transitional measure, the Minister of Municipal Affairs was allowed with the consent of the local municipality to make an order prior to July 26, 1992, to permit a severance under the will of a person who died prior to June 27, 1991.

RETROACTIVITY

In general, an amending statute is not retroactive unless expressly made so. Thus, the imposition of subdivision control province-wide on June 27, 1970, did not invalidate severances that had been completed prior to that date.

What of contracts that were still in the process of being completed when an amendment outlawed that type of transaction? While earlier authorities conflict, it would seem the matter has now been settled — such contracts will be enforceable. In each of *Miller v. Ameri-cana Motel Ltd.*, [1983] S.C.J. No. 15, [1983] 1 S.C.R. 229 and *Texaco Canada Inc. v. Bracci*, [1985] O.J. No. 2558, 51 O.R. (2d) 118 (H.C.J.), the owner of lands granted an option to purchase part of the lands. Subdivision control was subsequently imposed on the lands. In the first case, the Supreme Court of Canada held that in granting the option, the owner had effectively disposed of control of the fee simple (*i.e.*, ownership) in the lands at a time when it was permitted under the *Planning Act*; therefore, the option was enforceable. The Supreme Court of Ontario confirmed the same result in the *Texaco* case.

By similar reasoning, if an owner agrees to sell land (or grants an option) and before that agreement (or option) is completed, the owner acquires adjacent land, the agreement will remain enforceable. In other words, the owner cannot frustrate the original agreement to sell merely by acquiring adjacent land prior to completion of sale of the original lands.

EFFECT OF LAND REGISTRATION REFORM ACT, R.S.O. 1990, c. L.4

PLANNING ACT STATEMENTS

Section 42 of the *Registry Act*, R.S.O. 1980, c. 445 (introduced in April 1981 and repealed in 1984) required that all transfers contain either a consent under s. 29 of the *Planning Act*, or an affidavit verifying compliance with that Act made by one of the parties. The affidavit was not required where compliance was obvious on the face of the instrument (such as with a whole lot on a plan of subdivision). The affidavit, however, gave no protection to a person acquiring an interest in the land. If the *Planning Act* was breached, no interest would pass to the transferee, notwithstanding the existence of an affidavit of compliance. The onus was, therefore, on the transferee to ensure compliance throughout the period since the last general forgiveness of non-compliance on June 15, 1967.

The *Land Registration Reform Act*, R.S.O. 1990, c. L.4 ("LRRA") amended the *Planning Act* to add subs. 50(22), introducing a new scheme to assist title searchers in checking for compliance with the Act. Where the statements in Boxes 13 and 14 of a Transfer/Deed in Form 1 under the LRRA, R.R.O. 1990, Reg. 688, are signed by the vendor, the vendor's solicitor and the solicitor for the purchaser, that transfer and all previous conveyances affecting the land are deemed to comply with the *Planning Act*. If a breach has previously occurred, it will in effect be forgiven. There are serious penalties for those who deliberately sign Boxes 13 and 14 when they should not. But subsequent purchasers need not be concerned. It is not necessary to check for *Planning Act* compliance behind a transfer that has Boxes 13 and 14 completed. Furthermore, even if the transfer itself contravenes the Act inadvertently, it will nevertheless be deemed to be in compliance and the purchaser's lawyer will be saved from liability for negligence (see *Reeve-Burns v. Pelkman*, [1989] O.J. No. 1531, 70 O.R. (2d) 113 (Dist. Ct.), *Imrisek v. D'Ermo*, [1993] O.J. No. 1969, 14 O.R. (3d) 774 (Gen. Div.) and *Jacuniak v. Tamburro*, [2002] O.J. No. 1420, 59 O.R. (3d) 236 (S.C.J.)).

For registration purposes, the statements are optional and need not be completed. Where the statements are not completed, the next person dealing with the property will have to confirm that the *Planning Act* has been complied with back through the chain of title to a point when it is clear that there has been compliance with the *Planning Act*.

In the past, some solicitors expressed reluctance to sign the statements. This attitude is difficult to understand. As long as the solicitor and client have fulfilled their duties, completing the statements will reduce rather than increase potential liability, since there is deemed compliance with the *Planning Act*. In fact, commonly now the agreement of purchase and sale contains provisions requiring the statements to be completed.

LAND TITLES "QUALIFIED TITLE"

As discussed, the registration of a person as first registered owner with a qualified title under the *Land Titles Act*, R.S.O. 1990, c. L.5, is not subject to s. 50 of the *Planning Act* and, therefore, any previous breaches may be ignored. However, practitioners must review all transactions from and after the conversion of the lands to a qualified title to ensure s. 50 of the Act has been complied with.

APPLICATIONS FOR CONSENT

Under s. 53 of the *Planning Act*, municipal councils are empowered to hear applications and grant consents to conveyances that result in a severance. In most cases, the approving authority is the area municipality such as a region, county or district on the basis that proper planning should be done on a larger scale than would normally be achieved by a town or city. However, the area municipality can delegate its authority to a local municipal council.

The municipal council in turn may delegate its authority to grant consents to an appointed officer or to a committee of adjustment or land division committee.

Most have done so, usually to the same committee that had the authority prior to the Act being amended in 1983.

In giving a consent, the council or the committee has, under subs. 53(12), the same power to impose conditions as does the Minister in relation to plans of subdivision. These conditions could include the payment of special levies or the donation of lands for parks or roads. This latter condition is frequently imposed even though there are no immediate plans to widen the particular road that is fronting on that property. The acquisition of these strips will avoid the expense and difficulty of later expropriations.

The application for consent is made in a standard form prescribed under the Act as is the application fee. You will be required to supply a sketch showing the parcel to be severed and adjoining lands. A sketch prepared by the client will suffice; you will normally not wish to incur the expense of a surveyor until the consent has been obtained. In most cases, of course, you will ultimately have to obtain a reference plan in order to describe the land in the document which gives effect to the consent.

Notice of your application is given by the secretary-treasurer of the committee, usually by registered mail, to a number of municipal and provincial officials and to adjoining landowners. At the hearing, all interested parties may make representations to the committee. Some committees will make their decision on the spot; others will always reserve and make the decision later in private. In any event, the notice of the decision is usually sent by registered mail within a few days after the hearing date. The date of the decision is the date of mailing of that notice.

An appeal against a decision or of one or more of the conditions imposed may be made under subs. 53(39) by sending notice of appeal together with the prescribed fee by registered mail to the secretary-treasurer within 20 days of the date of the decision. If no notice is received, the decision is final. Otherwise, the appeal is made to the Ontario Municipal Board, which hears the entire matter again. The decision of the Board is final.

Once the decision has been made final and all the conditions have been satisfied, the clerk of the council or secretary-treasurer of the committee gives a certificate of the decision, usually by stamping it directly on the deed or other instrument. Subsection 53(42) of the Act provides that the certificate is conclusive and no action may be brought to question it.

The whole process from application to final decision will usually take a minimum of 8 to 10 weeks. Of course, more time may be added if the committee does not meet frequently, as is sometimes the case in smaller municipalities, or if the committee is very busy and you cannot get on the next agenda. If an appeal is taken to the Ontario Municipal Board, you may expect at least several months to be added to the process. The time required to obtain a consent may play havoc with the time periods agreed to in a transaction of purchase and sale. Certainly, sufficient time before closing should be allowed, and you may also wish to consider provisions for extending closing in the event the application does not proceed as expected.

REGISTERED PLANS OF SUBDIVISION

The other principal method of subdividing land is by registered plan of subdivision. This occurs where someone who has a large block of undeveloped land wishes to divide up the land into lots for sale. Prior to the Second World War, the only restrictions on the subdivision of lands were those found in the *Registry Act* and were really just registration requirements. Large areas of land were subdivided by developers, but few of the services were installed by them. The municipality then had to install the water mains, sewers, street lights, sidewalks and curbs. In many cases, this was done on a "local improvement" basis. This is a procedure whereby a municipality may borrow money for public services through the issue of debentures. The municipality then divides the cost of servicing the debenture among those properties benefited, on a frontage basis, and adds to the tax bill for each property its annual share of the debenture cost. During the Depression there were numerous debentures outstanding to pay for services which the municipalities could not pay off because there were no taxes coming in.

SUBDIVISION AGREEMENTS

The practice today is for the municipality to insist on developers installing all services at their cost before the municipality will accept and approve the subdivision. Section 51 of the *Planning Act*, as amended, sets out the procedure for obtaining approval of a plan of subdivision in great detail. Subsection (26) states that a municipality (or in the case of lands not within organized municipalities, the Minister of Municipal Affairs) may enter into agreements imposed as a condition to the approval of a plan of subdivision that will be enforceable against all subsequent owners of the subject land provided they have been registered against the title to the land.

When acting for a purchaser of a lot that is subject to a subdivision agreement, you must ensure that you comply with the agreement. This will be particularly so when the agreement requires an "occupancy certificate" to be issued by the municipality prior to your client moving into the house. In *Tabata v. McWilliams*, [1981] O.J. No. 3011, 33 O.R. (2d) 32 (H.C.J.), vard [1982] O.J. No. 3597, 40 O.R. (2d) 158 (C.A.), a solicitor was found to be negligent because he failed to discover or advise his client of the requirement for an occupancy certificate. The Court found that an inspection by the building inspector prior to issuing the certificate would have revealed a major crack in the foundation.

Normally, you will requisition evidence of compliance with the subdivision agreement from the vendor's solicitor. While the answer will often be to "satisfy yourself", you should insist upon delivery of evidence of compliance with such things as written approvals of plans. At the same time, however, you should write the municipality (usually the clerk's department) to enquire whether the agreement has been complied with to date. Since in many new subdivisions the developers' work will not be finished, you will also be interested to know whether the municipality holds sufficient security to ensure completion of their obligations.

ONE FOOT RESERVES

The municipality sometimes controls access to a subdivision by means of the "one foot reserve" (or 0.3 metres) until it is satisfied that all requirements of the subdivision have been completed. An examination of the plan during a search of title will often reveal such a strip at the ends of access streets. Since this strip is not shown as part of the street on the plan, it does not become a "public highway" under s. 57 of the *Surveys Act*, R.S.O. 1990, c. S.30, until the municipality passes and registers a by-law dedicating it as such. Under the subdivision agreement, the municipality will require the subdivider to convey the reserves to the municipality. Therefore, the municipality as owner will be able to control access.

On any plan where such a reserve appears in the Registry system, you must check the page in the abstract book for that plan entitled "Streets and Reserves" and there you will find whether or not the reserve has been dedicated. In the Land Titles system, there will be a PIN for the reserve.

In addition, similar reserves are also often created along the boundaries of some lands, for example, adjacent to busy streets. The purpose is to control access but, in these cases, on a permanent basis.

OFFICIAL PLANS

Section 14 of the *Planning Act* requires the local planning board to prepare an official plan, which is then submitted to the council for adoption. Council is required to send the draft plan to interested agencies for comment and to hold a public hearing with at least 20 days' notice at which anyone may make submissions. Council may adjust the plan to take account of comments received and may then adopt the plan by by-law. The plan must then be submitted to the Minister of Municipal Affairs for approval, except for a number of the regional municipalities where the regional council is now the approving authority.

The official plan is a statement of planning or development principles covering broad areas of the municipality in question. Under s. 24, no zoning by-law may be passed or public work undertaken by the municipality which does not conform with the official plan, or an amendment thereto which has been adopted by council but has not yet received final approval (provided the amendment receives final approval). This prohibition includes amendments to existing by-laws. Thus, a new by-law or amendment that is contrary to the existing official plan will require that the official plan also be amended. The procedure for amending the plan is the same as when it was originally adopted except that the council can initiate the process rather than the planning board.

ZONING BY-LAWS

Section 34 authorizes municipalities to pass by-laws prohibiting the use of land except for the purposes set out in the by-law. Although described in the Act as "restricted area by-laws", they are commonly known as land use control by-laws or zoning by-laws. It has been held in numerous cases that a by-law, once passed by council, is effective to defend against a building permit application brought after the by-law was passed, even though it may not come into force until, for example, an appeal has been dealt with by the Ontario Municipal Board.

Zoning by-laws divide the municipality into specific areas and the use to which you may put land or buildings within each zone is defined. They also contain such things as the required setback from the street, the size of the side lot allowance and the rear lot.

A zoning by-law is not retroactive. Under s. 34(9)(*a*) of the *Planning Act*, no by-law may prevent any use of land that was "lawfully used for such purpose on the day of the passing of the by-law, so long as it continues to be used for that purpose". A use that conforms to this section is known as a "prior" or "legal non-conforming use". To establish that a property being purchased has a legal non-conforming use is difficult; you must perform a historic search of the by-laws to ensure the use pre-existed a prohibition and then establish by affidavit or other evidence that such use was not discontinued at any time thereafter.

It was realized by the legislature that there should be some discretion in the application of these by-laws. For instance, if the by-law states that a house must be set back 25 feet from the street line, and you find from an examination of the survey that it is only 24 feet from the street line, you may apply to the local committee of adjustment for consent to a minor variance from the by-law. Under s. 45(1) of the *Planning Act*, this committee may authorize such minor variance as, in its opinion, is desirable for the appropriate development or use of the land, building or structure, provided that the committee is of the opinion that "the general intent and purpose of the by-law and of the official plan, if any, are maintained". A great variety of applications are heard by such committees, but in each case the variance must be minor. The committee's opinion as to what is minor will prevail. However, if you propose to change the use of the land entirely, or if you propose a major deviation from the standards of the by-law, then you will have to persuade the council to amend its by-law.

ZONING ENQUIRIES

When acting for a purchaser, you must enquire whether the existing property, including its buildings and your client's proposed use, comply with existing zoning restrictions. This will often be difficult and sometimes impossible for a solicitor to accomplish as the provisions of many by-laws are complex, and there may not be sufficient evidence readily available to check compliance. Additionally, you must ensure that you ask the right municipality. Many regional municipalities are given the power, under the Act establishing them, to zone within 150 feet of regional or metropolitan roads.

At a minimum, you should write the municipality to ask about compliance. Many municipalities will be helpful in supplying information. Others, unfortunately, are reluctant to supply any information, particularly since they can be held liable for misinformation; see, for example, the decision in *Grand Restaurants of Canada Ltd. v. Toronto (City)*, [1981] O.J. No. 2503, 32 O.R. (2d) 757 (H.C.J.), affd [1982] O.J. No. 3101, 39 O.R. (2d) 752 (C.A.).

If you have a survey of the property, you should either send it to the municipality for checking or check it yourself to see if such things as minimum frontages, set-back and side-yard allowances have been met.

SITE PLAN CONTROL

If a municipality has an official plan, it may pass by-laws under s. 41 of the *Planning Act* to designate areas of "site plan control". Such municipalities may then require prior approval of plans and the provision and maintenance of the facilities and matters permitted by subs. 41(7) as conditions of the development of land. Some of the facilities and matters dealt with in para. 41(7)(*a*) involve widenings of roadways abutting the developed lands, access ramps, curbings, offstreet vehicular parking and loading areas, driveways, walkways, grading, floodlighting, landscaping, garbage collection areas and conveyances to the municipality for public works. Section 41(7)(*a*)4.1 permits municipalities to require accessible facilities for persons with disabilities. As well, the municipality may approve the location of buildings, structures and other facilities on the site in addition to requiring perspective drawings and plans (including elevations and cross-sections) in certain specified cases. Agreements may be required to be entered into by the landowner respecting such matters, and such an agreement when registered will bind subsequent owners of the land.

Provision is made for an appeal to the Ontario Municipal Board by owners dissatisfied with the terms of the agreement required by the municipality or from the refusal of the municipality to approve their plans.

DEMOLITION CONTROL

Section 33 of the *Planning Act* empowers a municipality that has enacted a by-law describing standards of maintenance and occupancy of property to designate, in accordance with by-laws, areas of demolition control within the municipality. The effect of such designation is that within the area no residential property may be demolished without a permit issued by the council of the municipality. An appeal is permitted to the Ontario Municipal Board from the refusal of council to issue a permit. The council may not refuse the demolition permit where a building permit has been obtained to erect a new building on the site of the property proposed to be demolished, but in such case the permit to demolish may be issued on the condition that the new building be erected within such time as the permit specifies, and failing that, the owner of the property is liable to a monetary penalty. Provisions are included in subs. (10) for appealing to the Ontario Municipal Board against the conditions to be imposed and in subs. (11) for seeking relief from council under the circumstances where it is made to appear it is not feasible to comply with them. The demolition of residential property in an area of demolition control without having obtained a permit is made an offence under subs. (16), carrying a fine up to $50,000 for each dwelling unit contained on the property.

There is no provision for registration of a demolition control by-law. If you act for a client who intends to develop the property being purchased or tear down the existing buildings, it would be wise to enquire of the municipality if such a by-law exists. You might also consider making it a condition of the agreement of purchase and sale that no such by-law affects the land on closing.

BUILDING PERMITS

Even if you have managed to get a parcel of land severed and transferred to your client and it is zoned for the intended use, there is still one more obstacle before construction of the desired building can proceed. Section 34(1)4 and 6 of the *Planning Act* authorize the municipality to pass by-laws "[f]or regulating the type of construction and the height, bulk, location, size, floor area, spacing, character and use of buildings" and "[f]or requiring the owners or occupants of buildings or structures ... to provide and maintain loading or parking facilities". A lawyer is normally not involved at this stage; it is the job of architects to prepare plans that conform with the local building by-laws. Until such plans do conform, no building permit will be issued, and without a permit, your client cannot build on the land.

Under s. 8(3) of the *Building Code Act, 1992*, S.O. 1992, c. 23, the chief building official is given authority to issue staged permits (*e.g.*, for the foundation or any other stage of construction) prior to issue of a full permit, provided the owner enters into an agreement to, among other things, remove the construction and restore the site if the conditions of the agreement are not met and a full permit is not eventually obtained. The municipality may enforce the agreement and thereupon has a lien on the land for the cost of so doing; this lien has the same first priority as municipal taxes.

One issue you should be aware of relates to the performance of work without a proper building permit. Not infrequently owners and their contractors will do construction (including interior renovations) without a building permit, for reasons ranging from avoiding expense to avoiding realty tax reassessments to avoiding delays in construction. In the past, many municipal building officials, when they became aware of work done without a permit, would allow the default to be corrected by issuing a permit retroactively upon receipt of appropriate plans (and exercising discretion with respect to the extent of inspections, particularly if they knew the contractor and the general quality of his work). However, as a result of the decision in *Ingles v. Tutkaluk Construction Ltd.*, [2000] S.C.J. No. 13, [2001] 1 S.C.R. 298, where the City of Toronto was held liable for work improperly done and not fully inspected because it had already been covered up, you may expect less tolerance from building officials. You may expect them to require work to be uncovered so that full inspections can be performed. This can be a very expensive and disruptive process.

Therefore, when acting for a purchaser or mortgagee, where you have any indication that construction work has been done to the building, you should try to ensure that the appropriate permits were obtained and the work cleared after inspections.

ONTARIO BUILDING CODE AND PROPERTY STANDARDS BY-LAWS

The Ontario Building Code, set out in R.R.O. 1990, Reg. 61, pursuant to s. 19 of the *Building Code Act, 1992*, prescribes standards for the construction of buildings throughout Ontario. Note that the definition of "building" has been amended to include a sewage system, allowing municipalities to regulate the installation, operation and removal of septic systems. The Code has been held to "supersede all by-laws concerning the construction of buildings" (see *Minto Construction Ltd. v. Gloucester (Township)*, [1979] O.J. No. 4117, 23 O.R. (2d) 634 at 637 (Div. Ct.)). Nevertheless, the enforcement of the Code is delegated to the municipality. In addition, municipalities may still set their own standards for the maintenance of properties by the passing of by-laws under s. 31 of the *Planning Act*.

The Act allows for the issuance of various types of orders. These include orders requiring: the completion of demolition or construction (s. 8); general compliance with the Act or Building Code (s. 12); and work or demolition to be stopped (s. 14). In each case, if the required action is not taken by the owner in response to the order, the local municipality may undertake the work and charge its costs for doing so back to the owner, adding them to the tax roll and collecting them in the same manner as municipal taxes.

When acting for a purchaser of a property, you should write the municipality to ask about compliance of the property with the Ontario Building Code and the municipality's own property standards by-laws. Without doing an inspection, the municipality will only report the deficiencies of which it is aware. Although many solicitors refer to these as "work orders", this term may be too narrow. Your enquiry might be better if it asked the municipality to report any requirements it has in relation to the property since many requirements may not yet have evolved into an order to do work but will nevertheless bind the purchaser.

You will find that every municipality has a different procedure for such enquiries and charges different amounts for its reply. Some will assist by telephone, others will not. Some are quick to reply, others are very slow. While some will be generous with their information about the property, others such as the City of Toronto consider the information a secret to be shared only with the owner. You should ensure, if you can, that the purchase agreement includes a provision authorizing the release of such information by the owner (as do all real estate board forms). While it will often be a frustrating, time-consuming and sometimes expensive task to obtain the information, it is nevertheless one which you must perform. Remember that the standard form real estate board agreement of purchase and sale requires objections in regard to work orders to be made strictly within the time limit allowed in the contract.

ONTARIO HERITAGE ACT, R.S.O. 1990, c. O.18

The *Ontario Heritage Act* permits municipal councils and the Province to designate as historic buildings that are considered to be of historic or architectural value or interest. The municipality is required to maintain a register of properties that have been designated as well as other properties that are of interest, and to provide information from the register to all interested persons upon payment of a fee. Under s. 29(3), the council must serve notice on the owner of its intention to designate and also publish the notice in a local newspaper. An objection to the designation, which must be filed within 30 days, results in a hearing before a Conservation Review Board, which makes a recommendation to council. Ultimately, the council decides whether or not to designate. A by-law designating a property must be registered against title to that property.

A council is permitted to appoint a municipal heritage committee (sometimes called a "historical society") to assist it in heritage matters.

As indicated, the list may include properties in which the municipality is interested but which it has not designated, primarily because designation is a costly process. A property that has been listed cannot be demolished without 60 days' prior notice to the municipality. The building department will sound the alarm if an application is made affecting a listed property, with the result that the designation process may then be put in motion.

Service of notice of intention to designate a property voids existing permits to alter or demolish buildings on the property. Once designated, a property cannot be altered if the alteration is likely to affect the heritage attributes of the property unless the municipality consents. Further, the property cannot be demolished without the consent of the municipality. In either case, the municipality has 90 days to respond to an application. A refusal to permit alterations can be appealed to the Conservation Review Board whereas the appeal of a refusal to issue a demolition permit is to the Ontario Municipal Board. Remember, however, that the only power the Conservation Review Board has is to make recommendations to the municipal council, which has the ultimate power to decide.

In order to avoid an owner allowing a property to deteriorate, resulting in "demolition by neglect", a municipality is permitted to enact minimum maintenance standards by-laws. A failure to comply with such a by-law is not only an offence, but also entitles the municipality to undertake the necessary work and add the cost to the tax bill.

Section 37 of the Act contemplates the owner granting a "heritage easement" to the municipality, which will set out in detail the heritage attributes of the property that must be preserved. Although an owner would normally be reluctant to grant such an easement, it will usually arise in the context of obtaining permission to redevelop the property. The easement will be registered against title and will bind all future owners of the property.

Under s. 35 of the Act, a new owner of a designated property must give notice of change of ownership to the clerk of the municipality within 30 days of the change in ownership.

EXPROPRIATION

In Ontario, an amazing number of governmental bodies, boards and authorities have powers of expropriation. These powers are scattered throughout various statutes, both federal and provincial, and they can override any private property rights. The powers of expropriation contained in some 35 Ontario statutes have been somewhat restricted under the *Expropriations Act*, R.S.O. 1990, c. E.26, but this Act deals mainly with compensation. For guidance in dealing with procedures, compensation and valuation under this legislation, refer to John Coates and Stephen F. Waqué, *New Law of Expropriation* (Don Mills: Richard DeBoo, 1984).

For title purposes, the important thing to remember is s. 9(1) of the Act:

> 9(1) Where a proposed expropriation has been approved under this Act or under the *Ontario Energy Board Act, 1998*, the expropriating authority shall register, within three months after the granting of the approval, in the proper land registry office a plan of the land signed by the expropriating authority and by an Ontario land surveyor, and thereupon, but not otherwise, the land vests in the expropriating authority.

There can be no argument about that. Once the Ministry of Transportation, the local school board, the local municipality, the local hospital board or university registers such a plan, the land is theirs, free of the claim of the owner, the mortgagees, tenants and any other encumbrancers. This is not to say that they will not be compensated, but title has passed.

Under s. 39, the expropriating authority obtains possession of the land that has vested in such authority by serving a notice that it requires such possession.

The Act sets out many safeguards and the procedures under which the claim for compensation may be arbitrated, but remember that registering the plan by itself vests title.

AIRPORT ZONING REGULATIONS

Another topic that fits under the broad heading of governmental control is zoning regulations for airports by the federal Department of Transport. These are registered by the Department of Transport against all lands within a certain radius of such airports to control the height of buildings in the area of the airport. The allowable height increases as the distance from the end of the runway increases.

The information in the registered zoning regulations is difficult to understand. Unfortunately, Transport Canada does not respond to letter enquiries as to allowable building heights. Instead, you must now consult an engineer or surveyor to determine whether an existing or proposed building will meet the height restrictions.

CHAPTER 6

Status of Owner: Its Effect on Conveyancing

MARRIAGE

FAMILY LAW ACT

The *Family Law Act*, R.S.O. 1990, c. F.3, and its predecessor, the *Family Law Reform Act*, R.S.O. 1980, c. 152 (rep. S.O. 1986, c. 4, s. 71(1)), have effected significant changes to the law of property governing the relationship of husband and wife. Both statutes have gone a long way toward recognizing marriage as an "economic partnership". Under the present Act, the value of all property owned by either spouse is shared equally on termination of the marriage, subject to certain exceptions.

The *Family Law Act* continues to give special status to the "matrimonial home", a term and concept introduced in the *Family Law Reform Act*. This term is defined in s. 18(1):

> 18(1) Every property in which a person has an interest and that is or, if the spouses have separated, was at the time of separation ordinarily occupied by the person and his or her spouse as their family residence is their matrimonial home.

This definition is wide enough to include not only the city home, but also the summer cottage, for example, as a matrimonial home.

Note that the definition of matrimonial home changed slightly from when the previous legislation was enacted on March 1, 1986. Now, once a property ceases to be occupied as a matrimonial home, it loses that status. Under the *Family Law Reform Act*, provided a home was still owned at the time of termination of the marriage and had, at some point during the marriage, been used as a matrimonial home, it retained that status. This was the case even if, on the termination of the marriage, the family as a whole was no longer using the home.

Matrimonial homes also include (under s. 18(2)) housing units owned by a corporation where the ownership of the shares of such corporation entitles the owner of the shares to occupy the unit. This section may only have been meant to cover co-operatives where the right to occupy a unit is dependent upon the ownership of a share in the corporation owning the entire property. However, the section may also cover other situations, such as, for example, when someone puts the home in the name of a company in order to avoid the Act. If so, then you cannot dismiss the possibility that the Act applies simply because the property is owned by a company. The safest course when dealing with residential properties will be to treat them all as potential "matrimonial homes" unless the contrary can be demonstrated.

A property may also become a matrimonial home by registering a designation as such under s. 20 (note that more than one property can be so designated by both spouses). If the designation is signed by both spouses, any other property that is a matrimonial home (whether undesignated or designated by only one spouse) ceases to be one. If only one spouse signs, however, then the property so designated becomes a matrimonial home, but any other matrimonial home is not affected and remains as such. If you find a solo designation on title, your client should not acquire an interest in the property without either the other spouse's consent or a court order dispensing with it.

If a house is registered in one name only but is a matrimonial home, the spouse of the owner has two principal rights: the right of equal possession and the right to control disposition or encumbrance of the property. Both rights are dependent upon the continuation of the marital relationship and will cease to exist upon the termination of that relationship, either by death or divorce (s. 19(2)), except that the surviving non-owning spouse has a right to possession rent-free for 60 days after the death (s. 26(2)). The rights may also be terminated by a written separation agreement or by a court order.

The conveyancer must ensure that the spouse of the owner has consented to any disposition or encumbrance of a matrimonial home. The spouse should sign the transfer or charge giving his or her consent. If a transfer or charge is being electronically registered and as a result is not being manually signed, the spouse should sign the same acknowledgment and direction that the transferor or chargor has signed to evidence his or her consent (see Chapter 12 for a further discussion of the use of the acknowledgment and direction). If no consent is given, then under s. 21(2) the transaction may be set aside by court order.

If no spouse has signed the instrument, then the person acquiring an interest in the property in good faith and for value and without notice to the contrary may rely on a statement in the transfer or charge to the effect that:

1. the transferor/chargor is not a spouse;

2. the property is not ordinarily occupied by the transferor/chargor and his or her spouse as their family residence;

3. the spouses are separated and the property was not ordinarily occupied as their family residence at the time of separation;

4. some other property has been designated as a matrimonial home; or

5. the spousal rights in the home have been released under a written separation agreement (s. 21(3)).

It is not necessary for you to see the separation agreement; you may rely solely on the statement. However, you probably would want to see a registered designation of another property as the matrimonial home since that is a matter of public record.

The person who makes the statement is generally the transferor/chargor, but s. 21(4) of the Act also permits an attorney under a power of attorney to make the statement. The statement must be based on the attorney's personal knowledge and should expressly state that is the case.

Note that the acquirer of the interest must have no notice to the contrary. "Notice" has been held by the Court of Appeal to mean constructive notice, rather than actual notice (*Stoimenov v. Stoimenov*, [1985] O.J. No. 2310, 50 O.R. (2d) 1 (C.A.); followed in *Roby v. Roby (Trustee of)*, [2003] O.J. No. 3122, 43 R.F.L. (5th) 193 (S.C.J.)). You should question your client as to whether he or she has any knowledge of facts which hint at the existence of a matrimonial home. You, as the purchaser's or mortgagee's solicitor, should examine prior documents in your title search to see whether there is any indication of the existence of a spouse. If there is, you must enquire as to why that spouse is not signing the documents.

An interest in the matrimonial home that arises by "operation of law" is not covered by the requirement under s. 21 for the spouse's consent (see s. 21(5)). Therefore, an execution creditor will not be prevented from realizing on the interest of one of the spouses in a matrimonial home even though the other spouse had no prior knowledge of the liability giving rise to the judgment debt. This was confirmed by the Supreme Court of Canada in *Maroukis v. Maroukis*, [1984] S.C.J. No. 35, [1984] 2 S.C.R. 137, holding that the word "encumber" does not apply to an execution against one of the parties to a marriage.

However, where a lender and borrower intentionally create executions against a matrimonial home, they will be treated as "encumbrances", which require consent of the spouse under the Act. In *Walduda v. Bell*, [2004] O.J. No. 3071, 7 R.F.L. (6th) 205 (S.C.J.), a spouse borrowed money from her sister to finance her matrimonial litigation and then consented to judgment in favour of her sister, resulting in executions intended to tie up the matrimonial home and cause it to be sold. The court set the executions aside.

DOWER RIGHTS

The *Family Law Reform Act* abolished the common law right of a widow to dower except where such right was vested prior to the Act coming into force on March 31, 1978. It also repealed *The Dower Act*, R.S.O. 1970, c. 135 (S.O. 1978, c. 2, s. 70(2)), the background and effect of which is set out on pp. 61-62.

Although the right to dower was rarely exercised, it theoretically still may exist where a man has died and his widow has been exercising her dower rights since then. Because the right arose automatically on the death of a husband who owned real property, a person reviewing title where there has not been an express waiver of dower or a release signed by the wife of a deceased owner will need to be aware of those situations in which dower either did not exist or was avoided:

1. Joint tenancy: no dower rights attached to land held in joint tenancy.

2. Partnership: no dower rights attached to lands held as partnership property. This occurs because land is treated as personal property under s. 23 of the *Partnerships Act*, R.S.O. 1990, c. P.5, and not as realty.

3. Trustee held lands: where a married man held lands as trustee for someone else, neither his nor the beneficiary's wife had any dower rights under s. 1 of *The Dower Act*, but merely describing an owner as

"trustee" or "in trust" in a deed did not in itself avoid dower (*Seperich v. Madill*, [1946] O.J. No. 663, [1946] O.R. 864 (H.C.J.)).

4. Lands in a state of nature, *i.e.*, unimproved land: *The Dower Act*, s. 5.

5. Lands dedicated as streets and public highways: *The Dower Act*, s. 7.

6. Equitable estate in land: dower attached only to those lands where the husband owned the legal estate at some point during his marriage. When a man mortgaged his property, the legal estate passed to the mortgagee and the owner mortgagor was left with only the equity of redemption, *i.e.*, the right to demand the reconveyance of his legal title upon payment of the mortgage debt. If, during his marriage, a man owned only the equity of redemption, no dower attached: *Gardner v. Brown*, [1890] O.J. No. 138, 19 O.R. 202 (H.C.J.). Thus, if he bought land subject to a mortgage, or mortgaged his land before he married and then sold the land subject to that same mortgage, his wife had no dower right in that land. But if he was married and a discharge was registered before he sold the land, the land would become subject to dower rights even though he had already mortgaged it again. Also, if he died while holding just an equitable estate, his wife would have her dower interest in the property. When a man mortgaged his land during his marriage and his wife joined in to bar her dower, that bar operated only to the extent necessary to give full effect to the remedies of the mortgagee (*Re Luckhardt*, [1898] O.J. No. 73, 29 O.R. 111 (Div. Ct.)). If he sold the property so mortgaged without his wife joining in, she still would have her dower interest in the land except as against the mortgagee.

7. Divorce: a woman's right to dower in her husband's land ended upon their divorce.

8. Adultery: where a wife willingly left her husband and went away with her adulterer, she was barred from dower (*The Dower Act*, s. 8).

9. Insanity: where a wife was confined to a mental hospital when the husband bought land, he could sell it free of dower (*The Dower Act*, s. 12(1)). If she became of unsound mind and was confined to a mental hospital after he acquired land, a judge could dispense with dower (*The Dower Act*, s. 13(1)(*c*)).

10. Separation: where husband and wife were living apart or where the wife's whereabouts were unknown, he could apply for a judge's order dispensing with dower (*The Dower Act*, s. 13(1)(*a*) and (*b*)).

11. No Ontario residency: where a wife had not lived in Ontario since the marriage, she had no dower interest in Ontario lands (*The Dower Act*, s. 12(2)).

12. Conveyances to Uses: see pp. 15 and 39.

CHANGE OF NAME

Sometimes, there is a change in the name of a registered owner of property, most commonly in a woman's name as a result of marriage or divorce and, occasionally, pursuant to an order under the *Change of Name Act*, R.S.O. 1990, c. C.7. In all such cases, the transfer should include a statement that the transferor's name has changed with an explanation such as the following:

> The Transferor certifies that her name has been changed from Alice Hortense Smith to Alice Hortense Jones-Smith by virtue of her marriage to Wilbert Adam Jones on May 15, 1998.

In the case of an order under the *Change of Name Act*, a notarial copy of the order should be registered in the General Register under the *Registry Act*, R.S.O. 1990, c. R.20, s. 18(6)7. In the case of lands in the Land Titles system, it will be necessary to apply to amend the register to record the new name.

DEATH OF THE REGISTERED OWNER

JOINT TENANCY

Where land is registered in the names of two persons as joint tenants, and one of them dies, title to the land automatically devolves upon the survivor. Any attempt to deal with it in the will of the deceased party is ineffective.

For land registered under the *Registry Act*, no other action need be taken by the surviving joint tenant until the land is sold, mortgaged or leased. Then, in the instrument by which the land is dealt with, the death of the co-owner will be recited. A cautious purchaser might require some further evidence of death (such as the deposit of a copy of the death certificate), but there is no other legal requirement in the *Registry Act* for the transfer of the lands.

Under the *Land Titles Act*, R.S.O. 1990, c. L.5, one extra step must be taken. Section 123 of the Act provides for an application in the prescribed form to be submitted by the surviving joint tenant. The land registrar will then delete the name of the deceased joint tenant from the register, and the surviving joint tenant will be shown on the register as the owner.

The form of application to remove the name of a deceased joint tenant is Form 42, R.R.O. 1990, Reg. 690. The applicant must file with the application, evidence supporting same, including an affidavit by the applicant in Form 43, a certificate of death or copy of the letters probate or letters of administration of the deceased, and a succession duty consent (for deaths between January 1, 1970, and April 11, 1979). Under O. Reg. 44/78, no succession duty consent is required for joint tenants who were married, only for those who were not.

With the implementation of electronic registration and the amendments to the *Land Titles Act* and *Land Registration Reform Act* to allow such implementation, the Director of Titles issued Bulletin No. 2000-6 on December 20, 2000 to amend the practice to be followed in registering survivorship applications. Essentially, the Bulletin allows survivorship applications to be registered in the traditional manner using the completed Forms 42 and 43 which, of course, will require documentary evidence substantiating the death. In the e-reg system, there are two alternatives available to effect the registration. The traditional approach involves attendance at the actual land registry office and submission of the evidence for the application, usually an original or notarial copy of the death certificate, which will be registered in a general index of documents and assigned an index number. That index number must then be inserted into the e-reg survivorship application, which is filed electronically. The alternative is for the survivorship application to be electronically registered by a solicitor on the basis of compliance with law statements. This method does not require any evidence substantiating the death to be registered. Instead, a solicitor will make statements in the survivorship application as follows:

(a)   the applicant held the property as a joint tenant with the deceased;

(b)   by right of survivorship, the applicant is entitled to be the owner as a surviving joint tenant;

(c)   the deceased died on a certain date; and

(d)   a statement as to the family law status of the deceased and the applicant and as to whether the property at issue is a matrimonial home.

Of course, a solicitor will have to independently verify the facts supporting these statements and should obtain copies of the death certificate and other relevant documentation substantiating the statements made and keep them in his or her file. A solicitor should also require his or her client to sign an acknowledgment and direction which authorizes the survivorship applications to be electronically registered (the acknowledgment and direction is discussed in Chapter 12).

Sometimes a person who holds land in joint tenancy with another person will want to put an end to the automatic right of survivorship unilaterally. This may arise, for example, where a husband and wife have separated or divorced. The simple way to accomplish severance of a joint tenancy is to do a transfer of one owner's interest to himself or herself. In the Land Titles system, the transfer has to include a statement that the intention is to sever the joint tenancy; it is probably a good idea to do the same in the Registry system (and, in any event, the land transfer tax affidavit will likely contain such a statement). The result is to convert the joint tenancy into a tenancy-in-common. This procedure was confirmed in *Horne v. Evans*, [1987] O.J. No. 495, 60 O.R. (2d) 1 (C.A.).

A joint tenancy will also be severed by a mortgage of one joint tenant's interest.

Beware that joint tenants may unintentionally sever their joint tenancy by treating the property as tenants-in-common. In *Robichaud v. Watson*, [1983] O.J. No. 3046, 147 D.L.R. (3d) 626 (Ont. H.C.J.), a husband and wife, who were joint tenants but had separated, had exchanged "without prejudice" letters aimed at settling the amount to be paid by the husband to buy the wife's interest in the matrimonial home. The negotiations failed. However, after the husband subsequently died, the court found that the joint tenancy had been severed because the negotiations between them clearly indicated that they considered themselves as tenants-in-common. Several other cases referred to in this case have drawn the same conclusion.

A similar conclusion was reached by the Ontario Court of Appeal in *Bank of Montreal v. Bray*, [1977] O.J. No. 4277, 36 O.R. (3d) 99. The husband transferred his interest in the matrimonial home, previously held in joint tenancy, to his wife in what was subsequently found to be a fraudulent conveyance intended to defeat creditors. Although the conveyance was set aside, the Court was not prepared to reinstate the joint tenancy. The Court found that the conveyance was valid as between the parties even though it was void as against the creditors. In any event, the joint tenancy could not be restored because of the husband's intervening death.

If there are more than two joint tenants, a transfer by one of the joint tenants to himself or herself will only sever the joint tenancy for that tenant; the others will remain as joint tenants among themselves: *Williams v. Hensman* (1861), 70 E.R. 862.

ESTATE CONVEYANCING

One of the most confusing and troublesome areas in all conveyancing concerns problems arising out of the *Estates Administration Act*, R.S.O. 1990, c. E.22 (formerly known as *The Devolution of Estates Act*, R.S.O. 1970, c. 129). Very few solicitors can keep the various rules clear in their minds. The Act itself is difficult to follow.

The Act has three basic functions:

1. It sets out the manner in which property is to be distributed if there is no will.

2. It establishes that debts of the deceased are a lien on the property of the deceased and that this lien has priority over the interests of the persons beneficially entitled to the property.

3. It establishes that real property vests in the person beneficially entitled three years after the death of the deceased, even if the estate trustee (formerly known as an executor or administrator) does nothing. But the estate trustee may register a caution on title to the land which will postpone vesting for a further three years. This is to enable the estate trustee to properly dispose of the assets and pay off debts.

Thus, when searching title to land that was owned by someone who died, you have three main problems to consider:

1. When do the lands of the deceased, which have been devised to someone, become the property of that person, *i.e.*, when is the beneficiary entitled to sell the property?

2. When can an estate trustee sell the lands?

3. Will the purchaser get good title free from debts?

Note that the terminology for executors and administrators has been changed. Rules 74 and 75 of the *Rules of Civil Procedure*, as amended, now have a single name for both executors and administrators — the "estate trustee". Effective January 1, 1995, letters probate and letters of administration were replaced with a certificate of appointment of estate trustee (with or without a will, as the case may be). Letters probate and letters of administration issued prior to January 1, 1995, continue to be effective.

Vesting without a Deed

Intestacy — The estate trustee (formerly, the administrator) has three years within which to pay the debts of the deceased. But if, at the end of the three years, the deed still has not been registered in favour of those beneficially entitled (the widow and children for instance), then under s. 9, title to the lands vests in the widow and children. You would require a statement in the transfer by the persons dealing with the property that they are all the persons entitled to such property, *e.g.*, that they are the widow and two children and there are no other children.

Testacy — If the deceased, by will, devised a residence to a child and the estate trustee (formerly, the executor) did not transfer it, it would vest in the child at the end of three years. In this case, of course, you would know from looking at the will in whom the property is vested. However, if there is a power of sale in the will, express or implied, or if the property is given in trust to the estate trustee to carry out the testator's instructions, there will be no vesting and the estate trustee does not need to register any caution in order to preserve power to deal with the property (see *Nattress v. Levy*, [1946] O.W.N. 690, [1946] 4 D.L.R. 156 (H.C.J.) and *Caldwell v. LaMothe*, [1996] O.J. No. 1179 (Gen. Div.)).

Deeds under a Power of Sale

Power of Sale Where There Is a Will

1. Express power: The first thing to look for when examining the will of a deceased landowner is whether the will gave the estate trustee power to sell or dispose of the property. Usually, it does. If so, the estate trustee can sell the property without the consent of the beneficiaries, unless there is also a specific bequest of the subject property, in which case the consent of the beneficiary is required. Remember also that, as noted above, an express power of sale will prevent automatic vesting three years after death.

2. Implied power: If the will does not contain an express power of sale, but does contain a direction to the estate trustee to pay debts, or to do something else which obviously requires the property to be sold, there is an implied power of sale.

Power of Sale Under the *Estates Administration Act* — If there is neither an express nor implied power of sale under the will, the estate trustee may resort to the powers of sale under the Act. These are also available in case of intestacy.

1. Power of sale for purpose of paying debts (see ss. 16 and 17(1)): If a deed from an estate trustee states that the sale is for the purpose of paying debts, you are entitled to rely on that as evidence of authority to sell the property. In *Kinross Mortgage Corp. v. Central Mortgage & Housing Corp.*, [1979] O.J. No. 4034, 22 O.R. (2d) 713 (H.C.J.), it

was held that a recital in a deed that was given "for the purpose of administering the estate" was sufficient evidence of the authority of the estate trustee to convey.

2.   Power of sale for purpose of distributing the estate to the persons beneficially entitled (see subss. 17(1) and (2), as amended): If a will directs that a house be given to an estate trustee, and the estate trustee is further instructed to divide it among five children in equal shares, obviously the house will have to be sold and the proceeds divided. This can be done, but subs. 17(2) states that no such sale is valid unless the majority of the persons beneficially entitled to the house, representing together not less than one-half of all the interests therein, concur in the sale. If any one of the children is under 18 years of age, the Children's Lawyer must approve. The transfer must state that it is for the purpose of distribution, and the persons approving must sign together with the estate trustee.

3.   Transfer by estate trustee to the person beneficially entitled: The estate trustee may always carry out the direction of the testator by conveying the property to those beneficially entitled under the will.

Debts of the Estate

As mentioned, debts of the deceased are, under s. 5, a lien upon those lands which the testator has not specifically given to one or more heirs, that is, upon those lands forming part of the residue of the estate. Because of this, a purchaser's solicitor must ensure that either the debts have been paid, or that the land is released from the lien of debts. No debts will attach to the lands of a deceased in the following situations:

1.   Sale to pay debts: Since one of the purposes of the Act is to ensure payment of the deceased's debts, it is obvious that the lien for debts cannot apply to lands sold for the purpose of paying debts. Otherwise, no one would purchase.

2.   Power of sale in will: If the will expressly gives the estate trustee the power to sell the land, or even if the power of sale is only implied under the terms of the will, the land will be freed from the debts of the deceased upon exercise of the power.

3.   Sale for distribution purposes: If, under s. 17, the estate trustee sells the land with the consent of the majority of the beneficiaries in order to distribute the estate, the land will not be subject to debts.

4.   Judge's order: Lands that are conveyed to the beneficiaries within the three years following death will be freed from debts only if a court order is obtained prior to the conveyance. Otherwise, the lands remain subject to the debts forever in the hands of the beneficiaries, whether they obtained the lands by a conveyance from the estate trustee, or whether they vested under s. 9. However, a purchaser from the beneficiaries within the three-year period is protected where a court order has been obtained under s. 21.

An order can be obtained *nunc pro tunc* (now for then) where land has been transferred to a beneficiary without an order relieving it of the lien for debts and the beneficiary wants to sell the land within the three-year period. Evidence must be presented to the court that there are no debts or that there is adequate provision for their payment.

5. Expiry after three years: Except where the lands were conveyed to the beneficiaries within three years of death without a court order, the lien for debts expires at the end of three years after the death of the deceased. In any event, provided that your client is purchasing in good faith and without notice of any debts, you do not need to worry about debts being a lien in any case where the testator died more than three years ago, unless a creditor has registered a certificate of pending litigation or caution under s. 17(8)(*a*).

Section 125 of the *Land Titles Act* authorizes the land registrar to delete reference in the register to the unpaid debts of the deceased, or even to register a transfer to the person beneficially entitled to land without any reference to such debts, in cases where the transfer is registered within three years of the date of death of the deceased owner and evidence is produced that all debts have been paid and creditors have been notified.

Registration of Probate

It has been normal practice in recent decades to obtain and register probate of the will of a deceased who owned real property on death. However, up until the middle of the twentieth century, it was not uncommon for estate trustees merely to register the will itself as evidence of their authority to convey the land owned by the deceased, thus avoiding the expense of obtaining probate. Dramatic increases in probate fees have caused practitioners to re-examine the viability of using the will alone as the basis for conveying real estate owned by a deceased.

Section 18(6)1 and 2 of the *Registry Act* permits registration of both wills and letters probate (now a certificate of appointment of estate trustee with a will). It is clear law that the authority of estate trustees to act derives from the deceased's will and not from the appointment obtained by probating the will. Probate is useful in establishing beyond doubt that the will being relied on is indeed the last will of the deceased. Nevertheless, the court has confirmed that registration of a will alone will be sufficient as a basis for the estate trustees named therein to convey good title to the lands of a deceased (*Prinsen v. Balkwill*, [1991] O.J. No. 3645, 2 O.R. (3d) 281 (Gen. Div.)). Zalev J. quoted Middleton J.A. from *Hollwey v. Adams*, [1926] O.J. No. 123, [1926] 2 D.L.R. 960 at 510 (H.C.):

> [A]ny purchaser claiming title through or under the will is perfectly protected, for if there is an unregistered will it is void as against him, and those taking under this will would be left to their remedy against the vendor of the land.

Of course, it will also be necessary to deposit the death certificate on title in order to evidence the death of the registered owner.

Bulletin 93002, dated April 1, 1993, permits land registrars under the *Land Titles Act* to accept a transmission application without letters probate, provided that the application includes a notarial copy of the will, certificate of death, and an affidavit that the will has not been revoked by marriage or otherwise, that the testator was over 18, and that the value of the total estate does not exceed $50,000.

Frequently these days, a property may have been converted from the Registry system to the Land Titles system by the government (*i.e.*, Teranet). Special rules have been issued under Bulletin 2000-6 by the Director of Titles to permit a transmission application to be registered without a certificate of appointment of an estate trustee (thereby avoiding payment of probate fees) provided certain requirements are met. In order to take advantage of this exemption from the usual requirements, the application must include a copy of the will and an affidavit by the applicant or statements by the solicitor as follows:

1. that the property is a Ministry conversion from Registry to Land Titles;

2. that the transaction is the first dealing after the conversion of the property;

3. that the value of the estate is (enter value of estate);

4. attaching the same evidence as under the *Registry Act* with regard to the execution of the will and proof of death. If an affidavit of execution cannot be provided, a statement or affidavit made by someone who knew the deceased's handwriting may be used in lieu of the affidavit of execution. This should be someone of good standing within the community and must be someone who can state that he or she knew the handwriting of the testator, for example, a bank manager, an employer, or those individuals who can attest to an application for a passport. It cannot be a family member, a beneficiary or someone who can benefit from the estate;

5. that the will is the last will and that a certificate of appointment of estate trustee was not applied for; and

6. that the testator was of the age of majority at the time of the execution of the will, and that the will has not been revoked by the marriage of the testator or otherwise.

Finally, the applicant must provide a covenant to indemnify the Land Titles Assurance Fund (in case someone claims to have been wrongfully deprived of an interest in the land, for example, under a later will).

A deed or transfer must be signed by all of the estate trustees. It is well established that where there is more than one estate trustee, they must act unanimously and they cannot delegate their responsibilities (*Gibb v. McMahon*, [1905] O.J. No. 145, 9 O.L.R. 522 (C.A.), affd [1906] S.C.J. No. 14, 37 S.C.R. 362; *Willcocks v. MacLennan*, [1946] O.J. No. 153, [1946] O.W.N. 490 (C.A.)). However, the estate trustee may delegate a purely administrative act (*McLellan Properties Ltd. v. Roberge*, [1947] S.C.J. No. 31, [1947] S.C.R. 561). For example, a discharge of mortgage signed by someone under a power of attorney given by an estate trustee will probably be valid because the estate trustee, once the mortgage is paid, has no discretion to refuse to give a discharge (*Schiappa v. Baker*, [1980] O.J. No. 3581, 28 O.R. (2d) 380 (Co. Ct.)).

The procedures for the registration of transmission applications and transfers made by a personal representative of a deceased where the properties involved are subject to mandatory electronic registration are described in Bulletin No. 2000-6. As discussed in the context of survivorship applications, e-reg allows solicitors to make compliance with law statements to support a registration rather than file the evidence upon which such statements were made. The underlying evidence must still be obtained by the solicitor, but it is, subject to the qualifications that follow, simply kept in his or her file or referred to by listing a court file number.

For transmission applications, a solicitor must confirm by checking off the appropriate statements that appear when preparing an e-reg transmission application: (i) that the applicant is entitled to be the owner by law as an estate trustee, executor or administrator of the estate of the deceased; and (ii) as to the name and date of death of the registered owner. Reference must then be made either to a court file number and date by which a court appointed the applicant as estate trustee or to the fact that no such court appointment was applied for due to the fact that the total value of the estate is not more than $50,000. If this latter statement is made, a covenant to indemnify the Land Titles Assurance Fund is required to be filed with the Director of Titles using Form 54 from Regulation 690. Finally, a statement must be made as to whether the property is subject to the debts of the deceased or whether the debts have been paid in full.

In respect of the actual transfer of the property by the estate trustee, the e-reg system again relies upon compliance with law statements rather than affidavits, statutory declarations and the registration of supporting documents. The transfer must contain compliance with law statements to the effect that:

1. the transferor is entitled to transfer the property under the terms of the will, if any, the *Estates Administration Act* and the *Succession Law Reform Act*, R.S.O. 1990, c. S.26 or that the transfer is authorized by a court order for which a file number and date must be included;

2. title is or is not subject to spousal rights, and

3. the transferor has obtained the consent of all necessary parties or no such consent is required.

Again, a solicitor must retain in his or her file the materials upon which he or she was relying upon in making the above statements.

Family Law Act

The *Family Law Act* may affect the distribution of estate property where the deceased died after March 1, 1986, and left a spouse. If, for example, a widow owned less net family property than her deceased husband on the day before her husband's death, and did not contract out of the provisions of the Act, then the widow would be entitled to one-half of the difference between her net family property and that of her deceased husband, despite what the will or laws of intestacy say. The widow may choose to accept an equalization payment, and forego bequests made to her in the will or her entitlement on intestacy. Of course, if the will or laws of intestacy leave more than half of the difference to the widow, she will likely choose not to exercise her entitlement.

The surviving spouse has six months following the deceased's death to file an election with the Superior Court of Justice. During this time, the personal representative of the estate may not deal with estate assets, unless the surviving spouse gives written authorization or the court so orders. If no election is filed, the spouse is deemed to have chosen to take the entitlement arising under the will or on intestacy.

Despite these provisions, a purchaser of estate property need not conduct a search at the Court office to determine whether or not an election has been filed. A spouse's election is not, in the absence of a court order, an election to take a direct interest in the estate property, but it is an election to receive an amount of money of equivalent value. The court may order a conveyance of the property, but in that case, the order will be registered. A person acquiring an interest in the estate property may, therefore, safely ignore a claim by a surviving spouse to an interest in the property until registration of an order to that effect.

It is also usually unnecessary for the purchaser from an estate to ensure that a spouse's written consent is included in a transfer from an estate made within six months of death. Section 6(14) of the *Family Law Act, 1986* deals only with "distribution", which presumably means the transfer of estate assets to those entitled under the estate and does not include the sale of assets to a third party. Of course, the proceeds of sale would be subject to the restriction. Therefore, a purchaser need only be concerned to obtain a spouse's consent when purchasing from a beneficiary to whom the asset was transferred within the six-month period.

MENTAL INCOMPETENCY

A person has always been able to grant a power of attorney to another with power to deal with the grantor's property. However, in the past, the power would cease if the grantor became incompetent (for instance, through mental deterioration), which is exactly when the power might be most valuable. That problem was addressed with the introduction in 1979 of the *Powers of Attorney Act*, S.O. 1979, c. 107. Under that Act, a power of attorney continued to be valid if it contained a statement that it could be exercised notwithstanding the subsequent legal incapacity of the grantor.

Effective April 3, 1995, the relevant portions of the *Powers of Attorney Act*, R.S.O. 1990, c. P.20, were repealed (see S.O. 1992, c. 32, s. 24) and the *Substitute Decisions Act, 1992*, S.O. 1992, c. 30, was proclaimed into force. This Act contains the same concept of a "continuing power of attorney" allowing the attorney to use the power of attorney even though the grantor has since become legally incompetent provided the power of attorney "states that it is a continuing power of attorney" or "expresses the intention that the authority given may be exercised during the grantor's incapacity to manage property" (s. 7(1)).

The main difference between the *Powers of Attorney Act* and the replacement *Substitute Decisions Act* is that the former only required one adult witness to a properly executed power of attorney whereas the replacement Act requires two adult witnesses (not including the attorney, the attorney's spouse or the spouse or child of the grantor) for the power of attorney to be valid. However, s. 14

of the *Substitute Decisions Act* validates a continuing power of attorney conforming to the *Powers of Attorney Act* if it was executed before the Act came into force (*i.e.*, April 3, 1995) or within six months thereafter (*i.e.*, before October 3, 1995).

Although the *Powers of Attorney Act* has been substantially repealed, powers of attorney granted before the *Substitute Decisions Act* came into effect remain valid (s. 14).

Under the *Mental Health Act*, R.S.O. 1990, c. M.7, a person who is a patient of a psychiatric facility is required to be examined by a physician forthwith after admission as to whether he or she is capable of managing property (s. 54). If not, then the doctor issues a certificate which is sent to the Public Guardian and Trustee, who thereupon becomes that person's "statutory guardian of property" pursuant to s. 15 of the *Substitute Decisions Act*. Similarly, for non-patients whose capacity is being questioned, there is a procedure, under s. 16 of the *Substitute Decisions Act*, for an "assessor" to determine whether or not that person is capable of managing property. If the answer is no (and provided the person does not refuse), the Public Guardian and Trustee becomes the statutory guardian of property.

Formerly, there was a procedure for appointment of a "committee" by the court for persons found to be mentally incompetent or even for those not mentally incompetent but found incapable of managing their affairs.

In both cases, an attorney for that person under a continuing power of attorney can apply to replace the Public Guardian and Trustee (s. 17). So too can members of the immediate family of the incompetent person (although the attorney has priority). A certificate given by the Public Guardian and Trustee under s. 17(12) is proof of the guardian's authority. A notarial copy of that certificate should be deposited on title when the statutory guardian of property is dealing with an incompetent person's property.

The power of an attorney to deal with a person's property can be limited by restrictions stated in the power of attorney itself. A statutory guardian of property has unlimited power to deal with the person's property (s. 31(1)).

It is usual when receiving documents from an attorney dealing with land to require registration of a copy of the power of attorney and to obtain an affidavit that the power of attorney is in full force and effect and has not been terminated or revoked. Of great comfort is s. 13 of the *Substitute Decisions Act*, which provides that a person who acted in good faith and without knowledge of the termination or invalidity of a power of attorney can rely on the exercise of the power as being nevertheless valid.

MINORS

At common law, anyone under 21 years was classified as an infant (or, in today's parlance, a minor). The *Age of Majority and Accountability Act*, R.S.O. 1990, c. A.7, changed, effective as of July 28, 1971, the age at which a person ceased to be a minor in Ontario to 18 years. Section 4 of the Act provides that a reference to the age of 21 years in any Act of Parliament or Act of the legislature shall be read as a reference to the age of 18 years.

No contracts entered into by minors are enforceable against them except contracts for the supply of necessities. Even after minors reach adulthood, the contracts are still not enforceable against them unless they adopt the contracts or otherwise indicate that they consider themselves to be bound by them. Therefore, most agreements or documents signed by minors are voidable at their option. Likewise, transfers and charges made by infants are void. This is the reason for the inclusion of a statement in all transfers and charges that the transferor is at least 18 years old.

If you are not 18 years old, you cannot sell land without an order of the Superior Court of Justice obtained by an application under s. 59 of the *Children's Law Reform Act*, R.S.O. 1990, c. C.12, as amended, with notice to the Children's Lawyer (the official designated by the Act to look after the interests of minors).

Obviously, the way in which most minors obtain an interest in real estate is through the deaths of their parents. However, property left to children under 18 years or left to a trustee in trust for them cannot be sold without the concurrence of the Children's Lawyer, unless the trustee is given the express power to sell or has the implied power (to pay debts) or a court order has been obtained.

CORPORATE OWNERSHIP

CORPORATE STATUS

In order for a company to validly acquire, hold or convey land, it must, of course, be in existence. Sometimes, a person will enter into an agreement to purchase land "for a company to be incorporated". The purchaser does not want to go to the expense of incorporation until a deal has been made. Section 21 of the *Business Corporations Act*, R.S.O. 1990, c. B.16 provides that the liability of the person who entered into the contract ceases once the contract is adopted by the corporation. The adoption can be in writing or by conduct or action of the corporation (such as making a payment under the contract or taking title).

If a person enters into a contract in the name of a non-existent company (either because it has not been incorporated or because its charter has been cancelled), then that person will be personally liable under the contract (at least until the corporation is incorporated and adopts the contract as described above): see *1080409 Ontario Ltd. v. Hunter*, [2000] O.J. No. 2603, 50 O.R. (3d) 145 (S.C.J.). Upon adoption of the contract, however, even if it has previously been terminated, the corporation will be entitled to all of the benefits (including the right to sue for damages for breach of contract) as if it had been in existence at the time the contract was entered into: *1394918 Ontario Ltd. v. 1310210 Ontario Inc.*, [2002] O.J. No. 18, 57 O.R. (3d) 607 (C.A.).

Under the Act, a company can be dissolved voluntarily by its shareholders, or involuntarily by the Minister for failure to pay corporations tax or file the required annual returns. The Act now provides that, upon dissolution, any real property not disposed of is forfeited to the Crown (subs. 244(1), as amended). One saving exception is found in subss. 241(5) to (7) of the Act, which provides that a company dissolved by order of the Minister may be revived and the property will then be restored as if the company had never been dissolved (subject to the rights of anyone acquired during the period of dissolution). Revival applications cannot be brought more than 20 years after dissolution (subs. 241(5.1)). Sometimes, a company will be revived by a private Act passed by the legislature; in such case, the Act will similarly provide for restoration of the company's property to it.

The forfeiture of a corporation's property on dissolution will not defeat pre-existing rights such as a prior mortgage given by the corporation. Of course, the equity of redemption with its attendant rights, in the case of the exercise by the mortgagee of its power of sale, to an accounting and payment of the surplus, if any, will belong to the Crown as a result of the corporate mortgagor's dissolution. Subsection 242(3) of the Act requires that any proceeding against the company after its dissolution be served on the Public Guardian and Trustee. Subsection 242(4) requires a notice of sale under mortgage to be served on the Public Guardian and Trustee in the same manner as required by the *Mortgages Act*, R.S.O. 1990, c. M.40. The address of the Public Guardian and Trustee is:

Public Guardian and Trustee
595 Bay Street
Suite 800
Toronto, ON
M5G 2M6

Subsection 244(2) confirms that, if the notice of sale is given as required, the purchaser under power of sale will get good title. The Public Guardian and Trustee will, of course, as owner of the dissolved corporation's interest in the land, be entitled to an accounting of the sale proceeds and to payment of any surplus.

It is important that you verify that companies appearing as owners in the chain of title were in existence and capable of holding land at the time they acquired the property, while they held it, and when they conveyed it. If a corporation owning land was dissolved before it conveyed the land, the transferr will be void.

However, there may be circumstances, although, rare, where the transferee is protected — in *830990 Ontario Ltd. v. Rojas*, [2005] O.J. No. 1828, 27 R.P.R. (4th) 42 (S.C.J.), affd [2007] O.J. Nos. 4711, 4712, 2007 ONCA 842 (C.A.), a mortgagor was estopped from using a defence that the assignment was void where the corporate assignor had been dissolved on the basis that the mortgagor had received the benefit of the advances under the mortgage; it would be inequitable to permit her to avoid liability on this basis.

Because claims of the Crown were exempt from the 40-year rule under Part III of the *Registry Act* and from the title guarantee under s. 44 of the *Land Titles Act*, it is generally thought that the search for corporate ownership should extend back to the original Crown patent. However, some relief has been provided by an amendment to the Ontario *Business Corporations Act*, which states that a forfeiture on dissolution of a corporation is not effective against a purchaser for value where the dissolution occurred more than 20 years before registration of the transfer (see s. 244(3), S.O. 1994, c. 27, s. 71(32)). In other words, on a purchase, corporate searches need only be done against Ontario corporations owning the land in the 20 years prior to closing. When acting on a mortgage transaction, the search should be against corporations owning the land in the 20-year period before the deed or transfer to the borrower was registered.

Corporate searches can be performed either in person at the Companies and Personal Property Security Branch, 375 University Avenue, 2nd Floor, Toronto, ON or by computer through a service provider (such as Cyberbahn, Dye & Durham or Oncorp). The private-sector service providers charge a fee in addition to the government fee. To confirm corporate existence for companies incorporated prior to 1994, it will be necessary to obtain a microfiche from the Ministry; after that date, you have the added choice of confirming existence through a document list obtained online. You will be interested in the particulars of incorporation, the status of the company, and the date on which it was dissolved, if such is the case.

For a company that is selling or mortgaging land to your client, you may also obtain a Certificate of Status from the same office, for a fee. This certificate, however, tells you only the date of incorporation and that, as of the date of the Certificate, the company is a subsisting corporation.

Unfortunately, there are no similar time limitations on the effect of dissolution of corporations incorporated in jurisdictions other than Ontario. The *Canada Business Corporations Act*, R.S.C. 1985, c. C-44, s. 228 provides that for companies incorporated under that Act, undistributed property of a corporation at the date of dissolution vests in Her Majesty in right of Canada. Searches for federal companies are made at:

Corporations Canada,
9th Floor, Jean Edmonds Tower South
365 Laurier Avenue West
Ottawa, ON
K1A 0C8

Corporate profiles and Certificates of Compliance (equivalent to the Ontario Certificate of Status) are also available by computer at <http://www.corporations.ic.gc.ca>.

In summary, the general, but not universal, practice is to search for corporate ownership back to the Crown patent in both the Registry and Land Titles systems and then to check the status of corporate owners for the relevant periods of ownership, subject to the limitation of 20 years for Ontario corporations discussed above. Of course, for lands which have been converted from the Registry system to Land Titles Conversion Qualified (including thereafter to Absolute Title Plus), the parcel register for such properties, while noting that title is subject to s. 44(1) of the *Land Titles Act*, specifically excepts escheats or forfeitures to the Crown as a title qualification. As a result, no corporate searches need be done for corporations who owned the property prior to the date when title to the property was converted, which date is noted on the parcel. Corporate existence searches are only required for corporations who have owned the property from and after the conversion date.

EXTRA-PROVINCIAL CORPORATIONS ACT

Under the *Extra-Provincial Corporations Act*, R.S.O. 1990, c. E.27, all non-Canadian corporations (*i.e.*, those incorporated outside Canada) must have an extra-provincial licence to do business in Ontario. A corporation is deemed to be carrying on business if "it holds an interest, otherwise than by way of security, in real property situate in Ontario" (see s. 1(2)(*b*)).

If the corporation has been incorporated federally or in another province, it does not need a licence under the Act to carry on business in Ontario. However, if it has been incorporated in a foreign jurisdiction, a licence is required. The corporation must also have an agent for service located in Ontario. The agent's address will be the address for service to be completed in any transfer to the corporation.

A corporation in breach of the provisions of this Act is liable to a fine up to $25,000 and "every person acting as its representative in Ontario who authorized, permitted or acquiesced in such offence is also guilty of an offence and on conviction is liable to a fine of not more than $2,000" (see s. 20(2)). This may obviously include the solicitor who acts for a foreign corporation in purchasing Ontario land.

Section 22 gives express authority to a non-Canadian corporation with a licence to hold land. However, there is no provision that says that a conveyance to a corporation without a licence is void, nor does the Act provide for forfeiture of the interest held. Therefore, it is not necessary to check whether a non-Canadian corporation has a licence when dealing with land that is or has been owned by such a corporation. But absent such a check, it will be impossible for a solicitor to give an opinion, as is sometimes required in sophisticated transactions, that such a corporation is in good standing and does not contravene any laws.

Formerly, corporations which were not incorporated under the laws of Ontario, Quebec or Canada were required to obtain a licence to hold land under the *Mortmain and Charitable Uses Act*, R.S.O. 1980, c. 297. This statute was repealed by S.O. 1982, c. 12. The part dealing with charities was replaced by the *Charities Accounting Act*, R.S.O. 1990, c. C.10. The remainder of the Act providing for controls on corporate ownership of land was eventually supplanted by the *Extra-Provincial Corporations Act*. In searching title, you can safely ignore affidavits attached to old deeds under the *Mortmain and Charitable Uses Act*, which were required when the grantee was a corporation incorporated in a non-qualifying jurisdiction.

CHANGE OF CORPORATE NAME

Companies often change their corporate names for one reason or another. Sometimes they amalgamate with another company. If, in searching title, you find that a company took title as "Acme Stuffed Shirt and Puffed Cravat Co. Limited" and then, when it sold the property, it was called "Acme Funky Clothes Limited", you would require the registration in the general register of a notarial or certified copy of the articles of amendment issued to the company changing the name. These days, if you do not have the original articles of amendment, you can only obtain a certified microfiche from the Ministry. In this case, your notarial certificate can state that attached is "a paper copy made from a certified microfiche issued by the Minister of Consumer and Business Services". The issuance of the articles of amendment should be recited in the transfer.

In the Land Titles system, it will be necessary to apply to amend the register to change the name of the owner and to supply evidence of the change of name at the time of transferring the land. In doing so, you will have to supply a notarial or certified copy of the articles of amendment or amalgamation, as applicable. When applying for such an amendment under the e-reg system, it will be necessary to register the actual articles of amendment or amalgamation at the land registry office, where an index number will be assigned to the registration which can then be referred to in the Application to Change Name e-reg document.

INDOOR MANAGEMENT RULE

A company acts by resolutions passed at meetings of directors. The directors may, for example, resolve that the company sell its land and that the president and treasurer are authorized to execute the deed on behalf of the company. However, the purchaser's solicitor does not need to check that resolution. *Bona fide* outside persons dealing with the corporation are protected against deficiencies, provided the directors, officers and agents have been exercising powers and performing duties that are in the normal business of the corporation or usual for such persons to exercise. This is known as the "indoor management rule". The corporation is bound even if a resolution was not passed or the persons signing the document did not in fact have authority.

One word of caution: the indoor management rule may not be applicable in cases where a company is selling the whole or substantially the whole of the undertaking of the company. In this case, subs. 184(3) of the *Business Corporations Act* (R.S.O. 1990, c. B.16) and subss. 189(4) to (9) of the *Canada Business Corporations Act* require the passing of a special resolution plus such additional authorization as the articles of incorporation of the company may require. If acting for a purchaser from a corporation, you should satisfy yourself in this regard when advising on the agreement of purchase and sale. If the special resolution has not been passed, the agreement may not be binding.

CORPORATE DOCUMENTS REQUIRED BY MORTGAGEE

When your client is lending money to a corporation on the security of a mortgage on the corporation's lands, you want to be able to assure your client that the mortgage is valid and enforceable against the corporation. Therefore, it is standard practice to require production of the following:

1.   A notarial or certified copy of the articles of incorporation under which the company was incorporated. From this you can check the company name, its general powers and that there is no restriction on the statutory authority of the directors' borrowing power.

2. An officer's certificate that there is no restriction in the corporation's by-laws on the directors' statutory borrowing power.

3. For corporations under a statute which does not provide authority to the directors to borrow (*e.g.*, not incorporated under the Ontario or Canada *Business Corporations Act*), a certified copy of its general borrowing by-law. You want to check to see that the company is authorized under its by-laws to borrow money on the security of its land.

4. A certified copy of the resolution of directors authorizing this particular borrowing and empowering the vice-president and secretary (or whomever the directors designate) to execute the documents.

PARTNERSHIP

Two or more people may carry on business as partners and they may purchase land as partnership property. The rights of the parties *vis-à-vis* one another will be set out in the partnership agreement. The transfer to the partners should be to X and Y as partnership property.

It is important when taking a transfer from a partnership that all partners sign. The transfer should contain a declaration by at least one of the partners that: (a) the land was bought as partnership land; (b) the land was held as partnership land; and (c) the partners signing the transfer were, at the time of the purchase and during the course of ownership and at the present time, the only partners in the partnership.

When you see a transfer to partners, you should always check the registration under the *Business Names Act*, R.S.O. 1990, c. B.17. Formerly, the registration was required under the *Partnerships Registration Act*, R.S.O. 1970, c. 340, which has now been repealed; however, those registrations continued to be valid, but will by now have all expired. The new statute requires that persons associated in partnership shall not carry on business unless they register the names of all the partners by filing the form set out in regulations to the Act. The form sets out the names and addresses of all partners, the name under which they intend to carry on business and the time when the partnership was created. These declarations historically were registered in the land registry office for the county in which the partnership was to be established. All registrations under this Act are now centralized at:

Ministry of Government Services
Companies and Personal Property Security Branch
393 University Avenue, Suite 200
Toronto, ON
M5G 2M2

Unless the partnership agreement provides otherwise, land held as partnership property is held by the partners as tenants-in-common: see *Hegeman v. Rogers*, [1971] O.J. No. 1683, [1971] 3 O.R. 600 at 607-608 (H.C.J.). An interesting situation arose in *Agro Estate v. CIBC Trust Corp.*, [1999] O.J. No. 1714, 96 O.T.C. 140 (H.C.J.), where the owners were registered as joint tenants but the

Court found that they had in fact intended the property to be partnership property — in the result, Philp J. decided that the legal title passed to the surviving joint tenant in trust for himself and the estate of the deceased partner. In more normal circumstances, of course, the estate trustees of the deceased partner would be the ones to deal with transfer of the partner's interest in the land.

LIMITED PARTNERSHIP

A limited partnership is frequently used in the development and syndication of land. The limited partners have all of the tax advantages of owners of land, but their liability is limited. Title is normally registered in the name of a single general partner. Refer to the *Limited Partnerships Act*, R.S.O. 1990, c. L.16. Furthermore, s. 48(2) of the *Registry Act* requires that the transferee who is not a corporation be described by surname and at least one given name. This therefore precludes description of the transferee as a limited partnership. In any event, the Ontario Court of Appeal has concluded that the only entity legally capable of holding title to the real property of a limited partnership is the general partner (see *Kucor Construction & Developments & Associates v. Canada Life Assurance Co.*, [1998] O.J. No. 4733, 41 O.R. (3d) 577 (C.A.)). Transfers to a limited partnership should be to the general partner only, with or without reference to its role as general partner of the limited partnership (in Land Titles, the reference to the limited partnership will not be permitted).

Limited partnerships combine some of the features of partnerships and corporations. There are two kinds of partners:

1. general partners, who are personally liable for the full amount of the debts of the partnership just as partners are in a normal partnership; and

2. limited partners, who are liable for the debts of the partnership only up to the amount they have contributed to the capital of the partnership; in this respect they are similar to shareholders in a limited company or corporation whose liability for debts of the company is limited to their contribution to capital.

The important difference between a partnership and a limited partnership, so far as conveyancing is concerned, is that while in a partnership all partners must sign documents, in a limited partnership only the general partner is authorized to sign for the partnership. In the Land Titles system, a transfer or a charge must include a statutory declaration by the general partner that the transaction is for a partnership purpose within the meaning of s. 8 of the *Limited Partnerships Act*; otherwise, the document must be signed by all the partners. It would be sensible for a purchaser from a limited partnership of land under the Registry system to require the same practice to be followed.

To find out who are general partners, you must examine the declaration filed (pursuant to s. 3 of the Act):

Ministry of Government Services
Companies and Personal Property Security Branch
Registrar of Partnerships
393 University Avenue, Suite 200
Toronto, ON
M5G 2M2

To find out who are limited partners, and the amount of their contribution, you must examine the record required to be maintained at the partnership's principal place of business in Ontario.

TRUSTEES

Title to land is sometimes given to a person to hold as trustee for another. The reasons for so doing are varied, but the most common are to conceal the identity of the true owner or to avoid land vesting in a minor. It is usual to establish a trust by a written declaration of trust which will set out the powers and responsibilities of the trustee.

Although a trustee may act only within the terms of the trust, a purchaser need not be concerned about authority to act unless the purchaser has actual notice of the terms of the trust. The *Land Titles Act* does not recognize trusts, and the registered owner may deal with the land without any evidence of authority to do so (see p. 33).

A number of decisions have confirmed that the mere description of a grantor or mortgagor as a "trustee" or as holding "in trust" does not by itself constitute actual notice of the trust to anyone, including the person dealing directly with the person so described (*Hoback Investments Ltd. v. Loblaws Ltd.*, [1981] O.J. No. 2922, 32 O.R. (2d) 95 (H.C.J.); *Ignjatic v. McLennan*, [1981] O.J. No. 2923, 32 O.R. (2d) 104 (C.A.); *Cohen v. McClintock*, [1978] O.J. No. 3356, 19 O.R. (2d) 623 (H.C.J.)). But see *Martic v. Liban*, [1983] O.J. No. 2177, 19 E.T.R. 213 (Co. Ct.), where a detailed land transfer tax affidavit was held to give actual notice of the trust; in this case, the affidavit specifically identified the beneficiaries of the trust.

CHARITIES AND RELIGIOUS ORGANIZATIONS

CHARITIES

The *Mortmain and Charitable Uses Act* provided that land which was assured to a charity had to be sold within two years or it vested in the Public Trustee. This prevented a charity from accumulating land, for example, as an investment. But the restriction also applied to land actually used and occupied by the charity, although there was provision in this case for obtaining an order from the Supreme Court to sanction the retention of the land by the charity.

The Act was repealed in 1982 (S.O. 1982, c. 12) and replaced by an amendment to the *Charities Accounting Act*, R.S.O. 1990, c. C.10. This Act permits charities to hold land subject to the right of the Public Guardian and

Trustee (formerly the Public Trustee) to register a vesting notice. The Public Guardian and Trustee will do so for the purpose of selling such land if it is believed that the land has not actually been used by the charity for three years, is no longer required for the actual use and occupation of the charity and will not be required for such purpose in the immediate future. Any land which vested in the Public Trustee under the previous legislation is deemed to have been returned to the charity. Thus, as a purchaser, you need not be concerned about the charity's title to the land unless the Public Guardian and Trustee has actually registered notice.

RELIGIOUS ORGANIZATIONS

Many religious institutions are governed by special legislation, such as *The United Church of Canada Act*, S.O. 1925, c. 125. In general, however, the holding and disposition of land by religious organizations is governed by the *Religious Organizations' Lands Act*, R.S.O. 1990, c. R.23. In the event of conflict between this Act and special legislation, the special legislation overrides.

Under s. 2 of the Act, religious organizations are authorized to acquire land for certain specified purposes, such as a place of worship, a burial ground and a residence for its religious leader. The land is to be held in the name of trustees appointed by the organization and it automatically vests in their successors without a conveyance. The trustees may act only upon resolution of the organization. It will be important, therefore, to examine a certified copy of the resolution (which should be deposited on title) to determine the authority of the trustees.

Finally, it is to be noted s. 12(2) of the Act states that the provisions of the *Charities Accounting Act* regarding vesting in the Public Guardian and Trustee apply to lands not required for the actual occupation by the religious organization for a religious purpose.

CHAPTER 7

Easements and Restrictive Covenants

EASEMENTS

An easement is defined as a right in property belonging to someone else that benefits land owned by the person who has the easement. There are several types of easements that are found in ordinary day-to-day practice: the easement that the telephone company has over a strip of land at the rear of a house lot to install and maintain its lines; the easement one party has over a neighbour's property for a mutual driveway; the easement a cottage owner has across the farmer's land giving access to the highway; the easement for support that the parties on each side of a party wall have against the other. A right of way is simply a particular type of easement permitting passage over a particular strip of land.

METHODS OF CREATION

There are four ways an easement can be established:

1. *By express grant:* This is the most common and is dealt with in detail below.

2. *By implied grant:* These are easements that arise by law and in general, are necessary for the reasonable enjoyment of the benefited land. There are two principal types that are implied:

   (a) Right of way of necessity: If you own a parcel of land fronting on a highway which you sever, selling off the back half without explicitly giving the purchaser a right of way to the highway, the law will imply a right of way of necessity. However, if you sell off the front half without reserving a right of way to give yourself access to the highway, your parcel will be landlocked.

   (b) Right of mutual support: If you own a semi-detached house and your neighbour, who owns the other half of the house, decides to tear it down, your neighbour must not do anything that would cause your half to fall. Similarly, you must not excavate on your land so as to undermine your neighbour's building.

3. *Easements by prescription:* Section 31 of the *Real Property Limitations Act*, R.S.O. 1990, c. L.15, provides that an easement that has been enjoyed for 20 years without interruption or consent by the landowner cannot be defeated. If someone has used a short cut across a neighbour's

property registered under the *Registry Act* for 20 years to get to the back of his or her property, he or she may have established a permanent easement. To do so he or she must prove several things, including:

(a)   that the neighbour knew (or ought to have known) of the use;

(b)   that the neighbour did not give permission for the use;

(c)   that the neighbour had the right and power to stop the use. To explain, an owner who had leased his or her land before the user commenced is not in a position to stop the use because he or she has given exclusive possession of the land to the tenant; in this case, the period of prescription does not start until the lease terminates. Similarly, if the owner is under a disability (such as being an infant or being mentally incompetent), then a prescriptive right cannot be obtained;

(d)   that the neighbour refrained from stopping the use (*i.e.*, he acquiesced to the use);

(e)   that the use was "reasonably necessary for the better enjoyment" of his or her property (the benefitted, or dominant, tenement): see *Re Ellenborough Park* (1955), [1956] 1 Ch. 131 (C.A.). See also *Depew v. Wilkes*, [2002] O.J. No. 2987, 60 O.R. (3d) 499 (C.A.) where Rosenberg J.A. confirmed that parking adjacent to the dominant tenement was "connected with the normal enjoyment of the property" even though an alternative public area was available a couple of hundred of feet away;

(f)   that the use was continuous and without interruption — for example, the neighbour can prevent the period of prescription from running by locking a gate or by blocking the path once per year. However, note that s. 32 of the Act mandates that the person claiming the easement must acquiesce in the interruption for more than a year before it will be deemed to be an interruption; and

(g)   that the claimant to a prescriptive easement shows that the period of 20 years' use was "next before some action wherein the claim ... was or is brought into question" (s. 32).

4.   *Doctrine of lost modern grant:* As stated in *Ebare v. Winter*, [2005] O.J. No. 14, 26 R.P.R. (4th) 220 at para. 29 (C.A.): The doctrine of "lost modern grant" is a legal fiction that was created before the advent of statutory limitation periods to counteract the harshness of the common law rule that required proof of continuous use from time in memorial. The courts will sometimes accept this doctrine as a basis for finding in favour of an easement when a statutory prescriptive easement is not available as, for example, where a claim to a prescriptive easement has been lost because the claimant acquiesced in the interruption of it for more than one year or did not commence the action on a timely basis: see *MacRae v. Levy*, [2005] O.J. No. 313, 28 R.P.R. (4th) 291 (S.C.J.). See also *Henderson v. Volk*, [1982] O.J.

No. 3138, 35 O.R. (2nd) 379 (C.A.), where the Court of Appeal confirmed that the "doctrine of lost modern grant" was still available in Ontario, and that the requirements were exactly the same as for a prescriptive easement except that the 20-year period of use did not have to immediately precede the commencement of the action.

As noted above, a prescriptive easement is obtained only when the use has been without the consent of the owner. Permission given at the outset of the use will not, however, prevent the creation of a prescriptive right. The following quotation by MacKay J.A., in *Garfinkel v. Kleinberg*, [1955] O.J. No. 562, [1955] O.R. 388 at 394 (C.A.), is helpful:

> Where the right is claimed under *The Limitations Act*, consent to the user, unqualified as to time, will not be a bar to the owner of the dominant tenement obtaining a prescriptive right; if the user following the consent or permission is as of right by reason of the consent, and if the user continues for the full period of 20 years after the consent a prescriptive right is acquired under the statute; but permission asked and granted, periodic payments, or acknowledgment by the dominant owner that his user is not as of right, at any time during the 20-year period will prevent his acquiring a prescriptive right.

In other words, if a user, having obtained permission once, then continues to use the right of way for a continuous period of more than 20 years without anything further being said or done, that user will acquire a prescriptive easement over *Registry Act* lands (see, for example, *Cogan v. G.W.L. Realty Advisors Inc.*, [2000] O.J. No. 187, 30 R.P.R. (3d) 49 (S.C.J.) and *Block v. Trezzi*, [2001] O.J. No. 4143, 45 R.P.R. (3d) 139 (S.C.J.)). It is therefore important for a landowner who has given permission to renew that permission and obtain the user's acknowledgment periodically, at least once every 20 years, if he or she wishes to prevent a prescriptive easement from being created.

Of course, once land is registered under the *Land Titles Act* or has been transferred to the Land Titles system, a prescriptive easement cannot be acquired against that land (s. 51(1)). Nevertheless, the *Land Titles Act* excepts easements acquired prior to the date the land became subject to the Act. An interesting question arises regarding how the requirement to show an uninterrupted period of 20 years prior to the commencement of an action to secure a prescriptive easement applies when the land was transferred to the Land Titles system some time before the action was commenced — does the claimant have to show uninterrupted use for 20 years before the transfer plus the period after the transfer, or is the easement secured once the transfer to the Land Titles system occurs?

BASIC REQUIREMENTS

There are certain general requirements that must be met in order to create a legal easement (whether by prescription or by express grant). There must be a dominant and a servient tenement. The dominant tenement is the parcel of land which has the benefit of the easement; the servient tenement is the parcel over or through which the easement runs. You normally cannot have an easement which does not actually benefit a parcel of land. The easement must be reasonably "necessary" for the enjoyment of the dominant tenement: *Depew v. Wilkes* (cited above).

In addition, the dominant and servient lands must be owned by different parties or owned in a different capacity by the same person, and the purpose of the easement must be capable of forming the subject matter of a grant.

Of course, two parties can agree, by contract, to do something for one another; that is personal to the parties. An easement is something that "runs with the land", *i.e.*, when the dominant tenement is sold, the purchaser acquires the rights that the vendor had over the neighbour's land. When the servient tenement is sold, the purchaser is subject to those rights even though no mention of the easement is made in the transfer. (See s. 15 of the *Conveyancing and Law of Property Act*, R.S.O. 1990, c. C.34.)

An exception to the general rule that you cannot have an easement without a dominant tenement is found in s. 91(2) of the *Municipal Act, 2001*, S.O. 2001, c. 25), which states that "a public utility provided by a municipality does not have to be appurtenant or annexed to or for the benefit of any specific parcel of land to be valid." Another example is found in s. 27(1) amended by S.O. 1993, c. 23, s. 73(16)) of the *Ontario Water Resources Act*, R.S.O. 1990, c. O.40). That section expressly provides that easements in respect of water or sewage works in favour of the Ontario Water Resources Commission or any municipality having a contract with the Commission in respect of water or sewage works do not require dominant tenements to be enforceable.

If both the dominant and servient tenements are bought by the same person, the easement is said to merge. It disappears. Obviously, the owner of both parcels has no need of the easement.

PLANNING ACT, R.S.O. 1990, c. P.13

A consent under the *Planning Act* is generally required to transfer an easement over anything less than the whole of a parcel of land. A transfer of easement is an agreement that has the effect of granting the use of land for a period exceeding 21 years and is, therefore, covered by s. 50 of that Act. If parties want to create rights of way immediately without waiting for the *Planning Act* consent, then one device used is an agreement with a specified term of less than 21 years until the consent is obtained. Another method sometimes employed is to create a "blanket easement", that is, one covering the entire parcel of the transferor of the easement.

Note that under s. 9(1)(*b*) of the *Condominium Act, 1998*, S.O. 1998, c. 19, easements granted by or reserved to condominium corporations are exempted from the necessity of obtaining a consent. In addition, easements created in a condominium declaration are exempted by s. 40(5) of the *Land Titles Act*. Other exceptions include easements created by court order and expropriation.

GRANTS OF EASEMENTS

Grants of easements look much like any other transfer of land. There must be a proper description in accordance with O. Reg. 43/96 for both the dominant and servient lands. If an old metes and bounds description is being used (in the Registry system), then there must be a reference to the last registered instrument in which that description was used (subs. 61(2)). In accordance with subs. 61(3) of O. Reg. 43/96, the description is required to include the registration number of the deed, containing the same description that was most recently registered.

In the case of a separate transfer of an easement, Box 7 in the transfer will have to be amended by striking out "fee simple" and inserting "easement" instead. While the servient lands can be described in Box 5, the transfer should have attached to it a schedule that includes a description of the dominant tenement and describes the nature of the easement (for example, "a right of way in perpetuity for ingress and egress to and from the dominant tenement for pedestrians and vehicles").

As has been noted above, it is not necessary to describe an easement in a subsequent transfer of the dominant tenement since it will automatically be included because of s. 15 of the *Conveyancing and Law of Property Act*. However, it may have to be expressly set out if it is part of the description of the land under the *Land Titles Act* or in the electronic registration system. Even in the Registry system, it is probably wise to expressly include easements in the description of the land being transferred since that may avoid the potential of losing the easement after 40 years under Part III of the *Registry Act*, R.S.O. 1990, c. R.20.

Once described, the easement should thereafter be noted on title to both the servient and dominant tenements, thus ensuring that anyone searching title has notice of it. Refer to Bulletin 2005-03 for the procedures to record easements and releases of easements against the dominant and servient lands in both the Registry and Land Titles systems.

A right of way may also be established by reservation. To go back to the example of a person who did not reserve a right of way across the front half of the land that was sold, that person's transfer should have described the parcel being sold and then stated, "reserving unto the transferor, his heirs, successors and assigns, a right of way for passage and repassage of persons, vehicles and animals over: ...". Then, when the remaining property is sold, the transfer should mention the right of way, "together with a right of way: ...". Remember that a *Planning Act* consent may be required to validly reserve the easement.

In the older parts of cities where the houses are built close together, there are often mutual driveways. A deed to a house may include a description like this:

The whole of Lot 8, Plan 1972;

Together with a right of way over the southerly 4 feet 6 inches of the lands lying immediately to the north of the lands described herein;

And subject to a right of way over the northerly 4 feet 6 inches of the lands described herein.

In most new subdivisions, Bell Canada and the local Hydro Commission usually have easements over the rear four or six feet of each lot for their service lines. This must be brought to the attention of the purchaser client. There can be no interference with the hydro and telephone workers' right to enter onto the property to repair their lines, and certainly the owner cannot build on the affected strip of land.

However, some easements granted to Bell Canada and Ontario Hydro (now Hydro One Networks Inc.) may be void because no consents to the grants of easement were obtained as then required under the *Planning Act*. While no consent is required for a conveyance to Her Majesty in right of Canada or Ontario or to a municipal government, transfers to Bell Canada, which is a privately owned company, do not fall within these exceptions. When the *Planning Act* was re-enacted in 1983 (S.O. 1983, c. 1), Ontario Hydro was added to the list of exempt bodies under s. 50(3)(*d*) (in 1998 the exemption was amended to refer only to electricity distribution and transmission lines). However, prior transfers that contravened the Act were not forgiven. This invalidity may not, however, be of much practical consequence. Most of your clients will require electrical and telephone service and will not, therefore, wish to force the issue. Furthermore, prescriptive easements will, by now, likely have been obtained.

Easements for underground sewer and water lines can be very troublesome. They present one more reason to examine a survey carefully. A search of title will specify where the easement is. But then the survey must be examined to determine if the building or the garage has been erected over the easement.

Party walls are common in many cities, both in commercial buildings and in residential strip housing and semi-detached dwellings. Sometimes, there are actually party-wall agreements setting forth expressly the rights of the parties to maintain the wall. Even without an express agreement, the law will imply an easement of support requiring that the wall be maintained.

It may be useful to mention two problems that frequently arise respecting the use of easements. First, it is clear that an easement or right of way may not be used in order to access land that is not benefited by that easement or right of way. See, for example, the decision in *Gordon v. Regan*, [1985] O.J. No. 2282, 49 O.R. (2d) 521 (H.C.J.), affd [1989] O.J. No. 3233, 71 O.R. (2d) 736*n* (C.A.). In that case the owner of the dominant tenement purchased an additional adjoining parcel and constructed a garage on it; the Court would not permit the use of the right of way for automobiles to obtain passage to the garage. See also *Jengle v. Keetch*, [1992] O.J. No. 425, 7 O.R. (3d) 187 (C.A.), in which an owner leased a parcel of land which had the benefit of a right of way in order to gain access to his own land on the other side of the dominant tenement. The Court prohibited such use.

Second, owners of the servient tenement over which a right of way passes are often troubled by an increase in traffic over the right of way. Although the question will often involve difficult questions of fact, the issue turns on whether the volume of traffic or the nature of the user is within the original contemplation of the parties. A non-excessive increase in traffic will not be considered to breach the terms of the easement. See *Laurie v. Winch*, [1952] S.C.J. No. 48, [1953] 1 S.C.R. 49; *Donald v. Friesen*, [1992] O.J. No. 3263, 72

O.R. (2d) 205 (Dist. Ct.); and *Rudolph Furniture Ltd. v. 797574 Ontario Ltd.*, [1998] O.J. No. 4488 (Gen. Div.), vard [1999] O.J. No. 2735 (Gen. Div.).

ANCILLARY RIGHTS

An express grant of an easement will include ancillary rights where those rights are "reasonably necessary" for the use and enjoyment of the easement (even though such rights are not included in the grant). For example, in *Mackenzie v. Matthews*, [1999] O.J. No. 4602, 46 O.R. (3d) 21, the Court of Appeal confirmed a right of way to provide access to island properties included the right to install a dock and to have a vehicle turn-around area.

On the other hand, the Court of Appeal held, in *Fallowfield v. Bourgault*, [2003] O.J. No. 5206, 68 O.R. (3d) 417 at 422 (C.A.), that the ancillary rights must be necessary for the use or enjoyment of the easement, not just convenient or even reasonable. In that case, the appellants had erected a fence on their property that restricted, but did not entirely prevent access to, an easement area between the houses.

EXTINGUISHMENT

Once an easement is established, it cannot be easily lost. Indeed, the general principle of law is that an easement must be abandoned or released by the owner of the dominant tenement before it will be terminated. See, for example, *Jansons v. Iwanczuk*, [1991] O.J. No. 801, 17 R.P.R. (2d) 308 (Gen. Div.), where it was confirmed that mere non-use of a right of way will not by itself be considered an abandonment. In general, abandonment of an easement requires some action by the owner of the dominant tenement that demonstrates unequivocally an intention to abandon or terminate the easement. A very good summary of the principles regarding abandonment of easements is set forth in *Lywood v. Hunt*, [2009] O.J. No. 2101, 97 O.R. (3d) 520 at 529 (S.C.J.), supp. reasons [2009] O.J. No. 5801 (S.C.J.). See also *Fyfe v. James*, [2006] O.J. No. 325, 42 R.P.R. (4th) 221 (S.C.J.), where the right of way was held not to have been extinguished due to replacement with an alternate means of reaching the relevant properties. On the other hand, in *Overs v. ten Kortenaar*, [2006] O.J. No. 822, 46 R.P.R. (4th) 118 (S.C.J.), the actions of successive owners, who had not used a right of way for many years and who had planted trees and installed a fence without a gate, were taken to be an abandonment of the right of way.

Easements will also cease to exist where they have expired, where the servient land, including the easement, has been expropriated, or where the same party owns the dominant and servient lands (in which case, the easement is said to have "merged").

Practitioners should note that Bulletin No. 2005-02 was released on March 3, 2005 to clarify processes and guidelines with respect to easements under both the Land Titles and Registry systems. One important change is that the Ministry now expressly requires registrants to search servient lands to determine any prior interests relating to an easement.

ROAD ACCESS ACT

The *Road Access Act*, R.S.O. 1990, c. R.34, which came into force in 1978, gives statutory protection to persons using what might otherwise be referred to as a right of way of necessity (see p. 91). A claim to an "access road" is often coupled with a claim to a prescriptive easement in case one of them fails. An "access road" is defined in s. 1 as "a road located on land not owned by a municipality and not dedicated and accepted as, or otherwise deemed at law to be, a public highway, that serves as a motor vehicle access route to one or more parcels of land".

Section 2 prohibits any person from placing or maintaining an obstacle or barrier over an access road that prevents access to a parcel of land or a boat docking facility unless authorized by a judge's order or by written agreement of all persons affected by such barrier.

Subsections 2(3) to (6) set out the procedure for making application for closure of an access road.

Section 7 provides that a knowing contravention of s. 2 is an offence, and the Court "may order the person to remove the barrier or other obstacle" (s. 7(2)).

The courts have established a number of principles respecting the Act:

1.   The Act in effect authorizes the user to trespass on the land that the access road crosses. However, the right is only a temporary right and is limited to motor vehicle use.

2.   In order to be an "access road", there must not be alternate road access available. If there is, then the road is not an "access road" and no order is required to close it.

3.   The alternate road access must be available over an existing road. An unopened road allowance does not qualify.

See *Eaton v. Abram*, [1993] O.J. No. 2607, 15 O.R. (3d) 74 (Gen. Div.) and *2008795 Ontario Inc. v. Kilpatrick*, [2007] O.J. No. 3248, 86 O.R. (3d) 561 (C.A.).

Note that the Court of Appeal in the *Kilpatrick* case observed (but refrained from deciding) that users of an access road would not appear to have a defence to an application to close the road because of s. 3(1)(*b*), which states that a "judge may grant the closing order upon being satisfied that ... persons [using the road] do not have a legal right to use the road". This, of course, raises the question of whether the Act has any substantive effect.

RESTRICTIVE COVENANTS

A restrictive covenant bears some resemblance to an easement. Again there must be a dominant and a servient tenement, *i.e.*, one parcel of land which carries with it the benefit of the covenant and the other which carries the burden. A restrictive covenant can be described as a contract between two neighbouring landowners by which the covenantee, anxious to maintain the saleable value of the property, acquires the right to restrain the covenantor from putting the neighbouring land to certain specified uses.

Restrictive covenants were developed in the days before zoning by-laws. As an example, if Smith had a large parcel of land and sold off part to Jones, Smith may have required Jones to covenant not to use the land for industry. It is clear that, as between the two of them, there was a contract that the courts would enforce. It was not until the landmark case of *Tulk v. Moxhay*, [1848] 2 Ph. 774 (Ch. Div.), that the courts recognized the doctrine that both the benefit and the burden of that covenant would run with the land, *i.e.*, that Smith's transferee could sue Jones' transferee if the latter erected a factory on the land.

In order to successfully apply to court to enforce a restrictive covenant, there are certain requirements that must be kept in mind:

1. A restrictive covenant must be negative in nature. The courts will not force you to do a certain thing with your land, *e.g.*, paint your house pink. But a covenant that you will not paint your house blue might be enforceable. So, in setting up covenants you must be careful to state them in the negative. The following is a list of examples:

   (a) shall not use for a glue factory;

   (b) shall not build a fence over four feet high;

   (c) shall not construct a frame house;

   (d) shall not carry on any business.

   The Ontario Court of Appeal reaffirmed this principle in *Durham Condominium Corp. No. 123 v. Amberwood Investments Ltd.*, [2002] O.J. No. 1023, 58 O.R. (3d) 481 (C.A.), where the Court found that positive covenants will not bind subsequent owners. The Court felt itself bound by precedent even though it may make good commercial sense to change the rule. The appeal to the Supreme Court of Canada from this decision was discontinued ([2002] S.C.C.A. No. 208), and the case was cited with approval in *Brennan v. Dole*, [2000] O.J. No. 3904, 36 R.P.R. (4th) 32 (C.A.) and followed in *Innisfil 400 Group Ltd. v. Ontario*, [2007] O.J. No. 2863 (S.C.J.).

2. The covenant must actually benefit the dominant tenement.

3. The person suing to enforce a covenant must own the dominant tenement (*London County Council v. Allen*, [1914] 3 K.B. 642).

4. The owner wishing to enforce a restrictive covenant must establish that the benefit has in fact passed to him or her (as it does when a restrictive covenant "runs with the land").

There are three ways that the benefit of restrictive covenants runs with the land:

1. *Express annexation of the covenants to the dominant land:* A properly drafted restrictive covenant will clearly set out the restrictions and will clearly state that they are to be for the benefit of and appurtenant to specifically described land. Indeed, the dominant tenement must be described in the transfer creating a restrictive covenant (*Sekretov v. Toronto (City)*, [1972] O.J. No. 1883, [1972] 3 O.R. 534 (H.C.J.), vard [1973] O.J. No. 1885, [1973] 2 O.R. 161 (C.A.); *Thunder Bay (City) v. 1013951 Ontario Ltd.*, [2000] O.J. No. 1292, 32 R.P.R. (3d)

63 (S.C.J.), revd [2001] O.J. No. 962, 39 R.P.R. (3d) 196 (C.A.)). The dominant tenement must be identified in the document creating the restrictive covenant. In *Mohawk Square Developments Ltd. v. Suncor Energy Inc.*, [2007] O.J. No. 3552, 62 R.P.R. (4th) 100 (S.C.J.), the dominant tenement was not identified and the Court found the covenant to be merely personal to the original parties and not running with the lands. See also *Galbraith v. Madawaska Club Ltd.*, [1961] S.C.J. No. 43, [1961] S.C.R. 639.

The covenant should appear in a schedule to the transfer, such as:

> The transferee hereby covenants for himself, his heirs, successors and assigns, that he will not use the lands described herein for any purposes other than residential, which covenant is for the benefit of and shall run with the lands adjacent to the lands described herein and described in Schedule A.

Then, anyone purchasing the servient tenement will have notice of the covenant simply by searching the title. Anyone purchasing the dominant tenement will also have notice by searching the title. And the benefit of the covenant will accrue to a purchaser because it runs with the land.

One would assume that in order to properly establish a restrictive covenant that is to run with the land, the covenantor (being the transferee in the transfer) should execute the transfer and that the covenant should specifically be said to bind the heirs and assigns of the covenantor. However, in *Rowan v. Eaton*, [1927] O.J. No. 411, 60 O.L.R. 245 (C.A.), the registration of the deed by the grantee was deemed to be acceptance of the covenants by him, and notwithstanding the fact that the grantee did not execute the deed, the covenants were held to be binding upon the grantee and his heirs and assigns (see also *Cornish v. Kawartha Lakes (City)*, [2006] O.J. No. 2005, 44 R.P.R. (4th) 251 (S.C.J.)).

2.   *Express assignment of the covenant:* The original covenantee can expressly assign the benefit of the covenant in the transfer of the land.

3.   *Building scheme:* This is the most common method of creating restrictive covenants and is found in most new housing subdivisions. This type of restrictive covenant, which affects every lot in a subdivision, is actually a private scheme of town planning. The common interest of all parties living in that subdivision is to preserve the character and value of all the land in the subdivision. In a building scheme each purchaser of a lot in the scheme can sue, or be sued by, every other purchaser in the subdivision. It is enforceable by all owners, not just the original grantor. This is different from the situation where a landowner imposes a restrictive covenant on a specific parcel; there, only that parcel of land is benefited.

Five requisites of a building scheme were established by the English case of *Elliston v. Reacher*, [1908] 2 Ch. 374:

(a) Both plaintiff and defendant must have derived title from a common owner. Obviously, neighbours in a subdivision derived title from the original subdivider. See *Lakhani v. Weinstein*, [1980] O.J. No. 3836, 31 O.R. (2d) 65 (H.C.J.).

(b) The land must have been laid out in lots, subject to the restrictions, in a way consistent only with some general scheme of development.

(c) The restrictions must have been intended by the original subdivider to pass to the benefit of each purchaser.

(d) The purchasers must have bought land with notice of the scheme. Remember s. 74(1) of the *Registry Act*: "The registration of an instrument under this or any former Act constitutes notice of the instrument to all persons claiming any interest in the land, subsequent to such registration". See *White v. Lauder Developments Ltd.*, [1975] O.J. No. 2407, 9 O.R. (2d) 363 (C.A.).

(e) The geographic area to which the scheme extends must be well defined.

In most building schemes employed in Ontario, the original vendor reserves the right to waive or modify any of the restrictions as to one or more lots included in the scheme. There is authority to suggest that the reservation and exercise of a right such as this, as well as a failure to clearly define the extent of a scheme, invalidates the whole building scheme. In *Re Lankin*, [1951] O.J. No. 276, [1951] O.W.N. 821 (H.C.J.), Aylen J. held:

> It is my view that since The Canada Permanent Trust Company reserved the right to waive the restrictions with respect to any particular lot, the restrictions in question never constituted a building scheme which is now enforceable. ... There was no common scheme as a result of which these building restrictions were imposed for the simple reason that the trust company could, at any time, waive the restrictions with respect to any particular lot.

See also *Tepper v. 511825 Ontario Ltd.*, [2001] O.J. No. 2765, 42 R.P.R. (3d) 313 (S.C.J.), *Re Zierler*, [1957] O.J. No. 46, 8 D.L.R. (2d) 189 (H.C.J.) and *Osborne v. Bradley*, [1903] 2 Ch. 446.

Building schemes may be terminated because of the failure of owners within the scheme to observe the restrictions and to enforce them (see *Lafortune v. Puccini*, [1991] O.J. No. 447, 2 O.R (3d) 689 (Gen. Div.)).

There is one decision that runs contrary to all the principles stated above regarding the enforceability of restrictive covenants against subsequent owners of the affected land. In *Lakhani v. Weinstein*, [1980] O.J. No. 3836, 31 O.R. (2d) 65 (H.C.J.), Van Camp J. held that a restrictive covenant was binding on a subsequent owner merely because he had notice of it when he purchased the property, even though there was no valid building scheme. This decision was followed, reluctantly, on the basis of *stare decisis*, in *Tepper v. 511825 Ontario Ltd.*, [2001] O.J. No. 2765, 42 R.P.R. (3d) 313 (S.C.J.). The authors wonder, however, whether this decision would stand on appeal.

There is a dangerous clause in the standard printed forms of Agreement of Purchase and Sale: "Provided title is free from all encumbrances *except as to any registered restrictions or covenants that run with the land providing that such are complied with*" (emphasis added). But suppose the purchaser proposed to buy a house intending to:

1.   put in a swimming pool with a six-foot fence of solid board;

2.   park a camp trailer beside the house;

3.   rent one room to a brother-in-law; and

4.   carry on a real estate business in the basement.

Every one of these proposed uses may be forbidden under the restrictive covenants affecting title to the lot being purchased. Yet, the purchaser, in signing the standard agreement of purchase and sale containing the above clause, has agreed to accept title subject to any restrictions which are in compliance. It is therefore recommended that the words in italics above be deleted from all agreements. One should agree to buy only a title that is free from encumbrances.

In the usual situation where the purchaser has signed the agreement before asking for any advice from a lawyer and has agreed to accept covenants, all the lawyer can do is forward a copy of the restrictions to the client immediately after completing the search of title so that they do not later come as a great surprise.

Like easements, restrictive covenants merge if the dominant and servient tenements are purchased by the same person.

DISCHARGE OR MODIFICATION OF A COVENANT

At one time, there was nothing to prevent a restrictive covenant from running forever, as long as each purchaser of the servient tenement had notice. This tended to cause hardship because, through the years, the character of a particular district might have changed.

Thus, the legislature provided relief under s. 61(1) of the *Conveyancing and Law of Property Act*, R.S.O. 1990, c. C.34:

> 61(1) Where there is annexed to land a condition or covenant that the land or a specified part of it is not to be built on or is to be or not to be used in a particular manner, or any other condition or covenant running with or capable of being legally annexed to land, any such condition or covenant may be modified or discharged by order of the Superior Court of Justice.

You must prove to the judge that the benefit to the applicant greatly exceeds any possible detriment to the dominant tenement. An example of an order discharging restrictive covenants on this basis can be found in *Van Bork v. William Carson Holdings Ltd.*, [1998] O.J. No. 4523, 80 O.T.C. 40 (Gen. Div.).

Remember also that the *Conveyancing and Law of Property Act*, s. 22, voids any restriction made after March 24, 1950, concerning race, creed, colour, nationality, *etc.*

In many cases application to court is unnecessary because the covenants have time limits; they remain in force for a period of 20, 30 or 40 years from their original imposition. As well, restrictive covenants and building schemes expire automatically (unless re-registered) under s. 113 of the *Registry Act*, which provides for expiry of claims after expiry of the title search period, which is 40 years.

In a search of land under the Registry system, when you find restrictions on title that have expired, you may ignore them in your opinion on title (Your title notes should not ignore them; you want a record of the expiry date.) But you need not bother your client about them since they are no longer effective.

In a search of land under the Land Titles system, when you find restrictions that expired more than 10 years ago you may apply to the land registrar to have them removed from the register under s. 119(8) of the *Land Titles Act*, R.S.O. 1990, c. L.5. Otherwise, they remain on the register forever. The solicitor for the registered owner can make the necessary application and, upon payment of the fee, the land registrar automatically deletes reference to the restriction from the register.

If, in your Land Titles search, you find restrictions with no expiry date that have been registered for 40 years or more, the land registrar may delete them on application (s. 119(9)).

CHAPTER 8

Construction Liens

CONSTRUCTION LIEN ACT, R.S.O. 1990, c. C.30

A construction lien is a lien in favour of people who perform any work or service upon or who furnish any materials for construction, repair or alteration of a building. The lien attaches to the land upon which the construction takes place. It includes the right, in addition to ordinary creditor's rights, to sell the land and apply the proceeds to the debt.

There was no such lien at common law, nor is there one in England to this date. There, anyone doing work on another's land has just the ordinary rights of a creditor to sue in the courts on the contract of employment for the amount due. Obviously, in England, there is little chance of collecting. It takes months, maybe years, for an ordinary action to get into court, and by that time the owner may have sold the land and moved elsewhere. In Ontario, as in all other provinces of Canada and most states in the United States, construction or builders' lien legislation has been enacted for the protection of workers and suppliers.

CLAIM FOR LIEN

The right to the lien arises when the first work or service is performed (s. 15), but a lien claim is seldom registered at this stage. The carpenter, electrician, ready-mix concrete supplier or bricklayer usually expects to be paid and may even expect some delay. Many supply contracts call for payment 30 days after delivery. If that time goes by without payment, the supplier or worker must act.

Under the Act, construction liens will expire if they are not "preserved", *i.e.*, registered, within 45 days. However, the commencement (and, therefore, expiry) of this 45-day period varies with the type of lien claimant. Section 31 sets out the expiry periods, which are as follows:

1. For contractors (those who have privity of contract with the owner), the period starts to run on the earlier of:

    (i)   the publication of a certificate or declaration of substantial performance under s. 32; and

    (ii) the date the contract is completed or abandoned. Note that, under s. 2(3), a contract is deemed to be completed when the value of work remaining to be done or corrected is not more than 1 per cent of the contract price or $1,000 (whichever is less).

2.   Liens of other persons supplying services or materials (*i.e.*, subcontractors) will expire 45 days after the earliest of:

(i)   publication of a s. 32 certificate or declaration of substantial performance of the head contract;

(ii)   the date materials and services were last supplied under the subcontract; and

(iii) the date a subcontract is certified complete under s. 33.

Note that the concept of deemed completion under s. 2(3) has been found not to apply to subcontracts: *Woodmere (Credit Valley) Ltd. v. Sarcevich*, [1998] O.J. No. 2673, 40 O.R. (3d) 543 (C.A.).

A lien may be preserved (*i.e.*, registered) during the supplying of materials or services or at any time before it expires. Usually, you as lawyer will be asked on about the 44th day to prepare and file the claim for lien. The requirements of the form of this document are contained in s. 34(5). It must be verified by affidavit and a copy registered in the appropriate land registry office. Then, you should notify the owner of the land and the person liable on the contract in order to prevent progress draws being made under the contract without provision for your client's lien. You should also notify any encumbrancers apparent from the registered title and the general contractor if your claim is against a subcontractor. Mere registration is not enough; you must actually notify the owner or contractor in order to maximize your client's rights.

Usually, this action itself is sufficient to get your client paid. Once a lien claim is registered on title, the owner cannot sell the land until it is discharged. And, even more important in a large project, the owner will not get any more advances on a mortgage loan.

In some cases, if the owner disputes the amount claimed, or says that the work was not properly done, but is desperate to get ahead with the project, the owner may pay the amount claimed into court under s. 44(1) together with the lesser of $50,000 or 25 per cent of the claim on account of estimated court costs, and the court will then issue an order discharging the lien. The money is held in lieu of the lien on the land until a court action decides how much is really owing, but title is cleared.

LEASES

A contractor who does work for a tenant has a special problem. His lien will be limited to the leasehold interest of the tenant unless he first gives notice to the landlord under s. 19 and the landlord does not reply within 15 days with a notice that it will not be responsible for the work. A landlord may be prepared to allow the lien to attach to its freehold interest in the premises if the work will add value to the premises and the contractor will not otherwise proceed. If a lien is registered against the leasehold interest only, the landlord must give notice to the contractor of its intention to terminate the lease for non-payment of rent and the contractor may protect its claim by curing the default. However, the ability to realize the lien by selling the lease may encounter procedural difficulties (usually the landlord's consent is required) and the lease itself may have little value. A contractor working for a tenant usually finds little protection under the *Construction Lien Act*.

SUBSTANTIAL PERFORMANCE

There are detailed procedural rules set forth in s. 32 for certifying substantial performance of a contract. The test itself is set forth in s. 2 of the Act: the work must be ready for use or actually be used for its intended purpose, and the cost to complete the contract must not exceed the aggregate of the following percentages of the contract price:

1.   3 per cent of the first $500,000;

2.   2 per cent of the next $500,000; and

3.   1 per cent of the balance.

The certification is usually done by an architect or engineer employed by the owner to supervise the contract. If there is no such person, the owner and the contractor can jointly determine that substantial performance has been achieved and sign the certificate.

The crucial point to remember is that the time periods for lien registration do not begin to run until the certificate is published in a construction trade newspaper (usually the *Daily Commercial News*). This requirement is often not followed, especially with smaller contracts. In fact, many owners and contractors still follow the practice under the old *Mechanics' Lien Act*, R.S.O. 1980, c. 261, of releasing the holdback after the prescribed period has elapsed from the date of the certificate, without any publication of the certificate. The result is that the owner is taking the risk that subcontractors who are not paid may file valid lien claims after release of the holdback, and the owner will be liable for the holdback all over again.

It is important that the certificate be in the proper form (Form 6) and be properly issued. If not, it may not be valid and the lien period will not begin to run even if it is published (see *L.A. Legault Electric Ltd. v. 951034 Ontario Inc.*, [1995] O.J. No. 2064 (Gen. Div.).

GENERAL LIEN

If an owner enters into a single contract for improvements to more than one property, s. 20 permits a lien-holder to have a general lien against each property for the price of all services and materials supplied to all the properties.

The general lien overcomes the difficulty a supplier of materials and services might have in pinpointing the actual property that benefited from the materials or services. This problem occurs frequently in the case of subdivision housing construction.

The general lien must be registered against every property to which it is intended to apply. The general lien may be discharged against any property without disturbing its application to the rest of the properties.

LIENING CONDOMINIUM COMMON ELEMENTS

Condominium property presents a special problem when it comes to registering a construction lien. While it is simple to register a lien for work done in an individual unit (the lien is simply registered against that unit), there is some confusion over how you register against the common elements of a condominium where the work has been done for the condominium corporation, in view of the fact that the common elements and general index register no longer exists in the land registration systems.

First is the problem of description, which may be solved by referring to "all the units and common elements" of the identified condominium corporation (these together make up the "property" of the condominium). However, if the title has been automated, you may then have to list all the property identification numbers ("PINs") for the units, often an onerous and time-consuming job as well as one easily susceptible of typographical errors.

More important is the issue of who to list as "owner". Here practitioners disagree. Some believe it sufficient to list only the condominium corporation as owner, since it is clear that when you issue the certificate of action, you may sue the corporation alone as representative of the owners (s. 23(5)) of the *Condominium Act, 1998*, S.O. 1998, c. 19). Others, however, point out that the Act makes no such provision with respect to the original registration of the lien and it may be necessary to list all the owners of the individual units. This will obviously result in a great deal of subsearching cost and time required to prepare the lien (time which you may not have available given the lateness with which the claimant usually makes the decision to file the lien).

CERTIFICATE OF ACTION

If your client is still unpaid, and the lien has not been ordered discharged, then you must "perfect" the claim by commencing an action. The lien claim cannot be perfected unless it has been preserved. If an action has not been commenced within 90 days after the work has been substantially completed (*i.e.*, 45 days after the last day on which it could have been preserved under s. 31), and a certificate of that action registered on title, once again the lien "expires" (s. 36(2)).

DISCHARGING LIENS

It is usually easier to register a construction lien than it is to clear it from title, especially if a certificate of action has been registered. The procedure described in s. 41 of the Act has been confirmed by the Director of Titles in Registrars Bulletin No. 96002 issued on November 26, 1996.

If no certificate of action has been registered, then a release in the prescribed form will be sufficient to clear the lien from title. However, if a certificate of action has been registered, then it will be necessary to obtain a release from every person who has registered a lien, as well as everyone named as plaintiff in the certificate of action, before the liens and certificates will be removed from title. This is because of the possibility that the other liens may be "sheltering" under the registered certificate of action. In this case, the liens and certificates of action will be removed from title immediately in the Land Titles system. However, remember that, in the Registry system, they can only be ruled off two years later.

Otherwise, in order to get a lien and certificate of action off title, it will be necessary to obtain an order discharging the lien and vacating the certificate of action. Even then, it may not be possible to obtain the order unless you demonstrate by affidavit evidence that there are no other liens that can shelter under the registered certificate of action. This will be so even where the order is being obtained upon payment into court of the amount claimed and costs.

Under s. 46(1), any person may apply after two years for an order discharging the lien and vacating the certificate of action. The point of this provision is that an owner should not be prejudiced by a construction lien claimant who commences the action and then does nothing. If two years have gone by and no further action has been taken, the owner may apply *ex parte*, and the judge may vacate the certificate and discharge the lien.

HOLDBACK PROVISIONS

You must also remember the holdback provisions under s. 22. Anyone liable on a contract must hold back payment of 10 per cent of the amount owing until all liens relating to the holdback have expired.

The Act provides separate holdbacks for the work prior to substantial performance and for the finishing work (s. 22). Therefore, the initial holdback should not be released until 45 days after the publication of the certificate of substantial performance. The finishing holdback is released 45 days after total completion of the contract. In both cases, a prior subsearch is performed to ensure no liens have been registered.

There may be several levels of holdback. The owner pays the general contractor; the general contractor pays the subcontractor who has the contract for, for example, the floors and ceilings; the subcontractor in turn pays its suppliers and workers, the wage earners. Each of these should retain the statutory holdback of 10 per cent for 45 days, excepting of course payments to the workers. However, contractors will often rely on the owner's holdback to cover their liability. If at the end of 45 days no lien has been registered, the holdback may be paid out; but it cannot be paid in full if a lien has been registered. At the very least, the owner will retain enough to cover the lien and costs.

If an owner requires a title cleared immediately by an order of discharge, the owner must pay into court the full amount of the claim, plus costs, which often amount to as much as 25 per cent of the claim. Then, on the subsequent trial of the construction lien action, the court will determine the amount payable by the owner under the holdback provisions and will order the return of any excess to the owner: *James Dick Construction Ltd. v. Durham Board of Education*, [2000] O.J. No. 3278, 50 O.R. (3d) 308 (Div. Ct.). The actual holdback will then be divided among the lien claimants *pro rata*. This will often work a considerable hardship upon the owner because of the possibility of having to pay into court an amount far in excess of the amount of holdback required under the Act.

Nevertheless, the court will take the position that until the action is heard, there is no way of ascertaining the amount actually owing on the contract, and therefore, no way of knowing the amount of the holdback.

In the past, it was a common practice of contractors to register liens for the full amount of their contracts, even though the value of the work actually done was far less. Not only did they avoid the risk of registering for less than they were entitled, they also increased the pressure and their bargaining position with the owner who then had to post security for the entire amount plus costs in order to get the lien discharged by a court. To inhibit this practice, the Act now makes a person who registers a lien for a grossly exaggerated amount liable for the damages caused (s. 35), which of course could be very large, and also makes those who assist in registering it liable to an order for costs (s. 86(1)(*b*)). The latter provision strikes directly at the solicitor who prepares and registers the lien.

If the person liable on the contract does not hold back the required amount, that person will still be liable for that amount, with the possibility of having to pay twice. For example, assume the owner pays the general contractor in full, and the contractor in turn does not pay the subcontractor. The subcontractor files a lien. The owner will be liable to pay that lien up to the required 10 per cent holdback, even though payment has already been made to the general contractor. If, however, the owner had held back moneys as required under the Act, that money would entirely cover the liability.

EFFECT ON HOUSE PURCHASERS

What is the effect of all this on a prospective house purchaser? Is the purchaser liable for liens filed by persons working on that house?

If a purchaser agrees to buy a house that is under construction or renovation and closes when the work is complete, the purchaser will register the transfer after making a subsearch. If no liens are registered at that time, the purchaser is free of any such claim. Remember that the lien period may not have expired, but the provisions of ss. 70 and 71 of the *Registry Act*, R.S.O. 1990, c. R.20, govern priority of registration. The purchaser is "a *bona fide* purchaser for value without notice" of any claim, and, therefore, takes free from any subsequently registered construction lien. The subsequent registration of a lien will clutter the title but the purchaser will not be liable to pay any moneys to the lien claimant.

The situation is quite different where the purchaser agrees to purchase "according to sample". In new subdivisions, the purchaser chooses a vacant lot and then agrees to buy that lot, and the vendor agrees to erect a house exactly like the model, which may have a name or a number, for example:

> The vendor agrees that it will erect on the real property a dwelling of type P3270G Elevation C in accordance with plans and specifications filed with CMHC.

While this type of contract appears to bring purchasers within the definition of "owner" under s. 1(1) of the Act, they will not be subject to the holdback requirements so long as they fit within the definition of "home buyer" under s. 1(1). There are two key ingredients: first, they must not pay more than 30 per cent of the purchase price prior to closing, and second, closing must not occur until an occupancy certificate is issued by the municipality, or a certificate of completion and possession is issued under the *Ontario New Home Warranties Plan Act*, R.S.O. 1990, c. O.31.

TRUST FUNDS

Notwithstanding that a contractor has lost its lien rights, it still may have a claim to funds paid on account of the project. Sections 7 to 9 of the Act provide that funds paid to anyone (including the owner) in relation to a construction contract are to be held in trust for those who have done work or supplied materials because of the contract. For example, a mortgagee who applied funds advanced under a construction mortgage to pay down other indebtedness owed to it by the owner was held to have breached the trust provisions of the Act and ordered to make the funds available to those who worked on the project (see *G.C. McDonald Supply Ltd. v. Preston Heights Estates Ltd.*, [1992] O.J. No. 1634, 10 O.R. (3d) 409 (Gen. Div.)).

One special issue is worthy of note. Under s. 7(3) of the Act, after substantial performance has been certified, "any funds in the hands of the owner" are deemed to be trust funds for the benefit of the contractor until it is paid in full. This is a far-reaching principle. In *Structural Contracting Ltd. v. Westcola Holdings Inc.*, [2000] O.J. No. 2131, 48 O.R. (3d) 417 (C.A.), an owner of an office building was found to have breached its trust obligations when rents (including additional rents) received from tenants were used to pay operating expenses of the building rather than the contractor who had renovated the underground parking garage. As a result, since surplus revenues were not available, the principal shareholder and director of the corporate owner was held personally liable to pay the contractors.

Application of this principle could have bizarre results. As discussed below, in certain circumstances, a mortgage will have priority over a construction lien. However, use of rental income to make payments under that mortgage rather than to the contractor (which may well happen where there is a dispute as to the amount owing to the contractor) could render the owner and its principals personally liable to the contractor for breach of trust. If, on the other hand, the rental income is not applied to make the mortgage payments, default will occur and the property could be sold with the result that the lien claimant loses out totally.

This was the result in *Re Veltri Metal Products Co.*, [2005] O.J. No. 3217, 201 O.A.C. 79 (C.A.), where the company's assets were sold by court order and all the proceeds were paid to the secured creditors who had priority over the lien claimants. The Court of Appeal dismissed the trust claims of the lien claimants on the basis that the proceeds of sale were not received, nor did they come into the hands of the owner so as to trigger the trust provisions of the Act.

Unlike the holdback, which is held for the benefit of those who are two rungs down the contractual ladder, these trust funds are for the benefit of the person with a direct contractual relationship to the person holding the funds. The funds are therefore susceptible to set off (*i.e.*, reduction) by the owner or payor under

s. 12 if he or she believes on reasonable grounds that there are deficiencies or incomplete work that justify withholding or reducing payments to the recipient.

PUBLIC WORKS

If the project is a public work for the Crown in right of Ontario, a person who has a claim must send notice by registered mail to the appropriate office of the Crown setting out the nature and amount of claim prior to expiry of the lien period. The address for service is prescribed by regulation. Most commonly, notice will have to be sent to the Director of Legal Services for the Ministry who issued the contract. Other recipients are set forth in s. 1 of R.R.O. 1990, Reg. 175 (as amended). The actual addresses can be found on the Ontario Government website at <http://www.gov.on.ca>.

In the case of work on municipal streets or roads, notice is given by registered mail to the clerk of the municipality.

The claim forms a charge on the holdback. The claimant is not entitled to a lien against the land.

MORTGAGE PRIORITIES

Too often in the past, when things went wrong financially with a project, lien claimants who had contributed to the value of a property would receive nothing because a mortgage had priority over their liens. In the *Construction Lien Act*, provisions (found in s. 78) were introduced to alleviate this harsh result. In effect, the lender who finances the construction is subject to the same holdback requirements as the owner. If the lender does not ensure that the holdback is maintained, the lender's mortgage will lose priority to the liens to the extent of any deficiency in the holdback.

A mortgage created prior to the commencement of construction will have priority only to the extent of the lesser of the amount advanced under it and the value of the property, in both cases at the time construction commences (s. 78(3)). This provision, which runs contrary to the usual priority rules under the *Registry Act* and the *Land Titles Act*, R.S.O. 1990, c. L.5, prevents an owner from prejudicing the contractors who contribute to the value of the property by arranging and having the entire amount of a construction mortgage advanced prior to the commencement of construction. A stark example of this principle is found in *Park Contractors Inc. v. Royal Bank of Canada*, [1998] O.J. No. 5714, 38 O.R. (3d) 290 (Gen. Div.) where the contractor who performed environmental clean-up work on a property was given complete priority over a mortgage that had been properly advanced well before the work commenced because the Court found that the property had no value at the time the work commenced due to the contamination.

Non-construction loans are subject to the usual rules of priority provided that no liens are registered at the time of advance and the mortgagee has received no written notice of a lien (s. 78(4)). It is this provision that causes a mortgagee to subsearch before every advance even though the mortgage is not intended for construction purposes. As a result, the lender who is making several advances under its mortgage will get actual notice of a subsequently registered mortgage or other interest, thus losing the priority apparently given to all subsequent advances under a mortgage pursuant to s. 73 of the *Registry Act*.

It is important that a mortgagee not advance funds in the face of any registered lien, even when arrangements have been made to obtain a discharge of the lien out of the mortgage proceeds. This peculiar requirement arises out of the wording of s. 78(4) of the *Construction Lien Act*, which gives priority to all liens (whether registered or not) over an advance made in the face of a registered lien (see *Boehmers v. 794561 Ontario Inc.*, [1993] O.J. No. 1805, 14 O.R. (3d) 781 (Gen. Div.), affd [1995] O.J. No. 304, 21 O.R. (3d) 771 C.A.)). Charron J. of the Ontario Court (General Division) has given a full summary of this situation in *J. Sousa Contractor Ltd. v Kinalea Development Corp.*, [1994] O.J. No. 1465, 17 C.L.R. (2d) 94, affd [1996] O.J. No. 1337 (Div. Ct.). A mortgagee who discovers a registered lien (or has written notice of one) must insist that the borrower obtain and register a discharge employing personal funds before the advance under the mortgage is made. The Court of Appeal for Ontario upheld the lower Court's decision that a solicitor was negligent for advancing mortgage funds while a construction lien remained on title even though the solicitor had paid from the advance the full amount owing on that construction lien (see *Ron Miller Realty Ltd. v. Honeywell, Wotherspoon*, [1993] O.J. No. 4128, 16 O.R. (3d) 255 (C.A.)).

Because you can no longer be certain that a mortgage registered before any liens are registered has priority over those liens, a mortgagee when conducting a power of sale is now required in the Land Titles system to obtain an order discharging the liens and vacating all certificates of action. The same practice should presumably be followed with reference to *Registry Act* lands. The mortgagee proves its priority to the court, which then issues the appropriate order.

CHAPTER 9

Personal Property Security Act

More often than not, a real property practitioner involved in the purchase, sale, leasing or financing of land will find that there are interests in personal property that form part of the transaction. In the purchase of a house, the personal property may consist of furnishing or appliances, whereas in the purchase of a commercial or industrial property, there may be maintenance equipment, specialized operating system components or inventories of materials needed for the daily operation of the property, which the purchaser of the real property will also acquire or which a lender to that purchaser will want as security for its loan. Given this reality, a solicitor acting on any of these transactions must understand the statutory framework governing personal property and how it affects title to and the charging of the personalty involved.

The *Personal Property Security Act*, R.S.O. 1990, c. P.10 ("PPSA") governs the taking of security in personal property, including equipment, inventory, accounts and consumer goods such as automobiles, television sets, refrigerators, and stoves (sometimes called chattels), and referred to under the Act as collateral. The PPSA provides for a system of registration of security interests in personal property in Ontario. The PPSA does not, however, deal with title to personal property or create a statutory framework by which title to chattels can be determined. Unlike the *Land Titles Act*, R.S.O. 1990, c. L.5 and *Registry Act*, R.S.O. 1990, c. R.20 and their provisions relating to real property titles and the registers maintained to confirm ownership, there is no search that can be done under the PPSA to confirm that the person selling or charging its interest in personal property is the owner. Similarly, where the *Land Titles Act* and *Registry Act* create rules for establishing priorities among persons with registered interests in real property, the PPSA and the registry maintained thereunder cannot be as determinative of priorities since order of registration will not, of itself, determine priority. Still, the provisions of this Act must be understood not only to deal properly with personalty that accompanies real property being acquired or charged, but also to understand those areas where there is an overlap between real property law and personal property law.

The first step in the creation of a security interest in personal property is the entry into of a "security agreement". The security agreement may take different forms, such as a chattel mortgage, a conditional sale contract or an equipment lease with an option to purchase. For the purposes of the PPSA, the key is whether the agreement gives the creditor some kind of security interest in the collateral; if so, the security interest must be perfected under the PPSA either by registration or by taking possession of the collateral, in order to preserve the creditor's rights against other persons claiming an interest in the same goods.

A chattel mortgage is similar to a land mortgage in that the owner of the chattel conveys the legal title to the creditor as security for repayment of the loan. Under a conditional sale agreement, the purchaser does not get the legal title until all of the payments due are made. The purchaser has possession but the vendor has title.

REGISTRATION

Once a written security agreement is executed by the debtor, which agreement must contain a detailed description of the personal property involved, a secured party registers a "financing statement" under the PPSA in order to perfect the interest. The actual security agreement is never registered. The Act creates one centralized personal property security registry system where all registrations are made. It is an automated and electronic system. While paper registrations were previously allowed, effective August 1, 2007, the Personal Property Security Registration system became a fully electronic intake system with registration services available through the Internet at the ServiceOntario Access Now site found at <http://www.gov.on.ca>.

Registration "does not constitute constructive notice or knowledge to or by third parties of the existence of the financing statement" (s. 46(5)(*a*)). However, registration will, with certain exceptions, determine who has priority with respect to competing security interests in the same goods. In general, the first to register is entitled to priority.

Note that once a secured party registers a financing statement, that party is obligated to deliver a copy of it to the debtor within 30 days. Failure to do so results in a liability to pay a $500 "fine" to the debtor, collectable in Small Claims Court.

Only essential information is required to be entered into the electronic financing statement, including the borrower's name, address and date of birth, the lender's name and address, the registration period, classification of collateral and other specific information depending on the type of loan involved. Although not necessary, it is often desirable to include a detailed description of the collateral in order to avoid unnecessary enquiries in the future. For example, it will be helpful to indicate that the financing statement relates to a single project where it is given in connection with a construction loan or a site-specific mortgage.

Although it is a simple form to complete, its preparation should be undertaken carefully as, pursuant to s. 46(4), any error in its completion that is likely to mislead a person may invalidate its registration.

Except with respect to consumer goods, a secured party may register a financing statement either before or after the security agreement is signed by the debtor (s. 45(3)). One financing statement will suffice to perfect one or more security interests created or provided for in one or more security agreements between the same parties.

The PPSA permits different registration periods. A secured party may register a financing statement for a finite number of years, or for a perpetual period. (Note that the fee for perpetual registration, which is $500, is significantly higher than that for finite registration, which is $8 per year for one to 25 years.) Under s. 51(5) of the Act, if the collateral described in a financing statement is or includes consumer goods, then the financing statement shall be deemed to have a registration period of five years or less if so specified. All registration periods, including those with respect to consumer goods, may be extended or decreased by the registration of a financing change statement under s. 52(1).

Registrants must be careful and follow the registration requirements contained within the Act and its regulations, as any error could lead to the registration being invalid. Errors involving the name of the debtor have resulted in the most case law. Natural persons who are debtors must have their first name, middle initial, if any, and surname set out, followed by their date of birth. Corporate debtors must be identified by the name of the corporation set out in its articles of incorporation. If there is both a French form of name and an English form of name, or a combination thereof, both names must be set out. If the debtor is a general or limited partnership, the registered name under the *Business Names Act*, R.S.O. 1990, c. B.17 or *Limited Partnerships Act*, R.S.O. 1990, c. L.16, as applicable, must be used. For technical assistance, practitioners can access an application form, which can be completed and then sent to the Ministry of Government Services at the address below:

Companies and Personal Property Security Branch
PPSR Technical Support
393 University Avenue, Suite 200
Toronto, ON
M5G 2M2

The secured party should register a financing change statement to record any amendment to the registered information as the secured party becomes aware of the change, for example, in a name or address. This is also how amendments to, or discharges of the security agreement are recorded. The failure to register a financing change statement in certain circumstances will jeopardize the continued perfection of a security interest. If the debtor has changed names or transferred interest in the collateral to someone who assumes the security agreement, the secured party must register a financing change statement recording the new debtor's name within 30 days of learning of this change in order to preserve the rights.

A financing change statement must also be filed renewing the original registration before it expires. A renewal may be for any number of years except where the collateral is consumer goods in which case renewals are restricted to the same one- to five-year period as the original registration. If a secured party does not renew a registration before its expiry, the registration can be "reperfected" by registering a new financing statement rather than a financing change statement (see s. 52(2)). This "reperfection" gives the secured party continued perfection of its security interest from the date of the original registration of the financing statement that had expired; however, the new registration will not be effective against intervening registrants who have registered financing statements against the same collateral between the date of the original registration's expiry and the registration of the new financing statement. Priority will be lost to these registrants.

Land is immoveable and thus it is easy to organize registration systems under which searches are conducted in reference to the land. However, with chattels and other personal property, searches must be conducted on a "name" basis, that is, by searching against the name of the apparent owner or debtor. The difficulty is that there may be registrations affecting the chattels, which will not be disclosed unless you know the names of previous owners. It will be important to enquire as to the chain of ownership of the goods.

SEARCHES

Searches are conducted under the PPSA against individuals and business debtors, and in respect of motor vehicles by vehicle identification number via the Internet at the Government of Ontario website through Access Now. Telephone searches are also available. The fee for a verbal, printed or certificate response is $8 plus an extra $2 if the search was conducted by telephone. There are additional fees for Branch Office documents (including chattel mortgages and assignments of book debts, Central Office documents (including financing and financing change statements) and *Corporation Securities Registration Act*, R.S.O. 1980, c. 94 registrations. The information retrieved will depend on the type of property searched.

If your search discloses a registration that appears to affect chattels you are interested in, you have the right under the PPSA to require the secured party to give you a copy of the security agreement and a statement of account. If the secured party does not respond within 15 days of a request or gives an incorrect response, the secured party becomes liable for any resulting loss (s. 18(5)).

A solicitor acting for a purchaser of real property that includes chattels as part of the transaction, should search against the vendor under the PPSA to ensure that no one else claims a prior interest in those chattels. If the vendor is a corporation, a PPSA search should also be done on past names of the corporation and on any corporations that may have amalgamated with and are now continued with the corporation in its current form.

Once the search results are obtained, each outstanding registration will have to be reviewed to determine whether the personal property in the transaction at issue is affected. If, for example, in the purchase of an industrial building, equipment used in the building was being acquired together with the land, searches against the vendor that revealed security interests in the vendor's inventory will not be a concern and can be ignored. Similarly, registrations against the vendor where the equipment category is checked but where a description is then provided that clearly does not relate to the equipment being purchased, can also be ignored.

If the result of a PPSA search against a vendor reveals registrations, which do or may affect the personal property that is being acquired or charged in the transaction at hand, a purchaser or lender must ensure a discharge of the registrations that definitely relate to the collateral being acquired or charged is obtained. For general registrations against the entire class of a person's personal property, such as equipment, it is often expected that the vendor or borrower will approach the secured party in whose favour the general registration is made to obtain a "comfort" letter in which the secured party confirms that its interest in the vendor's equipment, for example, only relates to specific equipment or that it does not relate to the equipment at issue in the specific transaction at hand. Receiving such an estoppel letter comforts a purchaser or mortgagee and gives them assurances that the registrations in favour of such secured parties can be ignored.

As a last resort, s. 18(1) of the Act requires a secured party with an outstanding registration to produce information about the specific collateral it claims a security interest in and the debt that is secured by that collateral. This would allow a purchaser to satisfy itself in respect of the registration by reviewing the underlying security agreement or information derived therefrom.

Note that new subsections 56(2.2) and (2.3) have been added to the Act (by S.O. 2010, c. 16, Sched. 5) to permit a debtor to require a secured party to register a financing change statement to limit the collateral description in an already registered financing statement where the collateral description is broader than the security agreement provides. This will help debtors who are doing new financing to reduce future costs in obtaining waivers or "no interest" letters from existing secured parties.

PRIORITIES

Part III of the PPSA deals with perfection of security interests and priorities. As in the land registration systems, priorities are for the most part determined by the order of registration. However, unlike a mortgagee, a secured party who has registered may safely advance in the face of subsequent security agreements that have not been perfected by registration even though there is actual notice of them (s. 20).

There are complex rules to deal with other methods of establishing priority, such as taking possession of certain types of collateral. In addition, special status is accorded those who finance the purchase of chattels, so long as they register their security interest before the debtor obtains possession of the collateral or within 10 days after the collateral comes under the debtor's control. These are known as purchase-money security interests ("PMSI"). If the holder of a PMSI registers within the above time limit, the PMSI will have priority over any other security interest in the same collateral granted by the same debtor.

FIXTURES

Fixtures are chattels that have become attached to the land or buildings on the land in such a way so as to become part of the land. The manner and degree of affixation are two of several criteria that the common law considers in assessing whether a chattel has become a fixture (see *Stack v. T. Eaton Co.*, [1902] O.J. No. 155, 4 O.L.R. 335 (Div. Ct.)). If the criteria are not met, the chattel is still a chattel at common law; if the criteria are met, the chattel has been converted into a fixture, and therefore converted into realty.

The definition of "goods" in the PPSA, however, includes fixtures. This means that fixtures are personal property for the purposes of the PPSA but also real property at common law. As a result, there may be a conflict between those who claim an interest in the land and those who claim an interest in only the chattels that have become fixtures.

This conflict is addressed by s. 34(1) of the PPSA, which provides a set of rules for determining priorities between holders of perfected security interests in fixtures and persons claiming an interest in the real property to which the goods are affixed. Those rules are as follows:

    (a)   A creditor who obtained a security interest in goods under the PPSA prior to the goods becoming a fixture will have priority over anyone with an interest in the land, such as a mortgagee or the owner.

    (b)   On the other hand, a security interest in goods obtained by a creditor after the goods became fixtures will be subordinate and subject to any interest in the real property that existed at the time of the attachment of the goods to the real estate.

    (c)   A secured creditor who has a security interest in goods that have become fixtures may register a notice of security interest pursuant to s. 54 of the Act against title to the land to preserve its rights against subsequent purchasers or mortgagees.

    (d)   A mortgagee's subsequent advances under a mortgage that was registered before a creditor acquired a security interest in goods that have become fixtures, will also have priority over the PPSA creditor until the PPSA creditor registers a notice of security interest on title to the lands.

As a result, when acting for a purchaser or mortgagee of land, if a notice of security interest has not been registered and there is no actual notice of a security interest, you do not need to concern yourself about prior security interests in fixtures arising under the PPSA.

A secured party with a security interest in a fixture that has priority over persons with an interest in the real property may remove the fixture upon the default of the debtor under its security agreement. Pursuant to s. 34(3), such removal is permitted as long as the owner is reimbursed for any damage caused by the removal but not for any diminution in the value of the real property as a result of the removal. Prior to removing the fixture, the secured party must serve a notice on each person having an interest in the real property indicating its intention to remove the fixture after 10 days unless it is paid the outstanding obligation under the security agreement that gave rise to the security interest. If the obligation is not satisfied, the removal can proceed.

Finally, s. 56 of the Act requires a secured party to deliver a registerable discharge of a notice of security interest once the security agreement is performed. Failure to do so results in a $500 fine payable to the debtor whose land is still subject to the notice together with liability for any other damages incurred by the debtor as a result of the registration remaining.

ASSIGNMENT OF RENTS

Rents payable under real property leases represent another area of overlap between personal property law and real property law. A lease and the right to rents payable thereunder are interests in land and as such are often assigned by an owner to a mortgagee as collateral security to a mortgage by a security document known as a general assignment of rents. However, s. 4(1)(*e*) of the PPSA provides that the right to receive a payment under a lease and the assignment of that payment where the assignment does not transfer the assignor's interest in the real property falls within the scope of the PPSA. As a result, there may be a conflict between those secured claims in the income stream originating from leases that arise under the PPSA, and those that are created by real property registrations.

Section 36(1) of the PPSA attempts to resolve the conflict between the two systems. It provides that a security interest in any right to a payment under a lease perfected under the PPSA is subordinate to the interest of any person who acquires for value the lessor's interest in the lease or real property provided that the acquisition of the interest is registered in the applicable land registry office before the PPSA claimant registers a notice in the same land registry office. As a result, a purchaser for value of the real property without such notice acquires the right to receive the rents originating from leases of the property unencumbered by any security interest perfected under the PPSA.

Unfortunately, s. 36(1) only effects a subordination of the interest of the secured creditor under the PPSA to the purchaser of the real property. It does not deem the security interest to no longer be effective or cause the security interest to be discharged. While the subordination concept in s. 36(1) should suffice to allow a purchaser of real property to ignore the PPSA in determining what security interests affect rents being acquired and to concentrate on title searches alone, the fact is that the standard for most purchases is that title to all components of the property, including leases and rents, be acquired free and clear of all security interests and not just in priority thereto. As a result, real property practitioners involved in transactions where the income stream from rents is significant will not normally be satisfied with the subordination comfort contained in s. 36(1) and will search for outstanding PPSA interests that affect the rents and require their discharge. Furthermore, the fact that s. 73 of the Act states that the PPSA prevails over the *Registry Act* and *Land Titles Act* also causes practitioners to take a more conservative approach and require security interests in rents under the PPSA to be discharged to avoid any possible claim of priority by such secured creditors as a result of this paramountcy.

In mortgage transactions, registrations under both systems are required. A mortgagee will require registration of a general assignment of leases and rents on title to the property and will also register a financing statement to perfect the security interest in the rents created by that same general assignment. This allows the mortgagee to assert priority over other security creditors in those same rents in reliance on the normal PPSA priority rules contained in the Act for all perfected security interests and also on the provisions contained in s. 36.

REGISTERING SECURITY AGREEMENTS THAT AFFECT LAND

Normally, lenders taking a security interest in lands register a mortgage on title to the lands and, where there are rents involved, register an assignment of rents and leases on title to the lands as collateral security thereto. However, where there are significant personal property interests also to be secured, some of which affect fixtures, lenders may choose to use debentures or general security agreements as a single security document by which all interests, both real and personal, are charged. You may register a debenture or general security agreement against land if it contains a registerable description of the land. If the debenture or security agreement does not contain a registerable description, it will still be possible to register it by attaching it to a s. 25 declaration under the *Registry Act* or by registering a notice under s. 71 of the *Land Titles Act*.

To register a debenture or security agreement against land, you may use either Form 2 (Charge/Mortgage of Land) or Form 4 (Document General). In general, it is preferable to use Form 2 and attach the debenture or security agreement to it as a schedule. Remember to specify whether or not you want the charge terms implied under the *Land Registration Reform Act*, R.S.O. 1990, c. L.4 to apply. Electronic registration regulations also allow such agreements to be registered electronically.

CHAPTER 10

Real Estate Agents

While there is no legal requirement that an agent be involved in an agreement of purchase and sale or in a real estate transaction, most agreements and transactions that you will deal with do involve an agent. Most agreements for the purchase and sale of residential property use a printed form created by and for local real estate associations and their agents. In this chapter, certain matters concerning real estate agents' duties and their right to payment of commission are brought to your attention. A brief review of the *Real Estate and Business Brokers Act, 2002*, S.O. 2002, c. 30, Sched. C (the "Act") also follows.

LISTING AGREEMENT

The listing agreement is the contract between a property owner and a real estate agent. For the form of the listing agreement used by the Toronto Real Estate Board, please refer to Appendix 4. This contract sets out the terms on which the vendor is willing to sell. However, you should note that it is not an offer to sell and there is no legal requirement that the vendor accept any offer, even if the offer is on the terms set out exactly in the listing agreement.

The contract also contains an agreement as to the amount of commission to be paid, and the period during which the agent is authorized to sell the property. Under s. 11 of O. Reg. 580/05, passed pursuant to the Act, a listing period cannot be longer than six months unless the expiry date is prominently displayed and initialled. While previous agreements deemed the period to be extended for 90 days in the case of a purchaser who was introduced to the property or the vendor during the original listing period, the new Toronto Real Estate Board Listing Agreement allows the parties to agree to a specified extension period after the introduction. See *Terry Martel Real Estate Ltd. v. Lovette Investments Ltd.*, [1981] O.J. No. 3007, 32 O.R. (2d) 790, for a discussion by the Court of Appeal on the meaning of "introduction". This case involved a dispute between the two agents as to which one was entitled to the commission. The Court held that introduction of a person to a property means bringing the purchaser to the property for the first time. See also *Capital Real Estate Services Inc. v. Evangelisto*, [2002] O.J. No. 255 (S.C.J.) and *Hudson Highland Group Inc. v. Canada Life Assurance Co.*, [2007] O.J. No. 1878 (S.C.J.).

The extension clause is included to discourage an owner and a prospective purchaser from conspiring to avoid the agent's commission by postponing entering into a formal agreement of purchase and sale until a date beyond the expiry of the listing. The practical application of this extension clause is demonstrated in the case of *Royal LePage Real Estate Services Ltd. v. McArter*,

[2000] O.J. No. 349 (S.C.J.), affd [2002] O.J. No. 840 (Div. Ct.). At issue was the entitlement of an agent to a commission for a transaction where the agent had introduced a purchaser to the vendor during the currency of the listing agreement, but the purchase agreement was not signed until after it had expired but during the 90-day extension period, and the actual closing did not occur until after the 90-day extension had lapsed. In allowing the agent's claim for a commission, the Court held that the sale of the property to the purchaser was caught within the terms of the listing agreement's extension clause even though the sale of the property was not completed until the 90-day extension period had lapsed. The Court was of the view that entering into an enforceable purchase agreement during the extension period was sufficient to entitle the agent to a commission on the basis that the entry into such an agreement was akin to a sale that had been "effected" as required by the terms of the listing agreement.

The absence of a written listing agreement does not necessarily result in an obligation to pay a commission to an agent being avoided. In *Cash v. George Dundas Realty Ltd.*, [1973] O.J. No. 2158, 1 O.R. (2d) 241 (C.A.), affd [1975] S.C.J. No. 103, 59 D.L.R. (3d) 605, the Court held that an implied listing agreement existed where a vendor verbally agreed to pay an agent a commission if he found a purchaser. An agreement of purchase and sale was subsequently entered into and completed through the agent's efforts and as a result, the Court ruled that a commission was still payable.

However, in *Regional Group of Companies Inc. v. Assaly Construction Ltd.*, [2000] O.J. No. 2525, 34 R.P.R. (3d) 40 (S.C.J.), affd [2002] O.J. No. 724 (C.A.), the Courts refused to imply an agreement between a vendor and an agent. In this case, an exclusive listing arrangement was entered into between a vendor and an agent. A purchaser who had obtained information about the property for sale from the agent subsequently entered into an agreement to purchase the property and completed the transaction; however, the signing of the purchase agreement and the closing both occurred after the expiry of the 90-day holdover period and on very different terms than that contemplated by the original listing. In rejecting the agent's claim for a commission, the courts relied on s. 23 of the *Real Estate and Business Brokers Act*, R.S.O. 1990, c. R.4 (now repealed), which required a claim for a commission to be based on a written and signed listing agreement. The courts found no subsisting listing agreement in place and rejected the notion that any sort of equitable application of the said section was possible to allow recovery of the commission.

COMMISSION

Most forms of listing agreements contain the following provision:

I agree to pay you a commission of ___% of the sale price of my property on any sale or exchange from any source whatsoever effected during the currency of this agreement. ...

One of the leading cases on the interpretation of this clause is *Gladstone v. Catena*, [1948] O.J. No. 456, [1948] O.R. 182 (C.A.). At 190 O.R., Laidlaw J.A. quoted with approval comments of Lord Wright in *Luxor (Eastbourne) Ltd. v. Cooper*, [1941] A.C. 108 (H.L.):

> It may seem hard that an agent who has introduced a potential purchaser, able and willing to complete, should get nothing for what he has done, if, during the negotiations, the principal decides not to complete, according to his own pleasure and without any reason which *quoad* the agent is a sufficient excuse. But such is the express contract. And people in ordinary life do not seek the services of commission agents without a good prospect and intention of making use of them. The agent in practice takes what is a business risk.

The current listing agreement of the Toronto Real Estate Board ("TREB") has different commission language. It provides as follows:

> In consideration of the Listing Broker listing the Property, the Seller agrees to pay the Listing Brokerage a commission of ____% of the sale price of the Property or ____ for any valid offer to purchase the Property ...

The above language is similar to language found in some standard printed forms of agreement of purchase and sale, which often contain the following clause:

> The undersigned accepts the above Offer and agrees with the Agent above named in consideration for his services in procuring the said Offer, to pay him on the date above fixed for completion, a commission of ____% of an amount equal to the above mentioned sale price, which commission may be deducted from the deposit. I hereby irrevocably instruct my Solicitor to pay direct to the said Agent any unpaid balance of commission from the proceeds of the sale.

All careful solicitors acting for a vendor will change the agreement by deleting the words "on the date above fixed for completion" and substituting "on closing only" or "if and when this transaction is completed". Do not be misled by this seeming casualness about the commission clause; the wording is important and there are new cases every year in which agents sue to collect commissions on transactions that have not closed. From the agent's point of view, everything required by the contract was done; the agent introduced a willing purchaser to the owner on terms acceptable to the owner. If the owner subsequently declines to sell for some reason, and the agreement therefore is terminated, the agent still wants to be paid. In the case of *Nelson (Township) v. Stoneham*, [1957] O.J. No. 49, 7 D.L.R. (2d) 39, the Court of Appeal upheld the judgment of a lower court granting an agent his commission notwithstanding non-completion. In this case, the commission clause was the one quoted above without any amendment and Hogg J.A. had the following to say (at 43 D.L.R.):

> [W]hether an agent is entitled to a commission or not is dependent in each case upon the express terms of the particular contract with such agent. If the commission is to be paid upon the completion of the contract, then the mere procuring of an offer to purchase is not sufficient to entitle the agent to the commission. ... [I]n the case now under consideration, there is nothing said about

the commission being dependent upon the sale being effected or completed. ... The respondent [agent] was promised his commission if he procured for the appellant [owner] an offer for the land. ... It was not for effecting a sale, but for procuring the offer ... which was the consideration for the payment of the commission.

However, in a case before the Ontario Court of Appeal, *Leading Investments Ltd. v. New Forests Investments Ltd.*, [1981] O.J. No. 3112, 34 O.R. (2d) 175 (C.A.), which was affirmed by the Supreme Court of Canada (*sub nom. H.W. Liebig & Co. v. Leading Investments Ltd.*), [1986] S.C.J. No. 6, [1986] 1 S.C.R. 70, the vendor had signed a standard form listing agreement with the agent and subsequently had signed an agreement of purchase and sale that included the usual commission clause providing for payment on the date fixed for completion. Both courts held that the two documents must be read together and that the governing contract was the listing agreement. That agreement provided for payment of a commission on "any sale effected" during the currency of the listing. The courts held that the word "effected" meant sold; in other words, the sale needed to be completed before any commission was payable. See also *Royal Trust Corp. of Canada v. Christie*, [1984] O.J. No. 886, 23 A.C.W.S. (2d) 360 (Co. Ct.).

Interestingly, the current form of agreement of purchase and sale used by the Toronto Real Estate Board is much more clear. The clause on acceptance and commission now reads:

I, the Undersigned Seller, agree to the above Offer. I hereby irrevocably instruct my lawyer to pay directly to the brokerage(s) with whom I have agreed to pay commission, the unpaid balance of the commission together with applicable Harmonized Sales Tax (and any other taxes as may hereafter be applicable), from the proceeds of sale prior to any payment to the undersigned on completion, as advised by the brokerage(s) to my lawyer.

As is clear, the payment is stipulated to occur "on completion".

This is in contrast to the language quoted above in the standard TREB listing agreement, which refers to the commission being payable on procuring any valid offer. Given the decision in the *Leading Investments* case, which ruled that the listing agreement governed inconsistencies on commission terms between itself and the agreement of purchase and sale, practitioners must, if they get a chance before a client signs it, ensure that the listing agreement is amended to provide for payment of commissions only on closing of the sale.

Remember that the agent in most cases holds the deposit in a trust account as is required under s. 27 of the Act. Even if an agent does not go to court to collect the commission, it may well be difficult to persuade the agent to surrender the deposit if there is a dispute as to whether or not the commission is owing. For this reason, we suggest that the solicitor for the purchaser also has good reason to amend the commission clause.

There is no legal requirement as to the amount of a deposit, but in practice a real estate agent will usually persuade the purchaser to deposit an amount that will at least cover the agent's commission. This means that the agent will have no difficulty collecting the commission. If by chance the deposit is not sufficient, the agent is further protected by the inclusion of the direction to the vendor's solicitor to pay to the agent any unpaid balance. Annoying as it is for the solicitor to be put in the position of collecting the agent's commission, if it is a direction signed under seal and, provided that the solicitor receives the proceeds from the sale, the solicitor is probably bound by that direction.

In *Family Trust Corp. v. Morra*, [1987] O.J. No. 398, 60 O.R. (2d) 30 (Div. Ct.), a vendor was permitted to withdraw or rescind a direction to his solicitor to pay the agent's commission contained in a real estate board form of sale agreement, and the solicitor thereafter had no duty to pay to the agent. However, *Re/Max Garden City Realty Inc. v. 828294 Ontario Inc.*, [1992] O.J. No. 1080, 8 O.R. (3d) 787 (Gen. Div.) and *Re/Max Twin City Realty Inc. v. Do*, [2004] O.J. No. 2556 (S.C.J.), distinguished the *Morra* case on the basis that the agreement in that case was not under seal and there was no consideration given by the agent for the vendor's direction. In the *828294 Ontario* case, the agreement had a black circle with the word "Seal" under it; the Court held the direction was therefore enforceable and the vendor's solicitor was held to be liable for failing to ensure the commission was paid.

An agent's entitlement to a commission gets more complicated when a purchase agreement is entered into but, for some reason, is not completed. Even if a listing agreement or purchase agreement provides that a commission is not payable unless a sale is "effected", courts have awarded commissions to agents in circumstances where the closing has not occurred. For example, where a transaction does not close as a result of a breach by the vendor of the purchase agreement, courts have held that the vendor is liable to the agent for the commission that the agent would have otherwise earned on the transaction were it not for the vendor's breach, provided that the purchaser was ready to close. In both *Eades and Fenton v. Kukk*, [1972] O.J. No. 1798, [1972] 2 O.R. 802 (H.C.J.) and *Gill v. Pellington*, [1999] O.J. No. 1985, 25 R.P.R. (3d) 199 (S.C.J.), the Court held that the refusal of a vendor to close a transaction or the anticipatory breach by a vendor of a purchase agreement, both in circumstances where the purchaser was ready, willing and able to close, made the vendor liable to pay the agent the commission that would otherwise have been payable.

However, where a transaction does not close due to a purchaser's breach of a purchase agreement, an agent's ability to collect a commission will be determined by reference to the provisions of the listing agreement or purchase agreement and the triggering event specified (*i.e.*, procuring an offer, closing or effecting a sale). As we have seen earlier in this chapter, some courts interpret "sale" as meaning the entry into of a purchase agreement (due to the fact that beneficial title is transferred to the purchaser at that time), while others require the actual closing and registration of a transfer to occur.

DUTY OF AGENT TO VENDOR

One must always remember that a real estate agent is an agent for the vendor. This is confirmed by the very wording of the standard printed form. Yet, particularly where there is a multiple listing situation, a real estate agent is put in an impossible conflict of interest, which is well illustrated in *Canada Permanent Trust Co. v. Hutchings*, [1977] O.J. No. 1742, 3 R.P.R. 211 (Co. Ct.).

In that case, property was put on multiple listing for \$36,900. An agent (not the listing agent) showed the property to a client who had told the agent he wanted to spend between \$30,000 and \$38,000. An offer was prepared by the agent at \$33,000. The judge reviewed the evidence at length and stated (at 213 R.P.R.) that "[t]he price to be offered was arrived at after a discussion between the [purchaser and the agent] and it was obvious from the evidence that this was not the highest price that the [purchaser was] prepared to offer for the premises". The purchaser, in giving evidence, indicated that she had asked the agent if this would be a ridiculous offer and to that he apparently replied, "No, it would not be considered ridiculous". The judge stated that he was satisfied that the agent was aware that this was not the highest price the purchaser would pay.

There was a counter-offer at \$33,500, which was accepted by the purchaser; the vendor then changed his mind and refused to close. An action was commenced for specific performance and it was settled. Eventually, the sale was completed for \$33,500, and then the agent tried to collect his commission. The Court not only refused the agent his commission but allowed a counter-claim by the vendor for damages, and stated that the damages would be the difference between the highest price the purchaser would have paid and the price actually received.

Winter Co. Ct. J. (at 216 R.P.R.) emphasizes the agent's duty as follows:

> It is a common misconception among real estate agents and the public alike that the only duty of a real estate agent is to bring together a buyer and a seller at a price agreeable to both. It must be emphasized that a broker or agent should not and must not act on behalf of the vendor and purchaser. In that case his interest conflicts with his duty.

And (at 217 R.P.R.) he states that the vendors

> ... were entitled to full disclosure from [the agent] and he ought to have disclosed to them that the purchasers were prepared to pay a higher price or in any event, that this was not the highest offer that the purchasers were prepared to make.

See also *Wyne v. Martin*, [1968] B.C.J. No. 21, 62 W.W.R. 735 (S.C.), *D'Atri v. Chilcott*, [1975] O.J. No. 2208, 7 O.R. (2d) 249 (H.C.J.); and *Lewis v. Simcoe Real Estate Ltd.*, [1984] O.J. No. 2411, 33 R.P.R. 315 (Prov. Ct.).

The law is clear that real estate agents owe a fiduciary duty to their principals (vendors). This duty is a high one and goes well beyond a mere contractual obligation. In substance, the agents must at all times put the interests of their principals ahead of their own interests and must act with the utmost good faith. In *Raso v. Dionigi*, [1993] O.J. No. 670, 12 O.R. (3d) 580 (C.A.), an agent failed to disclose that the purchaser was the sister-in-law of the agent. The Court held that the vendors did not have to close, nor was the agent entitled to a commission.

However, in *Knoch Estate v. Jon Picken Ltd.*, [1991] O.J. No. 1394, 4 O.R. (3d) 385 (C.A.), the Court distinguished the duties of a selling agent acting for a purchaser from those of the listing agent. In this case, an agent was retained by a purchaser to find a new property. In the meantime, the agent learned of a property listed with another agent and arranged the sale of the property to a developer. While the negotiations between the vendor and the developer were ongoing (which subsequently culminated in an agreement of purchase and sale), the agent brought the property to the attention of the purchaser. Just before closing of the sale to the developer, the purchaser entered into an agreement to purchase the property from the developer at a substantially higher price than the developer was paying. The original vendor sued the selling agent, alleging that it had breached its fiduciary duty to the vendor by failing to disclose the existence of the ultimate purchaser and the fact that it was willing to pay a higher price.

The Court acknowledged that the selling agent was an agent of the listing agent, who owed a fiduciary duty to the vendor, but held that this relationship did not automatically impose a fiduciary duty on the selling agent. Griffiths J.A. held (at 398 O.R.) that:

> ... an agent in the position of Jenkins, as the selling agent, may be the agent of the vendor for limited purposes, which include authorization to present an offer to purchase and to receive notices to the vendor, as well as to make representations binding on the vendor. I would also agree that the selling agent is obligated not to deceive or mislead the vendor. But, in the absence of the characteristics of a true fiduciary relationship between the vendor and the selling agent, I do not think the law requires more of a selling agent than indicated above.

The first duty of an agent in a real estate transaction is to properly describe the property being sold, and to accurately set out the financing provisions. In *Charter-York Ltd. v. Hurst*, [1978] O.J. No. 2734, 2 R.P.R. 272 (H.C.J.), a real estate agent incorrectly described the boundaries of the farm that was the subject of the transaction. The purchaser refused to close and the Court refused to grant specific performance:

> Where a purchaser has been misled as to fundamental particulars by the vendor or his agent into purchasing something that he would otherwise have had no intention to purchase, the law is clear that there is no *ad idem* and hence no contract [at 278 O.R.].

LaBrosse J. stated (at 279 O.R.):

> In all such transactions, fundamental to the agent's contractual responsibility to the vendor was the duty to use reasonable care and skill to determine the exact property being sold.

Damages of up to $500,000 were awarded against the agent. (See also *449576 Ontario Ltd. v. Bogojevski*, [1984] O.J. No. 3184, 46 O.R. (2d) 161 (H.C.J.).)

An agent must, of course, also abide by contractual provisions specifically included in a listing agreement. Failure to do so will cause an agent to forfeit the commission, as in *Len Pugh Real Estate Ltd. v. Ronvic Construction Co.*, [1973] O.J. No. 2194, 1 O.R. (2d) 539 (Co. Ct.), vard (1975), 6 O.R. (2d) 454, 53 D.L.R. (3d) 71 (C.A.), where the agent failed to follow the vendor's instructions to vary the usual adjustment provisions in a purchase agreement, causing the vendor to accept an agreement without the change.

In *Apa v. McKay*, [1984] O.J. No. 1356, 28 A.C.W.S. (2d) 466 (H.C.J.), the real estate agent prepared an offer that misstated the terms of the mortgage to be assumed by the purchaser. The vendor failed to notice the error. The deal did not close and the vendor was successful in recovering not only damages for losses from the real estate agent, but also punitive damages. See also *Paul S. Starr & Co. v. Watson*, [1972] O.J. No. 1955, [1973] 1 O.R. 148 (C.A.) for another case where the agent's failure to properly draft a clause in a purchase agreement resulted in the agent losing his entitlement to a commission.

Finally, there is the situation where the agent is a purchaser or co-purchaser. In such situations, there is an even greater duty on the agent to the vendor. Specifically, the transaction "must be a righteous one and the price obtained must be as advantageous to the principal as any other price that the agent could, by the exercise of diligence on his principal's behalf, have obtained from a third person." See *Firoozi v. 809963 Ontario Ltd.*, [2005] O.J. No. 6233, 52 R.P.R. (4th) 93 at para. 99 (H.C.J.), reconsideration allowed [2006] O.J. No. 5317, 52 R.P.R. (4th) 115 (S.C.J.), citing *D'Atri v. Chilcott*, [1975] O.J. No. 2208, 55 D.L.R. (3d) 30 (H.C.J.).

DUTY OF AGENT TO PURCHASER

In *Avery v. Salie*, [1972] S.J. No. 42, 25 D.L.R. (3d) 495 (Q.B.), damages were awarded against an agent who was found to have been negligent because he did not check the particulars of an outstanding mortgage, and these particulars were in fact different than the vendor stated.

The doctrine of liability for negligent misstatement set out in *Hedley Byrne & Co. v. Heller & Partners*, [1963] 2 All E.R. 575, [1964] A.C. 465 (H.L.), is being used more and more in cases against agents. It was stated in *Chand v. Sabo Bros. Realty Ltd.*, [1977] A.J. No. 776, 81 D.L.R. (3d) 382 at 385 (T.D.), vard [1979] A.J. No. 828, 96 D.L.R. (3d) 445 (C.A.) as follows:

> I must consider the claim against the real estate agents based on their alleged breach of duty to the plaintiff on their negligent performance of a contract. The plaintiffs are relatively recent immigrants to Canada. This was their first purchase of a home and they were unfamiliar with the laws affecting such purchase. They, therefore, relied to a large extent on the real estate agent. However, the latter were agents of the vendor and there was no contractual undertaking with them towards the plaintiffs. But under the rule in *Hedley Byrne & Co. v. Heller & Partners Ltd.* ..., there was a duty to take care. Lord Morris of Borth-y-Gest stated as follows at 594 (All E.R.):
>
> > My lords, I consider that it follows and that it should now be regarded as settled that if someone possessed of a special skill undertakes, quite irrespective of contract, to apply that skill for the assistance of another person who relies on such skill, a duty of care will arise. ... Furthermore if, in a sphere in which a person is so placed that others could reasonably rely on his judgment or his skill or on his ability to make careful inquiry, a person takes it on himself to give information or advice to, or allows his information or advice to be passed on to, another person who, as he knows or should know, will place reliance upon it, then a duty of care will arise.
>
> . . . . .
>
> This principle applies in cases of real estate agents, there existing a quasi-fiduciary relationship between potential purchaser and a real estate company.

Olsen v. Poirier, [1978] O.J. No. 2729, 21 O.R. (2d) 642 (H.C.J.), affd [1980] O.J. No. 3489, 28 O.R. (2d) 744 (C.A.), concerns the purchase of a dairy farm in eastern Ontario by a recent immigrant to Canada. The immigrant was attracted to the purchase by an advertisement in a newspaper in Denmark placed by the real estate agent. The agent claimed to be an expert on dairy farms. The agent found the farm and negotiated an agreement, which was completed. Only after completion did the purchaser discover that the Ontario Milk Marketing Board had at that time a regulation that provided for reduction of the milk quota by 25 per cent in the event of a sale to anyone other than a member of the family. The Court ordered that the agreement should be rescinded and the purchaser's money returned. The Court found that the agent had made a negligent misrepresentation and ordered the full commission to be returned with costs.

Bango v. Holt, [1971] B.C.J. No. 119, 21 D.L.R. (3d) 66 (S.C.) deals with the negligence of an agent who was asked to find a "revenue producing property" for a purchaser. The agent found a property that was illegally being used as a duplex.

An agent is expected to know of recent changes to the law affecting the trade and to inform clients of them: *Cheng v. C.A. Fitzsimmons and Co.* (1982), 17 A.C.W.S. (2d) 153 (Ont. Co. Ct.).

Wong v. 407527 Ontario Ltd., [1996] O.J. No. 1030, 1 R.P.R. (3d) 245 (Gen. Div.), revd in part [1999] O.J. No. 3377, 26 R.P.R. (3d) 262 (C.A.) is another example of a situation in which an agent was found liable to a purchaser for the agent's negligence. In this case, the agent drafted a warranty in a purchase agreement intended to be a guarantee by the vendor in favour of the purchaser of the rents payable under leases of a property for the 12-month period after closing. Unfortunately, the vendor was a numbered company with no assets other than the property. The agent, in drafting the warranty, did not advise the purchaser of the risk of taking a warranty from an entity that would have no assets after closing, and did not draft the warranty to provide security for it. After closing, the purchaser was unable to collect rents from certain tenants and could not make up the loss upon enforcing the warranty. The Court held that, in such circumstances, a competent agent should have recognized the risk of accepting an unsecured warranty from such a vendor, and as a result, the agent was liable to the purchaser for losses incurred caused by his negligence.

Another very noteworthy case is *Soulos v. Korkontzilas*, [1997] S.C.J. No. 52, [1997] 2 S.C.R. 217, which involved an agent's representation of a purchaser interested in purchasing a commercial building. The agent submitted an offer for the purchaser to acquire the building, which the vendor signed back at a higher price. This counter-offer was rejected by the purchaser, but the purchaser submitted a further counter-offer. The vendor informed the purchaser's agent that this final offer would be acceptable. At this point, the agent deliberately withheld that information from the purchaser and, instead, arranged for his wife to submit an offer on the property at this negotiated price, which was accepted and which was later completed. Years later, the original purchaser learned of these events, brought an action against the agent for breach of fiduciary duty and sought to have the property transferred to him on the basis that the breach in question gave rise to a constructive trust. At trial, while the Court found there had been a breach by the agent of his fiduciary duty, the remedy requested was rejected because the evidence demonstrated that the agent had not been enriched by the acquisition as the agent had bought the property at its market value and that value had subsequently declined. The Court of Appeal reversed that decision, which was upheld by the Supreme Court of Canada. Both of the upper courts concluded that the facts of this case warranted a finding that a constructive trust requiring a reconveyance of the property by the agent to the purchaser had arisen regardless of whether or not the agent had been enriched by his conduct. Accordingly, the Court ordered the agent to transfer the property to the original purchaser.

Finally, in *Wemyss v. Moldenhauer*, [2003] O.J. No. 38, 7 R.P.R. (4th) 124 (S.C.J.), the agent was found negligent to the purchaser for failing to advise of an alteration to an inspection clause, even where the agent had been unaware of the alteration at the time. The purchaser had advised the agent about his concern with the home's septic system and that he wished to be able to get out of the deal if there was a problem with the system. The initial offer indicated that it was conditional on the purchaser obtaining an inspector's report satisfactory to the purchaser. That offer expired and the agent submitted a new offer. On signing back that offer, the inspection clause was altered to provide that it was conditional on the purchaser obtaining an inspector's report satisfactory to the purchaser that there were no structural defects. The addition of the term "structural defects" was not brought to the purchaser's attention. When the subsequent inspection report disclosed problems with the septic system, the purchaser instructed the agent to cancel the transaction and get his deposit back. It was only then that the purchaser and the agent realized that the clause had been altered. In awarding the purchaser his $50,000 deposit, the Court noted that the agent did not meet the standard of the reasonable care and skill expected of a real estate agent. In addition, the purchaser could not be found contributorily negligent for failing to read the counter-offer, as he was reasonably entitled to rely on his agent to have read and understood any changes that had been made.

However, there is a limit to the agent's responsibility. In *Hawkhead v. Sussex Realty Ltd.*, [1979] B.C.J. No. 961, 13 B.C.L.R. 289 (Co. Ct.), the Court found that an agent does not have a duty to advise on title. This was a case where a deal collapsed because the vendor was in such poor financial shape that he could not clear the title of the outstanding encumbrances. The frustrated purchaser sued the agent on the basis that the agent did not advise him of the deplorable state of the title to the property.

SELLER PROPERTY INFORMATION SHEET

Another document that is becoming common when a seller retains a real estate agent to market his or her home is a Seller Property Information Sheet ("SPIS"). The SPIS was developed by the Ontario Real Estate Association ("OREA") and has been distributed to real estate boards as a recommended document that agents should have sellers complete.

The SPIS contains several specific questions to be answered by the seller relating to the property being sold and its ownership, such as: whether the property is subject to encroachments/easements; what the zoning of the property is; whether the property's use is legal non-conforming; whether the property is subject to restrictive covenants; whether the property is connected to municipal services; whether the property is subject to flooding; whether the owner is aware of moisture or water problems; whether there is any lead plumbing on the property, *etc.* The SPIS often ends with the seller acknowledging that the SPIS will be made available to prospective purchasers. Often there is also an agreement by the seller to indemnify the broker from any liability associated with inaccurate information found on the SPIS.

The completion of the SPIS is not required by the *Real Estate and Business Brokers Act, 2002*, nor by the regulations passed thereunder. The Real Estate Council of Ontario also acknowledges on its website that a seller is not obliged to execute the SPIS. Nevertheless, OREA has promoted the SPIS and in fact, in many regions of Ontario, local real estate boards make completion of the SPIS a condition of allowing the seller's property access to the Multiple Listing Service system.

Many commentators have recognized the danger to a seller in completing an SPIS. Many court cases have been initiated by buyers and sellers where buyers sue sellers for unexpected discoveries as to the condition of a property found after closing, or where sellers sue buyers for failing to complete a transaction for something found before closing. It seems that with the addition of the SPIS, there are even more such cases. As one might expect, many of these cases are actions by buyers against sellers alleging that the seller made an inaccurate statement on the SPIS that was either deliberate, fraudulent or negligent and seeking damages as a result thereof. See *Kaufmann v. Gibson*, [2007] O.J. No. 2711, 59 R.P.R. (4th) 293 (S.C.J.), supp. reasons [2007] O.J. No. 3141 (S.C.J.) and *Riley v. Langfield*, [2008] O.J. No. 2028 (S.C.J.), supp. reasons [2008] O.J. No. 2816 (S.C.J.) for examples.

For practitioners representing sellers who have the opportunity to give advice to their clients before they sign the SPIS (which, more often than not, does not happen given the early state at which the SPIS is presented to, and signed by, a seller compared to when their lawyer is retained), the advice must be that the signing of the SPIS carries a great deal of risk. Many of the questions are complicated and not readily answered by a layperson; when answering, sellers are likely to be cursory in their statements, many probably just answering "yes" or "no". These factors can easily lead to inaccurate information that a buyer can take hold of, allege reliance on, and use to either launch an action or refuse to close if he or she uncovers contradictory circumstances. This results in a significant modification to the principle of *caveat emptor*, which puts the risk of undiscovered problems on the buyer absent fraud, negligent misrepresentation or failure to disclose latent defects by the seller.

For practitioners representing purchasers, the SPIS created by the seller and given to the buyer is obviously beneficial in that it arms the buyer with the seller's own admissions, which can be compared against the facts to form the basis of a *prima facie* case against a seller, using his or her own words, as to a dispute over a property's condition.

REAL ESTATE AND BUSINESS BROKERS ACT, 2002, S.O. 2002, c. 30, Sched. C

Real estate brokers and salespeople and their operations in Ontario are governed by the *Real Estate and Business Brokers Act, 2002*.

Section 4 of this Act prohibits trading in real estate by anyone unless he or she is a registered broker or salesperson. The only exceptions to this requirement are contained in s. 5. Those exceptions include executors or trustees selling under the terms of a will, auctioneers, solicitors and people selling their own real estate. To become registered as a salesperson in Ontario, you must first complete the Ontario Real Estate Association course of studies given at most community colleges. When you have successfully completed that course, you receive a certificate from the Real Estate Council of Ontario, and only then may you be employed by a real estate broker. To be registered as a salesperson, you must file with your application and fee, a certificate proving completion of the course, evidence of employment and a surety bond.

To become registered as a broker, you must have been a registered salesperson for a minimum of two years; as well, you must have completed other courses and you must file with your application the application fee and a surety bond.

Section 9 of the Act provides that unless a person is registered thereunder or is exempt from registration, an action for commission cannot be brought by that person.

Section 6 prohibits brokers or salespeople from trading in real estate until they have received written notice from the registrar that they are registered. Subsections 30(*b*) and (*c*) prohibit brokers from employing any unregistered person to trade in real estate on their behalf and prohibits them from paying any commission to such person.

Section 32 prohibits registrants from purchasing property for themselves unless they deliver a written statement to the vendor that they are brokers or salespeople, and the vendor acknowledges in writing the receipt of such statement. See *Sharma v. Hnatiuk*, [1987] O.J. No. 2594, 58 O.R. (2d) 345 (Dist. Ct.).

However, mere compliance with this section will not be sufficient to permit an agent who is purchasing from a vendor to collect a commission on the sale. See *George W. Rayfield Realty Ltd. v. Kuhn*, [1980] O.J. No. 3757, 30 O.R. (2d) 271 (H.C.J.), affd [1981] O.J. No. 2362, 31 O.R. (2d) 160 (C.A.). Galligan J. in his judgment again emphasizes the high duty of full disclosure that an agent owes to a vendor. The following appears at 277 O.R.:

> It may be that the notice in this case does amount to technical compliance with the provisions of [s. 32] of the Act as it now exists. However, in my opinion, it does in no way amount to compliance with or fulfilment of the high fiduciary responsibility that a real estate agent owes to his principal. The conflict between a purchaser's interest and that of a vendor is so great that, in my opinion, there must be the most complete disclosure by a real estate agent purchasing from his principal before it can be said that he has fulfilled his fiduciary responsibility to his principal.

In such a case, it is my opinion that the agent must give his principal the fullest disclosure of his knowledge of the real estate market in the area where the subject lands were situate. For example, if an agent had information that a property might even possibly be sold to some other purchaser at a higher price than that offered by the agent then that information must be brought to the attention of the principal so that the profit would be that of the principal rather than of the agent.

And again (at 278 O.R.):

A real estate agent dealing with his own client may not simply enter the market-place. The agent is in a position of great trust and he owes great trust to his principal. In my view, the simple disclosure that he was an agent, discloses the most abysmal ignorance of, or misconception of the very fundamental duties arising from the fiduciary relationship of a real estate agent to his principal. In my opinion, this agent was simply greedy. He wanted to purchase the property and he wanted to get a commission from the vendor as well.

In *Yared Realty Ltd. v. Topalovic*, [1980] O.J. No. 1195, 130 D.L.R. (3d) 625 (H.C.J.), a real estate agent entered into an agreement of purchase and sale "in trust" and evidence was adduced that the property was in fact being purchased for someone else and not for the agent personally. The agent did not comply with s. 32. Hollingworth J. held that the agent had sufficient interest in the property so that he was governed by s. 32. Therefore, his action for specific performance failed. See also *Raso v. Dionigi*, [1993] O.J. No. 670, 31 R.P.R. (2d) 1 (C.A.), where an agent was denied a commission where he failed to disclose to the vendor that a purchaser he had secured was in fact, his sister-in-law using her maiden name on the offer.

This obligation of disclosure has also been extended to situations where the agent has an interest in the vendor. In *489212 Ontario Ltd. v. Participative Dynamics Inc.*, [1997] O.J. No. 3856, 13 R.P.R. (3d) 32 (C.A.), the Ontario Court of Appeal held that an agent breached his fiduciary duty to his principal in failing to disclose to the purchaser his significant shareholdings in the vendor. This non-disclosure allowed the purchaser to rescind the purchase agreement and recover its deposit.

Section 36 of the Act is noteworthy in that it prohibits an agent from entering into an arrangement for the payment of a commission on the basis of the difference between the price at which the property is listed and the actual sale price. In fact, the commission must be calculated on a percentage basis or on a predetermined fixed price.

CHAPTER 11

The Agreement of Purchase and Sale

The agreement of purchase and sale is the basis of most routine real estate transactions. It is sometimes referred to as an "offer to purchase". Do not let this second term confuse you. In the law of contracts, every agreement is constituted by the acceptance of a valid offer. Therefore, when the purchaser submits an offer, it is an offer to purchase. When that offer is accepted, it constitutes an agreement or contract; in this case, it is an agreement of purchase and sale.

In most contracts, it is not essential that the agreement or contract be in writing. However, by s. 4 of the *Statute of Frauds*, R.S.O. 1990, c. S.19, an agreement for the sale of land must be in writing. No contract for the sale or purchase of land is enforceable against a party who has not signed a written memorandum thereof setting out the essential terms. In *McKenzie v. Walsh*, [1920] S.C.J. No. 68, 61 S.C.R. 312, the Supreme Court of Canada held that the essential terms of a contract for the sale of land were the identity of the parties, an accurate description of the property and the price to be paid. A specific closing date was not viewed by the Court as being essential. Similarly, in *Babcock v. Carr*, [1981] O.J. No. 3102, 127 D.L.R. (3d) 77 (H.C.J.), the Court held that an agreement identifying the parties, the price and the location and acreage of a property contained all the essential requirements for a contract and complied with the *Statute of Frauds* even though no closing date was mentioned.

The recent decision of the Court of Appeal in *Erie Sand and Gravel Ltd. v. Seres' Farms Ltd.*, [2009] O.J. No. 4179, 97 O.R. (3d) 241 demonstrates the Court's interpretation of the *Statute of Frauds* when dealing with oral agreements. The purchaser approached a vendor to negotiate the terms of purchase of a gravel pit. The parties orally agreed on the acreage of the property, its location, the price per acre, the deposit and the closing date. As a third party had a right of first refusal that would be triggered by the submission of a written offer, it was agreed that the purchaser would prepare a written offer, which it did, but that the vendor would not accept it until it first approached the third party to assess the likelihood that the third party would purchase the property on the same terms. After approaching the third party, the vendor concluded an arrangement to sell the property to that third party on terms that were less favourable to the vendor than those orally agreed upon with the first purchaser. The Court of Appeal upheld the trial judge's decision requiring the third party to transfer the property to the first purchaser. It rejected the third party's argument that the vendor and purchaser had no written agreement that was enforceable under the *Statute of Frauds* and instead found that all of the essential terms of the contract had been committed to writing, even though not accepted, and that there were acts of part performance that unequivocally took the agreement outside of s. 4 of the *Statute of Frauds*. Those acts included: delivery of the written offer; submission of a certified cheque; and the fact that the vendor knew that a written offer would trigger the third party's right of first refusal.

Occasionally, a client will come into your office with an informal memorandum similar to those considered in the above cases. Obviously, your client has not been reading the *Statute of Frauds*; perhaps your client just sat down at the kitchen table at someone's house or cottage and wrote out a version of the agreement they had come to and both parties signed the memorandum.

VENDORS AND PURCHASERS ACT, R.S.O. 1990, C. V.2

Such a memorandum will probably be lacking many of the details normally required in arranging the closing of a real estate transaction. The legislature has partly attended to this by s. 4 of the *Vendors and Purchasers Act*, which reads as follows:

4. Every contract for the sale and purchase of land shall, unless otherwise stipulated, be deemed to provide that,

   (*a*)   the vendor is not bound to produce any abstract of title, deed, copies of deeds or other evidence of title except such as are in the vendor's possession or control;

   (*b*)   the purchaser shall search the title at the purchaser's own expense and shall make any objections thereto in writing within thirty days from the making of the contract;

   (*c*)   the vendor has thirty days in which to remove any objection made to the title, but if the vendor is unable or unwilling to remove any objection that the purchaser is not willing to waive, the vendor may cancel the contract and return any deposit made but is not otherwise liable to the purchaser;

   (*d*)   taxes, local improvement rates, insurance premiums, rents and interest, shall be adjusted as at the date of closing;

   (*e*)   the conveyance shall be prepared by the vendor and the mortgage, if any, by the purchaser and the purchaser shall bear the expense of registration of the deed and the vendor shall bear the expense of the registration of the mortgage, if any;

   (*f*)   the purchaser is entitled to possession or the receipt of rents and profits upon the closing of the transaction.

Please note, however, that an informal memorandum signed by both parties, which is stated therein to be subject to a formal contract being completed is not binding on either party: *Eccles v. Bryant and Pollock*, [1948] Ch. 93 (C.A.). A contract to enter into a contract is not binding: *Von Hatzfeldt-Wildenburg v. Alexander*, [1912] 1 Ch. 284.

LORD'S DAY ACT, R.S.C. 1970, C. L-13

The federal *Lord's Day Act* used to be of critical importance in determining the validity of agreements of purchase and sale. That statute stated in s. 4 that it was not lawful for any person to sell or offer for sale or purchase any real estate on the Lord's Day. Consequently, a contract entered into on a Sunday was invalid.

However, on April 24, 1985, the Supreme Court of Canada ruled that this section, and the *Lord's Day Act* in general, was unconstitutional in that it infringed on the freedom of conscience and religion guaranteed by s. 2(*a*) of the *Canadian Charter of Rights and Freedoms*, and such infringement was not reasonable: *R. v. Big M Drug Mart Ltd.*, [1985] S.C.J. No. 17, [1985] 1 S.C.R. 295. In view of this, the Act was repealed with the enactment of the 1985 Revised Statutes of Canada. Now the fact that a contract is entered into on a Sunday does not affect its validity.

FORM OF AGREEMENT OF PURCHASE AND SALE

Usually, your clients will have entered into an agreement on a printed form prepared by a legal stationer or by the local real estate board.

Apparently, because it is printed, most people sign the form before consulting a lawyer and, in many cases, without even reading it. The purchase or sale of a house is the biggest transaction most people ever enter into, yet an amazing number blithely sign the agreement without ever calling on their lawyer for advice. Then they appear in their lawyers' offices asking them to solve problems arising out of that very agreement. These agreements are almost always prepared by real estate agents who, while trained and often expert in their own field, have little training or expertise in the complicated world of drafting legal documents.

For those cases where you are given an opportunity to advise on such an agreement before signing, or where you are called upon to draft such a standard form agreement, the following suggestions may be helpful. Please refer to the latest form of the Ontario Real Estate Association ("OREA") agreement of purchase and sale included as Appendix 4 hereto, which is the basis for the review that follows and whose provisions are reviewed below in the order in which they appear in that form.

PARTIES

There are two parties to the normal agreement: the purchaser and the vendor. Each of them should be properly identified and subsequently referred to in the agreement as defined, *e.g.*, "the Purchaser" or "the Vendor". If possible, you should make a quick search of title just to assure yourself that the party named as vendor is in fact the owner. Such a search is becoming easier and easier to do through the use of the Teraview database. If the owner is married, you might consider having the spouse join in the agreement with a covenant to execute the conveyance to release the interest of the spouse under the *Family Law Act*, R.S.O. 1990, c. F.3. Pursuant to s. 21(1) of the *Family Law Act*, one spouse cannot sell, mortgage or otherwise deal with a matrimonial home without the consent of the other spouse. A sale in contravention of this provision can be set aside unless a purchaser can demonstrate that he or she had no notice that the property was a matrimonial home. Paragraph 22 of the OREA form does contain a warranty that spousal consent is not necessary unless the spouse has executed the agreement, and the form contains a signing line where a spouse can indicate his or her consent. However, if this consent is not signed on assurances that no consent is necessary, and you have knowledge that the vendor is married, it may be worthwhile to insist on the other spouse's written consent. If this is a problem, the sooner it is revealed the better for all parties.

It is also important to recall the parties must have capacity to contract. Minors cannot ordinarily contract for the purchase or sale of property until they reach the age of 18 (see the *Age of Majority and Accountability Act*, R.S.O. 1990, c. A.7). Similarly, contracts entered into by mentally incompetent or incapacitated persons, while not automatically void as a result of a party's conditions, may be set aside if a court finds that the other party to the contract took advantage of the party with the incapacity. In *Junkin v. Junkin*, [1978] O.J. No. 3400, 86 D.L.R. (3d) 751 (H.C.J.), a retired man of diminished capacity agreed to sell his interest in a farm to his brother for a fraction of its value and was not represented by counsel during negotiations. The Court found that the brother and brother's solicitor had taken advantage of his condition in forcing him to complete the sale on such terms and ordered damages equal to the difference between the sale price and the property's fair market value. See also *Stubbs v. Erickson*, [1981] B.C.J. No. 1896, 34 B.C.L.R. 45 (S.C.), where the Court dismissed an action for specific performance against a vendor who was a chronic alcoholic and who had agreed to sell her house at a very low price, finding that the purchaser knew of her condition and predicament and took advantage of those facts in the transaction. Finally, pursuant to the provisions of the *Substitute Decisions Act, 1992*, S.O. 1992, c. 30 and the *Mental Health Act*, R.S.O. 1990, c. M.7, individuals may be declared mentally incompetent to manage their affairs, at which point they lose the capacity to contract. A committee or the Public Guardian and Trustee will be appointed to manage the individual's affairs and only they have the power to sell any real property owned by that individual.

If your client is making an offer on behalf of someone else, you must ensure that the agreement provides that your client has the right to assign the contract and escape its liabilities. If this is done, the benefits acquired, as well as the liabilities imposed, may be transferred to a third person. If there is no such provision, the benefits of the agreement may be assigned (see s. 53 of the *Conveyancing and Law of Property Act*, R.S.O. 1990, c. C.34), but your client will remain liable for any covenant contained in the agreement (see *King v. Urban & Country Transport Ltd.*, [1973] O.J. No. 2181, 1 O.R. (2d) 449 (C.A.)). If, for example, part of the purchase price is to be paid by way of a mortgage back to the vendor, then the purchaser cannot escape liability under the mortgage without obtaining the consent of the vendor. The purchaser could assign the agreement, but the vendor could insist that the original signing party be included as a guarantor on the mortgage. In *Roth (Trustee) v. Galway (Trustee)*, [1985] O.J. No. 1314 (H.C.J.), the Court found that a purchaser who claimed that he bought a property in trust for someone else was personally liable when a mortgage given back on the purchase went into default. The fact that the purchaser was noted as a trustee or acting in trust on all of the sale documents was not sufficient to relieve the individual from liability. The following clause might be included in an agreement to deal with trustee situations:

The Vendor acknowledges and agrees that the Purchaser has entered into this agreement as trustee for an unnamed principal (the "Principal") and that, upon the Purchaser delivering written notice to the Vendor of the name of the Principal, the Vendor will deal with the Principal as if it had been the original party to this agreement and thereafter [the named purchaser] shall have no personal liability hereunder.

Remember also that s. 53 requires notice of the assignment to be given to the vendor. This is confirmed in *DiGuilo v. Boland*, [1958] O.J. No. 602, [1958] O.R. 384 (C.A.), affd [1961] S.C.R. vii.

Where a corporation is a party to an agreement of purchase and sale, comfort can be taken in the "indoor management rule" in being assured that the party executing that contract has authority to bind the corporation. Section 19 of the *Business Corporations Act*, R.S.O. 1990, c. B.16 ("OBCA") and s. 18 of the *Canada Business Corporations Act*, R.S.C. 1985, c. C-44 ("CBCA") codify that rule for Ontario and Canada corporations, respectively. Pursuant to these provisions, a corporation cannot deny that a person held out as a director, officer or agent of the corporation was not duly appointed or authorized to enter into a contract which would be customary for a person with such authority to sign. Also, a corporation cannot assert that the articles, by-laws or any unanimous shareholder's agreement binding the corporation have not been complied with by the entering into of the contract. As a result, the other party to the contract, who does not otherwise have actual knowledge of any impropriety relating to the entry into of the contract by the corporation, is protected against claims of incapacity or lack of authority to contract which a corporation subsequently advances. Also note that pursuant to s. 18 of the OBCA, no one is deemed to have knowledge of the contents of any documents filed by a corporation with the provincial Companies Branch by reason only of their filing.

Section 184(3) of the OBCA does specifically consider the sale of real estate by a corporation and requires that a sale of property, other than in the corporation's ordinary course of business, which property constitutes "all or substantially all" of the property of the corporation, requires two-thirds of the corporation's shareholders to approve of the sale by resolution. For most companies, the sale of real estate will not be a transaction in the ordinary course of business but will be quite extraordinary. If the second test considering the substantiveness of the property to the company is met, the corporation is not allowed to sell the property without the special shareholders' resolution.

A purchaser buying from a corporation will not normally be in a position to assess whether property being sold by a corporation is being sold in the ordinary course or whether it constitutes all or substantially all of a corporation's property. If a purchaser does have knowledge as to such matters, it will require evidence that the shareholders' special resolution has been passed. If it does not have any knowledge, a purchaser is protected by the indoor management rule. After closing, reliance can be placed on s. 17(3) of the OBCA, which provides that "... no act of a corporation including a transfer of property ... is invalid by reason only that the act is contrary to its articles, by-laws, a unanimous shareholder agreement or this Act". As a result, failure to obtain a certified resolution of a corporation's shareholders does not affect the propriety of a transaction involving a corporation; however, if the opportunity to negotiate for the delivery of such a certificate presents itself, its request should be pursued for the sake of avoiding claims of impropriety.

If a purchaser is submitting an offer on behalf of a company to be incorporated, you will be interested in s. 21 of the OBCA, which provides that a corporation may adopt a pre-incorporation contract entered into in its name or on its behalf and thereupon the corporation is entitled to the benefits and is subject to the liabilities that were contracted in its name or on its behalf. The person who signed on its behalf ceases to be entitled to such benefits or to be subject to such liabilities. In acting for a person planning to sign a contract on behalf of a company not yet incorporated, you should advise this person of the possibility of personal liability in the event that the corporation does not adopt the contract within a reasonable time after it has been incorporated. See *Okinczyc v. Tessier*, [1979] O.J. No. 151, 8 R.P.R. 249 (H.C.J.), affd [1980] O.J. No. 283 (C.A.), where a purchaser "in trust" was held personally liable on an agreement to purchase when the company did not adopt the agreement (see also *1080409 Ontario Ltd. v. Hunter*, [2000] O.J. No. 2603, 50 O.R. (3d) 145 (S.C.J.)).

A person may avoid liability if a corporation does not subsequently adopt a pre-incorporation contract if that person makes it clear when entering into that contract that he or she is doing so in trust for that corporation and "without personal liability". In *Botwood Investments Ltd. v. Johnson*, [1982] O.J. No. 3235, 36 O.R. (2d) 443 (H.C.J.), the Court found that a purchaser entering into an agreement in that manner was absolved of personal liability (see also *Cha v. Chong*, [2004] O.J. No. 3006 (S.C.J.)). Also, the Court in *Roth (Trustee) v. Galway (Trustee)*, [1985] O.J. No. 1314 (H.C.J.), in finding a purchaser liable for defaulting under a mortgage given back to a vendor and refusing to accept a defence that the purchaser was only a trustee and not personally liable stated (at para. 12):

> In my opinion, a person who signs an Agreement of Purchase and Sale can only avoid personal liability therefor if, in the agreement, there are express and unequivocal words of qualification to this end. Those should at least immediately follow any use of the name and signature. But as well, to my mind, it would be better if, in addition, the agreement contained an express provision to the desired effect.

Please be aware, however, that the use of the "without personal liability" qualification in an agreement of purchase and sale, while relieving the contracting party of personal liability, will also deprive that person of the opportunity to sue for the benefits of the contract. See *Rothwell Corp. v. Amstel Brewery Canada Ltd.*, [1991] O.J. No. 2218, 6 O.R. (3d) 651 (Gen. Div.), where the Court dismissed an action by a purchaser who sought specific performance against a vendor. The person had entered into the contract "on behalf of an investor group". As such, the Court found the person had no personal liability and, as a result, was not entitled to advance an action against the vendor in its own name since the person had no personal interest in the contract.

In *1394918 Ontario Ltd. v. 1310210 Ontario Inc.*, [2002] O.J. No. 18, 57 O.R. (3d) 607, the Court of Appeal reviewed the law relating to pre-incorporation contracts in the context of s. 21 of the OBCA. It confirmed that where a corporation does not adopt a pre-incorporation contract, there was no one who could sue the vendor for any breach of that contract; after incorporation and adoption by the corporation of the contract, the corporation has status and standing to bring an action for damages against a vendor as it is then entitled to all benefits under the contract, including the right to a claim for damages.

When one of the parties to an agreement of purchase and sale is a partnership, any partner may bind the partnership if the transaction is in the partnership's ordinary course of business. A person dealing with that partnership may rely on the single partner's authority to bind the partnership unless he or she has knowledge otherwise (see s. 6 of the *Partnerships Act*, R.S.O. 1990, c. P.5). In *Manitoba Mortgage Co. v. Bank of Montreal*, [1889] S.C.J. No. 55, 17 S.C.R. 692, the Supreme Court confirmed that a real property transaction by a partnership may be completed by one partner on behalf of the others if such transactions are ordinarily part of its business; otherwise, if the real property transaction is not in the ordinary course of business of the partnership, one partner cannot bind the others and all partners must enter into the contract. As a result, when dealing with a general partnership, one should require all of the partners to sign the agreement of purchase and sale and have them include a representation, that they constitute all of the partners and have authority to bind the partnership. A search under the *Business Names Act*, R.S.O. 1990, c. B.17 is useful to verify who the partners of a partnership are as, pursuant to s. 2 of the Act, all partners of the partnership must register the name of the partnership. Although the failure of the partnership to register will not affect the ability of a partnership to carry on business or void any contract it enters into, most partnerships will register under the Act as failure to do so will prevent them from maintaining any proceeding in a court.

Where a limited partnership is a party to an agreement of purchase and sale, it is the general partners of the limited partnership who must execute the agreement, as it is only the general partners who can enter into contracts that bind the limited partnership pursuant to the *Limited Partnerships Act*, R.S.O. 1990, c. L.16. A search of the limited partnership's declaration filed at the office of the Registrar of Partnerships will reveal who the general partners are.

If you become aware that property is an estate asset, you must make further enquiries before preparing the agreement of purchase and sale. Examine the letters probate or letters of administration to see who is authorized to deal with the property. Does the estate trustee have power of sale? Has the property vested in the beneficiaries because it is now more than three years from the date of death? Is the estate selling for the purpose of distributing the proceeds to the beneficiaries? (See Chapter 6 for a discussion of these problems.) It is true, of course, that you can later check these matters and requisition that the proper parties join in the deed, but the agreement is not enforceable against the estate if the correct parties have not joined in the agreement (see *A. Harvey Hacker Builders Ltd. v. Akerfeldt*, [1964] O.J. No. 846, [1965] 1 O.R. 369 (H.C.J.), affd [1965] O.R. 182, 50 D.L.R. (2d) 130 (C.A.)). Also, no action can be pursued against the estate for lack of authority. Please note that an agreement of purchase and sale signed by an individual who dies before closing is still enforceable against the deceased's estate and all obligations of that person under the contract pass to the estate.

DESCRIPTION OF THE PROPERTY

The description must be very specific. If you are dealing with a house in a city, the municipal address will identify the house, but it does not give any indication of the size of the lot. You should show the side of the street and the frontage and depth of the lot on which the house is built. Your clients will be most unhappy to get a deed to a 35-foot lot when they thought they were buying a 70-foot lot. Often you will find measurements of frontage as "approximately" or "more or less". These terms are usually added by a careful vendor trying to build in a margin for error. How much of a deficiency will the courts consider is covered by the phrase "more or less"? When will they order specific performance?

Two Ontario cases illustrate the difficulty of advising a client in this regard: *Wilson Lumber Co. v. Simpson*, [1910] O.J. No. 56, 22 O.L.R. 452 (H.C.J.), and *Murphy v. Horn*, [1929] O.J. No. 58, [1929] 4 D.L.R. 693 (H.C.J.). In the *Wilson Lumber* case the property was described in the agreement as "... 250 Richmond Street, having a frontage on Richmond Street of 36 feet more or less by a depth of 110 feet more or less to a lane ...". The depth was in fact 98 feet 6 inches. The sale was for $12,000 and not a sum per foot. Meredith C.J. reviewed English law but approved the statement in an American case that "the words 'more or less' added to the statement of the depth, control that statement, so that neither party would be entitled to relief on account of a deficiency or a surplus unless in case of so great a difference as will naturally raise the presumption of fraud or gross mistake in the very essence of the contract". It was fairly easy for the court in this case to refuse the compensation for the deficiency, since the property was bounded on two sides by a street and on a third side by a lane. The purchaser received exactly what he contracted for.

In the *Murphy* case, the agreement described the property as "the ten acres more or less, being that part of farm 71 in the Township of Sandwich, West Essex County, Ontario, fronting on the fourth concession road between Dougal and Huron Mine Roads". In fact, the land consisted of ten arpents, an arpent being about five-sixths of an acre. The land was enclosed by a fence and, as in the *Wilson Lumber* case, it was a purchase for a set sum and not a sum per acre. Here the Court refused to follow the *Wilson Lumber* case, stating:

> The general principle is well established that where a misrepresentation is made by the vendor as to a matter within his knowledge, and even though it be founded on the honest belief in the truth of the representation, and the purchaser is misled by such misrepresentation, the purchaser is entitled to have the contract specifically performed, so far as the vendor is able to do so, and to have compensation for the deficiency.

This approach was followed by the Ontario Court of Appeal in *3999581 Canada Inc. v. 1394734 Ontario Inc.*, [2007] O.J. No. 1570, 282 D.L.R. (4th) 461, where due to an inadvertent error in description, the property was 12 per cent smaller than represented in the purchase agreement. The Court held that where there is a discrepancy between what the vendor agreed to convey and what it actually could convey, the purchaser is generally entitled to the remedy of specific performance with an abatement if the purchaser elects that remedy.

When drafting agreements, you will be safer if you bear in mind the interpretation of "more or less" by Raney J. in the *Murphy* case:

> I think the words "more or less" are not to be construed as the equivalent of "as estimated" or "as supposed" but are to be construed to mean, "about the specified number of acres", and is designed to cover such small errors as sometimes occur in surveys.

The decisions in *Bouskill v Campea*, [1976] O.J. No. 2112, 12 O.R. (2d) 265 (C.A.) and *Olszewski v. Trapman*, [2000] O.J. No. 2965, 35 R.P.R. (3d) 316 (S.C.J.) illustrate the courts' favouring of the approach in the *Murphy* case. In *Bouskill*, the Court of Appeal ruled that a variance in the depth of a lot by 11 feet was too great to be covered by the "more or less" qualification in the description where the depth was represented as being 172 feet. Similarly, in *Olszewski*, the Court allowed a purchaser to rescind an agreement where a lot whose acreage was stated as being 1.5 acres was actually 1.15 acres. The lot's density allowance would not allow the purchaser to build the improvements he had intended and, as a result, the Court held rescission was an appropriate remedy. The difference in area could not be ignored on the basis of the "more or less" qualification in the purchase agreement. The *Olszewski* case is useful in that it reviews other decisions on area discrepancies and comments on the ruling of the Court in light of the discrepancy at issue.

If you have a survey or legal description available, you should add to any short description "as more particularly described in the description (or shown on the survey) attached hereto as Schedule A". There is some risk in using the expression "as per vendor's deed" unless the parties are positive that there has been no change in the boundaries by way of sale or expropriation since the date of that deed and that, in fact, the vendor has good and marketable title to all of that land.

Charter-York Ltd. v. Hurst, [1978] O.J. No. 2734, 2 R.P.R. 272 (H.C.J.) involved negligence on the part of an agent in describing the land involved in a transaction, but it could just as easily have been a solicitor. In this case the Court ordered the agent to pay damages not to exceed $500,000. The agent did not accurately describe a farm property which was the subject of the agreement and as a result the Court (at 278 R.P.R.) refused to enforce the agreement:

> Where a purchaser has been misled as to fundamental particulars by the vendor or his agent into purchasing something that he would otherwise have had no intention to purchase, the law is clear that there is no *ad idem* and hence no contract. See *Sriven Bros. v. Hindley* (1913), 3 K.B. 564.

> After consideration of the facts of this case, I must conclude that there was no consensus *ad idem* as to the subject-matter of this transaction.

In *Rexhill Holdings Ltd. v. Maybird Investments Ltd.*, [1972] O.J. No. 1985, [1973] 1 O.R. 285 (H.C.J.), a purchaser refused to close and was claiming for the return of his deposit for two reasons, one of which was that the vendor was conveying more land than was described in the agreement. The agreement described the land as "part of East Half of Lot 20, Concession 7, having 54 acres and being the southwest corner of 17th Avenue and the 7th Line". In fact, the parcel consisted of 57.692 acres. Because the description did not say "54 acres more or less", the purchaser claimed it should not have to close because one party cannot unilaterally change the terms of the agreement. The Court reviewed a number of cases and was satisfied that the purchaser was getting what it bargained for. The obverse of this situation occurred in *Cottingham v. Cottingham*, [1885] O.J. No. 126, 11 O.A.R. 624 (C.A.), where a purchaser agreed to purchase a parcel of land for $3,100 and this parcel was stated to contain "100 acres more or less". Its area was actually 124.68 acres and the vendors proposed to convey 100 acres and withhold the extra 24.68 acres. The Court held that the agreement was for the purchase of the whole parcel and thus granted possession to the purchaser.

On the subject of the quantity of land purchased, Victor Di Castri, *The Law of Vendor and Purchaser*, 3d ed. (Toronto: Carswell, 1988), at 12-11, § 402, speaks of warranty:

> Warranty as to quantity. A statement of quantity in a description of the land sold does not *prima facie* import a warranty. Warranty is always a question of intention and the existence of that intention is a matter of fact to be determined by the totality of the evidence.

On the previous page, Di Castri deals with the Latin maxim *falsa demonstratio non nocet*, which is often referred to by the courts in this regard as follows:

> In the absence of fraud, a false description by way of addition may be disregarded, where the land is otherwise sufficiently described in or ascertainable from the contract and any relevant admissible parol evidence [see also *John Beattie Farms Ltd. v. Stevenson Estate*, [2004] O.J. No. 1177 (S.C.J.)].

Now all of this may be very interesting to legal scholars and lucrative to those lawyers who thrive on litigation. Surely, the minimum expected of a good conveyancing solicitor is to produce agreements which result in successful closings and not in litigation. If you are dealing with a parcel of land that is being purchased for a lump sum, you should describe it so that both parties are clearly aware of what they are buying and selling. If the parcel is bounded by streets, lanes, railway lines, rivers, fences or any other landmarks, reference to such should be included in the description. If the land is being purchased for development purposes, the parcel should be described as clearly as possible and it should be clearly stated that the price will be determined at $X per acre or $Y per square foot based upon a survey to be produced before closing. Your agreement could contain this clause to define the purchase price:

> The total purchase price is an amount equal to Sixty Thousand Dollars ($60,000.00) per acre (determined by survey as hereinafter provided) payable as follows:

Then, among the conditions insert the following:

> The total price shall have been determined on the basis of a certificate of an Ontario Land Surveyor satisfactory to the Purchaser, establishing the area of the Real Property.

In addition to the location, shape and size of the parcel of land, it is essential to properly describe any easements to which the land is subject. The obvious type of easement which must be referred to in the agreement is a mutual driveway, a party wall or a trunk sewer easement. If the vendor has neglected to mention one of these in the agreement, the purchaser would clearly be entitled to rescission. The situation is not as clear where the easement is for a footpath, roadway or overhead utility line which was clearly visible to the purchaser during the inspection of the property before submitting an offer.

The description of easements and exceptions is particularly important when dealing with cottage property. If access is over a right of way, be sure to describe it accurately in the agreement. And, if it is lakefront property, be sure to include an exception for the 66-foot reserve for road allowance along the lakeshore as part of the description. The purchaser who is by the terms of the agreement entitled to a title "good and free from all encumbrances", will not be forced to complete the purchase of a cottage erected, even in part, upon the 66-foot strip which the vendor does not own.

Normally, it is not necessary to include in the description of a property the buildings, fences and fixtures located thereon. Section 15(1) of the *Conveyancing and Law of Property Act* states:

> 15(1) Every conveyance of land, unless an exception is specially made therein, includes all houses, outhouses, edifices, barns, stables, yards, gardens, orchards, commons, trees, woods, underwoods, mounds, fences, hedges, ditches, ways, waters, watercourses, lights, liberties, privileges, easements, profits, commodities, emoluments, hereditaments and appurtenances whatsoever to such land belonging or in anywise appertaining. ...

It does not include chattels that are on or about the lands. When discussing an agreement of purchase and sale with either purchaser or vendor, be sure to ask if any chattels are to be included in the transaction and include a description of them in the agreement. At the same time, check to make sure that none of the buildings or fixtures is to be excluded.

PRICE

The price is settled between the parties and you can be of little assistance. However, the manner in which the price is paid should be amended to provide that it is to be paid by certified cheque or bank draft rather than by cash or "negotiable cheque" as is currently reflected on the OREA form. In certain circumstances, a purchaser may prefer to wire funds to the vendor and, accordingly, that alternative will have to be provided for by amending the OREA form to allow the purchase price to be tendered in that manner.

DEPOSIT

The next portion of the OREA form of agreement of purchase and sale requires that the purchaser indicate the amount of the deposit it is submitting with the offer or will submit once the offer is finally accepted. The person who will hold the deposit must also be indicated. In residential transactions, the listing agent usually holds the deposit in the belief that it is a neutral third party;

practically speaking, it is the agent's way of ensuring his or her sales commission is paid. In non-residential transactions, the practice varies and often the vendor's or purchaser's solicitor will hold the deposit.

The OREA form specifically provides that the deposit will be held in a non-interest-bearing account. When acting for a purchaser, this portion of the form should be amended to require the deposit to be invested in an interest-bearing account or investment certificate with interest to accrue to the benefit of the purchaser, such interest to be treated in the same manner as the deposit itself. Obviously, the farther off the date of closing is from the date of the submission of the deposit, the more important it is that the deposit is invested, preferably in a conservative investment certificate that pays the highest interest rate for the period of time until closing.

There is no rule on the amount to be submitted as a deposit. In residential transactions, agents will usually insist that an amount that covers their commissions be submitted as the deposit, as they are usually the party holding the deposit. This allows them to be paid immediately on the date of closing. Apart from this consideration, the amount of a deposit is often viewed as a reflection of the seriousness of the purchaser, especially where there are many conditions in the offer in the purchaser's favour or where the closing date is a long way off. A deposit which is too low may not be viewed by a vendor as sufficient to discourage the purchaser from defaulting, while a demand for a high deposit by the vendor will often be difficult for purchasers who are relying on financing in order to complete the transaction or who have such larger sums of money personally invested for fixed maturities that cannot be withdrawn earlier. If any advice can be given, it should be that the amount of the deposit be sufficient to demonstrate that a purchaser is serious about proceeding with the transaction and that he or she would not want to risk losing the amount submitted. Such seriousness should be all that a vendor should be looking for; more is not necessarily better when it comes to deposits, as we shall see later.

The deposit has two functions in the context of an agreement of purchase and sale: it is a partial prepayment that will be applied against the purchase price on closing and it is security given to the vendor to encourage the purchaser to complete the transaction or else risk its forfeiture. In reviewing the OREA standard form agreement, reference to the application of the deposit as a credit against the purchase price is specifically made; however, there is no mention of how the deposit is to be dealt with if the transaction does not close and no mention of the second function of the deposit as security. Accordingly, the OREA agreement or any agreement should deal specifically with the application of the deposit and all interest accrued therein in the event the transaction does not close. There are cases that have held that the deposit's function as security in the vendor's favour is implicit in the use of the word "deposit" and that a clause confirming that the deposit is forfeited to the vendor if the purchaser breaches the contract is not necessary (see *Shelson Investments Ltd. v. Durkovich*, [1984] A.J. No. 75, 34 Alta. L.R. (2d) 319 (Q.B.)). Nevertheless, it is recommended that a clause be specifically inserted into the agreement. While there are several variations on how such a clause should read depending on whether a vendor's slant or purchaser's slant is taken, an example of a clause that is a middle ground that should be inserted is as follows:

The Vendor and Purchaser acknowledge and agree that in the event this agreement is not completed as a result of the default of the Purchaser, the deposit and interest accrued thereon shall be forfeited to the Vendor; however, if this agreement is not completed for any other reason, the deposit and interest accrued thereon shall be immediately returned to the Purchaser without deduction and the party holding the deposit is hereby directed to do so.

With such a clause included in the standard OREA form, the deposit would be dealt with as follows in the circumstances listed below:

1. If the transaction is completed, the deposit is credited against the purchase price on closing.

2. If the purchaser refuses or does not close without any contractual or legal entitlement to do so, the deposit is forfeited to the vendor.

3. If the vendor refuses to close, the purchaser is entitled to the return of the deposit.

Where both the vendor and purchaser are in default, the courts have held that a purchaser should be entitled to the return of the deposit (see *Zender v. Ball*, [1974] O.J. No. 2123, 5 O.R. (2d) 747 (H.C.J.); *Dol v. Marlene Musclow Insurance Agency Ltd.*, [2006] O.J. No. 2230, 45 R.P.R. (4th) 297 (H.C.J.).

In spite of the above principles relating to deposits, purchasers who are faced with the forfeiture of their deposits often apply to court for relief against that forfeiture. One argument often used by purchasers to avoid the forfeiture is that notwithstanding their default, the vendor has not suffered any damages. This argument was rejected by the Ontario Court of Appeal in *De Palma v. Runnymede Iron & Steel Co.*, [1949] O.J. No. 495, [1950] O.R. 1, where the Court found that it was not necessary for a party to demonstrate it had suffered damages in an amount in excess of the deposit in order to retain it; the mere fact that the amount was given to it as a deposit relieved it of any obligation to account for the damages it suffered (see also *Impex Holdings Ltd. v. Princess Street Developments (Kingston) Inc.*, [1993] O.J. No. 200, 30 R.P.R. (2d) 51 (Gen. Div.)). Similarly, in *Liu v. Coal Harbour Properties Partnership*, [2006] B.C.J. No. 1983, 273 D.L.R. (4th) 508, the British Columbia Court of Appeal rejected a plaintiff's argument that a vendor be obliged to return a deposit of $391,000 where it was able to resell a property for a premium of approximately 30 per cent notwithstanding the plaintiff having defaulted under the purchase agreement.

There are cases in which the courts have granted at least partial relief against forfeiture where return of the full deposit would represent a windfall to the vendor. For example, in *Iyer v. Pleasant Developments Inc.*, [2005] O.J. No. 3407 (S.C.J.), revd [2006] O.J. No. 1319, 45 R.P.R. (4th) 147 (S.C.J.), the Small Claims Court refused to order the purchaser to return the $10,000 deposit and awarded the purchaser $9,300. The Court held that in the absence of any proof as to damages suffered, the keeping of the deposit would be "forfeiture, grossly disproportionate to the losses suffered, unconscionable and a case for relief from forfeiture" (see also *Tsui v. Zhao*, [2006] O.J. No. 3032 (S.C.J.)).

A noteworthy case to remember when considering the amount of the deposit and its forfeiture is the decision of the Privy Council in *Workers Trust & Merchant Bank Ltd. v. Dojap Investments Ltd.*, [1993] A.C. 573. In this case, the vendor required a deposit of 25 per cent of the purchase price upon entering into an agreement of purchase and sale. The deposit was delivered. The purchaser subsequently defaulted under the contract and the vendor retained the deposit. The purchaser applied to the Court for relief from forfeiture of the deposit. At trial, relief was denied. On appeal to the Court of Appeal, the Court allowed relief in part, finding that a deposit of 25 per cent was unreasonable, and ordered that the vendor only be entitled to retain a deposit that was usual in such transactions, which it found to be 10 per cent. The additional deposit taken was to be returned. The vendor appealed and the purchaser cross-appealed. The Privy Council held that in a contract for the sale of land, a reasonable amount given by a purchaser as a deposit to a vendor to secure its performance of the contract was acceptable and would be forfeited to the vendor if the purchaser breached the agreement. A deposit in such circumstances was not a penalty. However, where a vendor seeks and obtains a greater sum as a forfeitable deposit, the vendor must establish special circumstances justifying it and that it was therefore reasonable. The Privy Council ruled that the 25 per cent deposit was not justifiable and therefore the provision in the purchase agreement requiring its forfeiture was a penalty giving the court jurisdiction to grant relief. However, it disagreed with the Court of Appeal as to the extent of the relief and ordered all of the deposit returned, finding that since the vendor had not contracted for a reasonable deposit the whole deposit was repayable, with interest. The message from this case is certainly that more is not necessarily better when it comes to deposits.

It is also imperative that a purchaser remit a deposit within the time allowed to it to do so, especially when the agreement of purchase and sale provides that time is of the essence. A court will allow a vendor to terminate a contract where a purchaser is late in submitting the deposit, even if that tardiness is as short a period as two days, as in *1473587 Ontario Inc. v. Jackson*, [2005] O.J. No. 710, 74 O.R. (3d) 539 (S.C.J.), affd [2005] O.J. No. 3145, 75 O.R. (3d) 484 (C.A.).

BALANCE OF PURCHASE PRICE

The next issue to be dealt with in the printed form of the Agreement of Purchase and Sale is the terms of payment. The pre-printed form is organized such that a schedule is to be appended to add these terms. Most often, language will be required to deal with mortgages. There are four basic situations, with many variations.

Mortgage to Be Given Back to Vendor as Part of Purchase Price

Obviously, both parties to the agreement will require that the terms of the mortgage be stated clearly. Accordingly, the parties should, at a minimum, agree on the principal, interest rate, maturity, amortization period, calculation, priority and rights of prepayment applicable to the mortgage. If acting for a vendor, it is important to state in the agreement that the mortgage must be drawn on a form acceptable to the vendor. There are some offices which have had stationers print standard charge terms for them that include some unusual clauses. If it was stated clearly in the agreement that the vendor must approve the form, it would be an easy matter for the solicitor of the vendor to reject those clauses.

Some agreements set out the purchase price, a specific amount to be paid by deposit and the amount of cash on closing. These agreements then state that a mortgage will be given back for the balance due on closing. This practice is awkward and should be avoided. It will not only produce a mortgage in an odd amount, but the mortgage cannot be prepared in draft by the solicitor for the purchaser until the solicitor for the vendor prepares and delivers the statement of adjustments.

Existing Mortgage to Be Assumed as Part of Purchase Price

If you have a part in preparing an agreement of purchase and sale on behalf of a vendor, insist on seeing the mortgage document first. Even those clients who understand the difference between the amortization and the term may have faulty memories. And many clients seem to be baffled by interest calculations; they have no idea how much principal is actually owing at any time. If the agreement calls for a mortgage that matures in 2012, but in fact is due in 2009, or if the agreement calls for a mortgage on which there is $25,000 outstanding for principal, and in fact there is more or less than that amount, the purchaser may well refuse to close, or may insist on closing, and the vendor will be forced to pay the cost of making the mortgage comply with the contract: *Re Osterhout and Cada*, [1915] O.J. No. 381, 8 O.W.N. 30 (H.C. Div.). In *M&M Investments Ltd. v. Edwin Investments Ltd.*, [1991] B.C.J. No. 2898, 60 B.C.L.R. (2d) 181, the Court of Appeal allowed the purchaser to rescind a purchase agreement where the interest rate applicable to a mortgage to be assumed was 10½ per cent rather than 10¼ per cent as was set out in the purchase agreement. The Court of Appeal held that in most cases, the interest rate of a mortgage to be assumed is of "fundamental importance", entitling a purchaser to rescission if incorrect. Similarly, in *Garfreed Construction Co. v. Blue Orchid Holdings Ltd.*, [1976] O.J. No. 2377, 1 R.P.R. 79 (H.C.J.), the Court allowed a purchaser to rescind a purchase agreement where the outstanding principal was almost $18,000 more than that set out in the agreement. If there is actually less than that amount owing, the purchaser who wants to close will be forced to raise additional cash on short notice. This occurs most commonly when a client advises the agent of the amount owing as of the date the property is listed, and that amount appears in the agreement even though the transaction closes months later, after many further payments of principal have been made. Clearly, the amount of any mortgage to be assumed should be shown in the agreement as the amount owing as of the closing date.

However, if there is more principal outstanding than was stated in the agreement but the mortgage is open (unlike the situation in *Garfreed*), the court will not consider that a sufficient variation in the terms of the contract to relieve the purchaser from the obligation to close. Lieff J. in *Rexhill Holdings Ltd. v. Maybird Investments Ltd.*, [1972] O.J. No. 1985, [1973] 1 O.R. 285 (H.C.J.) stated that, since the mortgages to be assumed were fully open and could be easily reduced by the purchaser to the amount agreed to be assumed, there was no variation in the terms of the contract.

When dealing with a mortgage to be assumed, be sure that it does not contain a "due on sale" clause, being a provision that requires the mortgage to be paid off in full upon the sale of the property. Such a provision is less common in residential mortgages but is standard in all other mortgages. An example of a due on sale clause in a mortgage is as follows:

Provided that in the event of

(1)   the Chargor selling, conveying, transferring, or entering into any agreement of sale or transfer of the title of the Charged Premises to a purchaser, grantee or transferee not approved in writing by the Chargee; or

(2)   failure of such a purchaser, grantee or transferee to (a) apply for and receive the Chargee's written approval as aforesaid, (b) personally assume all the obligations of the Chargor under this Charge, and (c) execute an Assumption Agreement in the form required by the Chargee,

then at the option of the Chargee all moneys hereby secured with accrued interest thereon shall forthwith become due and payable.

The agreement of purchase and sale should be made conditional upon compliance with this provision and should outline whose responsibility and cost it will be to obtain the mortgagee's approval. In *Weeks v. Rosocha*, [1982] O.J. No. 3228, 36 O.R. (2d) 379 (Co. Ct.), revd [1983] O.J. No. 3040, 41 O.R. (2d) 787 (C.A.), the Court of Appeal held that a vendor was required to disclose the fact that a mortgage contained a due on sale clause if that mortgage was to be assumed by a purchaser, and the failure to deal with it in the purchase agreement entitled the purchaser to rescind the contract. See also *Lamperstorfer v. McDermott*, [1983] O.J. No. 2184, 30 R.P.R. 140 (Co. Ct.) for a case where the opposite result was justifiably reached in light of the specific facts of that case, and see *Griffiths v. Zambosco*, [1999] O.J. No. 2798, 103 O.T.C. 18 (S.C.J.), vard [2001] O.J. No. 2096, 54 O.R. (3d) 397 (C.A.)).

New Mortgage to Be Arranged to Provide Part of Purchase Price

Sometimes agents will prepare an agreement with a clause as follows:

... at the sale price of TWO HUNDRED THOUSAND, FIVE HUNDRED ($200,500) DOLLARS of lawful money of Canada, payable cheque TEN THOUSAND ($10,000) DOLLARS to the Agent for the Vendor as a deposit to be held by such Agent pending completion or other termination of the agreement and to be credited on account of the purchase money on closing, and the Purchaser agrees to pay a further sum of NINETY THOUSAND, FIVE HUNDRED ($90,500) DOLLARS in cash or by certified cheque to the Vendor on closing, subject to the usual adjustments. This offer is conditional upon the Purchaser or the agent obtaining a new first Mortgage for not less than ONE HUNDRED THOUSAND ($100,000) DOLLARS bearing interest at the rate of not more than 15 per cent per annum calculated semi-annually not in advance and repayable in blended monthly payments of about $1,246.16 including principal and interest and to run for a term of not less than 5 years.

This is incorrect. Between the vendor and the purchaser this is a cash transaction, and the full purchase price less the deposit, subject to the usual adjustments, is payable on closing. Of course, it must be subject to a condition that the purchaser obtain financing. Everyone knows that a new mortgage loan of $100,000 will not produce a net advance of $100,000. It should be clear that the inspection fees, solicitor's fees, solicitor's disbursements and the deduction of interest to the interest adjustment date are to be paid by the purchaser. Also, the condition should have an early expiry date. As written, the purchaser could walk away from the deal right up to and including the closing date. It amounts to nothing less than a free option. A condition in this form is also deficient because it does not state the manner in which notice of compliance or non-compliance is to be given. The following is suggested as a proper condition:

> This offer is subject to the following condition, compliance with which (unless the Purchaser shall waive such compliance) shall be a condition precedent to any obligation hereunder on the part of the Purchaser. The condition referred to is that the Purchaser shall have obtained a commitment, within ten (10) days of acceptance of this offer by the Vendor, for a first mortgage loan on the security of the real property for an amount not less than $100,000 bearing interest at the rate of not more than fifteen per cent (15 per cent) per annum repayable in blended monthly payments of principal and interest of about $1,246.16 to run for a term of five (5) years, all costs of which mortgage loan to be borne by the Purchaser. If the Purchaser has not notified the Vendor or the Vendor's solicitor in writing on or before 5:00 p.m. of the tenth day after acceptance of this offer by the Vendor that the Purchaser has been unable to obtain such mortgage loan, the Purchaser shall be deemed to have waived this condition.

Existing Mortgages to Be Discharged

The normal practice of solicitors when dealing with a mortgage to be discharged varies according to the mortgagee. If the mortgage is held by a bank or trust company or an insurance company, *i.e.*, an "institutional lender", the solicitor will normally close the purchase when presented with a statement from the mortgagee showing the amount required to obtain the discharge, together with a direction authorizing the purchaser to deduct from and pay out of the balance due on closing that amount directly to the mortgagee. The vendor's solicitor will then undertake to obtain and register the discharge.

Typically, the standard real estate board form of agreement of purchase and sale contains a clause that expressly provides for closing on the basis of the foregoing practice. Paragraph 12 of the OREA agreement contains such provisions. However, when dealing with a mortgage held by an individual or a private company, solicitors should insist upon the delivery of the executed discharge for registration on closing.

If the sale agreement does not contain the typical clause, you should be careful when dealing with institutional mortgages, especially in view of the decisions in *Fong v. Weinper*, [1973] O.J. No. 1956, [1973] 2 O.R. 760 (H.C.J.), *Garfreed Construction Co. v. Blue Orchid Holdings Ltd.*, [1976] O.J. No. 2377, 15 O.R. (2d) 22 (H.C.J.) and *McFadden v. Pye*, [1978] O.J. No. 3377, 22 O.R. (2d) 268 (H.C.J.). In these cases, the Court found that the production on closing of a statement by a mortgagee showing the amount required to discharge the mortgage, together with a certified cheque payable to the mortgagee for that amount, was not sufficient compliance with the agreement by the vendor "to discharge any existing mortgage ... on or before closing". In each case, the purchaser refused to close and the Court dismissed the vendor's action to forfeit the deposit.

Unless the agreement contains the typical clause referred to above, the following clause should be inserted by a solicitor acting for a vendor in any agreement of purchase and sale where there is a mortgage outstanding and it is the intention of the vendor that that mortgage be discharged using part of the balance due on closing:

> The Purchaser acknowledges and agrees that there is presently outstanding a mortgage in favour of A.B.C. Trust Company Limited and that the Purchaser will close this transaction upon production to the Purchaser of a statement from A.B.C. Trust Company Limited as to the amount required to obtain a discharge of that mortgage on the closing date together with a direction executed by the Vendor authorizing the Purchaser to pay that amount to the A.B.C. Trust Company Limited out of the balance due on closing and the personal undertaking of the vendor's lawyer to obtain and register the discharge of the mortgage within a reasonable period of time.

CONDITIONS

At this point in the OREA standard form agreement of purchase and sale, reference is made to schedules that are appended to the form for the purposes of adding supplementary provisions. One of the most common provisions to be added includes the conditions that must be satisfied before the purchaser will proceed with the transaction. Very often a purchaser will make an offer but it will be conditional upon some other occurrence. The most common example is a couple who want to move to a new house. They see a house they like and want to put in an offer, but if they do not sell their own house they will not have the money to close. Therefore, their obligation under the offer to purchase must be conditional upon the sale of their present house. When acting for this type of purchaser, the best form of condition is one stating that "this offer is conditional upon the purchasers completing the sale of their house at 10 Blank Street on or before the closing date set out herein". If acting for a vendor, this form is usually unacceptable because the vendor will not know until the closing date whether there is a sale or not. The normal condition will state that the offer is conditional upon the purchasers accepting an offer to purchase their present house within a specified time. You should point out the risk to the purchasers that once they have accepted an offer on their present house, they have a firm agreement to purchase the new house. If the purchaser of their present house, for any reason, does not complete that purchase, the agreement to purchase the new house is binding, and they may be forced to arrange temporary financing to complete the purchase while they find a new purchaser for their house.

Another very common condition already mentioned is the ability of the purchasers to arrange a mortgage loan. You can see how important it is that conditions be properly drafted; if not, the purchasers may be obligated to buy the property even if they do not have any money. At the very least, they will forfeit their deposit; they may also be sued for damages. But if the conditions are properly drafted, none of these penalties will arise. If they cannot sell their house, or raise a loan, they get their deposit back and the deal is terminated.

If you are acting for a vendor, you must point out the great disadvantage this type of offer has for the vendor. The vendor, anxious to move, accepts an offer subject to a condition that the purchasers must sell their house or raise a mortgage or any other condition (discussed below). If the purchasers cannot or do not comply with the condition, they just walk away and the vendor still has an unsold house.

You may be acting for someone who is buying property with some special use in mind; for example, the purchaser is buying a house to use as a boarding house or fraternity house; or the purchaser is buying a retail property to use as a convenience store; or the purchaser is buying vacant land on which to build an apartment; or the purchaser is buying 10 acres on which to construct a new factory building. It is essential to the purchaser in any of these situations, not only that the vendor can grant a clear title, but that the use the purchaser contemplates be allowed under the local zoning by-laws and title not be subject to any restrictive covenants preventing the particular use intended. Checking with the municipal office before signing the agreement may not be enough; zoning can and does change. You must, therefore, make the offer conditional upon there being no by-laws or restrictive covenants at the date of closing which could prevent the intended use. It might even be conditional upon obtaining a building permit for a specified number of suites in an apartment building.

If your client is buying a whole series of properties on a street for a land assembly, you may wish to make each offer conditional upon the completion of the others.

There are many other common conditions: engineering reports on soil conditions for the support of buildings, suitability of drainage, or sufficient flow of water from a well, for example. In residential transactions, it is almost always the case that a purchaser will make the agreement conditional on the result of a physical inspection of the home by a qualified expert being satisfactory to the purchaser. In a non-residential transaction, a purchaser almost always will make an agreement conditional on the completion of an environmental audit of the property in addition to the physical inspection.

Obviously, a vendor who has a popular property with many prospective purchasers is not going to be interested in a conditional offer; however, even vendors must recognize that any party who intends to finance the acquisition of a property must satisfy the mortgagee as to the physical and environmental condition of the property in order to obtain the loan, without which the transaction will not proceed.

Remember that, when dealing with land that is to be severed from lands to be retained by the vendor, you must make the agreement conditional upon compliance with s. 50 of the *Planning Act*, R.S.O. 1990, c. P.13. Otherwise, pursuant to s. 50(21), the agreement itself is not enforceable. Such a condition is considered a "true condition precedent" (a term discussed later) that cannot be waived by either party. Paragraph 15 of the OREA purchase agreement contains a condition to this effect as one of its standard provisions.

You should also consider at this stage whether the transaction could fall under the *Bulk Sales Act*, R.S.O. 1990, c. B.14, because it includes a sale in bulk of stock in trade out of the ordinary course of business. If so, the agreement should state that it will be completed in compliance with the terms of the *Bulk Sales Act*.

When drafting conditions, make it clear what the conditions are. It is not good enough to say, "The purchaser is to have 30 days to check the zoning". What is the condition there? Once the 30 days have passed, the condition has been fulfilled. The condition is that the purchaser be satisfied within 30 days of acceptance that the proposed use of the property is permitted by all applicable zoning by-laws.

Make it clear and certain when the condition is to be satisfied and how notice of compliance is to be given. In many cases, silence is deemed to be acceptance. If the condition has not been satisfied, give notice of the non-compliance in writing to the other party before the time expires or provide that silence is deemed to mean that the condition has not been satisfied.

Great care must be taken when drafting conditions. If you create what the Supreme Court of Canada referred to in *Turney v. Zhilka*, [1959] S.C.J. No. 37, [1959] S.C.R. 578, as a "true condition precedent", then it cannot be unilaterally waived. Where the obligations under the contract, for both parties, depend upon a future uncertain event that is in the control of a third party, until that event occurs, there is no right to performance on either side and no ability by either party to unilaterally waive the condition. Interestingly, the condition in *Turney* related to the approval of a plan of subdivision by the local municipality and did not specify for whose benefit the condition existed or who was required to satisfy the condition. While it could be argued that the lack of detail as to these matters explains the Court's ruling, the Supreme Court in several subsequent decisions where there was no such ambiguity consistently applied the *Turney* principle in deciding that a condition that relied upon a third party's decision or action was a true condition precedent rendering the agreement void if the condition was not satisfied, notwithstanding any purported waiver of the condition by either party (see *F.T. Developments Ltd. v. Sherman*, [1968] S.C.J. No. 91, [1969] S.C.R. 203; *O'Reilly v. Marketers Diversified Inc.*, [1969] S.C.J. No. 44, [1969] S.C.R. 741; and *Barnett v. Harrison*, [1975] S.C.J. No. 88, [1976] 2 S.C.R. 531).

As a result of these decisions, solicitors involved in drafting conditions for purchasers in purchase agreements had to be sure that their clients understood that the agreement could be void if a specific condition they wanted involving the satisfaction of a matter in a third party's control was not satisfied. In acting for a vendor, a solicitor had to make the vendor understand that the contract would terminate if the condition was not satisfied, even if the purchaser was content to proceed. The courts have continued to apply the *Turney* principle, as in *Goetz v. Whitehall Development Corp.*, [1978] O.J. No. 3277, 19 O.R. (2d) 33, where the Court of Appeal held that where there was a condition that certain events occur by a specific date and that date passed without the events occurring, the agreement expired, and the rights and obligations created by the agreement came to an end.

Since these decisions, courts have made more of an effort to distinguish between conditions that are true conditions precedent and those that are "simple" conditions, meaning that the party in whose favour they have been included can unilaterally waive them. In *Genern Investments Ltd. v. Back*, [1969] O.J. No. 1272, [1969] 1 O.R. 694 (H.C.J.), the Court held that although a zoning condition was a true condition precedent, the purchaser had drafted the condition to allow him to waive it, and the waiver right took the condition "outside the realm of a true condition precedent" as the purchaser had given himself the right to relinquish its benefit. In *Beauchamp v. Beauchamp*, [1972] O.J. No. 2054, [1973] 2 O.R. 43 (C.A.), affd (1974), 40 D.L.R. (3d) 160 (S.C.C.), the Court of Appeal held that a purchaser could unilaterally waive a financing condition even though the financing he had intended to obtain was not secured. The Court found that this condition was entirely for the purchaser's benefit and no prejudice was suffered by the vendor in allowing the purchaser to waive it as it simply meant the transaction could close, giving the vendor exactly what was contracted for. Similarly, in *Lestrange v. Juda*, [1973] O.J. No. 2316, 11 O.R. (2d) 702 (C.A.), the Court held that a condition in favour of the purchasers relating to the sale of their current home could be waived by them and was not a true condition precedent, but simply a one-way condition as it benefitted only the purchasers. Finally, *Smale v. Van der Weer*, [1977] O.J. No. 2427, 17 O.R. (2d) 480 (H.C.J.), is authority for the position that even a true condition precedent can be waived by both parties, and such a waiver may be inferred by the court if one party waives and the other, by proceeding with the transaction, "accepts" the waiver.

If your client, the purchaser, wants a property in any event and the conditions are inserted solely for your client's protection in the hope that they will force the vendor to obtain compliance, carefully draft the condition to make it clear that it may be waived by the purchaser and is inserted only for the purchaser. Examples are as follows:

> The agreement to be constituted by the acceptance of this offer is subject to the following conditions, compliance with all of which (unless the Purchaser shall in writing waive such compliance) shall be a condition precedent to any obligation hereunder on the part of the Purchaser and are included for the sole benefit of the Purchaser. The conditions referred to are that ...

> If such conditions are not complied with within the time aforesaid and such compliance is not waived as aforesaid, the Purchaser shall be entitled to the return of the deposit money without interest.

OR

> The Purchaser may terminate this agreement by written notice to the Vendor delivered to the Vendor on or before the ____ day of ____, 20__ if before that date [specific condition] has not occurred, in which event the deposit shall be returned without interest. This condition is included for the sole benefit of the Purchaser and may be waived by the Purchaser at her sole option.

It is preferable, of course, to specify the period of time within which the condition is to be satisfied. Where such detail is not included, the courts will imply a reasonable time for giving notice to a vendor as to the fulfillment of a condition (see *746396 Ontario Ltd. v. D'Elia*, [1998] O.J. No. 5321, 83 O.T.C. 315 (Gen. Div.)).

The practice has developed in recent years to include various conditions as to financing or condition of the building or ability to use for the purchaser's proposed use, all to be satisfied "in the Purchaser's sole discretion". The courts have refused to allow purchasers to walk away from their contractual obligations simply because they have changed their mind; the purchasers must be able to establish that they have used reasonable efforts to satisfy the condition and have been unsuccessful (see *Norfolk Motor Hotel (1974) Ltd. v. Graves*, [1989] N.S.J. No. 171, 91 N.S.R. (2d) 53 (C.A.); *Chan v. Hayward*, [1983] B.C.J. No. 1423, 44 B.C.L.R. 251 (S.C.); *BEM Enterprises Ltd. v. Campeau Corp.*, [1980] B.C.J. No. 115, 24 B.C.L.R. 244 (S.C.), vard [1981] B.C.J. No. 18, 32 B.C.L.R. 116 (C.A.); *Cox v. Alley*, [1991] B.C.J. No. 2002, 17 R.P.R. (2d) 283 (S.C.); *737985 Ontario Ltd. v. Essex Sanitary Plumbing and Heating Co.*, [1993] B.C.J. No. 1041, 31 R.P.R. (2d) 217 (Gen. Div.); *Eastwalsh Homes Ltd. v. Anatal Developments Ltd.*, [1993] O.J. No. 676, 12 O.R. (3d) 675 (C.A.)). Furthermore, the courts have ruled that even where an agreement provides that a matter could be considered at the sole discretion of a party, that party must act reasonably in exercising its discretion and do so in good faith; to allow a purchaser to do otherwise would be to convert an agreement of purchase and sale into an option to purchase (see *Allied Canadian Acquisition Corp. v. 1012689 Ontario Ltd.*, [2002] O.J. No. 289, 48 R.P.R. (3d) 43 (S.C.J.)).

The Ontario Court of Appeal had an opportunity to revisit these issues in *Marshall v. Bernard Place Corp.*, [2002] O.J. No. 463, 47 R.P.R. (3d) 1. In this case, the purchaser entered into an agreement to purchase a home that was conditional upon the inspection of the property by a home inspector and receipt of a report from the inspector that was satisfactory to the purchaser "in his sole and absolute discretion". The purchaser arranged for such an inspection and later received a report that the house was well built and required no major repairs. The report did note minor deficiencies that could be remedied at minor cost. Based on this report, the purchaser delivered a notice to the vendor that the condition was not satisfied and, as a result, the agreement was terminated. The vendor refused to return the purchaser's deposit, arguing that the purchaser could not rely on the condition given the minor nature of the deficiencies revealed by the home inspection.

At trial, the Court held that the purchaser was entitled to the return of his deposit (see [2000] O.J. No. 3321, 36 R.P.R. (3d) 153), which led to the appeal.

The Court of Appeal confirmed (at para. 16) that "discretion under contractual conditions subject to discretionary judgments ... must be exercised honestly and in good faith". The Court then referred to the Court of Appeal's decision in *Greenberg v. Meffert*, [1985] O.J. No. 2539, 18 D.L.R. (4th) 548 and approved of the analysis of Robins J.A. therein (at 554 D.L.R.):

> Provisions in agreements making payment or performance subject to "the discretion", "the opinion" or "the satisfaction" of a party to the agreement or a third party, broadly speaking, fall into two general categories. In contracts in which the matter to be decided or approved is not readily susceptible of objective measurement — matters involving taste, sensibility, personal compatibility or

judgment of the party for whose benefit the authority was given — such provisions are more likely construed as imposing only a subjective standard. On the other hand, a contract relating to such matters as operative fitness, structural completion, mechanical utility or marketability, these provisions are generally construed as imposing an objective standard of reasonableness ... In any given transaction, the category into which such a provision falls will depend upon the intention of the parties as disclosed by their contract. In the absence of explicit language or a clear intention from the tenor of the contract or the nature of the subject-matter, the tendency of the cases is to require the discretion or the dissatisfaction to be reasonable.

After its review of *Greenberg* and other decisions, the Court of Appeal in *Marshall* agreed (at para. 19) that "... the contract controls the standard to be applied to a sole discretion clause. The determination of whether a discretionary condition imposes a subjective or objective standard depends upon 'the intention of the parties as disclosed by their contract'". However, the Court insisted that whether or not the exercise of discretion is to be measured by an objective or subjective standard, the requirement of honesty and good faith applies. Furthermore, the Court confirmed (at para. 20) that:

> No contractual discretion is absolute, in the sense of authorizing the capricious or arbitrary exercise of the discretion. *Greenberg* confirmed that even a broadly stated contractual discretion is not "unbridled" and is subject to established limits.

Based on the above principles, the Court in *Marshall* found (at para. 21) that the home inspection report obtained by the purchaser provided

> an objective basis on which to assess the potential exercise of discretion under a discretionary property inspection condition. The intention of the parties, as reflected in the language of the condition, then determines the scope for subjective assessment of the materiality of the identified deficiencies.

In other words, the condition at issue, being the physical state of the home, was capable of an objective analysis. Once such an analysis reveals concerns, then the language of the condition will determine what latitude the party relying on the condition is given. In this case, the home inspection report did identify deficiencies which, although remediable at minimal cost, did on the facts carry with them certain risks and inconveniences. As a result, the report identified legitimate physical issues that were arrived at objectively. In light of these objective issues, the purchaser was entitled to exercise his discretion based on the wording of the contract, which in this case allowed the discretion to be exercised on a subjective basis. In other words (at para. 34):

> ... once the inspection report identified objective facts relating to deficiencies in the property, the expansive language of the inspection condition agreed to by the parties permitted the respondents to assess whether the risks, uncertainties and inconveniences associated with the deficiencies outlined in the report were acceptable, according to their own subjective circumstances and perspectives.

IRREVOCABILITY AND ACCEPTANCE

As mentioned in the opening paragraph of this chapter, most agreements of purchase and sale used in real property transactions involve an offer by one party to another party and the acceptance of that offer without any changes to it. The first step in the process is, of course, the preparation of the offer as either an offer by a purchaser to buy from an owner or an offer by that owner to sell to a third party. In either case, the offer is signed and dated by the party making the offer, which in the case of the OREA form occurs on the reverse of the form, and then presented to the other party. The completion of paragraph 1 of the OREA form is important to this process, as it is in this paragraph that the person making the offer indicates the period of time it remains open for acceptance, after which, if not accepted, the offer lapses. Note that the offer is usually stated as being irrevocable during this period which, at common law, is effective as long as there is consideration given by the other party. The requirement for consideration is usually satisfied by ensuring the party accepting the offer signs it under seal.

Once an offer is accepted, that acceptance must, of course, be communicated to the other party before the contract is considered complete and binding. Practically speaking, notices of acceptance are usually given through the real estate agents involved in the transaction; they are appointed by paragraph 3 of the OREA agreement for the purposes of receiving such notices on behalf of the parties.

Any changes to the terms of an offer by the party to whom it is presented for acceptance converts the offer to a counter-offer, which requires the original party who made the offer to accept the changes within whatever period of time the counter-offer provides for its acceptance.

CLOSING DATE

When completing paragraph 2 of the standard form agreement of purchase and sale, check that the closing date is not Saturday, Sunday or a statutory holiday. Because of chaotic conditions in many land registry offices on Fridays and at the end of a month, you should try to avoid those dates as well.

Note that paragraph 2 of the OREA form also provides that the vendor must deliver vacant possession of the property to the purchaser on closing. Obviously, if there are tenancies being assumed by a purchaser or other arrangements agreed to that would alter this requirement, the agreement must be amended to vary the vendor's obligations in this regard.

FIXTURES / CHATTELS / CONTRACTS

Paragraphs 4, 5 and 6 of the OREA standard form agreement of purchase and sale deal with what chattels are included, what fixtures are excluded and what contracts for rented equipment are to be assumed by the purchaser, if they are assumable.

Insofar as chattels are concerned, you must be specific and precise in listing what chattels are being sold to the purchaser with the property. In residential files, appliances and furniture will often be listed here; in non-residential files, the chattels that may accompany the sale will vary depending on the nature of the property being sold. Nevertheless, in both types of transaction, being precise and descriptive in listing the chattels (even listing serial numbers where available) will avoid disputes on closing as to what exactly was included. Also consider the fact that the OREA form does not deal with the condition of, title to or encumbrances that may affect chattels; all of its provisions relate to the real property. Accordingly, it is important for a purchaser's solicitor to add to the standard form assurances as to these matters insofar as the chattels are concerned, and of course to subsequently complete searches against the vendor under the *Personal Property Security Act*, R.S.O. 1990, c. P.10 to determine whether there are any security interests held by third parties in the vendor's chattels. The agreement should also be amended to require the vendor to deliver to the purchaser a bill of sale on closing evidencing the sale of the chattels.

Fixtures is another matter altogether and, in the context of the OREA form, is dealt with by making the parties agree as to what, if any, fixtures are excluded from the purchase price. You will recall that earlier in this chapter, reference was made to s. 15 of the *Conveyancing and Law of Property Act*, which provides that in every conveyance of land, all fixtures relating to the land are deemed included unless the parties specifically make an exclusion. As a result, it is in the vendor's interest to be specific in excluding any fixtures relating to a property that are not intended to be sold. Unfortunately, the law relating to what constitutes a fixture and at what point a chattel that is somehow affixed to realty loses its character as a chattel is confusing and often varies in each case depending on the chattel or item at issue. *Stack v. T. Eaton Co.*, [1902] O.J. No. 155, 4 O.L.R. 335 (Div. Ct.) sets out several general principles to distinguish chattels from fixtures. Often, the distinction is found in the degree of attachment (see *Credit Valley Cable TV/FM Ltd. v. Peel Condominium Corp. No. 95*, [1980] O.J. No. 3514, 27 O.R. (2d) 433 (H.C.J.)). Still, to avoid arguments, a vendor should err on the side of inclusion where there is any doubt as to whether something he or she considers a chattel and is not intending to sell with the property is a fixture, and list it in paragraph 5.

Paragraph 6 is meant to clarify what fixtures in a property are not owned by the vendor but are leased from a third party. In a residential situation, this usually applies to the hot water tank and/or furnace. In non-residential transactions, the likelihood that there will be components of the buildings and fixtures that are leased will be greater, as will the likelihood that there will be contracts for the provision of services or materials to the property generally. Such contracts, if important to the continued operation of the property, should be assigned to the purchaser, and this agreement will have to be augmented to deal with issues of obtaining the consent to assignment of such contracts and to allocating the responsibility for costs associated therewith. From a purchaser's perspective, it will also be important that certain contracts be cancelled by the vendor so that they are not inherited by the purchaser. The introduction of competition in the supply of gas and electricity to property owners and the contracts entered into by such parties in connection therewith is a perfect example of one area where purchasers will have to be careful in considering the opportunity or risk of assuming such contracts, depending on their terms and when they were entered into by the owner.

Note also that because of the requirement contained in the *Land Transfer Tax Act*, R.S.O. 1990, c. L.6 that all land transfer tax affidavits contain an apportionment of the total purchase price into that amount attributable to chattels and that amount attributable to land, buildings, fixtures and goodwill, it will be helpful if the parties agree to this apportionment in the agreement of purchase and sale. This will require two decisions on the part of the parties: first, which of the items included in the sale are in fact chattels and not fixtures; and second, what the value of those chattels is.

HARMONIZED SALES TAX

Harmonized Sales Tax ("HST") and its applicability to real property transactions is discussed in detail in Chapter 4. However, for the purposes of reviewing paragraph 7 of the OREA form of agreement, note that it gives the party preparing the offer the option of inserting whether HST is or is not included in the purchase price. For most residential transactions involving resales, the paragraph should provide that HST is included in the price as HST is not exigible on such transactions. However, there are no generalizations beyond the foregoing that can be made as to the applicability of HST to any transaction, and practitioners representing vendors and purchasers must be careful to deal with HST correctly to avoid further liability for HST. For example, in certain cases, where an owner uses a residence for business purposes, this may affect the exclusion given to that property insofar as HST is concerned. See also *Rive v. Newton*, [2001] O.J. No. 3226, 55 O.R. (3d) 175 (S.C.J.), affd [2003] O.J. No. 398 (C.A.), where a vendor and purchaser argued over the applicability of a clause similar to paragraph 7 of the OREA form and the Court was forced to analyze the particular type of land sold to arrive at a conclusion to the litigation. This case is another warning to practitioners to be aware of the manner in which HST is exigible in the context of every transaction.

For transactions involving lands that are not exempted from HST, the provisions in paragraph 7 of the OREA form are not adequate and should be supplemented to require the purchaser to pay HST unless evidence that the purchaser is an HST registrant and of his or her HST number is provided, as discussed in Chapter 4.

TIME TO SEARCH

Paragraph 8 of the OREA form of agreement of purchase and sale contains a clause common to most printed forms of such agreement. This paragraph gives the purchaser a set period of time within which to investigate title and "off-title" matters pertaining to the property, and to raise requisitions identifying any problems therewith. In reading the paragraph, note that there are two separate search periods. The first is for the title search and allows for a specific date to be inserted (usually between 15 and 30 days). The second period is given to investigate whether there are any work orders outstanding, whether the property's use is lawful and whether property insurance can be obtained for the property. These latter investigations must be completed and issues raised with the vendor within the 30-day period after title requisitions were due but, in any event, no later than five days before closing. In either case, requisitions must be delivered to the vendor within the allowable period and not just mailed: *Stykolt v. Maynard*, [1942] O.J. No. 438, [1942] O.R. 250 (H.C.J.).

The final sentence of paragraph 8 requires the vendor to execute any authorizations needed by the purchaser to complete its investigations as to "off-title" matters, investigations which usually involve writing to governmental authorities and obtaining from them information as to the status of the property's compliance with laws that the authority is responsible for administering, which information will often only be released if the vendor authorizes it. A written authorization should be one of the first things a purchaser's solicitor should obtain once he or she is retained on a purchase, given the time it takes to actually receive them and the lengthy time involved in then obtaining information from governmental authorities on the strength of these authorizations.

While the process of undertaking these title and off-title searches is dealt with elsewhere in this book, it is important to remember that once your searches are complete and the results are such that requisitions are required, such requisitions should thoroughly describe the nature of the problem and the factual background which led to the discovery of the problem, followed by the specific actions you require the vendor to take in order to correct the problem. A requisition should not be vague or lack the legal and factual basis for its submissions; it should read with the precision expected of a pleading in a court action to ensure that any application by a vendor under the *Vendors and Purchasers Act* for a ruling on the validity of the requisition does not result in the requisition being found to be unsupportable or lacking specificity. Replies to requisitions should be approached in a similar manner.

REPRESENTATIONS, WARRANTIES, FUTURE USE

It is good to point out to all parties signing an agreement of purchase and sale the standard clauses found in paragraphs 9 and 26 of the OREA form, which state that there are no representations, warranties or agreements other than those contained in the agreement in writing and specifically no representation or warranty as to any future intended use of the property. If a party was induced to enter into the agreement by any representation or other condition or warranty, this should appear in the agreement. Otherwise, by signing the standard agreement, the person is estopped from ever making any claim under that representation, condition or warranty.

Representations and warranties have become more and more common in recent years in agreements involving residential properties and are the norm in non-residential property transactions. The OREA form of agreement contains few representations and warranties and is drafted in a manner to require parties to supplement the agreement to add any representations and warranties agreed on by the parties.

Generally speaking, the purchaser will be most concerned with representations and warranties as it is the purchaser who will end up with the property after closing and who will have to "live with" the consequences. Given the verbal assurances often given by real estate agents in marketing a property and in light of the *caveat emptor* ("buyer beware") principle, it is largely through representations and warranties that a purchaser can ensure that remedies are available if the assurances turn out to be false.

Courts do distinguish between representations, warranties and conditions in agreements, and the differences are important in determining the rights and remedies of the party relying upon them. Basically, representations relate to past or present events that induce a party to enter into a contract, whereas warranties and conditions relate to future events and actually form part of the contract rather than serving as inducements in making the contract come into existence. Admittedly, all of these terms are frequently used interchangeably in agreements of purchase and sale.

The remedy available to a purchaser as a result of a vendor's breach of a representation will vary depending on whether the misrepresentation is considered innocent, negligent or fraudulent. Again, in very general terms, an innocent misrepresentation will only entitle a purchaser to rescind the contract before closing, while negligent misrepresentations will allow a purchaser to either rescind the contract or complete it and sue for damages. A fraudulent misrepresentation gives the purchaser even broader remedies. Insofar as warranties are concerned, the usual remedy is limited to the recovery of damages.

CONDITIONS AS TO GOOD TITLE

Paragraph 10 of the OREA form of agreement of purchase and sale is the key provision of the agreement governing the quality of title the vendor is required to deliver to the purchaser, and the obligation of the vendor to remedy title matters raised by the purchaser which derogate from that stated quality.

"Provided that the title is good..." is the basic condition of the agreement; if title is not good and free from all encumbrances except for those stated, there is no obligation on the purchaser to close. This is so even if this provision does not appear in the agreement of purchase and sale. Middleton J. in *McNiven v. Pigott*, [1914] O.J. No. 8, 22 D.L.R. 141 at para. 16 (H.C. Div.), vard [1915] O.J. No. 176, 22 D.L.R. 147 (C.A.), stated that "the principle is laid down that a contract for sale of land is merely upon condition, frequently expressed, *always implied*, that the vendor has a good title" [emphasis added].

The quality of title that the vendor must deliver to the purchaser pursuant to this clause was set out in *Zender v. Ball*, [1974] O.J. No. 2123, 5 O.R. (2d) 747 at 755, 51 D.L.R. (3d) 499 (H.C.J.), where Pennell J. states:

> The vendor must show a good title, that being a marketable title. A marketable title is one which can at all times and under all circumstances be forced upon an unwilling purchaser who is not compelled to take a title which would expose him to litigation or hazard.

He states (at 754 O.R.), citing *Joydan Developments Ltd. v. Hilite Holdings Ltd.*, [1972] O.J. No. 2008, [1973] 1 O.R. 482 (H.C.J.), as authority:

> Where the evidence supplied by a vendor falls short of showing good title, he cannot insist on completion, as a court will not force upon the purchaser anything less than a marketable title unless the purchaser has specifically contracted

otherwise. Therefore, where there is a valid objection to title which is not answered by the vendor nor waived by the purchaser, the agreement is by its terms void and the deposit should be returned.

By signing the standard form agreement, a purchaser does agree to accept title subject to certain encumbrances and qualifications. They are specifically listed as subparagraphs (a) to (d) in paragraph 10. These accepted qualifications are: (a) restrictive covenants, if in compliance; (b) agreements with municipalities or utility companies, if in compliance; (c) minor utility easements; and (d) any easements for sewers, drainage, public utilities, phone or cable lines or other services that do not materially affect the present use of the property. These qualifications are, generally speaking, sensible and are matters that a purchaser should accept, especially in residential transactions where, in most cases, these qualifications will be compatible with the purchaser's expectations for and use of the property. If no qualifications were allowed for such usual matters, almost every transaction would be subject to being terminated as a result of the existence of these matters. However, of these qualifications, the items listed in subparagraphs (a) and (d) are ones that may, in certain circumstances, merit deletion or modification when acting for a purchaser. Agreeing in advance to accept restrictive covenants of which a purchaser has no details can cause problems for the purchaser's intended or future use of the property. Issues of impairment of future uses also arise in subparagraph (d). In some situations, none of these qualifications may be acceptable, for example, when buying land for development purposes. In *Ridgely v. Nielson*, [2007] O.J. No. 1699, 53 R.P.R. (4th) 1 (S.C.J.), the Court allowed a purchaser to terminate a purchase agreement on the basis of the discovery of a significant sewer easement on the property, even though the easement did not affect the present use of the property and thereby should have been considered a permitted encumbrance based on the wording of paragraph (d) in the OREA form. The Court ruled that the purchaser's future intention to construct a pool and house extension were frustrated by the easement and were relevant factors to be considered. This decision does not seem consistent with the language in paragraph (d), which should only allow present uses, not future uses, to be considered in objecting to such easements. Practitioners are still urged to amend the permitted encumbrances where a purchaser's stated intended future uses may conflict with the encumbrances referenced, which will otherwise normally be forced on a purchaser.

Apart from the above qualifications, paragraph 10 does allow for other qualifications to be inserted into the agreement, and a vendor who knows of other qualifications that affect his or her title should add them as matters that a purchaser must accept; of course, the reply from a purchaser may be, as discussed above, that it is not fair to bind a purchaser to blindly accept title qualifications right from the start without having a chance to understand their full effect on the property.

The balance of paragraph 10 deals with the vendor's obligation in respect of requisitions made by the purchaser in accordance with the provisions of paragraph 8. As noted above in the *Zender* decision, the general principle has traditionally been that the failure of the vendor to answer a valid title objection will allow the purchaser to terminate the agreement of purchase and sale.

However, more recently the courts seem to have been applying less strict tests. In the Ontario Court of Justice decision in *Green v. Kaufman*, Brockenshire J. refused to allow a purchaser to avoid a contract because of a construction lien filed on the day of closing. He quoted with approval from *LeMesurier v. Andrus*, [1986] O.J. No. 2371, 54 O.R. (2d) 1 (C.A.), leave to appeal refused [1986] 2 S.C.R. v, where a driveway encroached slightly onto the neighbour's lot. The Court of Appeal in that case held that the test to be applied was whether the vendors were in a position to convey substantially what the contract called for. The Court quoted with approval: "Vendors and purchasers owe a duty to each other honestly to perform a contract honestly made", and "[t]he policy of the Court ought to be in favour of the enforcement of honest bargains". The defendant purchaser's appeal from the *Green* decision was dismissed: [1996] O.J. No. 4007 (C.A.).

Similarly, in *Toll v. Marjanovic*, [2002] O.J. No. 70, 46 R.P.R. (3d) 308 (S.C.J.), affd [2003] O.J. No. 2259, 10 R.P.R. (4th) 39 (C.A.), while the Court found that a purchaser's requisition to require a vendor to discharge a lease he granted over 1.59 per cent of his property to allow a neighbour to widen his driveway was valid, the nature of the defect was minimal and would not affect the use and enjoyment of the property and, as a result, did not allow the purchaser to terminate the agreement.

Two other cases dealing with condominium resales have held that a purchaser is not entitled to refuse to close a condominium purchase just because the municipality has advised of outstanding work orders against the entire building where the condominium corporation has taken reasonable steps to comply with the work orders. See *Ahuntsic Investments Inc. v. Cheng*, [1992] O.J. No. 2611, 28 R.P.R. (2d) 16 (Gen. Div.), affd [1994] O.J. No. 1274, 39 R.P.R. (2d) 38 (C.A.), and *Jasinski v. Trinchini*, [1994] O.J. No. 576, 113 D.L.R. (4th) 135 (Gen. Div.). See also *Boschetti v. Sanzo*, [2003] O.J. No. 5227, 26 R.P.R. (4th) 113 (S.C.J.), affd [2006] O.J. No. 3318, 49 R.P.R. (4th) 61 (C.A.), which related to the same condominium building at issue in the *Jasinski* case. The Court distinguished *Jasinski* and permitted the purchaser to refuse to close the sale on the grounds that the vendor had represented that there were no outstanding work orders, yet the bank had denied mortgage financing on the basis of there being existing work orders.

If the objection to title is material, it is no defence for the vendor to say that the purchaser was aware of the encumbrance when the purchaser signed the agreement: *Cato v. Thompson* (1882), 9 Q.B.D. 616. It is the vendor's obligation to make the title good unless the agreement has clearly stated exceptions to this obligation.

The last two sentences of paragraph 10 are known as the rescission clause or annulment clause, as the vendor is given the right to choose not to answer a requisition if the vendor is "unable or unwilling to remove, remedy or satisfy" the requisition. The result is that the agreement is terminated and the deposit is returned to the purchaser. The rescission clause rights are in addition to the rights given to a vendor to refuse to reply to requisitions that are not made within the requisition period set forth in paragraph 8 and to force a purchaser to accept title subject to the items listed in subparagraphs (a) to (d).

The justification for giving the vendor the right to rescind the agreement as a result of requisitions made by a purchaser is that vendors would otherwise be susceptible to claims for specific performance with an abatement in the purchase price if a vendor did not deliver the title promised through no fault of the vendor or through some action of a third party that the vendor did not control. Alternatively, a vendor could be faced with the expenditure of funds to correct title matters that is disproportionate to the funds to be received in closing the deal with the purchaser. In such circumstances, the rescission clause would allow a vendor to rescind the agreement if the purchaser does not waive the requisition rather than forcing the vendor to give the purchaser an abatement to compensate for the matter that was requisitioned or to spend large sums of money to correct the problem (see *Louch v. Pape Avenue Land Co.*, [1928] S.C.J. No. 53, [1928] S.C.R. 518).

While the reasoning behind the rescission clause as expressed by the Supreme Court in *Louch* is sensible, a reading of the clause in the OREA form makes it apparent that the clause is very broadly worded in allowing the vendor to decide that he or she is "unable or unwilling" to answer the requisitions. Such language could easily lead to abuse and away from the original intention behind the protection afforded to vendors. The courts quickly began to narrow and qualify the applicability of the clause. In *Hurley v. Roy*, [1921] O.J. No. 205, 50 O.L.R. 281 at 285 (C.A.), the Court stated:

> This provision was not intended to make the contract one which the vendor can repudiate at his sweet will. The policy of the Court ought to be in favour of the enforcement of honest bargains, and it should be remembered that, when a contract deliberately made is not enforced because of some hardship the agreement may impose on one contracting party, the effect is to transfer the misfortune to the shoulders of the other party, though he is admittedly entirely innocent.

Similarly, the Supreme Court in *Mason v. Freedman*, [1958] S.C.J. No. 34, [1958] S.C.R. 483 made it clear that a vendor seeking to rely on the rescission clause must act reasonably and in good faith and "not in a capricious or arbitrary manner". In other words, the vendor must make a legitimate attempt to remedy a defect in title or other problem raised by a requisition and demonstrate reasonable grounds for being unable or unwilling to do so. If the vendor acts in bad faith, the vendor cannot rely on the clause.

The decision of the Court in *11 Suntract Holdings Ltd. v. Chassis Service & Hydraulics Ltd.*, [1997] O.J. No. 5003, 36 O.R. (3d) 328 (Gen. Div.) contains a useful survey and discussion on the law surrounding the rescission clause and concludes that there are two main limitations on the vendor's ability to invoke the rescission clause. The first examines the vendor's conduct at the time the agreement of purchase and sale was entered into to determine whether the vendor was reckless in entering into the contract knowing of matters that he or she would have difficulty in remedying concerning the quality of title, but taking a chance nevertheless with no expectation of being able to deliver good title. The second examines what *bona fide* efforts a vendor takes to remedy title matters once requisitions are made.

When acting for a purchaser, it is often not acceptable to leave the vendor's obligation to convey good title subject to the risk of the invocation of the rescission clause by the vendor. For example, it is usually expected that the vendor will discharge all mortgages and it is recommended that a purchaser add a specific requirement of a vendor to obtain a discharge or other release or instrument clearing title to cover known problems. This obligation should override the rights of the vendor to invoke the rescission clause. Interestingly, older versions of the OREA forms once included as paragraph 4 a covenant of the vendor to discharge by closing all liens, charges and encumbrances. Unfortunately, the clause was drafted as being subject to the other provisions in the agreement and therefore was arguably subject to the rescission clause.

The approach recommended above did not help the purchaser in the case of *Toth v. Ho* (1998), 26 R.P.R. (3d) 76 (Gen. Div.). In that case, a specific provision was added to the agreement of purchase and sale obligating the vendor to discharge existing mortgages on closing. The purchaser subsequently requisitioned a discharge of such a mortgage, which was registered on title to the property. The mortgage in question, however, still had over two years left before it matured and was not open to prepayment. In order to obtain a discharge, the vendor discovered that the mortgagee was insisting on being paid the interest it would have earned for the balance of the term. Given the extent of the payment, the vendor invoked the rescission clause, arguing that it was unable to obtain the discharge in light of the extraordinary payment required by the mortgagee. Notwithstanding the fact that the agreement in question contained a specific obligation on the vendor to obtain a discharge, the Court upheld the vendor's right to rely on the clause on the basis that the requisition made to discharge the mortgage was a "requisition on title" as opposed to a "requisition of conveyance" and as such allowed the vendor to rescind the contract. The decision is not in keeping with the principle referenced earlier that a vendor who has acted recklessly in entering into an agreement knowing of existing impediments to giving good title to a purchaser, should not be entitled to rely on the rescission clause. In *Toth*, the vendor knew his mortgage was closed but still entered into an agreement to sell his property free of the mortgage without first clearing the matter with his mortgagee. In such circumstances, the vendor should not be allowed to rely on the clause. See the excellent annotation accompanying the *Toth* decision in the Real Property Reports, which further discusses the law surrounding the rescission clause and other nuances taken into consideration by courts in deciding whether a requisition entitles a vendor to invoke the rescission clause, including a discussion of the differences between "requisitions on title" versus "requisitions of conveyance".

The final sentence of paragraph 10 completes the arrangements set out in the agreement of purchase and sale relating to matters of title and requisitions by concluding that the purchaser is deemed to accept the vendor's title to the property except for matters raised and requisitioned within the allowable period to do so, and except for "any objection going to the root of title". If a requisition is not made within the period allowed for doing so, the courts have held that the purchaser cannot refuse to close and must accept title to the property subject to the issue raised in the requisition: *Todd v. Haslhofer*, [1983] O.J. No. 2995, 41 O.R. (2d) 409 (H.C.J.), affd [1986] O.J. No. 2994, 54 O.R. (2d) 127 (C.A.). There are exceptions to this general principle that allow objections to be raised after the requisition date, one of which is objections going to the root of title.

These are objections that question whether the vendor has any title at all or raise major concerns as to the underlying ability or authority of the vendor to convey title.

Another exception is for requisitions that relate to matters of conveyance. These are requisitions in respect of issues over which the vendor has control or that the vendor is entitled at law to have a third party remedy or rectify (such as obtaining the discharge of a mortgage). Where a requisition relates to a matter of conveyance, it can be brought after the requisition date (see *O'Neil v. Arnew*, [1976] O.J. No. 2412, 16 O.R. (2d) 549 (H.C.J.) and *Towne Meadow Development Corp. v. Chong*, [1993] O.J. No. 693, 30 R.P.R. (2d) 228 (Gen. Div.) for a discussion of these issues).

Notwithstanding the above exception, there is a lack of consistency in the decisions considering whether particular requisitions go to the root of title or are matters of conveyance and as a result, practitioners are encouraged to raise all requisitions before the requisition date expires rather than rely on these exceptions to justify an otherwise late requisition. In addition, remember that all of these exceptions only apply to requisitions on title. Requisitions that do not relate to title, such as ones relating to work orders or zoning matters, must always be brought within the time period allowed to raise them, which in the case of the OREA form is set out in paragraph 8. The Court of Appeal in *Cinram Ltd. v. Armadale Enterprises Ltd.*, [1996] O.J. No. 3901, 31 O.R. (3d) 257 has confirmed that requisitions relating to zoning are not normally considered matters of title. A similar confirmation was given by the Court of Appeal insofar as work orders are concerned in *Ahuntsic Investments Inc. v. Cheng*, [1994] O.J. No. 1274, 39 R.P.R. (2d) 38.

ELECTRONIC REGISTRATION

The introduction of electronic registration with the intention that it eventually becomes the only manner of registration, has required an addition to the agreement of purchase and sale to deal with the logistics of closing. Paragraph 11 of the OREA form was added to govern such logistics. It provides that where electronic registration is mandatory, the parties will cause their solicitors to enter into escrow agreements or document registration agreements ("DRA") in forms recommended by the Law Society of Upper Canada pursuant to which all documents and moneys required to complete the transaction will be tendered. The parties will then be required to await the completion and confirmation of all electronic registration before any money or documentation is released.

In the past and in registry offices where electronic registry is still not mandatory, the practice is of course for parties to exchange cheques, documents and the transfer/deed at the registry office and wait for registration to be completed before they release the closing deliveries. With electronic registration, no one has to leave their offices and as a result, the DRA allows parties to send documents and cheques to each other's solicitors in escrow pending the electronic registration of the transfer.

The Law Society has issued practice directives governing electronic registration which can be accessed on its website at <http://www.lsuc.on.ca>. Practice Directive 4 deals with the DRA and attaches as a schedule a recommended form of DRA to deal with basic transactions. The Law Society's form of DRA requires parties to confirm that all deliveries required by the purchase agreement have been made and are satisfactory, allocates responsibility for effecting electronic registration and for approving and electronically releasing instruments for electronic registration, allows parties to release cheques and documents from the escrow once electronic registration is completed, and also contemplates the possibility of a party choosing not to proceed and requiring electronic registration not to occur.

The Law Society form of DRA needs to be adapted to cover transactions that do not conform with the typical transaction. It is also advisable for parties to amend the form to deal with what happens if electronic registration cannot occur because the Teraview e-reg system is "down" or otherwise electronically inaccessible, which occurs from time to time. In the event of such system failures, parties should agree, if appropriate, to proceed to effect the electronic registrations on the next day when the system is again up and running.

PRODUCTION OF DOCUMENTS

Paragraph 12 concerning the production of documents in the standard printed form is quite clear and follows s. 4(*a*) of the *Vendors and Purchasers Act*. If you, as vendor, hold any documents, you must deliver them to the purchaser. If no documents are in the vendor's possession or control, there is no responsibility to produce them. From a purchaser's perspective, the clause may not be adequate insofar as obligations to provide surveys are concerned. A purchaser expecting that this clause will result in the delivery of an adequate survey may be disappointed. A purchaser expecting the vendor to provide a current or up-to-date survey must add a specific clause to this effect to ensure this happens.

Paragraph 12 also deals with the procedures surrounding the vendor's obligation to discharge institutional mortgages, which was discussed earlier in this chapter in the context of the payment of the purchase price.

RIGHT OF PURCHASER TO INSPECT PRIOR TO CLOSING

Most solicitors have always thought that unless a specific right is set out in the offer allowing the purchaser the right to inspect the property prior to closing, the purchaser has no right to carry out such an inspection. However, in *Harkness v. Cooney*, [1979] O.J. No. 4605, 131 D.L.R. (3d) 765 (Co. Ct.), involving an application under the *Vendors and Purchasers Act*, Costello Co. Ct. J. ruled that a purchaser has a right of inspection prior to closing.

Real Estate Board offers (paragraph 13 in the OREA form) usually state that the person named as purchaser has inspected the real property and, therefore, the offer may estop a purchaser from alleging that no inspection was made. If the purchaser was not satisfied with the inspection, then the purchaser should state in the offer that the offer is conditional on a further right to inspect, and the purchaser's satisfaction with such inspection, or that the offer is conditional on the purchaser's contractor submitting a report satisfactory to the purchaser as to the condition, repair status and strength of the structure in question. The problem with such a condition is that in the mind of the vendor, the offer is now reduced to an option, which the vendor may not be willing to accept. A purchaser, if concerned over the state of repair of the structure, should have the premises inspected by a professional prior to submitting the offer. Several companies now offer this service. They may be found in the Yellow Pages under "Building Inspection Service". If an inspection condition in the offer is being contemplated, then the time for such inspection should be short so that the offer may be confirmed by the purchaser within a day or two after acceptance.

BUILDING AT RISK OF VENDOR

Remember that at common law, unless otherwise stated, the risk of any loss or damage to buildings on the property is on the purchaser as beneficial owner. Thus, most printed forms of agreement of purchase and sale (paragraph 14 in the OREA form) contain a provision that reverses this position and provides that the buildings will remain at the risk of the vendor. If this clause does not appear in an agreement, then the purchaser must be advised to insure the premises. But in most cases, where the standard printed form is used, the vendor must maintain the insurance until closing.

From a purchaser's point of view, this single, short sentence that reverses the common law risk is hardly satisfactory in being able to deal with all of the changes that might affect a property between the date the agreement of purchase and sale is accepted and closing. While the balance of paragraph 14 discussed below deals with what happens if there is damage to the property, it does not deal with other risks, including changes in zoning, environmental problems, tenancy disputes, *etc*. While in most residential situations the provisions in paragraph 14 should suffice, transactions involving other properties (or even residential properties that are being purchased for income-generating reasons) may require that conditions be inserted in the agreement to ensure that the purchaser is allowed to terminate the agreement if certain essential and significant matters pertaining to the property have materially changed for the worse on the date of closing.

INSURANCE PROCEEDS

Under the usual printed form, in case of substantial damage to the buildings between the date of the signing of the agreement of purchase and sale and the date of closing, the purchaser has the option to cancel the agreement and demand the return of the deposit or to claim the proceeds of insurance and complete the transaction. However, in those situations where property is being sold for development and the buildings are to be demolished, the purchaser's right to terminate should be deleted.

What constitutes "substantial" damage is not clear from this provision and parties who require more certainty often amend this provision to define what substantial damage is and is not, usually by reference to a dollar amount which, if exceeded, constitutes substantial damage. Similarly, the option allowing a purchaser to still complete the transaction where there has been substantial damage and "take the proceeds" of insurance lacks precision and does not give the purchaser the certainty that he or she may need. Issues such as the sufficiency of the vendor's insurance, whether the insurance covers the peril that caused the damage, the threshold of deductions and whether the insurer will actually allow a cash payment to be made for the damage are not addressed. Unfortunately, the clause is rarely amended in residential transactions, probably because the likelihood of this contingency occurring is very low; still, a purchaser should be made aware of the provision's limitations.

PLANNING ACT

Every agreement for the purchase and sale of real property in Ontario should contain a provision similar to that contained in paragraph 15 of the OREA form, making the agreement subject to compliance with the *Planning Act*. This necessity is due to s. 50 of the Act, which prohibits conveyances of land that result in the subdivision of land that do not comply with its terms. The entry into an agreement of purchase and sale is specifically treated as a transaction caught within the s. 50 prohibition. Subsection 50(21) makes it clear that an agreement entered into in contravention of s. 50 is void as it does not create an interest in land; however, if the agreement is entered into subject to an express condition that the agreement is to be effective only if the provisions of s. 50 are complied with, the agreement is not affected by the voiding provisions in subs. 50(21). As a result, every pre-printed real estate board form contains a provision similar to paragraph 15 in the OREA form.

Also note that paragraph 15 goes on to provide that the vendor is responsible for obtaining any consent necessary under the *Planning Act* and actually agrees to proceed to obtain it at his or her expense by closing. From a vendor's point of view, the clause does not limit the vendor's obligations in proceeding with obtaining the consent, and arguably requires the vendor to exhaust all avenues of appeal if consent applications are initially rejected or if onerous conditions are imposed by a committee of subdivision in considering an application for consent. Accordingly, where a vendor or purchaser knows a consent will be needed for the transaction he or she is involved in, specific provisions and conditions should be inserted into the agreement to govern issues of timing, cost, appeals and satisfaction of conditions pertaining to applications for consent to severance.

From a vendor's perspective, the warning given in the preceding paragraph in leaving a *Planning Act* clause in the form set out in the OREA agreement of purchase and sale is fully warranted given the decision of the Court of Appeal in *John E. Dodge Holdings Ltd. v. 805062 Ontario Ltd.*, [2003] O.J. No. 350, 63 O.R. (3d) 304. In the purchase transaction in that case, the parties knew that a severance would be required to allow the purchaser to acquire the lands described in the purchase agreement. Paragraph 14 of the purchase agreement contained a clause on the *Planning Act* that is identical to that in the OREA form. The vendor applied for a severance and was granted one on the condition that it build an extension of a road next to the lands and convey the road to the municipality. As a result of this condition, the vendor terminated the agreement, arguing that the condition was unreasonable. The Court of Appeal rejected the vendor's position. In considering the extent of a vendor's obligation under a clause such as that in paragraph 15 of the OREA form, the Court explicitly rejected the vendor's position that the vendor needed only to act in good faith and use its best efforts to satisfy the condition. The Court found that the vendor was bound to either appeal the consent condition to the Ontario Municipal Board to obtain a variance of the decision or satisfy the condition.

WHO PREPARES DOCUMENTS

The wording of s. 4(e) of the *Vendors and Purchasers Act* is used in most printed forms, including in paragraph 16 of the OREA form. The deed or transfer is to be prepared at the expense of the vendor, and the mortgage, if any, at the expense of the purchaser. The usual practice is for the vendor's solicitor to prepare and attend to execution of the deed and the purchaser's solicitor to prepare and attend to execution of the mortgage.

In *Holmes v. Graham*, [1978] O.J. No. 3538, 21 O.R. (2d) 289, the Court of Appeal held that a purchaser is not required to close where the vendor tenders a deed that is not in registerable form, even where the land registrar as a convenience to the parties had agreed to accept the deed for registration upon the vendor's undertaking to produce and deposit a reference plan within six months.

Paragraph 16 also requires the parties and their solicitors to complete the statements on the transfer relating to the *Planning Act* if the purchaser so requires. As discussed in Chapter 5, the completion of the *Planning Act* statements should be requested in every transaction as it makes future searches affecting the property easier insofar as ensuring past *Planning Act* compliance.

RESIDENCY AND FAMILY LAW ACT

Paragraph 17 of the OREA form is another provision that should be in every agreement of purchase and sale. The requirements of the *Income Tax Act* relating to the sale of property by non-residents have been reviewed in Chapter 4. Without repeating in detail those requirements, this paragraph requires a vendor to either obtain the requisite clearance certificate from the Canada Revenue Agency exempting the property from tax or to provide a statutory declaration on closing confirming that the vendor is not a non-resident. If neither is provided, the purchaser is entitled to withhold from the purchase price and pay to the Canada Revenue Agency the amount required by the Act to satisfy the tax liability of the vendor under the Act.

Paragraph 22 of the OREA form pertaining to the *Family Law Act* has already been discussed in this chapter in the context of the parties to the agreement of purchase and sale. It is a warranty that spousal consent is not necessary unless the vendor's spouse has executed the agreement in the area provided for spousal consent.

ADJUSTMENTS

The clause dealing with adjustments appears in most printed forms substantially as it is set out in the *Vendors and Purchasers Act*, s. 4(*d*), although the printed forms now make it clear that all receipts or costs for the closing day itself shall be apportioned to the purchaser. This clause is very basic and meant to deal with only the most usual adjustments in the most usual transactions and should be amended to deal with transactions with additional adjustments.

TIME OF THE ESSENCE

It is essential that a clause appear somewhere in the agreement that time is of the essence of the agreement. Then, if either party defaults on the specified date for closing, the other party may immediately pursue remedies. If closing cannot take place on the specified date, it is important that an alternate date be fixed by the parties or their solicitors and that letters confirming that date be exchanged. These letters should confirm also that notwithstanding the delay, time is to remain of the essence. See *Syed v. McArthur*, [1984] O.J. No. 3235, 46 O.R. (2d) 593 (H.C.J.). You will have to satisfy yourself that the other party's solicitor has authority to extend the closing date. The printed form of agreement used by the Ontario Real Estate Association gives such authority in paragraph 20. To be safe, you should insist on the respective clients themselves agreeing in writing to the extension.

If the date for closing passes without such action being taken, it may well be difficult for your client to obtain an order for specific performance of the contract by the other party.

If the date for closing arrives and the other party is unable or unwilling to close, and a postponement is not agreed upon, you should protect your client's interest by demonstrating that time is of the essence and that your client is ready, willing, able and anxious to close. This is best accomplished by making formal tender on the other party.

The time of the essence clause is also relevant to all other dates in the agreement of purchase and sale. In *1473587 Ontario Inc. v. Jackson*, [2005] O.J. No. 710, 74 O.R. (3d) 539 (S.C.J.), affd [2005] O.J. No. 3145, 75 O.R. (3d) 484 (C.A.), a purchaser failed to pay a deposit within the five-day time period required by the purchase agreement and submitted it two days late. The deposit was refused by the vendor and it terminated the contract due to the purchaser's failure to remit the deposit within the allotted time. The Court upheld the right of the vendor to terminate, relying in part on the contractual provision that made time of the essence.

TENDER

The normal printed form states that "[a]ny tender of documents or money hereunder may be made upon Seller or Buyer *or their respective lawyers [and] [m]oney may be tendered by bank draft or cheque certified*" (emphasis added) by a chartered bank, trust company, Province of Ontario Savings Office, credit union or caisse populaire. It is important that those words in italics appear. At common law tender may be made only upon a party in person. It is usually impossible to ascertain where the defaulting party may be located on the date set for closing, but you can usually find the party's solicitor. Also, if the provision dealing with certified cheques does not appear, you will be required to tender in cash at great inconvenience and no little danger.

UREA FORMALDEHYDE FOAM INSULATION

Most real estate board forms contain a standard clause in which the vendor warrants that the property does not contain (or has not been insulated with) any urea formaldehyde foam insulation ("UFFI"). If you are consulted by the vendor before the agreement is signed, you should bring this clause to the vendor's attention and pay careful attention to the exact wording of it. Not only do you want to ensure that the property does not now contain any UFFI but, depending on the wording of the clause, it may be important to determine whether the property ever contained any UFFI which was later removed. Although the effect of UFFI on value has diminished in recent years, a purchaser may still be concerned if the property ever contained it since traces of it will remain even though removal has occurred.

Canada Mortgage and Housing Corporation, which caused the concern about UFFI originally by requiring a statutory declaration that no UFFI existed as a condition for its mortgage loan insurance, announced in January 1993 that the requirement no longer applies. As a result, the Ontario Real Estate Association had indicated that it would remove the clause from its standard form, but it remains as paragraph 23.

CONFLICT

The first sentence of paragraph 26 is important given the numerous recommendations in this chapter to add new provisions to the agreement of purchase and sale. It provides that any conflict or discrepancy between those additions and the pre-printed portions of the agreement will be decided by reference to the additions, which are deemed to supersede the pre-printed portions. Notwithstanding this provision, where additions are being included in a schedule to the standard form agreement of purchase and sale whose purpose is to change the manner in which the pre-printed paragraphs in the agreement deal with the topic, practitioners should, where appropriate, make it clear in that addition that the paragraphs being changed are either deleted or superseded, or should simply manually delete the pre-printed paragraph and have such deletion initialled by all parties.

COMMISSION CLAUSE

Note that in most printed forms the vendor irrevocably instructs his or her solicitor to pay to the real estate agent directly from the moneys received on closing the agent's commission agreed upon in the listing agreement. This payment must be made before any money is released to the vendor. The provision in the OREA form which appears after the signing lines for the purchaser is clear that the payment is required "on completion". Older versions of the form simply required the payment to be made on the date of closing, which is not acceptable from a vendor's point of view. Please review this provision in every agreement. There are many cases to indicate that agents fully believe that they are entitled to be paid their commission on the closing date set out in the agreement whether the transaction actually closes or not. So that there is no confusion on this point, you should in every case when acting for the vendor ensure that the commission is to be payable only if and when the transaction closes.

You might also wish to strike out the direction found in the fine print whereby the vendor's solicitor is instructed to pay any unpaid balance of commission from the proceeds of the sale. This direction is a great nuisance to a solicitor and is often forgotten. In those sales where the cheque for the balance due on the closing date is paid directly to the vendor and not by direction to the vendor's solicitor, the solicitor has no funds on hand out of which to pay the commission. This sometimes results in an unpleasant argument between agent and solicitor. More importantly, the courts have held that where such an irrevocable direction is given in such an agreement and the agreement is executed by the vendor under seal, the solicitor who ignores this direction will be liable to the real estate agent for any unpaid commissions (see *Family Trust Corp. v. Morra*, [1987] O.J. No. 398, 60 O.R. (2d) 30 (Div. Ct.) and *Re/Max Garden City Realty Inc. v. 828294 Ontario Inc.*, [1992] O.J. No. 1080, 8 O.R. (3d) 787 (Gen. Div.)).

For a discussion of whether or not an agent is entitled to a commission, see Chapter 10.

CERTIFICATE OF PENDING LITIGATION

As discussed in Chapter 15, where a purchaser alleges the breach of a purchase agreement by the vendor, an interim measure it often seeks to protect its interest in the property is the issuance of a certificate of pending litigation, which gets registered on title to the property to give third parties notice of the litigation. Such a registration effectively prevents any further dealing with the property pending the settling on the litigation. Given the harm caused to a vendor in having such a registration made against its property, it is sometimes the case in commercial agreements of purchase and sale that a provision is inserted where the parties agree that, regardless of the nature of any subsequent dispute by the parties resulting in the termination of the purchase agreement, the purchaser will be prohibited from registering a certificate of pending litigation. In *Lariat Land Development Inc. v. Loukras*, [2005] O.J. No. 1030, 29 R.P.R. (4th) 112 (S.C.J.), the Court ruled it will give effect to such clauses where they are clearly worded.

AMENDMENT TO OFFER

If an offer is submitted and the vendor changes some term, *e.g.*, the price, or the terms of the mortgage, or strikes out a condition, this change is obviously not binding on the offeror unless he or she agrees to it. The offer was not accepted as made. The real estate agent will tell you that the offer was "signed back". The agent returns with the agreement and asks for the purchaser's agreement to these changes. If the purchaser so agrees, the purchaser will initial them. What has actually happened is that a "counter offer" has been made. When this is done, the clause making the offer irrevocable by the purchaser should be altered by substituting the word "vendor" for the word "purchaser" and by extending the date, if necessary, to give the original offeror a chance to consider and accept the changes.

INTERPRETATION OF APPARENT ERRORS

In some cases, agreements are prepared quickly and inconsistencies occur between words and figures and between the printed form and a written addition. See *Halsbury's Laws of England*, 4th ed., Vol. 12, at 634:

> In the case of a difference between written words and figures, the written words as a general rule prevail, and in such a case evidence is not admissible to show that there was an omission from the written words. Where an instrument is in a printed form with written additions or alterations, the written words (subject always to be governed in point of construction by the language and terms with which they are accompanied) are entitled, in case of reasonable doubt as to the meaning of the whole, to have a greater effect attributed to them than the printed words, because the written words are taken as being intended to qualify the printed form, and because they are the terms selected by the parties themselves for the expression of their meaning, whereas the printed words are a general formula adapted equally to their case and that of all other contracting parties on similar occasions and subjects.

CHAPTER 12

Procedures in a Routine Transaction of Purchase and Sale

WHEN ACTING FOR A VENDOR

If you are fortunate, your clients have been in touch with you right from the time they decided to sell their home, cottage or other property. You will have advised them on the implications of the listing agreement with the agent, and you will have reviewed and discussed with them the terms of the offer to purchase before they accepted it. In most cases, however, the first time you hear about a deal occurs when your clients contact you to say that they have sold the property and that they want you to act for them. The agreement is signed, so you are bound by the terms agreed upon.

The first thing you should ask of your clients is to send or deliver to you existing title documents and information relating to the property or required for the preparation of the statement of adjustments, including the following:

1. the clients' copy of the deed or transfer to them when they bought the property. It is from this that you will get the description of the property;

2. plan of survey, if any (remember that the terms of a standard agreement of purchase and sale obligate the vendors to deliver only those documents in their possession. If they do not have a survey, then that is the end of it. If the purchasers require one, it is up to them to arrange and pay for it);

3. copy of any outstanding mortgages, together with the addresses of the mortgagees;

4. last year's and this year's realty tax bill;

5. if the house is oil heated, the size of the oil tank;

6. if there are tenants, a copy of the lease(s);

7. copies of any contracts relating to the property that the purchaser has agreed to assume; and

8. any other documentation or deliveries that the vendor has agreed to specifically provide to the purchaser.

Real estate agents make a practice of forwarding a copy of the agreement of purchase and sale to the solicitors acting on each side. In their covering letter, they will usually advise you of the name of the solicitor acting for the other party.

When you have the agreement before you, read it through carefully. Decide what it means, and if there is anything out of the ordinary, discuss it with your clients immediately. Make a practice of noting all of the relevant dates in your calendar, including the closing date, the requisition date and the date by which any conditions must be satisfied. This should prevent the embarrassment of suddenly discovering that you are not ready to close, or that you have not attended to completing matters relating to the satisfaction of a condition. In addition, a standard checklist should be prepared listing all of the facts pertaining to the transaction, and reminding you of the documents you must prepare and matters you must attend to in the course of bringing the transaction to its conclusion.

If you acted for the clients when they purchased the property, get your old file out of storage and keep it with the new one. If you did not act, ask if the clients still have their former solicitor's reporting letter. Either way, you should be able to tell if title is clear or, if not, what problems you face. If the property being sold is within the jurisdiction of a registry office where electronic registration is mandatory, a subsearch of title should be undertaken to examine the current state of title. Undertaking such a subsearch is even more important in circumstances where the property has been moved from the Registry system to the Land Titles system as part of the conversion of such titles being phased in by Teranet. Titles that have been converted by Teranet often contain qualifications as to certain matters that Teranet could not fully satisfy itself with and these qualifications will now appear on the parcel and likely be viewed by the purchaser as matters requiring action in order to remove them from the parcel. A common example of a qualification arising from such a conversion in the context of commercial properties is with a lease. In acting on the acquisition of a property while it was in the Registry system, notices of leases which appeared on title and which were expired or no longer affected the property were often dealt with by obtaining a statutory declaration from the vendor to that effect, as specific surrenders of the tenants' rights under such leases can not easily be obtained. Upon conversion, Teranet has often carried these leases onto the parcel notwithstanding the statutory declaration and as a result, a vendor is forced to make the necessary application under the *Land Titles Act*, R.S.O. 1990, c. L.5 to delete them. For reasons such as these, a subsearch should be undertaken to anticipate and deal with such problems in advance of receiving a requisition letter.

As you open the new file for this transaction, you should immediately forward a draft transfer to the solicitor for the purchaser, together with a copy of the survey, if available.

At this stage, you do not know how the purchaser intends to take title, so your draft transfer is prepared with the name of the grantee blank. The purchaser's solicitor must tell you how the purchaser will take title, *i.e.*, the exact spelling of the purchaser's name, the purchaser's date of birth and whether the purchaser will take alone, or jointly with a spouse, or in the spouse's name, or perhaps in the name of a company the purchaser owns. It is a courtesy to the other lawyer to get this draft out immediately so that the purchaser's lawyer can proceed with the search of title. At the very least, you should send the purchaser's lawyer a copy of the legal description and survey, if available.

If there are any mortgages outstanding on title, your next step is to write the mortgagee to ask for a statement showing the exact amount outstanding as of the closing date. There are two possible situations here:

1. If the purchaser has agreed to assume a presently outstanding mortgage, he or she will require evidence of the amount owing. If the mortgagee is an individual, the quickest method is to prepare the statement yourself from information given to you by your clients; mail this to the mortgagee and ask for it to be signed and returned to you. If it is an institutional mortgagee, write them asking for a statement "for assumption purposes". Be sure to quote their loan number if you know it. It should appear in some of the papers that your clients deliver to you.

2. If the mortgage is to be paid off by your clients on or before closing, write the mortgagee asking for a statement of the amount required to pay off the mortgage and ask the name of the mortgagee's internal payment officer or solicitor so you can make the necessary arrangements to pay off the outstanding balance and receive the discharge on closing.

In the case of a mortgage held by an individual, it is essential that the discharge be executed and available at closing. You should not expect anyone to close on your undertaking that you will, at some time in the future, produce and register a discharge of mortgage. Since the mortgagee might attempt to change the amount owing, might refuse to execute the discharge for some other reason, or might even die, you would be foolhardy to give an undertaking that the mortgagee will sign anything. However, in the case of a mortgage held by a bank, insurance company or trust company, it often is not possible to obtain a discharge before they have received the funds. In that case, the normal practice and requirement found in most standard form agreements of purchase and sale is to deliver to the purchaser a copy of the statement of the amount owing on the mortgage as issued by the mortgagee, together with a direction by the vendor to pay that amount directly to the mortgagee, and a personal undertaking by you to obtain and register the discharge. However, if you have any suspicion that the purchaser is looking for a way out of the deal, you should make special arrangements with the mortgagee to have the discharge delivered in escrow so as to be available at closing or, if that is not possible, advise your client to arrange "bridge financing" in order to have the discharge available for closing. See *Fong v. Weinper*, [1973] O.J. No. 1956, [1973] 2 O.R. 760 (H.C.J.), where the tender of a certified cheque and a mortgage statement was held not to be sufficient compliance with an agreement by the vendor to discharge any existing mortgage on or before closing.

If there are conditions to be satisfied or consents to be obtained as a prerequisite to closing, efforts should be undertaken to meet the conditions or to obtain the consents. If a severance is needed, applications must be made to the appropriate land division committee. If the property is occupied by commercial tenants, it may be necessary that you obtain acknowledgments from the tenants as to the facts of their tenancies, or "estoppel" certificates. As mentioned earlier, a review of the vendor's title and an updated subsearch of same may warn you as to title matters that require attention and that will likely be requisitioned by the purchaser's lawyer. If your vendor-client is a non-resident, arrangements will have to be made to obtain a clearance certificate from the Canada Revenue Agency ("CRA") in respect of income tax to avoid the withholding obligations that the purchaser will otherwise require, and which the agreement of purchase and sale stipulates occur absent such clearances. All of these matters and any other specific interim act explicitly provided for by the agreement of purchase and sale should be anticipated, attended to and organized between yourself and your client.

STATEMENT OF ADJUSTMENTS

When you have received the statements of the outstanding mortgages as well as all of the material from your clients, you can prepare the statement of adjustments. This is the statement from which you can calculate the balance due on closing, making adjustments for taxes and any other payments that affect the property. It may seem strange that in a transaction involving thousands of dollars you are concerned with pennies on adjustments; remember that this is the one part of the deal that your clients can clearly understand and can check. Nothing is more embarrassing than to have your clients phone and say that the adjustments do not add up. They then may begin to wonder whether they can have much faith in the rest of the work you are doing for them.

Most printed forms of agreement of purchase and sale stipulate that taxes, mortgage interest, utility charges, *etc.*, shall be adjusted as of the date of closing, with the closing date itself to be apportioned to the purchaser. In those cases where people write out their own contracts for the sale of property and omit any reference to adjustments, they are bound by s. 4(*d*) of the *Vendors and Purchasers Act*, R.S.O. 1990, c. V.2, which states that the contract shall be deemed to provide for such adjustments.

You should endeavour to prepare the statement of adjustments as early as possible for three reasons: (1) it will serve as a reminder to you of things that must be done; (2) your clients are always anxious to know exactly what they will receive on closing; and (3) the purchaser is just as anxious to know how much money needs to be raised.

If you are acting in a sale where the calculation of the statement of adjustments reveals a balance due on closing that is considerably in excess of the approximate amount shown in the agreement of purchase and sale, the sooner you get that statement to the purchaser's solicitor, the better for all concerned. The purchaser will need time to raise extra funds.

If the principal amounts outstanding on the mortgages to be assumed are substantially different than as shown in the agreement of purchase and sale, the purchaser may wish to terminate the agreement. In most cases, however, the purchaser will proceed. There are several reasons why such discrepancies occur. In many cases the vendor has only an approximate idea of the amount outstanding when the agreement is signed. In other cases, several principal payments may have been made between the date of the agreement and the date of closing, thus reducing the principal outstanding.

Sometimes, where the mortgage to be assumed is held by an institution, the mortgage requires monthly payments on account of realty taxes in addition to payments of principal and interest. The mortgagee will insist on having on hand sufficient funds by June or July, when taxes normally come due, to pay the full amount of those taxes. On a closing in March, April or May, there may be a substantial credit balance in the mortgagee's tax account which must be credited to the vendor on closing, thus increasing the cash that the purchaser will need to raise on closing.

Several computer programs are available for preparing statements of adjustment that have prompts built into them to draw out all information ordinarily required to complete the statement of adjustments. There is an example of a statement of adjustments later on in this chapter, broken down in great detail to help you understand how it is calculated.

"E. & O. E." stands for "errors and omissions excepted" and is inserted by solicitors to allow correction of the statement. It may help to ensure that the statement may be revised prior to the closing. However, it likely has no effect once the transaction is completed. To fully protect your clients against errors or other alterations in the adjustments discovered subsequent to closing, you should requisition and obtain on closing an undertaking of the other party to the transaction to readjust the statement of adjustments, if necessary.

Where it can be established, following closing, that as a result of a mutual mistake, the full amount of the purchase price was not paid, the vendor will be entitled to bring an action for the recovery of the balance of the purchase price; the closing will merge or extinguish the obligations of the purchaser under the agreement of purchase and sale only when evidence discloses that this was intended by the parties (*Handsaeme v. Dyck*, [1982] A.J. No. 1096, 20 Alta. L.R. (2d) 279 (Q.B.)).

You will find that the preparation of the statement of adjustments is a reminder of other things that should be attended to prior to closing.

Mortgages

Obviously, in the case of a transaction in which a mortgage is to be assumed, an attempt to prepare adjustments will remind you to obtain a mortgage statement from the mortgagee.

In the case where a mortgage is to be given back for part of the purchase price, you will be reminded to request a draft mortgage.

Property Insurance

It was once common for property insurance coverage to be transferred to the new owner on the sale of a home. Now most "homeowner's" or "comprehensive" policies cannot be transferred. Accordingly, no credit or debit entry is made on the statement of adjustments for property insurance. Nevertheless, you or your clients should notify your clients' insurance agent of the impending sale. Your clients may well have paid for a full year's worth of coverage and may be entitled to a refund of premium. It is advisable, however, to instruct the insurance agent not to terminate coverage until the sale is confirmed. If the transaction is delayed, your clients do not want to be without insurance coverage.

If your clients are taking back a mortgage for part of the purchase price, you will require evidence on closing that your clients' interest in the property is covered by insurance. You should notify the purchaser's solicitor that you will require such evidence as soon as possible, so that the purchaser may arrange coverage.

Taxes

When you are closing prior to the date on which the year's tax bill is issued, you will be forced to calculate the adjustment on the basis of last year's tax bill. If this happens, then you should prepare an undertaking for execution by your client to readjust if necessary, and request a similar undertaking from the purchaser.

Leases

If there are any leases to be assumed by the purchaser, you may be required to obtain acknowledgments or "estoppel" certificates from all tenants as to the amount of rent paid by them, the amount of prepayment, if any, and the expiry date of their leases. You must also prepare directions for execution by your clients informing all tenants of the sale and directing them to pay all further rents to the purchaser. Although the provisions of the *Conveyancing and Law of Property Act*, R.S.O. 1990, c. C.34 cause all leases to be assigned from a vendor to a purchaser upon the transfer of the property to which they relate without the need for any other agreement, it is common to prepare a specific document assigning the leases.

Utilities

When reviewing adjustments with your clients, you should remind them to arrange for the reading of the hydro, water and gas meters on the closing date. There will usually be no adjustment for any of these items. Consideration must also be given to any long-term contracts for the supply of gas and electricity that your client may have entered into and whether these contracts are to be assumed by the purchaser and any special adjustments made with respect to them.

Fuel Oil

It is common practice in sales of houses that are heated with oil for the vendor to fill the oil tank and charge in the adjustments for a full tank at the current price per litre. You should, therefore, remind your clients to "top up" their tank and also to check the size of the tank.

Chattels

If any chattels are being purchased, the amount payable for them should be added to the statement of adjustment and a bill of sale prepared to evidence their transfer.

Balance Due on Closing

The balance due on closing is arrived at by simply adding up the vendor's column and subtracting those items in the purchaser's column. Both columns must be equal in amount.

If, for any reason, the balance due on closing is to be paid to anyone other than the vendor, a note to this effect should appear on the adjustments so that the purchaser will know how to draw the cheque. You will be reminded to prepare the necessary direction for execution by the vendor authorizing this payment.

STATEMENT OF ADJUSTMENTS

Re: Adams sale to Brown of 13 Black Road, Goodtown
Adjusted as of May 31, 2010

		Allow Purchaser	Allow Vendor
Purchase price..			$250,000.00
Deposit..		$15,000.00	
First mortgage in favour of The Trust Company to be assumed by Purchaser			
Principal outstanding as of May 1, 2010	$125,000.00		
Interest at 10-1/2% per annum from May 1, 2010 to May 31, 2010 @ $35.96 per day	$1,114.76		
Allow Purchaser...		$126,114.76	
Second mortgage to be taken back by Vendor			
Allow Purchaser...		$25,000.00	
Realty taxes — 2010 taxes $2,400 paid in full	$2,400.00		
Vendor's portion 150 days @ $6.58 per day	$987.00		
Allow Vendor...			$1,413.00
Property insurance — purchaser to place own coverage. No adjustment.			
Fuel oil — 1,000 litres @ $0.50 per litre			
Allow Vendor...			$500.00
Hydro and water — no adjustment; final meter reading to be taken on closing			
BALANCE DUE ON CLOSING TO XY LAW FIRM			
as per direction..		$ 85,798.24	
....		$251,913.00	$251,913.00

E. & O.E.

MOVING TO CLOSING

While you have been preparing and forwarding the statement of adjustments and the draft transfer, the purchaser's solicitor should have been searching the title. When you receive the letter of requisitions, respond to it as soon as possible. Do not ignore requisitions, as so many do, until shortly before closing. Most requisitions can be answered, but it takes time to get releases, quit claim deeds and declarations and mortgage discharges executed by third parties. If requisitions are raised which cannot be answered, discuss them with your clients long before closing so that they have prior warning that the closing may be delayed or the agreement terminated. Also, have the courtesy to inform the purchaser's solicitor as soon as you discover that there is no available answer to a requisition so that instructions can be obtained from the purchaser.

Another reason for answering requisitions as soon as possible is to discover if there are any matters of title which may be dealt with by an application under the *Vendors and Purchasers Act*. This application will take some time and must be completed before closing. An applicant is not entitled to insist on a delay of closing in order to make application. One party may, in fact, be entitled to rely on the "time of the essence" clause in the agreement where the other has refused to close pending the outcome of an application.

It is particularly important that you warn your clients of such problems if they are planning to use the proceeds of the sale of this property to purchase a new property the same day. If there is any indication that closing will be postponed, give your clients all the notice possible so they can rearrange moving plans.

As discussed in Chapter 4, the sale of used residential housing is exempt from Harmonized Sales Tax ("HST") and as a result, there will be no obligation on the vendor to collect and remit HST in such circumstances. Where the transaction at hand involves property that is not exempt, such as commercial or industrial properties, HST is payable and it is the obligation of the vendor to collect it. Where the purchaser is an HST registrant and agrees to report on the transaction and self-assess to CRA, the vendor is relieved of the obligation to collect HST. It is normal for the purchaser to sign a certificate confirming that it is a registrant, disclosing its HST number, agreeing to self-assess and to indemnify the vendor in respect of any HST. It is imperative, however, that the vendor's solicitor verify the accuracy and currency of the purchaser's HST number. CRA maintains a website allowing solicitors to verify HST numbers and an enquiry to that site should be made by vendor's solicitors. In *Lee Hutton Kaye Maloff & Paul Henriksen v. Canada*, [2004] T.C.J. No. 429, 2004 G.T.C. 439, a purchaser gave a GST number to a vendor, which number had been cancelled by CRA. The vendor did not ascertain the validity of the number and completed the transaction without requiring payment of GST. CRA later assessed the vendor for the uncollected GST. The Court held that the vendor should have collected the GST and was not entitled to rely on the misrepresentation of the purchaser as to its GST registration status.

Make the appointment fairly early for the clients to come to your office to execute the transfer and any other documents required. Clients sometimes forget that documents must be signed and they are unavailable to sign when you need them. Before that meeting, clients should be asked about whether they own any interest in adjoining lands for the purposes of completing the *Planning Act*, R.S.O. 1990, c. P.13 statements on the transfer. Their spousal status should also be confirmed to determine what statement as to spousal status from the possible statements listed in Bulletin 86001 should be included and whether the client's spouse must be present to sign. Finally, their residency status should be confirmed to ensure that they are not non-residents and can sign a declaration to that effect, which declaration is a mandatory vendor's closing delivery. If they are non-residents, clearance certificates will have to be obtained (see Chapter 4).

If all requisitions have been answered and everything is in readiness, you should contact the purchaser's solicitor the day before closing to arrange a mutually convenient time to meet in the land registry office on the closing date. Personal meetings are obviously not necessary where electronic registration is in place, as discussed later in this chapter. If a mortgage is to be paid off, it is your responsibility to be sure that the solicitor for the mortgagee attends the land registry office at the same time to receive the balance due on the mortgage and deliver the discharge. Before leaving for the land registry office, check the file. Valuable time is wasted by solicitors or their clerks who rush off to the land registry office without ensuring that all documents are in the one file and properly executed. Then, be on time for your appointment. Produce your documents and obtain the certified cheque for the balance due on closing.

If the vendor is taking back a mortgage for part of the purchase price, the usual practice is to search for executions against the purchaser/mortgagor. However, you might consider the case of *Lang v. MacMillan*, [1958] O.J. No. 185, 13 D.L.R. 778 (H.C.J.), which indicates that such practice is unnecessary. In that case, a deed was given to the purchaser, who gave a mortgage back. The documents were registered in that order. In an action for foreclosure, an execution creditor, who had filed his execution against the purchaser prior to the purchase, claimed priority over the mortgage, arguing that his execution attached to the land in the time between registration of the two instruments. The court upheld the priority of the mortgage on the basis that it was given to satisfy the vendor's lien, which had priority over the execution. (See, however, the discussion concerning vendors' liens in Chapter 15.)

In all too many closings, it is discovered that matters that should have been attended to have been neglected, and undertakings are casually signed by solicitors, or their clerks, and accepted by the solicitor on the other side. Of course, the best rule is to give no undertakings ever, but that is a counsel of perfection. There are situations where undertakings are necessary, but in most cases the necessity of an undertaking could have been avoided by checking the file a day or so before closing. There is no point in accepting an undertaking from a solicitor for something that is beyond the solicitor's power to do, *e.g.*, obtain a discharge of mortgage from a third party (see *Polischuk v. Hagarty*, [1984] O.J. No. 3046, 49 O.R. (2d) 71 (C.A.)). Such an undertaking will be of little comfort to you or to your clients if the solicitor is subsequently unable to persuade the mortgagee to sign the discharge. Too many solicitors accept undertakings on closing so as not to delay or inconvenience a fellow lawyer, while ignoring their primary duty to their client. Rule 6.03(10) of the Rules of Professional Conduct reviews situations where undertakings should and should not be given. Undertakings signed by a lawyer on behalf of a client should only be given with the consent of the client and should explicitly state that the undertaking is given without any personal liability to the solicitor and his or her firm. Rarely, if ever, should a solicitor give his or her personal undertaking. If such an undertaking is absolutely necessary, he or she should be sure that the undertaking can be satisfied without the assistance of any other party.

After closing, you will arrange with the real estate agent to forward to you, or your clients, the balance of the deposit after deduction of the agent's commission.

It should no longer be necessary to notify the regional assessment office or the tax department of the municipality of the change in ownership so that future assessment notices and tax bills will go to the new owner, because the third copy of the Affidavit of Residence and of Value of the Consideration is delivered by the land registrar to the regional assessment office. However, that procedure is very slow and many municipalities request that you notify them of the change of ownership by letter to avoid a tax bill being misdirected, resulting in late payment penalties.

After closing, you should report in full to your clients. The final report should be quite detailed and include an accounting for all moneys, the particulars surrounding any mortgages taken back by the vendor as part of the purchase price and, of course, your account.

See the discussion later in this chapter regarding changes to the closing procedures described above as a result of the implementation of electronic registration.

WHEN ACTING FOR A PURCHASER

It is even more important in a purchase that you discuss the terms of an agreement of purchase and sale with your clients before it is signed. Unfortunately, you often do not have that opportunity. In any event, review the agreement fully with them to find out what they think it means.

As discussed in the context of acting for a vendor, it is important that upon being retained to act on a purchase, you complete a checklist that will guide you through the transaction and remind or prompt you to take the necessary steps in the proper order to arrive at completion. Much of the information you need to complete the checklist will come from the agreement of purchase and sale; other information will have to be provided by your client. The checklist should:

1.   identify the parties to the transactions and prompt you to ask your clients how they wish to take title (joint tenancy versus tenancy in common) and in whose name. If individuals will hold title, their dates of birth should be obtained as well as their full names (as middle names must be inserted in their entirety on the transfer if they are to be used). If a corporation will take title, your checklist should remind you to ask whether the corporation is registered for harmonized sales tax purposes and what that registration number is;

2.   highlight all of the relevant dates. This includes the closing date, requisition date and the date by which any conditions in the agreement of purchase and sale must be satisfied. These dates should be recorded in your business diary or other date reminder system you employ;

3.   list the municipal address, legal description and property identification number "PIN", if applicable, for the property;

4.   remind you to order and complete the various searches and other due diligence enquiries you are required to undertake in connection with the purchase, as further discussed below, and prompt you to note on

the checklist when the search or enquiry has been completed, reviewed and/or received;

5.   remind you to send out your requisition letter and preliminary report to your client on the results of your investigation and note the date such letters have been issued;

6.   prompt you to send authorizations to the vendor's solicitor allowing you to make searches with various governmental authorities of their records in respect of the property or the vendor, which searches are often not permitted without such authorizations;

7.   prompt you to contact the vendor's lawyer to obtain a survey of the property to the standards required by the agreement of purchase and sale and, if the survey is not recent or is otherwise unacceptable, to obtain instructions from your client on ordering a new survey;

8.   have you remind your client to arrange for insurance coverage for the property and, where any financing is being arranged in connection with the purchase, to obtain a certificate of insurance from the client's agent or broker which names the mortgagee and its interest in the property;

9.   anticipate that your client will likely be financing the acquisition and have you note from the agreement of purchase and sale whether your client is assuming or giving back a mortgage or whether a new mortgage will be arranged. Where a mortgage is to be assumed, the checklist should remind you to obtain an assumption statement from the mortgagee and determine whether the mortgagee's consent is required. If a new mortgage is to be arranged, a purchaser's lawyer often acts for that lender and your checklist should require you to ask your client who the mortgagee will be, at what branch and who the contact is. It should also remind you to obtain written instructions from that mortgagee accepting your dual role and prompt you to note conditions that must be fulfilled in order to obtain the advance;

10. list all of the documents to be prepared and signed by the purchaser and to be obtained from the vendor, as discussed further below;

11. allow you to calculate the funds you will require to complete the transaction by forcing you to list all of the components of the net cost for the acquisition and the sources of the funds; and

12. remind you to send a closing report to your client and to a new mortgagee and to list any post-closing matters to be resolved, often as a result of undertakings given or received on the closing.

The checklist should obviously list any other matters to be attended to by virtue of any additions to the agreement of purchase and sale. In this way, the checklist becomes a "road map" to guide you from the start of the transaction to its conclusion and will also serve as a reminder as to upcoming dates, information to be obtained from your client and matters that are being attended to by others.

One important reminder that should also be included on every checklist for a purchase transaction is to obtain the client's instruction as to obtaining title insurance. Rule 2.02(10) of the Rules of Professional Conduct requires a lawyer to advise the client of the options available in obtaining assurances on title, namely, between the traditional solicitor's opinion on title and title insurance. It is not mandatory that a client obtain title insurance, but the options should be presented and the legal and cost differences explained. Title insurance and its effect on closing procedures is described later in this chapter; however, for the time being, it is worth noting that your checklist should remind you that if title insurance is to be obtained, the title issuer's conditions and timelines must be met and you should note them thereon.

At this early stage in the transaction, contact should be made with the vendor's lawyer. A survey should be requested together with any other documents or deliveries that the agreement of purchase and sale requires the vendor to provide. The initial contact will have you ask for the enquiry authorizations referred to above to be signed, and you will also ask for a draft transfer and statement of adjustments to be provided as soon as possible.

The next stage in the transaction is to begin your enquiries, searches and general due diligence investigations. Often, where there are conditions in the agreement of purchase and sale, your client may not want you to begin any searches for fear of your efforts being wasted if the conditions are not satisfied. Still, remind your client that time is of the essence and that you need to be given enough time to complete your searches.

Begin your title search as soon as possible, including searches of adjoining lands for *Planning Act* compliance, execution searches, searches to confirm there is legal access to and from the property and a road allowance, and as to past corporate ownership of the property (see Chapter 16 for the search procedures). As mentioned, if there is no survey, or if the survey submitted is not recent, you should inform your clients. Get their instructions as to whether or not you should order an up-to-date plan of survey from a surveyor. If they decide not to go to the expense of ordering a new survey, make it clear that your title opinion will be subject to any encroachments or by-law infractions that might be shown by an up-to-date plan of survey. If you do not get these instructions in writing, you should put a memorandum of the conversation in your file. Review the survey to confirm that there are no encroachments and that the boundaries are consistent with the legal description and physical description of the property in the agreement of purchase and sale. Note the set-backs of the building on the property from the lot lines and obtain instructions from your client on any non-compliance with municipal by-laws governing set-back and other zoning matters. Also review the location of fences and retaining walls built along property boundaries to determine whether any variance in their locations could lead to claims of adverse possession. Finally, review the location of any easements in relation to the building and any other improvements on the property.

When you have completed your search of title, prepare your letter of requisitions carefully (see Chapter 16). Remember that your objective in submitting requisitions is to preserve and protect your clients' contractual rights: *Weeks v. Rosocha*, [1983] O.J. No. 3040, 41 O.R. (2d) 787 (C.A.). Then, see if you can find the answers to those requisitions yourself. Too many solicitors ignore letters of requisitions while careful and conscientious solicitors are forced to clear title whether they are acting for the purchaser or vendor.

You should make a preliminary search for executions at this time in the sheriff's office. If you find a similar name execution, you must request its removal prior to the end of the time period for making requisitions: *Koffman v. Fischtein*, [1986] O.J. No. 2992, 53 O.R. (2d) 671 (C.A.). On closing it will be necessary to have a new certificate just against the vendor. This will save you hours of frustration trying to satisfy yourself as to outstanding executions on the date set for closing.

Depending on the type of property the transaction involves, there are a number of "off-title" or municipal enquiries that are usual and should be made in connection with the acquisition of a property. Chapters 3 and 4 list dozens of statutes that affect real estate, and many of them implement compliance mechanisms that allow purchasers to make enquiries of the applicable governmental authority to determine whether there are any matters that are not in compliance, or payments required of the current owner that are in arrears. Some of the more common searches that should be undertaken in connection with almost every purchase of improved real property include:

1. writing to the local municipality for the status of realty taxes and local improvement charges, and obtaining a tax certificate to confirm the state of taxes;

2. searches for work orders and other directives of non-compliance, directed to the building department of the local municipality;

3. other work order searches to other applicable authorities that are relevant to the property (which can include the Fire Department, Health Department, Technical Standards and Safety Authority and the dozens of other authorities that can issue such orders, some of which are described in Chapters 3 and 4);

4. searches with the local conservation authority for confirmation as to whether any of its regulations affect the property and its use;

5. enquiries as to whether any agreements registered on title to the property in favour of municipalities, utility companies and any other entities are in compliance; and

6. enquiries with public utilities for the state of their account and enquiries with private utilities to have them note the anticipated change in ownership of the property to allow them to read the meter and to forward to you any documentation to be completed to allow services to be provided to the purchaser.

Consider if an enquiry should be made of Hydro One as to whether it has any unregistered easements in the land pursuant to s. 46 of the *Electricity Act, 1998*, S.O. 1998, c. 15, Sched. A. Certainly, you will wish to do so for rural land, but such easements can also exist in urban municipalities. Enquiries may be made online at <http://unregeasement.hydroone.com/lvr> for a fee.

It is absolutely essential that you satisfy yourself that the intended use and the location of the building on the lot comply with the appropriate municipal by-laws. There are a number of cases where solicitors have been found negligent for failing to ensure that the use of a property complied with municipal by-laws and regulations: *Wong v. Hassard*, [1985] O.J. No. 63 (C.A.). If you do not keep up-to-date copies of the by-laws in your office, you must check in each case with the municipal office. It is advisable to write to the clerk or the building commissioner of the municipality in which the land is situate, enclosing the survey and asking whether the siting of the building on the lot complies with local by-laws. The charge for this service varies from municipality to municipality. Many municipalities refuse to give any assurances on these matters and require you to satisfy yourself. This should be anticipated and instructions obtained as to the degree of zoning investigations to be independently conducted by you.

A number of searches related to corporate matters will also have to be undertaken. As discussed in Chapter 6, searches to ascertain the corporate status of companies in the chain of title during their respective periods of ownership will have to be completed to confirm there is no escheat issue. If the current owner is a corporation, a certificate of status should be obtained and additional searches undertaken to obtain confirmation that it is not insolvent or bankrupt. Where chattels or other personal property interests are being acquired together with the real property, searches for security interests registered against the vendor under the *Personal Property Security Act*, R.S.O. 1990, c. P.10 should be completed.

To the extent that any issues arise from any of the searches and enquiries that have been completed, those issues should be included in your requisition letter and action on their correction or remediation sought from the vendor.

While you are undertaking all of the above searches, it is often the case that your client will be attempting to satisfy certain conditions and you should keep yourself apprised of your client's progress in that regard. It is very common for conditions to be included as to the physical conditions of the buildings or homes on the property and as to the results of a building inspection or engineering report. When buying unimproved lands, purchasers will often have a condition in the agreement as to soil conditions and will commission geotechnical reports relating thereto. In commercial transactions, environmental audits are performed almost without exception to determine the environmental condition of the property. In all these cases, the purchaser's efforts to satisfy itself as to these matters will run parallel to your efforts in respect of legal due diligence. Remind your client of the time limitations within which to satisfy these conditions, and the need to make known to the vendor any objections arising from any reports received in keeping with the intent of the condition provisions granted to the purchaser in the agreement of purchase and sale.

Once conditions are waived or otherwise satisfied, attention needs to be paid to the preparation of closing documentation.

If a mortgage is to be given back as part of the purchase price, most standard form agreements of purchase and sale require the purchaser's solicitor to prepare the mortgage documents for the approval of the vendor's lawyer.

If a new mortgage is being arranged, check with the lender's internal mortgage officer or, where applicable, the solicitor for the mortgagee, from time to time to be sure that the mortgagee is satisfied with the title and other closing prerequisites and will be in a position to advance funds on the closing date. All mortgage documents should be reviewed and settled with the mortgagee or its solicitor. If you wish the proceeds of the mortgage to be paid to someone other than your clients, prepare the necessary direction and give the mortgagee's solicitor plenty of warning. If you as the purchaser's solicitor are also acting for the mortgagee, make sure that all information and documentation required by the mortgagee in its instructions to you has been obtained and is complete.

Similarly, if your client is assuming a mortgage, you should ensure that a statement is obtained from the mortgagee confirming the financial terms of the mortgage and the amounts outstanding. Confirmation should also be obtained as to what matters the mortgagee requires to be settled to effect the assumption (*i.e.*, evidence of insurance, automatic debit arrangements, *etc.*) and you should attend to them or confirm your client is doing so.

Apart from mortgage documentation, there are several documents that a purchaser's solicitor is responsible for preparing and/or reviewing. The most common documents of applicability to almost every purchase transaction are as follows:

1. The transfer will be prepared by the vendor's solicitor; have it reviewed and approved on the purchaser's behalf and in so doing, ensure that the vendor and his or her solicitors will be completing the *Planning Act* statements. This will also be a reminder to you to be prepared to complete the *Planning Act* statements so that you, as solicitor for the purchaser, can confirm the transaction complies with the subdivision control provisions of that Act.

2. A land transfer tax affidavit must be prepared and calculations made as to the amount of land transfer tax that will be payable.

3. The statement of adjustments will be prepared by the vendor's solicitor; it should be carefully reviewed and settled with the vendor's solicitor and be consistent with the arrangements in the purchase agreement governing those adjustments.

4. A statutory declaration of possession should be prepared in cases where the property is in the Registry system or where the property has been converted from Registry into Land Titles Conversion Qualified status ("LTCQ"). In both of these cases, claims of adverse possession are a concern and obtaining a declaration of possession may assist in rebutting any such third party claims. See *Alves v. Bechtel*, [2004] O.J. No. 5035, 28 R.P.R. (4th) 211 (S.C.J.), where the Court describes the legal position on statutory declarations and the rights of purchasers for incorrect assertions therein.

5. A bill of sale will be required to evidence the conveyance of any chattels to the purchaser.

6. If there are any tenants in occupancy of the property, it is normal for an agreement assigning the leases pertaining to such tenancies to be prepared along with a direction to the tenants to start paying rents to the purchaser from and after closing. If the agreement of purchase and sale requires that tenant acknowledgments be obtained, they should be prepared and sent to tenants, and reviewed once returned for any change made to them.

7. If your client will take title to the property in a name different from that identified in the agreement of purchase and sale, a direction to

that effect must be prepared to authorize the vendor's solicitor to engross the transfer in that manner.

8. You will be looking for evidence that the vendor has complied with the obligations of s. 116 of the *Income Tax Act*, R.S.C. 1985, c. 1 (5th Supp.) (either by obtaining a clearance certificate or by providing the necessary statutory declaration) to avoid a withholding obligation on the purchaser's part (see the detailed discussion on this requirement in Chapter 4).

9. You will also require evidence that the provisions of the *Family Law Act*, R.S.O. 1990, c. F.3 have been complied with, in the case of individuals, by ensuring that the necessary statements and signatures appear in the transfer, and in the case of any other entities, by receiving a statutory declaration that no spouse of an officer, director, partner, *etc.* uses the property as a matrimonial home.

10. In residential transactions, obtain any necessary assurances that the property is not subject to HST; in non-residential transactions, provide evidence that the purchaser is a registrant for the purposes of HST and provide the purchaser's registration number (see Chapter 4 for a detailed discussion of HST requirements).

11. Prepare or review documents prepared by the vendor that relate to requisitions you may have made.

At this point, it is important to be in contact with your clients to review any outstanding issues, then advise them as to the amounts needed from them to satisfy the purchase price, and to ensure they are available to sign all of the closing documents. It is also useful to inquire as to what arrangements have been made by the parties about the delivery of keys to the house. The safest and best practice from the point of view of a vendor is to deliver the keys with the transfer in the land registry office upon receipt of the balance due on closing. But this is inconvenient for your clients if they are moving on that day — the moving van would be at the house waiting to be unloaded and the keys would be at the land registry office, or at the solicitor's office. Probably the best compromise is for the vendor to leave the key with a trustworthy neighbour with instructions to release it only after receiving a call from the vendor's solicitor advising that the deal has closed. When acting for the purchasers, caution them against the risk of accepting and using the key to the house before you have closed. By taking possession they may be deemed to have waived any outstanding requisitions.

TITLE INSURANCE

A discussion of procedures to be followed in a routine purchase transaction would not be complete without considering the effect that title insurance has on those procedures. In residential transactions, it has become the preferred alternative to the traditional approach of the solicitor providing assurances on title matters through his or her opinion. It is often required by banks, trust companies and other lenders to protect their interests. As a result (and as mentioned earlier), a solicitor is obliged by the Rules of Professional Conduct to discuss this alternative with a client upon being retained by a client on a purchase transaction.

Title insurance is similar to other types of insurance with which clients are familiar, such as home or automobile insurance, and that comparison may be helpful in enabling a client to understand what title insurance is and whether they should instruct you to obtain it for them. The title insurance company agrees to compensate a purchaser for certain losses a purchaser may suffer as a result of specifically enumerated events or circumstances up to a maximum amount that is explicitly set out in the title insurance policy (usually the purchase price for the home). As with other forms of insurance, there are contractual provisions which, among other things, list exclusions and exceptions to coverage and impose other limitations. As there are several title insurance companies offering title insurance in Ontario, each with their own forms of policies, only general statements can be made about the coverage and limitation inherent in such policies and the general framework of such policies.

A title insurance policy for a residential property usually begins by confirming that the owner's title is insured in specifically described lands starting on a certain date (usually the date of closing), subject to exclusions, exceptions and conditions. The insurance covers losses incurred resulting from the title risks identified in the policy and for costs associated therewith (such as legal expenses) up to a maximum dollar limit.

The types of risks associated with ownership that are covered by the typical policy include:

1. a third party actually having title to the property;
2. improperly signed documents;
3. forgery and fraud, including forgery and fraud occurring after the date of the policy;
4. defective registration of an instrument;
5. lack of access;
6. a lack of marketable title allowing a subsequent purchaser or lender to refuse to complete a transaction involving the lands as a result of adverse matters or zoning violations that would have been revealed by a current survey;
7. any charge, lien or encumbrance affecting title;
8. violation of the subdivision control provisions of the *Planning Act*; and
9. work orders and encroachments.

In addition to the foregoing risks that are covered, a title insurer will also usually agree to pay all costs associated with a defence of the policy holder's title.

Every title insurance policy will contain exceptions to coverage, which exceptions will accord with those encumbrances to which your client has agreed to accept title pursuant to the terms of the agreement of purchase and sale, and which are registered against title on the date of closing. In other words, if there are easements, subdivision agreements and an assumed mortgage on title, and these encumbrances were acceptable to the purchaser on closing, no claim can be brought under the policy relating to losses suffered as a result of their existence.

In addition to the exceptions discussed above, most policies will exclude claims relating to environmental matters, expropriation proceedings and title problems caused by the owner or known to the owner but not disclosed to the insurer on the date that the policy was issued or that result in no loss to the owner.

Most policies will provide that the benefits of the policy apply as long as the policy holder owns the property or takes back a mortgage from someone who buys the property. Policies often allow the benefit of the policy to extend to purchasers of a mortgage taken back by the policy holder on a sale, to beneficiaries under a will upon the death of the policy holder and in other situations involving family law settlements.

As with most insurance policies, a title insurance policy requires any claims for compensation to be made promptly within strict time periods from the occurrence of the event giving rise to the claim or upon the policy holder becoming aware of circumstances affecting his or her title.

If a policy holder can prove his or her claim and substantiate the loss incurred as a result thereof, the policy gives the title insurer the right to decide on the approach to be followed in compensating the policy holder or challenging the claims asserted by a third party that are detrimentally affecting the policy holder. The title insurer has the option of negotiating a settlement among all parties, paying the third party in return for a release of its purported interest in the property insured, challenging the claim in court or paying the insured for the loss incurred to the limit of the policy. Note that there may be deductibles set forth in the policy in respect of certain types of losses that will reduce the recovery of the policy holder, and these deductibles need to be explained to your client.

Many policies provide for inflation coverage that increases the amount of the insurance coverage based upon an increase in the fair market value of the property over time. This inflation increase is not unlimited, and is often capped (usually at twice the original policy limit).

Again, the above discussion is of a general nature only, due to the number of insurers offering such coverage, and given the fact that insurers regularly update their policies to react to the market and compete for a greater share thereof. Practitioners must be familiar with these policies as they evolve so that they can properly advise their clients as to the title insurance alternative.

The benefits that title insurance offers to a purchaser vary depending on the circumstances of each transaction and the particular terms of a particular insurer's policy. Some of these benefits are as follows:

1. Less Searching — All title insurers allow a solicitor to ignore certain searches or inquiries that he or she would otherwise normally complete on a purchase transaction. The number of searches that can be dispensed with varies depending on the title insurer, and each insurer would have to be consulted as to its requirements in this regard, but, by avoiding such searches, the solicitor's time is saved, as is the fee usually charged by the municipality or other governmental authority for responding to the inquiry. Note, however, that a solicitor has been held to be liable for failure to obtain a verbal or written tax clearance

even though the purchasers had obtained title insurance: *Ruksc v. Hussein*, [2005] O.J. No. 5231 (S.C.J.).

2. Avoiding Surveys — Some title insurers will cover the risk of title defects that would have been discovered had a new survey been obtained or an old survey updated. Even where a purchaser was prepared to take such a risk anyway and would have opted not to get a new survey when purchasing the property, lenders are not that easy-going and will often require a new survey to complete a mortgage loan. Title insurance allows surveys to be dispensed with altogether and lenders will accept policies in lieu of surveys as a result of this protection, saving purchasers significant sums of money; however, each insurer's coverage must be examined to understand the limits of this survey coverage.

3. Insuring Existing Defects — In certain circumstances, a title insurer may be prepared to issue a special endorsement to its standard policy to cover a known title defect that would otherwise prevent a transaction of proceeding to closing. The title insurer, if the circumstances were acceptable to it, would underwrite the risk and may charge an additional premium relating to the endorsement. As a result, a transaction that was in trouble due to the defect may be saved if the purchaser accepts the insurance alternative to cover the risk of the known defect.

4. Broad Coverage — By covering risks such as fraud, forgery, errors in the Land Registry system and other similar items that could affect a person's title, title insurance offers protection against matters that are excluded from the traditional solicitor's opinion on title.

5. Post-Closing Events — Title insurance often covers risks that do not exist on the date of closing but that subsequently arise, for example, encroachments by others onto a property that relate to improvements constructed by neighbours after closing.

At present, the premiums charged by title insurers are relatively competitive for the average residential purchase transaction, with premiums in the $250 to $350 range where policies are to be issued to a purchaser and its lender. Disbursements that are avoided in many situations by choosing the title insurance alternative often make up for the cost of the premiums by themselves. The premium paid for title insurance is also a one-time fee and is not repaid annually to renew the policy. This is a difference that clients will have to be made aware of as they will be accustomed to the practice followed with home and auto insurance of paying annual renewal premiums.

If a client chooses the title insurance alternative, the procedures to be followed by a purchaser's solicitor vary from those described above. Certain searches no longer need to be conducted (depending on the insurer's specific requirements); new surveys may not be necessary and will not have to be reviewed. It will be necessary, however, to submit the necessary applications, prepare preliminary reports on title to the insurer and satisfy any condition of the insurer needed to have the policy issue to the purchaser and any lender on closing. All these requirements should be added to your checklist. In addition, the policy will have to be carefully reviewed to make sure it is correct in all respects and includes any special endorsements you may have negotiated. Your client's name, the legal description of the property and any specific title exception should be scrutinized in detail. Finally, arrangements with your client to obtain the moneys necessary to pay the premiums on closing will have to be obtained.

CLOSING THE DEAL

Now you have completed all your searches, your requisitions are all answered and tomorrow is the date for closing.

First, you must have your clients come to your office to execute any documents required of them and to deliver the cheque for the balance due on closing in accordance with the statement of adjustments. It must be a certified cheque or a bank draft. Furthermore, your office must obviously not issue a certified cheque (or any other cheque) out of its trust account unless the cheque from your clients to cover that amount is also certified.

At the same time, you should get from your clients a cheque payable to your firm to cover at least your disbursements and perhaps an advance on the fee. The disbursements on an average transaction would include the following: tax certificate, search, executions, work order search and other municipal enquiries, registration of transfer, registration of charge, land transfer tax and title insurance premiums, if applicable.

Land transfer tax is explained more fully in Chapter 4. However, as a quick reminder, the calculation is as follows: ½ of 1 per cent up to $55,000; plus 1 per cent from $55,000 to $250,000; plus 1½ per cent from $250,000 to $400,000; plus, where the property contains one or two single-family residences, 2 per cent on any excess over $400,000. In the City of Toronto, municipal transfer taxes are also payable with different rates applicable, as detailed in Chapter 4.

The following is a sample calculation of land transfer tax payable on the registration of a transfer of property purchased for $500,000 and containing a single-family residence. This calculation assumes the property is not in the City of Toronto:

0.5% of first $55,000	$275
1.0% of next $195,000	$1,950
1.5% of next $150,000	$2,250
2.0% of remaining $100,000	$2,000
Total land transfer tax	$6,475

Land transfer tax is paid by the person registering the transfer, usually the solicitor for the purchaser. You pay it together with the registration fee when you submit the document for registration. The land registry office will accept a solicitor's uncertified cheque for land transfer tax, but a client's cheque must be certified. The cheque is payable to the Minister of Finance. Of course, for transactions completed electronically, such taxes are collected by Teranet as discussed later in this chapter.

There is a procedure whereby you can take a transfer in advance of closing and pay the tax at the following address:

Ministry of Finance
Land Transfer Tax Branch
33 King Street West
Oshawa, ON
L1H 1A1

The transfer will be stamped to indicate that the land transfer tax has been paid. You would do this if, for some reason, your clients do not want the purchase price set out in the land transfer tax affidavit attached to the transfer in the local land registry office for their neighbours or anyone else to read. However, anyone can attend at the Branch and look at the file.

As noted in Chapter 4, Toronto purchasers will also be required to pay the Municipal Land Transfer Tax ("MLTT"). The MLTT will be collected at the same time the property transaction is registered and the provincial land transfer tax collected.

On the day before closing, you should call the solicitor for the vendor to make an appointment to meet in the land registry office to close. You, as solicitor for the purchasers, should arrive at the land registry office well before the appointed time to perform your subsearches.

It is all very well that six weeks previous, when you did your search, the vendor was the owner free and clear of encumbrances. But what if, in the meantime, the vendor has mortgaged the property, or a new execution has been filed, or someone has filed a construction lien against the property? You must protect your clients against the possibility of subsequent encumbrances by getting out the abstract book once again and seeing that there are no further entries, and by obtaining an up-to-date execution certificate against the vendor only. There is no need to get a certificate again for the predecessors in title since you already have that.

Even this final search is not sufficient. You will appreciate that in a busy land registry office hundreds of instruments are registered every day. It takes time for each of these instruments to be entered by the registrars and their deputies into the appropriate abstract books. They may be days or weeks behind. To cover that period, you must search the "day-book". This is a record kept by the land registry office of every document registered in the order of registration, giving registration number, date, the names of the parties and the lot and plan or lot and concession affected. This is a tedious search since you must go through these lists checking the names and the descriptions to see that the vendor's property is not affected.

In those cases where the search in the sheriff's office reveals an execution outstanding against a name similar to, or identical to, the vendor's, all too often the transaction is closed upon the vendor's solicitor giving an undertaking to produce a statutory declaration by the vendor that he or she is not the person named in the execution. You would be foolhardy to accept just that undertaking. The solicitor may or may not have authority to give such undertaking; it is often impossible to contact a client by telephone on moving day. Even if the vendor's solicitor has authority, you have no way of forcing the vendor to actually sign the declaration. And, if it is signed, it does not in any way affect the execution debtor's rights against the land if the declaration is false. You must first satisfy yourself that the execution does not affect the lands in question. You should contact the solicitor who filed the execution and find out as many details about the execution debtor as possible. It is often a simple matter to discover that the execution debtor and the vendor could not be the same; they have different spouses; they have lived at different addresses; they have different employers; or they are different ages.

This is not to say that you should not require the production of a statutory declaration by the vendor. It is further evidence, but you should not depend on it alone. If you had made your execution search before the closing date, you could have warned the vendor's solicitor of the problem and the vendor's solicitor could have obtained the declaration for delivery on closing.

When you have satisfied yourself as to subsearch and executions, you can sit down with the solicitor for the vendor and go through the procedure of closing.

Check all documents for proper execution. Check the tax bill and other material dealt with in the statement of adjustments. When satisfied that everything is in order, you hand over the certified cheque for the balance due on closing and receive and register the transfer. Naturally, you must register the transfer immediately after your last look at the day-book, so nothing else can be registered ahead of it.

Unless you have received a direction signed by the vendor authorizing you to make the cheque payable to someone else, it should be payable to the vendor.

Once the transaction has closed, it is important to note what post-closing matters remain outstanding. Usually, there will be undertakings that may have been given or received on closing that will have to be fulfilled. A common vendor's undertaking is to obtain a discharge of an institutional mortgage; as the purchaser's solicitor, you should follow up with the vendor's solicitor and make sure the undertaking is honoured.

The only matter left to be attended to is the reporting letters. There is always a reporting letter to be sent to the purchaser, but there also may be a requirement to deliver reporting letters to a mortgagee in connection with a loan or to a title insurer in connection with the issuance of title insurance. It is easy to set this chore aside for another day, and most solicitors do, but remember that your clients are very concerned about the purchase. Until you forward your report with the closing documents, they have no proof that you have completed the transaction for them. And until they receive your report, they do not have notice of the date for payment of their mortgage instalments or tax payments.

Even though it is time consuming, make the report as complete as possible. It serves several purposes. It is the only record your clients have of all the details of the taxes, mortgage, utilities, *etc.* It contains what you were retained for — your opinion of the state of title. Be sure that you make your opinion subject to all outstanding encumbrances and to those title deficiencies, if any, which have been discussed with and agreed to by your clients. The file copy of the report serves as a convenient record of the transaction for future reference.

One word of caution: your report should not contain the words, "I hereby certify that you have a good and marketable title ...". It should read, "In my opinion you have a good and marketable title ...". By certifying the title you may become a guarantor of that title, and may therefore be liable to your clients if, for example, it is subsequently discovered that a document in the chain of title is a forgery. If you have given your opinion as to title, you could only become liable if you have been negligent in the performance of your duties in the transaction.

If your client has instead chosen to obtain title insurance, no opinion will be given; instead, the original title insurance policy will accompany your closing report and it will be that policy that your client will look to insofar as all assurances on title are concerned.

ELECTRONIC REGISTRATION

The introduction of electronic searching and registration in Ontario in recent years requires that the closing procedures discussed earlier in this chapter be modified where the property concerned is within a jurisdiction where electronic registration is mandatory. The changes are, in fact, quite dramatic and, for the first time, require solicitors to equip their offices with compatible computer systems and to subscribe to Internet communication systems in addition to simply learning the different procedures.

The statutory framework by which electronic registration has been introduced and by which it is governed has been discussed in Chapters 1 and 2. A review of some of the regulations and directives that affect electronic registration and searching have also been addressed in those chapters. The discussion that follows relating to closing procedures can only be properly understood by reviewing those earlier chapters. In addition, much of what has previously been reviewed in this chapter, relating to closing procedures to be followed in respect of transactions where the property does not fall within a jurisdiction where electronic registration is mandatory, is still important to understand as there is still a need to prepare, review and obtain statements of adjustment and other closing documents that are not registered. However, given that it is the intention of Teranet to eventually implement mandatory electronic registration throughout Ontario and therefore dispense with the visit to the registry office that, until now, has been the essence of closing a real estate transaction, an understanding of the procedures a solicitor must follow in closing an electronic registration (or "e-reg") property matter is essential in adapting to this new system.

The more significant concepts introduced by the e-reg system that most affect closing procedures are:

1. Registration documents are not printed or produced on paper but are electronic creations.

2. Registration documents are not signed; instead, solicitors obtain directions from clients to release documents for registration.

3. Registration is effected electronically by all concerned parties releasing registration documents for registration via e-mail communications.

4. Attendance at a registry office is dispensed with; instead, solicitors enter into escrow agreements known as document registration agreements,

pursuant to which funds and non-registration documents are exchanged in advance of electronic registration.

5.   Supporting documentation that previously had to accompany registration documents (for example, the various affidavits in support of a transfer under power of sale) no longer are registered; instead, the supporting documentation is held by a solicitor in his or her file and that solicitor includes "compliance with law statements" in the applicable registration document, which can be relied upon by the other solicitors to the transaction and by solicitors searching title to that property in the future (in the same way that completed *Planning Act* statements allow solicitors to avoid searching for past *Planning Act* compliance).

6.   Final searches (for executions and new entries) and payments (of registration fees and land transfer tax) previously conducted at the registry office are completed or effected online.

The practical effect that these changes have on the actual closing mechanics will be discussed below.

Teranet requires Teraview users to be licensed in order to access the system. Each licence will grant varying degrees of access to the system. Lawyers can obtain the most comprehensive licence, allowing them to conduct searches, make registrations and make compliance with law statements. Non-lawyers can obtain licences that allow them to simply do searches and/or effect registrations that do not require compliance with law statements.

Each user is given a personalized USB key that must be used to gain access to the system. The key requires the user to insert his or her password upon logging onto the system, which identifies the user to the system and records the user's identity each time a registration is completed or a statement of law certification is made by that user. This allows Teranet to trace every registration and statement to an individual. Rule 5.01(3) of the Rules of Professional Conduct passed by the Law Society of Upper Canada prohibits a lawyer from allowing any person to use his or her key or password, and makes lawyers responsible for ensuring that non-lawyers in their offices who are licensed to use the system do not similarly allow others access to the system through keys assigned to them.

Once a solicitor has been retained to act on a property transaction, inputting the property identification number ("PIN") for that property will allow the solicitor to gain access to the parcel register for the property and complete the title search for it. If your client's records do not disclose the PIN, Teraview allows you to search by legal description, municipal address and owner to determine the PIN. When Teraview is first accessed for that purpose, the system will allow a user to assign and enter a docket number under which all future accesses and registrations can be tracked to assist in posting the disbursements incurred for each access to a file. Title searching using the e-reg system is discussed in detail in Chapter 16.

In a typical purchase and sale transaction, it often makes more sense for the purchaser's solicitor to prepare the draft transfer. Since the purchaser's solicitor must access Teraview to search title to the property, he or she can use that opportunity to quickly prepare the transfer. When the PIN for the property is inserted in the appropriate box of the electronic transfer, the system will automatically complete most of the other sections of the transfer by drawing upon the information in the system as to the legal description, current owner, municipal address, *etc.* The purchaser's solicitor can then insert the name of the purchaser and complete any remaining sections of the document (such as the consideration). In each case, the system will prompt the user to complete any remaining sections and often offer alternative suggestions as to each respective section's completion. Once complete, the information in the transfer will be used by Teraview to prepare the land transfer tax affidavit, again prompting the user as to the completion of each section for which additional information is required.

Once the transfer is complete, it must be e-mailed to the Teranet user acting for the vendor, in which e-mail the purchaser's solicitor will grant access to the document to such user. This often requires that a call be made to the other solicitor to confirm who will be reviewing the transfer and to obtain their e-mail address on the system. The vendor's solicitor will then have an opportunity to review the draft transfer and make any required changes. When both solicitors are satisfied as to the final form of the transfer, each of them logs onto the system and notifies the system that the document is complete or, in other words, "signs" the document for completeness. This notification is the first "electronic signature" required from each party's solicitor before the transfer is ready for electronic registration.

As mentioned earlier, the e-reg system eliminates the need for supplementary affidavits, statutory declarations and other supporting materials that otherwise would have had to accompany an instrument at the time of registration. In the case of a transfer under power of sale, for example, the sale papers required under the *Mortgages Act*, R.S.O. 1990, c. M.40 are not included with the transfer. The sale papers must still be prepared and executed by the appropriate parties but they are simply retained in the solicitor's file. For the purposes of the transfer itself, the solicitor relies upon the sale papers in his or her file to make a statement in the transfer that all statutory requirements have been fulfilled to allow the transfer under power of sale. In fact, once you have chosen to complete a transfer under power of sale (which choice will be offered by the e-reg system) the compliance of law statement will be automatically displayed for the solicitor's acceptance, for which a further electronic signature will be required by the solicitor making the statement. As mentioned earlier, Teraview will only allow Ontario solicitors in good standing who are licensed with Teranet to complete compliance with law statements. Teranet will be updated by the Law Society as to its membership and each lawyer's status to allow the system to deny access to non-lawyers or suspended/disbarred lawyers insofar as such compliance statements are concerned.

The legislation that introduced the e-reg system allows solicitors to rely upon compliance of law statements without the need for reviewing the underlying materials upon which such statements are based.

The next procedural change of consequence in the e-reg system is the lack of client signatures on the transfer, or any registration document for that matter. As there is no paper copy of a transfer prepared, and as access to the e-reg system is restricted, clients do not physically or electronically sign registration documents. However, in order to ensure solicitors have authority from clients to proceed with transactions, which authority would have previously been demonstrated by the client affixing his or her signature to a document, the e-reg system creates an acknowledgment and direction that is intended to be printed and presented to a client for execution to evidence a client's instructions to complete a transaction.

In a purchase and sale transaction, the solicitor for the vendor will produce an acknowledgment and direction that will specifically authorize the release for registration of the transfer (a printed copy of the electronic version thereof being attached), will have the vendor acknowledge the accuracy of the information thereon, will authorize the lawyer to enter into a document registration agreement on the client's behalf (which agreement is discussed below) and will contain a confirmation from the client as to his or her identity and as to the import of releasing the transfer for registration electronically. This direction and acknowledgment, once signed, should be kept in the solicitor's file to evidence the client's instructions. When dealing with an individual, remember to have the client's spouse sign the acknowledgment and direction, where applicable, to evidence spousal consent to the transfer in accordance with the provisions of the *Family Law Act*, R.S.O. 1990, c. F.3 as, once again, the transfer registered electronically will only have a completed statement as to such matters, which a vendor's solicitor must demonstrate can be supported by an actual acknowledgment from the spouse.

An acknowledgment and direction should be signed in every situation where a party is releasing an interest in real property or where information is being registered electronically based on client statements. A purchaser's solicitor must also have a client execute a paper copy of the land transfer tax affidavit to support the electronic version registered with the transfer, with the former being maintained in the solicitor's file. Similarly, if a vendor must obtain a discharge of a mortgage or other instrument from title and arrangements have been made with the mortgagee or other party to have the vendor's solicitor electronically effect the discharge or release, that solicitor must have an acknowledgment and direction signed to evidence the instruction received by that party to release or discharge the rights they enjoy.

In using an acknowledgment and direction as the basis for proceeding with a transaction absent client signatures on the actual registration documents, practitioners should keep in mind that in certain situations, it will be necessary for a solicitor to prepare additional documentation to make up for the lack of client signatures on registration documents. For instance, on its website, the Law Society of Upper Canada <http://www.lsuc.on.ca> lists in its practice guidelines for electronic registration the example of a guarantee of a chargor's obligations under a charge. While a solicitor acting for a chargee can still prepare a charge in an electronic format and identify a guarantor in the charge, it is not sufficient that the guarantor simply execute the acknowledgment and direction that is executed by the chargor to authorize its registration. A separate paper form of guarantee should be signed by the guarantor to evidence the obligations of the guarantor in respect of the guarantee (see Practice Guideline 5 issued by the Law Society and found on the website noted above). Practitioners must use their discretion in the circumstances of a particular transaction to determine whether it is important to supplement an acknowledgment and direction with additional documentation to further substantiate the intention of the parties in respect of contractual commitments that often go beyond the simple conveyancing matters for which the e-reg system was designed.

Once all registration documents have been signed for completeness and each solicitor to the transaction has had his or her respective clients execute the appropriate acknowledgment and direction relating to the documents to be registered, the manner in which the parties proceed to closing is different under the e-reg system. There is no longer any meeting at the registry office where documents and cheques are exchanged pending the physical registration of the transfer. There is, in fact, no need for a meeting at all. Instead, the solicitors for each party to a transaction enter into an escrow arrangement through the document registration agreement ("DRA") on behalf of their clients, which arrangement has been authorized in the acknowledgment and direction. Furthermore, as discussed in Chapter 11, most standard form realtor forms of agreements of purchase and sale (see paragraph 11 of the OREA form) have been augmented to specifically provide for the respective solicitors of the vendor and purchaser to enter into a DRA to deal with closing mechanics.

The Joint Committee on Electronic Registration of Title Documents of the Law Society of Upper Canada and Canadian Bar Association — Ontario has prepared a standard form DRA to be used by practitioners, a copy of which is included as Appendix 1. As one can see by reviewing the DRA, the key provisions of the DRA are as follows:

1. All closing documents and moneys are to be exchanged in accordance with the terms of the agreement of purchase and sale and held in escrow by the parties' solicitors.

2. The purchaser's solicitor is given responsibility for the registration of the e-reg documents unless the box provided for in the DRA is checked, shifting the responsibility to the vendor's solicitor.

3. The solicitor not registering the e-reg documents agrees to electronically release the e-reg documents for registration once he or she receives all of the deliveries required to be delivered pursuant to the terms of the agreement of purchase and sale. Once the e-reg documents are released, the non-registering solicitor is authorized to release the closing documents that he or she has received in escrow following the earlier of (i) receipt of notice from the other solicitor that registration has been completed; or (ii) the closing time referred to in the agreement of purchase and sale, unless a notice is given by the registering solicitor that he or she will not be registering the e-reg documents.

4. The registering solicitor agrees to register the e-reg documents provided that he or she has received all of the deliveries required to be delivered to his or her client under the terms of the agreement of purchase and sale and provided that a notice is not sent by any party that the registration is not to proceed.

5. Any party may give notice to the other prior to registration being effected that they choose not to proceed with registration, in which event all documents are returned without prejudice to the rights of the parties under the agreement of purchase and sale.

The form of DRA recommended by the Joint Committee may require modification depending on a particular transaction and the number of parties to the transaction, and will evolve to keep up with the practical realities of closing procedures. For example, DRAs often contain a provision where the parties agree that if the e-reg documents cannot be registered due to a system malfunction or due to the system not being accessible to users, the closing documents will continue to be held pending accessibility to the system.

The events that occur on the actual day of closing under the e-reg systems are revealed, in part, in the DRA. The vendor's solicitor will have delivered the closing documents that are not to be registered to the purchaser's solicitor, and the purchaser's solicitor will have delivered those non-registration closing documents executed by his or her client to the vendor's solicitor together with a certified cheque for the closing proceeds. All of the documents and cheques are received and held in escrow. Once both solicitors have confirmed to one another that they are satisfied with the closing deliveries due to them, the vendor's solicitor logs onto the system, accesses the e-reg transfer and authorizes its release for registration. Upon being informed by the vendor's solicitor that the transfer has been released for registration, the purchaser's solicitor will then log onto the system, access the transfer and select the registration function. Teraview will then prompt the user to complete a subsearch of the property to allow the user to confirm that there have been no further registrations on title. If there have been further registrations, the purchaser's solicitor can usually review these online to determine whether they are problematic. Occasionally, such registrations are not immediately accessible online and contact needs to be made with Teranet to have the instrument "loaded" onto the system in order to retrieve them. There are also situations where instruments cannot be loaded onto the system quickly enough to accommodate closing deadlines and, in such circumstances, attendance at the registry office is necessary in order to obtain the instrument.

Once the purchaser's solicitor is satisfied with the subsearch results, he or she will instruct the system to proceed with registration. Teraview will then automatically search executions and allow the user to print a sheriff's certificate. If executions are clear, the registration will be completed. The purchaser's solicitor will then contact the vendor's solicitor to confirm the registration, at which point all documents and cheques are released from the escrow imposed by the DRA.

Insofar as the payment of land transfer tax, municipal land transfer tax and registration fees is concerned, the registering solicitor will, upon first registering with Teranet as a licensed user of Teraview, have established a bank account and given Teranet authorization to automatically debit from that account land transfer tax amounts and registration fees payable in connection with transactions completed via the e-reg system each day. A solicitor will usually have received from a client amounts necessary to cover land transfer taxes and registration fees, and these amounts will be deposited or transferred to the Teraview account for the debit that Teranet will initiate at the end of the day. The Law Society prohibits trust accounts from being subject to any automatic debit arrangements and, as a result, has implemented special rules that can be found on the Law Society's website setting forth the type of account to be created by members and how it is to be managed.

The description of the procedure to be followed in the context of the registration of a transfer in the e-reg system would have to be duplicated to deal with other registrations that are often required in completing a typical purchase and sale transaction. The vendor's solicitor may, at the same time, be coordinating the registration of a discharge of mortgage with the vendor's lender, which will require a separate acknowledgment and direction and a DRA that the vendor's solicitor, purchaser's solicitor and discharging lender's solicitor are all parties to. Similarly, the purchaser may be arranging financing for the acquisition and as a result, the purchaser's solicitor and purchaser's lender's solicitor will be coordinating the preparation and registration of e-reg charges using the same procedures. The e-reg system accommodates all of these parties and allows documents to be electronically created and registered in sequence so that the interest of each party is protected. Practitioners will find the Electronic Registration Procedures Guide published by the Ministry of Government Services to be helpful in providing the technical step-by-step assistance and details applicable to all the varied registrations practitioners need to make in the context of a real estate practice, which are too numerous to set out in this chapter.

The Law Society of Upper Canada issues Residential Real Estate Transaction Practice Guidelines, accessible on its website, that practitioners should review to understand what the Law Society views as a solicitor's responsibility in such transactions. These form part of the more comprehensive Real Estate Practice Guide issued in June 2010, which can also be found on the Law Society's website.

CHAPTER 13

Acting for the Purchaser of a Condominium Unit

Condominiums are now a familiar concept in Ontario. We are all aware of the basic idea of condominium: the ownership by a purchaser of a "unit" in a project, whether it be a townhouse in a row of townhouses, or an apartment in a high-rise building, together with ownership by the owners in the project as tenants in common of all the common elements of the project. Ontario's statute governing condominiums is the *Condominium Act, 1998*, S.O. 1998, c. 19, which was proclaimed into force on May 5, 2001. The Act applies to all condominiums, whether created before or after that date.

The *Condominium Act, 1998* and the declaration and by-laws of the condominium corporation, which is created by the registration of the declaration and the description, provide an administrative framework for the management of the project and the common elements. Each unit owner is a member of the corporation and is entitled to vote at corporation meetings. It is at these meetings of unit owners that the board of directors is elected and major decisions concerning the operation, management and maintenance of the project are undertaken. Only unit owners or their mortgagees may vote.

Before attempting to advise a client in connection with a condominium purchase, you will want to read the *Condominium Act, 1998*. You may also want to refer to one of the textbooks on the Act: J.R. Gardiner, *The Condominium Act, 1998: A Practical Guide* (Toronto: Canada Law Book, 2001); H. Herskowitz and M.F. Freedman, *Condominiums in Ontario: A Practical Analysis of the New Legislation* (Toronto: Law Society of Upper Canada and Ontario Bar Association, 2001); A. Loeb, *The Condominium Act: A User's Manual*, 3d ed. (Toronto: Carswell, 2009).

This chapter is intended to direct your attention to some of the practical problems that a solicitor for a prospective purchaser of a condominium unit should deal with.

GENERAL CONCEPTS

When acting for first-time purchasers of a condominium unit, you must take the time to explain the concept of condominium. They have usually been led to believe that they are buying a housing unit, and that they will have all the same rights and privileges, and the same opportunity to participate in the appreciation of property values, as if they were buying a detached house on its own lot, but that they are to be spared the routine maintenance problems of a homeowner. It is your responsibility to point out that while they will have title to a unit, the boundaries of which will be set out in the declaration, their use and enjoyment of that space will be limited and restricted by a number of factors that are not present in the purchase of a traditional house on its own lot.

DECLARATION

The declaration is the basic document creating the condominium corporation. It contains a description of the units, an allocation by percentage of the ownership of the common elements, and an allocation of the obligation to share in the common expenses (also by percentages). It may also include rules restricting the use of the unit and the common elements. There may be special provisions dealing with recreational facilities. The registration of the declaration along with the description in the Land Registry Office creates the condominium corporation.

You must ensure that the unit being transferred is the one your clients think they are buying. That can usually only be done by reference to the condominium plans.

In reviewing the declaration in order to advise your clients, there are certain points which may require special attention. First, the allocation of common expenses should usually be consistent with the percentage interest in the common elements specified in the declaration. Second, the purchasers will want to know the boundaries of the unit and those parts of the common elements of which they have exclusive possession. This may include parking spaces. Finally, any restrictions on sales or leases of the units set forth in the declaration must be brought to their attention.

Section 7(4) of the *Condominium Act, 1998* permits a declaration to contain "conditions or restrictions with respect to the occupation and use of the units or common elements". In residential condominiums, it is typical to find restrictions limiting use to residential. A classic point of contention arises over restrictions on pets. There are conflicting decisions on whether a prohibition against pets contained in a declaration is permitted. In two decisions, a prohibition against pets (and, in particular, dogs) was found to be enforceable: *Peel Condominium Corp. No. 78 v. Harthen*, [1978] O.J. No. 3422, 20 O.R. (2d) 225 (Co. Ct.) and *Waterloo North Condominium Corp. No. 186 v. Weidner*, [2003] O.J. No. 2496, 65 O.R. (3d) 108 (S.C.J.). However, in *215 Glenridge Ave. Ltd. Partnership v. Waddington*, [2005] O.J. No. 665, 75 O.R. (3d) 46 (S.C.J.), Quinn J. held (at para. 17) that "if any part of a declaration conflicts with subsection 58(1) [of the *Condominium Act*] it is void and unenforceable". That section deals with rules respecting the use of common elements and units and requires that they be reasonable. The decision is astonishing and had no authorities cited to support the conclusion.

BY-LAWS

The condominium corporation's by-laws are usually similar to the by-laws of any corporation or club. They set forth the rules for running the corporation, specifying the number of directors, quorums, notice of meetings and so on. A by-law must be passed by the board of directors and confirmed at a general meeting by a majority of the owners. Before it is effective, a copy certified by an officer of the condominium corporation must be registered in the land registry office under s. 56(10) of the *Condominium Act, 1998*.

RULES AND REGULATIONS

The directors of the condominium corporation may pass rules under s. 58 of the Act "respecting the use of common elements and units", but the rules must be reasonable: *Sudbury Condominium Corp. No. 3 v. Lebel*, unreported, Bolan D.C.J., July 24, 1985 (Ont. Dist. Ct.). In *Waterloo North Condominium Corp. No. 31 v. Indico Ltd.* (1984), 23 A.C.W.S. (2d) 545 (Ont. Co. Ct.), a rule limiting the number of domestic animals that could be kept in any unit was found to be beyond the power of the condominium corporation. Also note that restrictions on children living in adult lifestyle condominiums were found to be contrary to law: *York Condominium Corp. No. 216 v. Dudnik*, [1991] O.J. No. 638, 3 O.R. (3d) 360 (Div. Ct.). Note, however, the discussion above regarding restrictions contained in declarations.

A rule only becomes effective 30 days after notice to each owner, subject to a meeting being demanded by 15 per cent of the owners to reconsider the rule.

If any owner or occupant of the property breaks the rules or fails to observe the Act, declaration or by-laws, the corporation or an owner or a mortgagee may apply to the Ontario Court (General Division) for an order directing compliance under s. 134, provided that mediation and arbitration under s. 132 are first attempted and have failed.

COMMON ELEMENTS

The common elements are all those parts of the condominium that do not form part of the units. In a high-rise these include, for example, the entrance lobby, hallways, elevators, heating system, roof and structure of the building. In a townhouse project, they may include the lands, private driveways and party walls.

Certain parts of the common elements may be designated for exclusive use by various owners. For example, backyards and balconies often form part of the common elements, but are reserved for the exclusive use of the owners of the adjacent units. Parking spots in the garage may be assigned to particular units, although frequently the parking areas are now divided into separate "units" to facilitate the allocation and sale of parking spaces to meet the different requirements of various owners.

COMMON EXPENSES

The condominium corporation is responsible for the cost of operating and maintaining the condominium development. To cover its costs, the corporation collects monthly contributions from the unit owners in the proportions set out in the declaration. These costs are called common expenses and will likely include maintenance and repair of the common elements, the cost of insurance, cleaning, gardening, snow removal, management, legal and accounting fees. The monthly amount will be one-twelfth of an annual budget estimate.

If an owner fails to make the monthly common expense payments, the corporation has an automatic lien against the owner's unit under s. 85(1) of the Act. To preserve the lien, the corporation must register a notice against title to the unit within three months. If the corporation gives notice by registered mail to the mortgagees of the unit before registration of the lien, then the lien will have priority over the mortgages. If the notice is given after registration, then the priority is limited to the three months of arrears arising immediately prior to registration. (Note that the old distinction between a residential condominium and others has been eliminated. Priority is now granted both for residential and non-residential condominiums.) One registration is sufficient to cover all subsequent defaults until a discharge is registered.

Note that the lien can only be claimed against the unit in respect of which the default occurred and not against other units not in default but owned by the same owner: *York Condominium Corp. No. 482 v. Christiansen*, [2003] O.J. No. 343, 64 O.R. (3d) 65 (S.C.J.).

All unit mortgages are deemed to include a provision permitting the mortgagee to collect the common expenses and to pay them to the corporation. Some institutional lenders operate common expense accounts in the same manner as they do tax accounts. They do so particularly because of the possibility that the lien for common expenses may obtain priority over their mortgages.

INSURANCE

Because the condominium corporation is responsible under s. 89(1) for repair of both the common elements and the units after damage has occurred, the corporation is required to carry replacement cost insurance covering both the units and common elements against major perils. However, the owners are solely responsible for insuring the improvements made to units. Thus, the owners, while not having to carry fire insurance on their entire unit, should take out insurance on their contents and decoration. Remember that the major part of fire damage in most instances will be to those items classified as improvements, such as wallpaper, rugs and painting.

Most insurance companies now have packages designed specifically for condominium unit owners. However, to avoid a lack of coverage resulting from confusion as to the responsibility to cover a particular item, it may be wise for owners to place their insurance through the corporation's insurance agent with instructions to cover whatever the corporation has not.

The corporation will normally have an insurance trust agreement under which a trustee is designated to receive and disburse insurance proceeds. This will avoid the chaos that would result if the insurance company had to make the proceeds payable to all the owners.

REPAIRS

In general, the corporation is responsible for maintenance of the common elements and owners are responsible for their units. The declaration may, however, require owners to maintain part of the common elements. For example, it is common to oblige owners to maintain those parts of the common elements of which they have exclusive use, such as apartment balconies or backyards adjacent to a townhouse.

When damage occurs, such as that caused by fire, s. 89(1) makes the corporation responsible for the repair of both the common elements and the units, although this obligation does not include the improvements made to the unit by the owners. Owners will be responsible for the damage they do to the common elements, except to the extent that the damage is covered by insurance.

RESERVE FUND

To ensure that condominium owners set aside funds to meet repair and replacement costs, every corporation is required under s. 93 of the Act to maintain a reserve fund with annual contributions from the owners. A new condominium corporation (*i.e.*, one registered after the Act came into force) is required to conduct a reserve fund study within the first year after registration of the declaration and description. Thereafter, the studies must be updated every three years.

The owners' contributions to the reserve fund must be at least 10 per cent of their annual common expenses or the amount recommended by the reserve fund study, whichever is greater. This is a sensible practice which supplies an increasing fund of money available to replace deteriorating common elements. It is common for the developer of a new condominium project to require the purchasers initially to contribute a lump sum payment equal to one to three months of common expense payments in order to establish the reserve fund.

LEASES

Unless the declaration restricts their rights to do so, owners may lease their units as they would any other property. If a significant number of owners in any project decide to rent out their units, this may create conflict with the resident owners who feel that tenants, not having the same stake in the property, will not put as much effort or expense into the upkeep of the property. Special rules in this regard apply to the original developer who must specify in the disclosure statement to the nearest 25 per cent how many units are intended for rent. Section 78(1)1 obliges the developer to take all reasonable steps to sell the other residential units, and owners may apply to a court under s. 134 to prevent any attempt by the developer subsequently to lease units that were originally intended for sale.

A special provision (s. 51(6)) has been included in the Act to protect owners who occupy their residential units. If more than 15 per cent of the units are "owner-occupied" (meaning the unit has not been leased in the previous 60 days), those owners are entitled to elect one director to the board. The other owners have no vote with respect to that one position. Of course, all owners are entitled to vote for all other positions on the board.

Owners who rent out their units are required under s. 83 to give notice to the corporation, including the tenant's name and the owner's address and a copy of the lease.

Note that a lease by a purchaser during the interim occupancy period will not be protected by the *Residential Tenancies Act, 2006*, S.O. 2006, c. 17, once the agreement of purchase and sale has been terminated; thereafter, the tenant is merely a tenant at will and the right of occupancy can be terminated by the developer: *Symphony Place Corp. v. Angelini*, [1992] O.J. No. 93, 7 O.R. (3d) 151 (Gen. Div.). The situation may be different if the lease was consented to or approved by the developer.

MANAGEMENT AGREEMENT

The condominium corporation, which has the responsibility of managing the common elements, will frequently enter into a management agreement with a company to assume these responsibilities for a fee. Initially, of course, the developer will hire the management company while still in control of the project.

In the early history of condominiums in Ontario, it quickly became apparent that some developers took advantage of their initial control to set up management agreements between the condominium corporation and either themselves or related companies for long periods of time on terms very favourable to the management company. In this way they could ensure continuing profit to themselves although the condominium owners might not get the service they wanted or deserved.

The Act now provides that a management agreement entered into when the developer still controls the project can be terminated at any time by the board of directors by passing a resolution under s. 111 and giving 60 days' notice to the other party to the contract. There is no time limit for exercising this right. Similar provisions apply to any contract for the continuing supply of goods and services and leases of common elements for business purposes, except that the board must act within 12 months after the turnover meeting. Thus, if the terms of the developer's management agreement are unfavourable or the service is not good, the new owners may now make their own arrangements.

PURCHASE OF NEW UNITS

The *Condominium Act, 1998* contains numerous rules relating to the first-time purchase of residential units from the developer. These rules were thought to be necessary because of a number of abuses by condominium builders. Under the Act, the person who registers the declaration (usually the developer), is called the declarant; until the condominium is registered, that person is known as the proposed declarant.

AGREEMENTS TO PURCHASE

In the purchase of a new unit, the purchasers and their solicitors are faced in almost every case with a form of agreement of purchase and sale that has been printed by the declarant. Since there may be dozens, scores or even hundreds of units in the development, the declarant will be reluctant to amend the form of agreement to permit special clauses for individual purchasers. Naturally, you should still review the agreement for your clients if you have the chance, although it may be difficult to negotiate changes to it.

The agreement will contain the usual provisions found in most agreements to purchase residential property, including clauses covering the purchase of the unit and the transfer of title, the assumption of mortgages, the payment of deposits and the balance of the purchase price. It will also contain provisions in anticipation of "closing" occurring before the registration of the condominium plan, which is required in order to be able to transfer title. Since construction will be completed sooner than the documentation creating the corporation, the vendor will attempt to provide for closing at the earliest possible date that construction will permit. Frequently, however, delays occur resulting from construction or even sales or financing difficulties. Therefore, the agreement will also contain provisions permitting the postponement of closing for occupancy purposes and the ultimate transfer of title. In an attempt to control the length of these delays, s. 79(1) of the Act requires the declarant to take all reasonable steps to register the declaration "without delay".

Section 6 of O. Reg. 165/08 under the *Ontario New Home Warranties Plan Act*, R.S.O. 1990, c. O.31 requires that the vendor attach to the agreement of purchase and sale either the *Condominium Home Addendum (Tentative Occupancy Date)* or the *Condominium Home Addendum (Firm Occupancy Date)* and furnish proof to Tarion that this has been done. The Addenda set forth a set of rather complicated rules respecting delays in the occupancy date for a new condominium home. In general, a vendor must specify either a tentative or a firm occupancy date and, if it was a tentative date, then by a subsequent notice, establish a firm occupancy date. The vendor may extend the firm's occupancy date by notice but must pay the purchaser compensation unless the extension is by mutual agreement or is due to causes beyond the vendor's control (strikes, fire, flood, acts of God or civil insurrection). The compensation is for the purchaser's out-of-pocket expenses resulting from the delay to a maximum of $7,500 in total (including $150 per day for living expenses). You should refer to the appropriate Addendum if needed to determine whether a delay in occupancy is within the acceptable limits and whether the vendor owes the purchaser costs for an unacceptable delay.

DISCLOSURE STATEMENT

The declarant must give to the purchasers a copy of a document called a disclosure statement which sets forth the information specified in s. 72, including, among other things, a description of the property and its proposed amenities (including a schedule for completion of the amenities), a copy of the declaration, by-laws, rules, a description of contracts that the corporation has entered or will be entering into, a copy of the budget for the year following registration and a copy of the insurance trust agreement (if there is one).

The purchasers have the right under s. 73 to withdraw from the agreement at any time within 10 days after they receive the disclosure statement or an executed copy of the agreement of purchase and sale, whichever is later. In order to rescind, the purchaser sends a written notice which must be received by the declarant within the 10-day period. This provision is intended to allow purchasers a "cooling-off" period after they have agreed to purchase and received complete information about the project.

If there is subsequently a material amendment to the information, purchasers have a further 10 days in which to rescind the agreement to purchase.

There have been a variety of decisions in the past few years regarding whether changes in circumstances relating to condominium projects require the delivery of an amended disclosure statement, thus triggering the purchasers' right to rescind. These cases resulted from purchasers' attempts to escape their contracts in a falling real estate market. In the leading decision, the Ontario Court of Appeal, in *Abdool v. Somerset Place Developments of Georgetown Ltd.*, [1992] O.J. No. 2115, 10 O.R. (3d) 120 at 139, confirmed that the test was one of materiality and that the onus was on the purchaser to

> establish objectively that had the information that was not disclosed, or that was inaccurately or insufficiently disclosed, been properly disclosed in the disclosure statement at the time it was delivered to the purchaser, a reasonable purchaser would have regarded the information as sufficiently important to the decision to purchase that he or she would not likely have gone ahead with the transaction but would instead have rescinded the agreement before the expiration of the ten-day cooling off period.

This approach has been codified in the new Act in the definition of "material change" in s. 74(2).

Note that a condominium purchaser may have more than the statutory right to rescind. In *Rogers Cove Ltd. v. Sloot*, [1991] O.J. No. 1937, 28 A.C.W.S. (3d) 1089 (Gen. Div.), Langdon J. found that, although the attempt to rescind by the purchaser was exercised too late under the Act, the changes to the project were so material that the vendor "intended ultimately to convey something materially different from that for which Sloot had contracted" and accordingly held that Sloot had an equitable right to rescind his contract.

You should also be aware that, under s. 133(2) of the Act, both a purchaser and the condominium corporation have a right to recover damages from the declarant if they have relied upon a material statement in the disclosure statement that is false, deceptive or misleading, or if the disclosure statement omits material information that is required to be provided under the Act.

DEPOSITS

Pursuant to s. 81, all deposit moneys (including "reservation deposits") must be held in trust by the declarant's solicitor or by a prescribed trustee unless the declarant delivers prescribed security to the purchasers to protect these deposits.

Under s. 22 of O. Reg. 48/01, the protection given by the Tarion Warranty Corporation under the *Ontario New Home Warranties Plan Act* for the first $20,000 paid to the declarant is considered to be "prescribed security" for the purposes of the Act, and the declarant may therefore use this money as his or her own. Otherwise, the declarant may provide an insurance policy to the purchaser that guarantees repayment if necessary for the deposits (known as "excess deposit insurance"), although this method is not often used.

The declarant is required under s. 82 to pay interest to residential purchasers on all sums received to the date the unit is available for occupancy. The declarant may choose to pay the interest on that date or on closing (either by payment or by giving a credit on the statement of adjustments). If the declarant chooses the closing date, then it must on closing pay interest on the interest earned up to the occupancy date. The interest rate is prescribed pursuant to s. 19 of O. Reg. 48/01 to be 2 per cent below the one-year mortgage rate of the Bank of Canada at the end of March and September in each year.

A purchaser may not contract out of this section; an agreement to waive the interest payable by the declarant is ineffective: *Grandby Investments Ltd. v. Wright,* [1981] O.J. No. 3040, 33 O.R. (2d) 341 (H.C.J.), and *Dunkelman v. Neighbourhood Developments Ltd.,* [1985] O.J. No. 496 (H.C.J.).

BUDGET

The declarant must deliver to the purchasers a copy of the budget covering the year immediately following registration of the declaration and description. If the budget proves to be low, the declarant is liable under s. 75(2) to pay the deficiency for that year to the condominium corporation. This provision was intended to discourage the declarant from deliberately underestimating the cost of operating the condominium to assist in sales.

INTERIM OCCUPANCY AGREEMENT

Until the declaration is registered, there is no title to a unit which can be transferred to a purchaser. Construction, however, will be sufficiently complete to permit occupancy at an earlier date, and because the declarant is anxious to have the project occupied to cover carrying costs and to facilitate mortgage advances, the agreement of purchase and sale will often require the purchasers to make the entire down payment and to move in at the earliest possible stage. During the period prior to the transfer of title, the purchaser's occupancy will be governed by an agreement known as an "interim occupancy agreement", usually appended as a schedule to the agreement of purchase and sale.

The relationship between the declarant and purchasers during this time is subject to the *Residential Tenancies Act, 2006,* with certain minor variations. First, there are special provisions set out in subss. 80(6) and (7) of the *Condominium Act, 1998* restricting the obligations of the declarant as landlord to the same obligations that the condominium corporation will have after registration of the declaration. The section also permits the declarant to withhold consent to an assignment of the occupancy agreement. Second, s. 58(1)4 of the *Residential Tenancies Act, 2006* permits an order to be obtained terminating occupation of the unit by the purchasers when the agreement of purchase and sale has been terminated. This has been confirmed, for example, in *Whitby Harbour Development Corp. v. Cater*, [1992] O.J. No. 1201, 23 R.P.R. (2d) 25 (Gen. Div.), where Macfarland J. held that rescission by the purchasers ended their right to occupy. Furthermore, it has been held in that case and in *Symphony Place Corp. v. Angelini*, [1992] O.J. No. 93, 7 O.R. (3d) 151 (Gen. Div.) that tenants of purchasers have no higher protection than the purchasers and that, as regards the developer, such tenants are merely tenants at will once the purchase agreement has been terminated.

The monthly interim occupancy payments that purchasers must pay after they occupy the units are limited under s. 80(4) to the aggregate of the realty taxes, common expenses and interest at the prescribed rate (*i.e.*, the Bank of Canada rate for a one-year mortgage) on the unpaid balance of the purchase price. Note that, under s. 80(3), the purchaser can elect to pay the whole price on taking occupancy but the election must be made in the initial 10-day rescission period. These limitations were intended to prevent the declarant from making a profit during the occupancy period; otherwise, the declarant might not be very anxious to transfer title promptly. See *Hashim v. Costain Ltd.*, [1986] O.J. No. 408, 54 O.R. (2d) 790 (H.C.J.).

BLANKET MORTGAGES

Many standard developers' agreements require the purchasers to accept title to their units subject to the original mortgage or mortgages given by the developer to finance construction of the project. The vendor undertakes to obtain and register a discharge of the mortgage after closing. The danger in this procedure is that the developer will not pay the mortgage and indeed may go bankrupt before the mortgage has been paid. The mortgagee may then realize on the mortgagee's security by foreclosing or by selling all of the units, with the result that the purchasers may lose their entire down payment. The purchasers will have lost the protection given by the Ontario New Homes Warranty Program for the first $20,000 because title has passed and it is therefore no longer a "deposit". In at least one instance, the Law Society's insurers have determined that a solicitor was negligent when he did not advise his client of these risks even though the agreement had been signed without his advice.

The unfortunate practice by developers requiring purchasers to close notwithstanding the blanket mortgage is unnecessary in view of ss. 13 and 14 of the Act. Under s. 13, a blanket mortgage is only enforceable against individual units after registration of the declaration, rather than against the property as an entirety. A partial discharge of each unit may be obtained under s. 14(2) by paying directly to the mortgagee that portion of the mortgage balance equal to the percentage share of the common expenses attributable to that unit under the declaration: *511666 Ontario Ltd. v. Confederation Life Insurance Co.*, [1985] O.J. No. 2324, 50 O.R. (2d) 181 (H.C.J.). When acting for purchasers of a new condominium unit, you should make every attempt to ensure that a payment is made directly to the mortgagee. In that way, a partial discharge can always be obtained.

In many instances, the declarant will wish to reserve a vendor's lien to cover the balance of the first mortgage advances that will not be received until occupancy of the unit and transfer of the title. Notice of this lien may be registered on the title. In addition, because the declarant has received credit for the entire mortgage, the purchasers may also be required to pay interest to the declarant on the unadvanced portion of the mortgage until the declarant receives the final draw.

SUMMARY OF PROCEDURES WHEN ACTING FOR PURCHASERS OF A NEW UNIT

The following is a short list of steps that you should take in a normal straightforward purchase of a unit from a developer:

1. When consulted by clients prior to submitting their offer, review and advise your clients about the following:

   (a) the agreement of purchase and sale;

   (b) the occupancy agreement (if applicable);

   (c) the disclosure statement, including the declaration, description, by-laws, management agreement and insurance trust agreement; and

   (d) the budget.

2. Recommend to your clients that they review the condominium documentation, particularly the declaration, by-laws, rules and budget.

3. Search title:

   (a) If the declaration has not been registered, then there will be little point in searching the title at this time, except perhaps to discover financial trouble that the registration of liens and mortgages might indicate. You do not need to concern yourself with problems in the prior chain of title even if, because the Land Titles system was not available (as was the case in some areas prior to 2009), the land was registered under the Registry system and s. 78(10) of the *Registry Act*, R.S.O. 1990, c. R.20 required a Certificate of Title under the *Certification of Titles Act*, R.S.O. 1990, c. C.6 (now repealed) prior to registering the condominium. In most cases, you need only search the title after you have been advised that the condominium is registered.

   (b) If the declaration has been registered, then you must search the parcel register for the unit, which will include registration details of the following:

      (i) easements and the original encumbrances affecting the entire property;

      (ii) the declaration (which includes a description of the unit and the common elements as well as any exclusive use common elements) and the by-laws;

        (iii)   any easements and any encumbrances affecting all the units (*e.g.*, blanket mortgage, construction liens, *etc.*); and

        (iv)   the ownership of the unit together with any mortgages, liens, and leases affecting only that unit.

4.   If the condominium is not registered before closing, arrange for delivery of the balance due on closing and occupancy agreement in return for the keys.

5.   Obtain a tax certificate.

6.   Do the usual searches regarding utilities, by-law compliance and subdivision agreement compliance.

7.   Arrange for execution by your clients of the following:

    (a)   affidavit under the *Land Transfer Tax Act*, R.S.O. 1990, c. L.6;

    (b)   assumption agreement (of mortgage), if applicable.

8.   Do a subsearch immediately prior to closing.

9.   Ensure that there are no executions against the vendor or the condominium corporation.

10.   Obtain the following from the vendor:

    (a)   transfer;

    (b)   mortgage;

    (c)   statement of adjustments; and

    (d)   status certificate (see below)

11.   Register the transfer.

12.   Subsequent to closing, ensure that the vendor's lien (if applicable) is removed (see p. 305).

PURCHASE OF RESALE UNITS

Many of the problems faced in the purchase of new units from the developer do not exist in regard to the purchase of a resale unit. Normally, the condominium will already have been registered and the dangers described above will be resolved. You will, of course, have to follow the usual procedures for any purchase of real estate, including those set out in the preceding summary.

One item relating to adjustments on closing deserves special mention. The real estate board standard form agreement for resales of condominium units provides that the reserve (or contingency) fund will not be adjusted. This is sensible as the fund represents depreciating assets that will one day require repair or replacement, such as the roof or heating system (see p. 299). The fund, therefore, forms part of the value of the unit and should be accounted for, if at all, in the purchase price.

STATUS CERTIFICATES

As previously mentioned (see p. 297-98), the owner of each unit must contribute to the common expenses, usually in proportion to the percentage ownership of the common elements. Although your title search of the unit will disclose a registration made by the corporation in order to preserve its lien for unpaid common expenses beyond the three-month period provided in s. 85(2) of the *Condominium Act, 1998* you must obtain a status certificate (formerly known as an "estoppel certificate") from the corporation to ensure that payments are up-to-date. Section 76(6) states that the certificate "binds the corporation ... as against a purchaser or mortgagee of a unit who relies on the certificate". This is an improvement on the old Act, which stated that the certificate was binding only in favour of the person who requested it.

The status certificate used must be Form 13 under O. Reg. 48/01, for which the corporation may charge a fee not exceeding $100. In addition to showing the status of common expense payments, the certificate also discloses the balance in the reserve fund, any anticipated increases in common expenses and any actions by or against the corporation. This is important information to your clients.

The corporation must attach copies of various documents to the estoppel certificate, including the last annual financial statements of the corporation and its current budget, the declaration, by-laws and rules, the management and other agreements, and the most recent reserve fund study. This is an inexpensive way for you to acquire copies of these documents if the vendor does not have them, rather than by paying for copies from the land registry office.

CHAPTER 14

Representing Purchasers of New Homes

AGREEMENTS OF PURCHASE AND SALE

Ideally, a purchaser's solicitor should be given the opportunity to review the agreement of purchase and sale before the purchaser signs on the dotted line. However, that seldom happens in the case of resale properties, and even less frequently in the purchase of new homes. From time to time, particularly in and around Toronto, it is a seller's market and new homes are sold faster than they can be built. If a purchaser is not willing to sign the agreement of purchase and sale there and then in the vendor's office, there are plenty of other purchasers who will.

Consequently, the solicitor's role, even when the market slows down, frequently is to explain the agreement to the purchasers after the fact, when it may be too late to change some of the clauses that are not favourable to the purchaser. Nevertheless, purchasers should be made aware of exactly what they have contracted to do.

STANDARD FORM CONTRACT OF PURCHASE AND SALE

The first thing to realize is that the agreement of purchase and sale has been drawn up by the builder/vendor and is generally extremely one-sided. The agreement requires careful scrutiny to realize the full impact of the small print. This burden may be alleviated somewhat if the Building Industry and Land Development Association ("BILD") (formerly, the Greater Toronto Home Builders' Association ("GTHBA")) standard agreement of purchase and sale for new homes has been used. A copy of this agreement is included in the book as Appendix 5.

This form of agreement was drawn up by the GTHBA in an effort to improve the building industry's image. The GTHBA sought to come up with a contract that was easy for consumers to understand and was fairer to them than previous forms often used by builders. The effort was successful in that regard and the BILD agreement is now widely used throughout Ontario by BILD members. The form, originally created in 1987 and last updated in 2010, can be obtained by members of BILD and printed with the builder's name and logo, but BILD's name and logo must also appear. The text may not be printed differently, though changes can be made in a schedule.

Tarion Warranty Corporation ("Tarion"), the administrator under the *Ontario New Home Warranties Plan Act*, R.S.O. 1990, c. O.31 requires that all agreements of purchase and sale for newly constructed homes include an Addendum on the prescribed form. Previously, the terms of these Addenda were incorporated in bold in the BILD form of agreement but now the appropriate Addendum is simply attached as a schedule. The various forms of Addenda are discussed below.

The present form of the BILD agreement is balanced and generally fair to both parties. Certainly, the adoption of the BILD standard form contract has made review by lawyers simpler and faster, just as standard forms have in the resale market. Nevertheless, there are still several paragraphs to which you should pay close attention. If possible, you should try to change some of these provisions to make them more favourable to your client. At the very least, you should warn your client of their content.

Paragraph 1(a) — Deposit

Given the price of today's houses, particularly in Toronto, vendors often demand deposits, perhaps paid in installments, that exceed $40,000. However, the Ontario New Home Warranties Plan (discussed below) provides protection for only the first $40,000 for freehold properties or homes built under contract ($20,000 for condominium units, as discussed in Chapter 13). If your client's deposit exceeds that amount, your client should be made aware that he or she could lose the excess if the builder goes bankrupt before the deal closes.

If you are reviewing the agreement prior to execution, you should attempt to gain your client some additional protection if the deposit exceeds the prescribed limit. You could request that the amount of the deposit over and above the protected maximum be held in trust by the vendor's lawyer or the real estate agent; that the vendor obtain excess deposit insurance; or that the excess be secured by a letter of credit or personal guarantee from the vendor's principal. For new condominiums, of course, all excess deposits must be held in trust by someone other than the vendor until prescribed security (*i.e.*, insurance) is provided to the purchaser (see Chapter 13). However, this protection is not required for purchasers of new homes that are not condominiums.

Your odds of succeeding in this attempt are low: most vendors will refuse to provide additional comfort to the purchaser. However, to limit your own liability in the event the vendor goes bankrupt, you should make an effort on your client's behalf, as well as inform your client of the risks inherent in depositing more than the protected limit.

The standard agreement does not specify who is to receive the interest on the deposit. Since the deposit is paid directly to the vendor, it usually keeps the interest. Insert a clause specifically saying that the purchaser is to receive the interest earned on the deposit prior to closing.

Paragraphs 6 and 7 — Mortgage Provisions

If the purchaser does not do everything needed to obtain mortgage financing, the purchaser will have defaulted under the agreement, and the vendor may terminate the agreement. The purchaser will not only lose the deposit, but may also be liable to the builder for the cost of extras.

Paragraph 6(a) requires the purchaser to provide the vendor with a copy of a mortgage commitment for at least 75 per cent of the purchase price within 20 days of execution of the agreement. If he or she does not, then paragraph 7 deems the failure to be a material default by the purchaser and the vendor may terminate the agreement and return the deposit. If the purchaser is paying all cash without financing, then paragraph 6(b) requires the purchaser to produce evidence from his or her bank or trust company proving his or her ability to pay.

Paragraph 8 — Adjustments

Paragraph 8 incorporates a Schedule 2 to the agreement detailing adjustments to the purchase price. These adjustments must be reviewed carefully and discussed with your client. Schedule 2 contemplates the possibility of the vendor charging the purchaser for a wide variety of things including various construction items, municipal development levies, the Law Society levy, a survey, various administrative and closing costs and any reduction in the HST rebate recoverable by the vendor as a result of extras or upgrades ordered by the purchaser. The adjustments possible are very extensive and can significantly increase the overall cost to your client. Remember that these costs may not have been anticipated and may not be covered by the financing arranged by the purchaser. It is very important that the purchaser be made aware of these costs at the earliest opportunity so that he or she has the opportunity to ensure there are sufficient funds for closing.

Paragraph 9 — Modifications

Pursuant to this paragraph, the purchaser agrees to abide by any minor modifications to the plans required by the developer or municipality. If your client insists on having a house built exactly as represented on the plans, you must amend this paragraph.

Paragraph 10 — Construction

Purchasers sometimes object to this paragraph when they are made aware of it. A big attraction of buying a brand new home is the opportunity to select the colour and type of finishing materials. This paragraph permits the vendor to substitute alternate materials of at least equal quality, provided the value of the property is not diminished and the dwelling is not substantially altered. Furthermore, if the colours or materials selected by the purchaser become unavailable during construction, the purchaser has a certain time limit within which to choose new colours and materials, failing which the vendor will make the selection for the purchaser.

Paragraph 11 — Completion

The purchaser almost always closes and moves into a new home before it is totally finished. According to the standard form contract, the dwelling is deemed to be completed when all interior work has been substantially completed so that the building may be reasonably occupied. The purchaser is not permitted to hold back any funds on closing for uncompleted work.

Paragraph 8(a) of the Tarion Addendum requires the vendor to produce an occupancy permit if the municipality issues them or a certificate by the vendor that occupancy requirements under the Building Code have been met. Otherwise, the Addendum provides for delay of closing with compensation payable if applicable.

Remember the decision in *Tabata v. McWilliams*, [1981] O.J. No. 3011, 33 O.R. (2d) 32 (H.C.J.), vard [1982] O.J. No. 3597, 40 O.R. (2d) 158 (C.A.). In that case the purchaser's solicitor had been informed, as the result of a routine enquiry, that no occupancy permit had been issued, but closed the purchase anyway without following up on this requirement and without discussing it with his client. The basement wall subsequently collapsed. It turned out that there had been no building inspections; if performed, they might have uncovered the faulty design and construction, which were not in compliance with the Building Code. The solicitor was held to be negligent.

Paragraph 12 — Pre-delivery Inspection

The purchaser must go through the home with the vendor's representative prior to closing to verify that the dwelling has been completed in accordance with the agreement. Any deficiencies are noted on the Certificate of Completion and Possession.

While the vendor will be responsible for completing and correcting any deficiencies noted, the Home Warranty Program provides the purchaser with an assurance that the vendor's responsibilities will be fulfilled. Builders who fail to deliver the completed form to Tarion within 15 days of a home's possession may see a change in their terms and conditions of registration.

Paragraph 13 — Title

The vendor is obliged to provide a foundation survey at least 14 days prior to closing. You may want to modify this to provide that the vendor do so more than 20 days before closing to assist you with your title search and requisitions. Similarly, you will want to make sure that being able to search title up to 15 days before closing is adequate.

Paragraph 15 — Risk

If the house is damaged, the vendor is obliged to repair it and complete the sale, and is entitled to extension of dates including the closing date, but only if it gives the appropriate notice in accordance with paragraph 7(b) of the Tarion Addendum attached to the sale agreement.

Paragraph 18 — Assignment

The agreement may not be assigned to anyone other than the purchaser's spouse without the vendor's written consent. The intent of this paragraph is to prevent speculation.

Paragraph 26 — Harmonized Sales Tax

Either the word "includes" or the word "excludes" has to be deleted from this paragraph. If the purchase price includes the Harmonized Sales Tax ("HST"), then the purchaser promises that the purchaser or someone related to him or her will be the first to occupy the house as a primary residence. This enables the vendor to obtain the available HST rebate (which the purchaser assigns to the vendor). Note that these provisions prevent the acquisition of the house as an investment for rental purposes.

Paragraph 30 — Default

This is an all-encompassing provision, giving the vendor the right to terminate the agreement, keep the deposit and pursue other available remedies if the purchaser breaches the agreement in any way. Any breach, no matter how minor, is enough to cause the deal to fall apart, with no notice to the purchaser. You will want to amend this paragraph to give the purchaser notice and a reasonable opportunity to remedy a breach. If you are seeing the agreement after it has been signed, advise your client to adhere strictly to the time limits and other requirements of the contract.

Schedule 3 — Privacy

The BILD agreement includes a schedule under which the purchaser consents to the collection of personal information by the vendor and the provisions of it to others for various purposes such as completing the transaction, completing construction of the dwelling (by giving the information to suppliers and tradespeople) and for marketing of future projects by the vendor and its affiliates. The schedule is in addition to paragraph 39, which permits the vendor to obtain credit reports about the purchaser.

ONTARIO NEW HOME WARRANTIES PLAN

Builder registration and new home enrolment in a warranty program first became mandatory in Ontario in 1977 under the *Ontario New Home Warranties Plan Act*. In 1984, the name of the corporation administering the program was changed to the Ontario New Home Warranty Program. In 2004, it became Tarion Warranty Corporation.

The Act is intended to ensure that all new home buyers receive minimum construction warranties from the vendor. Note, however, that the Act does not replace or abolish common law warranties such as an implied warranty of fitness. Indeed, the Act preserved such rights under s. 13(6), which declare the statutory warranties to be "in addition to any other rights the owner may have". This conclusion was confirmed in *Carleton Condominium Corp. No. 109 v. Tartan Development Corp.*, [1995] O.J. No. 619, 22 O.R. (3d) 718 (Gen. Div.).

REGISTRATION

Every builder and vendor of new homes in Ontario must be registered under the Act. Failure to register could result in a $100,000 fine for a corporation and a $25,000 fine for an individual or director.

Every new home offered for sale in Ontario must also be enrolled under the program after a building permit is obtained and before construction is started. The enrolment fee depends on the sale price and ranges from $325 to $750 per dwelling, plus HST. This fee is frequently one of the additional costs passed on to the purchaser under the agreement of purchase and sale.

You should ensure that both the vendor and the building are registered. Of course, the building may not yet be enrolled under the plan if a building permit has not yet been obtained.

The Act requires that vendors register before selling any new homes. That raises the question whether a purchaser can escape an agreement that was entered into before the vendor registered under the Act (as sometimes happens) on the basis that it was an illegal contract. After a couple of contradictory decisions of the lower courts, the Ontario Court of Appeal has decided that such contracts are enforceable: see *Beer v. Townsgate I Ltd.*, [1997] O.J. No. 4276, 36 O.R. (3d) 136 (C.A.).

PROTECTION UNDER THE ACT

Deposits by purchasers on freehold or contract homes are protected to a maximum of $40,000. As mentioned above, purchasers should be advised not to deposit any more than this amount.

The other warranties relate to construction. They cover five situations: incomplete work, defects in workmanship and materials, water penetration, major structural defects and delays in closing.

The incomplete work allowance applies to purchasers who have title to the property and who are occupying it. Tarion will compensate the purchaser for any incomplete work up to the greater of 2 per cent of the sale price and $5,000.

The warranty against defects in workmanship and materials commences on the date the purchaser becomes the registered owner of the house and continues for two years after possession. The maximum compensation is $300,000.

The warranty against water penetration through the basement or foundations lasts for two years after possession.

There is a further warranty against major structural defects (to a maximum of $300,000) that lasts for seven years from the date of possession. "Major structural defect" is defined in s. 1 of the *Administration of the Plan Regulation*, R.R.O. 1990, Reg. 892 as:

> any defect in work or materials,
>
> (a) that results in failure of the load-bearing portion of any building or materially and adversely affects its load-bearing function, or
>
> (b) that materially and adversely affects the use of such building for the purpose for which it was intended ...

TARION ADDENDUM

Pursuant to Builder Bulletin 46 issued by Tarion, every agreement of purchase and sale for a new house must have attached to it one of the prescribed forms of Addenda published by Tarion. Depending on circumstances, the vendor will choose one with a firm closing date or one with a tentative closing date, and it may also choose one with a couple or more conditions than the other.

Statement of Critical Dates

The provisions regarding tentative and firm closing dates, extensions and notices required, termination rights as a result and purchaser's compensation are complicated and require careful reading. Following is a brief (and incomplete) summary.

The vendor must complete a section in the Addendum specifying either a firm or tentative closing date and an outside closing date (which cannot be more than 365 days after the firm closing date or the second tentative closing date, whichever is earlier). If it fails to complete these dates, the vendor cannot enforce the agreement against the purchaser. Furthermore, if the closing does not occur by the outside closing date specified, then the purchaser has a 30-day window in which to terminate the agreement.

There are detailed notice requirements by the vendor to the purchaser in order to extend the dates. Failure to give the required notice will result in a tentative date becoming the firm closing date.

The vendor may extend closing beyond a firm closing date subject to the purchaser's right to terminate if it is beyond the 365-day period and to payment of compensation for the purchaser's costs caused by the delay, including $150 per day for living costs to a maximum of $7,500.

Unavoidable Delay

The vendor is entitled to extensions of the various closing dates as a result of unavoidable delay caused by events beyond the vendor's reasonable control (such as strikes, fire, pandemics and so on). However, the vendor must give notice of the event causing the delay within 10 days after its occurrence (failure to do so means no extension) and the extension is only for the period from the date the purchaser receives the notice and the date that the cause of the delay ends.

Early Termination Conditions

The vendor must set forth any conditions that the agreement is subject to and is limited to the list of conditions set forth in Schedule A to the Addendum that the vendor has chosen. These include *Planning Act*, R.S.O. 1990, c. P.13 and other governmental approvals, achieving a specified threshold of sales by a specified date, obtaining construction financing satisfactory to the vendor and being satisfied that the purchaser has the financial resources to complete the purchase. The vendor must specify a date or dates by which the conditions are to be satisfied, which must be at least 90 days before the firm closing date.

Occupancy Requirements

The vendor must provide the purchaser with a certificate of occupancy if such are issued by the chief building official of the municipality or, if not, then a signed written confirmation by the vendor that the dwelling meets the occupancy requirements under the Ontario Building Code.

PROCEDURE

Prior to closing, the vendor will provide the purchaser with a Homeowner Information Package issued by Tarion and arrange a pre-delivery inspection to identify construction deficiencies and incomplete items. These will be noted on a Certificate of Completion and Possession which sets forth the date of possession (which is also the date warranty coverage begins). The purchaser's signed receipt for the package and the completed certificate are required to be filed by the vendor with Tarion within 15 days.

The purchaser may submit an initial warranty claim with Tarion for incomplete or deficient items within 30 days after the possession date. The purchaser may submit another claim form within the last 30 days of the first year after possession. Thereafter, the owner may submit a claim form before the end of the second year after possession. Generally, the vendor has 120 days within which to correct the items listed, failing which the purchaser can involve Tarion. Ultimately, if the vendor does not fix the items (and they are legitimate), Tarion will arrange to have them fixed.

Finally, the owner may submit a claim with Tarion for major structural defects prior to the end of the seventh year after possession. Tarion will work directly with the owner to settle these claims.

Although the warranties run with the land (that is, they benefit and are enforceable by subsequent owners), there is an important procedural issue to be aware of. In *Liddiard v. Tarion Warranty Corp.*, [2009] O.J. No. 4912, 99 O.R. (3d) 656 (Div. Ct.), the Court denied a claim for damages because the owners who commenced the claim no longer owned the home at the time of the appeal (it was sold by the mortgagee under power of sale). The Court held that the benefits of the warranty vested in the person owning the property. It observed that the vendor could make arrangements with the purchaser to adjust for outstanding claims.

CONSTRUCTION LIENS

The *Construction Lien Act*, R.S.O. 1990, c. C.30, is dealt with more fully in Chapter 8. Nevertheless, there are a few provisions dealing directly with new homes which should be highlighted here.

You should advise your purchaser client about the dangers of being classified as an "owner", rather than a "home buyer" under the Act. Construction lien claimants can look to an owner for payment of their claims, but not to a home buyer. A home buyer is not an owner, provided the home buyer has not paid more than 30 per cent of the purchase price prior to closing, and the home is not conveyed until it is ready for occupancy.

Accordingly, the purchaser should not pay more than 30 per cent of the purchase price as a deposit and for extras before closing. Verify that that is the case before closing. Moreover, ensure that the home is ready for occupancy on closing, generally by instructing your client to perform the final inspection and complete the Certificate of Completion and Possession prior to closing.

CHAPTER 15

Remedies on Default

Not all real estate transactions are completed. For one reason or another — a wild fluctuation in house prices, a change of plans, or a change of heart — one of the parties may decide not to go through with the deal between the time the agreement was signed and the scheduled closing date. This chapter focuses on the consequences for your clients if they default for no legitimate reason, and the remedies available to the non-defaulting party.

It is beyond the scope of this book to advise on litigation procedures, but we can briefly describe some of the remedies available.

For more information, there are a number of reference sources available on this topic: Paul M. Perell and Bruce H. Engell, *Remedies and the Sale of Land*, 2d ed. (Toronto: Butterworths, 1998); F. Paul Morrison, "The Purchaser's Remedies" and C. Clifford Lax, "Specific Performance or Damages for the Vendor" in *Remedies and the Sale, Mortgaging and Leasing of Land*, Canadian Bar Association (Ontario, 1987); Victor Di Castri, *The Law of Vendor and Purchaser*, 3d ed., looseleaf (Toronto: Carswell, 1989-); Earl A. Cherniak, "Remedies: Specific Performance" and Laurence A. Pattillo, "Remedies: Damages for Breach of a Contract of Sale of Land" in *The Fundamentals of Real Estate Litigation* (Insight Educational Services, 1988); and *Default and Remedies in Real Estate Transactions* (Insight Educational Services, 1990).

CHOICE OF REMEDY

The remedy you advise your clients to select will depend, of course, not only on the remedies available to them, but also on the outcome they wish to achieve. Basically, they have three choices: they can treat the contract as though it never happened and ask that both parties be placed back in their original positions; they can demand that the contract be carried through to completion as intended; or they can claim damages in lieu of, or in addition to, performance of the contract. If your clients are the vendors, they have a fourth option, which is to consider the contract cancelled and keep the purchaser's deposit.

There is no need for an innocent party to make a specific choice as to the relief sought until the time of trial; inconsistent remedies may be pleaded in the alternative. However, selection of a particular remedy may preclude a certain course of action, and your clients ought to be so advised. For instance, if your vendor clients are seeking specific performance of the contract, they may not sell the property to anyone else pending judgment.

TENDER

Except where there has been an anticipatory breach, the non-defaulting parties must be able to establish to the court that, on the original closing date, they were ready, willing and able to close. Good tender is the best evidence of that fact.

Proper tender involves presenting the other party with all that is required to close the deal. In the case of the purchasers, they must present the vendor with the exact amount payable: *Mus v. Matlashewski*, [1944] M.J. No. 32, [1944] 4 D.L.R. 522 (C.A.). Even if the purchasers have not received the draft transfer or statement of adjustments from the vendor, they should attempt to make good tender by presenting the vendor with what they estimate to be the amount due on closing: *Dacon Construction Ltd. v. Karkoulis*, [1964] O.J. No. 737, [1964] 2 O.R. 139 (H.C.J.).

However, where the other party has made it clear that they have no intention of closing the deal (anticipatory breach), it is not incumbent on the party not in default to tender. The law does not require a meaningless ritual to be performed: *Stewart v. Ambrosino*, [1977] O.J. No. 2277, 16 O.R. (2d) 221 (C.A.); *Mondino v. Mondino*, [2004] O.J. No. 1132, 18 R.P.R. (4th) 200 (S.C.J.); *DeFranco v. Khatri*, [2005] O.J. No. 1890, 30 R.P.R. (4th) 192 (S.C.J.). Moreover, the party who is unwilling or unable to close may not rely on the "time of the essence" clause when the innocent party does not tender: *Bethco Ltd. v. Clareco Canada Ltd.*, [1985] O.J. No. 2677, 52 O.R. (2d) 609 (C.A.).

Defective tender will not necessarily rule out a remedy, particularly where the flaw is the result of some action of the defendant. In *Syed v. McArthur*, [1984] O.J. No. 3235, 46 O.R. (2d) 593 (H.C.J.), the plaintiff purchaser tendered the amount called for in the statement of adjustments prepared by the vendor, which amount subsequently proved to be wrong. Pennell J. held (at 601-602) that the discrepancy "[did] not justify the court in magnifying a slight defect and using it as an excuse for a refusal to decree specific performance".

For an excellent discussion of the problems of tendering, refer to M.A. Gross, "A Practitioner's Guide to the Law of Tender", *Canadian Bar Journal*, 12 (October 1969), at 282. See also *Zender v. Ball*, [1974] O.J. No. 2123, 5 O.R. (2d) 747 (H.C.J.).

LIENS

Once the agreement of purchase and sale has been signed and the deposit paid, each party has a lien on the property. In the case of the vendor, the lien is for the amount of the purchase price yet unpaid (purchase price less deposit and any payments of purchase money made prior to closing). The lien will continue until the purchase price is paid or something else happens to vacate the lien (*e.g.*, the contract is rescinded).

The purchasers' lien is for the amount of the deposit, plus any other funds they advance on account of the purchase price prior to closing. As soon as the purchasers receive any indication that the vendor may be unwilling to complete the deal, they should register their interest, as evidenced by the agreement of purchase and sale, on title to the property. Bulletin 2000-2 sets out the requirements for registration under the *Land Titles Act*, R.S.O. 1990, c. L.5. In this case, a caution is used which must set out the date of closing and have a land transfer tax affidavit attached. Remember that the caution expires 60 days after registration and cannot be renewed. Instead, the purchaser must commence an action and obtain a certificate of pending litigation (formerly known as a *lis pendens*) pursuant to s. 103 of the *Courts of Justice Act*, R.S.O. 1990, c. C.43 to continue to protect the claim against title. Note that full land transfer tax is payable on the total purchase price when registering notice of the agreement (see p. 109).

Because a certificate of pending litigation is such an effective limitation on the vendor's right to dispose of the property, s. 103(4) of the *Courts of Justice Act* was added to prevent abuse. This subsection states that any registrant of a certificate who does not have a reasonable claim to an interest in the land will be liable for any damage the property owner sustains as a result of the registration. Note that, if damages are an adequate remedy, a certificate of pending litigation should not be registered, or the registrant may be liable: *Pete & Martys (Front) Ltd. v. Market Block Toronto Properties Ltd.*, [1985] O.J. No. 564, 37 R.P.R. 157 (H.C.J.).

SETTING THE CONTRACT ASIDE

Your clients may be able to walk away from an aborted transaction if they can establish that there was no deal in the first place. In order to do so, they will have to prove that there was something amiss with the contract itself.

That is not easy to do, unless your clients were minors, mentally incompetent or intoxicated at the time they signed the agreement. Any of these conditions may preclude your clients from entering into a binding contract.

Your clients may also be able to set the contract aside if they can establish that one of the other "essentials" for a binding agreement, besides the capacity to contract, was missing: for example, intention, offer and/or acceptance, or consideration. See *Maida v. Dalewood Investments Ltd.*, [1985] S.C.J. No. 27, [1985] 1 S.C.R. 568. Similarly, the contract may be unenforceable if the *Statute of Frauds*, R.S.O. 1990, c. S.19, has been breached. Also, the court will not enforce a contract if it is found to be illegal — such was the case in *Bemister v. Patterson*, [2007] O.J. No. 3839, 229 O.A.C. 203 (C.A.), where the purchaser (an experienced realtor) enticed the vendor to agree to sell a new house to his wife although he knew that the builder's consent was required and that it would not be forthcoming. Usually, however, when a real estate agent or a lawyer is involved to ensure proper procedure is followed and a deposit is paid, it is difficult to defeat the contract.

Even if there is a binding contract, events subsequent to its execution may make it unenforceable. For example, the agreement of purchase and sale may contain a condition precedent which is not satisfied. The purchasers may have inserted a clause making the agreement conditional on financing. They try but are unable to find anyone to lend them the money. The purchasers are not responsible for the failure of the condition if they have proceeded in good faith, so they may terminate the agreement. Or perhaps the purchasers' solicitor conducts a title search and finds a title defect. The purchasers requisition the removal of the defect, but the vendor is unable or unwilling to comply. In that case, the purchasers may terminate the agreement.

RESCISSION

When the contract is rescinded, the parties are released from their contractual obligations. In true rescission, they are restored to their respective pre-contractual positions. In other words, the purchasers' deposit is returned to them.

Rescission is a response to a contract which should never have been executed in the first place. It seeks to negate an agreement entered into under inequitable circumstances, such as duress, undue influence, illegality, fraud, misrepresentation, mistake or frustration.

After closing, the purchasers' right to rescission may be restricted by *caveat emptor* and the doctrine of merger.

CANCELLATION OF THE CONTRACT

Unlike rescission, cancellation of the contract does not put the parties back in exactly the same position they were in prior to execution of the contract. The one big difference is that the vendor is generally entitled to keep the purchasers' deposit. Consequently, while the vendor might move to have the contract declared cancelled, this is not a remedy that the purchasers will normally pursue, unless it is to avoid a greater penalty, such as damages.

SPECIFIC PERFORMANCE

Specific performance is exactly that: actual performance of the contract as the parties originally intended. In order for the equitable relief of specific performance to be awarded, there must be absolutely no uncertainty in determining what was contracted for, the contract must be capable of enforcement, and there must be no suggestion that enforcement of the contract would be unconscionable.

SPECIFIC PERFORMANCE FOR THE VENDORS

The discretionary remedy of specific performance has historically been rarely awarded to vendors: damages have generally been found to be adequate. The more common course of action for innocent vendors is to resell the property and then claim any loss from the defaulting purchasers. The vendors may also claim damages arising from the failed sale, *e.g.*, legal fees, from the original purchaser: *Dobson v. Winton & Robbins Ltd.*, [1959] S.C.J. No. 58, [1959] S.C.R. 775.

Of course, it is certainly open to the vendor to claim specific performance as an alternative remedy. In *Landmark of Thornhill Ltd. v. Jacobson*, [1995] O.J. No. 2819, 25 O.R. (3d) 628, the Court of Appeal awarded specific performance to a vendor of a condominium unit, holding that in the particular case damages were not an adequate remedy. A similar finding was made in *Dick v. Dennis*,

[1991] O.J. No. 2347, 20 R.P.R. (2d) 264 (Gen. Div.), where a vendor could not resell a condominium unit because the market was so poor that virtually nothing was selling and the property was difficult to value because of its uniqueness; the Court concluded that awarding damages would not achieve the basic rule, namely, that the vendor should be put in the same position as if the contract had been performed.

Keep in mind, though, that even if a vendor has claimed specific performance, the vendor may still have a duty to mitigate unless "some fair, real and substantial justification for his claim to [specific] performance" is found: *Asamera Oil Corp. v. Sea Oil & General Corp.*, [1978] S.C.J. No. 106, [1979] 1 S.C.R. 633. However, in an unreported decision released on November 24, 1995 (Court file No. C8963), the Ontario Court of Appeal held that "there is no obligation to mitigate in an action for specific performance".

Vendors may also maintain actions for specific performance with compensation to the purchaser (abatement) for any deficiency, provided that the vendors have not disentitled themselves to relief with "unclean hands". The deficiency must be small and immaterial: the courts are reluctant to order purchasers to buy a property which is less than they bargained for (see *Orchard v. Fournie*, [1982] O.J. No. 3464, 38 O.R. (2d) 636 (C.A.); *LeMesurier v. Andrus*, [1986] O.J. No. 2371, 54 O.R. (2d) 1 (C.A.)).

SPECIFIC PERFORMANCE FOR THE PURCHASERS

Purchasers are entitled to demand that vendors honour their agreements. However, damages are generally pleaded as an alternative remedy and there may be cases where a claim for specific performance either is or ought to be abandoned before trial. Again, specific performance is an equitable remedy which will only be ordered when damages will not suffice.

Purchasers, like innocent vendors, have a duty to mitigate. If they have the funds to purchase a suitable alternative property following default, the law says that they must do so. However, if there is something unique about the property in question, the purchasers are entitled to adhere to their claim for specific performance. This will depend on the facts of the case. The Supreme Court of Canada has now confirmed that realty is not always unique (unless it can be shown to be) and, as a general rule, damages will suffice: *Semelhago v. Paramadevan*, [1996] S.C.J. No. 71, [1996] 2 S.C.R. 415. Courts have found the requisite level of "uniqueness" where the land is especially suitable for the use proposed, such as a hotel: *John E. Dodge Holdings Ltd. v. 805062 Ontario Ltd.*, [2001] O.J. No. 4397, 56 O.R. (3d) 341 (S.C.J.), affd [2003] O.J. No. 350, 63 O.R. (3d) 304 (C.A.). Another fact situation supporting an order for specific performance occurred in relation to a family-held cottage that had been part of a community of cottages for many years: *Bernstein v. Brudner*, [2007] O.J. No. 1440 (S.C.J.).

There are situations where an order for specific performance is so unlikely, it is hardly worth pleading. Chief among these are instances where the plaintiffs cannot demonstrate that they are blame-free, that they have performed all that was required of them under the contract, or that they were ready, willing and able to close. Also, if the property was being purchased for investment, rather than residential purposes, the courts seem more likely to find that damages are a more appropriate remedy than specific performance: *Domowicz v. Orsa Investments Ltd.*, [1994] O.J. No. 2489, 20 O.R. (3d) 722 (Gen. Div.); *Heron Bay Investments Ltd. v. Peel-Elder Developments Ltd.*, [1976] O.J. No. 1403, 2 C.P.C. 338 (H.C.J.), but see *Bashir v. Koper*, [1983] O.J. No. 2507, 40 O.R. (2d) 758 (C.A.).

The purchasers may obtain specific performance even where the vendor is not able to convey the property as agreed. The purchasers may choose to buy whatever the vendor has, with an abatement of the purchase price: *Goyal v. 619908 Ontario Ltd.*, [1987] O.J. No. 904 (H.C.J.).

DAMAGES

Damages are awarded to innocent parties when they want to affirm the contract and be placed in the same financial position as if the contract had been performed. In that case, damages compensate them for the loss of the bargain.

Of course, damages may also be awarded in addition to specific performance, or when the plaintiff has accepted the defendant's repudiation of the contract.

DAMAGES FOR THE VENDORS

The purpose of damages is to place vendors, so far as it is possible by money, in the same position in which they would have been if the contract had been performed. Vendors should generally attempt to mitigate their loss by relisting the property for sale as soon as possible. Vendors' damages will include, for example, the differential in the sale prices and any additional legal fees. Other costs might include maintenance and carrying costs, as well as property taxes paid on and after the scheduled closing.

Assume the vendors have contracted to buy another house following the sale of their present home to the purchasers. If the purchasers default, they will either have to borrow money to close that purchase or breach the agreement in which they are purchasers. The costs resulting from either keeping or breaching this agreement will be recoverable from the original purchaser if it can be shown that the defaulting purchasers knew or ought reasonably to have known that the vendors intended to purchase a new property with the proceeds of sale: see *Kasekas v. Tessler*, [1989] O.J. No. 644, 4 R.P.R. (2d) 110 (C.A.).

Where the purchasers repudiate the contract without justification, the general rule is that the deposit is forfeited to the vendors: *Heck v. Matthis*, [1970] O.J. No. 1625, [1971] 1 O.R. 105 (C.A.); *CXL Universal Holdings Inc. v. Century 21 Harvest Realty Ltd.*, [2007] O.J. No. 372, 154 A.C.W.S. (3d) 977 (S.C.J.). The vendors' right to the deposit does not depend on proof. Even if the vendors later sell the property for more than was originally agreed, the purchasers will not get the deposit back. As a practical matter, however, the deposit is usually held by the real estate agent, and the agent will not release it to the vendors unless the purchasers consent to the release or it is ordered by a court. This is not a question of law; the agent simply does not want to be caught in the middle of the dispute.

In order to keep a deposit, it must be reasonable in amount, given the circumstances. It must not be punitive in nature. If it is too large or too great a percentage of the purchase price, then the courts will order its return. Generally, a deposit not exceeding 10 per cent will be considered reasonable, although amounts in excess of that may be considered reasonable if the circumstances justify it. In *Porto v. Di Domizio*, [1996] O.J. No. 22, 50 R.P.R. (2d) 113 (Gen. Div.), the Court held that only the original deposit of $10,000 could be kept and ordered the return of the second deposit of $150,000 (together, the deposits equalled 31.25 per cent of the purchase price).

DAMAGES FOR THE PURCHASERS

The purchasers' measure of damages was traditionally based on the difference between the price contracted for in the original agreement of purchase and sale and the market price on the day of the breach, which is usually the date set for closing.

For some time, the purchasers' damages were limited by the rule in *Bain v. Fothergill* (1874), L.R. 7 H.L. 158, [1874-1880] All E.R. Rep. 83 (H.L.), when that case was whole-heartedly adopted by the Supreme Court of Canada in *Ontario Asphalt Block Co. v. Montreuil*, [1916] S.C.J. No. 6, 52 S.C.R. 541. The *Bain* case limited purchasers' damages to recovery of their deposit, with interest, plus the costs of investigation of title. Cases since then have limited the rule. In *A.V.G. Management Science Ltd. v. Barwell Developments Ltd.*, [1979] S.C.J. No. 30, [1979] 2 S.C.R. 43, Laskin C.J.C. expressed *in obiter* that *Bain* should no longer be followed in Canada. In *Mitchell v. Nagoda*, [1985] O.J. No. 482 (H.C.J.), Steele J. echoed that sentiment and rejected the *Bain* argument.

The use of price difference as a method of assessing damages produced some problems, however. Prices may rise significantly in a short period of time. By trial, the purchasers may not be able to purchase a comparable property with the money from damages. This issue was dealt with in *Wroth v. Tyler*, [1973] 1 All E.R. 897, [1973] 2 W.L.R. 405 (Ch. Div.), where the Court found that damages should be calculated as of the date of trial. This decision was accepted in Canada in *Metropolitan Trust Co. of Canada v. Pressure Concrete Services Ltd.*, [1973] O.J. No. 2075, [1973] 3 O.R. 629 (H.C.J.), affd [1975] O.J. No. 2408, 9 O.R. (2d) 375 (C.A.), and in *Billie v. Mic Mac Realty (Ottawa) Ltd.*, [1977] O.J. No. 1747, 3 R.P.R. 48 (H.C.J.). The issue has now been conclusively resolved by the Supreme Court of Canada in *Semelhago v. Paramadevan*, [1996] S.C.J. No. 71, [1996] 2 S.C.R. 415, stating that damages should be calculated as of the date of trial.

As in the case of the vendors, consequential damages or losses that the purchasers experience due to the vendors' breach may be recoverable. The purchasers will have to provide proof as to the amount of the loss. The court will also consider the factors of causation and remoteness to determine whether the expenses are recoverable.

Note as well that, if the vendors have been guilty of fraud or negligent misrepresentation, the purchasers may receive damages in recognition of the cost of correcting the defect or the loss in value of the property: *Lowe v. Suburban Developers (Sault Ste. Marie) Ltd.*, [1962] O.J. No. 622, [1962] O.R. 1029 (C.A.); *De Michele v. Peterkin*, [1985] O.J. No. 542, 37 R.P.R. 173 (H.C.J.).

CHAPTER 16

Searching Titles

HOW TO FIND THE LEGAL DESCRIPTION

If you are acting for the purchaser of land, your basic duty is to determine that the vendor has title to the land the purchaser has agreed to buy, free and clear of encumbrances and title defects other than those agreed to in the agreement of purchase and sale. The whole point of hiring a lawyer to handle a real estate purchase is to obtain the lawyer's title opinion. And this opinion must be based upon a search of title.

We will assume that your office is acting for the purchaser of land. You have received a copy of the agreement of purchase and sale, and it specifies the number of days from the date of acceptance that you have to complete your title search and submit requisitions. If the agreement of purchase and sale is silent with respect to the time within which to search title, s. 4(*b*) of the *Vendors and Purchasers Act*, R.S.O. 1990, c. V.2, provides that the purchaser has 30 days within which to search title and submit requisitions.

If the agreement deals with vacant land, it will usually describe the parcel by reference to the lot and plan or concession. In these cases, you can immediately proceed to the land registry office and start your search.

If the agreement deals with residential property, chances are that the property will be described by municipal address only. Your first step should be to contact the solicitor for the vendor (the agent can tell you who it is), requesting a legal description of the property so you can commence your search. Do not rely too much on this. That solicitor may not yet have received the vendor's legal documents, or for some reason the vendor's solicitor may not reply to you. It is no defence for you, if you have not made your search and submitted your requisitions within the prescribed time, that the other lawyer did not give you the description. It is your duty to find it.

The local municipal assessment department will have a short description, for example, "W 50 feet Lot 10, Plan 1490", but many of these offices will not give out this information over the telephone. You must attend in person.

In some land registry offices, you may find large maps that show the outline of various plans of subdivision superimposed upon the street layout, and from this you can find out the legal description.

The foregoing applies mostly to lands under the Registry system. For lands under the Land Titles system, you will have to determine the parcel and section number to obtain the right parcel register.

For land that has been designated under the automated recording and property mapping part of the *Land Registration Reform Act*, R.S.O. 1990, c. L.4, Part II, it will be necessary to determine the property identification number ("PIN"), which is similar to the parcel number system used in the Land Titles system. The land registry office has large- and small-scale maps that are used for this purpose.

SEARCHES UNDER THE REGISTRY SYSTEM

With the lot and plan number in hand, you are ready to commence your search.

First, for *Registry Act*, R.S.O. 1990, c. R.20 lands, ask at the counter in the land registry office for the abstract index for the concession or the registered plan in which the land is located. If it is on a plan, you should also obtain a copy of the plan.

Check for one-foot reserves at the end of streets. Next, find the page in the abstract book for the lot on the plan that you are searching. If you are searching a whole lot, then you will be interested in every instrument abstracted for that lot. If you are searching only part of the lot, check the thumbnail description set out in the right-hand column of the abstract to see which instruments affect your land. If there is any doubt as to whether or not the instrument affects your land, you must check it. Most deposits will fall into this category.

You should prepare your abstract, a "solicitor's abstract", by copying from the book everything that appears there relating to your land.

If the plan was registered more than 40 years ago, follow the abstract back at least 40 years prior to the closing date of your transaction (see Chapter 1). As a result of the decision of the Supreme Court of Canada in *Fire v. Longtin*, [1995] S.C.J. No. 83, [1995] 4 S.C.R. 3, it has been concluded that you need not go back further than 40 years.

It is not sufficient just to make a "name search", *i.e.*, to follow the chain by following the names back through the years. You must check any reference on the abstract to a description that could in any way affect the parcel you are searching. This includes a deliberate search of the description of neighbouring lands that form part of the same lot as you are searching to make sure there is no encroachment. There is no need for a full search of adjacent lands; just check the earliest and latest descriptions shown for those parcels.

Remember that certain mortgages and discharges were formerly ruled off the abstract index in red by the registrar when the discharge was 10 years old. More recently, the discharge is noted on the page beside the entry of the mortgage. Most conveyancers find it very helpful to make a note in their abstract of such mortgages since they are often referred to in other documents, and if there is no mention of the mortgage in the abstract, it will be confusing to another person who needs to check it back at the office. However, the abstract index has sometimes been recopied by the land registrar, in which case the abstract is cleaned up and references to deleted instruments are omitted.

Always bear in mind during this often tedious procedure that the object of the title search is to determine the state of title. Your object in preparing the abstract at the land registry office is to make it absolutely clear to anyone else who may want to check your abstract and pass on the title just what the title situation is. Your abstract is not just for today for the purpose of preparing requisitions, but also for the day, perhaps one year, five years or 15 years from now, when your client is reselling the property and the new purchaser's solicitor discovers some problem on title. In those cases, it is comforting to pull the old file and find the answer right there in a complete title search.

It is not enough, of course, just to copy down what appears in the abstract. Until recently, there were seven columns in an abstract index containing the following information only: the registration number of the instrument; the date on the instrument; its date of registration; the type of instrument; the grantor; the grantee; and an abbreviated description of the land affected by the instrument. (Now there are six columns; the date of the instrument has been eliminated from the abstract index.) To find out what the instrument is really about, or the true description of the lands, or whether or not the parties have actually executed properly, *etc.*, you must examine the instrument itself.

Often the instrument refers you to other documents that do not appear in the abstract, for instance, letters probate, power of attorney, or articles of amendment whereby a company's name is changed. All of these are registered in the General Register since they do not contain a description of specific lands. These instruments must also be examined and their contents noted.

It is standard practice to use abbreviations in these notes:

S.F.C.A.	*Short Forms of Conveyances Act*
(1) to (2) in f.s.	grantor to grantee in fee simple
Hab.	habendum
4 u.c.	four usual covenants
R. 3 b.d.	release. party of third part barred dower
S & S (1) and (3)	signed and sealed by grantor and party of third part
Aff ex age	affidavit of execution and age

For anything other than these routine details, you should copy particulars out in full so that the search will indicate exactly what each instrument has accomplished and any deficiencies to which it is subject.

It is particularly important that you make a readable copy of the description of the lands in each document and of the spelling of the parties' names. If the spelling is different in the typed portion than in the signature, you must look for an explanation. If the description is different than in the previous document, there must be an explanation.

Some of the most difficult title searches involve little pieces of cottage or farm property. It could be that, because until recently much of this land had little value, little care was taken; it is also unfortunately true that much conveyancing in the country areas was done by persons without legal training. Little attention was paid to detail and, therefore, in many cases, descriptions make no sense at all.

When dealing with cottage properties, your search should also indicate whether the property has access to a public road either directly or through a right of way connecting the parcel with the nearest road allowance.

Many problems arising out of faulty descriptions are gradually being solved because most registrars are refusing to accept for registration documents that do not have proper descriptions. As well, reference plans are usually required for new descriptions.

When you are dealing with a mortgage that has been discharged, there is no point in laboriously copying out the repayment terms. But notes on a mortgage that is still outstanding must clearly indicate all terms and privileges, unless you know it will be discharged.

Occasionally, you may come to a title where it is not necessary to go back 40 years. If title has been certified under the *Certification of Titles Act*, R.S.O. 1990, c. C.6 (now repealed), you need not go beyond the date that is shown in the certificate. From that date forward, however, your search will be quite normal. Another statutory root of title is a deed under the *Veterans' Land Act*, R.S.C. 1970, c. V-4 (see Chapter 3), although an argument has been raised that the *Veterans' Land Act* should not be relied on to commence a title search as it is a federal statute and so *ultra vires*. Tax deeds were once considered good roots of title; unfortunately, this is not so any longer.

The automation of the Land Registry system by which every parcel of land is mapped and assigned a PIN as a first step before it is converted by Teranet to Land Titles Conversion Qualified ("LTCQ") is important to understand insofar as its effect in performing searches under the Registry system is concerned.

In the process of reviewing titles in the Registry system for eventual conversion into an LTCQ title, Teranet will often take a property in the Registry system, map it, create a parcel and assign it a PIN before its actual conversion. A practitioner reviewing such a PIN will see that the letter "(R)" will follow the PIN to denote that the property is still in the Registry system.

The parcel created for a Registry PIN will identify a description for the property by referencing the legal description in the last registered transfer of the property, which instrument will be noted on the parcel together with the apparent owners of the property based on that transfer.

All instruments and other registrations that affect the property identified in the PIN that were made prior to the date of the creation of the PIN, must be searched manually using the paper records of the land registry office as described earlier. All documents registered after the date of the PIN's creation are listed on the automated parcel and accessed via the PIN. This is known as the parcelized day forward registration system ("PDFR").

Properties in PDFR must therefore be searched manually and then reference must be had to the PIN and the parcel it references to uncover new registrations that will only be abstracted on the automated parcel. Remember, however, that the lands being searched are still governed by the Registry system, whether or not a PIN has been assigned to them, and the implementation of the PDFR for such lands does not cause the title to be guaranteed by the Ministry. Such a guarantee will only be applicable when the lands are fully converted into LTCQ, at which time the PIN for a property previously in PDFR will be amended to remove the "(R)" designation at the end and replace it with an "(LT)".

The approach used by the land registry office with respect to abstracting discharges of mortgages also changes with the implementation of the PDFR system. As a result of amendments to s. 56 of the *Registry Act*, discharges of mortgages are effective either by lining out the mortgage on the paper abstract or by the registrar making an entry on the automated parcel to the effect that the mortgage is deleted. If the mortgage is registered on the paper abstract and the discharge is registered after the property to which it relates has been brought into PDFR, the land registrar may, in place of ruling out the mortgage on the paper abstract, note the deletion of the mortgage on the automated parcel for the property. Manual deletions and entries confirming deletions are both effective.

SEARCHES UNDER THE LAND TITLES SYSTEM

If the property is in the Land Titles system, your job will in some respects be much easier. Here you just make notes from the register as it stands or obtain a copy of the register. You must still obtain a copy of the plan and you must still examine mortgages and agreements to find out specific terms. But in theory you do not go back behind the current entries in the register.

Unfortunately, the system has a few flaws. A Land Titles certificate of absolute title does not affect claims by the Crown, and this means, *inter alia*, the rights of the Crown in land that has escheated to the Crown because the charter of the corporate registered owner has been cancelled. Therefore, you must search back in the chain of title (even into the Registry system) to get the names of any corporations that owned the land so you can make enquiry from the Ministry of Government Services to ascertain whether all such corporations were still in existence on the date when they transferred title.

Remember also that you cannot rely on the land registrar's certificate as indicating compliance with the *Planning Act*, R.S.O. 1990, c. P.13. However, as discussed in the *Land Registration Reform Act* section of Chapter 1, these exceptions do not apply to an LTCQ title. Properties whose titles have been converted or are shown as LTCQ only require searches relating to *Planning Act* compliance and as to corporate subsistence for the period after the date the title was converted into LTCQ, which conversion date will be shown right on the parcel.

OUT-OF-TOWN SEARCHES

If you are dealing with property in municipalities other than your own, you have three alternatives:

1. Go to the local land registry office and do the search in the usual way.

2. Write to a local law firm and ask them to do the search as your agent and report to you. Before doing this, you should inform your clients and get their consent. Presumably they retained you because they felt you had some special ability.

3.   Write to the local land registrar and ask for a Registrar's Abstract. This is an abstract prepared by the land registrar under the registrar's signature and seal, certifying that all of the documents affecting your parcel of land are listed. The registrar will copy all the information shown in the abstract books. But the abstract does not tell you anything about the instruments themselves. Before giving your opinion on title, you must check copies of the instruments. The land registrar will supply you with copies of all instruments upon request, but this can be expensive.

If your out-of-town land is in the Land Titles system, you can order a Certificate of Search that will tell you everything you could find by examining the register in person.

However, there may be problems in relying on a Registrar's Abstract or Certificate of Search. Neither will provide the information for an adjoining land search if required to ensure compliance with the *Planning Act*. They may also not provide you with a complete list of corporate owners in order to permit a search to ensure that no forfeiture of the land occurred due to cancellation of a corporate charter.

AUTOMATED SEARCHING

The gradual automation of all title records by Teranet has today reached the point where one can say that the method by which titles are searched has changed dramatically. It is no longer a function of attending at the applicable land registry office with pen and paper in hand and photocopier at the ready; instead, for properties that have been automated and especially for those properties converted into the LTCQ system, a solicitor's office is where the search is conducted and the pen, paper and photocopier have been replaced by the personal computer and printer.

The Law Society of Upper Canada has in its practice directives to solicitors relating to electronic title searching and electronic registration recognized that a real estate practitioner cannot effectively practise in this area without automating his or her office. It strongly urges practitioners to become familiar with hardware and software configurations required by Teranet in order to operate in the Teraview system and to equip their offices accordingly. For those practitioners who may have resisted the automation of their offices in general respects, the practice of real estate will no longer give them an option as eventually, all land registry records will be searched, and registrations made, electronically.

Assuming a user has the necessary computer equipment, he or she must first be licensed with Teranet to access the Teraview system. Licensing allows Teranet to identify who is accessing the system and to determine the level of access each user should be given with a view to monitoring the security of the system. Access can be given to do searches only, or to search and to register documents. Only an Ontario solicitor in good standing will be granted a licence for the latter type of access. At the same time, arrangements will be finalized with Teranet to create an account from which title searching fees incurred while online will be debited. A valid removable storage device must be obtained by the licensee, which must be inserted into the computer and which identifies the user to the system. The user's passcode will be contained within the device. It is only by using both the device and the passcode on that device that access is achieved. A "valid" storage device, such as a flash drive, must be no more than 1024 MB, and must not contain more than one profile.

Once you are logged onto Teraview and choose the e-Reg icon, the screen will offer various options. You will normally want to click on the "Administration" button on the menu bar, which will allow you to create a docket against which all disbursements incurred for the title search to be performed will be posted. In this way, numerous searches on varying properties can be performed in one sitting by simply creating a new docket for each search. The docket is saved by the system to allow its retrieval the next time the system is used for that file. Once a search is complete, the system allows you to print a detailed Docket Summary that records the fees incurred and lists the particular searches or registrations made that resulted in the fees.

You must then choose the land registry office in which the property to be searched is located, again by selecting "Administration" from the menu bar and following the "Change LRO" prompt until the desired land registry office name is displayed. To begin a search, select "Property" from the menu bar and then choose the reference by which the search is to be performed. The system will allow you to search properties by reference to its PIN, by its municipal address, by its registered owner, by instrument number, by condominium number and by plan of subdivision. One of these alternatives, together with the prompt that the system offers you, will allow you to locate the desired property. If your information about the property is incomplete or incorrect and does not allow for any of the above searches to be used, you can always choose to "Search by Map". This allows you to locate the property by going through a successive series of maps that start by displaying a general area and become more specific as the geographic area is more narrowly defined.

Once the property to be searched is located on the screen and is selected from among the other properties that your search may have revealed, the "Search Results" window is displayed. The window will display four tabs and a PIN "tree". In most cases, the "PIN Details" tab will be displayed, which will display the PIN, will indicate whether the PIN is for a land titles or registry property, will indicate whether the PIN is active and will give an address and property description. To see the parcel register, highlight the PIN and click on the "Parcel Register" button at the bottom of the screen. The parcel register for the property will then be displayed. A new set of tabs will be offered to allow you to have the system display the owner for the parcel, the instruments registered against the parcel, any land registry office remarks made in connection with the parcel, the qualifications applicable to the parcel and whether the PIN has been consolidated from other PINs. By accessing all of the tabs, you can obtain all of the information that appears on a parcel register. The parcel register can also be printed, which gives you a copy of the parcel with all the information from all of the tabs.

Opening the "Instruments" tab displays all of the instruments registered against the parcel, with particulars as to registration number, date of registration and instrument type given, followed by a notation as to whether the instrument is certified, noted with a "C". If the "C" is present for any instrument it means that the instrument has been certified. If the parcel is in Land Titles, all government guarantees apply to it. If the parcel is in Registry, the "C" indicates that it has been checked. If there is a "D" beside an instrument, it means that the instrument has been deleted. If an instrument has only recently been registered, it will often be the case that it will not yet have been certified and is in the process of being checked for certification. If there is a problem with the registration, the "C" will not be attached to it until the problem is resolved and reliance cannot be placed on such an instrument during this interim period.

From the list of instruments, you can highlight any that are to be reviewed and the system will display it. It can then be printed. Given Teranet's on-going task of imaging all instruments registered in all land registry offices, it may be that a certain instrument that you want to review has not yet been entered into the system. In such circumstances, Teranet will have to be contacted to have the instrument scanned in so that it can be reviewed. If the instrument you want to review has not been certified, it can only be obtained by physically attending at the applicable land registry office or by ordering the instrument by courier through Teranet. Plans can be similarly accessed and printed, though full-size copies can only be obtained at the registry office itself.

Assuming that you have retrieved the parcel register and reviewed and/or printed all of the instruments on it, you can return to the screen where the PIN details were first displayed and obtain boundary and adjacent lands information by accessing other tabs. The next tab, which is entitled "Map", will illustrate a portion of the PIN map on which the property you are searching is found. The map will highlight the property in a darker colour and then illustrate all neighbouring lands and their respective PINs.

By choosing the "Adjacent" tab, all properties that share a boundary with the property you are searching will be displayed, together with their respective PINs. This will allow you to review each adjacent PIN for the purposes of establishing *Planning Act* compliance. Each adjacent PIN can be retrieved in the same manner described above.

If the lands you are searching are in the LTCQ system, it is likely that a complete search of the lands and adjoining lands for *Planning Act* compliance can be completed in the manner described above. This is because LTCQ titles do not contain qualifications that force practitioners to perform *Planning Act* searches back to 1967 or to undertake searches to ascertain whether all corporations in the chain of title were subsisting during their respective periods of ownership. LTCQ titles only require searchers to investigate such matters from the period after the conversion of the title to LTCQ, which will be a relatively recent date and, as a result, completing *Planning Act* searches will often be possible by simply accessing the "Adjoining" tab and reviewing the PINs that are displayed. Similarly, at least for the near future, it will be easy to determine from the Teraview system which corporations have owned the property from the date of conversion, so that a search in the Corporations Branch of the Ministry of Government Services can be done to establish each such corporation's subsistence.

If the lands being searched are not in the LTCQ system but indicate a Land Titles Absolute title, the *Planning Act* and escheat exceptions to title do not apply, meaning that full *Planning Act* searches back to 1967, where applicable (as discussed in Chapter 5), and searches for all corporations in the chain of title must be completed. Those searches cannot be completed online. As such searches require that historical information on properties be obtained, attendance at the applicable land registry office is required. Even for LTCQ titles, practitioners have found that information as to historical ownership of a property is important to undertake certain municipal inquiries (such as searches with the Ministry of Environment). Practitioners must be aware of these limitations and understand that the current state of implementation of automation will often still require attendance at the registry office for limited purposes, in order for a title search to be complete.

The description of the automated title searching procedures above can only be properly appreciated by logging onto the system and undertaking an actual search. Teranet offers practice sessions and training courses for new subscribers to help orient users to the system. Teranet also publishes a Reference Guide that is helpful to new users.

EXECUTIONS

You should search in the office of the sheriff of the county or judicial district for executions long before the closing date. There is nothing more frustrating than to go to closing and then search executions, and to have your closing delayed because at the last minute you discover executions that may affect your title.

Similarly, if your land is in the Land Titles system, check for executions against the registered owner at the land registry office. The land registrar will not accept a transfer unless the registrar is satisfied that there are no executions outstanding against the transferor.

In the Registry system, to be protected under the 40-year rule, you should search executions against everyone named as owner in your abstract for the full 40-year period.

Remember that an execution filed with the sheriff creates a lien only against those lands owned by the person named in the execution at and after the time of filing. The lien binds the land from that time on, so it is essential that you do not close until you have removed that lien.

An execution filed against a person in 1987 has no effect on the house that the person used to own if it was sold in 1985. By checking the date of filing the execution against the date of registration of the transfer of property, you can ignore many executions reported to you by the sheriff.

The most usual type of execution is one against a similar name. You find in your search that the property was owned by Robert J. Adams. The sheriff reports an execution against one Robert J. Adams and the filing date is during Adams' ownership of the property. The usual answer is that the Robert J. Adams against whom the execution is filed is not the Robert J. Adams who owned the property. The solicitor for the vendor should produce a statutory declaration by the Adams on title to that effect. You should satisfy yourself that this is so. If you go to the sheriff's office, you can find out the name of the plaintiff who filed the execution and who acted as the plaintiff's solicitor. You should contact that solicitor explaining your problem and asking for any information on the Adams that that solicitor sued. If the solicitor tells you that this Adams was around 25 years of age with bright red hair, was unmarried and lived in an apartment, and you know from your investigations that the Adams on title was 63, bald, married and lived in the house that is the subject of the transaction for 25 years, then obviously that execution will not affect you. You should still require a declaration to be deposited on title by Robert J. Adams stating the above facts, because by the time your client sells the house again that information may not be so readily available and the execution may still be filed.

What if the sheriff makes a mistake and does not include in the certificate some executions that are filed and that form a lien against the land that your client has just purchased? It is likely that your client is precluded from suing the sheriff under the *Public Authorities Protection Act*, R.S.O. 1990, c. P.38, s. 142 of the *Courts of Justice Act*, R.S.O. 1990, c. C.43 and s. 5(6) of the *Proceedings Against the Crown Act*, R.S.O. 1990, c. P.27: *Sokolowska v. Ontario*, [2004] O.J. No. 6072 (S.C.J.).

As part of the automation of title searching described earlier in this chapter, execution searching has also been automated to allow Teraview licensees to search for executions using their desktop computers. Upon accessing the Teraview network, you can elect to search the Ministry of the Attorney General's writs database called "WritSearch" rather than proceeding into the Province of Ontario Land Registration and Information System ("POLARIS") database. Once again, you simply open or create a docket against which writ searching fees will be noted, choose the enforcement office in which the search is to be performed and type in the name of the person or entity to be searched. The search results will be displayed. If the search is clear, a certificate can be printed. If the search is not clear, the screen will display the execution numbers that are outstanding, any of which may be highlighted in order to instruct the system to provide you details of the execution. A new window will then appear listing various information relating to the writ and allowing you the option of selecting various tabs entitled "Debtor", "Creditor", "Solicitor", "Comments" and "Costs" to extract more information. Alternatively, you can elect to print all of the writ's details by selecting that option.

SURVEY

The next big area for requisitions is the survey. The title may be perfect, executions clear and all taxes paid in full, but an up-to-date plan of survey may show that the house is partly built on the neighbour's property, or that the neighbour's fence or garage encroaches five feet into the backyard, or that the location of the house on the lot does not comply with the local building or zoning by-laws.

Therefore, a plan of survey is essential to a complete search of title. If no plan of survey is in existence, or if the plan of survey is very old, contact the clients immediately and point out the importance of a current plan of survey. Remember the fine print in the agreement of purchase and sale: the vendor has no responsibility to hand over any document that the vendor does not have. If your clients decide (as most do) that they will not pay the cost of a new survey, try to get confirmation in writing from them. And be sure that in your reporting letter you make your opinion "subject to any encroachments, by-law infractions or other discrepancies which an up-to-date plan of survey might reveal".

Occasionally, the survey will reveal encroachments by the buildings being purchased onto property owned by the municipality. Remember that adverse possession cannot be obtained against highways. Other than by removing the encroachment, the problem can sometimes be solved by obtaining an "encroachment agreement" with the municipality. Ordinarily, the encroachment must be relatively minor. The agreement allows the encroachment to remain until such time as the municipality requires the land for its own purposes. If appropriate, you should requisition this agreement from the vendor.

As discussed in Chapter 12, title insurance is often obtained in cases where there is an older survey and a client does not want to pay for the cost of a new survey. Title insurance will usually protect a purchaser from defects that would have been disclosed had an up-to-date survey been obtained. The cost for the premium will often be less than the cost of obtaining the new survey and, in addition, the payment of the premium will give the purchaser the other protection afforded by the policy relating to title matters generally. This approach to dealing with old surveys is also usually acceptable to mortgagees who finance property acquisitions. Lenders usually require that surveys be recent but will forgo that requirement if they are given the benefit of a title insurance policy that extends to possible defects that would be disclosed by an up-to-date survey.

REQUISITIONS AND METHODS OF CLEARING TITLE DEFECTS

Once your search is complete, you must decide if the title is acceptable to you and if it complies with the terms of the agreement of purchase and sale. If it does, then you can proceed to close without any further problems.

If, however, the title is deficient, you must submit your letter of requisitions, and you must do it within the time set out in the agreement. Remember that the requisitions must be delivered within the specified time, not just mailed: *Stykolt v. Maynard*, [1942] O.J. No. 438, [1942] O.R. 250 (H.C.J.). The fax machine and e-mail are now of great assistance in ensuring that requisitions are submitted properly when time is running short.

All requisitions should be submitted in proper form so they can be used in an application under the *Vendors and Purchasers Act*, R.S.O. 1990, c. V.2. You should set out the number of the instrument, its date, its description, what it purports to do and what it is lacking. Then, you should clearly set out what you require as a solution to the problem, for example:

Instrument Number 125946 North York is an Executors' Deed dated June 16, 1964, and registered July 10, 1964, from the executors of the estate of James Smith, deceased, to Christopher Robin. This deed does not contain a release of dower by the widow of James Smith. REQUIRED production and registration on title of a release of dower by the widow, or in the alternative, evidence that James Smith died unmarried or a widower.

Now that the vendor's solicitor knows the problem, the solicitor can check the old file to see if there is some obvious answer that you have overlooked. Then the vendor's solicitor can consider how to get the answer. Perhaps the solicitor's files contain a declaration by some member of the family of James Smith that his wife predeceased him and he did not remarry.

If the solicitor gives an answer that you do not think is sufficient and that you refuse to accept, either of you may then make application to a judge under the *Vendors and Purchasers Act*. The application sets out in full your requisition and the vendor's solicitor's reply. Then, the judge must decide whether the answer is sufficient at law. If the judge decides that the answer is sufficient, a copy of the formal order so stating will be registered on title and you may then proceed to close, safe in the knowledge that this problem has been resolved.

If the judge decides the answer is not sufficient, then your clients will be entitled to back out of the deal and demand the return of their deposit since the title is not free and clear of encumbrances as contracted for in the agreement of purchase and sale.

Victor Di Castri in *The Law of Vendor and Purchaser*, 3d ed., looseleaf (Toronto: Carswell, 1989), states at 9-12, §313, that a vendor must not only make a good registered title, but

> must also remove all "clouds" on his title, including under this term any instrument registered under a Registry Act *ex facie* valid and which generates a claim of title and casts doubt or suspicion on the title, or is calculated to embarrass the owner in disposing of the property or in maintaining his title.

In *Danby v. Stewart*, [1979] O.J. No. 4085, 23 O.R. (2d) 449 at 451 (H.C.J.), Maloney J. confirmed that "[i]t is still the law of this Province that a purchaser cannot be compelled to purchase a clouded title or 'buy a lawsuit'".

Motions under the *Vendors and Purchasers Act* are surprisingly rare. Normally, title requisitions are answered. Sometimes the answer is not the one you wanted but it is a sufficient answer: the declaration of possession.

Remember that under the *Real Property Limitations Act*, R.S.O. 1990, c. L.15, 10 years' adverse possession makes good title. Therefore, the vendor may produce a declaration stating that he or she has been in possession and occupation of the lands since 1973 or 1988 or other date, as long as it is 10 years or more prior to closing, that the vendor's possession was undisturbed throughout by any claim and that the vendor has made no acknowledgment to anyone of any right. Remember, though, that a 10-year possessory title is no answer to requisitions concerning interests of the Crown.

Be careful in relying on another solicitor to answer your requisitions. Unfortunately, all too many solicitors practising in the real estate field do not answer your requisitions. Your clients are not going to be interested in your problems. Therefore, you should always do what you can to clear up the title on your own. For those things you cannot do yourself, do not assume that the other solicitor will do them for you. Contact the other solicitor and keep pursuing them. And if you are not successful, warn your clients in plenty of time so you can get instructions.

It may be that your clients will accept the risk of taking title subject to the outstanding problem on the basis that time will cure it; perhaps in a few more years the deficiency will be beyond the 40-year period, or next year there will be 10 years' undisturbed possession. In other cases, there may be a "good holding title" (see Chapter 1). In these cases, try to get instructions from your clients in writing or, at the very least, confirm to them by letter your understanding of their instructions so that they cannot complain later that you have obtained a faulty title for them.

This might be the place to mention that, while your duty to your clients is to protect them in every way possible, it is only common sense to protect yourself against your clients as well. For this reason, you should make records of discussions with clients and confirm any change of instructions in writing. Clients have short memories; when they decide to sell and the problem is still outstanding, they tend to forget that they instructed you to ignore it. It is of great comfort to have a record of those instructions on file. Of course, your opinion on title must also be subject to the outstanding problem. It is convenient at that time to be able to refer back to a letter in which the clients agreed to these instructions.

CHAPTER 17

Legal Description of Land

The way in which we describe parcels of land in Ontario today requires an understanding of old practices adopted when Upper Canada was first surveyed, combined with the relatively recent changes introduced to improve the quality and reduce the complexity of such descriptions. With the even more recent changes brought about by the automation of Ontario's land registry system, it also requires an understanding of the Province of Ontario Land Registration and Information System ("POLARIS") and how it further assists in achieving its objective of descriptive clarity.

METES AND BOUNDS DESCRIPTIONS

The description of lands using metes and bounds has traditionally been the most common method utilized in conveyancing documents to establish the boundaries of a parcel of land. Admittedly, given changes introduced to the *Registry Act*, R.S.O. 1990, c. R.20 and *Land Titles Act*, R.S.O. 1990, c. L.5 requiring the replacement of metes and bounds description with reference plans, such descriptions are becoming less and less common and will eventually be eliminated altogether. However, it is still important today to have an understanding of how to describe lands by metes and bounds. Many such descriptions are still used and are still acceptable. Moreover, even with the mapping and indexing of all lands and the conversion of Registry titles into Land Titles Conversion Qualified ("LTCQ"), the current description of a parcel of land is often still made by reference to metes and bounds. As a result, even if you will never have to prepare a new description using metes and bounds, you must be able to verify and understand existing metes and bounds descriptions found in current instruments or those that appear in the chain of title.

When solicitors dealt with large parcels of undeveloped farm lands, the description was simple. Such parcels were usually described as they were originally patented: the whole of Lot 10, Concession VI, Township of Blackacres; or the North half of Lot 5, Concession XI, Township of Osgoode; or even the North half of the East half of Lot 3, Concession VII, Township of Whiteland. The latter method was sometimes known as a description by "aliquot section".

The traditional form of wording used to begin descriptions was as follows:

ALL AND SINGULAR that certain parcel or tract of land and premises situate, lying and being in the Township of Blackacres, in the County of Goodhope and being composed of the whole of Lot 10, in Concession VI of the said Township.

Now, it is not necessary to include the usual "All and singular ..." preamble.

A description of the whole or aliquot part of a lot was simple to prepare and, after checking the township map in the local land registry office to ascertain the shape, size and location of that lot and concession, it was easy to explain to a client exactly what land was involved.

A problem arose when one attempted to carve a specific parcel out of that concession lot. To do this, you had to describe the parcel using a metes and bounds description (subject to the requirement for reference plans referred to below). If you were dealing with a parcel having a frontage of 50 feet on the road allowance and a depth of 100 feet at the southwest corner of the lot, a proper description would be the following:

> Part of Lot 10, Concession VI, in the Township of Blackacres, County of Goodhope, more particularly described as follows:
>
> COMMENCING at the southwest angle of Lot 10;
>
> THENCE northerly along the westerly limit of the Lot a distance of 100 feet to a point;
>
> THENCE easterly parallel to the southerly limit of the Lot a distance of 50 feet to a point;
>
> THENCE southerly parallel to the westerly limit of the Lot a distance of 100 feet, more or less, to a point in the southerly limit of the Lot which point is distant 50 feet measured easterly along the southerly limit from the place of commencement;
>
> THENCE westerly along the southerly limit a distance of 50 feet, more or less, to the place of commencement.

Anyone reading that description could easily sketch the parcel without confusion.

BEARINGS

Rectangular parcels with boundaries parallel to original lot lines present no problems. When you deal with parcels that do not have parallel boundaries, you enter the confusing world of bearings. The preparation of descriptions using bearings is the work of a surveyor, but a conveyancer must be able to interpret and check such descriptions. Bearings are actually similar to compass directions in that they define the relationship of the line to north or south. Directions are always given as east or west of north and east or west of south. For example, "N 16°W" on a survey may be written "North 16° West" and means a line that is 16° west of north; "S 65° 17'E" may be written "South 65° 17 minutes East" and means a line that is 65 degrees 17 minutes east of south.

A circle contains 360 degrees (°); a degree contains 60 minutes ('); a minute contains 60 seconds ("). Each quarter of the circle contains 90 degrees. You can see that the diagonal line when proceeding toward the top of the page has a bearing of 30 degrees east of north (N 30°E). When you are proceeding along the line toward the bottom of the page, the line has a bearing of 30 degrees west of south (S 30°W). Thus, every line has two bearings depending on which direction you are heading.

You may use either words or symbols to designate degrees, minutes and seconds. To avoid confusion, you may not use symbols to designate distances such as feet and inches.

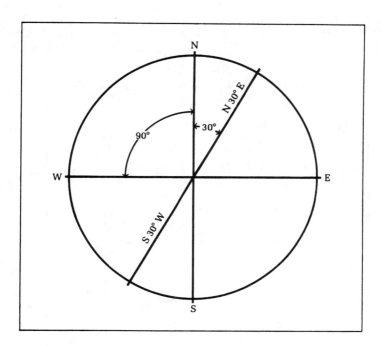

The next description is illustrated on p. 344.

Part of Lot 5, Concession XI, in the Township of Osgoode, County of Badlands, more particularly described as follows:

PREMISING that the westerly limit of the road allowance between Concessions XI and XII has a bearing of North 45° 11' West and relating all bearings herein thereto;

COMMENCING at a point in the westerly limit of the road allowance distant 632.56 feet measured on a bearing of South 45° 11' East along the westerly limit of the road allowance from the northeast angle of Lot 5;

THENCE South 37° 16' 25" West a distance of 125.63 feet to a point;

THENCE South 44° 03' 40" East a distance of 101.67 feet to a point;

THENCE North 42° 10' 57" East a distance of 125.17 feet, more or less, to a point in the said westerly limit of the road allowance;

THENCE North 45° 11' West along the westerly limit of the road allowance a distance of 115 feet, more or less, to the place of commencement.

It will no doubt seem odd that even in a description so accurate that the measurements are given to hundredths of feet, you still find the expression "more or less". The point is that the description must completely enclose the parcel of land; there can be no gaps. In the example above, the line running from west to east along the south of the parcel must get to a point in the westerly limit of the road allowance, so the measurement is said to be more or less. Similarly, when the description proceeds northerly along the road, the measurement is not as important as the fact that the line must reach the "place of commencement".

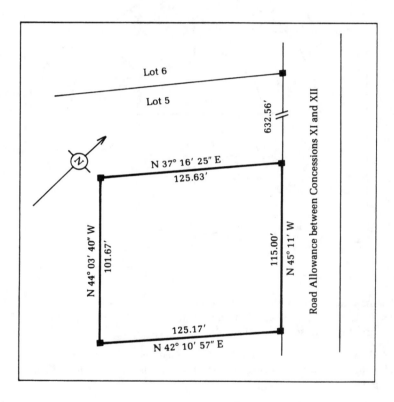

SUBDIVISION PLANS

Metes and bounds descriptions as above were used to describe single parcels of land within a concession lot. However, if a farmer or developer proposed to sell off a number of parcels for the construction of houses, such descriptions became unwieldy. In these situations, a plan of subdivision was often registered to facilitate descriptions pursuant to the provisions of the *Planning Act*, R.S.O. 1990, c. P.13 (see Chapter 5). Now, of course, in order to subdivide land in this fashion, you must register a plan of subdivision.

A plan of subdivision is a detailed plan illustrating the dimensions of each lot on the plan together with the dimensions and bearings of all internal streets. Each lot is given a number. From then on a particular parcel of land would be described, for example, as Lot 76, Plan 4543, Township of Osgoode, County of Goodhope.

Many of these lots on plans were, for one reason or another, further divided and once again were done by a metes and bounds description of a part of a lot on a plan.

REFERENCE PLANS

A long-term program to improve description of land was instituted under the *Registry Act* in 1964 with the introduction of the concept of "reference plans". They are surveys that show the boundaries of the parcel of land, including various appropriate internal divisions (the different parts of the parcel then being numbered) and that have been filed in the land registry office and given a numerical designation such as 64R-9876.

The need for reference plans arose from the existence of many descriptions that were so vague, complex or inaccurate that it was almost impossible to tell what land was being described. Now, you must file a reference plan for every new parcel of land unless the land registrar exempts you from that requirement having regard to the circumstances. In addition, you may be required to provide a reference plan if the land registrar considers the description to be vague or complex. You may be able to persuade the registrar to let you use a vague or complex description one more time on condition that it will be stamped as not being acceptable for any future registrations.

Reference plans when filed are numbered in consecutive order and given a prefix consisting of the land registry office number and the letter "R" to indicate the nature of the plan. Thus, a plan in the land registry office for the Registry Division of Toronto will be designated as Plan 64R-9876. Often, these plans are referred to as "R-Plans".

If you are dealing with a large parcel of land in which various parties have interests in parts of the total parcel, you will find such a reference plan to be of great assistance. For instance, a shopping centre may consist of parcels of land owned by different parties and there may be easements and leases to be registered against parts of those parcels. Metes and bounds descriptions of each piece would be confusing. It is much easier and clearer to all parties to file a detailed survey of the total parcel and describe portions thereof as: Parts of Lots 16, 17, 18, 19 and 20, Plan 2932, City of Toronto, more particularly described as Parts 7, 8 and 9, Plan 64R-9876.

Always bear in mind that this is a reference plan only; its only purpose is for convenience of description. It is not a plan of subdivision under the *Planning Act*.

STATUTORY REQUIREMENTS

REGISTRY ACT

The basic statutory provision governing legal descriptions for lands in the Registry system is contained in s. 25. It provides that no instrument may be registered unless it contains:

(a)   a reference to the lot or part lot on the plan or concession it affects;

(b)   a registrable description of the land it affects, unless such a description of the same land is already recorded in the abstract index; and

(c)   the property identification number ("PIN"), if any has been assigned.

The requirements contained within paragraph (b) above will be discussed later in reviewing the regulations governing legal descriptions.

There are exceptions to the above rules. Sections 25(3)(*d*) and (*e*) of the *Registry Act* allow an instrument or court order to be registered on title against lands even where the instrument or court order does not contain a proper description of the lands, provided that a statement accompanies the instrument or court order made by one of the parties to the instrument or action, or their solicitor, confirming that the instrument does affect the lands and setting forth the proper legal description for the lands.

Section 80 deals with the circumstances in which a reference plan is required. It provides that no transfer, conveyance of mortgage shall be registered unless:

(a)   the land is the whole part remaining to the owner described in a previous conveyance to the owner;

(b)   the land is the whole of a lot or block on a plan of subdivision, judge's plan or a municipal plan;

(c)   the land is the whole of a Part on a previously recorded reference plan; or

(d)   the land is shown on a new reference plan.

Moreover, s. 81 provides that where the land registrar is of the opinion that the legal description contained in an instrument tendered for registration is complex or vague, he or she may require a reference plan to be deposited to describe the land.

LAND TITLES ACT

The *Land Titles Act* contains provisions similar to those in the *Registry Act*. Section 140 provides that all lands "shall be described in such manner as the land registrar considers is best calculated to secure accuracy". Pursuant to s. 142, no instrument shall be registered unless it contains:

(a)   a reference to the parcel number, if any, of the land it affects;

(b)   a reference to the lot or part lot on the plan or concession it affects;

(c)   where the instrument purports to deal with part of a parcel, a registrable legal description of the land it affects; and

(d)   the PIN for the land, if assigned.

There is no complementary provision to that in the *Registry Act* which allows an instrument or court order not containing a registrable legal description to still be registered on the basis of a solicitor's statement as to the lands the instrument or order were meant to affect.

Section 150 deals with the need for reference plans. It is narrower than the similar provision in the *Registry Act*. It provides that no transfer or charge of land shall be registered unless a reference plan has been deposited to describe the lands being transferred on charged. This reference plan requirement does not apply if:

(a) the whole of the lands in the parcel are being dealt with;

(b) the whole of a lot or block on a registered plan of subdivision is being dealt with; or

(c) the lands are described according to a previously registered reference plan.

ONTARIO REGULATION 43/96

You should also be aware also of the various requirements for acceptance of descriptions for registration as set out in O. Reg. 43/96, as amended, which, while promulgated under the *Registry Act*, also applies to lands governed by the *Land Titles Act*. A knowledge of the Ontario practice established by this regulation will prevent the embarrassment and delay of having instruments rejected for registration by the land registrar because the descriptions do not comply with its provisions.

This regulation is very detailed and has parts dealing with general requirements for all plans and specific requirements for strata plans, reference plans, plans of subdivision and expropriation plans, all of which will, more often than not, be more of a concern to surveyors creating such plans than to solicitors. Part VIII of this regulation complements the provisions found in s. 21 of the *Registry Act* and s. 141 of the *Land Titles Act*, which relate to the automation of all lands by their mapping and division into blocks and properties that are then assigned a PIN in keeping with the POLARIS system.

The requirements that will most often affect you insofar as descriptions are concerned are contained in Part XII of the regulation. Of those requirements, pay particular attention to those described below, as they will be more relevant to your day-to-day practice:

1. A description shall mention every lot affected by the instrument (s. 53(2)). It is not acceptable to describe five lots by saying "Lots 4 to 8 inclusive"; you must say "Lots 4, 5, 6, 7 and 8". There must also be a reference to the appropriate plan or concession, as the case may be.

2. Where the description gives the bearings of lines in degrees, the origin of the bearings must be stated in the description (s. 55(1)(*a*)). You will see an example of this in the description on p. 343, where the bearings were all related to the stated bearing of the road allowance.

3. Where any boundary of a parcel is a curved line, the description of that curve must include the arc length, the radius, the chord length and the chord bearing (s. 55(1)(*b*)). The sketch below and the following excerpt from a description will assist you to understand each of these terms.

> THENCE South 75° West a distance of 180 feet to an iron bar marking the beginning of a curve to the right having a radius of 115 feet;
>
> THENCE in a northwesterly direction along the curve having a chord distance of 163 feet, a chord bearing of North 60° West, an arc distance of 180.64 feet to an iron bar marking the end of the curve;
>
> THENCE North 15° West a distance of ...

4. Where the description is of part of a lot, the description must refer to at least one of the corners of the lot and must give the distance from that corner to an angle of the part being described (s. 55(1)(*c*)). An example of the application of this rule is also found in the description on p. 343, where the distance from the point of commencement to the corner of the concession lot is given.

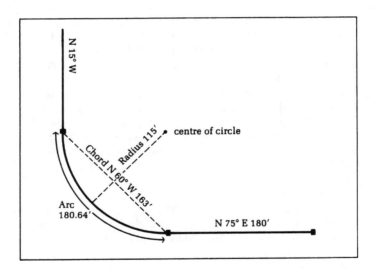

5. Symbols may not be used for the words "feet" and "inches", but symbols may be used for the words "degrees", "minutes" and "seconds" (s. 55(1)(*d*)).

6. Words may not be abbreviated or contracted except that the capital letters "N", "E", "S" and "W" may be substituted for "North", "East", "South" and "West" with respect to bearings in degrees (s. 55(1)(*d*)).

7. A description of land must not describe land by exception (s. 57). Such descriptions by exception were common prior to the enactment of this regulation, for example, "... all of Lot 10, Concession IV, except that portion thereof previously conveyed by instrument number 123456". Now, you must prepare a reference plan of the parcel you are dealing with. There are exceptions to this prohibition:

    (a) if you are repeating a description contained in an instrument registered before July 1, 1964;

    (b) if the land excepted is a parcel completely surrounded by the land described in the instrument;

    (c) if the land excepted is a designated Part on a reference or an expropriation plan;

    (d) if the land excepted is the whole of the land shown on a registered plan of subdivision; or

    (e) if the land excepted is the right of way of a railway company, or is a public street, road or highway that was laid out by an original survey or shown on a registered plan.

8. A description may not describe a boundary solely by reference to the registration number of a registered instrument, for example: "Thence westerly along the southerly limit of Lot 9 to the easterly limit of the lands described in instrument registered as number 987654" (s. 58). However, you may still refer to the registration number of a registered instrument provided you also include measurements and comply in all other respects with the regulations.

9. You must employ imperial units or metric units. The subdivision of these units requires decimals to describe fractions, except that you may continue to use inches where the description is the same as in a previous instrument (s. 59).

10. A description must include reference to the municipality, county, district or regional municipality, as applicable. Where the name of the municipality in which the parcel is situated has for any reason changed since the last previously registered conveyance, both the old name and the new name must be included in the description (s. 54); for example, "... situate, lying and being in the Town of Halton Hills in the Regional Municipality of Halton (formerly the Town of Acton in the County of Halton) ...".

11. You may still describe land as "the west half of Lot 3, Concession VI" or "the Southeast quarter of Lot 14, Concession 11" if it was so described in the original Crown Patent and no adjacent part of the same lot is owned by the person dealing with such part (s. 63(*d*)).

12. You may still describe land as "the North half of Lot 47 according to Registered Plan Number 2000" if it was previously so described in a registered instrument (s. 63(*c*)).

13. When dealing with part of a street or highway that has been stopped up or closed, the description shall also refer to the by-law or other instrument by which the street or highway was stopped up or closed and to the registration number of the by-law or other instrument (s. 63(*h*)).

14. Notwithstanding any of the foregoing, a description may repeat an otherwise unacceptable description if you are preparing an administrator's or executor's deed repeating the description contained in the deed to the deceased person, or if you are preparing an assignment of a lease or mortgage repeating the description in the lease or mortgage (s. 64(3)).

As mentioned above, practitioners should review this regulation in its entirety to become familiar with all of its requirements insofar as legal descriptions are concerned.

PROPERTY IDENTIFICATION NUMBER

Both the *Registry Act* and *Land Titles Act* require that where a PIN has been assigned to a property, it may be used in any document to be registered and be considered as part of the legal description. Chapter 16 discusses the way in which one locates the PIN and discusses the manner in which the PIN indexing system applies to lands in both the Registry system and the Land Titles system.

It is true that once the Land Registry system is fully automated and electronic registration is mandated everywhere, title searching will be accomplished by accessing the PIN and legal descriptions will be automatically imported into documents simply by inputting the PIN. The PIN indexing makes the Land Registry system easier to use and helps eliminate the human error associated with the reproduction of legal descriptions. However, it is not a substitute for understanding a legal description and confirming that the lands that are supposed to be the subject of a transaction match those actually described in conveyancing documents. While the overall manipulation of the system becomes easier and more streamlined using this indexing system, practitioners should avoid becoming casual in describing properties. There is a risk that practitioners begin using the PIN alone as the property's description or that the PIN together with a municipal address becomes a shorter way to describe a property. These inclinations should be avoided and practitioners must be vigilant in using the actual legal description to describe properties and not taking the PIN shortcut.

CHAPTER 18

Proper Execution of Documents for Registration

INDIVIDUALS

SEALS NOT REQUIRED

Seals have never been required to register instruments under the Land Titles system. Individuals once had to affix a seal to instruments registered under the Registry system, but this practice was dispensed with following enactment of the *Land Registration Reform Act*, R.S.O. 1990, c. L.4 ("LRRA") (see s. 13).

From time to time, in a Registry system search of title, documents are discovered which lack a seal. Occasionally, solicitors requisition a correcting deed properly sealed on the basis that a document without a seal cannot by definition be a deed. In reply to such a requisition, you should refer to *First City Trust Co. v. Canada Mortgage and Housing Corp.*, [1984] O.J. No. 896, 32 R.P.R. 36 (Co. Ct.); *Procopia v. D'Abbondanzo*, [1973] O.J. No. 1977, [1973] 3 O.R. 8 (H.C.J.), vard (*sub nom. Procopio v. D'Abbondanzo*), [1975] O.J. No. 2316, 8 O.R. (2d) 496 (C.A.); *Linton v. Royal Bank of Canada*, [1966] O.J. No. 1102, [1967] 1 O.R. 315 (H.C.J.); and *Re Sandilands* (1871), 6 L.R.C.P. 411 at 413 (C.P.): "To constitute a sealing, neither wax, nor wafer, nor a piece of paper, nor even an impression is necessary".... A document being a deed from the outset that purports to be "signed, sealed and delivered" is a deed when executed even though there is no evidence of sealing. The maxim *omnia praesumuntur legitime facta donec probetur in contrarium* applies: "all things are presumed to have been done legitimately, until proven otherwise".

Unfortunately, Misener J. took a contrary view in *South-West Oxford (Township) v. Bailak*, [1990] O.J. No. 3307, 75 O.R. (2d) 360 (Gen. Div.), in which he refused to enforce a contract that was purportedly signed under seal but on which there was no evidence of a seal (a seal was needed to extend the limitation period beyond the normal six years). Misener J. held that the words were not sufficient by themselves. This approach was endorsed by the Court of Appeal in *872899 Ontario Inc. v. Iacovoni*, [1998] O.J. No. 2797, 40 O.R. (3d) 715 (C.A.).

These differing approaches may have been settled by the following excerpt from the Supreme Court of Canada decision in *Friedmann Equity Developments Inc. v. Final Note Ltd.*, [2000] S.C.J. No. 37, [2000] 1 S.C.R. 842 at para. 36:

Today, while the creation of a sealed instrument no longer requires a waxed impression, there are still formalities which must be observed. At common law, a sealed instrument, such as a deed or a specialty, must be signed, sealed and delivered. The mere inclusion of these three words is not sufficient, and some indication of a seal is required: see, e.g., *872899 Ontario Inc. v. Iacovoni* (1998), 163 D.L.R. (4th) 263 (Ont. C.A.). To create a sealed instrument, the application of the seal must be a conscious and deliberate act. At common law, then, the relevant question is whether the party intended to create an instrument under seal.

AFFIDAVIT OF WITNESS NOT REQUIRED

The signature of an individual on either a Land Titles or Registry system instrument is usually not required to be witnessed. The instrument will be accepted for registration even if the signature is illegible. Note that the person signing the document may use initials in place of full given names in the signature, even if the name is set out in full in the instrument.

However, if an individual signs by making his or her mark, or if the person cannot read, an affidavit of subscribing witness must be added by the witness stating that the witness saw the individual execute the document by making the mark "X" after the individual had read the document, or after it had been read to that person and he or she seemed to understand it. The witness does not sign beside the signing party's signature; the witness' affidavit is contained in a separate schedule. The affidavit must identify the witness as such and must state the signing party's name (see Bulletin No. 93007).

NO AFFIDAVIT OF AGE AND SPOUSAL STATUS

As mentioned in Chapter 1, an affidavit of age and spousal status is no longer required. Rather, the Transfer, Charge and Document General forms now include statements regarding age and spousal status. A document made under the LRRA will be denied registration if it includes an affidavit of age and spousal status and it was executed on or after April 1, 1985.

CORPORATIONS

When a corporation executes an instrument, the corporate seal or a statement by the signing officers that they have authority to bind the corporation must also appear. The capacity of the signing officers is also usually set out, but an instrument will not be refused registration if that information is missing. The name of each signing officer must be typewritten or printed legibly near the signature.

ESTATE TRUSTEES

Instruments signed by persons in their capacity as estate trustees should indicate that capacity after their signature, for example:

"John Brown"

"Mary Smith"

Estate trustees of the Estate of Peter Brown.

It may be that an estate trustee will also be signing the document in a personal capacity to release some personal interest in the estate.

When a person is signing as as estate trustee, no statement as to age or spousal status is required. Of course, if the estate trustee is also signing in a personal capacity, the normal statements are required.

ELECTRONIC REGISTRATION

For any transaction involving lands within the boundaries of a Land Registry Office where electronic registration is mandatory, the proper execution of a document for registration is that it not be executed at all. With the implementation of Part III of the LRRA, Land Registry Offices are phasing out the traditional paper registrations, and replacing them with electronic registrations. As paper is dispensed with, so are the methods of executing registration documents as discussed earlier in this chapter.

Section 21 of the LRRA makes it clear that despite any statute or rule of law, where electronic registration has been mandated, no document dealing with an interest in land need be in writing or be signed to be effective. Section 22 reinforces this reality by stressing that where a document is produced both in an electronic format and in a traditional paper format, the electronic document prevails over the written form of the document. As a result, transfers, charges and other registration documents are prepared simply by inputting information into the Teraview system. Once the system acknowledges that the document is complete, it will allow authorized users of the system to electronically "sign" a document for completeness and release, at which time it is registered.

Dispensing with signatures was the next logical step to the elimination of affidavits of execution by the LRRA in 1984. As a result of taking this next step, the Land Registry system no longer relies on the signatures of the parties to a transaction to validate the system, but instead restricts who may use and effect registrations to maintain its integrity, and requires those restricted users to ensure that they have authority from the actual parties to the documents before they proceed with registration.

The elimination of signatures on documents that are electronically registered has also meant, in most cases, the elimination of signatures on supporting materials that are required to accompany such registrations. Section 24 of the LRRA provides that any requirement to have an affidavit, declaration, statement or other written evidence accompany a registration document is satisfied where the Director of Land Registration permits such evidence to be electronically submitted, even though such affidavit, *etc.* is not in writing and has not been signed. The method chosen to implement this provision is to use statements in electronic registrations to replace affidavits, which statements can be relied upon by other parties without requiring any further evidence to substantiate the matters to which the statements make reference.

An example that illustrates the impact of this change is the case of a transfer under power of sale. Such a transfer will contain many statements, made by the transferor and the transferor's solicitor, all of which may be relied upon by the transferee without any signature or paper evidence to support the statements. There will be a statement that the transferor transfers the land. There will also be a statement as to age and spousal status (where the transferor is an individual). If the transferor is a corporation, there will be a statement that the individual signing for the corporation has the authority to bind the corporation. There may be statements as to compliance with the *Planning Act*, R.S.O. 1990, c. P.13. Finally, there will be statements as to default and as to the serving of notices to those entitled to receive notice under the *Mortgages Act*, R.S.O. 1990, c. M.40, as would have traditionally appeared in affidavits and statutory declarations. On the passing of the *Ministry of Government Services Consumer Protection and Service Modernization Act, 2006*, which received Royal Assent on December 20, 2006, new statements are required as of April 7, 2008. If the new statements are not included after that date, an error message will appear. The retired and new statements are set out in full in Bulletin 2008-02.

As mentioned above, the only "signing" of any registration document that occurs is electronic "signing" of a document for completeness and then for release. This electronic "signature" allows the Teraview system to record the identity of the Teraview user who approved the preparation of the document and then consented to its registration. Using the example of the transfer, the solicitor for each of the transferor and transferee must "sign" the document as to completeness when they are both content with its form and content. On the day of closing, the transferor's solicitor will "sign" the document for release and the transferee's solicitor will then "sign" the transfer to effect its registration.

While it is true that the Teraview electronic registration system has eliminated the need for signatures on documents, signatures are still required as between a solicitor and his or her client to evidence the authority given to the solicitor by the client to proceed with the electronic registration. This is accomplished by way of a direction. For every registration document, Teraview allows a user to print a direction, to which is appended a paper copy of the document to be registered. This direction should be presented to a client for signature to evidence the client's approval to proceed with the document's registration. See Chapter 12 for a more detailed discussion of this requirement.

POWER OF ATTORNEY

People often find it impossible or inconvenient to execute instruments dealing with their land. They may be planning to be absent from the country, or they may be ill, or they simply may not wish to be bothered signing documents. In any such case, they may execute a power of attorney appointing someone else their attorney to execute documents on their behalf. A power of attorney may be very specific as to the acts the attorney is authorized to do, or it may be a very general power authorizing the attorney to do all business actions. If you are considering a title in which an instrument was executed by an attorney, examine the power of attorney carefully to assure yourself that the attorney had authority to perform that act.

Powers of attorney are now governed not only by common law but also by the *Powers of Attorney Act*, R.S.O. 1990, c. P.20, and the *Substitute Decisions Act, 1992*, S.O. 1992, c. 30, which was proclaimed into force on April 3, 1995.

Although a power of attorney need not be in any specific form, there are forms prescribed under both Acts. A power of attorney executed under the *Powers of Attorney Act* must be witnessed by at least one witness and contain a statement that the witness is not the attorney or the spouse of the attorney. A power of attorney under the *Substitute Decisions Act, 1992* requires two witnesses and a statement that they are not the attorney, the spouse of the attorney or the donor or a child of the donor. However, powers of attorney that comply with the *Powers of Attorney Act* executed prior to October 3, 1995 (*i.e.*, six months after proclamation of the *Substitute Decisions Act, 1992*) are grandfathered.

Powers of attorney are often used in cases of mental incompetency. To be effective for this purpose, a power of attorney must include the following statement:

> In accordance with the *Powers of Attorney Act*, I declare that this power of attorney may be exercised during any subsequent legal incapacity on my part.

Inclusion of this statement makes it a "Continuing Power of Attorney" under the *Substitute Decisions Act, 1992*.

Before the *Substitute Decisions Act, 1992*, a power of attorney was effective as soon as it was signed. Under this new Act, a power of attorney can be made contingent upon a future event, such as the occurrence of mental incompetency. This may, however, create a new conveyancing problem, *i.e.*, a requirement for proof of the occurrence of the event giving rise to the effectiveness of the power of attorney being used to execute documents.

However, if a certificate of incompetency is issued under the *Mental Health Act*, R.S.O. 1990, c. M.7, then the Public Guardian and Trustee automatically becomes the "Statutory Guardian for Property" of that person, superseding any power of attorney. The attorney (under the *Substitute Decisions Act, 1992*) may apply to replace the Public Guardian and Trustee. Otherwise, only a limited group of people (*e.g.*, close family members) may apply to replace the Public Guardian and Trustee.

A power of attorney may be registered in the general register under s. 18(6) of the *Registry Act*, R.S.O. 1990, c. R.20, or in the land titles office under s. 41 of R.R.O. 1990, Reg. 690. The government has published a form of Continuing Power of Attorney for use under the *Substitute Decisions Act, 1992* that is printed on both sides of short (8½" × 11") paper in blue ink. Notwithstanding these deficiencies, Bulletin No. 94001 issued by the Ministry of Consumer and Commercial Relations (now the Ministry of Government Services) instructs land registrars to accept the form for registration when it is attached to a completed Form 4, Document General.

No instrument executed by an attorney may be registered unless the original, a true copy or a notarial copy of the power of attorney is registered in the same land registry office and the date of registration and the registration number of the power of attorney is endorsed on the instrument.

When an attorney signs an instrument, the signature should be in ink. Under that signature should appear the words "as attorney for" the signing party:

Name(s)	Signature(s)
Jones, John Frederick	"Alan K. Morrison"
by his attorney	as attorney for
Alan K. Morrison	John Frederick Jones

Where the attorney executes an instrument, the attorney must include a statement in the instrument that, to the best of his or her knowledge and belief, the power of attorney is still in full force and effect and that the donor was at least 18 years old when the power of attorney was executed. There is no need for the attorney to state his or her own age when executing an instrument or the power of attorney itself.

Normally, a power of attorney ceases to be valid on the death of the grantor of the power. The reason for this is that the attorney has no more power or capacity to act than does the grantor. However, the grantor may expressly provide in the power of attorney that the power survives the grantor's death. As well, any act done pursuant to a power of attorney without knowledge of the death of the grantor is valid.

Powers of attorney are registered electronically in the e-reg system. Section 4(*i*) of O. Reg. 19/99 under the LRRA lists the electronic registration requirements for any document that is registered in reliance on the authority of a power of attorney as follows:

> 4. A document submitted for electronic registration, other than a power of attorney or a revocation of a power of attorney, shall contain,
>
> . . . . .
>
> (*i*)   if the document is made by an attorney acting under a power of attorney given by a donor that is not a corporation,
>
>> (i)   a statement by the attorney that, to the best of the attorney's knowledge and belief,
>>
>>> (A)   the donor was at least 18 years old and had the legal capacity to give the power when giving it, and

(B)   the power is in full force and effect,

(ii)   a statement by the solicitor submitting the document confirming that the solicitor has reviewed the power with the attorney who has confirmed that,

    (A)   the attorney is the lawful party named in the power,

    (B)   the attorney is acting within the scope of the authority granted by the power,

    (C)   to the best of the attorney's knowledge, information and belief, the power was lawfully given and has not been revoked, and

    (D)   if the attorney is a corporation, the person signing the document at the time the document was made was in the stated position at the corporation and had the authority to bind the attorney, and

(iii)   the registration number and date of the power;

(*i*.1)   if the document is made by an attorney acting under a power of attorney given by a donor that is a corporation,

(i)   a statement by the attorney that,

    (A)   to the best of the attorney's knowledge and belief, the power is in full force and effect,

    (B)   the attorney is acting within the scope of the authority granted under the power, and

    (C)   the attorney has the authority to bind the donor, and

(ii)   the registration number and the date of the power;

Insofar as the content of the power of attorney itself, s. 39.1 of the amended regulation provides as follows:

39.1(1) A power of attorney submitted for electronic registration shall contain,

(*a*)   a statement of the type of the document;

(*b*)   statements setting out the effect of the document;

(*c*)   the date that the preparation of the document was completed;

(*c*.1)   a statement by the party completing the document that the party has the authority to complete the document;

(*d*)   the date that the land registrar received the document for registration;

(*e*)   the names of the parties to the document;

(*e*.1)   a statement by the party who applies to have the document registered electronically specifying whether the party is the donor or the donee of the power;

(*f*)   an address for service, including the postal code, for the person claiming or obtaining an interest under the document or for the person's solicitor;

(*g*)   the name, address, telephone number and fax transmission number of the person who prepared the document;

(*h*)   the name, address, telephone number and fax transmission number of the person who submitted the document;

(*i*)   if the document is made by a corporation, a statement by the person acting for the corporation that the person is authorized to bind the corporation;

(j)   all other information that the Director considers necessary to establish the interest claimed by the parties to the document;

(k)   a statement whether the power is for a limited purpose or a general purpose; and

(l)   an image, in electronic format, of the original executed and witnessed power or of a notarial or certified copy of the original.

As with other e-reg documents, once a user accesses the Teraview system and selects the power of attorney document for completion, the system delivers automatic prompts requiring the user to provide the necessary information to complete the power of attorney. A user will be asked to enter the name of the party giving the power of attorney, the purpose for which the power is given and the name of the person appointed to act as attorney.

Recently, many practitioners have expressed concerns over the method of registering a power of attorney in the e-reg system. Many believe the system causes a donor to create one power of attorney to deal with real property matters and a second power of attorney for other matters. Usually, the traditional paper power of attorney is the only document created by a donor to deal with the delegation of such powers. The e-reg system's requirements arguably result in the creation of a second power of attorney simply to accommodate the registration system. Many practitioners would prefer that the paper power of attorney be the only power of attorney and have urged Teranet to allow for the paper registration of a notarial copy of the power of attorney, as is the practice in land registry offices where e-reg is not mandatory.

Some of these concerns were addressed in Bulletins 2009-01 and 2009-02, which were issued by the Ministry to detail the practical implementation of the regulations and to help practitioners understand what Teraview would require in order for powers of attorney to be registered and for documents that rely on a power of attorney to be registered. One of the most noteworthy changes is the introduction of a power of attorney index for each registry office. Powers of attorney and any partial or total revocation of a power of attorney must be registered in this index. Upon registration, the document is given a registration number; that number is then recited in the document being registered on title that relies on the authority of the power of attorney. Practitioners must now review any power of attorney by searching the index to retrieve the power of attorney referenced in any document and to ensure a revocation has not subsequently been filed in the index. Searches can be conducted in the index by reference to instrument number, donor name and attorney name.

LAND TRANSFER TAX AFFIDAVIT

In addition to the affidavits already referred to, all transfers tendered for registration must have an Affidavit of Residence and Value of the Consideration under the *Land Transfer Tax Act*, R.S.O. 1990, c. L.6, attached thereto. Of course, in the e-reg system, the land transfer tax affidavit is not signed but is electronically filed. See Chapter 12 for a further discussion of the treatment of this affidavit under the e-reg system.

UNILATERAL EXECUTION OF DOCUMENTS

Most documents on title are conveyances, charges or quit claim deeds from one party to another party, but they are executed only by the first party, *i.e.*, the transferor or chargor. Many transfers contain conditions or covenants on the part of the transferee, who does not sign, and all charges contain provisos and conditions that affect the chargee. Is the party to such an instrument bound by the conditions, restrictions and provisos contained therein if this party does not signify acceptance of same by executing the document? See *Halsbury's Laws of England*, 3d ed., Vol. 2, at 357:

> Where a person named in some deed, whether as a party thereto or not, has, without executing the deed, accepted some benefit thereby assured to him, he is obliged to give effect to all the conditions on which the benefit was therein expressed to be conferred; and he must, therefore, perform or observe all covenants or stipulations on his part which are contained in the deed, and on the performance or observance of which the benefit conferred was meant to be conditional. For example, a mortgagee who has made a loan on mortgage, but has not executed the mortgage deed (which has been executed by the mortgagor only), is bound to give effect to a proviso therein contained for reduction of the rate of interest on punctual payment, or for allowing the loan to remain on the mortgage for a certain term.

See also *Rowan v. Eaton*, [1927] O.J. No. 411, [1927] 2 D.L.R. 722 (C.A.).

WHO MAY SWEAR AFFIDAVITS

The *Commissioners for Taking Affidavits Act*, R.S.O. 1990, c. C.17, names certain persons who automatically, by virtue of their office or position, become commissioners for taking affidavits, for example, all judges and local registrars of the Ontario Superior Court of Justice; all solicitors; all clerks and treasurers of municipalities; all members of the provincial legislative assembly.

The *Registry Act*, s. 31(1), states that every land registrar and deputy land registrar is *ex officio* a commissioner for taking affidavits for use under that Act relating to land in that registry division.

The *Land Titles Act*, R.S.O. 1990, c. L.5, s. 22, states that the land registrar may administer an oath for any of the purposes of that Act.

Under s. 4 of the *Commissioners for Taking Affidavits Act*, anyone over 18 years of age may apply for a commission. These are usually issued as limited commissions authorizing the commissioner to swear affidavits in the performance of duties for a specific employer, and they are good for a period of three years but may be renewed.

A notary public is appointed by the Lieutenant Governor under the *Notaries Act*, R.S.O. 1990, c. N.6, and is empowered by s. 4 to exercise the powers of a commissioner for taking affidavits in Ontario. The appointment of notaries (other than for lawyers) expires after three years, but they can be reappointed.

PROPER PROCEDURE IN TAKING AFFIDAVITS

Section 9 of the *Commissioners for Taking Affidavits Act* requires the person administering an oath to do so "in the manner required by law". Sections 16 and 17 of the *Evidence Act*, R.S.O. 1990, c. E.23, provide various methods of taking an oath for an affidavit. Although these sections appear permissive, it is suggested that an oath should be taken in the manner set out.

EVIDENCE ACT

Sections 16 and 17(1) of the *Evidence Act* state:

16. Where an oath may be lawfully taken, it may be administered to a person while such person holds in his or her hand a copy of the Old or New Testament without requiring him or her to kiss the same, or, when the person objects to being sworn in this manner or declares that the oath so administered is not binding upon the person's conscience, then in such manner and form and with such ceremonies as he or she declares to be binding.

17(1) A person may, instead of taking an oath, make an affirmation or declaration that is of the same force and effect as if the person had taken an oath in the usual form.

For taking a statutory declaration, the following form is prescribed by s. 43 of the *Evidence Act* and s. 41 of the *Canada Evidence Act*, R.S.C. 1985, c. C-5:

I, ... , solemnly declare that (*state the fact or facts declared to*), and I make this solemn declaration conscientiously believing it to be true and knowing that it is of the same force and effect as if made under oath.

Declared before me

at the   of

this   day of   , 20

   A Commissioner, *etc.*

Although the requirements are somewhat imprecise and the practice, particularly on busy days, is extremely casual, one should bear in mind the seriousness of the duty, both of the person making the affidavit or declaration and of the person administering the oath.

COMMISSIONERS FOR TAKING AFFIDAVITS ACT

Sections 9 and 10 of the Commissioners for Taking Affidavits Act state:

9. Every oath and declaration shall be taken by the deponent in the presence of the commissioner, notary public, justice of the peace or other officer or person administering the oath or declaration who shall satisfy himself or herself of the genuineness of the signature of the deponent or declarant and shall administer the oath or declaration in the manner required by law before signing the jurat or declaration.

10. Every commissioner, notary public, justice of the peace or other officer or person administering an oath or declaration who signs a jurat or declaration without the due administration of the oath or declaration is guilty of an offence and on conviction is liable to a fine of not more than $2,000.

CRIMINAL CODE

The following are relevant sections of the *Criminal Code*, R.S.C. 1985, c. C-46:

131(1) ... every one commits perjury who, with intent to mislead, makes before a person who is authorized by law to permit it to be made before him a false statement under oath or solemn affirmation, by affidavit, solemn declaration or deposition or orally, knowing that the statement is false.

. . . . .

(2) Subsection (1) applies whether or not a statement referred to in that subsection is made in a judicial proceeding.

. . . . .

132. Every one who commits perjury is guilty of an indictable offence and liable to imprisonment for a term not exceeding fourteen years.

. . . . .

138. Every one who

(*a*) signs a writing that purports to be an affidavit or statutory declaration and to have been sworn or declared before him when the writing was not so sworn or declared or when he knows that he has no authority to administer the oath or declaration,

(*b*) uses or offers for use any writing purporting to be an affidavit or statutory declaration that he knows was not sworn or declared, as the case may be, by the affiant or declarant or before a person authorized in that behalf, or

(*c*) signs as affiant or declarant a writing that purports to be an affidavit or statutory declaration and to have been sworn or declared by him, as the case may be, when the writing was not so sworn or declared,

is guilty of an indictable offence and is liable to imprisonment for a term not exceeding two years.

AFFIDAVITS SWORN OUTSIDE ONTARIO

Occasionally you will prepare a document that must be completed outside Ontario, be it overseas, in the United States or even in another province of Canada. To be acceptable for registration, the affidavits on a document that are sworn outside Ontario can be sworn before one of the following:

1. a commissioned officer on full-time service in the Canadian forces, who must note rank and unit below his or her signature;

2. the head of a municipality, who must note the office held below his or her signature and impress the seal of the municipality on the document;

3. an officer of any of Her Majesty's diplomatic or consular services, who must impress the seal or stamp of the office held on the document; or, most commonly,

4. a notary public, who must impress the official seal on the document.

See ss. 44 and 45 of the *Evidence Act*, and s. 31(2) of the *Registry Act*.

Although in practice you usually insist that affidavits sworn out of the province be sworn before one of the foregoing, there is authority in s. 45(1)(*d*) of the *Evidence Act* for such affidavit to be sworn before "a commissioner for taking affidavits" without any further evidence of such commissioner's capacity.

Apparently, the Ontario form of affidavit is unique in the world. If you do not pencil in on the form the exact place for each person to sign and the place for the notary's seal, the document invariably comes back incomplete.

In most other jurisdictions, parties appear before a notary, who then signs a statement that he or she saw the party sign the document. Unfortunately, this does not comply with the *Registry Act* or the *Land Titles Act*, so the document must be returned to be signed again. You may think it looks absurd to put pencilled messages with arrows all over your document, for example: "Jones signs here"; "witness signs here"; "fill in witness's name here"; "notary signs here and affixes seal here". Nevertheless, it seems to be the only way one can be sure of getting a document back from a foreign jurisdiction in registrable form.

CHAPTER 19

Financing Land: A Miscellany

There is a large body of law respecting mortgages in Ontario, both case law and textbooks. Even a summary of that law is beyond the scope of this work, although a discussion of mortgage remedies is attempted in the following chapter. What follows is simply a short discussion of some of the terms and expressions that a newcomer to the mortgage field might find confusing, as well as a discussion of some issues related to mortgages.

MORTGAGES

Clients often speak of going out to "get a mortgage" when they really mean they are seeking a loan and they will give a mortgage on some real estate (usually their house) as security for the repayment of the loan. The landowner ("mortgagor") executes the mortgage document that once included a grant of the fee in that land to the lender ("mortgagee"). Since the enactment in 1984 of the *Land Registration Reform Act*, R.S.O. 1990, c. L.4 ("LRRA"), a mortgage (now known as a "charge") does not result in the transfer of any estate or interest in the land (s. 6(1)). Instead, the charge merely creates a security interest in the land. That security interest is discharged on payment of the principal and interest owing on the loan in accordance with the charge document.

Despite the fact that the legal estate does not pass to the mortgagee on the execution of a charge or mortgage, s. 6(3) of the LRRA specifies that "a chargor and chargee are entitled to all the legal and equitable rights and remedies that would be available to them if the chargor had transferred the land to the chargee by way of mortgage".

When the vendor of a property takes a mortgage as part of the purchase price, it is a "purchase money mortgage". The vendor is said to have taken a "mortgage back". The vendor holds the mortgage as security for payment of the balance of the purchase price. In some cases, the transfer will reserve a "vendor's lien" for the outstanding balance of the purchase price, which lien is to be collaterally secured by a mortgage. When acting for a purchaser in such a situation, be sure that any transfer referring to such a vendor's lien states that the registration of a discharge of the collateral mortgage will serve as an effective discharge of the lien. Many solicitors refuse to accept a transfer containing any reference to a vendor's lien unless the agreement of purchase and sale authorized it.

In regard to the question of priorities, it was made clear in *Thompson v. Harrison*, [1927] O.J. No. 55, 60 O.L.R. 484 (H.C.J.), that under s. 73 (now s. 71) of the *Registry Act*, R.S.O. 1990, c. R.20, priority of registration under the Act prevails regardless of the vendor's lien, at least where the first mortgagee did not have notice of the unpaid purchase price. In that case, the mortgage given to satisfy the vendor's lien was left unregistered until after the registration of a subsequent mortgage given by the purchaser. The subsequent mortgage was held to have priority over the mortgage back. Furthermore, although a vendor will retain a vendor's lien even if a mortgage is taken back to secure the unpaid purchase price, that vendor's lien will not have priority over a first mortgage registered and advanced on closing even where the first mortgagee had actual notice that part of the purchase price remained unpaid: *Silaschi v. 1054473 Ontario Ltd.*, [2000] O.J. No. 1399, 48 O.R. (3d) 313 (C.A.). See, however, *Durbin v. Monserat Investments Ltd.*, [1978] O.J. No. 3414, 20 O.R. (2d) 181 (C.A.), where a mortgage registered before the deed to the mortgagor was held not to have priority over the purchase money mortgage.

A purchase money mortgage is obviously the cheapest loan a purchaser can get. There is no inspection fee, no solicitor's fee and no requirement for a survey. The purchaser gets a loan for the full face amount of the mortgage.

Contrast this type of mortgage with the situation where a prospective purchaser arranges a mortgage loan from a third party. The third party could be a rich uncle, a mother-in-law, or a bank, insurance company or trust company.

Normally, a property owner seeking a mortgage loan will make an application to an institutional lender on that company's prescribed form. The prospective lender will send an appraiser to evaluate the property and it will obtain a credit report on the borrower. If, on the basis of the property appraisal and the credit report, the lender decides to proceed with the loan, the lender will issue a "mortgage commitment" to the borrower that sets out the terms of the loan. If the borrower agrees with the terms, the borrower will sign one copy of the commitment.

At this stage the lender will instruct its solicitor to proceed with the legal requirements. That solicitor must make a complete search of title, check for unregistered liens and for by-law compliance just as if the solicitor were acting for a purchaser, since the lender will require a solicitor's opinion as to the state of the title and as to the validity and priority of the mortgage. It is also that solicitor's responsibility to prepare the mortgage document and arrange for its execution and registration.

For these services, the solicitor naturally expects to be paid and the lender is not going to pay for the privilege of loaning money. Thus, the total costs of the mortgage, including the appraisal fee, the mortgagee's legal costs and the cost of a survey, if one is required, will be the responsibility of the borrower and will often be deducted from the advance of the loan.

CONSTRUCTION AND COMPLETION LOANS

If the security for a mortgage loan is property on which new construction is to take place, the loan may be advanced in one of two ways depending on the terms of the commitment. If it is a "completion loan", the borrower constructs the new building; when it is completed, the lender will make an inspection and, if satisfied, will advance the total amount of the mortgage loan (after deducting the costs noted above). This type of loan is also known as "permanent financing". In the meantime, however, the borrower must somehow arrange to construct the building with his or her own money or through some type of interim or "construction loan".

Few builders or developers can afford to tie up their capital in construction, and bridge financing is expensive. So the usual type of construction loan calls for progressive draws or advances. The first advance might be made when the foundation is complete; a second advance when the frame is complete; a third when the roof is on, and a final one when the building is complete, depending on the terms of the commitment.

This adds slightly to the cost of the loan, since the lender may wish to make an inspection before each advance, and the lender's solicitor will subsearch title and executions at each advance to ensure the priority of the advances. Once again, the borrower pays the cost of the extra inspections and subsearches.

BLENDED PAYMENT MORTGAGES

Until the Second World War, almost all mortgage loans were repaid by periodic payments of principal (usually quarterly), plus a payment of interest on each payment date on the amount of principal then outstanding. With each payment of principal, the amount owing is reduced and, therefore, the next interest payment is also reduced.

Today, most mortgages are repaid by monthly "blended payments" that include principal and interest. The total amount of the payments remains constant throughout the term of the loan, but the portion of each payment attributable to interest decreases as the principal is reduced while the portion of each payment attributable to principal increases.

When dealing with blended payment mortgages, a lender must be sure that the repayment clause complies with the requirements of s. 6 of the *Interest Act*, R.S.C. 1985, c. I-15 as replaced by S.C. 2001, c. 4, s. 92:

> 6. Whenever any principal money or interest secured by mortgage on real property or hypothec on immovables is, by the mortgage or hypothec, made payable on a sinking fund plan, or on any plan under which the payments of principal money and interest are blended or on any plan that involves an allowance of interest on stipulated repayments, no interest whatever shall be chargeable, payable or recoverable on any part of the principal money advanced, unless the mortgage or hypothec contains a statement showing the amount of the principal money and the rate of interest chargeable on that money, calculated yearly or half-yearly, not in advance.

This would be important if, for instance, you were instructed to prepare a blended payment mortgage that called for interest to be calculated monthly. The Act does not prohibit this; it just requires that the mortgage also contain a statement showing what that monthly interest rate would be if calculated half-yearly, not in advance. Note that the penalty for non-compliance is severe: "no interest whatever shall be chargeable".

Two cases have created confusion in the meaning of "blended payments". Both *Kilgoran Hotels Ltd. v. Samek*, [1967] S.C.J. No. 72, [1968] S.C.R. 3, and *Miglinn v. Castleholm Construction Ltd.*, [1974] O.J. No. 2081, 5 O.R. (2d) 444 (C.A.) contain bald statements that periodic payments including principal and interest are not "blended" payments within the meaning of s. 6 of the *Interest Act*. No rationale is offered, nor is the conclusion necessary for the decision in either case. However, there is a very clear statement in a Supreme Court of Canada decision: "principal and interest are *blended* only if the deed does not disclose the true rate of interest payable" (*Ferland v. Sun Life Assurance Co. of Canada*, [1974] S.C.J. No. 49, [1975] 1 S.C.R. 266). Therefore, the safe course will always be to provide for calculation of interest on an annual or semi-annual basis.

For a review of cases decided under ss. 6 and 7 of the *Interest Act*, see M.A. Waldron, "Sections 6 and 7 of the Canada Interest Act: Curiouser and Curiouser" (1984) 62 Can. Bar Rev. 146. See also *Lacroix v. Bank of Montreal*, [2004] O.J. No. 4775, 28 R.P.R. (4th) 285 (S.C.J.) and *Pramco II, LLC v. Boblo Developments Inc.*, [2010] O.J. No. 1925, 2010 ONCA 336 (C.A.).

CALCULATION OF INTEREST

"Simple" interest is anything but simple. Most people assume that the way to calculate how much interest is owing for a particular period is to multiply the principal by the applicable interest rate and pro-rate the result for the period in question, by dividing the result either by 12 months or by 365 days, and multiplying by the number of months or the number of days in the period. This will be true if the interest is calculated on a monthly or daily basis. However, it will not be true if the calculation is required to be on an annual or semi-annual basis.

If interest is to be calculated on an annual basis, say at 12 per cent per annum, but payments are monthly, then the calculation has to take into account the fact that the lender has received part of its total annual interest in advance and will be deemed to have re-invested it at the same rate — the lender is only entitled to have received a total of 12 per cent at the end of the year, including the deemed interest on the periodic payments during the year. In order to achieve this result, therefore, the actual effective interest rate will be somewhat lower than 12 per cent. These are calculations for an accountant or actuary and are beyond the skill level of most legal practitioners. They must rely on computer programs to determine amortized payments and interest paid. It is important to remember the requirement under s. 6 of the *Interest Act* that mortgages having amortized payments must include a statement of the interest rate calculated annually or semi-annually — a provision that interest be calculated monthly or daily in such mortgages runs the risk that no interest at all can be collected.

The foregoing result was confirmed by the decision in *Morenish Land Development Ltd. v. Metropolitan Trust Co.*, [1979] O.J. No. 4041, 23 O.R. (2d) 1 (C.A.).

VARIABLE RATE MORTGAGES

In periods of fluctuating or low interest rates, investors tend to put their funds in shorter and shorter term deposits with the result that mortgage lenders experience difficulty in finding funds to lend on long-term mortgages at fixed rates. In response, lenders tend toward mortgages of ever shorter terms and with floating or variable rates of interest tied to the lender's prime lending rate.

However, many homeowners on limited budgets cannot cope with the fluctuating monthly payments that go with changes in interest rates. To meet their needs, most institutional lenders offer a "variable rate mortgage" with a fixed monthly payment. The mortgage provides that if interest rates go down there will be larger payments on account of principal. On the other hand, if interest rates increase so that the fixed monthly payment does not cover the interest accrued for the previous month, then the shortfall will be added to the principal. The mortgagor may thus owe more at the end of the mortgage than was borrowed in the first place.

BLANKET OR WRAP-AROUND MORTGAGES

Sometimes a property will be subject to a relatively small first mortgage with a low interest rate. A purchaser may naturally be tempted to try to preserve the benefit of this low rate, but will be faced with the difficulty and expense of obtaining second mortgage financing to make the purchase possible. In the past, some mortgage lenders have accommodated this desire by giving a loan based on a "blanket" or "wrap-around" mortgage.

The principal amount of this type of mortgage includes the outstanding principal balance of the first mortgage, although the entire amount is not immediately advanced. The second mortgagee promises to make payments under the first mortgage so long as the second mortgage is kept in good standing. If the first mortgage matures during the term of the second mortgage, the mortgagee will pay it off and obtain a discharge. Thus, the second mortgage will become a first mortgage.

In the past, second mortgages of this type have required payment of interest on the entire original principal amount at the second mortgage rate. Presumably, this rate would be lower than a regular market rate for second mortgages because of the interest saving on the amount secured by the first mortgage. However, it has now been decided that the second mortgagee may charge interest only on the amount actually advanced under the mortgage: *Wagner v. Argosy Investments Ltd.*, [1979] O.J. No. 3148, 7 R.P.R. 305 (Dist. Ct.), and *LaPointe v. Robinson Holdings Ltd.*, [1984] B.C.J. No. 3204, 8 D.L.R. (4th) 750 (S.C.).

The term "blanket mortgage" is also used in a different context to describe mortgages that cover more than one and usually all of the mortgagor's properties.

INTEREST RATE BUY-DOWNS

In times of high interest rates, vendors frequently arrange mortgage financing at less than current market rates in order to facilitate sales. They do so by prepaying part of the interest that the mortgagee demands with the result that the annual rate during the term can be reduced. This method is called an "interest rate buy-down".

Lenders will not, of course, permit an unlimited reduction of the interest rate. They will be concerned about the ability of the borrower to meet increased payments at the end of the term or to repay the loan.

AMORTIZATION AND TERM

The "term" of a mortgage is the period of time during which the principal must be fully repaid. The term ends on the due date or "maturity date".

The word "amortization" is used only when dealing with blended payment mortgages. It refers to the period of time that would be required to pay all of the principal and interest under the mortgage assuming a fixed monthly payment. For example, a $100,000 mortgage loan with interest at 6.5 per cent per annum calculated half-yearly, not in advance, will be fully repaid (amortized) by monthly payments of $632.07 each month for three years. Thus, there is a three-year amortization and a three-year term. But a mortgage loan for the same amount of principal and the same amount of interest with monthly payments in the same amount may be due in five years. Thus, there is a three-year amortization and a five-year term. In any case, where the term is for a shorter period than the amortization, there will be a large payment of principal payable on the due date since the loan will not be fully amortized. That final payment is sometimes referred to as a "balloon payment".

So, term is the time during which the loan is to be repaid. Amortization is the time during which, if blended payments were to continue to be made, the loan would be fully paid off without a balloon payment at the end. Software programs are readily available to produce amortization schedules from most computers. The schedule usually shows in three columns the amount of each payment that goes for interest, the amount that goes for principal and the amount outstanding on the mortgage after each payment is made.

NATIONAL HOUSING ACT MORTGAGES

This legislation was an effort by the federal government to pump more money into the housing field. The government does not actually put up the money. The money is loaned by approved lenders under the *National Housing Act*, R.S.C. 1985, c. N-11 ("NHA") — usually banks, insurance and trust companies. But the repayment of the loan is guaranteed to the lender by the federal government's agency, the Canada Mortgage and Housing Corporation ("CMHC"). A fund is held by CMHC to which a borrower contributes — the "mortgage insurance fee". Out of this fund CMHC reimburses the lender for any mortgage loan that is not repaid.

ASSIGNMENT OF MORTGAGE/TRANSFER OF CHARGE

A lender who holds a mortgage (charge) as security may sell that security at any time. The lender receives whatever consideration has been agreed upon from the purchaser and then delivers a "transfer of charge" (formerly an assignment of mortgage) under which the lender transfers to the purchaser (or transferee) the charge against the mortgaged land, together with all rights against the mortgagor (chargor) to collect the outstanding principal and interest.

The price the lender receives for the mortgage may be more or less than the outstanding principal balance of the mortgage. It will be more if interest rates have fallen so that the investment is now a good one. It will be less if interest rates are higher than the current mortgage rate, in which case the lender is said to have accepted a "discount". In this way, the purchaser of the mortgage increases the effective rate of return under the mortgage. Discounting a mortgage is commonly done by a vendor who finds it necessary to take back a mortgage in order to sell a house, but who needs the cash immediately.

Remember that, for an assignment of mortgage to be fully effective, notice of the assignment must be given to the mortgagor (see s. 53(1) of the *Conveyancing and Law of Property Act*, R.S.O. 1990, c. C.34). The failure to give notice has been raised as a defence in a number of power of sale cases. The courts have held that a Notice of Sale under Mortgage reciting the assignment is sufficient notice of the assignment: *967305 Ontario Ltd. v. North American Trust Co.*, [1996] O.J. No. 517, 28 O.R. (3d) 212 (Gen. Div.); *Manco Inc. v. Wojnowski*, [1998] O.J. No. 3857, 76 O.T.C. 233 (Gen. Div.). However, in *Lee v. Korea Exchange Bank of Canada*, [1999] O.J. No. 2296, 44 O.R. (3d) 366 (S.C.J.), Cullity J. refused to confirm the propriety of a sale under power of sale completed by the assignee of a mortgage where the assignment was made after the Notice of Sale was issued and no notice of the assignment was given to the mortgagor; see also *Emedi v. McMaster*, [1982] O.J. No. 2304, 25 R.P.R. 41 (H.C.J.). But in *490352 Ontario Inc. v. ASAAPV Financial Corp.*, [1985] O.J. No. 384, 1 C.P.C. (2d) 36 (H.C.J.), the Court upheld a power of sale where the assignment was given after the Notice of Sale was issued and notice of the assignment was given to the mortgagor.

The law has been further confused on this point by the decision in *Alltricor Financial Management Inc. v. Nu-Port Homes Inc.*, [2003] O.J. No. 185, 7 R.P.R. (4th) 33 (S.C.J.), in which O'Driscoll J. stated that "a mortgagee cannot rely on power of sale proceedings commenced by a mortgagee prior to assignment where no notice of such assignment has been given, *and where it fails to comply with Form 1 in that it fails to provide notice of the assignment*" (emphasis added). In this case, the Form 1 Notice could not have referred to this assignment since the assignment occurred after the Notice was issued. In our opinion, an assignment of the mortgage after the sale proceedings are commenced should not invalidate those sale proceedings so long as notice of the assignment is given so that those entitled to redeem know whom to pay. However, the *Alltricor* decision throws this into doubt.

Often when a person holds a mortgage (*i.e.*, is the mortgagee), and wants to borrow money, this person gives an assignment (transfer) of that mortgage as security for the loan. The assignment contains a provision for reassignment to the original mortgagee upon repayment of the debt. In the past, this type of transaction sometimes took the form of a "mortgage of a mortgage". Since January 1, 1971, however, neither a mortgage of a mortgage nor a discharge of a mortgage of a mortgage may be registered without a judge's fiat under s. 58 of the *Registry Act*.

Sometimes, when a mortgagor or other person interested in the property pays off a mortgage, the mortgagor or person will wish to obtain an assignment of the mortgage rather than a discharge. Consequently, the mortgagor or other person will be able to step into the shoes of the mortgagee and maintain priority for the amounts secured by the mortgage over other claims against the property. See the *Mortgages Act*, R.S.O. 1990, c. M.40, s. 2. The decision in *Hallman Brierdale Ltd. v. Anton*, [1979] O.J. No. 4320, 25 O.R. (2d) 509 (H.C.J.) confirms the right of a mortgagor to demand an assignment rather than a discharge when the mortgagor has paid the mortgagee in full. Similarly, under s. 2 of the *Mercantile Law Amendment Act*, R.S.O. 1990, c. M.10, a surety or other joint debtor who pays a debt is entitled to an assignment of the security held for that debt.

BONUS

The term "bonus" is usually used to describe an extra payment of interest required before a mortgagee will accept a prepayment of principal: *Gullett v. Income Trust Co.*, [1985] O.J. No. 200, 11 O.A.C. 178 (C.A.); *Broome v. Rea*, [1987] O.J. No. 2036, 43 R.P.R. 110 (Dist. Ct.). In *Lodge v. Canada Mortgage and Housing Corp.*, [2007] O.J. No. 135, 57 R.P.R. (4th) 272 (S.C.J.), the Court confirmed that a mortgagee was entitled to demand payment to cover its lost future interest on a closed mortgage as a condition of agreeing to an early discharge of the mortgage.

Traditionally, mortgages often include a clause that requires a mortgagor who has defaulted in payment of principal under the mortgage to either give three months' notice or to pay three months of interest before he or she will be permitted to cure the default. The provision mimics s. 17 of the *Mortgages Act*.

Historically, it was thought that a mortgagee could not insist on payment of this bonus as a condition of curing a default because it was considered by the courts to be a penalty and therefore unenforceable under s. 8 of the *Interest Act: 459745 Ontario Ltd. v. Widerview Holdings Ltd.*, [1987] O.J. No. 359, 59 O.R. (2d) 361 (H.C.J.). More recently, however, the courts have permitted mortgagees to enforce the provision, although the rules are confusing and require careful attention. See *Mintz v. Mademont Yonge Inc.*, [2010] O.J. No. 660, 91 R.P.R. (4th) 303 (S.C.J.).

In brief, s. 17 of the *Mortgages Act* applies to every mortgage and overrides any inconsistent provision in the mortgage. It gives a mortgagor the option of giving three months' notice or paying a bonus of three months' interest as a pre-condition of curing the default. This will apply both before and after maturity of the mortgage as long as the mortgagee has not commenced enforcement proceedings. However, if a mortgagee has issued a notice of sale, then s. 17 of the *Mortgages Act* does not apply because the payment is now a requirement imposed by the mortgagee and is no longer an option of the mortgagor (instead of giving three months' notice). On the other hand, the mortgagee may require payment of a three months' bonus, but only if the mortgage contains a clause permitting that. For a summary of the relevant cases on these rules, see *Ialongo v. Serm Investments Ltd.*, [2007] O.J. No. 789, 54 R.P.R. (4th) 310 (S.C.J.).

PREPAYMENT PRIVILEGE

When a mortgage is said to be "open", it will contain a privilege such as the following:

> Provided that the mortgagor, when not in default hereunder, shall have the right to pay the whole or any part of the principal outstanding hereunder at any time or times without notice or bonus.

Often a mortgage that permits payment before the scheduled maturity date will require the mortgagor to pay an amount to compensate the mortgagee for the interest lost to the maturity date; this is sometimes called a "yield maintenance payment" and will usually discount the total amount to reflect the early receipt of the payment.

There have been cases dealing with the question of whether or not a prepayment clause survives when the original mortgage agreement is extended. Assume the original mortgage contained a full prepayment privilege. However, when the mortgage was renewed, the extension agreement did not contain reference to the prepayment privilege. In *Cloval Developments Inc. v. Koledin*, [1983] O.J. No. 3261, 44 O.R. (2d) 261, the Court of Appeal held that the right to prepay was lost. Therefore, if a prepayment privilege is desired, it must be repeated or referred to in the renewal agreement.

RIGHT TO REDEEM AFTER FIVE YEARS

Even if a mortgage does not contain a prepayment privilege, there are statutory rights, contained in s. 18 of the *Mortgages Act* and s. 10 of the *Interest Act*, to pay the amount due for principal and interest at any time after five years from the date of the mortgage upon payment of three months' interest in lieu of notice. It has been held that the mortgagor may not elect to give notice but must pay the bonus: *Hone v. London Life Insurance Co.*, [1981] O.J. No. 2987, 32 O.R. (2d) 619 (H.C.J.). This relief will only have effect, of course, where the term of the mortgage is longer than five years (a rare occurrence these days).

The question of whether or not there is a right to prepay has arisen in the context of mortgage renewals. Suppose the original term of the mortgage was for less than five years, but a renewal agreement was entered into, making the total term of the mortgage more than five years from the date on which the mortgage originally commenced. In *Royal Trust Co. v. Potash*, [1986] S.C.J. No. 58, [1986] 2 S.C.R. 351, the Supreme Court of Canada upheld the mortgagee's position that the renewal agreement could not be ignored and that the mortgagor was not entitled to prepay the mortgage at any time following the fifth anniversary of the original date of the mortgage.

Note, however, that the statutory right to redeem does not extend to mortgages given by corporations. In the past, most mortgages with a term in excess of five years were given by incorporated builders or developers, who then sold the new house to an individual purchaser who assumed the mortgage. In one case where the term was for 17 years and, in order to avoid the prepayment privilege, a lender insisted on lending to a corporation and subsequently consented to a transfer of the property to the individual principals of the company, the British

Columbia Supreme Court held that the prepayment privilege was still not available: *Wall v. Maritime Life Newbury Assurance Co.*, [1992] B.C.J. No. 270, 64 B.C.L.R. (2d) 358.

A number of cases have confirmed that the statutory right to prepay after five years is not available even where the corporation, to the knowledge of the mortgagee, held the property in trust for individuals (*Litowitz v. Standard Life Assurance Co. (Trustee of)*, [1996] O.J. No. 3816, 30 O.R. (3d) 579 (C.A.), or where the borrower was a limited partnership with individuals owning the limited partnership units: (*Kucor Construction & Developments & Associates v. Canada Life Assurance Co.*, [1998] O.J. No. 4733, 41 O.R. (3d) 577 (C.A.)). Recently, it was confirmed that a non-profit corporation that gave a mortgage in order to further its charitable purpose could not avail itself of the statutory five-year prepayment right (*Lodge v. Canada Mortgage and Housing Corp.*, [2007] O.J. No. 135, 57 R.P.R. (4th) 272 (S.C.J.)).

However, if a mortgage is given jointly by a corporation and an individual, then the statutory right to prepay may be exercised: see the *Litowitz* decision referred to above.

DISCHARGE OF A MORTGAGE

Many people assume that when they have made the last payment on their mortgage, that is all they must do. They do not realize that, until the discharge (Form 3, Discharge of Charge/Mortgage, R.R.O. 1990, Reg. 688) is registered on title, the mortgage is still outstanding for title purposes. The lender or its solicitor prepares the discharge and charges a fee that the mortgagor must pay. Then the discharge must be registered in the land registry office and the mortgagor must pay the registration fee. Note that *Franceschina v. Guaranty Trust Co. of Canada*, [1984] O.J. No. 3343, 48 O.R. (2d) 62 (Dist. Ct.) states that if the discharge of mortgage is prepared by the mortgagor's solicitor, there is no fee owing to the mortgagee's solicitor.

The delivery of a discharge by the mortgagee will not necessarily extinguish the mortgagee's rights under the mortgage. A mortgagee may still claim payment from the mortgagor after the mortgage has been discharged where, by mutual mistake, less than the full amount of the mortgage was paid: *Shiner v. Varadeff*, [1975] O.J. No. 2239, 7 O.R. (2d) 684 (Co. Ct.).

Where the parties cannot agree on the amount left owing to discharge a mortgage, the mortgagor can pay into court the amount the mortgagee alleges is due and can receive a discharge order pending resolution of the dispute: *Schrittwieser v. Morris*, [1987] O.J. No. 1046, 62 O.R. (2d) 177 (H.C.J.).

ASSUMPTION AGREEMENT

When A borrows from B and gives a mortgage as security, the mortgage contains a promise by A to pay the principal and interest, and this promise is called the "covenant". The borrower is free to sell the property, subject to the mortgage (in effect selling the equity of redemption) at any time and the purchaser assumes the obligations, under the mortgage.

Section 20 of the *Mortgages Act* permits a mortgagee to sue the present owner of the equity of redemption where the present owner has agreed to indemnify the original mortgagor under the mortgage. The agreement to indemnify need not be clearly expressed but can be implied from the circumstances of the sale. It was held in *384846 Ontario Ltd. v. 705464 Ontario Inc.*, [1997] O.J. No. 1291, 12 R.P.R. (3d) 42 (Gen. Div.) that there is a presumption that s. 20 applies unless there is clear evidence to the contrary. Therefore, if you wish to avoid the application of s. 20, you should include an express statement in the transfer that the transferee is not assuming the mortgage and, in the land transfer tax affidavit, do not list the existing mortgage as being assumed. Rather, put the outstanding mortgage debt in the line for liens to which the transfer is subject or in the line for "other valuable consideration" and explain below that the property is subject to a mortgage that the transferee is not assuming.

The liability of the purchaser will end once the property is resold. Of course, the mortgagee will always have the right to sue the original mortgagor on the basis of the mortgage contract signed: *Malaviya v. Lankin*, [1985] O.J. No. 2701, 53 O.R. (2d) 1 (C.A.). However, the mortgagee is entitled only to obtain a judgment against one or the other, not against both.

The liability of the original mortgagor who has sold the property may be extinguished upon renewal of the mortgage by the new owner depending on the wording of the mortgage. In *Citadel General Insurance Co. v. Iaboni*, [2004] O.J. No. 2912, 71 O.R. (3d) 817 (C.A.), the Court found that both the mortgagors and the guarantors were not liable where a mortgage had been renewed (and not merely extended), because the mortgage specifically stated that extensions would not affect the liability of the original mortgagors but did not include renewals in that provision.

Developers of new subdivisions will usually make an arrangement with the mortgage lender to be released from the covenant in the mortgage upon the purchasers executing "assumption agreements" by which they contract directly with the mortgagee to make the payments under the mortgage. This arrangement is necessary for the developer to avoid the accumulation of vast contingent liabilities which would then hamper subsequent attempts to obtain financing for new projects.

Because the covenant of the original mortgagor remains outstanding if a release is not granted, you should always remind any clients selling property on which they were the original mortgagor of this continuing liability. You may be able to obtain a release of the covenant from the mortgagee if you can produce an assumption agreement from the purchaser.

NOVATION

"Novation" is said to occur when a new contract is created in place of the old. It sometimes arises with respect to mortgages in the context of assumption agreements and renewals.

If it can be concluded that a new arrangement has been made in substitution for the old, then a novation has occurred. For example, the mortgagee may enter into a renewal agreement of an existing mortgage with a subsequent owner of the property or an assumption agreement with a purchaser and, in doing so, as is often the case, may vary some of the terms of the mortgage. There is the possibility that the courts may conclude that the mortgagee has accepted the new arrangement in complete substitution for and satisfaction of the old arrangement, in which case a novation will have occurred and the old debtor (and guarantors) will thereby be released. In addition, there may be issues with respect to loss of priority to interests in the land that have arisen since the original mortgage was put in place.

It may be difficult to conclude whether or not novation has occurred since it is always a question of fact. The Supreme Court of Canada has enunciated three principal requirements for novation to occur as follows:

1. The new debtor must assume the complete liability.

2. The creditor must accept the new debtor as a principal debtor and not merely as an agent or guarantor.

3. The creditor must accept the new contract in full satisfaction of and substitution for the old contract.

See *National Trust Co. v. Mead*, [1990] S.C.J. No. 76, [1990] 2 S.C.R. 410.

The mere entering into of renewals or extensions, even with changes in the terms of the mortgage, will not necessarily mean that novation has occurred. See, for example, *Riley v. Investors Group Trust Co.*, [1999] O.J. No. 3580 , 91 A.C.W.S. (3d) 485 (C.A.) and *Household Realty Corp. v. Freeman*, [2000] O.J. No. 57, 29 R.P.R. (3d) 221 (S.C.J.). In both cases, the Court concluded that a mere extension of mortgage in which there was not a material adverse change in the terms would not result in novation and that the original guarantor and covenantor remained liable.

However, you should proceed cautiously and keep the possibility of novation in mind when acting for a mortgagee and dealing with a subsequent owner of the property with respect to the mortgage. The determination that a new contract has been executed in complete substitution for the old may mean that the mortgagee will lose the benefit of the covenant to pay by the original mortgagor as well as any by a guarantor. Consider also whether the determination that novation has occurred will cause a problem with respect to priorities. If there is a guarantee, consider obtaining the concurrence of the guarantor to ensure that novation will not result in a loss of the guarantee.

GUARANTEES

The wording of a guarantee is of great significance to the continuing liability of a guarantor where there is an extension or renewal of the mortgage that has been guaranteed. At common law and in equity, the liability of a guarantor could be extinguished if there was a material alteration to the terms of the mortgage upon renewal or extension without the guarantor's consent. However, the courts have held that it is permissible for a guarantor to contract out of these protections. The decision in *AGF Trust Co. v. Muhammad*, [2005] O.J. No. 1, 73 O.R. (3d) 767 (C.A.) contains a good summary of previous cases on this subject and concludes that a guarantor will remain liable where the guarantee provides that the liability will continue "until the mortgage moneys are fully paid and satisfied".

LIMITATIONS

Limitation periods relevant to mortgage actions are complicated and confusing. Mortgages are subject to the *Real Property Limitations Act,* R.S.O. 1990, c. L.15 (which was left over without change from the previous *Limitations Act* when the law respecting other limitation periods was reformed under the *Limitations Act, 2002,* S.O. 2002, c. 24, Sched. B).

In general, a mortgagee must commence an action within 10 years after default occurs. However, an action to collect interest only must be brought within six years (see s. 17). Both periods will, of course, be extended if a payment or written acknowledgment of the debt is given. Actions to realize on the security of the mortgage (*i.e.,* foreclosure or power of sale) must be commenced within 10 years of default of payment of either principal or interest (see s. 22).

Determining when default has occurred can be particularly difficult in respect of collateral mortgages. A "collateral mortgage" usually describes a mortgage given to secure an obligation not directly set out in the mortgage, for example, a separate promissory note or a guarantee. The issue is whether default under the mortgage occurs immediately when there is default under the primary obligation or only when demand is made under the mortgage. The answer will depend on whether the mortgage obligation is conditional on demand being made, in which case the limitation period will not commence until the demand is made.

The issue is particularly important in the case of a demand mortgage. At common law, the limitation period runs from the date that the mortgage is granted, not from the date of demand (unless the obligation to pay does not arise until demand is made). The *Limitations Act, 2002* was amended in 2007 to change this common law principle to a two-year limitation period for demand obligations, but this amendment does not apply to mortgage obligations because they are governed by a different statute. Therefore, in a true demand mortgage, the 10-year limitation period begins to run when the mortgage is granted, whereas under a collateral mortgage, the period only begins to run when demand is made: *Mortgage Insurance Co. of Canada v. Grant*, [2009] O.J. No. 3769, 99 O.R. (3d) 535 (C.A.).

BOND MORTGAGES/TRUST DEEDS

The terms "bond mortgages" and "trust deeds" are used interchangeably. When it is necessary for a company to borrow a large amount of money, it may be difficult to find a single lender to lend the full amount, while it is easy to find several parties who will each lend a portion of the total amount. In such a situation, a mortgage to a number of parties would be unwieldy. So the borrower gives a bond mortgage or trust deed to a trustee who holds title to the property in trust for the several lenders. The trustee issues bonds to each of those lenders as security for their loan in an amount equal to their respective contributions to the total loan.

When the borrower paid the total amount of the loan plus the interest called for in the bond mortgage, historically the borrower was entitled to receive from the trustee a "release and reconveyance", whereby the trustee released the borrower from the many obligations contained in the bond mortgage and reconveyed the land to it. Now this is accomplished by a standard form discharge of mortgage.

If a borrower defaults under its obligations, the trustee may take possession of the property and operate it for the benefit of the bondholders, or the trustee may sell the property and divide the proceeds among the bondholders.

SALE/LEASEBACK

A manufacturing company may require capital for expansion. It has many choices: it may borrow from the bank; it can attempt to obtain a mortgage loan; it can sell shares; it can sell bonds under a bond mortgage; or it can sell the factory site and lease it back from the purchaser.

Under the last mentioned method — "sale/leaseback" — the company receives the full current market value of the factory and the land on which it is built. It also receives a long-term lease of the property from the purchaser. Thus, it has the necessary cash and it still has occupation of its factory to carry on business. The purchaser, of course, is looking for a return on the investment. The purchaser wants to get the money back over a period of time, together with interest. The rental to be paid by the vendor/lessee will be calculated just as a blended mortgage payment is calculated by using amortization tables.

In order that the investor can be sure of receiving that return on the investment without any expenditures, the lease must be a "net lease". Although there are endless variations, under the purest form of net lease, the tenant must continue to pay all the costs of operating and maintaining the building just as when the tenant was the owner. In addition to the basic rent, the tenant pays the realty taxes, fire insurance premiums, utility charges and the cost of all maintenance and repairs. There is no exception in the repair covenant for reasonable wear and tear or even for destruction in case of fire. It is the tenant's responsibility to rebuild the premises. The tenant can use the proceeds of the fire insurance to apply to the cost of repairs or rebuilding.

Meanwhile, the owner's income continues unabated month after month. Thus, the amount of the basic rent is the owner's net return. Contrast this method with the position of an apartment building owner who knows the net return only after deducting from the rents received the taxes, insurance, utilities, repairs and maintenance costs that had to be paid.

A further advantage to the investor in a sale/leaseback situation is that at the end of the term of the lease the investor owns the property and can use it in any desired way.

CONVERTIBLE MORTGAGES

During inflationary times with high interest rates, lenders often require more than the fixed-rate of return that the standard mortgage offers. Borrowers, on the other hand, may find a floating rate of interest results in an ever-present danger of default. Sometimes, they will agree upon a "convertible mortgage" as the means to meet their respective needs. Simply put, the major difference between this and the usual fixed-rate mortgage is that the borrower grants the lender an option to purchase the property at a fixed price, usually equal to the market value of the property at the beginning of the term of the mortgage. In this way the lender is entitled to the benefit of any increase in the value of the property over the term while also receiving regular interest payments during the same period. Typically, the amount advanced under the mortgage will be close or equal to the value of the property, the interest rate charged will be low compared to current market rates and the term will be relatively long, for example, 10 to 20 years. The borrower, on the other hand, retains ownership and may therefore claim capital cost allowance (depreciation) for tax purposes. In many respects, a convertible mortgage transaction resembles a sale, with the main difference being that the transfer of title is postponed.

There is one serious legal concern relating to this type of mortgage. Over a century ago, the courts instituted a doctrine against creating clogs on the equity of redemption, under which they disallowed any device that prevented the mortgagor from getting the property back after the mortgagor's obligations had been discharged under the mortgage. An option to purchase in favour of a mortgagee was found to be a clog and therefore void, since the mortgagee could avoid the judicial and statutory protections given to a mortgagor who defaulted under the mortgage by simply exercising the option to purchase.

However, the doctrine was created before the era of income tax and high interest rates. These factors have helped induce creative techniques in mortgage financing, including convertible mortgages. In recent years, the courts have been prepared to accept as valid, options which are given as a collateral advantage to the lender by a sophisticated borrower of relatively equal bargaining strength: *BCE Development Corp. v. Cascade Investments Ltd.*, [1987] A.J. No. 1123, 56 Alta. L.R. (2d) 349 (C.A.); *Dical Investments Ltd. v. Morrison*, [1989] O.J. No. 666, 68 O.R. (2d) 549 (H.C.J.), revd [1990] O.J. No. 2160, 75 O.R. (2d) 417 (C.A.). To be found valid, however, it is most important that the option must not be intended as an available remedy in the event of default.

PARTICIPATION MORTGAGES

Another type of mortgage obtained by lenders in times of high inflation is a "participation mortgage". The mortgage provides that the lender is entitled to share with the borrower in the income from the property or in the increase in the value of the property over the term. If the property is not sold at the end of the term, there may be provision for an appraisal to determine the lender's share.

One issue that arises particularly with regard to these types of mortgages but also in relation to all mortgages is s. 347 of the *Criminal Code*, R.S.C. 1985, c. C-46, which makes it a criminal offence for a mortgage to require payment of "interest" at a rate in excess of 60 per cent per annum. "Interest" is defined broadly for this purpose and has been interpreted to include all costs to the borrower, including commitment fees, legal costs, bonuses and other charges: *677950 Ontario Ltd. v. Artell Developments Ltd.*, [1992] O.J. No. 1548, 93 D.L.R. (4th) 334 (C.A.), affd [1993] S.C.J. No. 61, [1993] 2 S.C.R. 443. The rate of return is to be determined with reference to the contracted term of the mortgage and not some shorter period that may result from an earlier prepayment by the mortgagor: *Nelson v. C.T.C. Mortgage Corp.*, [1984] B.C.J. No. 3161, 16 D.L.R. (4th) 139 (C.A.), affd [1986] S.C.J. No. 35, [1986] 1 S.C.R. 749.

Where a mortgage is found to provide for interest in excess of the criminal rate, the court may be prepared to sever one or more provisions of the mortgage in order to bring the total rate within the maximum permissible rate of 60 per cent per annum and, in some cases, may be prepared to change the interest rate. Thus, in *Transport North American Express Inc. v. New Solutions Financial Corp.*, the Supreme Court of Canada reversed a decision by the Ontario Court of Appeal and applied "notional severance" to reduce the effective interest rate of 60.1 per cent in the contract to 60 per cent ([2004] S.C.J. No. 9, [2004] 1 S.C.R. 249, revg [2002] O.J. No. 2335, 60 O.R. (3d) 97 (C.A.)).

INDEPENDENT LEGAL ADVICE

A topic that has attracted increasing judicial attention is the desirability, or indeed requirement, that family members of the borrower who join in a mortgage transaction to assist the borrower, obtain their own separate legal advice from an independent lawyer. Sometimes, it is a spouse or parent who is giving a mortgage on the family home to support a business loan or a family member who is giving a guarantee. Often, the lender will make it a condition of the loan that a certificate of independent legal advice be obtained from a different lawyer who is not acting on the loan transaction, confirming that the nature and effect of the mortgage or guarantee was explained to and understood by the family member who is giving the assistance.

There have been a number of cases in recent years in which courts have denied recovery to the lender on a mortgage or guarantee because the person signing the mortgage did not receive independent legal advice. The most notorious of these decisions is found in *MacKay v. Bank of Nova Scotia*, [1994] O.J. No. 2498, 20 O.R. (3d) 698 (Gen. Div.), in which Lederman J. held at 709:

> A bank, however, cannot escape its responsibility by merely recommending independent legal advice in this situation. It must insist on it. If the customer refuses, the obtaining of a waiver of independent legal advice cannot ameliorate the circumstances. The plaintiff should have been advised in no uncertain terms that if she did not obtain independent legal advice then the bank would decline the loan.

In other cases, lawyers acting for lenders have been found to have been negligent or to have breached a fiduciary duty for not ensuring that independent legal advice was given to a relative of the borrower who was giving assistance in the transaction. See, for example, *Shoppers Trust Co. v. Dynamic Homes Ltd.*, [1992] O.J. No. 2000, 10 O.R. (3d) 361 (Gen. Div.), and *Premier Trust Co. v. Beaton*, [1990] O.J. No. 2169, 1 O.R. (3d) 38 (Gen. Div.).

However, note the decisions in *Bank of Montreal v. McCabe*, [1998] O.J. No. 724, 77 A.C.W.S. (3d) 536 (Gen. Div.) and *Upper Valley Dodge Chrysler Ltd. v. Cronier Estate*, [2005] O.J. No. 5097, 205 O.A.C. 238 (C.A.). In the former,

Murphy J. held that the bank did not have an obligation to recommend independent legal advice and that the loss was due to the defendant's own carelessness, and in the latter, the Court of Appeal held that while it would have been better if the mortgagor had obtained independent legal advice, the loan constituted a considerable benefit and she would have signed it even with the benefit of such advice.

In *Toronto-Dominion Bank v. Figliozzi Estate*, [2000] O.J. No. 3215, 99 A.C.W.S. (3d) 237 (S.C.J.), Hollett J. adopted, as obligations imposed by law, the recommendations of Fran Weisberg set forth in a paper delivered by her to the Canadian Bar Association (Ontario) entitled, "Principles and Practical Steps in the Giving of Competent Independent Legal Advice". In summary, those steps are as follows:

1. Open a file.

2. Ensure the client understands what you are saying about the nature and effect of the documents.

3. Obtain an independent interpreter if the client does not speak English (or you are not fluent in the client's language).

4. Get the appropriate financial disclosure for the transaction, even if that results in delay.

5. If you do not know the client, ask for identification.

6. Enquire about duress or undue influence if the client appears anxious to proceed with a bad bargain.

7. Do not act for both the lender and a guarantor.

8. Canvass the possibilities of obtaining security for the giving of a guarantee or collateral mortgage without corresponding consideration.

9. If you advise against this transaction and the client still wants to proceed, ensure you have a witness to your advice.

10. Keep a careful docket of your time.

11. Accept payment of your account only from the client.

12. Send a reporting letter.

Finally, if the guarantor or other accommodation party refuses to obtain independent legal advice, ensure that you have that person read and sign a clearly worded waiver. The foregoing will help to keep you from being a defendant when the guarantor subsequently attempts to repudiate the guarantee.

CHAPTER 20

Mortgage Default Proceedings

From time to time, we encounter periods of declining property values during which mortgage defaults are more common. It is important to know the choice of remedies available to mortgagees and the advantages and disadvantages of each. In addition, because the task will usually fall to the real estate practitioners, it is essential to have an understanding of the basic procedures in conducting a sale under the power of sale contained in the mortgage.

DEFAULT

The most common and obvious form of default under a mortgage is the failure to make principal and interest payments when they are due. Most mortgages, however, contain many pages of covenants by the mortgagors relating to such things as repairs, insurance, taxes, construction liens, waste and so on, all of which relate to matters important to mortgagees who are concerned about the maintenance of their security. The failure of the mortgagors to perform any one of these obligations will usually permit the mortgagees to accelerate payment of the principal under the mortgage or to sue for specific performance or damages. In most mortgage forms, the wording of the power of sale begins: "provided that upon default of payment ...". It has been confirmed by the Court of Appeal that failure to pay taxes is a default in payment enabling the exercise of the power of sale: see *Royal Trust Corp. of Canada v. 880185 Ontario Ltd.*, [2005] O.J. No. 1651, 30 R.P.R. (4th) 165 (C.A.); *Glassworkers Social Club v. Forestgate Leasing Inc.*, [1998] O.J. No. 2798, 40 O.R. (3d) 606 at 608 (C.A.).

Of course, the failure to pay the principal balance on maturity is a default under the mortgage. Sometimes mortgagors will want to keep interest current while they look for a new mortgage loan. Mortgagees can accept such payments without fear of it being deemed to have effected a renewal (*NN Life Insurance Co. of Canada v. 568554 Saskatchewan Ltd.*, [1993] S.J. No. 626, 115 Sask R. 136 (Q.B.)).

In general, mortgagees may exercise any of the remedies available to them immediately upon default being made. However, to exercise a power of sale, whether under the terms of a mortgage or under Part II of the *Mortgages Act*, R.S.O. 1990, c. M.40, default must have continued for at least 15 days before the notice of sale may be issued (ss. 26(2) and 32).

REMEDIES UPON DEFAULT

A wide range of remedies are open to mortgagees upon default being made under their mortgages, depending on the circumstances of the default. The following is a list of some of these remedies with a brief commentary on some of the advantages and disadvantages of each, but before discussing the remedies available to the mortgagee, brief mention should be made of two statutes that can delay any action taken by the mortgagees.

PRIVACY

A new and potentially very difficult issue has arisen that may seriously hamper the ability of some mortgagees to realize on their security. In *Citi Cards Canada Inc. v. Pleasance*, [2011] O.J. No. 15, 2011 ONCA 3 at para. 22, the Ontario Court of Appeal has held that "financial information pertaining to a debtor ... is 'information about an identifiable individual'" and is therefore protected under the *Personal Information Protection and Electronic Documents Act*, S.C. 2000, c. 5. Most mortgagees who do not hold a first mortgage will want to know how much they have to pay to obtain discharges of prior mortgages in order to be able to deliver clear title to a purchaser or to have the purchaser assume the prior mortgages.

In the *Citi Cards* case, the creditor was attempting to enforce a judgment by having the sheriff sell the property and so the Court suggested that the mortgagor be cross-examined in the existing litigation in order to obtain the necessary information. However, in most power of sales, there is no litigation and, therefore, it may add considerable time and expense to obtain the information.

It is suggested that the mortgagees add provisions to their mortgages whereby the mortgagor consents to the provision to the mortgagee of information about prior ranking indebtedness. The Act permits consents to be given to allow a creditor to obtain personal information so long as the purpose is reasonable.

BANKRUPTCY AND INSOLVENCY ACT

Section 244 of the *Bankruptcy and Insolvency Act*, R.S.C. 1985, c. B-3 ("BIA") (s. 244 en. S.C. 1992, c. 27, s. 89(1), am. 1994, c. 26, s. 9) states:

> 244(1) A secured creditor who intends to enforce a security on all or substantially all of
>
> (a)   the inventory,
>
> (b)   the accounts receivable, or
>
> (c)   *the other property*
>
> of an insolvent person that was *acquired for, or is used in relation to, a business* carried on by the insolvent person shall send to that insolvent person, in the prescribed form and manner, a notice of that intention. (emphasis added)

The period of the notice (known as a Notice of Intention to Enforce Security) is 10 days unless the debtor consents (after the notice is given) to earlier enforcement. The prescribed form is a simple one setting forth the names of the debtor, the secured creditor, the total secured indebtedness and a warning that enforcement is intended to be taken.

Note the emphasized parts of the section. The notice is required only if the debtor is insolvent; however, if the mortgage is not being paid, the mortgagee must assume that the mortgagor is insolvent. Further, the notice is required only in relation to business assets and therefore will not usually apply in the case of a house mortgage. Be cautious on this point, since even a house can be used in relation to a business of the debtor.

Rule 124 of the *Bankruptcy and Insolvency General Rules*, C.R.C. c.368 requires that the notice must be in prescribed form and shall be served, or sent by registered mail or courier, or, if agreed to by the parties, by electronic transmission.

It appears that the notice, when required, may be given concurrently with the mortgage notice of sale. In *Prudential Assurance Co. (Trustee of) v. 90 Eglinton Ltd. Partnership*, [1994] O.J. No. 868, 18 O.R. (3d) 201 at 213 (Gen. Div.), Farley J. held (at para. 29) that the BIA notice did not "act as an 'add on' or extension of every common law, statutory or contractual notice" but rather was "in the nature of a minimum notice". Nevertheless, it is safer to give the notice prior to issuance of the notice of sale under mortgage.

It is uncertain as to the effect of a failure to give the notice when required. The only remedy mentioned in the BIA is that the court may restrain a sale or other enforcement until the prescribed notice has been given (s. 248, en. S.C. 1992, c. 27, s. 89(1)). Current practice does not require a mortgagee to prove that the BIA notice has been given, although it remains to be seen if a court will overturn a sale or proceedings leading to a sale by reason of the failure to give the notice. In *Bank of Montreal v. Negin*, [1996] O.J. No. 4194, 31 O.R. (3d) 321 (C.A.), the bank did not wait the full 10 days after issuing a BIA notice; however, the Court of Appeal did not think that this merited any redress since no prejudice to the mortgagor had occurred. This decision was followed in *AGF Trust Co. v. Muhammad*, [2005] O.J. No. 1, 73 O.R. (3d) 767 (C.A.).

Although a detailed discussion is beyond the scope of this book, you should be aware of the right of insolvent persons under the BIA to make a "proposal" to their creditors. A proposal is in effect a formal plan by the debtors to restructure their indebtedness in order to avoid bankruptcy. Usually, the debtors propose that their creditors accept various compromises in order to make the best of a bad situation. If the debtors file a proposal with the court or file notice of their intention to file a proposal within 10 days after a secured creditor gives the BIA notice of its intention to enforce its security, then all actions by the secured creditor are stayed until the proposal is filed and voted on, or the time for filing the proposal expires. The proposal must be filed within 30 days, although the court can (and often does) extend that period to a maximum of six months. If 10 days have elapsed after the secured creditor's BIA notice was given, then it is too late for the debtors to file a proposal or notice of their intention to do so, and the secured creditor may proceed without further interference.

Once a proposal is filed, the creditors are divided into appropriate classes (for example, secured versus unsecured creditors, landlords and so on) and each class votes on the proposal. If the proposal is defeated, the debtor automatically becomes bankrupt. If the proposal is approved, it is binding on all the debtor's creditors, although anyone may subsequently apply to the court to have the proposal annulled because the debtor has defaulted under it, in which case the debtor also automatically becomes bankrupt.

FARM DEBT MEDIATION ACT

The purpose of the *Farm Debt Mediation Act*, S.C. 1997, c. 21 (replacing the *Farm Debt Review Act*) is to facilitate the making of arrangements between farmers in financial difficulty and their creditors. All secured creditors who intend to realize on their security are obliged to give the farmer at least 15 business days' notice of their intention (s. 21) including advising the farmer of his or her right to apply for a stay of proceedings under s. 5. An insolvent farmer can apply for a 30-day stay of proceedings against the secured creditors (ss. 5 and 7(1)). This stay may be extended to a total of 120 days (s. 13). During this period, the administrator under the Act prepares a report of the farmer's financial affairs and then appoints a mediator to attempt to reach an acceptable arrangement between the farmer and his or her creditors (s. 10).

The foregoing notice must be given even before the notice of sale under mortgage. Failure to give the notice will invalidate proceedings taken toward a sale. Section 22(1) states that "any act done by a creditor in contravention of section 12 [stay of proceedings] or 21 [notice] is *null and void*" (emphasis added). A notice of sale given prior to the issuance of the notice under the Act will be treated as a nullity and not capable of being rescued by a subsequent court order: See *M&D Farm Ltd. v. Manitoba Agricultural Credit Corp.*, [1999] S.C.J. No. 4, [1999] 2 S.C.R. 961.

One of the difficulties facing a creditor who intends to enforce its security is whether the debtor is a "farmer". The definition in s. 2 of the Act includes individuals, corporations and partnerships "engaged in farming for commercial purposes". That could include hobby farmers. Mortgagees may not even realize that they are dealing with a "farmer" and are therefore caught by the Act. However, if the debtor has leased his land or made it available to a third party to conduct the farming operations (even a related party such as a wholly owned subsidiary), then the debtor will not be subject to the Act and the creditor may proceed without regard to it (see *R.S.W.H. Vegetable Farms Inc. v. Bayerische Landesbank Girozentrale*, [2009] O.J. No. 4284, 58 C.B.R. (5th) 281 (S.C.J.). Further, minor incidental farming use by mortgagors will not qualify them as "farmers" (see *Moyer v. Polsin*, [1992] O.J. No. 2468, 11 O.R. (3d) 216 (Div. Ct.)).

What is a creditor to do in the face of these uncertainties? The practical answer, if there is any suspicion that the mortgagor may be a "farmer", is to serve the notice under s. 21(1) of the Act with the express comment that the mortgagee is reserving its right to challenge an application for a stay in proceedings if the mortgagor cannot establish that he or she is a genuine "farmer" pursuant to the Act.

What is a purchaser to do? If there is no question that the mortgagor is a farmer, then the purchaser must insist on being satisfied that the notice under s. 21(1) of the Act was given. While s. 21(2) of the Act protects a "person who purchased the property in good faith from the creditor", failure to confirm that the notice was given will mean that the purchaser was not acting in good faith (see the *R.S.W.H. Vegetable Farms* case cited above). However, if the purchaser acting reasonably, did not know that the mortgagor was a farmer, he or she will be protected.

ACCELERATION OF MORTGAGE DEBT

The mortgage will always provide that, upon default, whether in the payment of principal or interest or in the performance of some other obligation, the mortgagee has the right to demand immediate payment of all the principal and interest due under the mortgage. However, the mortgagee's right to do so has been restricted by ss. 22 and 23 of the *Mortgages Act*.

Under s. 22, a mortgagor has a limited right to put the mortgage back into good standing by paying the mortgage arrears, or by performing the covenant in default. However, the mortgagor must do so before a sale of the property under the mortgage or before the commencement of an action to enforce the rights of the mortgagee. An agreement to sell the mortgaged property constitutes a "sale" within the meaning of s. 22(1) and will therefore usually terminate the mortgagor's rights to put the mortgage into good standing: *Theodore Daniels Ltd. v. Income Trust Co.*, [1982] O.J. No. 3315, 37 O.R. (2d) 316 (C.A.); *Mission Construction Ltd. v. Seel Investments Ltd.*, [1973] O.J. No. 1890, [1973] 2 O.R. 190 (H.C.J.); *Van Minnen Construction Ltd. v. Murphy*, [1977] O.J. No. 2524, 19 O.R. (2d) 125 (H.C.J.); *Artibello v. Standard Trust Co.*, [1983] O.J. No. 2966, 41 O.R. (2d) 150 (H.C.J.); *Montreal Trust Co. of Canada v. Raptis*, [1994] O.J. No. 2790, 21 O.R. (3d) 350 (Gen. Div.). See, however, the discussion regarding the effect of making the sale agreement conditional on not being redeemed below at p. 402.

Even after commencement of an action, provided there has been no sale, recovery of possession or final foreclosure, the court has the discretion under s. 23 to permit the mortgagor to put the mortgage back into good standing by paying the arrears and costs into court. The parties may not be in agreement as to what constitutes "costs". If that is the case, the mortgagee is obliged to have the costs assessed before the mortgagor is required to pay them. Under s. 43(3), the costs are payable 10 days after assessment (*Royal Trust Corp. of Canada v. E.R. Kwinch Investments Ltd.*, [1984] O.J. No. 3065, 44 O.R. (2d) 593 (Master)). Costs have been found to include not just legal costs, but all costs incurred by the mortgagee in the exercise of the power of sale (*Color Cove Ltd. v. Canada Permanent Trust Co.*, [1986] O.J. No. 2939, 55 O.R. (2d) 87 (Div. Ct.)). However, costs may not go so far as to cover those incurred by a mortgagee personally in defending an action brought by a mortgagor for improper conduct of sale (*Strawrene Ltd. v. Kay*, [1986] O.J. No. 738, 55 O.R. (2d) 429 (H.C.J.)).

INCREASED INTEREST RATE

Section 17 of the *Mortgages Act* permits a mortgagor who has defaulted in the payment of principal to cure the default by paying the overdue principal plus a three months' bonus of interest or to give the mortgagee three months' notice that the payment will be made. The notice to the mortgagee must specify the date that payment will be made and set forth the interest on the overdue principal at the mortgage rate that will be paid on that date. This procedure has now been approved by the Ontario Court of Appeal in *Mastercraft Properties Ltd. v. EL EF Investments Inc.*, [1993] O.J. No. 1704, 14 O.R. (3d) 519. The purpose of the section is to allow the mortgagee time to arrange for reinvestment of the principal so paid, or at least to compensate the mortgagee for lost interest while arrangements to reinvest the money are made.

Note, however, that the mortgagee may not require that a three-month bonus always be paid as a condition of accepting payment; the mortgagee must allow the mortgagor the option to give the notice instead. This occurs because s. 8 of the *Interest Act* prohibits penalties on default (*Tomell Investments Ltd. v. East Marstock Lands Ltd.*, [1977] S.C.J. No. 91, [1978] 1 S.C.R. 974; *Parkhill v. Moher*, [1977] O.J. No. 2436, 17 O.R. (2d) 543 (H.C.J.); *459745 Ontario Ltd. v. Wideview Holdings Ltd.*, [1987] O.J. No. 359, 59 O.R. (2d) 361 (H.C.J.)).

Various schemes have been attempted by mortgagees to avoid the effect of s. 8 with a view to encouraging prompt payment. Most have failed. For example, a provision in a mortgage that increased the interest rate after maturity was held to be unenforceable (*Beauchamp v. Timberland Investments Ltd.*, [1983] O.J. No. 3279, 44 O.R. (2d) 512 (C.A.)). A mortgage cannot be interest free until maturity and thereafter require interest if the principal is not repaid (*Pemberton Realty Corp. v. Carter*, [1975] B.C.J. No. 1144, 58 D.L.R. (3d) 478 (S.C.)). A mortgage may not provide for a lower rate of interest if payments are made on time (*Weirdale Investments Ltd. v. Canadian Imperial Bank of Commerce*, [1981] O.J. No. 2934, 32 O.R. (2d) 183 (H.C.J.)). However, a provision for an increase in the interest rate one week before maturity was held to be enforceable by the British Columbia Supreme Court in *Raintree Financial Ltd. v. Bell*, [1993] B.C.J. No. 2845, 85 B.C.L.R. (2d) 82, as was a provision for an increased rate one month prior to maturity (see *Reliant Capital Ltd. v. Silverdale Development Corp.*, [2006] B.C.J. No. 1028, 42 R.P.R. (4th) 39 (C.A.) and *Granville Savings & Mortgage Corp. v. Pekich*, [1995] A.J. No. 275, 46 R.P.R. (2d) 72 (Master)).

FORECLOSURE

Under the historical concept of a mortgage, mortgagors granted the legal title of their property to the mortgagees. (The *Land Registration Reform Act*, R.S.O. 1990, c. L.4, has abolished this doctrine, although s. 6(3) preserves all the historical rights and remedies under a mortgage.) In centuries past, mortgagees actually went into possession of the land and acted as if they were the owners until the debt was repaid, at which point the mortgagees were obliged to reconvey the land to the borrowers. If the mortgagors failed to make a payment, or were late by even one day, then the mortgagees were relieved of their obligation to reconvey. This harsh result was subsequently softened by the

English courts of equity, which imposed rules of fairness on the mortgage contract and permitted the mortgagors time to remedy their default. This right to redeem the mortgage became known as the "equity of redemption". If the mortgagors failed to redeem the mortgage within the time limits imposed by the courts, they were, upon the court's order, thereafter foreclosed from exercising their equity of redemption.

Foreclosure involves a detailed procedure under the *Rules of Civil Procedure*, R.R.O. 1990, Reg. 194 (Rule 64). In brief, mortgagees first issue and serve claims for foreclosure on the mortgagors and all subsequent encumbrancers whom they wish to foreclose. The action may be defended by any one or more of the defendants, either on the merits or by filing a notice desiring the opportunity to redeem ("D.O.R.") or a notice desiring sale ("D.O.S."). The latter document indicates a desire to have the property sold under the court's supervision, while the former means the defendant wants to be allowed time by the court to redeem the mortgage.

A hearing before the Superior Court of Justice follows, at which point a judgment for foreclosure is usually obtained (because there is seldom a defence on the merits) with a reference to a Master to settle the accounts (that is, to determine the amount owing on the mortgage and to set the priorities of those entitled to redeem).

If someone has asked for a sale and posted the required deposit for costs, the court will direct that a sale be attempted. If no one has filed a notice D.O.S. or if an attempted sale has proved abortive, the court will then set the period of redemption, which will usually be 60 days unless someone can convince the judge that it should be shorter or longer in the circumstances.

At the end of the redemption period, if no one has redeemed or obtained an order extending the period for redemption, mortgagees may apply for a final order of foreclosure (often known as an "F.O.F."), which they will then register on title. Even then the mortgagors or any of the other defendants may apply to reopen the action and further extend the period for redemption. An application to extend the period will usually be granted provided that the mortgagees have not done something that would prevent them from returning the land intact (such as selling or mortgaging it).

Once the foreclosure is completed with the registration of an F.O.F., the mortgagees become the owners of the property and may deal with it as they please.

Foreclosure as a remedy offers the following advantages:

1. The proceedings are conducted under the supervision of a court with the result that the mortgagees have the court's protection and mortgagors may be prevented from frivolously delaying the proceedings.

2. The mortgagees may ultimately become the owners of the property and may thereafter retain any profit made on its sale. Note, however, the case of *Ontario Housing Corp. v. Ong*, [1987] O.J. No. 111, 58 O.R. (2d) 125 (H.C.J.), affd [1988] O.J. No. 1151, 63 O.R. (2d) 799 (C.A.). In that case, the mortgagee obtained default judgment for immediate foreclosure. However, the judgment was signed one day

too early, and the mortgagee was compelled to hand over to the mortgagor the substantial profit it had made on the sale.

POWER OF SALE UNDER A MORTGAGE

The mortgage contract usually permits mortgagees to sell the mortgaged property upon default. The mortgagees have the right to convey the legal title or equity of redemption (whatever has been mortgaged to them) to a third party purchaser and to apply the sale proceeds to their outstanding debt. If the sale proceeds are less than the mortgage debt (including costs), then they have the right to sue the mortgagors for the deficiency. If the sale produces a surplus, then they are obligated to turn it over to the next encumbrancer in line behind them or, if none, then to the mortgagors. Naturally, they have an obligation to render an accounting to those interested in the property upon completion of the sale, so that they may confirm the proper disposition of the proceeds.

Because of this duty to account, mortgagees also have an obligation to obtain the best price available for the property in the circumstances. Failure to do so will render them liable to subsequent encumbrancers and the mortgagors in an action for the deficiency from the price that they should have obtained on the sale.

Numerous cases in Ontario and elsewhere attempt to elucidate the duty of mortgagees to make a proper sale. In *Cuckmere Brick Co. v. Mutual Finance Ltd.*, [1971] 2 All E.R. 633, [1971] 2 W.L.R. 1207 (C.A.), Lord Salmon of the English Court of Appeal held:

> I accordingly conclude, both on principle and authority, that a mortgagee in exercising his power of sale does owe a duty to take reasonable precaution to obtain the true market value of the mortgaged property at the date upon which he decides to sell it.

Mortgagees are entitled to look after their own interests but they must not do so wilfully at the expense of others (*Canada Mortgage and Housing Corp. v. Canplex Corp.*, [2008] O.J. No. 86, 66 R.P.R. (4th) 67 (S.C.J.)). However, it has been conclusively established that mortgagees do not have a duty to mitigate their losses: *Manufacturers Life Insurance Co. v. Granada Investments Ltd.*, [2001] O.J. No. 3932, 150 O.A.C. 253 (C.A.). Therefore, mortgagees can choose when they want to sell and, while they must use reasonable precautions to obtain the true value of the property, they do not have to be concerned about protecting the mortgagor's interests.

Throughout the conduct of a sale under power of sale, the mortgagees must always act defensively with an eye to the potential attack by others demanding after completion that they make up an alleged deficiency. There is very little opportunity to correct mistakes made in the conduct of the proceedings, with the result that mortgagees may find themselves vulnerable to an attack at a later date, at which point they are unable to do much to protect themselves. It is essential that mortgagees and their solicitors conduct the sale with the utmost care in order to minimize the possibility of liability at a later date. Remember that mortgagees are accountable not only to the owner but to all subsequent encumbrancers.

For an excellent summary of the duties of mortgagees in the conduct of enforcement proceedings, as well as receivers appointed by them, see *Silven Properties Ltd. v. Royal Bank of Scotland,* [2003] EWCA Civ 1409, [2004] 4 All E.R. 484 (C.A.).

The exercise of a contractual power of sale often offers many advantages over other remedies available to a mortgagee:

1. The procedure can be very quick and inexpensive. Mortgagees are able to sell the property after the prescribed 35 days' notice given after 15 days of default.

2. Once an agreement of purchase and sale has been entered into by the mortgagees, the mortgagors have no further right to redeem or to put the mortgage back into good standing (*Mission Construction Ltd. v. Seel Investments Ltd.,* [1973] O.J. No. 1890, [1973] 2 O.R. 190 (H.C.J.); *Hornstein v. Gardena Properties Inc.,* [2006] O.J. No. 2757, 212 O.A.C. 203 (C.A.))

However, mortgagees must be aware that once they serve a notice of sale demanding payment of the entire mortgage amount, they cannot refuse to accept payment by the mortgagors (*Cruso v. Bond,* [1882] O.J. No. 139, 1 O.R. 384 (C.A.)). See also *Wycliffe Humberplex Ltd. v. Humberplex Developments Inc.,* [2009] O.J. No. 3709, 83 R.P.R. (4th) 205 (C.A.).

Mortgagors have been known to deliberately default on a mortgage that is not open for prepayment solely for the purpose of luring the mortgagees into issuing a notice of sale so that the mortgagors may then prepay the mortgage.

STATUTORY POWER OF SALE

When a mortgage does not contain any power of sale provisions, mortgagees may rely upon the power of sale provided under Part II of the *Mortgages Act.* A notice of sale may be given after 15 days' default. Although s. 26(1) seems to allow a sale after 45 days' notice, note that s. 24 confers a power of sale only after three months of default. Therefore, the mortgagees will not be able to enter into an agreement to sell until at least three months after default, although they can give the requisite notice at a much earlier date. The notice is in the same statutory form as with a private power of sale.

Note that if a sale under Part II is by way of public auction, mortgagees may, under s. 24(1), be able to purchase the mortgaged property for their own benefit, contrary to the general rule (see *infra,* pp. 401-402). However, in W.B. Rayner and Richard H. McLaren's text, *Falconbridge on Mortgages,* 4th ed. (Toronto: Canada Law Book, 1977), at 704 and 742, the authors express some doubt on this point, reasoning that the section only authorizes the mortgagee to purchase for resale.

POSSESSION

Upon default, mortgagees may recover possession of the mortgaged premises from the owner and any subsequent encumbrancers. This right is based upon the old theory of a mortgage being a conveyance of the legal title to the property that entitled the grantee to possession of the property. Of course, the mortgagees' right to possession against the mortgagors also extends to any person who claims under the mortgagors and whose interest arises subsequent to the mortgage.

Possession will normally be recovered under a writ of possession obtained pursuant to Rule 60.10 of the *Rules of Civil Procedure*.

Often, mortgagees will not wish to obtain vacant possession of the mortgaged property, but rather will wish to receive the rents from the property. Under the implied charge terms, mortgagors agree to "attorn" to the mortgagees, that is, to become the tenants of the mortgagees on the default and to turn over all of the rents being received by the mortgagors. Thus, mortgagees will serve a notice of attornment on the mortgagors and those tenants of the property whose leases are prior to the mortgage. A tenant who continues to pay the mortgagor risks being liable again to the mortgagee for the same rent.

As mentioned before, mortgagees are entitled to possession as against tenants under leases subsequent to the mortgage. Mortgagees will technically not be entitled under the mortgage to require the payment of rent to them by a subsequent tenant. They may, however, be able to force that tenant to enter a new lease with them or else be evicted.

Often mortgagees will avoid the latter problem by obtaining an assignment of rents and leases as collateral security to the mortgage. When the mortgagors default, the mortgagees merely give notice to the tenants of the assignment requiring future rents to be paid to the mortgagees. This assignment should be registered in the land registry office in order to establish priority over any other claimants, such as an assignee of book debts who will have registered under the *Personal Property Security Act*, R.S.O. 1990, c. P.10 ("PPSA"). The PPSA gives priority to assignees of a lease who have registered in the land registry office (see p. 207); however, it is customary, out of extra caution, to also register notice of the assignment under the PPSA in case the assignment is treated as one of rents only and which therefore needs to be registered under the PPSA to preserve its priority.

Having either obtained vacant possession or control of the rents, mortgagees are called mortgagees in possession. They thereupon assume extensive and sometimes onerous obligations with regard to the maintenance and operation of the property. For example, they must exercise reasonable care in maintaining the property, and they must not allow it to deteriorate. They may have to expend their own money in making repairs, which they can add to the mortgage debt. After deducting their expenses in maintaining and operating the property from the income from the property, they should apply the balance to outstanding interest, costs and principal under the mortgage. They will be required to account to the mortgagors and subsequent encumbrancers for the rents received and expenditures made. They should therefore keep careful records.

The prospect of taking possession of residential premises will be of particular concern to mortgagees. Having done so, they are deemed by Part V of the *Mortgages Act*, s. 47, to be "landlords" under the *Residential Tenancies Act, 2006*, S.O. 2006, c. 17, and will have the landlords' obligations to the tenants under the tenancy agreement and that Act, including for example, the obligation under s. 20 to maintain the premises "in a good state of repair and fit for habitation". In addition, the mortgagee, and a purchaser from him or her, are liable for the last month's rental deposit usually paid by the residential tenants even though the mortgagee has not received such payments. In *Top Link Investments Ltd. v. Hutchinson*, [1997] O.J. No. 5125, 37 O.R. (3d) 107 (Gen. Div.), Ground J. held that the combined effect of ss. 82 and 88 of the *Landlord and Tenant Act*, R.S.O. 1990, c. L.7 (now ss. 105 and 18, respectively, of the *Residential Tenancies Act, 2006*), made the purchaser of residential premises from a mortgagee under power of sale liable for these security deposits. Note that s. 27 of the *Mortgages Act* provides for repayment to residential tenants of their security deposits to the extent there are proceeds left after payment of all secured creditors. Successor landlords are not liable for payments in excess of the last month's rental deposits unless they actually receive the moneys. Furthermore, purchasers under power of sale will not be liable for prior defaults by mortgagors including, for example, illegal rents paid prior to taking possession (*981673 Ontario Ltd. v. Jessome*, [1994] O.J. No. 3039, 21 O.R. (3d) 343 (Gen. Div.)).

With one exception, mortgagees of rented residential premises cannot evict the tenants except for the causes listed in Part V of the *Residential Tenancies Act, 2006* (such as non-payment of rent). If the mortgaged property is a single-family home, then, under s. 53 of the *Mortgages Act*, the tenancy can be terminated on 60 days' notice if the purchasers undertake in writing that the home will be occupied by them or their immediate family. Mortgagees can also apply under s. 52 of the *Mortgages Act* to set aside the tenancy on the basis that it was entered into to prejudice their interests.

Mortgagees will wish to review their position carefully before taking possession of residential premises, including consideration of the state of repair and the anticipated strategy for further realizing upon their security.

ACTION ON THE COVENANT

Because a mortgage is a contract for the repayment of a loan, usually with interest, mortgagees will, on default, have the right to sue the mortgagors on their covenant to repay the debt. This right may be exercised on the day following the date a payment was due, but not made. The mortgagees may sue only for the overdue payment or, if the mortgage so provides, they may accelerate the principal and sue for all the money secured by the mortgage.

In most cases, judgment can be obtained quickly as there will usually be no substantial defence available to the mortgagors. After judgment, the mortgagees will obtain and file a writ of seizure and sale with the sheriff and may then levy execution for recovery from all of the mortgagors' assets, and not just the mortgaged property.

The persons signing the mortgage as mortgagors will remain liable to the mortgagees on their covenant to repay, even though the mortgaged property has been conveyed. As this fact is not well understood by the public, it is important to bring it to the attention of your clients when they sign the mortgage, or when they sell the property subject to the mortgage. There have been cases recently where solicitors have been held liable to their clients for failure to so advise them.

In addition to being able to sue the persons who sign the mortgage, mortgagees have been given the right under s. 20 of the *Mortgages Act* to sue the grantee of the equity of redemption (*i.e.*, the current owner). However, they may not sue both; recovery of judgment against one will release the other. The right given under s. 20 is also limited to those purchasers of the property who are obligated to indemnify the mortgagors in the circumstances. Therefore, the grantee may avoid liability on the covenant by expressly refusing to indemnify the vendor in the agreement to purchase.

To establish privity of contract and thus create a continuing liability on the covenant to repay, mortgagees will sometimes require that purchasers of a property execute an assumption agreement in favour of the mortgagees in respect of the mortgage. This will most often occur in the case of new subdivisions, where the builder will want to be released from its covenant to avoid accumulating massive contingent liabilities over the years. However, this may well result in a novation.

Suing on the covenant only avoids the necessity of accelerating the mortgage debt as in foreclosure and power of sale proceedings. The mortgagees may wish to pursue this remedy when they suspect the mortgagors are deliberately defaulting under the mortgage in the hope that the mortgagees will accelerate the debt with the result that the mortgagor may prepay the loan. In addition, the mortgagees have the right to sue on the covenant when there has been a sale under power of sale but the proceeds were not enough to satisfy the mortgage debt. Remember also that a foreclosure action usually includes a claim on the covenant. Mortgagees will be able to pursue this remedy even after a final order of foreclosure so long as they are in a position to return the mortgaged property to the mortgagor intact.

DISTRESS

The right to distrain is the right to seize the goods of a debtor, sell them and apply the proceeds to the debt.

A mortgagee's right to distrain against the goods of the mortgagor may result from a contractual provision of the mortgage or from the creation of a landlord and tenant relationship between the mortgagor and the mortgagee (see the foregoing discussion regarding attornment).

In the former case, most mortgages in Ontario provide that the mortgagee may distrain for arrears of interest. In the latter case, distress was the common law right of a landlord against a tenant for arrears of rent.

In Ontario, the mortgagee's right to distrain may not be allowed in cases of residential property because of the abolition of distress for residential tenancies under s. 40 of the *Residential Tenancies Act, 2006*. However, this restriction may apply only where the mortgagee has gone into possession and may not affect the mortgagee's contractual right to distrain.

MORTGAGEE MAY PERFORM COVENANT

The mortgage document usually provides that the mortgagee may, on default by the mortgagor, perform the mortgagor's covenant and either demand immediate payment of the cost of so doing, or add it to the mortgage debt. If added to the mortgage debt, the cost will bear interest at the mortgage rate. If reimbursement is demanded, the mortgagee will have all the other remedies available on default of payment.

In *Boyer v. Fox*, [1980] O.J. No. 3667, 29 O.R. (2d) 330 (H.C.J.), Holland J. held that a notice of sale could only be issued for default of payment of an instalment of principal or interest and not for failure to perform some other covenant, such as a failure to pay taxes. He therefore issued an injunction preventing the resulting sale. However, in both *Royal Trust Corp. of Canada v. 880185 Ontario Ltd.*, [2005] O.J. No. 1651, 30 R.P.R. (4th) 165 and *Glassworkers Social Club v. Forestgate Leasing Inc.*, [1998] O.J. No. 2798, 40 O.R. (3d) 606, the Ontario Court of Appeal held that a failure to pay taxes constituted a "default of payment" under the mortgage and the mortgagee was entitled to exercise its power of sale. In any event, the mortgagee could pay the taxes itself, demand payment from the mortgagor and then commence its sale proceedings. In the alternative, the mortgagee could simply accelerate the principal by demanding payment from the mortgagor and then exercising its power of sale. See also *H & S Bookspan Investments Ltd. v. Axelrod*, [1984] O.J. No. 3317, 47 O.R. (2d) 604 (H.C.J.), and *Royal Trust Corp. of Canada v. 880185 Ontario Ltd.*, [2005] O.J. No. 1651, 198 O.A.C. 235 (C.A.), wherein *Boyer v. Fox* was expressly held to have been wrongly decided.

POWER OF SALE PROCEEDINGS

In the early 1990s, there was a dramatic increase in the number of cases involving powers of sale under mortgage. This reflected difficult economic times and certainly was directly related to high and fluctuating interest rates. Since a defence on the merits is most often not available, mortgagors are forced into attempts to attack mortgagees on procedural grounds in the hope of delaying or upsetting an attempted realization of the security. Ultimately, all that mortgagors who have defaulted can hope for is delay to permit a reorganization of their financial affairs or a return of better economic times.

Mortgagees must exercise the utmost care in the conduct of a private power of sale. If they make an error, not only may they be liable to the mortgagors for a deficiency, but they may also find themselves burdened with contractual obligations under an agreement to sell without the ability to complete. Part III of the *Mortgages Act* requires notice of sale to be served under very precise rules prior to any sale; neglecting to observe those rules, sometimes even in very minor respects, may result in the complete failure of a sale. It is often not possible to salvage an agreement to sell by re-serving the notice; you must terminate the agreement. As with a breach of the *Planning Act*, R.S.O. 1990, c. P.13, the results of a mismanaged sale proceeding can be devastating. The opportunities to cure a defect in the notice procedure and bring an existing agreement to sell back to life are limited.

The following is a brief summary of suggested steps to be followed in the exercise of a power of sale. For fuller discussions, please refer to *Handbook on the Power of Sale under a Mortgage and Debenture*, 3d ed. (Insight Educational Services, 1988); the Law Society of Upper Canada's Programme on Mortgage Remedies 1985; and James S. Hilton, "Enforcement of Mortgage Security" in *Real Estate and Landlord and Tenant 1986-87* (Bar Admission Course materials).

WHEN MAY NOTICE BE SERVED?

Section 32 of the *Mortgages Act* requires that notice of sale may not be given until default has continued for at least 15 days. If a notice is given prior to this time, it will be a nullity (*Baresyd Enterprises Ltd. v. Csizmadia*, [1981] O.J. No. 2257, 23 R.P.R. 60 (Co. Ct.); *Windy Ridge Developments Inc. v. Norris*, [2006] O.J. No. 1618, 43 R.P.R. (4th) 268 (S.C.J.)). An injunction will be issued to prevent a sale when the notice is served prior to the lapse of the 15-day period (*Steffen v. Toronto Dominion*, [1980] O.J. No. 1383 (H.C.J.)).

You must first establish that default triggering the power of sale has occurred and when it occurred; this procedure is an easy task when the default consists of failure to pay on a specified date. As mentioned before (see p. 381), most mortgages provide for default in payment of principal or interest. With demand mortgages it may be difficult to establish the precise date of default; the debtor must be given a reasonable time after demand to pay (*Mister Broadloom Corp. (1968) Ltd. v. Bank of Montreal*, [1983] O.J. No. 3271, 44 O.R. (2d) 368 (C.A.)). The length of "reasonable time" depends on all the circumstances.

LENGTH OF NOTICE

Section 32 of the *Mortgages Act* reads as follows:

> 32. Where a mortgage by its terms confers a power of sale upon a certain default, notice of exercising the power of sale shall not be given until the default has continued for at least fifteen days, and the sale shall not be made for at least thirty-five days after the notice has been given.

The courts have held that the date specified in the notice of sale for repayment must be at least 35 days after the date of service of the notice; if it is any less, then the notice will be found to be a nullity (*371802 Ontario Ltd. v. Schramm*, [1979] O.J. No. 4423, 26 O.R. (2d) 550 (H.C.J.)). A notice which specifies the 35th day after the notice was mailed is acceptable (*Timmerman v. Central Guaranty Trust Co.*, [1992] O.J. No. 632, 8 O.R. (3d) 669 (Gen. Div.)).

Section 34 of the *Mortgages Act* deems notice to be given on the day it was mailed by registered mail. A controversy developed under the *Family Law Reform Act*, R.S.O. 1980, c. 152, because of its provision that mailed notices were deemed to have been given five days later. Section 22(3) of the *Family Law Act*, R.S.O. 1990, c. F.3 (as amended) now makes it clear that a mortgagor's non-owning spouse is not entitled to any greater notice period to redeem the property.

In preparing a notice of sale, you should still allow extra time beyond the minimum 35 days. Section 31(2) (as amended) of the *Mortgages Act* indicates that you may rely on the abstract of title or parcel register and a sheriff's certificate as of "the time specified" on the day preceding mailing the notice of sale. Unfortunately, there does not appear to be any guidance as to what "the time specified" is. To be safe, you should conduct a subsearch after you send out the notice of sale to ensure that you served everyone who registered an interest on the day before. If someone did register, then you will want to send a copy of the notice to that person and still have at least 35 days left before the date specified in the notice.

In *Morra v. Aloe*, [1971] O.J. No. 1545, [1971] 2 O.R. 532 (H.C.J.), Galligan J. held that you do not need to serve execution creditors who file after notice is first given to the mortgagor. However, while procedures in the Registry and Land Titles offices ensure their records are updated immediately, there may still be some concern that an execution may not appear on a certificate immediately after it is filed. It is suggested that you update your search after serving the mortgagor. As noted above, if you allow extra time, you will be able to serve additional copies on new encumbrancers appearing upon an update of your searches. This may also be a convenient method of proceeding, especially with out-of-town properties. Note that nothing in the Act requires that the notice of sale be sent to all the subsequent encumbrancers on the same day. Presumably, however, they should all get the same notice.

WHOM DO YOU SERVE?

You must serve the following people:

1. All those appearing from the abstract index or the parcel register and a sheriff's certificate to have an interest in the mortgaged property. You will only serve those subsequent in interest to the mortgagee (s. 31(1) (as amended) does not require notice to "persons having an interest in the mortgaged property prior to that of the mortgagee"). The Ontario Court of Appeal has decided that notice of sale need not be served on guarantors if they have not made any payments under the mortgage since they do not have an interest in the property: *Canadian Financial Co. v. First Federal Construction Ltd.*, [1982] O.J. No. 3108, 34 O.R. (2d) 681 (C.A.), leave to appeal refused [1982] S.C.C.A. No. 393, 35 O.R. (2d) 224*n*. See also *394363 Ontario Ltd. v. Fuda*, [1984] O.J. No. 3436, 49 O.R. (2d) 672 (H.C.J.), affd (1986), 54 O.R. (2d) 443 (C.A.), leave to appeal refused (1986), 56 O.R. (2d) 608*n* (S.C.C.). Nevertheless, it may be good practice to serve guarantors, especially where the mortgagee intends to sue the guarantors for any deficiency after the sale. It has been held that the original mortgagor must be served because he or she continues to have an interest in the property, either because the mortgagor has made payments under the mortgage or because of the right to claim

against it if called upon to perform the mortgagor's covenant under the mortgage: *General Trust Corp. of Canada v. Di Carlo*, [1993] O.J. No. 2366, 16 O.R. (3d) 221 (Gen. Div.); *Baresyd Enterprises Ltd. v. Csizmadia*, [1981] O.J. No. 2257, 23 R.P.R. 60 (Co. Ct.); *National Trust Co. v. Hoffman*, [1983] O.J. No. 3183, 43 O.R. (2d) 412 (H.C.J.).

2. The Crown or other public authority where the mortgagee has received written notice of a statutory lien.

3. Any other people who gave the mortgagee notice in writing of their interest. The courts have held that actual notice of a claim is not enough; the mortgagee must have received a notice in writing.

In addition, you must be mindful of s. 22 of the *Family Law Act*, which provides that the spouse of an owner is equally entitled to any notice of sale. Because of the difficulty of determining the marital status at the time of giving notice of a husband and wife who owned the property jointly, the practice has developed of giving notice to "the spouse" of each. Master Sandler suggested, in *Maritime Life Assurance Co. v. Karapatakis*, [1979] O.J. No. 4181, 24 O.R. (2d) 311 (Master), that the mortgagees must make reasonable enquiry as to the identity of the spouse. However, this suggestion appears to have been influenced by the fact that the case was for foreclosure and required personal service. In addition, it is to be noted that the *Land Titles Procedural Guide* approves the practice of sending notice to "the spouse" of the owner, and it has been implicitly approved in several cases.

If you fail to serve someone, then that person's interest cannot be affected by any sale under the mortgage. As provided in s. 31(1) of the *Mortgages Act*, the mortgagee may propose to sell the property subject to that interest even though the interest is subsequent to the mortgage. In the alternative, you may be able to obtain a quit-claim from the encumbrancer that you failed to serve. The danger is that your entire notice may be found invalid. The safest course is, except for tenants you wish to retain, to serve everyone in sight; it will not hurt you to serve too many people.

Unfortunately, a notice of sale will not be sufficient by itself to wipe out subsequently registered construction lien claims because of the possibility that the lien may have priority over the mortgage (see Chapter 8). Therefore, it will be necessary to obtain orders in the lien actions to get the liens off title (*Bernard J. Kamin Ltd. v. Blue Mountain Capital Corp.*, [1990] O.J. No. 348, 72 O.R. (2d) 264 (Dist. Ct.)).

MANNER OF GIVING NOTICE

Section 33(1) of the *Mortgages Act* reads as follows:

33(1) A notice of exercising a power of sale shall be given by personal service or by registered mail addressed to the person to whom it is to be given at the person's usual or last known place of address, or, where the last known place of address is that shown on the registered instrument under which the person acquired an interest, to such address, or by leaving it at one of such places of address, or where the mortgage provides for personal service only, by personal service, or, where the mortgage provides a specific address, to such address.

The Court of Appeal has held that sending the notice to the address for service listed in the mortgage is sufficient for compliance with s. 33: *CIBC Mortgage Corp. v. Chopra*, [1997] O.J. No. 3458, 35 O.R. (3d) 362. However, the Court specifically declined to say whether using that address would be sufficient if the "mortgagee knows that the proposed method of service will not bring the notice to the attention" of the intended recipient. There have been two other cases in which the notices were found to have been properly served where they were sent to the addresses shown on the mortgage even though the mortgagee was aware of other addresses for the mortgagor: *Confederation Trust Co. v. Mac-Don Builders Inc.*, [1990] O.J. No. 1859, 75 O.R. (2d) 278 (Gen. Div.); *Alessandria Real Estate Investments Ltd. v. Toronto-Dominion Bank*, [1991] O.J. No. 2339, 6 O.R. (3d) 536 (Gen. Div.).

In view of the foregoing, it is important that you make enquiries from the mortgagees as to what addresses they may have for the mortgagors or anyone else who is entitled to notice. In *Hal Wright Motor Sales Ltd. v. Industrial Development Bank*, [1975] O.J. No. 2259, 8 O.R. (2d) 76 (Dist. Ct.), the mortgagee's solicitor apparently did not ask his client for the mortgagor's address and sent the notice to the mortgaged property. The notice was held to be a nullity and the impending sale was enjoined.

You should enquire from the mortgagees about their latest correspondence with the mortgagors, if any. Check the mortgage for any addresses. It may also be wise to check available public records for addresses, such as the telephone directory and corporate information records at the Companies Branch. The recommended approach is to serve all encumbrancers at all addresses known for them, including in care of their solicitors. The notice is effective on the day that it is mailed by registered mail, even if it is subsequently returned unopened (*Wood v. Bank of Nova Scotia*, [1980] O.J. No. 3625, 29 O.R. (2d) 35 (C.A.)).

You may serve lien claimants and execution creditors by sending the notice to their solicitors.

There were previous uncertainties about what the effect of a dissolution of a corporate mortgagor was on the rights of a mortgagee to enforce its mortgage. The *Business Corporations Act*, R.S.O. 1990, c. B.16 was amended in 1998 to remove the uncertainties. Section 242(4) requires the mortgagee who commences a power of sale against a corporation that has been dissolved to serve the notice of sale on the Public Guardian and Trustee at the following address:

Public Guardian and Trustee
800-595 Bay Street
Toronto, ON
M5G 2M6
Attention: Corporate Legal Services

Section 244(4) makes it clear that no notice to the Public Guardian and Trustee is required if the dissolution of the corporate mortgagor occurs after the issuance of the notice of sale. Of course, in either case, the Public Guardian and Trustee will be entitled to demand an accounting from the mortgagee and will be entitled to a surplus if there is one.

FORM OF NOTICE

The *Mortgages Act* requires notice of sale to be in the form printed at the end of the Act. Although minor deviations from the form will not affect its validity, you should attempt to follow it as closely as possible. Be extremely careful in setting out the amounts due under the mortgage; you should be as detailed as possible. Note, however, that the amounts to be specified are as of the date of the notice, although you may wish to include a note of the *per diem* rate of interest to assist in the calculation of the payment required to redeem the mortgage. A subsequent payment that does not bring the mortgage completely into good standing will not invalidate your notice (*Aloi v. Spencer*, [1980] O.J. No. 3681, 29 O.R. (2d) 435 (H.C.J.); *Glassworkers Social Club v. Forestgate Leasing Inc.*, [1998] O.J. No. 2798, 40 O.R. (3d) 606 (C.A.)).

The purpose of the notice is to alert subsequent encumbrancers of the jeopardy to their interest in the mortgaged property and to permit them to pay. If the notice is misleading, confusing or incorrect, it will be set aside. The following are examples of notices which were found to be invalid:

1.   The date as specified in the notice was fewer than 35 days after the date of service of the notice (*371802 Ontario Ltd. v. Schramm*, [1979] O.J. No. 4423, 26 O.R. (2d) 550 (H.C.J.)).

2.   A notice must be sent to the mortgagor's address known by the mortgagee, and not to the mortgaged property (*Hal Wright Motor Sales Ltd. v. Industrial Development Bank*, [1975] O.J. No. 2259, 8 O.R. (2d) 76 (Dist. Ct.); *National Trust Co. v. Hoffman*, [1983] O.J. No. 3183, 43 O.R. (2d) 412 (H.C.J.)).

3.   Reference to the power of sale under Part II of the *Mortgages Act* was not deleted in a notice of sale (*Comrie Lumber Co. v. Tomlinson Construction Services Ltd.*, [1977] O.J. No. 2200, 15 O.R. (2d) 613 (H.C.J.)).

4.   A notice identified the default as being under the third and fourth mortgages when in fact the default was under the second and third mortgages (*Munro v. Pago Developments Ltd.*, [1979] O.J. No. 4362, 26 O.R. (2d) 37 (H.C.J.)).

5.   A notice was not manually signed (*Botiuk v. Collison*, [1979] O.J. No. 4429, 26 O.R. (2d) 580 (C.A.)).

6.   A notice did not identify the capacity of the person signing on behalf of the mortgagee (*Salciccia v. Reid*, [1978] O.J. No. 3501, 21 O.R. (2d) 10 (H.C.J.)).

7.   A notice issued and served prior to an agreement between the mortgagor and the mortgagee for different repayment terms and conditions, and subsequent default to the mortgagor under new terms was held to be invalid and a new notice of sale was required (*Paul Horvat Investments Ltd. v. Goldcrown Holdings Ltd.*, [1989] O.J. No. 989, 26 R.P.R. 36 (H.C.J.)).

8. A notice did not give separate amounts for principal and interest, and applicable other items including taxes, insurance and costs were defective (*Morgan v. Canada Trust Co.*, [1983] O.J. No. 3072, 42 O.R. (2d) 246 (H.C.J.), but see *Ginsberg v. Morgan Estate*, unreported, Flinn Co. Ct. J., May 4, 1984 (Ont. Co. Ct.), where notice was held not to be defective and purchaser's title was not impeached).

9. A notice stated that municipal taxes were owing when the taxes had been paid by the receiver from the revenues (*Grenville Goodwin Ltd. v. MacDonald*, [1988] O.J. No. 1437, 65 O.R. (2d) 381 (C.A.)).

10. A notice set out the wrong amount owing (*Alessandria Real Estate Investments Ltd. v. Toronto-Dominion Bank*, [1991] O.J. No. 2339, 6 O.R. (3d) 536 (Gen. Div.); *Sliwinski v. Marks*, [2005] O.J. No. 1018, [2005] O.T.C. 198 (S.C.J.)).

The following are examples of notices that were held to be valid:

1. A notice identified the property by municipal address only and did not include a legal description (*Koutoulakis v. Aaron*, [1980] O.J. No. 174, 4 A.C.W.S. (2d) 336 (H.C.J.)).

2. A notice was sent only once to a person who was both a guarantor and a third mortgagee (*Royal Trust Corp. of Canada v. Roughley*, [1979] O.J. No. 4498, 27 O.R. (2d) 318 (Div. Ct.)).

3. A notice did not include taxes and did not follow Form 1 as authorized by the Act (*Ilich v. R. Glisich Real Estate Ltd.*, [1984] O.J. No. 200 (H.C.J.).

4. A notice set out only the total amount owing without a detailed calculation (*Hornstein v. Gardena Properties Inc.*, [2006] O.J. No. 2757, 212 O.A.C. 203 (C.A.). The Court held that, if amounts were in dispute, they could be dealt with in a subsequent accounting.

NO INTERMEDIATE PROCEEDINGS

Having served the notice of sale, you must be extremely careful not to do anything during the notice period that might contravene s. 42 of the *Mortgages Act*, which prohibits "further proceedings" during that period. This restriction is based on the principle that any action by the mortgagee might prejudice the mortgagor's ability to redeem the mortgage. For example, if the mortgagee enters into an agreement to sell the property, even if it is conditional on the mortgage not being redeemed, the mortgagee may have found the only purchaser to whom the mortgagor could have sold the property in order to raise the money to pay off the mortgage. A sale was enjoined where a mortgagee advertised the property during the notice period (*Smith v. Brown*, [1890] O.J. No. 84, 20 O.R. 165 (Ch. Div.)). More recently, Ground J. refused to grant relief to a mortgagor where the mortgagee had listed the property and entertained offers during the notice period, although it is noteworthy that the issue was not raised until after the sale had closed. Ground J. noted that the only remedy for breach was to declare the intermediate proceeding a nullity, and that there was no "transaction" at hand that could be enjoined (*Municipal Savings & Loan Corp. v. 819035*

Ontario Ltd., [1995] O.J. No. 1695, 55 A.C.W.S. (3d) 1059 (Gen. Div.)). A mortgagee was not entitled to sue for possession during the notice period (*Lee v. Guettler*, [1975] O.J. No. 2487, 10 O.R. (2d) 257 (C.A.)). Changing the locks on the mortgaged premises and serving notices of attornment of rent during the redemption period have been held to contravene s. 42 (*Bank of Nova Scotia v. Barnard*, [1984] O.J. No. 3218, 46 O.R. (2d) 409 (H.C.J.)). However, an assignment of mortgage is not a "further proceeding" under s. 42 (*490352 Ontario Inc. v. ASAAPV Financial Corp.*, [1985] O.J. No. 384, 1 C.P.C. (2d) 36 (H.C.J.)). As well, s. 42 does not preclude an order of *nunc pro tunc* ("now for then") (*McKenna Estate v. Marshall*, [2005] O.J. No. 4394, [2005] O.T.C. 905, 37 R.P.R. (4th) 222 (S.C.J.)).

The consequence of a breach of s. 42 may be that the further proceeding will be set aside (*Jones v. Torgis*, [1978] O.J. No. 3632, 22 O.R. (2d) 123 (Master)). On the other hand, where a mortgagee commenced an action at the same time as issuing a notice of sale, the Court held this to be an irregularity and granted an order *nunc pro tunc* giving leave for the action retroactively (*McKenna Estate v. Marshall*, [2005] O.J. No. 4394 (S.C.J.). The notice of sale is not voided by a breach of s. 42 (*Sierra Garden Homes Ltd. v. 668417 Ontario Ltd.*, [1990] O.J. No. 2273, 1 O.R. (3d) 446 (Gen. Div.)). Nevertheless, you must be careful. Because the "further proceeding" may have prejudiced the mortgagor's ability to redeem, the sale itself may be stayed.

ASSIGNMENT OF MORTGAGE

The assignment of the mortgage after a notice of sale has been issued may create a problem for the assignee in being able to complete a sale. There have been a number of cases where the courts have enjoined a sale because the mortgage was assigned after the notice of sale was issued but, in each case, no notice of the assignment was given to the mortgagor. See p. 369 for a discussion of these cases. Since the purpose of the notice of sale is to tell the mortgagor formally how much is owing and whom to pay, it seems obvious that it is necessary to give notice of the assignment to the mortgagor and to all others to whom the notice was issued.

ACCEPTANCE OF PAYMENTS AFTER NOTICE

The courts have held that acceptance of payments made under a mortgage after a notice of sale has been issued does not invalidate the sale proceedings: *Wood Street Developments Inc. v. AGB Halifax Enterprises*, [1997] O.J. No. 1376, 33 O.R. (3d) 220 (Gen. Div.); *Glassworkers Social Club v. Forestgate Leasing Inc.*, [1998] O.J. No. 2798, 40 O.R. (3d) 606 (C.A.). The result is different only if the acceptance of payments can be construed as an agreement by the mortgagee to amend the mortgage payment terms: *Botiuk v. Collison*, [1979] O.J. No. 4429, 26 O.R. (2d) 580 (C.A.).

HOW TO CURE A DEFECTIVE NOTICE

The opportunities to remedy a notice of sale that is defective in form or manner of service are limited. Usually, the only thing to be done is to re-serve the notice. This will not only be embarrassing and expensive, but may also be impossible if you have already contracted to sell the property. However, there are two methods by which you may remedy the situation:

1. Arrange to obtain a quit-claim or other appropriate release from the subsequent encumbrancers. This may be possible where you can demonstrate that the encumbrancer has no hope of recovery from the property, even if the encumbrancer manages to avoid this sale.

2. Apply to the court for an order dispensing with notice of sale under s. 39 of the *Mortgages Act*. The court may be inclined to grant such a request where it can be shown that no prejudice will likely result to subsequent encumbrancers. For example, you may be able to prove that they probably already knew of the default and the mortgagee's intention to realize on his or her security, and that a further delay would not result in any greater recovery.

It is even possible to obtain an order dispensing with notice *nunc pro tunc* in respect of a completed sale earlier in the chain of title where there is some obvious defect in the proceedings that raises a question as to the validity of the sale. Although normally the application would be brought by the mortgagee, it could also be brought by the current owner on the basis that he or she is included under the definition of "mortgagee" in the *Mortgages Act* as a person deriving title under the original mortgagee.

CONDUCT OF SALE

Mortgagees should always be concerned that they may be required to prove that they obtained the best price for the property under the circumstances. They can establish value by obtaining appraisals, by having a number of offers to purchase the property that show what willing purchasers were prepared to pay, or by ensuring that all those who might be interested in purchasing had an opportunity to bid. Appropriate and timely advertising is probably the surest way of meeting this obligation. As mortgagees cannot control how many people will make offers, and appraisals do not always determine value with precision, how can the mortgagees be criticized if they made the property available to all those who might be interested?

The mortgagees must decide in each case the best method of marketing the property. If they are prudent, they will choose to list the property with an experienced agent, hold a public auction or invite tender bids. In the latter two cases, they will normally set a reserve equal to the amount owing to them on account of principal, interest and costs. In addition, they will set conditions of sale resembling the ordinary terms of an agreement of purchase and sale. Finally, they will usually specify that the highest or any bid will not necessarily be accepted. Sometimes a public auction or tender invitation is held in order to draw out those interested in the property so that later private negotiations may be undertaken.

While in most respects, the agreement of purchase and sale will be identical to an ordinary agreement to sell the property, two special considerations are raised:

1.   Should the agreement specify that the vendors are mortgagees and the sale is being conducted pursuant to their power of sale contained in the mortgage? While this specification will alert the purchasers as to the form of the documentation that they will be receiving, there may be a concern that knowledge of the nature of the sale will depress the sale price, exposing the mortgagees to criticism. Nevertheless, *Hausman v. O'Grady*, [1986] O.J. No. 1449, 61 O.R. (2d) 96 (H.C.J.), affd [1989] O.J. No. 852, 67 O.R. (2d) 735 (C.A.) held that there is no requirement to suppress the fact that the sale is being made by the mortgagee.

2.   Should the completion of the agreement be conditional on the mortgage not being redeemed? Most mortgagees would rather be redeemed than sell, since they will then bear no risk. However, it may be difficult to find purchasers who are prepared to expend the effort and expense in attempting to purchase only to be deprived at the last moment. You will recall that an agreement to sell normally extinguishes mortgagors' rights to redeem or put the mortgage back into good standing (see p. 389). There are a number of conflicting decisions as to the effect of a condition included in a sale agreement making a sale agreement conditional on the mortgagor not redeeming the mortgage. There is a line of cases permitting the mortgagor to take advantage of such a condition even though the mortgagor was not a party to the agreement: *National Trust Co. v. Saad*, [1997] O.J. No. 1815, 33 O.R. (3d) 419 (Gen. Div.); *Miranda v. Wong*, [1986] O.J. No. 231, 36 A.C.W.S. (2d) 247 (H.C.J.); *Nalisa Investments Ltd. v. National Bank of Canada*, [1980] O.J. No. 643, 3 A.C.W.S. (2d) 341 (H.C.J.). More recently, however, the Court of Appeal refused a mortgagor's application where the sale agreement was subject to the mortgagor's right to redeem "up to the time of waiver or expiration of all rights of termination or fulfillment of all conditions": *Logozzo v. Toronto-Dominion Bank*, [1999] O.J. No. 4088, 45 O.R. (3d) 737 at para. 14 (C.A.). Borins J.A. expressed his doubt as to the correctness of the decision in *Saad* but decided on other grounds, namely, that a mortgagor could not enforce the benefit of a clause in a contract to which he was not a party, and further that he had not tendered the amount due prior to the sale agreement being entered into. In *1391748 Ontario Inc. v. Royal Bank of Canada*, [2001] O.J. No. 1849 (S.C.J.), Somers J. held that an agreement that permitted the mortgagee to terminate if the mortgage was redeemed was not a conditional agreement and therefore refused an injunction application by the mortgagor.

In proceeding to sell the property, mortgagees may have to consider the timeliness of obtaining possession of the property from mortgagors, especially if a purchaser will want vacant possession on closing. They cannot attempt to obtain possession during the notice period. If they wait until after, they may have difficulty in obtaining possession in time for a fixed closing date. It may, therefore, be easiest to obtain possession prior to issuing the notice of sale.

WHO MAY BUY?

In general, anyone other than the mortgagee who is selling may purchase the property. This includes a subsequent encumbrancer who will also be entitled to receive the designated share of any surplus realized (*Harron v. Yemen*, [1883] O.J. No. 155, 3 O.R. 126 (C.A.)). If the mortgagor purchases, it will be treated as a redemption of the mortgage and will not affect the position of subsequent encumbrancers (see *Falconbridge on Mortgages*, at 744).

Frequently, mortgagees want to know whether they or someone related to them (including a company owned by them) can purchase the property. The answer is clear that if the mortgagees themselves purchase the property, it will be treated as if nothing happened, leaving the mortgagors' equity of redemption intact (*Farrar v. Farrar's Ltd.* (1888), 40 Ch. D. 395 (Ch. Div.)). In *Hunter v. Thoma*, [1981] O.J. No. 649, 9 A.C.W.S. (2d) 114 (H.C.J.), Cromarty J. held (at para. 43) that, "A sale under power of sale by a mortgagee who holds in trust for certain persons to those persons is no sale". A sale to a corporation owned by a mortgagee or someone else related to the mortgagee will also not extinguish the mortgagor's equity of redemption (*665456 Ontario Ltd. v. Barelan Management Inc.*, [1990] O.J. No. 657, 72 O.R. (2d) 705 (C.A.)).

COMPLETION OF SALE

The documents delivered on closing include the following:

1. A transfer containing recitals of the mortgage, the existence of default, the issuance of notice and the exercise of the power of sale contained in the mortgage. Under s. 5(1)3 of the *Land Registration Reform Act*, R.S.O. 1990, c. L.4 (as amended), only trustee covenants are implied in transfers by chargees.

2. The statutory declarations referred to in s. 35 of the *Mortgages Act*, consisting of:

    (a) a declaration as to default by the mortgagees or their solicitor dated as close as possible to closing;

    (b) a declaration of service with the original post office receipt as an exhibit; and

    (c) a declaration by the mortgagees or their solicitor that the sale complies with Part III of the Mortgages Act.

These declarations together form "conclusive evidence of compliance" with Part III and should therefore be deposited on title.

In the Land Titles system, the documents consist of a transfer reciting that the transferor is the registered owner of the charge and that the transfer is pursuant to the power of sale and in accordance with Part III, and "Sale Papers" made up of an application for registration and the same type of declarations referred to in item 2 above. The declaration as to default must detail the priority claimed over other encumbrances on the register which are to be deleted.

If the land being sold is in the automated registration system, then the above-mentioned statutory declarations are replaced with statements in the transfer to be registered electronically.

Section 36 of the *Mortgages Act* offers great comfort to a purchaser under a power of sale. It says that the purchaser's title is "not liable to be impeached" if the declarations referred to in s. 35 are obtained. There are, however, some limits on this protection.

Section 36 does not become effective until the purchase is completed (*Hal Wright Motor Sales Ltd. v. Industrial Development Bank*, [1975] O.J. No. 2259, 8 O.R. (2d) 76 (Dist. Ct.)). Furthermore, Vannini D.C.J. quoted (at para. 47) with approval from Falconbridge: "The protection of the statute, as well as that usually provided in express powers of sale, extends only to purchasers, without notice, actual or constructive, of any impropriety or irregularity".

In *Botiuk v. Collison*, [1979] O.J. No. 4429, 26 O.R. (2d) 580 (C.A.), the purchaser was denied the protection of s. 36 where the notice of sale was found invalid because it was not signed. Therefore, a purchaser's solicitor must be careful to ensure the regularity of the power of sale proceedings by checking the sale documentation against the information from the searches.

APPLICATION OF PROCEEDS

In order to complete the sale, the mortgagee may have had to pay or apply part of the sale proceeds to satisfy claims having priority over its mortgage, such as prior mortgages and realty taxes. These will of course be permitted to be deducted or recovered from the sale proceeds. In addition, there may be governmental claims which must be paid; for example, the Minister of National Revenue has a statutory super-priority for unremitted employee source deductions and Goods and Services Tax (now Harmonized Sales Tax). This was confirmed in *MCAP Service Corp. v. Hunter*, [2007] O.J. No. 429, 50 R.P.R. (4th) 161 (C.A.).

The proceeds realized from a sale under mortgage are applied first to the costs of the sale, then to the outstanding indebtedness under the mortgage and then, if there is a surplus, it should be applied to subsequent encumbrances in the order of their priority. The remaining balance, if any, belongs to the mortgagor.

If the mortgagor has any doubt as to who is next entitled to the surplus resulting from a sale, the mortgagor may pay the money into court under the *Trustee Act*, R.S.O. 1990, c. T.23.

SALE UNDER A DEBENTURE

Section 41 of the *Mortgages Act* provides that Part III requiring notice of sale does not apply to "a mortgage given by a corporation to secure bonds or debentures". Presumably, the legislature thought that statutory protections were not required for persons who were sophisticated enough to enter into debenture transactions; they could negotiate their own notice requirements for inclusion in the debenture.

There is some doubt, however, as to what constitutes a mortgage given to secure bonds or debentures. In *Diegel & Feick Inc. v. Donia Consulting Corp.*, [1980] O.J. No. 713, 35 C.B.R. (N.S.) 134 (H.C.J.), a case involving a power of sale under a debenture which contained no notice provisions, Eberle J. held that s. 41 precluded the application of Part III to the sale. However, in *Ramardo Mines Ltd. v. Canadian Imperial Bank of Commerce*, [1980] O.J. No. 716, 2 A.C.W.S. (2d) 302 (H.C.J.), Eberle J. was intrigued by an argument that to fit within s. 41, there had to be two separate documents — a mortgage and a debenture. He did not need to reach any conclusion. In these authors' view, this argument should not succeed; a debenture is simply a corporate promise to pay, while a mortgage involves the pledge of property to secure that promise to pay. Surely, there is no difference whether these concepts are included in one document or two.

The Electronic Registration Procedures Guide confirms the ability of a debenture holder to sell without notice under Part III of the *Mortgages Act*.

Although debenture holders or the receivers appointed by them under the debenture have a power of attorney to act on behalf of the company giving the debenture, it is suggested that the exercise of a power of sale should be done by the debenture holders themselves or on their behalf. If the company itself sold, then it would do so subject to all encumbrances. Therefore, a sale under a debenture relying on the power of attorney given by the company may not have the desired effect of eliminating subsequent encumbrances.

APPENDIX 1

Document Registration Agreement

<u>DOCUMENT REGISTRATION AGREEMENT</u>

BETWEEN:

_____

(hereinafter referred to as the **"Purchaser's Solicitor"**)

AND:

_____

(hereinafter referred to as the **"Vendor's Solicitor"**)

RE: _____ (the **"Purchaser"**) purchase from _____ (the **"Vendor"**) of _____ (the **"Property"**) pursuant to an agreement of purchase and sale dated _____ , as amended from time to time (the **"Purchase Agreement"**), scheduled to be completed on _____ (the **"Closing Date"**)

FOR GOOD AND VALUABLE CONSIDERATION (the receipt and sufficiency of which is hereby expressly acknowledged), the parties hereto hereby undertake and agree as follows:

Holding Deliveries In Escrow

1. The Vendor's Solicitor and the Purchaser's Solicitor shall hold all funds, keys and closing documentation exchanged between them (the "Requisite Deliveries") in escrow, and *shall* not release or otherwise deal with same except in accordance with the terms of this Agreement. Both the Vendor's Solicitor and the Purchaser's Solicitor have been authorized by their respective clients to enter into this Agreement. Once the Requisite Deliveries can be released in accordance with the terms of this Agreement, any monies representing payout funds for mortgages to be discharged shall be forwarded promptly to the appropriate mortgage lender.[1]

---

[1] Solicitors should continue to refer to the Law Society of Upper Canada practice guidelines relating to recommended procedures to follow for the discharge of mortgages.

Advising of   2.   Each of the parties hereto shall notify the other as soon
Concerns with   as reasonably possible following their respective receipt of
Deliveries   the Requisite Deliveries (as applicable) of any defect(s) with
                  respect to same.

Selecting   3.   The Purchaser's Solicitor shall be responsible for the
Solicitor   registration of the Electronic Documents (as hereinafter defined)
Responsible   unless the box set out below indicating that the Vendor's
for   Solicitor will be responsible for such registration has been
Registration   checked. For the purposes of this Agreement, the solicitor
                  responsible for such registration shall be referred to as the
                  "Registering Solicitor" and the other solicitor shall be referred
                  to as the "Non-Registering Solicitor":

                  Vendor's Solicitor will be registering the   ☐
                  Electronic Documents

Responsibility   4.   The Non-Registering Solicitor shall, upon his/her receipt
of Non-   and approval of the Requisite Deliveries (as applicable),
Registering   electronically release for registration the Electronic Documents
Solicitor   and shall thereafter be entitled to release the Requisite
                  Deliveries from escrow forthwith following the earlier of:

and   a)   the registration of the Electronic Documents;

Release of   b)   the closing time specified in the Purchase Agreement
Requisite   unless a specific time has been inserted as follows
Deliveries by   [_____ a.m./p.m. on the Closing Date] (the
Non-   **"Release Deadline"**), and provided that notice
Registering   under paragraph 7 below has not been received; or
Solicitor   c)   receipt of notification from the Registering Solicitor
                        of the registration of the Electronic Documents.

                  If the Purchase Agreement does not specify a closing time
                  and a Release Deadline has not been specifically inserted the
                  Release Deadline shall be 6.00 p.m. on the Closing Date.

Responsibility of Registering Solicitor	5. The Registering Solicitor shall, subject to paragraph 7 below, on the Closing Date, following his/her receipt and approval of the Requisite Deliveries (as applicable), register the documents listed in Schedule "A" annexed hereto (referred to in this agreement as the **"Electronic Documents"**) in the stated order of priority therein set out, as soon as reasonably possible once same have been released for registration by the Non-Registering Solicitor, and immediately thereafter notify the Non-Registering Solicitor of the registration particulars thereof by telephone or telefax (or other method as agreed between the parties).
Release of Requisite Deliveries by Registering Solicitor	6. Upon registration of the Electronic Documents and notification of the Non-Registering solicitor in accordance with paragraph 5 above, the Registering Solicitor shall be entitled to forthwith release the Requisite Deliveries from escrow.
Returning Deliveries where Non-registration	7. Any of the parties hereto may notify the other party that he/she does not wish to proceed with the registration[2] of the Electronic Documents, and provided that such notice is received by the other party before the release of the Requisite Deliveries pursuant to this Agreement and before the registration of the Electronic Documents, then each of the parties hereto shall forthwith return to the other party their respective Requisite Deliveries.
Counterparts & Gender	8. This Agreement may be signed in counterparts, and shall be read with all changes of gender and/or number as may be required by the context.
Purchase Agreement Prevails if Conflict or Inconsistency	9. Nothing contained in this Agreement shall be read or construed as altering the respective rights and obligations of the Purchaser and the Vendor as more particularly set out in the Purchase Agreement, and in the event of any conflict or inconsistency between the provisions of this Agreement and the Purchase Agreement, then the latter shall prevail.

---

[2] For the purpose of this Agreement, the term "registration" shall mean the issuance of registration number(s) in respect of the Electronic Documents by the appropriate Land Registry Office.

Telefaxing
Deliveries &
Providing
Originals if
Requested

10.   This Agreement (or any counterpart hereof), and any of the closing documents hereinbefore contemplated, may be exchanged by telefax or similar system reproducing the original, provided that all such documents have been properly executed by the appropriate parties. The party transmitting any such document(s) shall also provide the original executed version(s) of same to the recipient within 2 business days after the Closing Date, unless the recipient has indicated that he/she does not require such original copies.

Dated this _____ day of _____, 20_____ .

Name/Firm Name of Vendor's
Solicitor

Name/Firm Name of Purchaser's
Solicitor

_____

_____

_____

_____

_____

_____

Name of Person Signing

Name of Person Signing

_____

_____

(Signature)

(Signature)

Note: This version of the Document Registration Agreement was adopted by the Joint LSUC-CBAO Committee on Electronic Registration of Title Documents on _March 29, 2004_ and posted to the web site on _April 8, 2004_.

Reprinted with permission of the Law Society of Upper Canada.

APPENDIX 2

Listing Agreement

OREA Ontario Real Estate Association

Listing Agreement
Authority to Offer for Sale

Form 200
for use in the Province of Ontario

This is a **Multiple Listing Service® Agreement** ⬭ *(Seller's Initials)* **OR** **Exclusive Listing Agreement** **EXCLUSIVE** ⬭ *(Seller's Initials)*

BETWEEN:

BROKERAGE:...

....(the "Listing Brokerage") Tel.No. (..........).........................

SELLER(S):...(the "Seller")

In consideration of the Listing Brokerage listing the real property **for sale** known as......................................

....(the "Property")

the Seller hereby gives the Listing Brokerage the **exclusive and irrevocable** right to act as the Seller's agent,

commencing at 12:01 a.m. on the..day of....................................., 20............,

until 11:59 p.m. on the...day of......................................, 20............ (the "Listing Period"),

Seller acknowledges that the length of the Listing Period is negotiable between the Seller and the Listing Brokerage and, if an MLS® listing, may be subject to minimum requirements of the real estate board, however, in accordance with the Real Estate and Business Brokers Act (2002), **if the Listing Period exceeds six months, the Listing Brokerage must obtain the Seller's initials.** ⬭ *(Seller's Initials)*

to offer the property **for sale** at a price of: Dollars (CDN$)..

....Dollars

and upon the terms particularly set out herein, or at such other price and/or terms acceptable to the Seller. It is understood that the price and/or terms set out herein are at the Seller's personal request, after full discussion with the Listing Brokerage's representative regarding potential market value of the Property.
The Seller hereby represents and warrants that the Seller is not a party to any other listing agreement for the Property or agreement to pay commission to any other real estate brokerage for the sale of the property.

1. **DEFINITIONS AND INTERPRETATIONS:** For the purposes of this Listing Agreement ("Authority" or "Agreement"), "Seller" includes vendor, a "buyer" includes a purchaser, or a prospective purchaser, and a "real estate board" includes a real estate association. A purchase shall be deemed to include the entering into of any agreement to exchange, or the obtaining of an option to purchase which is subsequently exercised. This Agreement shall be read with all changes of gender or number required by the context. For purposes of this Agreement, anyone introduced to or shown the Property shall be deemed to include any spouse, heirs, executors, administrators, successors, assigns, related corporations and affiliated corporations. Related corporations or affiliated corporations shall include any corporation where one half or a majority of the shareholders, directors or officers of the related or affiliated corporation are the same person(s) as the shareholders, directors, or officers of the corporation introduced to or shown the Property.

2. **COMMISSION:** In consideration of the Listing Brokerage listing the Property, the Seller agrees to pay the Listing Brokerage a commission
of............................% of the sale price of the Property or...
for any valid offer to purchase the Property from any source whatsoever obtained during the Listing Period and on the terms and conditions set out in this Agreement **OR** such other terms and conditions as the Seller may accept.
The Seller further agrees to pay such commission as calculated above if an agreement to purchase is agreed to or accepted by the Seller or

anyone on the Seller's behalf within............................. days after the expiration of the Listing Period **(Holdover Period)**, so long as such agreement is with anyone who was introduced to the Property from any source whatsoever during the Listing Period or shown the Property during the Listing Period.
If, however, the offer for the purchase of the Property is pursuant to a new agreement in writing to pay commission to another registered real estate brokerage, the Seller's liability for commission shall be reduced by the amount paid by the Seller under the new agreement.
The Seller further agrees to pay such commission as calculated above even if the transaction contemplated by an agreement to purchase agreed to or accepted by the Seller or anyone on the Seller's behalf is not completed, if such non-completion is owing or attributable to the Seller's default or neglect, said commission to be payable on the date set for completion of the purchase of the Property.
Any deposit in respect of any agreement where the transaction has been completed shall first be applied to reduce the commission payable. Should such amounts paid to the Listing Brokerage from the deposit or by the Seller's solicitor not be sufficient, the Seller shall be liable to pay to the Listing Brokerage on demand, any deficiency in commission and taxes owing on such commission.
All amounts set out as commission are to be paid plus applicable taxes on such commission.

3. **FINDERS FEES:** The Seller acknowledges that the Brokerage may be receiving a finder's fee, reward and/or referral incentive, and the Seller consents to any such benefit being received and retained by the Brokerage in addition to the commission as described above.

INITIALS OF LISTING BROKERAGE: ⬭ **INITIALS OF SELLER(S):** ⬭

Form 200 Revised 2011 **Page 1 of 3**

4. **REPRESENTATION:** The Seller acknowledges that the Listing Brokerage has provided the Seller with information explaining agency relationships, including information on Seller Representation, Sub-agency, Buyer Representation, Multiple Representation and Customer Service.
The Seller authorizes the Listing Brokerage to co-operate with any other registered real estate brokerage (co-operating brokerage), and to offer to pay

the co-operating brokerage a commission of......................% of the sale price of the Property or..

.... out of the commission the Seller pays the Listing Brokerage.

The Seller understands that unless the Seller is otherwise informed, the co-operating brokerage is representing the interests of the buyer in the transaction. The Seller further acknowledges that the Listing Brokerage may be listing other properties that may be similar to the Seller's Property and the Seller hereby consents to the Listing Brokerage listing other properties that may be similar to the Seller's Property without any claim by the Seller of conflict of interest. The Seller hereby appoints the Listing Brokerage as the Seller's agent for the purpose of giving and receiving notices pursuant to any offer or agreement to purchase the property. Unless otherwise agreed in writing between Seller and Listing Brokerage, any commission payable to any other brokerage shall be paid out of the commission the Seller pays the Listing Brokerage, said commission to be disbursed in accordance with the Commission Trust Agreement.

MULTIPLE REPRESENTATION: The Seller hereby acknowledges that the Listing Brokerage may be entering into buyer representation agreements with buyers who may be interested in purchasing the Seller's Property. In the event that the Listing Brokerage has entered into or enters into a buyer representation agreement with a prospective buyer for the Seller's Property, the Listing Brokerage will obtain the Seller's written consent to represent both the Seller and the buyer for the transaction at the earliest practicable opportunity and in all cases prior to any offer to purchase being submitted or presented.

The Seller understands and acknowledges that the Listing Brokerage must be impartial when representing both the Seller and the buyer and equally protect the interests of the Seller and buyer. The Seller understands and acknowledges that when representing both the Seller and the buyer, the Listing Brokerage shall have a duty of full disclosure to both the Seller and the buyer, including a requirement to disclose all factual information about the Property known to the Listing Brokerage.

However, the Seller further understands and acknowledges that the Listing Brokerage shall not disclose:
  - that the Seller may or will accept less than the listed price, unless otherwise instructed in writing by the Seller;
  - that the buyer may or will pay more than the offered price, unless otherwise instructed in writing by the buyer;
  - the motivation of or personal information about the Seller or buyer, unless otherwise instructed in writing by the party to which the information applies or unless failure to disclose would constitute fraudulent, unlawful or unethical practice;
  - the price the buyer should offer or the price the Seller should accept; and
  - the Listing Brokerage shall not disclose to the buyer the terms of any other offer.

However, it is understood that factual market information about comparable properties and information known to the Listing Brokerage concerning potential uses for the Property will be disclosed to both Seller and buyer to assist them to come to their own conclusions.

Where a Brokerage represents both the Seller and the Buyer (multiple representation), the Brokerage shall not be entitled or authorized to be agent for either the Buyer or the Seller for the purpose of giving and receiving notices.

MULTIPLE REPRESENTATION AND CUSTOMER SERVICE: The Seller understands and agrees that the Listing Brokerage also provides representation and customer service to other sellers and buyers. If the Listing Brokerage represents or provides customer service to more than one seller or buyer for the same trade, the Listing Brokerage shall, in writing, at the earliest practicable opportunity and before any offer is made, inform all sellers and buyers of the nature of the Listing Brokerage's relationship to each seller and buyer.

5. **REFERRAL OF ENQUIRIES:** The Seller agrees that during the Listing Period, the Seller shall advise the Listing Brokerage immediately of all enquiries from any source whatsoever, and all offers to purchase submitted to the Seller shall be immediately submitted to the Listing Brokerage before the Seller accepts or rejects the same. If any enquiry during the Listing Period results in the Seller accepting a valid offer to purchase during the Listing Period or within the Holdover Period after the expiration of the Listing Period, the Seller agrees to pay the Listing Brokerage the amount of commission set out above, payable within five (5) days following the Listing Brokerage's written demand therefor.

6. **MARKETING:** The Seller agrees to allow the Listing Brokerage to show and permit prospective buyers to fully inspect the Property during reasonable hours and the Seller gives the Listing Brokerage the sole and exclusive right to place "For Sale" and "Sold" sign(s) upon the Property. The Seller consents to the Listing Brokerage including information in advertising that may identify the Property. The Seller further agrees that the Listing Brokerage shall have sole and exclusive authority to make all advertising decisions relating to the marketing of the Property for sale during the Listing Period. The Seller agrees that the Listing Brokerage will not be held liable in any manner whatsoever for any acts or omissions with respect to advertising by the Listing Brokerage or any other party, other than by the Listing Brokerage's gross negligence or wilful act.

7. **WARRANTY:** The Seller represents and warrants that the Seller has the exclusive authority and power to execute this Authority to offer the Property for sale and that the Seller has informed the Listing Brokerage of any third party interests or claims on the Property such as rights of first refusal, options, easements, mortgages, encumbrances or otherwise concerning the Property, which may affect the sale of the Property.

8. **INDEMNIFICATION AND INSURANCE:** The Seller will not hold the Listing Brokerage responsible for any loss or damage to the Property or contents occurring during the term of this Agreement caused by the Listing Brokerage or anyone else by any means, including theft, fire or vandalism, other than by the Listing Brokerage's gross negligence or wilful act. The Seller agrees to indemnify and save harmless the Listing Brokerage and any co-operating brokerage from any liability, claim, loss, cost, damage or injury, including but not limited to loss of the commission payable under this Agreement, caused or contributed to by the breach of any warranty or representation made by the Seller in this Agreement or the accompanying data form. The Seller warrants the Property is insured, including personal liability insurance against any claims or lawsuits resulting from bodily injury or property damage to others caused in any way on or at the Property and the Seller indemnifies the Brokerage and all of its employees, representatives, salespersons and brokers (Listing Brokerage) and any co-operating brokerage and all of its employees, representatives, salespersons and brokers (co-operating brokerage) for and against any claims against the Listing Brokerage or co-operating brokerage made by anyone who attends or visits the Property.

9. **FAMILY LAW ACT:** The Seller hereby warrants that spousal consent is not necessary under the provisions of the Family Law Act, R.S.O. 1990, unless the Seller's spouse has executed the consent hereinafter provided.

10. **VERIFICATION OF INFORMATION:** The Seller authorizes the Listing Brokerage to obtain any information affecting the Property from any regulatory authorities, governments, mortgagees or others and the Seller agrees to execute and deliver such further authorizations in this regard as may be reasonably required. The Seller hereby appoints the Listing Brokerage or the Listing Brokerage's authorized representative as the Seller's attorney to execute such documentation as may be necessary to effect obtaining any information as aforesaid. The Seller hereby authorizes, instructs and directs the above noted regulatory authorities, governments, mortgagees or others to release any and all information to the Listing Brokerage.

INITIALS OF LISTING BROKERAGE: ( )   **INITIALS OF SELLER(S):** ( )

11. USE AND DISTRIBUTION OF INFORMATION: The Seller consents to the collection, use and disclosure of personal information by the Brokerage for the purpose of listing and marketing the Property including, but not limited to: listing and advertising the Property using any medium including the Internet; disclosing Property information to prospective buyers, brokerages, salespersons and others who may assist in the sale of the Property; such other use of the Seller's personal information as is consistent with listing and marketing of the Property. The Seller consents, if this is an MLS® Listing, to placement of the listing information and sales information by the Brokerage into the database(s) of the appropriate MLS® system(s), and to the posting of any documents and other information provided by or on behalf of the Seller into the database(s) of the appropriate MLS® system(s). The Seller acknowledges that the MLS® database is the property of the real estate board(s) and can be licensed, resold, or otherwise dealt with by the board(s). The Seller further acknowledges that the real estate board(s) may: distribute the information to any persons authorized to use such service which may include other brokerages, government departments, appraisers, municipal organizations and others; market the Property, at its option, in any medium, including electronic media; compile, retain and publish any statistics including historical MLS® data which may be used by board members to conduct comparative market analyses; and make such other use of the information as the Brokerage and/or real estate board deems appropriate in connection with the listing, marketing and selling of real estate.

In the event that this Agreement expires or is cancelled or otherwise terminated and the Property is not sold, the Seller, by initialling:

⬭ **Does**   ⬭ **Does Not**

consent to allow other real estate board members to contact the Seller after expiration or other termination of this Agreement to discuss listing or otherwise marketing the Property.

12. SUCCESSORS AND ASSIGNS: The heirs, executors, administrators, successors and assigns of the undersigned are bound by the terms of this Agreement.

13. CONFLICT OR DISCREPANCY: If there is any conflict or discrepancy between any provision added to this Agreement (including any Schedule attached hereto) and any provision in the standard pre-set portion hereof, the added provision shall supersede the standard pre-set provision to the extent of such conflict or discrepancy. This Agreement, including any Schedule attached hereto, shall constitute the entire Agreement between the Seller and the Listing Brokerage. There is no representation, warranty, collateral agreement or condition, which affects this Agreement other than as expressed herein.

14. ELECTRONIC COMMUNICATION: This Listing Agreement and any agreements, notices or other communications contemplated thereby may be transmitted by means of electronic systems, in which case signatures shall be deemed to be original. The transmission of this Agreement by the Seller by electronic means shall be deemed to confirm the Seller has retained a true copy of the Agreement.

15. SCHEDULE(S)..and data form attached hereto form(s) part of this Agreement.

THE LISTING BROKERAGE AGREES TO MARKET THE PROPERTY ON BEHALF OF THE SELLER AND REPRESENT THE SELLER IN AN ENDEAVOUR TO OBTAIN A VALID OFFER TO PURCHASE THE PROPERTY ON THE TERMS SET OUT IN THIS AGREEMENT OR ON SUCH OTHER TERMS SATISFACTORY TO THE SELLER.

....   DATE...................................   ....
(Authorized to bind the Listing Brokerage)   (Name of Person Signing)

THIS AGREEMENT HAS BEEN READ AND FULLY UNDERSTOOD BY ME AND I ACKNOWLEDGE THIS DATE I HAVE SIGNED UNDER SEAL AND HAVE RECEIVED A TRUE COPY OF THIS AGREEMENT. Any representations contained herein or as shown on the accompanying data form respecting the Property are true to the best of my knowledge, information and belief.

SIGNED, SEALED AND DELIVERED I have hereunto set my hand and seal:

....   ⚫ DATE...................................   ....
(Signature of Seller)   (Seal)   (Tel. No.)

....   ⚫ DATE...................................   ....
(Signature of Seller)   (Seal)

SPOUSAL CONSENT: The undersigned spouse of the Seller hereby consents to the listing of the Property herein pursuant to the provisions of the Family Law Act, R.S.O. 1990 and hereby agrees that he/she will execute all necessary or incidental documents to further any transaction provided for herein.

....   ⚫ DATE...................................   ....
(Spouse)   (Seal)

DECLARATION OF INSURANCE

The broker/salesperson...
                                              (Name of Broker/Salesperson)

hereby declares that he/she is insured as required by the Real Estate and Business Brokers Act (REBBA) and Regulations.

....
(Signature(s) of Broker/Salesperson)

APPENDIX 3

Measurement Conversion Table

1 chain	= 4 rods	= 22 yards	
	= 100 links	= 66 feet	= 20.1168 metres
1 link	= 7.92 inches	= 0.66 feet	= .2012 metres
1 rod, pole or perch	= 25 links	= 16.5 feet	= 5.0292 metres
1 furlong	= 40 rods	= 660 feet	
	= 1/8 mile	= 10 chains	= 201.168 metres
1 mile	= 320 rods	= 80 chains	
	= 1,760 yards	= 5,280 feet	= 1.6093 kilometres
1 acre	= 10 sq. chains	= 160 sq. rods	= 4,046.86 sq. metres
	= 43,560 sq. feet	= 4,840 sq. yards	= .40468 hectares
1 square mile	= 640 acres		= 2.59 square kilometres
			= 259.0080 hectares
1 metre	= 3.2808 feet	= 1.0936 yards	
1 kilometre	= 3,280.8 feet	= 1,093.6 yards	= .6214 miles
1 square metre	= 10.76 sq. feet		
1 hectare	= 107,641 sq. feet		= 2.4711 acres
1 gallon	= 4.546 litres		
1 litre	= 0.22 gallon		

APPENDIX 4

Agreement of Purchase and Sale

OREA Ontario Real Estate Association **Agreement of Purchase and Sale** Form **100**
for use in the Province of Ontario

This Agreement of Purchase and Sale dated this.................................... day of .... 20........

BUYER,.., agrees to purchase from
(Full legal names of all Buyers)

SELLER,.., the following
(Full legal names of all Sellers)

REAL PROPERTY:
Address.. fronting on the .... side

of.. in the ....

and having a frontage of .... more or less by a depth of .... more or less

and legally described as ....

.... (the "property").
(Legal description of land including easements not described elsewhere)

PURCHASE PRICE: Dollars (CDN$)...

....Dollars

DEPOSIT: Buyer submits ....
(Herewith/Upon Acceptance/as otherwise described in this Agreement)

.... Dollars (CDN$).......................................

by negotiable cheque payable to.. "Deposit Holder"
to be held in trust pending completion or other termination of this Agreement and to be credited toward the Purchase Price on completion.
For the purposes of this Agreement, "Upon Acceptance" shall mean that the Buyer is required to deliver the deposit to the
Deposit Holder within 24 hours of the acceptance of this Agreement. The parties to this Agreement hereby acknowledge that,
unless otherwise provided for in this Agreement, the Deposit Holder shall place the deposit in trust in the Deposit Holder's
non-interest bearing Real Estate Trust Account and no interest shall be earned, received or paid on the deposit.

Buyer agrees to pay the balance as more particularly set out in Schedule A attached.

SCHEDULE(S) A...**attached hereto form(s) part of this Agreement.**

1. **IRREVOCABILITY:** This Offer shall be irrevocable by .... until .... a.m./p.m. on
    (Seller/Buyer)

    the .... day of .... 20........., after which time, if not accepted, this
    Offer shall be null and void and the deposit shall be returned to the Buyer in full without interest.

2. **COMPLETION DATE:** This Agreement shall be completed by no later than 6:00 p.m. on the .... day

    of ...., 20......... . Upon completion, vacant possession of the property shall be given to the
    Buyer unless otherwise provided for in this Agreement.

3. **NOTICES:** The Seller hereby appoints the Listing Brokerage as agent for the Seller for the purpose of giving and receiving notices pursuant
    to this Agreement. Where a Brokerage (Buyer's Brokerage) has entered into a representation agreement with the Buyer, the Buyer hereby
    appoints the Buyer's Brokerage as agent for the purpose of giving and receiving notices pursuant to this Agreement. **Where a
    Brokerage represents both the Seller and the Buyer (multiple representation), the Brokerage shall not be entitled
    or authorized to be agent for either the Buyer or the Seller for the purpose of giving and receiving notices.** Any
    notice relating hereto or provided for herein shall be in writing. In addition to any provision contained herein and in any Schedule hereto,
    this offer, any counter-offer, notice of acceptance thereof or any notice to be given or received pursuant to this Agreement or any Schedule
    hereto shall be deemed given and received when delivered personally or hand delivered to the Address for Service provided in the
    Acknowledgement below, or where a facsimile number is provided herein, when transmitted electronically to that facsimile number.

    FAX No. .... (For delivery of notices to Seller)   FAX No. .... (For delivery of notices to Buyer)

    INITIALS OF BUYER(S): ( )   **INITIALS OF SELLER(S):** ( )

Form 100   Revised 2011   **Page 1 of 5**

4. **CHATTELS INCLUDED:**..
....
....
....
Unless otherwise stated in this Agreement or any Schedule hereto, Seller agrees to convey all fixtures and chattels included in the Purchase Price free from all liens, encumbrances or claims affecting the said fixtures and chattels.

5. **FIXTURES EXCLUDED:**...
....

6. **RENTAL ITEMS:** The following equipment is rented and **not** included in the Purchase Price. The Buyer agrees to assume the rental contract(s), if assumable: ....

7. **HST:** If the sale of the property (Real Property as described above) is subject to Harmonized Sales Tax (HST), then such tax shall be .... the Purchase Price. If the sale of the property is not subject to HST,
   (included in/in addition to)
   Seller agrees to certify on or before closing, that the sale of the property is not subject to HST. Any HST on chattels, if applicable, is not included in the purchase price.

8. **TITLE SEARCH:** Buyer shall be allowed until 6:00 p.m. on the .... day of..................................., 20......., (Requisition Date) to examine the title to the property at Buyer's own expense and until the earlier of: (i) thirty days from the later of the Requisition Date or the date on which the conditions in this Agreement are fulfilled or otherwise waived or; (ii) five days prior to completion, to satisfy Buyer that there are no outstanding work orders or deficiency notices affecting the property, and that its present use (...) may be lawfully continued and that the principal building may be insured against risk of fire. Seller hereby consents to the municipality or other governmental agencies releasing to Buyer details of all outstanding work orders and deficiency notices affecting the property, and Seller agrees to execute and deliver such further authorizations in this regard as Buyer may reasonably require.

9. **FUTURE USE:** Seller and Buyer agree that there is no representation or warranty of any kind that the future intended use of the property by Buyer is or will be lawful except as may be specifically provided for in this Agreement.

10. **TITLE:** Provided that the title to the property is good and free from all registered restrictions, charges, liens, and encumbrances except as otherwise specifically provided in this Agreement and save and except for (a) any registered restrictions or covenants that run with the land providing that such are complied with; (b) any registered municipal agreements and registered agreements with publicly regulated utilities providing such have been complied with, or security has been posted to ensure compliance and completion, as evidenced by a letter from the relevant municipality or regulated utility; (c) any minor easements for the supply of domestic utility or telephone services to the property or adjacent properties; and (d) any easements for drainage, storm or sanitary sewers, public utility lines, telephone lines, cable television lines or other services which do not materially affect the use of the property. If within the specified times referred to in paragraph 8 any valid objection to title or to any outstanding work order or deficiency notice, or to the fact the said present use may not lawfully be continued, or that the principal building may not be insured against risk of fire is made in writing to Seller and which Seller is unable or unwilling to remove, remedy or satisfy or obtain insurance save and except against risk of fire (Title Insurance) in favour of the Buyer and any mortgagee, (with all related costs at the expense of the Seller), and which Buyer will not waive, this Agreement notwithstanding any intermediate acts or negotiations in respect of such objections, shall be at an end and all monies paid shall be returned without interest or deduction and Seller, Listing Brokerage and Co-operating Brokerage shall not be liable for any costs or damages. Save as to any valid objection so made by such day and except for any objection going to the root of the title, Buyer shall be conclusively deemed to have accepted Seller's title to the property.

11. **CLOSING ARRANGEMENTS:** Where each of the Seller and Buyer retain a lawyer to complete the Agreement of Purchase and Sale of the property, and where the transaction will be completed by electronic registration pursuant to Part III of the Land Registration Reform Act, R.S.O. 1990, Chapter L4 and the Electronic Registration Act, S.O. 1991, Chapter 44, and any amendments thereto, the Seller and Buyer acknowledge and agree that the exchange of closing funds, non-registrable documents and other items (the "Requisite Deliveries") and the release thereof to the Seller and Buyer will (a) not occur at the same time as the registration of the transfer/deed (and any other documents intended to be registered in connection with the completion of this transaction) and (b) be subject to conditions whereby the lawyer(s) receiving any of the Requisite Deliveries will be required to hold same in trust and not release same except in accordance with the terms of a document registration agreement between the said lawyers. The Seller and Buyer irrevocably instruct the said lawyers to be bound by the document registration agreement which is recommended from time to time by the Law Society of Upper Canada. Unless otherwise agreed to by the lawyers, such exchange of the Requisite Deliveries will occur in the applicable Land Titles Office or such other location agreeable to both lawyers.

12. **DOCUMENTS AND DISCHARGE:** Buyer shall not call for the production of any title deed, abstract, survey or other evidence of title to the property except such as are in the possession or control of Seller. If requested by Buyer, Seller will deliver any sketch or survey of the property within Seller's control to Buyer as soon as possible and prior to the Requisition Date. If a discharge of

INITIALS OF BUYER(S): ◯   **INITIALS OF SELLER(S):** ◯

Form 100   Revised 2011   **Page 2 of 5**

any Charge/Mortgage held by a corporation incorporated pursuant to the Trust And Loan Companies Act (Canada), Chartered Bank, Trust Company, Credit Union, Caisse Populaire or Insurance Company and which is not to be assumed by Buyer on completion, is not available in registrable form on completion, Buyer agrees to accept Seller's lawyer's personal undertaking to obtain, out of the closing funds, a discharge in registrable form and to register same, or cause same to be registered, on title within a reasonable period of time after completion, provided that on or before completion Seller shall provide to Buyer a mortgage statement prepared by the mortgagee setting out the balance required to obtain the discharge, and, where a real-time electronic cleared funds transfer system is not being used, a direction executed by Seller directing payment to the mortgagee of the amount required to obtain the discharge out of the balance due on completion.

13. **INSPECTION:** Buyer acknowledges having had the opportunity to inspect the property and understands that upon acceptance of this Offer there shall be a binding agreement of purchase and sale between Buyer and Seller. **The Buyer acknowledges having the opportunity to include a requirement for a property inspection report in this Agreement and agrees that except as may be specifically provided for in this Agreement, the Buyer will not be obtaining a property inspection or property inspection report regarding the property.**

14. **INSURANCE:** All buildings on the property and all other things being purchased shall be and remain until completion at the risk of Seller. Pending completion, Seller shall hold all insurance policies, if any, and the proceeds thereof in trust for the parties as their interests may appear and in the event of substantial damage, Buyer may either terminate this Agreement and have all monies paid returned without interest or deduction or else take the proceeds of any insurance and complete the purchase. No insurance shall be transferred on completion. If Seller is taking back a Charge/Mortgage, or Buyer is assuming a Charge/Mortgage, Buyer shall supply Seller with reasonable evidence of adequate insurance to protect Seller's or other mortgagee's interest on completion.

15. **PLANNING ACT:** This Agreement shall be effective to create an interest in the property only if Seller complies with the subdivision control provisions of the Planning Act by completion and Seller covenants to proceed diligently at his expense to obtain any necessary consent by completion.

16. **DOCUMENT PREPARATION:** The Transfer/Deed shall, save for the Land Transfer Tax Affidavit, be prepared in registrable form at the expense of Seller, and any Charge/Mortgage to be given back by the Buyer to Seller at the expense of the Buyer. If requested by Buyer, Seller covenants that the Transfer/Deed to be delivered on completion shall contain the statements contemplated by Section 50(22) of the Planning Act, R.S.O.1990.

17. **RESIDENCY:** Buyer shall be credited towards the Purchase Price with the amount, if any, necessary for Buyer to pay to the Minister of National Revenue to satisfy Buyer's liability in respect of tax payable by Seller under the non-residency provisions of the Income Tax Act by reason of this sale. Buyer shall not claim such credit if Seller delivers on completion the prescribed certificate or a statutory declaration that Seller is not then a non-resident of Canada.

18. **ADJUSTMENTS:** Any rents, mortgage interest, realty taxes including local improvement rates and unmetered public or private utility charges and unmetered cost of fuel, as applicable, shall be apportioned and allowed to the day of completion, the day of completion itself to be apportioned to Buyer.

19. **PROPERTY ASSESSMENT:** The Buyer and Seller hereby acknowledge that the Province of Ontario has implemented current value assessment and properties may be re-assessed on an annual basis. The Buyer and Seller agree that no claim will be made against the Buyer or Seller, or any Brokerage, Broker or Salesperson, for any changes in property tax as a result of a re-assessment of the property, save and except any property taxes that accrued prior to the completion of this transaction.

20. **TIME LIMITS:** Time shall in all respects be of the essence hereof provided that the time for doing or completing of any matter provided for herein may be extended or abridged by an agreement in writing signed by Seller and Buyer or by their respective lawyers who may be specifically authorized in that regard.

21. **TENDER:** Any tender of documents or money hereunder may be made upon Seller or Buyer or their respective lawyers on the day set for completion. Money may be tendered by bank draft or cheque certified by a Chartered Bank, Trust Company, Province of Ontario Savings Office, Credit Union or Caisse Populaire.

22. **FAMILY LAW ACT:** Seller warrants that spousal consent is not necessary to this transaction under the provisions of the Family Law Act, R.S.O.1990 unless Seller's spouse has executed the consent hereinafter provided.

23. **UFFI:** Seller represents and warrants to Buyer that during the time Seller has owned the property, Seller has not caused any building on the property to be insulated with insulation containing ureaformaldehyde, and that to the best of Seller's knowledge no building on the property contains or has ever contained insulation that contains ureaformaldehyde. This warranty shall survive and not merge on the completion of this transaction, and if the building is part of a multiple unit building, this warranty shall only apply to that part of the building which is the subject of this transaction.

24. **LEGAL, ACCOUNTING AND ENVIRONMENTAL ADVICE:** The parties acknowledge that any information provided by the brokerage is not legal, tax or environmental advice.

25. **CONSUMER REPORTS: The Buyer is hereby notified that a consumer report containing credit and/or personal information may be referred to in connection with this transaction.**

26. **AGREEMENT IN WRITING:** If there is conflict or discrepancy between any provision added to this Agreement (including any Schedule attached hereto) and any provision in the standard pre-set portion hereof, the added provision shall supersede the standard pre-set provision to the extent of such conflict or discrepancy. This Agreement including any Schedule attached hereto, shall constitute the entire Agreement between Buyer and Seller. There is no representation, warranty, collateral agreement or condition, which affects this Agreement other than as expressed herein. For the purposes of this Agreement, Seller means vendor and Buyer means purchaser. This Agreement shall be read with all changes of gender or number required by the context.

27. **TIME AND DATE:** Any reference to a time and date in this Agreement shall mean the time and date where the property is located.

INITIALS OF BUYER(S): ( )   **INITIALS OF SELLER(S):** ( )

28. **SUCCESSORS AND ASSIGNS:** The heirs, executors, administrators, successors and assigns of the undersigned are bound by the terms herein.

SIGNED, SEALED AND DELIVERED in the presence of: IN WITNESS whereof I have hereunto set my hand and seal:

....   ⬤ DATE.............
(Witness)   (Buyer)   (Seal)

....   ⬤ DATE.............
(Witness)   (Buyer)   (Seal)

I, the Undersigned Seller, agree to the above Offer. I hereby irrevocably instruct my lawyer to pay directly to the brokerage(s) with whom I have agreed to pay commission, the unpaid balance of the commission together with applicable Harmonized Sales Tax (and any other taxes as may hereafter be applicable), from the proceeds of the sale prior to any payment to the undersigned on completion, as advised by the brokerage(s) to my lawyer.

SIGNED, SEALED AND DELIVERED in the presence of: IN WITNESS whereof I have hereunto set my hand and seal:

....   ⬤ DATE.............
(Witness)   (Seller)   (Seal)

....   ⬤ DATE.............
(Witness)   (Seller)   (Seal)

SPOUSAL CONSENT: The Undersigned Spouse of the Seller hereby consents to the disposition evidenced herein pursuant to the provisions of the Family Law Act, R.S.O.1990, and hereby agrees with the Buyer that he/she will execute all necessary or incidental documents to give full force and effect to the sale evidenced herein.

....   ⬤ DATE.............
(Witness)   (Spouse)   (Seal)

CONFIRMATION OF ACCEPTANCE: Notwithstanding anything contained herein to the contrary, I confirm this Agreement with all

changes both typed and written was finally accepted by all parties at...................a.m./p.m. this...day

of..., 20............ .   ...
                                                                                          (Signature of Seller or Buyer)

INFORMATION ON BROKERAGE(S)

Listing Brokerage... Tel.No.(.............)................

Co-op/Buyer Brokerage.. Tel.No.(.............)................

ACKNOWLEDGEMENT

I acknowledge receipt of my signed copy of this accepted Agreement of Purchase and Sale and I authorize the Brokerage to forward a copy to my lawyer. | I acknowledge receipt of my signed copy of this accepted Agreement of Purchase and Sale and I authorize the Brokerage to forward a copy to my lawyer.

.... DATE............   .... DATE............
(Seller)   (Buyer)

.... DATE............   .... DATE............
(Seller)   (Buyer)

Address for Service.................   Address for Service.................
..............Tel.No.(.........).........   ....Tel.No.(.........).........
Seller's Lawyer.......................   Buyer's Lawyer.......................
Address................................   Address................................
(..........)............ (..........).... (..........)............ (..........)....
        Tel.No.   FAX No.   Tel.No.   FAX No.

FOR OFFICE USE ONLY   **COMMISSION TRUST AGREEMENT**

To: Co-operating Brokerage shown on the foregoing Agreement of Purchase and Sale:
In consideration for the Co-operating Brokerage procuring the foregoing Agreement of Purchase and Sale, I hereby declare that all moneys received or receivable by me in connection with the Transaction as contemplated in the MLS® Rules and Regulations of my Real Estate Board shall be receivable and held in trust. This agreement shall constitute a Commission Trust Agreement as defined in the MLS® Rules and shall be subject to and governed by the MLS® Rules pertaining to Commission Trust.

DATED as of the date and time of the acceptance of the foregoing Agreement of Purchase and Sale.   Acknowledged by:

....
(Authorized to bind the Listing Brokerage)   (Authorized to bind the Co-operating Brokerage)

OREA Ontario Real Estate Association

Schedule A
Agreement of Purchase and Sale

Form 100
for use in the Province of Ontario

This Schedule is attached to and forms part of the Agreement of Purchase and Sale between:

BUYER,.., and

SELLER,..

for the purchase and sale of ....

.... dated the .... day of ...., 20......... .

Buyer agrees to pay the balance as follows:

This form must be initialed by all parties to the Agreement of Purchase and Sale..

INITIALS OF BUYER(S): ⬭   **INITIALS OF SELLER(S):**

APPENDIX 5

Agreement of Purchase and Sale

AGREEMENT OF PURCHASE AND SALE

OFFER

1. Through _____ as agent for the Vendor,
_____ ("the Purchaser")
hereby offers to purchase the proposed Lot / Part of Lot No _____ as shown on the attached plan, in the
_____ of _____ (the "Real Property"), which Real Property shall include the house to
be constructed thereon pursuant to this Agreement, including those features described in Schedule _____, (collectively the
"Dwelling"), being Type _____ Elevation _____ from _____
_____ (the "Vendor") on the terms and conditions contained in this Agreement, for
$ _____ (the "Purchase Price") payable:

(a) By payment to the Vendor of $ _____ , plus further deposits, if any, (collectively
the "Deposit") payable to the Vendor by cheque, with a date calculated from the date of this Offer or dated as set forth below or in an
attached schedule marked "Deposit";

Days/Date:	_____	Amount:	_____
Days/Date:	_____	Amount:	_____
Days/Date:	_____	Amount:	_____
Days/Date:	_____	Amount:	_____
Days/Date:	_____	Amount:	_____

(b) By payment of the balance of the Purchase Price, as adjusted pursuant to Paragraph 8, to the Vendor on Closing by bank draft or
cheque certified from a Canadian Chartered Bank, trust company or credit union.

SCHEDULES AND ADDENDUM

2. Schedule(s) 1, 2, 3 and _____ attached to this Agreement
form a part of the Agreement (collectively the "Schedules"). TARION Warranty Corporation's ("TARION') 'Statement of Critical Dates'
and 'Addendum to Agreement of Purchase and Sale' (the "Addendum"), together with the appendix to the Addendum containing
Additional Early Termination Conditions (if appended thereto) are attached to this Agreement and form a part of the Agreement. The
Purchaser confirms it has read and agrees to be bound by the Schedules, the Statement of Critical Dates, the Addendum and the
appendix to the Addendum containing Additional Early Termination Conditions (if appended thereto).

CLOSING

3. The date that this Agreement is to be completed (the "Closing") is defined at page 3 of the Addendum.

ACCEPTANCE

4. This offer shall be irrevocable by the Purchaser until 11:59 p.m. on the _____ day of _____ , 20_____ , after which
time, if not accepted , this offer shall be null and void. If accepted, this offer shall constitute a binding Agreement of Purchase and Sale.

SIGNED, SEALED AND DELIVERED this _____ day of _____ , 20_____ in the presence of

Witness

_____ Purchaser _____

_____ Purchaser _____

The Vendor hereby accepts the above offer. DATED at _____ this ____ day of _____ , 20_____

Per: _____   Per: _____

{Name(s)} _____   _____ Authorized Signing Officer(s)

Vendor		Purchaser	
Address		Address	
Tel:		Tel:	
Fax:		Fax:	
Email:		Email:	

Vendor's Solicitor:		Purchaser's Solicitor:	
Address		Address	
Tel:		Tel:	
Fax:		Fax:	
Email:		Email:	

BILD

2

SCHEDULE "1"

DEFINITIONS
5.   (a)   "Developer": means any predecessor in title to the Real Property who has entered into obligations with the Municipality for subdivision or servicing of the Real Property or any other party who may otherwise have the right as between it and the Vendor over architectural control of the Dwelling.
  (b)   "Municipality": means any municipal corporation, whether local or regional, having jurisdiction over the Real Property.
  (c)   "Levy" or "Levies" means all levies, development charges, education development charges, parkland levies or any impost or other charges imposed by a Municipality or private or public utility corporation in respect of the Real Property.

FINANCING
6. Within 20 days after the execution of this Agreement, the Purchaser shall deliver to the Vendor:
  (a)   a mortgage commitment from a bank, trust company or other financial institution for at least 75% of the Purchase Price; or
  (b)   evidence from a bank, trust company or other financial institution, indicating that the Purchaser has sufficient funds and is able to close this transaction without registering a mortgage against the Real Property. If the Vendor determines in its sole and unfettered discretion that the evidence provided to it pursuant to this Paragraph 6(b) is insufficient or not acceptable for the purposes of Closing, the Purchaser shall deliver a mortgage commitment for at least 75% of the Purchase Price to the Vendor within 20 days of request.

7. The Purchaser acknowledges and agrees that the failure of the Purchaser to deliver the documentation described at Paragraph 6 within the time periods described therein, shall be considered a material default of this Agreement.

ADJUSTMENTS AND DEPOSITS
8.   The Purchase Price shall be increased or adjusted as of Closing or deposits paid as set out in sections _____ of Schedule 2.

The date of Closing itself shall be apportioned to the Purchaser. If there are chattels involved in this transaction, the allocation of value of such chattels shall be estimated where necessary by the Vendor and retail sales tax may be collected and remitted by the Vendor.

The Purchaser agrees to pay after Closing any charges for water, hydro, fuel and other services. The parties agree to readjust any of the items in Schedule 2 where appropriate after Closing.

MODIFICATIONS- AND PLANNING ACT COMPLIANCE
9.   The parties shall accept minor modifications which the Developer or Municipality may require, including walkouts, narrowed driveway entrances, decks, side porches or a reverse layout (mirror image). If the Real Property is a lot on a plan of subdivision which has not yet been registered, lot sizes or dimensions are also subject to change without notice provided they are not substantially varied.

This Agreement is conditional upon the Vendor obtaining compliance at its own expense with the subdivision control provisions (Section 50) of the Planning Act.

CONSTRUCTION
10. The Vendor agrees that it will complete the Dwelling in accordance with the plans and specifications available for viewing by the Purchaser at the Vendor's sales office. All work will be perform ed in a workmanlike manner, free from defects in material and in compliance with the Ontario Building Code. All Construction Lien Act claims for materials or services supplied to the Vendor shall be the responsibility of the Vendor. Notwithstanding the foregoing the Vendor may substitute other materials of at least equal quality for those specified and may alter the plans and specifications, provided that such substitution or alteration shall not materially diminish the value of the Real Property or substantially alter the Dwelling.

If the stage of completion of the Dwelling permits, the Purchaser may be requested by the Vendor to select certain colours and materials from the Vendor's samples. If any selection of the Purchaser is not reasonably available during construction so that the Vendor by seeking to obtain it would be delayed in the construction of this or other dwellings, the Vendor shall notify the Purchaser and provide an opportunity to the Purchaser to make or approve an alternate selection of at least equal quality from the Vendor's samples. If the Purchaser has not made or approved selections within ten days of written request by the Vendor in the case of original selections, or seven days of written request in the case of an alternate selection, the Vendor may exercise all of the Purchaser's rights to colour and material selection and such selections by the Vendor shall be binding on the Purchaser.

The Purchaser will not enter the Real Property unless accompanied by a representative of the Vendor. When entering the Real Property, the Purchaser agrees to abide to the Occupational Health and Safety Act regulations including safety gear for head and foot or any other apparel as required by the Vendor.

Hot water heater and tank and all or part of the furnace and any other equipment as identified elsewhere in this Agreement and Schedules will not be included in the Purchase Price if rented.

Extras shall be paid for in advance, together with applicable HST, and such payment shall not be refunded if this transaction is not completed by reason of the Purchaser's default. If this Agreement is ended in circumstances in which the Deposit is to be returned to the Purchaser, any amount paid for extras shall also be returned. If an extra is omitted, the Purchaser shall be credited with the amount which the Purchaser was charged for it and this credit shall be the limit of the Vendor's liability.

OCCUPANCY & COMPLETION
11. For the purpose of Closing, the Dwelling shall be deemed to be completed when all interior work has been substantially completed so that the Dwelling reasonably may be occupied, notwithstanding that there may remain exterior work to be completed including, but not limited to, painting, driveway, grading, sodding and landscaping. There shall be no holdback or deduction on Closing for uncompleted work. The requirement that the Vendor deliver evidence to the Purchaser that the Dwelling is ready for occupancy prior to Closing is described at Paragraph 8(a) of the Addendum.

TARION WARRANTY CORPORATION
12. (i) The parties hereto agree that the Purchaser or the Purchaser's designate (being a person designated by the Purchaser in writing as having authority to complete the Pre-Delivery Inspection and sign the PDI Form and CCP, in a form acceptable to the Vendor) shall meet with the Vendor's representative at the date and time designated by the Vendor within 7 days prior to the date of Closing, in order to conduct a pre-delivery inspection of the Dwelling (hereinafter referred to as the "Pre-Delivery Inspection"), and to list all incomplete, deficient or missing items with respect to the Dwelling on TARION's Pre-Delivery Inspection Form ("PDI Form") and to complete and sign the PDI Form and TARION's Certificate of Completion and Possession ("CCP"), in the forms prescribed from time to time by (and required to be completed pursuant to the provisions of) The *Ontario New Home Warranties Plan Act* R.S.O. 1990, as amended, and the regulations promulgated thereunder.
(ii)   It is further understood and agreed that the most current version of TARION's Homeowner Information Package ("HIP") shall be delivered to the Purchaser by the Vendor no later than the date of the Pre-Delivery Inspection, and that the HIP is also available for the Purchaser's review or possession at any prior time, directly from TARION. The Purchaser, or the Purchaser's designate agrees to execute and provide to the Vendor TARION's Confirmation of Receip t form acknowledging the Purchaser's receipt of the HIP forthwith upon the receipt of same.
(iii)   The Purchaser hereby irrevocably nominates and appoints the Vendor to be its lawful attorney in the Purchaser's name in order to

3

execute the PDI Form, the CCP and/or the Confirmation of Receipt form in the event the Purchaser fails to do so when required by the terms hereof.

TITLE

13. Title to the Real Property shall be good and free from encumbrances except that it may be subject to subdivision or other agreements, covenants and restrictions (which restrictions may include the power to waive or vary), easements, licenses and rights required by the Vendor, Developer, Municipality or other affecting authorities including utilities, all of which the Purchaser shall accept provided there does not exist default under any and provided that the Purchaser's use of the Real Property for residential purposes is permitted. The Purchaser shall satisfy himself or herself as to compliance with such matters and any releases specifically contemplated in such agreements may be obtained by the Vendor subsequent to Closing. Title may also be subject to easements for maintenance or encroachment required for adjoining properties and to the encroachments permitted thereby. If any of the foregoing easements, restrictions or rights are required to be created after Closing the Purchaser shall execute any documents needed. The rights of re-entry referred to in Paragraph 17 shall also affect title and these rights as well as any of the above may be contained in the transfer delivered to the Purchaser.

Municipal subdivision agreements regulate development. The Purchaser should inquire of the Municipality on whether the applicable subdivision agreement contains special warnings, construction or servicing requirements, easement, fences or berms or other matters affecting the Real Property.

The Purchaser shall be allowed until fifteen (15) days before the date of Closing to examine the title at his or her own expense and if, within that time, any valid objection to title is made in writing to the Vendor, which the Vendor is unable or unwilling to remove and which the Purchaser will not waive, this Agreement shall notwithstanding any intermediate act or negotiations, be at an end and the Deposit shall be returned without interest or deduction and the Vendor shall not be liable for any damages or costs whatever. Save as to any valid objections so made within such time or going to the root of title, the Purchaser shall be conclusively deemed to have accepted the title of the Vendor to the Real Property. The Purchaser is not to call for the production of any title deeds, or other evidence of title except as are in the possession of the Vendor.

The Vendor shall provide a foundation survey of the Real Property at least 14 days before closing.

PRIOR MORTGAGES

14. Title to the Real Property may be encumbered by mortgages not to be assumed by the Purchaser on Closing. The Purchaser agrees to accept the Vendor's written undertaking to remove such encumbrance on title within a reasonable time after Closing if accompanied by,
(i) a written statement from the mortgagee of the amount required to be paid to obtain a discharge of the Real Property together with a direction from the Vendor permitting payment to that mortgagee of such amount by the Purchaser; or
(ii) written confirmation by the mortgagee that a discharge will be available without any action or payment on the part of the Purchaser or Vendor;
(iii) together with an undertaking by the Vendor's solicitors to remit to the mortgagee any funds directed to it pursuant to (i) above and to register any such discharge when received by them.

RISK

15. The Dwelling shall remain at the Vendor's risk until Closing. If the Dwelling is damaged prior to Closing, the Vendor shall repair the damage, finish the Dwelling and complete the sale, subject to any Unavoidable Delay, as such term is defined at Page 3 of the Addendum.

TRANSFER

16. The transfer shall be prepared by the Vendor's solicitors at the Vendor's expense and shall be registered forthwith on Closing by the Purchaser at his or her expense. The Purchaser agrees to advise the Vendor's solicitors, at least fifteen (15) days prior to the date of Closing, as to how the Purchaser will take title to the Real Property and of the birth dates of any parties taking title to the Real Property.

Title may be conveyed directly from the Developer to the Purchaser. If it is, and if the Vendor so requests, the Purchaser shall execute an acknowledgement that the Developer is not the builder and has no liability to the Purchaser as such.

AFTER CLOSING

17. The Ontario New Home Warranty shall constitute the Vendors' only warranty, express or implied, in respect of any aspect of construction of the Dwelling and further shall be the full extent of the Vendor's liability for defects in materials or workmanship or damage, loss or injury of any sort, whether arising in tort or in contract. **THE PURCHASER IS URGED TO REVIEW THE WARRANTY, PARTICULARLY ITS EXCLUSIONS,** and to be aware that the Vendor is not liable for loss or damage to any landscaping, furnishing or improvement by the Purchaser caused either by any defect for which the Vendor is responsible or by the remedying of such defect. The Purchaser shall care for sod, shrubs and other landscaping provided by the Vendor or Developer and shall replace any of it that dies.

The Purchaser shall not alter the grading or drainage pattern of the Real Property in any way and shall not construct any fences, pools, patios, sheds, or similar structures prior to final grading approval without the Vendor's consent. Some settlement of the lands is to be expected and the Purchaser shall repair minor settlement.

The Vendor reserves the right of re-entry for itself, the Developer and the Municipality for the completion of grading and the correction of any surface drainage problems or the completion of any other matter required by the subdivision agreement. The Vendor may re-enter to remedy at the Purchaser's expense any default by the Purchaser. The Vendor may also re-enter to complete any outstanding work.
The Purchaser acknowledges the following:
a) the Vendor shall not be liable for any damaged or diseased trees on the Real Property however caused and that the Purchaser assumes full responsibility for care, removal and replacement of such trees, provided that no trees may be removed from the Real Property except in conformance with the provisions of the municipal subdivision or other agreement affecting the Dwelling;
b) the Vendor will rectify any major settlement once only, and such work, unless of an emergency nature, will be completed when seasonably feasible and according to the Vendor's work programme and availability of materials and tradesmen's services. The Vendor is not responsible for any damage to the Dwelling which the Vendor considers of a minor nature by reason of such settlement;
c) final lot grading and sodding may not be completed until the year following the year of occupancy, and the Purchaser agrees that the timing for the completion of same shall be at the Vendor's sole discretion subject to Tarion Bulletin 42;
d) the Developer has agreed to provide and pay for paved roads, curbs, street lighting, sanitary and storm sewers and such other private or public services along the public highway as required by the Municipality or the municipal subdivision agreements, and that such are the responsibility of the Developer and not the Vendor; and
e) a sidewalk, if any, will be installed by the Developer in accordance with the appropriate municipal subdivision agreement.

NON ASSIGNABLE

18. This Agreement is personal to the Purchaser and may not be assigned other than to the Purchaser's spouse without the Vendor's written approval. Prior to closing, the Purchaser covenants that it shall not advertise or list or enter into an agreement to sell the Real Property for resale without the Vendor's prior written approval in its sole discretion.

CLOSING AND TENDER

19. The parties waive personal tender and agree that failing other mutually acceptable arrangements, tender may be validly made if the tendering party attends at the Registry Office in which the title to the Real Property is recorded at 4:00 o'clock p.m. on the date of Closing and for a period of one-half hour thereafter shall be ready, willing and able to close or alternatively, the tender may be validly made upon the designated solicitors for the party being tendered upon. The parties agree that payment must be made or tendered by bank draft or cheque certified by a Canadian Chartered Bank, trust company or credit union. Mortgages not being assumed by the

4

Purchaser need not be paid by the Vendor, only arrangements made to do so in accordance with paragraph 14 in which case the Purchaser should complete the transaction.

The Purchaser agrees that keys may be released to the Purchaser at the construction site or sales office on Closing. The Vendor's advice that keys are available shall be a valid tender of possession of the Real Property to the Purchaser.

WHOLE AGREEMENT
20. The parties acknowledge that there is no representation, warranty, collateral agreement or condition affecting the Agreement or the Real Property except as contained in this Agreement. Any statement or representation made by real estate agents or employees of the Vendor or contained in any sales brochures or in any other document shall not be legally binding upon the Vendor unless contained in this Agreement. This Agreement may not be amended other than in writing.

INTER-PRETATION
21. This Agreement is to be read with all changes of gender or number required by the context. Time shall in all respects be of the essence. All headings are for convenience of reference only and have no bearing or meaning in the interpretation of any particular clause in this Agreement.

RESIDENCY AND FAMILY LAW ACT
22. The Vendor represents that it is not a non-resident for the purposes of Section 116 of the Income Tax Act, Canada, and that spousal consent is not necessary to this transaction under the provisions of the Family Law Act.

NO REGISTRATION
23. The Purchaser confirms that this Agreement does not create an interest in the Real Property. The Purchaser will not at any time register or permit to be registered on title to the Real Property, this Agreement or a notice or assignment or transfer thereof or a caution, purchaser's lien or certificate of pending litigation or any encumbrance or cloud or other document whatsoever, and any such registration shall permit the Vendor to exercise any of its remedies set forth in this Agreement or at law, including the right of the Vendor to terminate this Agreement subject to the provisions of the Ontario New Home Warranties Plan Act, whereupon the Deposit may, in addition to any other remedy hereunder or at law available to the Vendor, be forfeited as liquidated damages.

ELECTRONIC REGISTRATION
24. If electronic registration of documentation at the Land Registry Office is in effect on the date of Closing, the following terms and conditions shall form part of this Agreement:
i)   The Purchaser shall retain a solicitor in good standing with the Law Society of Upper Canada to represent the Purchaser with respect to this Agreement;
ii)   The Purchaser shall direct his/her solicitor to execute an agreement as reasonably required by the Vendor's Solicitor (the "Solicitor's Agreement") establishing the procedure for completion of this Agreement;
iii)   The Purchaser and Vendor acknowledge that the delivery of documents and/or money may not occur contemporaneously with the registration of the Transfer/Deed of Land and may be delivered in escrow pursuant to the Solicitors' Agreement.
iv)   If the Agreement cannot be completed in escrow pursuant to the Solicitors' Agreement, the Purchaser's solicitor shall attend at the offices of the Vendor's Solicitor at such time as directed by the Vendor's solicitor or as mutually agreed upon to complete the Agreement.
v)   Paragraph 19 is hereby amended to provide that tender shall have been validly made by the Vendor when the "Completeness Signatory" for the Transfer/Deed of Land has been electronically "signed" by the Vendor's solicitor and same shall be satisfactory evidence that the Vendor is ready, willing and able to complete the sale.

GRADING
25. The Purchaser covenants that it will not at any time before or after Closing, without the prior written consent of the Vendor and the Developer, interfere with any drainage ditch completed by the Developer or take any steps which may result in the alteration or change of any grading or drainage or removal of soil or top soil in contravention of the Developer's obligations under the applicable subdivision agreement. In such event, the Vendor or the Developer may enter upon the Real Property and correct such grading and remove any such obstructions at the Purchaser's expense to be paid forthwith upon demand. This covenant may be included in the Purchaser's transfer at the option of the Vendor.

The Purchaser further acknowledges that settlement may occur due to soil disturbance and conditions including areas affecting walkways, driveways and sodded areas. The Vendor agrees to rectify such settlement problems as and when required by the Municipality or the Developer subject to the Purchaser's obligation to assume the cost of removing and re-installing any driveways or walkways installed by the Purchaser.

H.S.T.
(delete one)
26. (a) The Purchase Price includes/excludes H.S.T., calculated at the prevailing rate as of the date of this Agreement and has been determined taking into account the H.S.T. rebate, being the new housing rebates, refunds, credits or the like (collectively the "Rebate"), that are permitted pursuant to the statutes and regulations that are enacted and passed in order to implement the H.S.T (the "H.S.T. Legislation"). If H.S.T. is included, the Purchaser assigns to the Vendor all the Purchaser's rights to the Rebate and shall execute and deliver to the Vendor on or before Closing any assignments, directions, applications, consents, declarations, undertakings and other documents, pursuant to the H.S.T. Legislation and/or required by the Vendor to enable the Vendor to apply for and receive the Rebate and a statutory declaration in a form satisfactory to the Vendor confirming that:
  (i)   The Purchaser is acquiring the Real Property for use as the primary place of residence of the Purchaser, an individual related to the Purchaser or a former spouse of the Purchaser; and
  (ii)   The Purchaser or a person related to the Purchaser will be the first individual to occupy the Real Property as a place of residence.
(b) In the event that the Purchaser takes any action or makes false representations that would disentitle it from receiving the Rebate, it shall indemnify the Vendor from any loss of such rebate and the amount of such loss shall be credited to the Vendor on Closing if discovered prior to Closing, or paid to the Vendor if discovered after Closing.

The Purchaser acknowledges that the purchase of any extras or upgrades herein may result in the reduction of the Rebate otherwise payable to the Vendor. In such event, the Vendor shall, on Closing, receive a credit on the statement of adjustments for such reduction (the "Rebate Reduction").

UPGRADES, SELECTIONS & CHANGES
27. (a)   The Purchaser is advised that exterior elevation, appearances and finishings will be similar to pictures or renderings but may not necessarily be identical.
(b)   The Purchaser acknowledges and agrees that various types of flooring, such as carpets, marble, tile and/or hardwood floors in the Dwelling may result in different heights (to be established by the Vendor in its sole discretion) in the transitional areas between them, and that the Vendor may use appropriate reducers in the area.
(c)   Variations from Vendor's samples may occur in finishing materials, kitchen and vanity cabinets, floor and wall finishes due to normal production process.
(d)   The Purchaser acknowledges Vendor's advice that at Vendor's discretion door swings may be different from those indicated on brochures, and agrees to accept door swings as adjusted at Vendor's discretion.
(e)   The Purchaser is notified that the number of steps to the front or rear entrances may be increased or decreased depending on final grading.
(f)   The Purchaser acknowledges that the finishing materials contained in any model suite, customer service office, or sales office are for display purposes only, and may not reflect the actual type, quality or grade of materials and/or finishes included in the Dwelling.
(g)   The Purchaser acknowledges that any hardwood flooring installed in the Dwelling is made of a natural material which is subject to normal shrinkage, board separation and expansion due to changes in humidity for which the Purchaser agrees is not the responsibility of the Vendor.

SUCCESSION
28. This Agreement shall be binding upon the heirs, executors, administrators, successors and permitted assigns of each party.

5

NOTICE

29. Any notice required to be given pursuant to this Agreement may be given personally or sent by email, fax, courier or registered mail to the Purchaser or the Vendor or to the Purchaser's or Vendor's Solicitor at the address/contact numbers identified on page 1 of this Agreement. If either party wishes to receive written notice under this Agreement at an address/contact number other than those identified on page 1 of this Agreement the party shall send written notice of the change of address/contact number to the other party. Written notice given by one of the means identified in this paragraph is deemed to be given and received in accordance with paragraph 15(b) of the Addendum, provided that in respect of electronic transmission, the sender does not receive notification that the transmission did not go through.

DEFAULT

30. In case of material default or breach of this Agreement by the Purchaser, the Deposit and any other amounts paid by the Purchaser shall be forfeited to the Vendor, irrespective of any other right, cause of action or remedy to which the Vendor may be entitled.

31. Time shall be of the essence.

WAIVER

32. No waiver by the Vendor of any breach of covenant or default in the performance of any obligation hereunder or any failure by the Vendor to enforce its rights herein shall constitute any further waiver of the Vendor's rights herein, nor shall any waiver constitute a continuing waiver unless otherwise provided.

NON-MERGER

33. The Purchaser's covenants and agreements herein shall not merge on Closing but shall remain in full force and effect according to their terms, notwithstanding the conveyance of title to the Real Property and the payment of the Purchase Price.

FURTHER ASSURANCES

34. The Purchaser will execute such other documents and assurances to carry out the intention of this Agreement, and will deliver same upon, prior to or after Closing, as may be required by the Vendor.

PLANNING APPLICATIONS

35. The Purchaser acknowledges that applications may be made to obtain minor variances or other planning or development approvals in respect of the Real Property, the residential development upon which the Real Property is situate or any nearby residential developments marketed by the Vendor and the Purchaser hereby covenants and agrees that it shall not oppose any such applications and the Purchaser further acknowledges and agrees that the covenant may be pleaded as an estoppel or bar to any opposition or objection raised by the Purchaser thereto.

CLOSING DOCUMENTS

36. The Purchaser acknowledges that the Vendor is not required to deliver "hard" or paper copies of the documentation pertaining to the Closing of the herein transaction, draft or otherwise, to the Purchaser or the Purchaser's solicitor (the "Closing Documentation"). The Vendor or the Vendor's representatives may, at their option, deliver to the Purchaser or the Purchaser's solicitor any or all of the Closing Documentation by email and/or by website. If delivered by website, the Closing Documentation shall be made available for download on an internet website designated by the Vendor and access to such website shall be effected by way of a confidential password to be provided to the Purchaser and/or the Purchaser's solicitor.

EXTENSION

37. The Vendor may unilaterally extend a Firm Closing Date or Delayed Closing Date, as the case may be, for one (1) Business Day to avoid the necessity of tender where a Purchaser is not ready to close on the Firm Closing Date or Delayed Closing Date, as the case may be. The parties hereto acknowledge that delayed closing compensation will not be payable for such period and that the Vendor may not impose any penalty or interest charge upon the Purchaser with respect to such extension. 'Firm Closing Date', 'Delayed Closing Date' and 'Business Day' are defined in the Addendum.

ASSIGNMENT

38. The Vendor shall have the right to assign this Agreement, provided that any such assignee shall be bound by all of the covenants made by the Vendor herein, in which event the Vendor shall thereupon be released from all obligations hereunder.

CREDIT REPORT

39. The Purchaser acknowledges having been notified by the Vendor that a consumer report containing credit and/or personal information may be applied for, obtained or referred to in connection with this transaction and the Purchaser hereby consents to same and to forthwith execute any documents and authorizations required by the Vendor in this regard.

SUBORDINATION

40. The Purchaser agrees that this Agreement shall be subordinated to and postponed to any mortgage(s) arranged by the Vendor and any advances made thereunder from time to time or liabilities secured thereunder and to any agreements, easements, licenses, rights covenants and restrictions referred to herein to which title to the Real Property may be subject. The Purchaser agrees to execute all necessary documents and assurances to give effect to the foregoing as requested by the Vendor.

SEVERABILITY

41. If any provision of this Agreement or the application thereof to any person or circumstances, to any extent, be invalid or unenforceable, then the remainder of this Agreement or the application of such provision to persons or circumstances other than those to which it is held invalid or unenforceable shall not be affected thereby and each provision of this Agreement shall be valid and enforced to the fullest extent permitted by law.

       *   *   *

6

SCHEDULE "2"   **ADJUSTMENTS AND DEPOSITS**

(a)   any charges paid to a utility for the connection and/or energization of services or the installation of meters not to exceed $_____ plus HST;

(b)   the enrolment fee required pursuant to the TARION Warranty Corporation not to exceed $_____ plus HST;

(c)   realty taxes, adjusted on the Vendor's reasonable estimate as though the Dwelling were fully completed, the Real Property separately assessed and the taxes paid. (THE PURCHASER IS ADVISED that the Mortgagee may require a deposit to be paid to it to establish a tax account not to exceed $_____ and further, that the Municipality may issue a realty tax bill for supplementary assessment following Closing, which taxes may be in addition to those adjusted with the Vendor, and wholly or partly the responsibility of the Purchaser.)

(d)   an amount equal to the unused portion of any insurance premium relating to the Real Property where the policy has been arranged by the Vendor and is to be assumed by the Purchaser;

(e)   costs incurred by the Vendor as set forth below:

     (i)   boulevard landscaping up to a maximum of $_____ plus HST;

     (ii)   asphalt paved driveway up to a maximum amount of $_____ plus HST;

     (iii)   any charges imposed upon the Vendor or its solicitors by the Law Society of Upper Canada upon registration of the Transfer/Deed of Land or Charge/Mortgage of Land described as a transaction levy or similar charge, which is currently $65.00 plus HST;

     (iv)   any Levy imposed in respect of the Real Property; **OR**

         any increase of an existing, or imposition of a new Levy in respect of the Real Property between the date this Agreement is executed and the date upon which a building permit for the erection of the Dwelling is issued;

     (v)   the cost of preparing a foundation survey of the Dwelling not to exceed $_____ plus HST.

(f)   a damage deposit for the Purchaser's covenants contained in paragraph 25, in the amount of $_____ to be refunded to the Purchaser without interest, upon municipal assumption of the subdivision services and return of any security deposit given by the Vendor to the Developer or the Municipality;

(g)   an administration fee of Two Hundred ($200.00) Dollars plus HST for any cheque delivered to the Vendor not accepted by the Vendor's bank for any reason;

(h)   an administration fee of $_____ plus HST for the delivery of notices to the Purchaser and/or the Purchaser's solicitor as required pursuant to the Addendum;

(i)   the amount of $_____ plus HST for completing the Closing via electronic registration;

(j)   any charge imposed by the Municipality for new municipal numbering for the Real Property; and

(k)   the Rebate Reduction, if any.

7

SCHEDULE "3" PURCHASER'S CONSENT TO THE COLLECTION AND LIMITED USE OF PERSONAL INFORMATION

For the purposes of facilitating compliance with the provisions of any applicable Federal and/or Provincial privacy legislation (including without limitation, the Personal Information Protection and Electronic Documents Act S.C. 2000, as amended), the Purchaser hereby consents to the Vendor's collection and use of the Purchaser's personal information necessary and sufficient to enable the Vendor to proceed with the Purchaser's purchase of the Real Property, including without limitation, the Purchaser's name, home address, e-mail address, telefax/telephone number, age, date of birth, and in respect of marital status only for the limited purposes described in subparagraphs (c), (d), (h), (i) and (j) below, and in respect of residency status, and social insurance number only for the limited purpose described in subparagraph (i) and (j) below, as well as the Purchaser's financial information and desired design(s) and colour / finish selections, in connection with the completion of this transaction and for post-closing and after-sales customer care purposes, and to the disclosure and/or distribution of any or all of such personal information to the following entities, on the express understanding and agreement that the Vendor shall not sell or otherwise provide or distribute such personal information to anyone other than the following entities, namely to:

(a) the Vendor's sales agents, and any companies or legal entities that are associated with, related to, affiliated with the Vendor, other future real estate developers that are likewise associated with, related to or affiliated with the Vendor (or with the Vendor's parent/holding company) and are developing one or more other real property developments or commercial properties that may be of interest to the Purchaser or members of the Purchaser's family, for the limited purposes of marketing, advertising and/or selling various products and/or services to the Purchaser and/or members of the Purchaser's family;

(b) one or more third party data processing companies which handle or process marketing campaigns on behalf of the Vendor or other companies that are associated with, related to or affiliated with the Vendor, and who may send (by e-mail or other means) promotional literature/brochures about new real property developments and/or related services to the Purchaser and/or members of the Purchaser's family;

(c) any financial institution(s) providing (or wishing to provide) mortgage financing, banking and/or other financial or related services to the Purchaser and/or members of the Purchaser's families;

(d) any private lender(s) or financial institution(s) or their assignee or successor, providing (or wishing to provide) financing, or mortgage financing, banking and/or other financial or related services to the Vendor, the Tarion Warranty Corporation and/or any warranty bond provider, required in connection with the development and/or construction financing of the Real Property;

(e) any insurance companies providing (or wishing to provide) insurance coverage with respect to the Property (or any portion thereof), including without limitation, any title insurance companies providing (or wishing to provide) title insurance to the Purchaser or the Purchaser's mortgage lender(s) in connection with the completion of this transaction;

(f) any trades/suppliers or sub-trades/suppliers, who have been retained by or on behalf of the Vendor (or who are otherwise dealing with the Vendor) to facilitate the completion and finishing of the Real Property and the installation of any extras or upgrades ordered or requested by the Purchaser;

(g) one or more providers of cable television, telephone, telecommunication, security alarm systems, hydro-electricity, chilled water/hot water, gas and/or other similar or related services to the Real Property (or any portion thereof), unless the Purchaser advises the Vendor in writing not to provide such personal information to an entity providing security alarm systems and services;

(h) any relevant governmental authorities or agencies, including without limitation, the Land Titles Office (in which the Real Property is registered), the Ministry of Finance for the Province of Ontario (i.e. with respect to Land Transfer Tax), and Canada Revenue Agency (i.e. with respect to HST);

(i) Canada Revenue Agency, to whose attention the appropriate interest income tax information return and/or the non-resident withholding tax information return is submitted (where applicable), which will contain or refer to the Purchaser's social insurance number or business registration number (as the case may be), as required by Regulation 201(l)(b)(ii) of The Income Tax Act R.S.C. 1985, as amended, or for the benefit of the Vendor or its related or parent company where the Purchaser has agreed to provide financial information to the Vendor to confirm the Purchaser's ability to complete the transaction contemplated by the agreement of purchase and sale, including the Purchaser's ability to obtain sufficient mortgage financing;

(j) the Vendor's solicitors, to facilitate Closing of this transaction, including the closing by electronic means via the Teraview Electronic Registration System, and which may (in turn) involve the disclosure of such personal information to an internet application service provider for distribution of documentation.

(k) the Vendor's accountants and/or auditors who will prepare the Vendor's regular financial statements and audits;

(l) the Vendor's solicitors for the purposes of facilitating closing of the transaction or enforcement of the Vendor's rights under the Agreement of Purchase and Sale; and

(m) any person, where the Purchaser further consents to such disclosure or disclosures required by law.

SCHEDULES

Vendors may add Schedules including further or alternate provisions about: *(Any such Schedules should be initialled by the parties.)*

- *Features Schedule (referred to in paragraph 1)*
- *Deposit (referred to in paragraph 1 (a)*
- *Adjustments and Deposits (continuation of Schedule 2, if applicable)*
- *Site Plan or other plans*

- *Warning clauses required by subdivision agreements or other provisions in subdivision agreements affecting particular lots.*
- *Restrictive covenants or other title matters of note.*
- *Resale/assignment restrictions before closing*
- *Agency disclosure*

8
APPENDIX TO ADDENDUM
Additional Early Termination Conditions – Page 1

ADDITIONAL CONDITION #1
Description of the Early Termination Condition:
The Purchase Agreement is conditional upon confirmation by the Vendor that it is satisfied the Purchaser has the financial resources to complete the transaction based on the information set forth in Section 6 of the Purchase Agreement. This condition is for the benefit of the Vendor and may be waived by the Vendor in its sole discretion. The date by which this condition is to be satisfied or waived by the Vendor is noted below and is a maximum of 60 days following the signing of the Purchase Agreement.

The Approving Authority (as that term is defined in Schedule A) is:
There is no Approving Authority for this Early Termination Condition.

The date by which Condition #1 is to be satisfied is the _____ day of _____ , 20 _____,

ADDITIONAL CONDITION #2 (IF APPLICABLE)
Description of the Early Termination Condition:
_____
_____
_____
_____

The Approving Authority (as that term is defined in Schedule A) is:
_____

The date by which Condition #2 is to be satisfied is the _____ day of _____ , 20 _____.

ADDITIONAL CONDITION #3 (IF APPLICABLE)
Description of the Early Termination Condition:
_____
_____
_____
_____

The Approving Authority (as that term is defined in Schedule A) is:
_____

The date by which Condition #3 is to be satisfied is the _____ day of _____ , 20 _____.

ADDITIONAL CONDITION #4 (IF APPLICABLE)
Description of the Early Termination Condition:
_____
_____
_____
_____

The Approving Authority (as that term is defined in Schedule A) is:
_____

The date by which Condition #4 is to be satisfied is the _____ day of _____ , 20 _____.

ADDITIONAL CONDITION #5 (IF APPLICABLE)
Description of the Early Termination Condition:
_____
_____
_____
_____

The Approving Authority (as that term is defined in Schedule A) is:
_____

The date by which Condition #5 is to be satisfied is the _____ day of _____ , 20 _____.

ADDITIONAL CONDITION #6 (IF APPLICABLE)

Description of the Early Termination Condition:
_____
_____
_____
_____

The Approving Authority (as that term is defined in Schedule A) is:
_____

The date by which Condition #6 is to be satisfied is the _____ day of _____ , 20 _____.

9
APPENDIX TO ADDENDUM
Additional Early Termination Conditions – Page 2

ADDITIONAL CONDITION #7 (IF APPLICABLE)
Description of the Early Termination Condition:

_____
_____
_____
_____

The Approving Authority (as that term is defined in Schedule A) is:

_____

The date by which Condition #7 is to be satisfied is the _____ day of _____ , 20 _____.

ADDITIONAL CONDITION #8 (IF APPLICABLE)

Description of the Early Termination Condition:

_____
_____
_____
_____

The Approving Authority (as that term is defined in Schedule A) is:

_____

The date by which Condition #8 is to be satisfied is the _____ day of _____ , 20 _____.

ADDITIONAL CONDITION #9 (IF APPLICABLE)
Description of the Early Termination Condition:

_____
_____
_____
_____

The Approving Authority (as that term is defined in Schedule A) is:

_____

The date by which Condition #9 is to be satisfied is the _____ day of _____ , 20 _____.

ADDITIONAL CONDITION #10 (IF APPLICABLE)
Description of the Early Termination Condition:

_____
_____
_____
_____

The Approving Authority (as that term is defined in Schedule A) is:

_____

The date by which Condition #10 is to be satisfied is the _____ day of _____ , 20 _____.

ADDITIONAL CONDITION #11 (IF APPLICABLE)
Description of the Early Termination Condition:

_____
_____
_____
_____

The Approving Authority (as that term is defined in Schedule A) is:

_____

The date by which Condition #11 is to be satisfied is the _____ day of _____ , 20 _____.

Index